MANIA
An Evolving Concept

MANIA
An Evolving Concept

Edited by

Robert H. Belmaker, M.D.
Jerusalem Mental Health Center
Jerusalem, Israel

and

H.M. van Praag, M.D., Ph.D.
University Hospital
Academisch Ziekenhuis Utrecht
Utrecht, The Netherlands

SP MEDICAL & SCIENTIFIC BOOKS

SPECTRUM PUBLICATIONS, INC.
175-20 Wexford Terrace, Jamaica New York 11432

Library of Congress Cataloging in Publication Data

Main entry under title:

Mania, an evolving concept.

   Includes index.
   1. Affective disorders. I. Belmaker, R. H.
II. Praag, Herman Meir van. [DNLM: 1. Psychoses,
Manic-Depressive. WM207 M2773]
RC537.M35   616.89   80-78
ISBN 0-89335-115-6

DEDICATION

We dedicate this book to the city in which it was conceived.

Contributors

DOV R. ALEKSANDROWICZ, M.D.
Shalvata Psychiatric Center
Hod Hasharon, Israel

NANCY C. ANDREASEN, M.D.
University of Iowa
Iowa City, Iowa

J. ANGST, M.D.
Psychiatrische Universitatsklinik
Zurich, Switzerland

WILLIAM ANNITTO, M.D.
New York University Medical Center
New York, New York

R.H. BELMAKER, M.D.
Jerusalem Mental Health Center
Jerusalem, Israel

GABRIELLE A. CARLSON, M.D.
Neuropsychiatric Institute
Los Angeles, California

W.T. CARPENTER, JR., M.D.
Maryland Psychiatric Research Center
Baltimore, Maryland

DONALD COHEN, M.D.
Yale University
New Haven, Connecticut

WILLIAM CORYELL, M.D.
University of Iowa
Iowa City, Iowa

JOHN M. DAVIS, M.D.
Illinois State Psychiatric Institute
Chicago, Illinois

HAIM DASBERG, M.D.
Jerusalem Mental Health Center
Jerusalem, Israel

DAVID L. DUNNER, M.D.
Harborview Medical Center
Seattle, Washington

MARGIT FISCHER, M.D.
Aarhus Psychiatric Hospital
Aarhus, Denmark

DINSHAH GAGRAT, M.D.
VA Center
Wood (Milwaukee), Wisconsin

ELLIOT GERSHON, M.D.
NIMH
Bethesda, Maryland

SAMUEL GERSHON, M.D.
N.Y.U. School of Medicine
New York, New York

KATHLEEN HALL
New York State Psychiatric Institute
New York, New York

DAVID JANOWSKY, M.D.
University of California
San Diego, California

URIREL LAST, M.D.
Hebrew University
Jerusalem, Israel

YAKOV LERNER, M.D.
Eitanim Psychiatric Hospital
Doar Na Shimshon, Israel

THOMAS LOWE, M.D.
Yale University
New Haven, Connecticut

JULIEN MENDLEWICZ, M.D.
Universitaires de Bruxelles
Bruxelles, Belgium

A. KAPLAN DE NOUR, M.D.
Hadassah Hospital
Jerusalem, Israel

MORTIMER OSTOW, M.D.
Riverdale, New York

ROBERT M. POST, M.D.
NIMH
Bethesda, Maryland

H.M. VAN PRAAG, M.D.
University Hospital
Utrecht, The Netherlands

ROBERT F. PRIEN, PH.D
NIMH
Rockville, Maryland

RONALD RIEDER, M.D.
NIMH
Bethesda, Maryland

T.W. ROBBINS
University of Cambridge
Cambridge, England

B.J. SAHAKIAN
University of Cambridge
Cambridge, England

HERZL SPIRO, M.D.
Wisconsin College of Medicine
Milwaukee, Wisconsin

JOSEPH H. STEPHENS, M.D.
Maryland Psychiatric Research Center
Baltimore, Maryland

STEVEN D. TARGUM, M.D.
NIMH
Bethesda, Maryland

H.Z. WINNIK, M.D.
Jerusalem, Israel

GEORGE WINOKUR, M.D.
University of Iowa
Iowa City, Iowa

Contents

Introduction

Mania: An Evolving Concept aims to be a 23-chapter comprehensive textbook on manic illness. While numerous books have appeared in recent years on depression, mania has been much less written about. Yet, as a clinical problem, it can be argued that mania is more acute, more demanding of doctors' time, more disruptive of society, and more difficult to treat. There is less research with manic patients than with depressive patients, since manic patients are less cooperative and often aggressive. Yet, somehow, psychiatry has developed, in our view, a set of comfortable assumptions about mania that could never be promoted about depression without vociferous dissent.

In depression, it is widely recognized that differential diagnosis based upon apparent sadness and problems in living is difficult; that there are numerous subtypes; that etiology may be sociological, psychological, biological, or all three combined; that genetic factors are involved in some cases but not in others; that drug treatments are better than placebo but often fail; that psychotherapy and sociotherapy may be useful but need further research; and that no single biochemical correlate has yet been truly proven.

With regard to mania, the complexity of knowledge somehow becomes too much to bear. Many clinicians and researchers act as if they believe that mania—at least mania of all psychiatric illnesses—is easily and always reliably diagnosable; has a clear genetic etiology and specific biochemical pathogenesis; can be treated effectively with a unique drug that corrects the underlying defect; is not a relevant subject for complex psychological and sociological speculation or treatment; and always has an excellent prognosis.

The present volume was assembled with a request to each chapter author that he rethink some of the common assumptions about mania. Effort was made to assemble the widest range of views and to demand that chapter authors confront opposing views presented in other chapters. In some cases, this textbook is the first clear exposition of doubt or retraction of dogmas: Chapters 2 and 3 reveal that the prognosis of mania is not always excellent. Chapters 7 and 8 suggest that X-linkage of manic-depressive illness is not proven, although several general psychiatry texts quote this as an established fact. Chapter 11 declares firmly that lithium is *not* specific for manic-depressive illness, although textbooks said so until just recently. Chapter 12 reviews the literature and finds that lithium is *not* clearly effective in inhibiting amphetamine-induced euphoria in animal models of mania, although this claim too is widely accepted as fact. Chapter 13 emphasizes the heresy that dopamine, and not noradrenalin or serotonin, may be the biochemical mediator of mania.

INTRODUCTION

This book could be very unpopular among those that need to feel that mania is a very clear illness with a well-defined course and etiology, about to become psychiatry's third breakthrough after syphilis psychosis and pellagra psychosis. This book does not repeatedly declare how much amazing progress has been made. Progress has indeed been made and the book aims to document this progress. However, the emphasis is on all the open questions.

A final word should be said about the conception of this book, its intellectual history and location of editing. The book was conceived during the sabbatical of Herman van Praag in Jerusalem 1976–77. In his contact with the Lithium Clinic, headed by R. H. Belmaker at the Jerusalem Mental Health Center–Ezrath Nashim, it was noted that mania, as compared with depression, seemed to evidence more frequently in Jerusalem than in van Praag's native Holland. Indeed, a study by Elliot Gershon in 1975 had found that bipolar illness represented about 45 percent of admissions for affective disorder in Jerusalem, compared with 20 percent reported by Perris in Sweden, for example; i.e. every other depressed patient in Jerusalem is bipolar, whereas only every fifth depressed patient in Sweden is bipolar. Discussions on this phenomenon between the editors ranged from the "Mediterranean personality" to Tay-Sachs disease. It was natural, therefore, that Israeli psychiatrists and researchers are well-represented in this volume, along with the internationally known researchers whose chapters are a must in every book on affective disorder. The editors have also wondered whether Jerusalem might represent a natural laboratory for the study of mania and bipolar illness, and whether the high incidence of mania in Jerusalem might somehow provide a key to understanding some of the complexities of the illness' causes.

R. H. Belmaker
H. M. van Praag

MANIA
An Evolving Concept

CHAPTER 1

Mania: Disease Entity
or Symptom Cluster

R. H. Belmaker and H. M. van Praag

Research and therapy in mania have usually been based on a concept of mania as a pathologic process that defines a disease entity, manic-depressive illness (Winokur et al., 1969). Considerable effort is expended at clinical conferences aimed at deciding whether a particular patient is a manic-depressive or a schizophrenic. The assumption is that such diagnosis has therapeutic, prognostic, and genetic implications. What is the evidence underlying this assumption that manic-depressive illness and schizophrenia are separate disease entities? The oft-quoted "anemia" model emphasizes that different anemic illnesses have overlapping symptomatology but different underlying pathogenesis, prognosis, and treatment. Iron-deficiency anemia and sickle cell anemia thus have overlapping symptoms, but every physician learns the crucial importance of differentiating the two illnesses. Based on this model, psychiatric clinicians often argue about whether a patient with mixed manic and schizophrenic features is "really" a manic-depressive or a schizophrenic. Yet an equally valid model in medicine is that of the collagen vascular or rheumatoid illnesses. These offer a gradient in symptomatology, with a gradient in prognosis, treatment response, and genetic factors. The correlations among clinical phenomenology (symptoms) and prognosis, treatment response, and family history of illness are quite imperfect, though they exist.

Is the collagen-vascular-disease model more appropriate to the major psychoses? Most authors agree that the phenomenology of mania greatly overlaps that of schizophrenia, and that many delusions and even hallucinations are consistent with a diagnosis of mania (Lipkin et al., 1970). Carlson and Goodwin (1973) report that a large fraction of their manic patients reached delusional, hallucinatory stages, and that such phenomena are not restricted to "atypical" cases. Carpenter and Strauss (1974) have reported a high frequency of first-rank Schneiderian symptoms of schizophrenia in manic patients, and Taylor and Abrams (1977) have reported the common occurrence of catatonia in manic-depressive illness. Welner et al. (1977) have recently challenged the assumption that manic-depressive illness has a uniformly good prognosis, and Bleuler (1968), several years ago, emphasized the variable and often remitting clinical course of schizophrenia. With regard to treatment outcome, few theoreticians have come to grips with the apparent effectiveness of neuroleptics in mania (Shopsin et al., 1975; Belmaker et al., 1976b; Wyatt and Torgow, 1976) and even in some forms of depression (Simpson et al., 1972). Lithium has been occasionally claimed to be specific for manic-depressive illness (Gershon, 1968; Hekimian et al., 1969), and Carlson and Goodwin (1973) emphasize that even the most psychotic, hallucinated patients in their series of manic patients responded to lithium therapy to the same degree as the more classic manic patients, whose disorder was limited to mood symptoms. However, Schou (1954, 1968) noted that "atypical" (usually schizophrenic) features were associated in a graded way with reduction in the apparent effectiveness of lithium treatment. Rimon and Rakkolainen (1968) reported similar findings, as did Murphy and Beigel (1974), who stated that "paranoid-destructive" manic patients respond more poorly to lithium therapy than "elated-grandiose" manic patients.

The genetic data, on the other hand, would seem to support a specific illness model for manic-depressive illness and schizophrenia. Kety (1977) studied the biological relatives of a group of schizophrenic patients who had been adopted away at a very early age. He compared the biological relatives of the schizophrenic adoptees with the biological relatives of a matched group of nonschizophrenic adoptees. While he found significantly higher rates of schizophrenia and schizoid conditions in the biological relatives of the schizophrenic adoptees than in the biological relatives of the controls, he did *not* find excess of affective disorder or remitting psychosis in the relatives of the schizophrenic patients. Thus it seemed that the genetic predisposition to schizophrenia is distinct from that of affective disorder or acute "schizo-phreniform" psychosis. Mendlewicz and Rainer's recent adoption study (1977) of manic-depressive illness found not a single case of schizophrenia in the reared-apart relatives of bipolar manic-depressives. Moreover, evidence for X-linkage of manic-depressive illness would support a specific disease model (Mendlewicz et al., 1972; Fieve et al., 1973), although schizoaffective illness may also sometimes be X-linked (Belmaker and Wyatt, 1976; Baron, 1977).

The above discussion should not be taken as an indication that the anemia model is wrong and the collagen-vascular-disease model correct. The data are far from all in. Yet it seems crucial to tolerate this ambiguity of models and to prevent premature closure. Research based on an uncritical acceptance of one of the models can be both theoretically misleading and clinically useless.

As an example, consider the question of lithium therapy of schizoaffective disorders: Some authors have questioned the existence of such conditions and feel that most such conditions should be subsumed as part of the syndrome of bipolar manic-depressive illness (Procci, 1976). On the other hand, two key studies (Prien et al., 1972; Johnson et al., 1968) reported that lithium treatment is inferior to neuroleptic treatment in the treatment of excited schizoaffective states, and thereby some researchers concluded that mixed conditions might best be lumped in with schizophrenia, schizoaffective type (DSM II, 1968). Single-drug comparison of lithium versus neuroleptic in schizoaffective illness is clearly based on a disease entity model, as the researcher gives nature the opportunity to say yes or no to the question, Is lithium superior to neuroleptic in a particular disease entity? A gradient or continuum model would ask, Does lithium add benefit in mixed conditions already treated with neuroleptic? A recently completed double-blind con- trolled trial of lithium plus haloperidol vs. placebo plus haloperidol in schizoaffective illness found marked benefit for lithium (Biederman et al., 1979). This benefit was not even suspected in the single-drug comparison studies mentioned above. A disease entity model, searching for an answer as to whether schizoaffective illness belongs to manic-depressive illness (Procci, 1976) or to schizophrenia (DSM II, 1968), expects to find one drug superior in such cases in a way that supports classification of those cases with either schizophrenia or manic-depressive illness. A gradient or continuum model, however, would immediately have made the need for a drug combination study apparent. If schizophrenia and manic-depressive illness do exist in mixed forms with fully mixed etiology and pathophysiology, then a mixture of treatments may sometimes be necessary (as much as our prejudice against polypharmacy rightly objects). A similar dilemma has occurred in research and treatment of delusional depression, where it has only recently been realized that such patients respond poorly to tricyclic antidepressants, even if their history and course are consistent with a diagnosis of depression (Glassman et al., 1975, 1977). A continuum model would stimulate research on neuroleptics and neuroleptic-tricyclic antidepressant combinations in such cases even though such combinations do *not* seem useful in sad or apathetic chronic schizophrenic patients (Hollister et al., 1963).

Further developments in biochemical etiologies of the psychoses may someday make the above discussion irrelevant if a specific biochemical cause of manic-depressive illness and another specific cause of schizophrenia are discovered. Even if polymorphic in clinical phenotype, such biochemical causes might be expected to be reliable guides for treatment response and prognosis. That is, some genotypic manic-depressives may have clinical phenomenology similar to that of schizophrenia, but if the anemia model is correct, these cases should have treatment response and prognosis consistent with the underlying pathogenesis. However, it is of interest to note that the most exciting, though far from proven, biochemical genetic marker in psychosis research today is *not* specific for manic-depressive illness vis-à-vis schizophrenia. Reduction in platelet MAO activity has been reported in schizophrenia (Wyatt et al., 1973) and to a lesser but overlapping and qualitatively similar degree in manic-depressive illness (Murphy et al., 1974). Such nonspecificity should not lead to an out-of-hand rejection of the role that reduced platelet MAO may play in the pathogenesis of schizophrenia and manic-depressive illness (Murphy et al., 1974; Belmaker et al., 1976a). Until the state of knowledge is much more advanced, researchers must be able to shift between disease entity models and continuum models in designing research strategies in psychosis. It is especially saddening to see some researchers so convinced of the validity of particular diagnostic criteria that they project the attitude that "anyone who doesn't do it this way doesn't know how to diagnose mania." We have in front of us a fruit called psychosis, and we don't know whether it's a citrus that will divide itself into separable sections or an apple that we must divide along arbitrary lines. The present volume is an attempt to review and assemble the most recent information on mania, and perhaps to suggest which future research might be most tasty if mania is cut up like an apple and which research might be more appetizing if mania is served up like a citrus. Final decisions on the nature of the internal structure of the fruit are neither promised nor possible.

REFERENCES

Baron, M. Linkage between an X-chromosome marker (deutan color blindness) and bipolar affective illness. *Arch. Gen. Psychiat.* 34, 721–725 (1977).

Belmaker, R.H., and Wyatt, R.J. Possible X-linkage in a family with varied psychoses. *Israel Ann. Psychiat. Rel. Discip.* 14, 345–353 (1976).

Belmaker, R.H., Ebbesen, K., Ebstein, R.P., and Rimon, R. Platelet monoamine oxidase in schizophrenia and manic-depressive illness. *Brit. J. Psychiat.* 129, 227–232 (1976a).

Belmaker, R.H., Ebstein, R.P., Schoenfeld, H., and Rimon, R. The effect of haloperidol on epinephrine-stimulated adenylate cyclase in humans. *Psychopharmacology* 49, 215–217 (1976b).

Biederman, J., Lerner, Y., and Belmaker, R.H. Combination of lithium plus haloperidol in schizoaffective disorder: A controlled study. *Arch. Gen. Psychiat.* 36, 327–333 (1979).

Bleuler, M. A 23-year longitudinal study of 208 schizophrenics and impressions in regard to the nature of schizophrenia. In *Transmission of Schizophrenia*. D. Rosenthal and S.S. Kety, eds. Pergamon Press, Oxford (1968), pp. 3–12.

Carlson, G., and Goodwin, F.K. The stages of mania: A longitudinal analysis of the manic episode. *Arch. Gen. Psychiat.* 28, 221–228 (1973).

Carpenter, W.T., and Strauss, T.S. Cross-cultural evaluation of Schneider's first-rank symptoms of schizophrenia: A report from the International Pilot Study of Schizophrenia. *Am. J. Psychiat.* 131, 682–687 (1974).

Diagnostic and Statistical Manual of Mental Disorders II. Washington D.C., American Psychiatric Association (1968).

Fieve, R.R., Mendlewicz, J., and Fleiss, J.L. Manic-depressive illness: Linkage with the Xg blood group. *Am. J. Psychiat.* 130, 1355–1359 (1973).

Gershon, S. Use of lithium salts in psychiatric disorders. *Dis. Nerv. Syst.* 29, 51 (1968).

Glassman, A., Kantor, S., and Shostak, M. Depression, delusions and drug response. *Am. J. Psychiat.* 132, 716–719 (1975).

Glassman, A.H., Perel, J.M., Shostak, M., Kantor, S.J., and Fleiss, J.L. Clinical implications of imipramine plasma levels for depressive illness. *Arch. Gen. Psychiat.* 34, 197–204 (1977).

Hekimian, L.J., Gershon, S., Hardesty, A.S., and Burdock, E.I. Drug efficacy and diagnostic specificity in manic-depressive illness and schizophrenia. *Dis. Nerv. Syst.* 30, 747 (1969).

Hollister, L.E., Overall, J.E., Meyer, F., and Shelton, J. Perphenazine combined with amitryptiline in newly admitted schizophrenics. *Am. J. Psychiat.* 120, 591–592 (1963).

Johnson, G., Gershon, S., and Hekimian, L.J. Controlled evaluation of lithium and chlorpromazine in the treatment of manic states: An interim report. *Comp. Psychiat.* 9, 563–573 (1968).

Keyt, S.S. Genetic aspects of schizophrenia: Observations on the biological and adoptive relatives of adoptees who become schizophrenic. In *The Impact of Biology on Modern Psychiatry.* E.S. Gershon, R.H. Belmaker, S.S. Kety, and M. Rosenbaum, eds. Plenum, New York (1977), pp. 195–206.

Lipkin, K.M., Dyrud, J., and Meyer, G.G. The many faces of mania. *Arch. Gen. Psychiat.* 22, 262–267 (1970).

Mendlewicz, J., Fleiss, J.L., and Fieve, R.R. Evidence for X-linkage in the transmission of manic-depressive illness. *Jama* 222, 1624–1627 (1972).

Mendlewicz, J., and Rainer, J.D. Adoption study supporting genetic transmission in manic-depressive illness. *Nature* 268, 327–329 (1977).

Murphy, D.L., and Beigel, A. Depression, elation, and lithium carbonate response in manic patient subgroups. *Arch. Gen. Psychiat.* 31, 643–648 (1974).

Murphy, D.L., Belmaker, R.H., and Wyatt, R.J. Monoamine oxidase in schizophrenic and other behavioral disorders. *J. Psychiat. Res.* 11, 221–247 (1974).

Prien, R.F., Caffey, E.M., and Klett, C.J. A comparison of lithium carbonate and chlorpromazine in the treatment of excited schizoaffectives. *Arch. Gen. Psychiat.* 27, 182–189 (1972).

Procci, W.R. Schizoaffective psychosis: Fact or fiction? *Arch. Gen. Psychiat.* 33, 1167–1176 (1976).

Rimon, R., and Rakkolainen, V. Lithium iodide in the treatment of confusional states. *Brit. J. Psychiat.* 114, 109–110 (1968).

Schou, M., Juel-Nielson, N., and Stromgren, E. The treatment manic psychoses by the administration of lithium salts. *J. Neurol. Neurosurg. Psychiat.* 17, 250–260 (1954).

Schou, M. Special review: Lithium in psychiatric therapy and prophylaxis. *J. Psychiat. Res.* 6, 67–95 (1968).

Shopsin, B., Gershon, S., Thompson, H., and Collins, P. Psychoactive drugs in mania. *Arch. Gen. Psychiat.* 32, 34–42 (1975).

Simpson, G.M., Amin, M., Angus, J.W.S. Edwards, J.G., Go, S.H., and Lee, J.H. Role of antidepressants and neuroleptics in the treatment of depression. *Arch. Gen. Psychiat.* 27, 337–345 (1972).

Taylor, M.A., and Abrams, R. Catatonia: Prevalence and importance in the manic phase of manic-depressive illness. *Arch. Gen. Psychiat.* 34, 1223–1225 (1977).

Welner, A., Welner, Z., and Leonard, M.A. Bipolar manic-depressive disorder: A reassessment of course and outcome. *Comp. Psychiat.* 18, 327–332 (1977).

CHAPTER 2

The Diagnosis of Mania

William T. Carpenter, Jr., and Joseph H. Stephens

Historical Review of the Concept

Manic-depressive disorders have been known since antiquity (Zilboorg, 1944). Arieti (1974) discusses the teachings of the second-century physician Aretaeus, who not only described the symptomatology of mania and melancholia, but also noted a relation between the two states. Aretaeus observed that young people are more susceptible to mania and older people to melancholia, and that although the two states are related, mania is not always an outcome of melancholia. The contributions of Kraepelin were thus anticipated by at least seventeen centuries. Aretaeus described the intermittent character of the illness as well as the guilt-ridden, and self-sacrificing attitudes of the melancholic as contrasted with the gay and overactive behavior of the manic. The teachings of Aretaeus were ignored over the centruies, and it was not until 1851 that Falret (1929) again described the condition, characterizing its circular and intermittent nature. Kraepelin (1921) was influenced by the work of Falret and conceived the concept of manic-depressive psychosis as one syndrome that included simple mania, the periodic and circular insanities, and most cases of melancholia. His concept also included some less severe affective moods that were considered rudiments of the more severe cases. He believed that these different sydromes had common fundamental features and a uniformly benign prognosis. He also believed that the different syndromes could not be easily differentiated and might even replace one another in the same patient. Thus, both in his dementia praecox and in his manic-depressive psychosis, outcome was an important nosological characteristic. It was, however, not until 1899, in the sixth edition of his *Textbook of Psychiatry,* that Kraepelin used the term "manic depressive insanity." Most readers of Kraepelin in English are

7

familiar only with the eigth edition of his textbook, published in 1913 in German and in 1921 in English translation. The more important English translations of Kraepelin are now again available in facsimile reprints, and the modern reader will find Kraeplin's description of manic states unsurpassed. However, it is not at all certain whether or not the manic state that Kraepelin has so lucidly described should be considered a definable disease or a symptom complex on one end of a continuum that stretches from "pure" affective syndromes through a range of schizoaffective syndromes to schizophrenia. Kendell (1975) has suggested that psychotic illness may eventually come to be represented in dimensional terms rather than continue to be classified as discrete types. He believes that further studies may serve only to blur diagnostic distinctions rather than to clarify them. Strauss (1973) also discusses continuum models of psychopathology, but he would expect further study to clarify what dimensions and points along continuum are best used in categorizing patients.

Lewin (1931) has described two types of thought process used by scientists in considering the data of their observation. In the first, labeled "Aristotelian," the scientist conceives of his data as consisting of discrete, separable instances capable of being defined in such a way that each instance falls into no more than one of several possible categories. This mode of thought is well suited to a primitive scientist who has to make order out of diversity. Lewin labeled his second category of scientific thought process "Galilean." In this category, instances are conceived as falling along a number of continua, and covariation is not only possible but expected. Wolpert (1977), in his monograph on manic-depressive illness, states his belief that the classification of diseases as embodied in DSM-II (1968) remains primitive and Aristotelian rather than Galilean in that it does not tolerate ambiguity of models. Actually, the lack of clear-cut operational definitions in nosologic systems such as ICD-8 (World Health Organization, 1967) and DSM-II leads to considerable diagnostic ambiguity despite offering discrete classes of psychopathology. DSM-III (1978) remains Aristotelian in the discreteness of its categories, but in other areas it is Galilean in its tolerance of ambiguity, its interest in covariance along several axes, and its acceptance of intermediate concepts, such as schizoaffective disorders listed separately from schizophrenic and affective disorders. At any rate, present-day descriptive concepts of mania, whether Aristotelian or Galilean, do not represent impressive advances since the time of Kraepelin. Important gains have been made in other aspects of mania, such as genetics, psychobiology, and therapeutics. Despite the extensive investigation of mania, it is still not possible to identify patients with mania in absolute terms, and no ancillary diagnostic procedures can validate a diagnosis of mania in the individual patient. Variables such as family history and pharmacologic responsivity are critical in establishing group differences and lend support to conceptualizing mania as an affective disorder discrete from schizophrenia and other psychotic illnesses. Nonetheless, the behavior associated with mania clearly overlaps that observed in some other psychiatric disorders and in nonpathologic deviations of normal behavior.

In summary, we conceptualize the manic patient within the broad context of a medical model (see Engel, 1977, for a discussion of the socio-psycho-biomedical model), but regrettably note that diagnosis (in most instances) rests on the clinician's observation of the individual patient's disordered thinking, feeling, and acting during illness episodes, in the pattern of illness, and in relation to psychopathologic depression. The disturbed behavior associated with mania can easily be conceptualized on a continuum. However, the pattern of illness, the genetic data, and to some extent, the results of biochemical, psychophysiologic, and pharmacologic investigations favor conceptualizing mania as a subgroup of affective disorders discrete from other classes of psychiatric illness. We accept this latter position, but are mindful that the data are not unequivocal and that the overlap among groups is extensive.

DESCRIPTION OF THE BEHAVIOR AND THE ILLNESS

When mania is used as a descriptive term, it connotes excessive mental and physical activity manifest in many ways, but with a surprising consistency across patients. Physical manifestations include more movement, more talking, pressured speech, increased volume of speech, increased wakefulness, agitation, inability to remain still, abrupt and repetitive movements, threatening gestures, and assaultive or dominating behavior. Mental overactivity (a descriptive rather than an explanatory concept) is manifest by expansiveness of mood and thought; increased rapidity in thinking processes; pressured expression of thought; heightened sense of endurance; perceived high energy; increasingly self-referential and grandiose, tangential, circumstantial speech; failure to filter trivial stimuli; and an inability to maintain focus.

In manic illness there may also be garbled speech, clang associations, neologisms, belligerency, development of hallucinations, and delusions of a frantic quality. The mood is dysphoric, often elated and depressed simultaneously or in rapid sequence, irritable and agitated, but with less anxiety than is usually associated with severe and perplexing mental disturbance. The mood is labile, and sudden changes are common. Rage, delight, irritation, depression, and euphoria appear and disappear inexplicably.

Premorbid development is not consistently impaired, but past history may include characterologic or episodic depressive illness or mood swings. Earlier hyperactive behavior may be reported. Normal development is compatible with a diagnosis of mania, and the impaired premorbid development associated with process schizophrenia is unexpected in the manic patient. For individual manic patients, the history may include early and critical losses of significant objects, particularly the death of a parent. It may also include a history of high expectation. The family may reveal depressive and manic patients, and is much less likely to reveal relatives with schizophrenia. Simiilarly, certain nationalities and ethnic groups, such as Scandinavians and Jews, may have a higher prevalence. However, most of these variables are not established as critical to the pathogenesis of mania, and many will be absent in any particular individual manifesting manic behavior.

DIFFERENTIAL DIAGNOSIS OF MANIA

As with other conditions that will present with a clinical urgency, the diagnostician utilizes the cross-sectional psychopathologic picture extensively. There are no pathognomonic signs or symptoms of mania.

Fifty years ago, Bleuler (1924) wrote, "There are no specific signs of the affect psychoses; everything occurring in manic depressive insanity can also be seen in other diseases." Schneider (1959) also could find no symptom of first rank in mania. The same is true today. The many pathologic manifestations associated with mania cannot be considered highly discriminating of the diagnosis. The diagnosis is suggested by the overall constellation of behavior and the inability to rule in other illnesses to explain the manic behavior. A patient acutely manifesting many of the above symptoms who had recently ingested street drugs would be suspected of having a drug-induced toxic psychosis rather than mania. Another patient manifesting many of the above symptoms—but who had a family history of schizophrenia and an incomplete recovery from several prior psychotic episodes, and whose development of the psychotic episode had made it difficult to understand particular psychotic features in terms of mood disturbance—could be diagnosed schizophrenic.

Neither Kraepelin (1921) nor Bleuler (1924) would have disagreed with the DSM-III draft (1978), which states that the essential feature of a manic episode is a distinct period when the predominant mood is either elevated and expansive or irritable, and is associated with other symptoms of the manic syndrome, which include hyperactivity, excessive involvement in activities without recognizing the high potential for painful consequences, pressure of speech, flight of ideas, inflated self-esteem, decreased need for sleep, and distractability.

It is, of course, relatively easy to differentiate manic psychosis from illnesses that do not have manic features. The important and difficult differential is between mania and other acute psychoses. Episodic behavioral dyscontrol phenomena (Monroe, 1970), the reactive psychoses of Scandinavia (McCabe, 1975), the acute schizophrenias, the brief psychotic reactions, and drug-induced psychotic states all share features in common with mania. For most of these conditions, there is no definitive laboratory validation of the condition. The differential is best made by considering multiple features simultaneously. The greatest error is caused by a single-minded focus on a few symptoms. For example, if Schneider's first-rank symptoms are taken as sufficient indication of the presence of schizophrenia, then a substantial number of manic patients will be misclassified (Carpenter et al., 1973; Carpenter and Straus, 1974). Similarly, if mania is diagnosed simply on the presence of severe agitation, pressured speech, and expansive mood, then many patients with other acute psychotic syndromes will be misclassified. Drug-induced conditions are differentiated by a history of ingestion, by laboratory confirmation, by subsidence of symptoms within the expected time course of drug effect. Organic psychosyndromes are differentiated by careful mental status examination, EEG, neuropsychological and other ancillary diagnostic techniques.

The diagnosis is most difficult in the initial illness episode. If a constellation of manifest psychopathology suggesting mania occurs with a clear sensorium, an absence of those special forms of hallucinations and delusions highly discriminating of schizophrenia (Carpenter and Straus, 1974), and no evidence incriminating drugs or seizure like phenomena, a tentative diagnosis of manic psychosis is given. If history reveals good premorbid development, family history of affective disorders, or a pattern of past mild mood disturbance, confidence in the diagnosis increases. It appears wise, however, to reach final diagnostic conclusions only after the illness is established as episodic (bipolar or unipolar) with good or only modestly disturbed interepisode functioning. Manic episodes responsive to lithium therapy and depressive episodes responsive to ECT or antidepressant pharmacotherapy are reassuring. A lack of expected therapeutic response or of good interepisode functioning in the early stages of illness raises diagnostic doubts but by no means negates a diagnosis of mania. Parentheticallly, symptomatic improvement with these therapies and good recovery do not rule in a diagnosis of affective disorder or preclude assignment to other classes. The assessment of therapeutic response in the individual patient is tentative, since we are dealing with illnesses that are episodic in nature and with patients who may be responding to placebo effects or to unspecified environmental support. If a manic patient improves following a few days of lithium therapy, and deteriorates with cessation of lithium therapy, the evidence is strongly supportive of a manic diagnosis. This is the best example of specific diagnostic information from pharmacotherapy effect in single cases with functional psychoses. Physostigmine in anticholinergic psychosis is another example, but in this instance is an organic psychosyndrome.

The psychiatric diagnostician is entitled to exceptional confidence in diagnosing manic-'depressive illness when the typical past history compliments the cross-sectional picture. If the patient has had it before, we can pronounce the fact that he is having it again, and this can be done with reliability and presumed validity rivaling any in medicine. This bears more than an incidental relation to the fact that investigators can thrive in these diagnostic waters while they flounder in the uneven seas of schizophrenia.

PREDICTORS OF COURSE AND OUTCOME

It is far easier to devise criteria for operational identifications of diagnoses that have fairly high reliability than it is to devise a diagnostic nosology that can be externally validated. As Feinstein (1977) points out, we can engage in two distinctly different types of nosological reasoning: The first is merely to form names or denominations for the observed evidence; the second is to draw inferences from the observed evidence, arriving at inferential titles representing entities that have not actually been observed. The inference can occur by reasoning backward to an etiologic or pathogenetic cause preceding the ailment, or by a forward prediction that estimates the prognosis or predicts the best type of treatment. Noting that his is "an alleged expert in nosology unfettered by intimate knowledge of psychiatric practice," Feinstein urges that in gearing psychiatric nosology to an inferential anchor, we concentrate on verifiable inference, such as response to treatment, but particularly on natural prognosis and clinical course.

In the field of schizophrenia, there are numerous studies on the natural prognosis and long-term course of the disorder (Stephens, 1978). This is not true in the affective disorders, especially in regard to mania. Kraepelin (1921) characterized manic-depressive disease as not eventuating in a diagnosis of dementia praecox and usually not becoming chronic. Bleuler (1924) wrote, "Concerning the general prognosis little can be said as yet." Recent follow-up and prognostic studies in manic-depressive illness are less optimistic about the natural course of the illness than earlier ones in spite of the marked psychopharmacologic advances that have resulted in a decrease in the frequency and severity of attacks.

In general, patients suffering from manic-depressive illness with episodes of mania tend to have a more severe illness than manic-depressive patients with depression only (Welner et al., 1977b; Bratfos and Haug, 1968; Winokur, 1970; Perris, 1968). Perris (1966) has shown that patients who have no attacks that are other than manic are unusual. Rennie (1942), in a large follow-up study, found that only 25% of patients with an initial manic episode had no subsequent illness. No one has disputed the commonly accepted findings that almost all patients with manic episodes also have depressive episodes at some time.

Winokur (1975) has compared two groups of bipolar patients, those presenting at admission with their first manic episode, and those who were admitted for mania but had had previous manic episodes. Those with the previous history of manic episodes were less likely to have episodes of mania subsequent to the index admission. This surprising finding was interpreted to suggest that as a group, bipolar patients are likely to suffer a flurry of episodes that will then die out in time. Pollack (1931), however, gives evidence that manic episodes have a high tendency to recur.

Tsuang and Winokur (1975) compared long-term follow-ups of patients diagnosed for mania, depression, or schizophrenia by the St. Louis criteria (Feighner et al., 1972). Approximately one quarter of the depressed and manic patients were rated as showing severe psychiatric disability on 35-year follow-up, while about half of the schizophrenics were rated severely disabled. It should be noted that the diagnostic scheme for schizophrenia used included past history variables that could be considered either predictors or markers of chronicity. Carpenter et al. (1978) suggest that classification systems that predict chronic illness in schizophrenia probably, wittingly or unwittingly, utilize markers of chronicity as diagnostic criteria. This is not a criticism of nosology, but rather a clarification of the difficulty in using course and outcome to validate an illness and to distinguish one illness from another. If the St. Louis criteria required similar chronicity for diagnosis, the three groups might have been even less distinct at 35-year follow-up. A case in point is the report by Welner et al. (1977a). Six months of illness were required for a diagnosis of schizoaffective schizophrenia. Long-term follow-up revealed a chronic course in a majority of their patients, a sharp contrast to follow-up results with acute schizoaffective patients.

Unlike unipolar depression, unipolar mania has received little attention, no doubt due to its rarity. Abrams and Taylor (1974) have presented evidence in support of the conclusion that unipolar mania is clinically homogeneous with bipolar manic-depressive illness, with no distinguishing psychopathologic or treatment features for the manic psychosis.

The prognostic significance of manic symptoms in the functional psychoses remains the subject of controversy. The Welner et al., study mentioned above found no significant correlation between the presence or absence of manic or depressive symptoms and the course of illness or extent of later deterioration. Nearly three quarters of their patients had a chronic course, usually with deterioration.

Little work has been done in examining premorbid variables as outcome predictors in manic illness. Since premorbid features are decisive in establishing prognosis in schizophrenia and related psychoses (Stephens, 1978; Vaillant, 1963; Astrup and Noreik, 1966; Strauss and Carpenter, 1974a), one assumes that inattention to these variables in mania is based on the failure to observe a frequently occurring pattern of developmental dysfunction in this illness.

Bromet et al. (1974) and Rosen et al. (1969) have presented evidence suggesting that predictors of outcome in schizophrenia, such as poor social functioning prior to the onset of the disorder, do not predict outcome in other psychiatric illnesses. The study of Strauss et al. (1978) of a heterogeneous group of first admissions, however, suggests that this is not the case. Other investigators have also indicated that variables significantly correlated with outcome in schizophrenia are also significantly correlated with outcome for other diagnostic groups, including neuroses (Sims, 1975) and borderline patients (Carpenter et al., 1977a)

Two of the most widely used premorbid adjustment scales are the Elgin Prognostic Scale and the Phillips Scale. Garmezy (1968), in particualr, has extensively studied those two prognostic scales, and points out that they have such low ceilings that most nonschizophrenics and normals score at the extreme reactive end of the scales. However, Wittman and Steinberg (1944), using the original Elgin Prognostic Scale on 156 manic-depressives, showed that the predictive value of the scale scores was significantly higher than the staff members' clinical judgments as to prognosis. The authors concluded that the prognosis in the functional psychoses depends mostly upon factors inherent in the indivicual rather than upon the treatment. The present situation is, no doubt, different since major breakthroughs in therapeutics have occurred. There have been no published attempts to validate these preliminary findings with manic-depressive patients using the Elgin or Phillips scales. Unfortunately, the statistical deficiencies of the original report make it difficult to interpret.

One of us studied 350 patients discharged from the Phipps clinic between 1948 and 1960 with a diagnosis of schizophrenia, schizoaffective reaction, or paranoid state (Stephens, et al. unpublished data). These patients were retrospectively rediagnosed using Research Diagnostic Criteria (RDC [Spitzer et al., 1977]). These patients, on all of whom long-term follow-up data were available, were also rated on the Elgin Scale. All ratings were done without knowledge of the follow-up. Table 1 gives the new RDC diagnoses and associated follow-ups. Two things are of note: Only 17 (5%) of the patients were rediagnosed as pure affective disorders, although 82 (23%) were rediagnosed schizoaffective (22% of these had originally been diagnosed as schizoaffective). This is a surprising consistency in diagnosis. It is also to be

Table 1.

Diagnosis by RDC	N	Follow-Up		
		Recovered	Improved	Unimproved
Schizophrenia	164	26	74 (45%)	64 (39%)
Schizoaffective, manic	25	5 (20%)	16 (64%)	4 (16%)
Schizoaffective, depressed	57	17 (30%)	26 (46%)	14 (24%)
Unspecified psychosis	81	23 (28%)	47 (58%)	11 (14%)
Major or minor depression	17	8 (47%)	6 (35%)	3 (18%)
Other nonpsychotic	6	2 (33%)	3 (50%)	1 (17%)
Total	350	81 (23%)	172 (49%)	97 (28%)

noted that the follow-up for the schizophrenic patient is worse than for the other disorders. This may be due partly to the requirement that schizophrenia signs have to last at least two weeks from the onset of a noticeable change in the subject's usual condition, whereas the other diagnoses require only a week's duration. However, depressive symptoms in this particular sample are also correlated with a favorable prognosis. By stepwise regression analysis, it was determined that 10 of the Elgin items gave a better prediction of follow-up than the standard 20 items. Six of these 10 items are purely premorbid adjustment items, while 4 are cross-sectional items. Table 2 indicates that in schizophrenia as well as the other diagnoses, the premorbid score is more predictive of outcome. In the schizoaffective patients, affective disorder patients, and those with unclassified nonpsychotic conditions, the cross-sectional score is not predictive. Once again, we have evidence that the longitudinal picture is of extreme importance in predicting outcome. It appears that this may be true in the affective disorders as well as in

Table 2.

Correlation r between Elgin scores and follow-up	N	Elgin Premorbid Items	Elgin Cross-Sectional Items
Schizophrenia	164	.53†	.33†
Schizoaffective	82	.56†	.20 (n.s.)
Unspecified psychoses	81	.41†	.29*
Other diagnoses	23	.69†	.25 (n.s.)

*p < .01
†p < .001

schizophrenia, although this study is only indirectly related to manic psychosis in that the "manic" cohort is diagnosed as schizoaffective, not manic-depressive.

It is fair to close this section by calling for further study of premorbid predictors in mania. In the meantime, several working "conclusions" are permissible. First, common sense and experience with other functional psychoses suggest that significant impairment in premorbid functioning will worsen the prognosis in mania. The type of social adaptation presently highlighted in prognostic scales appears reasonably intact in most manic patients. Hence, its usefulness as a prognosticator may be limited to the minority of cases where a range of impairment is found. Second, the conceptual emphasis on good premorbid and outcome in manic-depressive disease may have prevented adequate attention to a more chronic subgroup. Chronic course has clearly been described in manic psychosis, as has early morbid development. We may have been unduly tautologic as the concept of mania developed. The oft-cited proclivity of many to overdiagnose schizophrenia and underdiagnose affective disorders no doubt has credence, and chronic forms of affective disorders are prime candidates for this error. We are mindful, of course, that the usual concern is with acute psychoses. Third, if one assumes that course and outcome is heterogeneous in manic psychosis, then the search for predictors will be renewed and should include variables related to object loss, pattern of coping with loss, cyclothymic personality features, and age and type of onset, as well as those variables found useful in other psychoses.

DISCUSSION OF PROBLEMS WITH CURRENT DIAGNOSTIC APPROACHES AND NOSOLOGIC CONCEPTS OF MANIA

Morrison and Flanagan (1978) believe that the most frequent diagnostic error made in psychiatry today is the diagnosis of schizophrenia in a patient who actually has a primary affective disorder, frequently of the bipolar type. Pope and Lipinski (1978), after an extensive literature review, conclude that overreliance on so-called schizophrenic symptoms taken alone or in cross-section has resulted in overdiagnosis of schizophrenia and underdiagnosis of affective illnesses, particularly mania. However, the pendulum may swing too far, and there is reason to be concerned with the problem of overdiagnosis of affective disorders in general. It is difficult to say to what extent this applies to mania in particular. Considerable attention to developing stringent criteria for a diagnosis of schizophrenia has not been accompanied by a similar effort to develop stringent criteria and a narrow definition of manic-depressive illness. The past problem of too many affective-disorder patients diagnosed as schizophrenic may be replaced by a future problem of too many nonaffective psychotic patients diagnosed as affective disorder. This will always be a problem when there are neither pathognomonic manifestations nor ancillary tests to establish the diagnosis.

The problem is also a reaction to earlier overdiagnosing of schizophrenia. Another factor is lithium therapy and prophylaxis. The presence of an effective and reasonably safe treatment for manic conditions has encouraged the use of manic diagnoses. Baldessarini (1970) demonstrated a remarkable increase in the number of patients diagnosed manic-depressive coincident with the introduction of lithium treatment at the Phipps Psychiatric Clinic. When we err in diagnosis, we believe it better to err toward affective disorders and away from schizophrenia, since the treatment is more specific, more successful and less dangerous in the affective disorders. If we rank psychiatric diagnoses in a hierarchy of the problems caused by erroneous treatment, schizophrenia heads the list, with affective disorders well behind. From a clinical vantage, it is surely better to maintain a schizophrenic patient on lithium than a manic-depressive patient on dopamine-blocking neuroleptic drugs. However, this clinical contingency should not permit us to abrogate a responsibility to the careful delineation of each nosologic entity. A further cautionary note is a reminder that manic conditions are responsive to neuroleptic medication. Dopamine-blocking drugs are antipsychotic, not antischizophrenic. Patients with manic symptomatology who respond to neuroleptic medication should not be suspected of having schizophrenia on that basis, nor should they be considered for maintenance neuroleptic medication. An unfortunate consequence of trends toward avoiding hospital-ization or rapid discharge of admitted patients is to be misled diagnostically by rapid symptom reduction with antipsychotic drugs.

Another problem associated with pressures to quickly classify and treat is an inattention to past history. Not only is past history often the most informative diagnostic datum in manic conditions, but it also reveals to what extent the patient has impairments in functioning between episodes. We have reached the clinical nadir of paying precious little attention to manic patients' nonpharmacologic therapeutic requirements. The maintenance of family, interpersonal, and occupational functioning following symptom reduction is a critical issue with many manic patients, although intrapsychic and interpersonal consequences are not as pervasive or severe as those found in schizophrenia. The past history is, of course, critical in establishing need for and response to maintenance lithium therapy.

Interest in the longitudinal course of psychiatric illness implies conern, not only with past history, but also with the evolution of the illness during the future. It is easily forgotten that both Kraepelin *and* Bleuler emphasized the need for prolonged and exact observation of the patient before making a diagnosis with conviction. Carlson and Goodwin (1973) have written on the need to make use of longitudinal sequential analysis of changing symptoms, rather than of simple cross-sectional enumeration of symptoms, if we are to increase diagnostic clarity in manic patients. As discused above and as reviewed by Skodal et al. (1976), there appear to be no pathognomonic symptoms of schizophrenia capable of establishing with complete reliability the differential diagnosis between a schizophrenic psychosis and an affective psychosis. The functional conditions that are currently called chronic schizophrenia, acute schizophrenia reaction, mania, bipolar and unipolar depression, and hysterical psychosis can all present with the same syndrome. In order to distinguish underlying illnesses from one another, it is necessary to abandon total reliance on symptoms for diagnosis and to look more closely at the longitudinal course as obtained from a detailed past history. Strauss and Carpenter (1974b) have challenged the concept that certain symptoms designate certain diseases, validated by poor outcome. They have suggested abandoning the unitary concept of schizophrenia as a disease, and have recommended thinking in terms of a confluence of factors, such as symptoms, chronicity, and underlying personality characteristics, that exist and have meaning independently of one another. It is equally appropriate to think in terms of confluence of factors in considering patients presenting primarily with manic symptoms. Implementation of a multaxial system in DSM III should have the sanquine effect of redirecting the attention of American psychiatrists to aspects of human funtioning currently neglected in the evaluation and treatment of the manic patient. We may take a fresh look at chronicity and interepisode functioning in manic patients.

CONCLUDING COMMENTS

The clarity of mania as a nosologic concept and the apparent ease in identifying the manic patient have had two contrasting effects relevant to this chapter on diagnosis. First, with validity and reliability of classification presumed, investigators found manic and manic-depressive illness ripe for study. For some years, genetic, ontogenetic, psychodynamic, and family/cultural issues were studied. With the advent of lithium therapy and the emerging methods of biological psychiatry, recent attention has focused on psychopharmacologic, neurobiologic, and genetic investigations. It can even be said that mania has been overstudied if measured against attention given to the more perplexing, prevalent, and severe illnesses classified as schizophrenia. As reflected in subsequent chapters, these studies have contributed significantly to our understanding of manic illness, and have had the important effects of stimulating acquisition of new information relevant to brain physiology and neuropharmacology and of spawning new methods in clinical psychobiology.

The second effect has been less rewarding. Descriptive studies have received less attention, and some unwarranted clinical assumptions have gone unchallenged. Several examples are here mentioned in concluding this chapter:

1. Important changes in the clinical manifestation and natural course of illness have been documented in several psychiatric syndromes and illnesses (Grinker 1973; Bleuler, 1968). This issue is not well studied in mania except as relevant to effects of pharmacotherapy. Whether there is less "chronic mania" today than at the turn of the century is uncertain. If so, drug effects have not been distinguished from other causes of changing patterns in psychopathology.

2. It is valuable to note important group differences in course of illness between process schizophrenia and manic-depressive illness. However, this conceptual distinction has been misapplied in individual cases. There is a proclivity in many settings to consider chronic functional psychoses as schizophrenia and acute functional psychoses as affective disorders. Many have criticized the practice of overdiagnosing schizophrenia, but this has implied the inappropriate inclusion of acute or episodic psychotic patients under the rubric of schizophrenia. It may also be noted that chronic manic-depressive patients with deterioriating function and/or lengthy hospitalization may be diagnosed as schizophrenic, thus obscuring the chronicity-associated affective disorders in many instances. The episodic manic patient will frequently show deterioration in work and social functioning, intellectual underachievement, a degree of anhedonia between episodes, disturbed pattern of interpersonal relating with difficulty sustaining intimacy, and other illness effects difficult to distinguish from features of schizophrenia, substance abuse, borderline personality, and other psychiatric conditions.

3. The extent to which acute psychotic conditions are mislabeled "manic-depressive" clouds the concept on the other end of the acute/chronic dimension. While this diagnostic mistake is often not therapeutically harmful, it is an impediment to evolving a valid nosology. It has become fashionable to apply stringent criteria in identifying schizophrenic patients while using nonstringent criteria for affective disorders (e.g., overactivity and euphoria for mania, and first-rank symptoms, prognostic measures, course of illness, etc., for schizophrenia). We agree that schizophrenia has been too broadly defined in some centers, but little good will accrue from making the same error with manic-depressive illness. The fact is that the nosology and classification techniques for acute psychotic conditions (excluding organic psychosyndromes) is not satisfactory. Affective disturbance and flagrant psychotic symptoms are common to all. When past history, family history, course, and treatment-response data fail to sufficiently clarify diagnosis, it is best to defer diagnosis and treat the patient empirically.

4. The study of variables associated with diagnosis (in contrast to diagnostic variables per se) may be enhanced by using set criteria of highly specifiable signs and symptoms or clearly delineated course of illness. The RDC (Spitzer et al., 1977) are an example. However, nosologic investigations and those studies aimed at clarifying the diagnostic process are not well served by reliance on such criteria. The phenomenon of psychotic illness is far too complex and personal to be adequately perceived within a narrow set of observations. The clinician deals with a subjective phenomenon, and his judgments are subjective. Highly specifiable criteria lend themselves to crispness of defintion, but do not alter the subjective nature of diagnosis. Reliability of clinical judgments are sometimes enhanced, but difficult to specify, phenomena such as poor rapport and incomprehensiveness in speach can also be reliably judged and usefully applied to diagnosis (Carpenter et al., 1973). Reliance on a few specified sign and symptom variables may assist the investigators in taking a first look at a hypothesized enzyme abnormality, but it will not help the psychiatric phenomenologist in understanding and classifying the psychopathologic disturbances is his purview. The problems associated with oversimplified description of complicated clinical phenomena have been put in clear relief, with the use of psychotic relapse and/or hospital readmission as sufficient criteria to assess treatment efficacy in schizophrenic outpatients. The result is an extraordinarily limited body of information on the actual impact of maintainence neuroleptic therapy on core schizophrenic pathology (Carpenter et al., 1977b). Similarly, focus on symptomatic manifestations in illness episodes associated with assumption of good interepisode functioning has made us inattentive to some forms of manic illness (i.e., chronic) and some aspects of pathologic functioning.

5. The psychiatric phenomenologist (evolving a concept of mania) and the clinician (identifying cases of mania) have the task of *describing* and *understanding* behavioral manifestations of illness. To clarify without understanding betrays the observational foundations of our specialty. An important current dilemma around which this point can be discussed is the classification of patients with mixed schizophrenic and affective features. Schizoaffective schizophrenia (and, presently, schizoaffective disorder as a separate class) provides a useful wastebasket for this diagnostic dilemma. Useful, because assigning uncertain cases to this category has two benefits: First, it increases homogeneity within affective and schizophrenic classes by reducing false positive inclusions. Second, it highlights a syndrome(s) requiring further study. However, some diagnosticians now advocate using this category whenever symptoms associated with schizophrenia coexist with symptoms associated with affective disorders. This approach ignores the fact that none of the symptoms in question are pathognomic of either disorder. Severe affective disturbance is routinely noted in early episodes of schizophrenic illness, and flagrnat psychotic symptoms, including Schneider's first-rank symptoms, have been reported in most empiric studies of manic and severe depressive disorders. When determining that a patient has evidence "suggesting" the presence of each disorder, the diagnostician should use a detailed historical approach to ascertain the likelihood that one set of

symptoms can account for the other. If a recurrent illness pattern is already established, and manifest psychopathology, course, and treatment response weigh heavily in favor of either schizophrenia or affect disorder, the clinician should conclude that another episode of the same illness is present. If past episodes are not informative, the diagnosis can rest on the temporal and psychological relation between the two phenomena (e.g., affective-type symptoms and schizophrenic-type symptoms). If one phenomenon can explain the other, the clinician need not resort to a schizoaffective diagnosis. A depressed patient may gradually isolate himself, feeling profoundly undeserving and unloved. A suspician that people do not like him may be transformed into a belief that people avoid him because of a foul odor and because his brain is signaling them to avoid the danger of his presence. The death of a friend is attributed to some dark force working through the patients' body without his intention. The emergence of this later symptomatology is not sufficient to dislodge the patient from an affective-disorder diagnosis if the early features of this illness give strong support to a depressive diagnosis.

6. A diagnosis of mania has many implications about one's past, future, treatment, biology, etc.—more, in fact, than most psychiatric diagnoses. This does not mean, however, that the diagnosis per se is a sufficient guide to a comprehensive treatment plan. In addition to the major role of lithium salts in treatment, the psychiatrist must consider a range of other interventions, including psychosocial techniques, family work occupational guidance, use of other medication in management, genetic counseling, and others.

Manic psychosis is an intriguing clinical phenomenon. Despite the wide variability in psychopathologic manifestation, mania is a more homogeneous disease entity than most psychiatric disorders. Manic patients share many features in common, including behavior, therapeutic response patterns, genetic vulnerability, course of illness, and some biochemical and psychophysiological attributes. Relative ease in identifying patients, together with cohort homogeneity, has made mania an attractive illness for study. Despite these features, important issues remain to be clarified relevant to nosology. We can anticipate progress in defining the limits to be implied by a manic diagnosis, in determining the relation of mania to other episodic psychoses, in assessing the validity of a schizoaffective (manic-type) category, and in determining the full range and pattern of course and outcome in mania.

REFERENCES

Abrams, R., and Taylor, M.A. Unipolar mania: A preliminary report. *Arch. Gen. Psychiat.* 30, 441–443 (1974).

Arieti, S. Affective disorders. In *American Handbook of Psychiatry.* S. Arieti, ed. Basic Books, New York (1974).

Astrup, C., and Noreik, K. *Functional Psychoses Diagnostic and Prognostic Models.* Charles C. Thomas, Springfield, Illinois (1966).

Baldessarini, R. Frequency of diagnosis of schizophrenia versus affective disorders from 1948 to 1968. *Am. J. Psychiat.* 127, 759–763 (1970).

Bleuler, E. *Textbook of Psychiatry.* Macmillan, New York (1924).

Bleuler, M. A 23-year longitudinal study of 208 schizophrenics and impressions in regard to the nature of schizophrenia. In *The Transmission of Schizophrenia* D. Rosenthal and S. Kety, eds. Pergamon, Oxford (1968).

Bratfos, O., and Hang, J.O. The course of manic depressive psychosis. *Acta Psychiat. Scand.* 44, 89–112 (1968).

Bromet, E., Harrow, M., and Kasl, W. Premorbid functioning and outcome in schizophrenics and nonschizophrenics. *Arch. Gen. Psychiat.* 30, 203–207 (1974).

Carlson, C.A., and Goodwin, F.K. The stages of mania: A longitudinal analysis of the manic episode. *Arch. Gen. Psychiat.* 28, 221–228 (1973).

Carpenter, W.T., Jr., Bartko, J.J., Strauss, J.S., and Hawk, A.B. Signs and symptoms as predictors of outcome: A report from the International Pilot Study for Schizophrenia. *Arch. Am. J. Psychiat.* 135, 940–945 (1978).

Carpenter, W.T., Jr., Gunderson, J.G., and Strauss, J.S. Considerations of the borderline syndrome: A longitudinal comparative study of borderline and schziophrnic patients. In *Borderline Personality Disorders: The Concept, The Syndrome, The Patient,* P. Hartocollis, ed. International Universities Press, New York (1977a).

Carpenter, W.T., Jr., Strauss, J.S., and Muleh, S. Are there pathognomonic symptoms in schizophrneia? An empiric investigation of Schneider's first-rank symptoms. *Arch. Gen. Psychiat.* 28, 847–852 (1973).

Carpenter, W.T., Jr., McGlashan, T.H., and Strauss, J.S. The treatment of acute schizophrenia without drugs: An investigation of some current assumptions. *Am. J. Psychiat.* 134, 14–20 (1977b).

Carpenter, W.T., Jr., and Strauss, J.S. Cross-cultural evaluation of Schneider's first-rank symptoms of schizophrenia: A report from the International Pilot Study of Schizophrenia. *Am. J. Psychiat.* 131, 682–687 (1974).

Corbett, L. Clinical differentiation of the schizophrenic and affective disorders: A comparison of the Bleulerian and phenomenologic approaches to diagnosis. In *Psychiatric Diagnosis: Explorations of Biological Predictors,* H.S. Akiskal, and W.L. Webb, eds. S.P. Medical and Scientific Books, New York (1978).

DSM-II Diagnostic and Statistical Manual of Mental Disorders. American Psychiatric Association, Washington (1968).

DSM-III Draft. American Psychiatric Association, Washington (1978).

Engel, G.L. The need for a new medical model: A challenge for biomedicine. *Science* 196, 129–136 (1977).

Falret, J.P. *Lecons.* Quoted in O. Koerner, Die Artzliche Kenntnisse, in *Ilias and Odysse* (1929).

Feighner, J.P., Robbins, E., Guze, S.B., Woodruff, R.A., Winokur, G., and Munoz, R. Diagnostic criteria for use in psychiatric research. *Arch. Gen. Psychiat.* 26, 57–63 (1972).

Feinstein, A.R. A critical overview of diagnosis in psychiatry. In *Psychiatric Diagnosis,* V.M. Rakoff, H.C. Stancer, and H.B. Kedward, eds. Brunner-Mazel, New York (1977).

Garmezy, V. Process and reactive schizophrenia: Some conceptions and issues. In *The Role and Methodology of Classification in Psychiatry and Psychopathology,* M. Katz, J. Cole, and W. Barton, eds. U.S. Government Printing Office, Washington (1968).

Grinker, R. Changing styles in psychotic and borderline states. *Am. J. Psychiat.* 130, 151–152 (1973).

Kendell, R.E. *The Role of Diagnosis in Psychiatry*. Blackwell Scientific, Oxford (1975).

Kraepelin, E. *Manic Depressive Insanity ad Paranoia*. Livingstone, Edinburgh (1921).

Lewin, K. The conflict between Aristotelian and Galilean modes of thought in contemporary pychology. *J. Gen. Psychiat.* 5, 141–177 (1931).

McCabe, M.S. Reactive psychoses: A clinical genetic investigation. *Acta Psychiat. Scand. Suppl. 259* (1975).

Morrison, J.R., and Flanagan, T.A. Diagnostic errors in psychiatry. *Comp. Psychiat.* 19, 109–117 (1978).

Monroe, R. *Episodic Behavioral Disorders: A Psychodynamic and Neurophysiologic Analysis*. Harvard Univ. Press (1970).

Perris, C., ed. A study of bipolar (manic depressive) and unipolar recurrent depressive psychoses. *Acta Psychiat. Scand. Supp. 194* (1966).

Perris, C. Course of depressive psychoses. *Acta Psychiat. Scand.* 44, 238–248 (1968).

Pollock, H.M. Recurrence of attacks in manic depressive psychoses. *Am. J. Psychiat.* 11, 567–574 (1931).

Pope, H.G., and Lipinski, J.F. Diagnosis in schizophrenia and manic depressive illness: A reassessment of the specificity of schizophrenic symptoms in the light of current research. *Arch. Gen. Psychiat.* 35, 811–828 (1978).

Rennie, T.A. Prognosis in manic depressive psychoses. *Am. J. Psychiat.* 98, 801–814 (1942).

Rosen, B., Klein, D.F., Levernstern, S., and Shahinian, S.P. Social competence and post-hospital outcome among schizophrenic and non-schizophrenic psychiatric patients. *J. Ab. Psychol.* 74, 401–404 (1969).

Schneider, K. *Clinical Psychopathology*. Translated by M.W. Hamilton. Grune & Stratton, New York (1959).

Sims, A. Factors predictive of outcome in neurosis. *Brit. J. Psychiat.* 127, 54–62 (1975).

Skodal, A., Buckley, P., and Salamon, P. The ubiquitous symptoms of schizophrenia. *Comp. Psychiat.* 17, 511–516 (1976).

Spitzer, R.L., Endicott, J., and Robbins, E. *Research Diagnostic Criteria (RDC)*. New York Biometrics Research, New York State Psychiatric Institute (1977).

Stephens, J.H. Long term prognosis and follow-up in schizophrenia. *Schiz. Bull.* 4, 25–47 (1978).

Stephens, J.H., Goldberg, J., Ota, K., and Carpenter, W.T. Hospitalized schizophrenics retrospectively diagnosed by six diagnostic systems (unpublished).

Strauss, J.S. Diagnostic models and the nature of psychiatric disorder. *Arch. Gen. Psychiat.* 29, 445–449 (1973).

Strauss, J.S., and Carpenter, W.T., Jr. The prediction of outcome in schizophrenia. II. Relationships between predictor and outcome variables: A report from the WHO International Pilot Study of Schizophrenia. *Arch. Gen. Psychiat.* 31, 37–42 (1974a).

Strauss, J.S., and Carpenter, W.T., Jr. Characteristic symptoms and outcome in schizophrenia. *Arch. Gen. Psychiat.* 30, 429–434 (1974b).

Strauss, J.S., Kokes, R.F., Carpenter, W.T., Jr., and Ritzler, B.Z. The course of schizophrenia as a developmental process. In *Nature of Schizophrenia: New Findings and Future Strategies*. L.C. Wynne, R.L. Cromwell, and S. Matthysse, eds. Wiley, New York (1978).

Tsuang, M.T., and Winokur, G. The Iowa 500: Field work in a 35-year follow-up of depression, mania, and schizophrenia. *Can. Psychiat. Assoc. J.* 20, 359–365 (1975).

Vaillant, G.E. The natural history of the remitting schizophrenias. *Am. J. Psychiat.* 120, 367–375 (1963).

Welner, A., Croughan, J., Fishman, R., and Robins, E. The group of schizoaffective and related psychoses: A follow-up study. *Comp. Psychiat.* 18, 413–421 (1977a).

Welner, A., Welner, Z., and Leonard, M. A. Bipolar manic-depressive disorder: A reassessment of course and outcome. *Comp. Psychiat.* 18, 327–332 (1977b).

Winokur, G. Natural history of the affective disorders (manias and depressions). *Sem. Psychiat.* 2, 451–463 (1970).

Winokur, G. The Iowa 500: Heterogeneity and course in manic depressive illness (bipolar). *Comp. Psychiat.* 16, 125–131 (1975).

Wittman, M.P., and Steinberg, L. Follow-up of objective evaluation of prognosis. *Elgin State Hospital Papers* 5, 216–227 (1944).

Wolpert, E. A., ed. *Manic Depressive Illness: History of a Syndrome.* International Universities Press, New York (1977).

World Health Organization. *Manual of the International Statistical Classification of Diseases, Injuries, and Causes of Death,* Vol. 1, 8th ed. World Health Organization, Geneva (1967).

Zilboorg, G. Manic depressive psychoses. In *Psychoanalysis Today,* S. Lorand, ed. International Universities Press, New York (1944).

CHAPTER 3

Diagnosis, Family, and Follow-up Studies

William Coryell and George Winokur

A major reason to delineate an illness and to determine its relationship to other illnesses is the practical usefulness of the final formulation. In the area of clinical management, a useful diagnosis allows the prediction of short- and long-term outcome, including response to various treatment interventions. In the area of psychiatric research, a useful diagnosis remains stable over time and can be externally validated by such findings as specific genetic factors. Of course, a prerequisite to the above is diagnostic reliability.

RELIABILITY

Mania may be considered an independent entity or part of a continuum including schizophrenia. Resolution of the question of which alternative is more useful requires several steps. The issue of diagnostic reliability is necessarily the first of these. Data from follow-up, treatment, or family studies that indicate that an independent concept of mania is most useful are meaningless if mania and schizophrenia are not reliably distinguished. Likewise, an argument in favor of schizoaffective illness as an autonomous third psychosis cannot be made if diagnosticians do not agree as to its presence.

A number of factors may influence apparent diagnostic reliability. One of the few studies attempting to quantify sources of unreliability concluded that two thirds of their disagreements using a DSM-II classification scheme were due to inadequacy of nosology as opposed to patient or diagnostician inconsistencies (Ward et al., 1962). Subsequent work has shown that this inadequacy can be corrected to a significant extent by the use of operational criteria (Spitzer et al., 1975b). Still other work has explored the effect on apparent reliability of the training of interviewers (Coryell et al., 1978), the structuring of interviews (Weitzel et al., 1973), and the design of reliability studies (Helzer et al., 1977).

Also important is the statistic with which reliability is expresses. Many current researchers in the area of reliability use the kappa statistic, which takes chance agreement into account (Helzer et al., 1976; Sandifer et al., 1964; Spitzer et al., 1976; Cloninger et al., 1978). Values for kappa range from 0 to 1.0, representing chance and perfect agreement respectively. Spitzer has suggested that kappa values exceeding 0.75 might be considered indicative of good reliability, and those below this value as indicative of fair (.50 to .75) or poor (less than .50) reliability) Spitzer et al., 1976). A low kappa value, then, indicates poor reliability but does not reveal the causes. These causes may involve factors other than nosology.

Several studies that in their design have taken these other factors into account have shown that mania and schizophrenia are among the psychiatric diagnoses that can be reliably assessed. Table 1 presents kappa values from several of these studies. These data indicate that mania can be diagnosed with a high degree of reliability, while figures for schizophrenia, though somewhat lower, are still in the fair to good range. Results from the two studies by Spitzer using RDC criteria indicate poor reliability for the diagnosis of schizoaffective disorder (Spitzer et al., 1975a; Spitzer et al., 1975b). The Helzer study did not incorporate such a category (Helzer et al., 1977). The fact, however, that the exclusion of undiagnosed patients (N = 30) markedly increased kappas for schizophrenia and affective disorders but not for the other diagnoses is evidence that the poor reliability of the undiagnosed category was mainly the result of problems in distinguishing atypical schizophrenia from atypical mania or depression.

Table 1. Kappa Values for Selected Diagnoses

	Study		
Diagnosis	Helzer et al., 1977 (N = 101)	Spitzer et al., 1975b (N = 120)	Spitzer et al., 1975b (N = 68)
Mania	.82	.83	.93
Schizophrenia	.58	.73	.80
Schizoaffective	—	.33	.48 (manic type)
Undiagnosed	.19	.45	—

FOLLOW-UP STUDIES

A continuum model incorporating at one extreme a manic syndrome(s) predictive of remission and at another a schizophrenic syndrome(s) featuring chronicity and often deterioration would, if useful, show in mixed states a quantitative relationship between the symptoms and courses characteristic of the extremes. In other words, in a case with symptoms of both schizophrenia and mania, a prognosis could be calculated from an algebraic sum of the respective symptoms, schizophrenic symptoms being weighted in one direction and manic symptoms in another. Alternatively, if the concept of schizophrenia and manic disorder as two or more discrete entities is preferable, then the outcome predicted by either syndrome would be relatively independent of admixtures from the other.

Few follow-up studies involving patients with both affective and schizophrenic symptoms have clearly distinguished patients with only manic symptoms from those with depressive symptoms past or present. There is, however, evidence that unipolar mania is neither common (Perris and d'Elia, 1966) nor autonomous from bipolar mania (Abrams and Taylor, 1974). One of the remaining difficulties in interpreting this literature, then, is the possibility that manic and depressive symptoms affect prognosis in a significantly different fashion. In fact, however, those studies that distinguish between manic and depressive symptoms show that they affect the likelihood of recovery in a similar direction. For these reasons, the effect on prognosis of affective symptoms inclusive of *both* mania and depression will be discussed unless the study in question allows more specifity.

Table 2 illustrates the varying degrees of success of efforts to define features of prognostic significance in the area of schizophrenia. The arbitrary label of "nontypical schizophrenia" used here subsumes a list of syndromes. These syndromes have in common the presence of features associated with the likelihood of remission, a prognosis not typical of schizophrenia as it has traditionally been defined. In addition to the variability of diagnostic nomenclature, follow-up length, and classification of follow-up status, the designs of these studies fall into several groups to be discussed below. Despite such differences among these studies, they have consistently demonstrated the beneficial effect of affective symptoms on prognosis in patients who also display schizophrenic symptoms.

Most authors have, at or near the time of follow-up, retrospectively assessed initial symptomatology. This method has obvious practical advantages. Unfortunately, the distribution of clinical features falsely rated as absent is unknown under these circumstances.

Some retrospective studies have assessed the prognostic value of large or unspecified numbers of factors. Stephens et al. (1966) assessed the ability of a possible 54 prognostic factors to differentiate between 50 good outcome and 50 poor outcome schizophrenics selected from a larger group of 350 patients given a clinical diagnosis of either schizophrenia or paranoid state. "Depression" and "guilt" were among the 11 factors to significantly differentiate the

Table 2.

Study	Follow-up Length	Term	N	Status (%)	Follow-up Category	Status (%)	N
						Typical Schizophrenia	
		Nontypical Schizophrenia					
Morrison et al., 1973	1–15 yrs x̄ = 3.2	Schizophreniform	289	22	Recovered ever	8	183
				40	Social recovery	19	
				51	Ill without remission	78	
				12	Deteriorated	13	
Johanson, 1958	10–18 yrs	Uncertain schizophrenia	27	42	0–1 (recovered)	2	82
				53	2–4	60	
				5	5–6 (deteriorated)	38	
Eitinger et al., 1958	5–15 yrs	Schizophreniform	44	23	Complete remission	0	110
				52	Much improved	2	
				14	Improved	10	
				23	No effect	88	
Clark and Mallett, 1963	3 yrs	Schizoaffective	17	18	Symptom-free	11	76
				29	Symptomatic	14	
				53	Rehospitalized	72	
Vaillant, 1964	2–15 yrs	Good prognosis		80	Remission	21	
				20	Invalidism	79	
Stephens and Astrup 1965	4–14	Nonprocess	120	96	Recovered or impaired	47	73
				4	Unimproved	53	
Vaillant, 1964	1–2	Good prognosis	28	64	Full remission	10	72
				25	Social remission or not schizophrenic	36	
					Schizophrenic and social-disabled	54	

two groups at the $p < .01$ level. Kant (1941) compared the presenting features of 39 "deteriorated" and 30 recovered schizophrenic patients. Though he did not directly discuss affective symptoms as the differentiating factors, he elsewhere proposed a subclassification of the recovered group (Kant, 1940). Only one classification, containing five cases with a catatonic picture, and one case with an "acute paranoid reaction" were not described as featuring prominent manic or depressive symptomatology.

A variation in the above design that has potential to further refine prediction involves the initial selection of subjects on the basis of presence of one or more signs of known prognostic value. Factors predicting outcomes that are favorable relative to others within this "good prognosis" group are then assessed. In a 6 to 18-year follow-up, Holmboe and Astrup (1957) selected 255 patients with Langfeldt process symptoms, and a time span between onset of the first psychotic symptom and hospitalization of less than six months. While blind to outcome, the authors assigned the patients to one of six groups on the basis of presenting symptoms. "Depression" and "excitation" syndromes comprised two of the three groups associated with a better outcome.

Affective symptoms have also been included in predetermined groups of clinical features then shown to have prognostic significance at follow-up. In a 4- to 14-year follow-up with a cohort of 334 inpatients possibly inclusive of patients cited in the above study, Stephens and Astrup (1965), while blind to outcome status, classified patients as process or nonprocess schizophrenics after Leonhardt. Traits consistent with nonprocess schizophrenia included presence of manic-depressive psychosis in near relatives, and in patients, "presence of symptoms resembling an affective disorder." Four percent of the nonprocess schiqophrenics were classified as unimproved on follow-up in contrast to 53% of the process group. Vaillant (1964), in a 2- to 15-year follow-up of 72 patients, correctly predicted outcome expressed dichotomously in over 80% of the cases. The seven prognostic signs used included "depressive symptoms" and a family history of psychotic depression.

In a prospective short-term study, Taylor and Abrams (1975) used the presence or absence of a number of nonaffective signs to describe good and poor prognosis groups. Thus, good prognosis patients had an onset of less than three months and two of a possible four features, including a precipitating event, clouded consciousness, broad affective range, and/or a good premorbid adjustment. Their good prognosis group (N = 64), with a remission or marked improvement rate at time of discharge of 84%, met criteria for mania in 50% of the cases. The poor prognosis group (N = 24) had only 17% marked improvement rate and satisfied criteria for mania in only 12% of cases. In another short-term prospective study Vaillant (1964) again tested the prognostic value of seven "good prognostic" criteria with a cohort of 103. The success rate was almost identical to that obtained with a long-term retrospective study cited above.

Croughan et al. (1974) examined the quantitative effect of affective symptoms in a more direct manner. In a retrospective chart study, they discussed 204 consecutive admissions with a discharge diagnosis of "schizo-affective," "schizo-phreniform" or "related disorder" and two or more items from a list of psychotic thought and behavior symptoms. The course of illness was considered "discernible" in 54% of the cases. These patients tended to have an unremitting course whether or not they had a quantity of affective symptoms sufficient to meet Feighner criteria. A 5-year follow-up of the 63% of this cohort within a 10-mile radius substantiated this finding (Welner et al., 1977). The average length of illness at index admission for the original group, however, was approximately 7½ years. It is quite possible that substantial chronicity is a more powerful predictor of subsequent chronicity than are affective symptoms in such patients.

The weight of the evidence, then, indicates that the presence of affective symptoms in individuals otherwise designated as schizophrenic alters the prognosis in a direction characteristic of affective illness. Though this might be taken as evidence supporting a continuum concept, it might also be considered an argument for redefining the boundaries of affective and schizophrenic illness as discrete entities. Resolution of this dilemma in terms of follow-up data requires a series of additional pieces of evidence. Do schizophrenic symptoms in the presence of an otherwise affective syndrome result likewise in a corresponding decrease in likelihood of remission? If so, is the relationship between quantity of schizophrenic symptoms and corresponding prognosis discontinuous? If such quantitative symptomatic thresholds cannot be demonstrated, boundaries for discrete entities cannot be defined, and evidence would favor the continuum concept as most useful. There are several follow-up studies that incorporate groups with varying mixtures of schizophrenic and affective symptoms. They fail, however, to answer the above questions satisfactorily for reasons cited below.

A follow-up study involving the "Iowa 500" group of patients showed the course of 284 patients with "schizophreniform illness" to be intermediate in terms of recovery over a 2 to 18-year period between that of schizophrenia and affective disorder, both unipolar and bipolar (Morrison et al., 1973). This group, however, was comprised of individuals with discharge chart diagnoses of schizophrenia who failed to meet the fairly restrictive Feighner critera. The presence of affective symptoms, inadequate duration, and a prior history of alcoholism are all incompatible with these criteria. Subsequently, a subgroup of 84 of the original 284 schizophreniform patients were designated as "atypical schizophrenia" by the presence of either affective symptoms or a previous episode of remitting psychiatric illness (Tsuang et al., 1976). Outcome for this group differed significantly from that for the schizophreniform and schizophrenia groups in terms of percent recovered (see Table 3). The difference between the bipolar affective disorder group and the atypical schizophrenia group failed to reach significant levels, however. Because of the sampling criteria used, the "atypical schizophrenics" here represent for the most part the schizophreniform cases excluded from the schizophrenia category on the basis of affective symptomatology and inadequate duration. On the other hand, most "atypical" cases were excluded from an affective disorder category because of inadequate duration only and not because of schizophrenic symptomatology* (a minimum duration of one month was required). Within the discrete entity concept, then, these data can be considered supportive of both a narrower definition of schizophrenia and a broader definition of affective disorder than those used by the psychiatric staff at Iowa Psychopathic Hospital between 1934 and 1944. Since the relative quantities of schizophrenic symptoms in the affective disorder and "atypical" groups are not given, however, no conclusions can be drawn for or against a continuum concept.

Table 3.

Diagnostic Group	N	% Recovered Ever		
Bipolar A.D.	87	54		
			NS	
Atypical schizophrenia*	85	44		
			$p < .05$	$p < .001$
Schizophreniform	284	22		
		$p < .05$		
Schizophrenia	183	8		

*Subsample of schizophreniform group.

It should be emphasized that data used in the above two studies were obtained exclusively from chart review. Results, therefore, are tentative. Ongoing 30- to 40-year personal follow-up data considering several different outcome categories are consistent with the above findings (M. Tsuang, personal communication). With the exception of occupational disability, outcome values for the atypical schizophrenia group consistently resemble those for the bipolar affective disorder group more than those for the schizophrenia group. The prognosis for the atypical schizophrenia group, however, is also consistently worse than that for the bipolar group. Reasons for this finding remain unclear.

There is little additional information of relevance available from studies exclusively concerned with prognosis of the affective disorders. As mentioned

---

*Personal communication.

previously, many of the earlier studies did not distinguish bipolar from unipolar patients. Robins and Guze (1972) reviewed 21 studies with follow-ups of at least one year, and found only three in which this distinction had been made (Perris and d'Elia, 1966; Rennie, 1942; Lundquist, 1945). Two of these studies employed a somewhat circular design in which the typicality of the course subsequent to initial evaluation influenced the selection of follow-up material (Perris and d'Elia, 1966; Lundquist, 1945). Other workers presented data on follow-up studies of bipolar patients selected without reference to follow-up course, but did not specifically address clinical features predictive of chronic symptomatology or social impairment (Morrison et al., 1973; Lundquist, 1945). MacDonald (1918), in an early follow-up study of 451 patients including 152 manics, implicated age of onset, duration of index episode, and "innate constitutional defects" as factors relevant to chronicity, but did not mention possible relevance of other clinical features. The design and length of follow-up was not specified. In a discussion of 12 manics with duration exceeding 5 years selected from a review of 2,000 cases of mania, Wertham (1928) stated that those patients lacked "an admixture of constitutional schizophrenic features." He cited, without reference to data, a "manic constitution" and "psychobiological rigidity" as possible predictors of chronic mania. Other authors have reported their clinical impression that cyclothymia is associated with chronicity in affective illness (Kraepelin, 1921).

The extensive literature on "good prognosis schizophrenia," then, is not balanced in quantity by work concerning "poor prognosis mania." This may be the result of traditional diagnostic practices that have weighed various features thought to implicate schizophrenia more heavily than coexisting affective symptoms in given patients. Presumably, as a result of such findings as those listed above, more recently developed definitions of these illnesses tend to assign more importance to affective symptoms in arriving at the final diagnosis. Several studies have demonstrated the resulting overlap between concepts of "good prognosis schizophrenia" and affective illness, operationally defined. McCabe et al. (1972) screened consecutive admissions for subjects having an acute onset and at least one schizophrenic symptom as defined by Langfeldt. These criteria have been used by a number of studies to define schizophrenic groups (Clayton et al., 1968; Johanson, 1958; Stephens et al., 1966). Subjects were divided into good and poor prognostic groups on the basis of length of onset and premorbid features. By research criteria (Feighner et al., 1972), 68% of the good prognosis group had a present or previous depression, while 46% had an ongoing or previous mania. Corresponding figures in the poor prognosis group were 12% and 0%. Taylor, as mentioned above, presented similar findings using admission diagnoses of residents to obtain the "schizophrenic" samples (Taylor and Abrams, 1975).

Other work has shown that various sets of recently developed operational criteria have classified a number of individuals as having affective disorder who also display symptoms that might have earned them the status of schizophrenic by more traditional diagnostic methods. Abrams and Taylor (1976) collected 55 patients from consecutive admissions on the basis of the presence of at least one symptom of catatonia, a state traditionally associated with schizophrenia. The authors diagnosed 62% of these patients as having mania and 5% as having depression by their research criteria. In a similar study involving a consecutive series of 117 hallucinated patients, Goodwin et al. (1971) classified 28 as having affective disorder by criteria of Cassidy et al. (1957) and Clayton et al. (1965). One half of these patients reported two or more voices discussing them. Finally, Schneiderian first-rank symptoms, at one time advanced as pathonomic for schizophrenia, were found in 23% of patients classified as manic by IPC criteria in the International Pilot Study for schizophrenia (Carpenter and Strauss, 1974).

Factors other than the development of sets of operational criteria influence diagnostic practices. Kendell demonstrated marked differences in the rate of diagnoses of affective disorder between Britain and America before operational criteria came into wide use in either country (Kendall et al., 1971). Baldessarini (1970) studied the rates of diagnoses of schizophrenia and mania depressive illness at one hospital over a 25-year period, and noted that these rates fluctuated markedly in a reciprocal fashion. One of two marked increases in the diagnostic rate of mania coincided with the advent of lithium therapy.

Efforts to bring existing follow-up literature to bear on the mania/schizophrenia continuum issue, therefore, are vastly confounded by nosological confusion. The literature is, in addition, inadequate in scope and awaits the demonstration of the effect, or lack of it, of schizophrenia-like symptoms on outcome in individuals otherwise meeting criteria for mania.

DIAGNOSTIC STABILITY

If mania and schizophrenia represent quantitative or qualitative variations of a single more general illness, as the continuum model would imply, then the number of individuals manifesting symptoms of mania at one end of the continuum would be likely to contain significant numbers of individuals who at another point in time would manifest a schizophrenic syndrome. This would at least be suggested by analogy with syndrome manifestations of such continuum illnesses in medicine as diabetes or neurosyphilis.

The small amount of literature available on this subject suggests that such diagnostic instability is unusual. The rate of diagnostic revision is consistently low across several studies (see Table 4). Lundquist (1945), in a 10-1 to 30-year follow-up of manic patients, cited only nine cases requiring diagnostic revision to schizophrenia on follow-up. Of the 100 manic patients so diagnosed by research criteria in the Iowa 500 series mentioned above, 66 had inpatient or outpatient follow-up spanning one year or more at the same institution, and in only six cases was there a subsequent revision of diagnosis to schizophrenia (Winokur, 1974). Coryell subsequently examined diagnostic revision in all patients admitted to the same hospital between the years 1920 and 1971 receiving, during any admission, the diagnosis of mania. Of the 94 patients (such patients with more than one admission), the diagnosis of mania was followed by the diagnosis of schizophrenia in eight cases (unpublished data).

Table 4.

Study	N	Length of Follow-up	% Manics with Subsequent Diagnosis of Schizophrenia
Lundquist, 1945	103	10–30 yrs	9%
Winokur, 1974	66	1–20 yrs	9%
Coryell*	94	1–26 yrs	8%

Unpublished data.

FAMILY STUDIES

Given the lack of other external validators for use in the formulation of psychiatric disease concepts, data from family history studies have special relevance. A number of the expectations following logically from either the discrete entity concept or the continuum concept can be tested against existing data.

Failure to find strong diagnostic concordance between probands and first-degree relatives would be inconsistent with the discrete entity concept. If such concordance was found, then certain patterns might nevertheless suggest the appropriateness of a continuum concept. For instance, if mania and schizophrenia were considered respectively to be milder and more severe expressions of the same underlying illness, then a polygenetic theory of transmission would predict that more mania would be found in the families of schizophrenics than in the families of manics. Findings by Winokur et al. (1972) in a study involving the Iowa 500 group mentioned above are inconsistent with these formulations. These authors made diagnoses of first-degree relatives from family history information originally obtained by admitting physicians. Efforts were made to avoid bias in these assessments by previous removal of information as to sex, diagnosis, outcome, or year of admission. The distinction between schizophrenia and affective illness in family members was made on the basis of age of onset and apparent course of illness. There were significant associations between proband diagnoses and family history of morbid risk for the same illness for both schizophrenic and affective disorder probands (see Table 5). Furthermore, neither the morbidity risk for affective disorder in the family members of schizophrenic probands nor that for schizophrenia in the family members of affective disorder probands exceeded population prevalences for these illnesses. Evidence against operation of a "halo effect" in the original collection of family history data is the fact that more affective disorder than schizophrenia was found in the primary relatives of schizophrenic probands.

Table 5. Illness Among First-Degree Relatives

Proband Diagnosis	Schizophrenia		Affective Disorder	
	N	Morbid Risk %	N	Morbid Risk %
Schizophrenia (N = 200)	13	2.11	32	5.50
Mania (N = 100)	5	1.15	37	11.28
Unipolar depression N = 225)	5	.41	123	14.32
All 1° A.D. (N = 325)	10	.62	160	13.50

In harmony with the conclusions of many follow-up studies, familial patterns of probands with nontypical schizophrenia suggest that such syndromes are more closely allied to the affective disorders than to schizophrenia. Table 6 presents data from several studies comparing the family histories of typical and nontypical schizophrenic probands in terms of respective morbidity risk for schizophrenia and affective disorder among first-degree relatives. Typical and nontypical schizophrenics are consistently distinguished by the morbidity risk for affective disorder in their respective families. The first two studies also gave family history patterns for probands with affective disorder (Tsuang et al., 1976; Tsuang et al., 1977). When these patterns were compared with those of the nontypical schizophrenic families, no significant differences were noted in morbidity risk for either schizophrenia or affective disorder. The fact that morbidity risk for schizophrenia rarely distinguishes proband groups may reflect a combination of diagnostic heterogeneity among proband groups and the overall low incidence of schizophrenia across all family groups. Selection criteria by McCabe et al. required that poor prognosis schizophrenics have at least a two-year duration of illness and a poor premorbid adjustment (McCabe et al., 1971). The resulting group of patients was probably more homogeneous than the schizophrenics satisfying Feighner criteria used in other studies, and therefore more strongly associated with a family history of schizophrenia.

Table 6. Differences in Morbidity Risks for First-Degree Relatives When Typical and Nontypical Schizophrenics are Compared

Proband Diagnosis (N)	Schizophrenia	Affective Disorder
Atypical schizophrenia (85) vs. schizophrenia (200) (Tsuang et al., 1976)	N.S.	$P < .001$
Schizoaffective (53) vs. schizophrenia (200) (Tsuang et al., 1977)	N.S.	$p < .001$
Good prognosis (53) vs. poor prognosis (25) (McCabe et al., 1971)	$p < .027$	$p < .0048$

Other workers have used population prevalence for purposes of comparison. Welner and Stromgren (1958) investigated 315 siblings in a group of 71 schizophreniform probands, so designated on the basis of good outcome. The rate of schizophrenia was significantly lower than the lowest rate among siblings of typical schizophrenics cited in other studies.

The consistency of conclusions of this and other work dealing with family studies of subjects with nontypical schizophrenic syndromes is more remarkable when the lack of constancy in the definitions of such syndromes between studies is considered. Welner and Stromgren (1958) included selected patients "presenting several common schizophrenic symptoms" with an absence of "autism." The Iowa 500 cohort included only those patients satisfying Feighner et al. criteria (1972) while Tsuang et al. (1977) used DSM-II criteria to define schizoaffective illness. The good prognosis probands of McCabe et al. (1971) and Fowler (1972) all had at least one symptom of a possible 11 considered indicative of schizophrenia by Astrup and Noreik (1966), in addition to an acute onset and good premorbid history. Taylor and Abrams (1975) used the diagnosis of admitting residents plus several other nonaffective prognostic factors. Finally, Clayton et al. (1968) required probands to satisfy the concept of schizophrenia as defined by Langfeldt, in addition to having at least one affective symptom. All of these authors concluded that the family history of patients so described suggested an association with affective disorder rather than with schizophrenia.

A THIRD PSYCHOSIS

A review of the relevant follow-up literature has failed to provide adequate evidence that either the continuum or the discrete entity concept is the more useful prognostically. This failure may, of course, be due to insufficiencies listed above. There are several reasons to believe that work with more power to resolve this issue is forthcoming. One is the recent growth of attention paid to nosological clarity. Another is the increased pressure to rigorously study the functional psychoses, which has, at least in part, resulted from the relatively recent development of more effective and specific therapies.

The data presented regarding diagnostic stability and genetics are clearly more harmonious with the discrete entity concept. Certain of these data, however, suggest that the "discrete entities" as they are presently defined warrant revision pending further information. A significant and fairly consistent proportion of manics subsequently becomes schizophrenic (Table 4). Family history studies indicate that affective and atypical schizophrenic cohorts may be contaminated with "process" schizophrenia. Given the patterns of past findings and follow-up studies, it is unlikely that nosological and design rigor employed in the future studies will eliminate outcome heterogeneity within diagnostic entities. It is possible that the addition of a third entity will be necessary to further reduce such heterogeneity.

A number of authors have made cases for reactive psychosis as a separate illness. While this entity may eventually gain wider acceptance, it appears unlikely that it will be applicable to syndromes resembling mania. Winokur et al. (1969) reviewed the few reported cases of "reactive mania" and found them for the most part to be attributable to organic factors. McCabe (1975), in a relatively recent and comprehensive study of reactive psychosis, chose to include the presence or past history of mania as one of his exclusion criteria.

Leonhard chose the term "cycloid psychoses" to distinguish a group of syndromes distinct from manic-depressive illness or schizophrenia (Leonhard, 1960). Later, Perris (1974) chose the same term, while Mitsuda (1967, 1972) used "atypical schizophrenia" to designate somewhat similar syndromes. Among the features common to these three descriptions are the frequent presence of affective symptoms (both mania and depression), an episodic course, an acute onset, presence of precipitating factors, and a clouding of consciousness. All three authors have asserted that this third psychosis breeds true. Out of 26 monozygotic schizophrenic twin pairs collected by Mitsuda,

14 were concordant for any schizophrenia. Seven pairs were composed of "typical" cases and seven other pairs were composed of "atypical" or "intermediate" schizophrenia cases. There were no twin pairs containing both an atypical or intermediate schizophrenia case and a typical case. Unfortunately, none of these authors have explicitly stated inclusion and exlusion criteria, nor have they made diagnostic assignments of family members while blind to proband diagnosis.

The category of "undiagnosed" is available for designating those patients who fall outside of the concepts of mania and schizophrenia being used. This category has the major disadvantage of conveying only the information that the subject so diagnosed did not fit the clinician's classification system. There is some evidence that manic syndromes are unlikely to be designated as undiagnosed in clinical practice. Welner applied research criteria to 263 inpatient charts carrying a discharge diagnosis of "undiagnosed" (Welner, 1972). Of the 173 charts receiving a research diagnosis, only six were manic. In regards to schizophrenia, it has been shown that the more restrictive diagnostic systems leave large numbers of psychotic patients undiagnosed (Morrison et al., 1973). The recent development of explicit criteria for schizoaffective illness found in the RDC (Spitzer et al., 1975a) is likely to allow an increase rate of classification of such patients. Whether this designation in reality conveys more information of prognostic significance than the category of "undiagnosed" remains to be seen. The possibility that it might, however, seems to justify its provisional use.

REFERENCES

Abrams, R., and Taylor, M.A. Unipolar mania. *Arch. Gen. Psychiat.* 30, 441–443 (1974).
Abrams, R., and Taylor, M.A. Catatonia: A progressive clinical study. *Arch. Gen. Psychiat.* 33, 579–581 (1976).
Astrup, C., and Noreik, F. *Functional Psychosis.* Charles C. Thomas, Springfield, Illinois (1966), pp. 133–134.
Baldessrini, R.J. Frequency of diagnoses of schizophrenia versus affective disorders form 1944 to 1968. *Am. J. Psychiat.* 127, 759–763 (1970).
Carpenter, W.T., and Strauss, T.S. Cross-cultural evaluation of Schneider's first-rank symptoms of schizophrenia: A report the International Pilot Study of Schizophrenia. *Am. J. Pschiat.* 136, 6 (1974).
Cassidy, W.L., Flanagen, N.B., Spellman, M., and Cohen, M. Clinical observations in manic-depressive illness. *JAMA* 164, 1535–1546 (1957).
Clark, J.A., and Mallett, B.L. A follow-up study of schizophrenia and depression in young adults. *Brit. J. Psychiat.* 109, 491–499 (1963).
Clayton, P.J., Pitts, F.N., Jr., and Winokur, G. Affective disorder. IV. Mania. *Compr. Psychiat.* 6, 313–322 (1965). Clayton, P.J., Robin , L., and Winokur, G. Family history studies. III.

Schizoaffective disorder, clinical and genetic factors including a one to two year follow-up. *Compr. Psychiat.* 9, 31–49 (1968).

Cloninger, C.R., Miller, J.P., Wette, R., Martin, R.L., and Guze, S. The evaluation of diagnostic concordance in follow-up studies. I. A general model of causal analysis and a methodological critique. *J. Psychiat. Res.* (submitted for publication, 1978).

Coryell, W., Cloninger, C.R., and Reich, T. Diagnostic reliability: Use of non-physician interviewers. *J. Nerv. Ment. Dis.,* (in press, 1978).

Croughan, J.L., Welner, A., and Robins, E. The group of schizoaffective and related psychosis—critique, record, follow-up and family studies. II. Record studies. *Arch. Gen. Psychiat.* 31, 632–637 (1974).

Eitinger, L., Laane, C.L., and Langfeldt, G. The prognostic value of the clinical picture and the therapeutic value of physical treatment in schizophrenia and the schizophreniform states. *Acta Psychiat. Neurol. Scand.* 33, 33–53 (1958).

Feighner, J.P., Robins, E., Guze., Woodruff, R.A., Winokur, G., and Munoz, R. Diagnostic criteria for use in psychiatric research. *Arch. Gen. Psychiat.* 26, 57–63 (1972).

Fowler, R.C., McCabe, M.S., Cadoret, R.J., and Winokur, G. The validity of good prognosis schizophrenia. *Arch. Gen. Psychiat.* 26, 182–185 (1972).

Goodwin, D.W., Alderson, P., and Rosenthal, R. Clinical significance of hallucinations in psychiatric disorders. *Arch. Gen. Psychiat.* 24, 76–80 (1971).

Hawk, A.B., Carpenter, W.T., and Strauss, J.S. Diagnostic criteria and five-year outcome in schizophrenia. *Arch. Gen. Psychiat.* 32, 343–347 (1975).

Helzer, J.E., Clayton, P.J., Pambakian, R., Reich, T., Woodruff, R.A., and Reveley, M.A. Reliability of psychiatric diagnosis. II. The test/retest reliability of diagnostic classification. *Arch. Gen. Psychiat.* 34, 136–141 (1977).

Helzer, J.E., Robins, L.N., Taibleson, M., Woodruff, R.A., Reich, T., and Wish, E.D. Reliability of psychiatric diagnosis. I. A methodological review. *Arch. Gen. Psychiat.,* (Submitted March 19, 1976).

Holmbee, R., and Astrup, C. A follow-up study of 255 patients with acute schizophrenia and schizophreniform psychoses. *Acta Psychiat. Neurol. Scand. Suppl. 115*32, 11–16 (1957).

Johanson, E. A study of schizophrenia in the male. *Acta Psychiat. Neurol. Suppl. 125* 33, 23–47 (1958).

Kant, O. Types and analyses of the clinical pictures of recovered schizophrenics. *Psychiat. Quart.* 14, 676–694 (1940).

Kant,O. A comparative study of recovered and deteriorated schizophrenic patients. *J. Nerv. Ment. Dis.* 93, 616–624 (1941).

Kendell, R.E., Cooper, J.E., Gourlay, A.J., Copeland, J.R.M., Sharpe, L., and Gurland, B.J. Diagnostic criteria of American and British psychiatrists. *Arch. Gen. Psychiat.* 25, 123–130 (1971).

Kraepelin, E. *Manic Depressive Insanity and Paranoia.* Arno, New York (1921), pp. 159–164.

Leonhard, K. Die atypische psychosen und kleist lehre von den endogenen psychosen. In *Psychiatrie der Gagenwart,* Vol. II, H.W. Gruhle, R. Jung, W. Mayer-Gross, and M. Muller, eds. Springer, Berlin (1960), p. 147.

Lundquist, G. Prognosis and course in manic-depressive psychoses. A follow-up study of 319 first admissions. *Acta Psychiat. Neurol. Suppl. 35* (1945).

MacDonald, J.B. Prognosis in manic-depressive insanity. *J. Nerv. Ment. Dis.* 47, 20–30 (1918).

McCabe, M.S. Reactive psychoses. *Acta Psychiat. Scand. Suppl. 259* (1975).

McCabe, M.S., Fowler, R.C., Cadoret, R.J., and Winokur, G. Familial differences in schizophrenia with good and poor prognosis. *Psychol. Med.* 1, 326–332 (1971).

McCabe, M.S., Fowler, R.C., Cadoret, R.J., and Winokur, G. Symptom differences in schizophrenia with good and poor prognosis. *Am. J. Psychiat.* 128, 1239–1243 (1972).

Mitsuda, H. *Clinical Genetics in Psychiatry.* Igaku-Shoin, Tokyo (1967), pp. 68–74.

Mitsuda, H. Heterogeneity of schizophrenia. In *Genetic Factors in Schizophrenia,* A.R. Kaplan, ed. Charles C. Thomas, Springfield, Illinois (1972).

Morrison, J., Winokur, G., Crowe, R., and Clancy, J. The Iowa 500. The first follow-up. *Arch. Gen. Psychiat.* 29, 678–682 (1973).

Perris, C. A study of cycloid psychoses. *Acta Psychiat. Scand. Suppl. 253* (1974).

Perris, C., and d'Elia, G. A study of bipolar (manic-depressive) and unipolar recurrent depressive psychoses. *Acta Psychiat. Scand. Suppl. 194* 153–165 (1966).

Rennie, T.A. Prognosis in manic-depressive psychoses. *Am. J. Psychiat.* 98, 801–814 (1942).

Robins, E., and Guze, S.B. Classification of affective disorders: The primary-secondary, the endogenous-reactive, and the neurotic-psychotic concepts. In *Recent Advances in the Psychobiology of the Depressive Illnesses: Proceedings of a Workshop Sponsored by the NIMH,* T.A. Williams, M.D. Katz, and J.A. Shield, Jr., eds. U.S. Government Printing Office (1972).

Sandifer, M.G., Pettus, C., and Quade, D. A study of psychiatric diagnosis. *J. Nerv. Ment. Dis.* 139, 350–356 (1964).

Spitzer, R.L., Endicott, J., and Robins, E. Clinical criteria for psychiatric diagnosis and DSM-II. *Am. J. Psychiat.* 132, II (1975a).

Spitzer, R.L., Endicott, J., Robins, E., Kuriansky, J., and Gurland, B. Preliminary report of the reliability of research diagnostic criteria (RDC) applied to psychiatric case records. In *Psychopharmacology,* S. Gershon, and R. Beer, eds. Raven, New York (1975b), pp. 1–47.

Spitzer, R.L, Fleiss, J.L., and Endicott, J. Problems of classification: Reliability and validity. Presented at the meeting of the American College of Neuropsychopharmacology, New Orleans, December (1976).

Stephens, J.H., and Astrup, C. Treatment outcome in "process" and "non-process" schizophrenics treated by "A" and "B" types of therapists. *J. Nerv. Ment. Dis.* 140, 449–456 (1965).

Stephens, J.H., Strup, C., and Mangrum, J.C. Prognostic factors in recovered and deteriorated schizophrenics. *Am. J. Psychiat.* 122, 116–1121 (1966).

Taylor, M.T., and Abrams, R. Manic-depressive illness and good prognosis schizophrenia. *Am. J. Psychiat.* 132, 741–742 (1975).

Tsuang, M.T., Dempsey, G.M., Dvoredsky, A., and Struss, A. A family history study of schizo–affective disorder. *Biol. Psychiat.* 12, 331–338 (1977).

Tsuang, M.T., Dempsey, G.M., and Rauscher, F. A study of "atypical schizophrenia". *Arch. Gen. Psychiat.* 33, 1157–1160 (1976).

Vaillant, G.E. Prospective prediction of schizophrenic remission. *Arch. Gen. Psychiat.* 11, 509–518 (1964).

Ward, C.H., Beck, A.T., Mendelson, M., Mock, J.E., and Erbaugh, J.K. The psychiatric nomenclature: Reasons for disagreement. *Arch. Gen. Psychiat.* 7, 60–67 (1962).

Weitzel, W.D. Morgan, D.W., Guyden, T.E., and Robinson, J.A. Toward a more efficient mental status examination: Free-form or operationally defined. *Arch. Gen. Psychiat.* 28, 215–218 (1973).

Welner, A., Croughan, J., Fishman, R., and Robins, E. The group of schizo-affective and related psychoses: A follow-up study. *Compr. Psychiat.* 18, 413–422 (1977).

Welner, A., Liss, J.L., and Richardson, M. Undiagnosed psychiatric patients. *Brit. J. Psychiat.* 120, 315–319 (1972).

Welner, A., and Stromgren, E. Clinical and genetic studies on benign schizophreniform psychoses based on a follow-up. *Acta Psychiat. Neurol.* 33, 377–399 (1958).

Wertham, F.I. A group of benign chronic psychoses: Prolonged manic excitements. With a statistical study of age, duration and frequency in 2000 manic attacks. *Am. J. Psychiat.* 9, 13–78 (1928).

Winokur, G. Diagnostic stability over time in schizophrenia, mania and depression. *New Eng. J. Med.* 290, 1027 (1974).

Winokur, G., Clayton, P., and Reich, T. *Manic-Depressive Illness.* C.V. Mosby, St. Louis (1969).

Winokur, G., Morrison, J., Clancy, J., and Crowe, R. The Iowa 500. II. A blind family history comparison of mania, depression, and schizophrenia. *Arch. Gen. Psychiat.* 27, 462–464 (1972).

CHAPTER 4

Twin Studies and Dual Mating Studies in Defining Mania

Margit Fischer

In psychiatry, diagnoses are based mainly on symptoms and to a certain extent on the course. The typical manic patient has elated mood, psychomotor overactivity, and lack of normal inhibitions. The clinical picture can vary from a somewhat elated, overtalkative person with a lot of brilliant ideas to a person who is in constant activity, hardly sleeps, spends money, buys thing, writes letters. Occasionally he might be violent and sometimes he has delusions, often of a megalomaniac type. It has most often a fairly acute onset and an episodic course with full remission between episodes (which may include severe depressions). Similarly, one could describe the typical schizophrenic patient as a person with thought disorder of various kinds, feeling somebody or something is influencing his mind, sometimes with paranoid delusions, often hallucinated, a person who gradually loses drive and initiative, and becomes emotionally isolated. His behavior may become bizarre and his movements stereotyped. Often the onset is insidious, and the course shows several psychotic episodes with only partial remissions. Around the "typical" patient are a cluster of patients with a fairly similar clinical picture, but we also find patients with some typical schizophrenic symptoms as well as clearly affective symptoms, the so-called schizoaffective or atypical psychoses.

Different studies have used slightly different criteria for the diagnosis of schizophrenia and manic-depressive psychosis, but to an extent the delineation is arbitrary and some variation unavoidable. A more widespread and consistent difference in criteria can make it impossible to compare studies from different countries. The U.S.-U.K. study (Kramer, 1961; Cooper at al., 1969) demonstrated some of these differences.

Diabetes mellitus may illustrate the complex relationship between etiology and symptoms. The initial symptoms are often tiredness, increased thirst, polyuria, loss of weight, and pruritus. With our present knowledge, an examination of sugar in blood and urine will give the diagnosis. We can also relate and explain some of the symptoms, such as the thirst, polyuria, and loss of weight, as a direct effect of the insufficient production of insulin in the Langerhans islands. We have here a clear link between symptoms and pathology. However, the relationship between etiology and symptoms is more obscure. The lack of production of insulin could be genetically determined, but the same symptoms would appear if the pancreas were destroyed by an infection or a tumor. The relationship between the late-coming symptoms (e.g., blindness) and etiology is even more complex.

If we translate this into psychiatry, it means that some symptoms may be the direct effect of a specific brain pathology. For instance, the psychomotor overactivity in mania could be caused by malfunction of some specific cell. Some of the other manic symptoms may also be directly related to this malfunction, while others may develop as a consequence of the primary symptoms. Similarly, one could imagine some typical schizophrenic symptoms as related to a specific pathology. In both cases, the specific malfunction could be genetically determined or caused by a brain abnormality.

FAMILY STUDIES

Family studies give empirical risk figures for relatives of probands with a specific disorder. Family studies do not separate the chromosomal inheritance from the social inheritance, and can therefore not prove whether a specific disease is genetically determined.

Table 1 shows the incidence of psychoses in relatives of manic-depressive probands (Zerbin-Rüdin, 1967). In the table unipolar and bipolar manic-depressives were not separated, but combined figures from Angst (1966) and Perris (1966) show that the incidence of affective psychoses in siblings of

Table 1. Incidence of Psychoses in Relatives of Manic-Depressive Probands

	Manic-Depressive	Schizophrenia
Parents	10–13%	0.5%
Siblings		
a. Both parents normal	5–7%	1%
b. One parent manic-depressive	15–20%	1%
Children	10–15%	2%

bipolar probands was 22%, and only 13% in siblings of unipolar depressive probands.

Angst (1966) included in his examination 73 probands with schizoaffective psychosis (Misch-psychosen). He underlines that the mixture is in symptomatology more than in etiology. Those who started with depressive symptomatology and ended up having a schizophrenic picture were genetically close to schizophrenic probands. Those who started with a schizophrenic symptomatology and later developed manic-depressive psychosis seemed to be a mixture of manic-depresseve and schizophrenic as far as the etiology is concerned, determined by examination of relatives. Taken together, it showed that the incidence of psychoses in parents and siblings was manic-depressive 6%, schizophrenia 7%, schizoaffective 7%.

Table 2. Offspring of Two Psychotic Parents (After Elsässer, 1952)

Diagnosis† of Parents	Total Offspring*	Schiz.	Man.-Depr.	Atyp.	?
S × S (34 pairs)	96	30	—	—	—
M × M (20 pairs)	47	2	21	1	3
S × M (19 pairs)	68	12	12	1	3
A × S (23 pairs)	91	9	2	3	2
A × M (21 pairs)	55	—	11	9	—
A × A (17 pairs)	67	8	9	16	3

*Older than age 16.
†S = schizophrenic; M = manic-depressive; A = atypical.

DUAL MATING STUDIES

A special kind of family studies is the examination of offspring of two psychotic parents. Table 2 shows results of Elsässer's study (1952), based on Schulz (1940) and Kahn (1923) and his own probands. It appears from the table that all psychotic children of two schizophrenic parents are schizophrenic, and nearly all psychotic children of manic-depressive parents are manic-depressive. The mating schizophrenia + manic-depressive gives the result that half of the psychotic children are manic-depressive and the other half schizophrenic. Matings where one of the parents has an atypical psychosis give a more varied result, and the mating of two atypical psychoses shows that some of the children are schizophrenic, some manic-depressive, and some atypical. From the total material it appears that approximately 25% of the offspring were psychotic, another 25% had nonpsychotic syndromes, and around 50% were normal. Some bias cannot be excluded, as the examiner was not "blind," but the results as they are indicate strongly that the two major psychoses segregate rather than mix (the figures are not age-corrected).

A major recent study of the children of two psychotic parents was published by Kringlen (1978). Table 3 shows the distribution of psychotic offspring according to the diagnoses of the parents. The findings are in good accordance with thos of Elsässer. A Russian dual mating study (Moskalenko, 1972, referred by Gottesman and Shields, 1976) found that 33/57 offspring of two schizophrenic parents were schizophrenic. Only 5 of the 57 were found to be within normal limits.

Table 3. Psychosis in the Offspring of Two Psychotic Parents, Distribution by Diagnosis of Parents and Offspring (Kringlen, 1978)

Parents	No. of Couples	No. of Offspring					
		Schiz.	React.	M - D	Suic.	Bord.	Total
Schiz. + Schiz.	8	5	1	—	—	—	25
Schiz. + React.	20	3	1	—	—	3	42
Schiz. + M - D	6	2	—	—	—	—	12
M – D + React.	4	—	—	1	—	—	9
React. + React.	9	—	1	—	1	1	28
M – D + M – D	1	—	—	—	—	—	5
Total	48	10	3	1	1	5	121

Erlenmeyer-Kimling (1968, 1975) has, in her prospective study of children of two schizophrenic parents, reported that so far the age-corrected risk for psychiatric hospitalization is 32%. Not all were definite schizophrenics, but all had a hospital diagnosis of psychosis.

TWIN STUDIES

Twins can be monozygotic or dizygotic. Monozygotic (MZ) twins are derived by division of one fertilized egg cell and are therefore genetically identical, while dizygotic (DZ) twins are derived from two fertilized egg cells, and their genetical equipment is therefore not more alike than siblings in general. As number of environmental factors will influence a pair of monozygotic and a pair of same-sexed dizygotic twins similarly, the proportion of affected MZ and DZ pairs in an unselected series can throw light on the relative contribution of environment and heredity regarding the trait or the disorder in question. If the proportion of MZ concordant pairs is significantly higher than the proportion of concordant DZ pairs, it can be assumed that genetic factors are responsible wholely or partly for the development of the trait or the disorder. However, it says nothing about how they may be transmitted.

Comparison of the environment to which the sick and the healthy twin of a MZ discordant pair have been subjected may give information about what factors were responsible for the difference in phenotype.

Some theoretical objections against the method as used in psychiatry have been put forward. Price (1950) emphasizes the natal and prenatal conditions that in MZ twins may account for dissimilarities usually ascribed to later environmental influence.

The assumption that the number of environmental factors is similar in MZ and DZ pairs may also be correct only to some degree. The reaction from other people, including the parents, may be more alike toward two MZ twins than toward two DZ twins, as they themselves are more alike. Further, the role division often seen in twins, where one is more dominant and the other more submissive, may contribute to enlarge the difference between two MZ twins. However, the examinations of twins grown up apart tend to show

Table 4. Pairwise Concordance Rates in the Major Twin Studies of Affective Psychoses

Author	MZ Pairs		DZ Pairs	
	N	% Concordance	N	% Concordance
Luxenburger (1928) (Germany)	3	67	13	0
Rosanoff et al. (1934) (U.S.A.)	23	70	67	16
Essen-Möller (1941, 1971) (Sweden)	8	25	3	0
Slater (1953) (U.K.)	8	50	30	24
Kallmann (1946) (U.S.A.)	27	93	55	24
DaFonseca (1959) (U.K.)	21	71	39	38
Kringlen (1967) (Norway)	6	33	20	0
Allen et al. (1974) (U.S.A.)	15	33	34	0
Bertelsen et al. (1977) (Denmark)	55	58	52	17
	27*	63*	35*	23*

* Including typical manic-depressives only.

that these factors do not have a major impact (Shields, 1962; Juel-Nielsen, 1965).

Table 4 shows the concordance rate in the major twin studies in affective psychoses.

The concordance rate for affective psychoses is, on average, 60–70% in MZ pairs, and in DZ pairs probably around 25%. In both cases the concordance rate in MZ pairs is significantly higher than in DZ pairs, and thus indicates strongly a hereditary factor in the etiology.

In most of the twin studies, discordant MZ pairs have been scrutinized in order to find possible environmental differences that could explain why one twin fell ill and the other did not. In schizophrenia particularly, this has been studied, and Pollin and Stabenau (1968) collected a series of discordant twins with this objective. There seems to be some evidence that the twin who later becomes schizophrenic is usually the submissive partner, usually has a slightly lower IQ, more often has had a difficult birth, and perhaps was the smaller of the twins. However, it is difficult to evaluate these findings, especially after the latest report (Belmaker et al., 1974), in which 25% of Pollin and Stabenau's discordant twins have become concordant.

THE DANISH TWIN STUDIES

The material is based on a cross-checking of birth register and the Central Psychiatric Register. The Psychiatric Twin Register comprises all same-sexed twin pairs born in Denmark during the period 1870–1920 who were not broken by death of one or both twins before the age of 6 and where one or both twins has been hospitalized for a mental disorder or has committed suicide. The description of the twin register is available in Hauge et al. (1968). Dupont et al. (1974) have described the Central Psychiatric Register. A detailed description of the sampling, zygosity, diagnosis, examination of twins and relatives, etc., are given elsewhere (Fischer, 1973; Bertelsen et al., 1977).

Table 5 shows the distribution by the Danish Psychiatric Twin Register. The study of the schizophrenic twins (Fischer, 1973) focused partly on the etiology, partly on the possible environmental factors. The concordance rates for MZ and DZ twins were, respectively, approximately 50% and 20%.

There is only one MZ pair where a diagnosis of schizophrenia in one twin and manic-depressive psychosis in the other twin could be questioned. However, the author diagnosed both as schizophrenic. A summary of the case history for this pair will be given in the appendix to this chapter (pair #143).

The study of the twins with affective psychosis was undertaken by Bertelsen, who published a summary of some of his findings in 1977. I am most grateful for the personal communications he has given me to elucidate

Table 5. The Danish Psychiatric Twin Register
(1975 composition)

Diagnosis	No. of Pairs
Schizophrenia	73
Manic-depressive psychosis	110
Paranoid psychoses	12
Reactive/neurotic depressions	43
Neuroses other than depressive	17
Personality disorders and abusus	46
Other diagnoses	48
Suicides without further psychiatric classification	46
Total	395

some special points and for his permission to publish these data. His study is of great importance; the methodology is as perfect as possible. He has personally investigated the twins and their relatives, his material is sufficiently large to permit conclusions to be drawn, case material is available (so far unpublished) for all the twins, and they can be divided into unipolar and bipolar affective psychosis. The pairwise concordance figures for MZ and same-sexed DZ twins before dividing the material into unipolar and bipolar psychosis are, respectively, $30/55 = 58\%$ and $9/52 = 17\%$.

The pairwise concordance rate for the bipolar twins only appears in Table 6. Approximately three fourths of the MZ and one fifth of the DZ twins are concordant, and including pairs with partial concordance, all but one of the MZ and half of the DZ twins are concordant.

Table 6. Pairwise Concordance Rate
for Bipolar Twin Probands.
(Bertelsen et al., 1977)

Level of concordance*	MZ	DZ
C_1	21 (75%)	7 (20%)
$C_2 + C_3$	6 (21%)	10 (29%)
Discordant	1 (4%)	18 (51%)
Total	28	35

* C_1: co-twin: Affective psychosis.
  C_2: co-twin: Psychosis other than affective.
  Severe affective personality disorder.
  Committed suicide.
  C_3: co-twin: Neurosis.
  Personality disorder other than affective.
  Abusus.
  Discordant: co-twin: Mentally normal.

There are 28 MZ pairs with at least one bipolar proband. Twenty-one of them are concordant for affective psychosis. Fourteen of the co-twins have had both manic and depressive episodes, seven co-twins have had depressive episodes only. In only one pair was the diagnosis of affective psychosis in one MZ twin and schizophrenia in his co-twin arguable. The author concluded that both were atypical manic-depressive. A summary of the case history of this pair is given in the appendix to this chapter (pair #21).

These concordance figures are based on detailed case notes as well as personal examination whenever possible. In 16 of the 21 concordant bipolar MZ pairs, both twins had been hospitalized for an affective psychosis, while the diagnosis of the remaining 5 is based on personal examination by the author. Furthermore, the material had the advantage that the youngest twins were about 55 years old when examined, so that age correction is hardly necessary.

In Table 7 the material of MZ bipolar twins is distributed according to the diagnosis of the proband and the co-twin, with emphasis on subtype of affective psychosis. It appears that a schizoaffective psychosis was probable in three cases. In the first the co-twin was unipolar depressive, in the second he

Table 7. Distribution of MZ Twin Pairs Where the Proband Twin Has Unipolar Mania or Bipolar Manic-Depressive Psychosis According to Subtype in Proband and Co-twin

Diagnosis of proband twin	? Schizophrenia	? Atypical manic-depr. psych	Unipolar depression	Bipolar man-depr.	Atyp. man-depr. (N)	Atyp. man-depr. (S)	Affective person. disorder	Normal	Total
Unipolar Mania	1	—	—	—	—	—	—	—	1
Bipolar manic-depressive	—	4	12	—	—	2	1		19
Atyp. manic-depressive N (with neurotic symptoms)	—	2	2	—	—	1	—		5
Atyp. manic-depressive S (with schizophrenia-like hallucinations and delusions)	—	1	1	—	1	—	—		3
Total	1	7	15	—	1	3	1		28

was bipolar manic-depressive, while in the third pair both twins had a schizoaffective psychosis. In one case, as mentioned previously, one twin had a unipolar mania and the other possibly schizophrenia. However, unfortunately, the information available makes it difficult to decide whether the co-twin had an atypical affective psychosis or schizophrenia.

The material was also examined to see whether the concordance rate was different for MZ twins where the proband had had a typical manic episode and where the proband had only had a hypomanic episode. There was no difference between the two groups.

Clinically one cannot distinguish between two patients with endogenous depression where one has the same genotype as bipolar manic-depressive and the other a "unipolar genotype," but as it appears from the concordance rates, there must be a difference in the genotype or the group may be heterogeneous.

The material was also divided according to handedness in order to examine a possible relationship between handedness and concordance. The total number of MZ pairs where one was right-handed and the other was left-handed was relatively small, only 14%. From this material there is no indication that handedness and concordance rate are related in affective psychosis. Information regarding handedness of the schizophrenic twin sample is, unfortunately, not available.

DISCUSSION

Studies into the etiology of schizophrenia and mania leave no doubt that in both a genetic component is involved, but exactly how it is involved and what is inherited is still unknown. It could be one or several genes, it could be dominant or recessive, but there is also the possibility that schizophrenia and manic-depressive psychosis, like retinitis pigmentosa and muscular dystrophy, can be inherited in different ways in different families.

The majority of the evidence presented previously in this article points in the direction that whatever is genetically transmitted, it is one thing in schizophrenia and another in affective psychosis. Of all the cases examined in the Danish twin studies, only the two pairs described in the appendix are possible examples of mania and schizophrenia in a single monozygotic twinship, and the two examples are not typical cases of the variant illnesses.

The schizoaffective psychosis presents a special problem. From the existing evidence it is reasonable to believe that this syndrome covers at least three different disease entities: In some the etiological factor is the same as in schizophrenia, in some the same as in affective psychosis, and finally in a small group there is an etiology different from both schizophrenia and affective psychosis.

REFERENCES

Allen, M.C., Cohen, S., Pollin, W., and Greenspan, S.I. Affective illness in veteran twins. A diagnostic review. *Am. J. Psychiat.* 131, 1234–1239 (1974).

Angst, J. Zur Aetiologie und Nosologie endogener depressiver Psychosen. *Monogr. Gesamtgeb. Neur. Psychiat.* 112 (1966).

Belmaker, R.H., Pollin, W., Wyatt, R.J., and Cohen, S. A follow-up of monozygpotic twins discordant for schizophrenia. *Arch. Gen. Psychiat.* 30, 219–222 (1974).

Bertelsen, A., Harvald, B., and Hauge, M. A Danish twin study of manic-depressive disorders. *Brit. J. Psychiat.* 130, 330–351 (1977).

Cooper, J., Kendell, R.E., Garland, B.J. Cross-national study of diagnosis of the mental disorders: Some results from the first comparative investigation. *Am. J. Psychiat. Supp. 125* 21 (1969).

Da Fonesca, A.F. Affective equivalents. *Brit. J. Psychiat.* 109, 464–469 (1963).

Dupont, A., Videbech, T., and Weeke, A. A cumulative national psychiatric register. *Acta Psychiat. Scand.* 50, 161–173 (1974).

Elsässer, G. *Die Nachkommen geisteskranker Elternpaare.* George Thieme, Stuttgart (1952).

Erlenmeyer-Kimling, L. Studies on the offspring of two schizophrenic parents. In *The Transmission of Schizophrenia,* D. Rosenthal and S.S. Kety, eds. Pergamon, Oxford (1968).

Erlenmeyer-Kimling, L. A prospective study of children at risk for schizophrenia. In *Life History Research in Psychopathology 4,* R. Wirt, G. Winshur and M. Roff, eds. Univ. of Minnesota Press, Minneapolis (1975).

Essen-Möller, E. Psychiatrische Untersuchungen an einer Serie von Zwillingen. *Acta Psych. et Neur. Scand. Suppl. 23* (1941).

Essen-Möller, E. Twenty-one psychiatric cases and their MZ co-twins: A thirty-year follow-up. *Acta Genet. Med. et Gemell.* 19, 315–317 (1970).

Fischer, M. *Genetic and environmental factors in schizophrenia.* Munksgaard, Copenhagen (1973).

Gottesman, L.I., and Shields, J. A critical review of recent adoption, twin and family studies of schizophrenia. *Schizo. Bull.* 360 (1976).

Hauge, M., Harvald, B., Fischer, M., Gotlieb Jensen, K., Juel–Nielsen, N., Raebild, I., Shapiro, R., and Videbech, T. The Danish twin register. *Acta Genet. Med. et Gemell.* 17, 315–332 (1968).

Juel-Nielsen, N. Individual and environment. *Acta Psychiat. Scand. Suppl. 183* (1965).

Kahn, E. Studien uber Vererbung und Entstehung geistiger Störungen. *Monogr. Gesamtgeb. Neur. Psychiat.* 36 (1923).

Kallman, F.J. The genetic theory of schizophrenia: An analysis of 691 schizophrenic twin index families. *Am. J. Psychiat.* 103, 309 (1946).

Kramer, M. Some problems for international research suggested by observations on differences in first admission rates to mental hospitals in England and Wales and of the United States. In *Proceedings of the Third World Congress of Psychiatry,* Toronto (1961) pp. 153–160.

Kringlen, E. *Heredity and Environment in the Functional Psychoses.* Heineman, London (1967).

Kringlen, E. Adult offspring of two psychotic parents with special reference to schizophrenia. In *Proceedings from the Second Conference on Schizophrenia,* Rochester (1978, in press).

Luxenburger, H. Vorläufiger Bericht uber psychiatrische Serienuntersuchungen an Zwillingen. *Zeitschrift f. ges. Neur. Psychiat.* 116, 297–326 (1928).

Moskalenko, V.D. A comparative study of families with one or two schizophrenic parents (cited by Gottesman and Shields, 1976). *Zhurnal Neuropatologii, Psikhiatrii imeni S.S. Korsakova* 72, 86–92 (1972).

Perris, C. A study of bipolar (manic-depressive) and unipolar recurrent depressive psychoses. *Acta Psychiat. Scand. Suppl. 194* (1966).

Pollin, W., and Stabenau, J. Biological, psychological and historical differences in a series of monozygotic twins discordant for schizophrenia. *J. Psychiat. Res.* 6, 317–332 (1968).

Price, B. Primary biases in twin studies. *Am. J. Human Genet.* 2, 293–352 (1950).

Rosanoff, A.J., Handy, L.M., Plesset, I.R., and Brush, S. The aetiology of so-called schizophrenic psychoses with special reference to their occurrence in twins. *Am. J. Psychiat.* 91, 247–286 (1934).

Schulz, B. Kinder schizophrener Elternpaare. *Zeitschrift f ges. Neur. Psychiat.* 168, 1–3 (1940).

Shields, J. *Monozygotic twins brought up apart and brought up together.* Univ. Press, New York (1962).

Slater, E. (with the assistance of J. Shields). Psychotic and neurotic illnesses in twins. *Medical Research Council Special Report Series* No. 278, Her Majesty's Stationery Office, London (1953).

Zerbin-Rüdin, E. Endogene Psychosen. In *Humangenetik Band V,* 2. George Thieme, Stuttgart (1967).

Appendix

Case histories of the only two twin pairs from the Danish twin studies in which one twin may have schizophrenia and the other manic-depressive psychosis.

PAIR #143

The paternal grandfather committed suicide at the age of 82, and a paternal uncle likewise committed suicide, at the age of 68. Another paternal uncle had been an inmate of a mental hospital, diagnosis schizophrenia. The father, who was described as a portly, jolly person, had a tendency to brood if anything upset him, and this moodiness could, at times, develop into what was described as depressions.

The twins were numbers 3 and 4 of 7 siblings. Their birth was uncomplicated. Their natures were very different, Adam being the quieter and the more reserved; he was also very musical. Hjalmar, on the other hand, was more open and impetuous.

HJALMAR

After leaving school, Hjalmar stayed at home for some years. He was not particularly religious-minded, and ran rather "wild" at times, consorting with casual girl friends. His father died when he was 19, and it was then observed that he began to be "nervous," absent-minded and irritable. When he was 20, he left home and obtained employment on a farm not far away. During the year of this employment, he often used to complain to Adam that he was overworked, and that he felt tired and it was all too much for him. In the end he returned home to his mother. The year after, his youngest sister, to whom he had been very closely attached, died. Thereafter, his symptoms increased, he kept isolated, he never lifted a finger, and he gave the impression of being almost apathetic.

As his symptoms still increased, he was admitted to a private mental home, where he stayed for about 2 months, after which his symptoms abated and he was discharged (the case report was not forthcoming). The next 2 years he spent at home, partly helping on the farm, and partly, with ability and success, trading in cattle. Without known specific reason, his symptoms returned, this time in the forms of withdrawal and increasing suspiciousness, particularly toward his mother, whom he finally suspected of wishing to poison him.

First admission, aged 23 years, diagnosis schizophrenia.

Duration of stay in hospital, 5 years.

On admission he was calm and oriented. He stated that his food had been poisoned. He had auditory hallucinations and waved his arms about in a strange fashion. At times he seemed anxious. He was subsequently described as hysterical, foolish, agitated, and untidy, and as having a number of hypochondriacal delusions, but without any specific mood.

Aftert 1½ years in hospital, he was treated with cardiasol shock. Contemporaneous with this treatment, his condition improved. When spoken to, he appeared lucid and oriented and seemed to have some insight into his disease. An attempt was made to discharge him, but 2 weeks later he was readmitted with the same symptoms as previously. After 5 years in hospital, he returned to his home, where his family agreed to take care of him.

His discharge lasted 11 years, during which time he lived on a brother's farm. He helped a bit with the farm work, but according to information supplied by the family, he was constantly psychotic.

Second admission, aged 39 years, diagnosis schizophrenia.

Duration of stay in hospital, 6 years.

FOLLOW-UP 1966

Hjalmar was under care in a home to which he had been transferred after discharge from hospital. For the most part he was idle. He did not read, but watched television now and again. He seemed to be passive, smiling vacantly, and his mood seemed almost neutral. His memory, as far as his family was concerned, was completely satisfactory. During the interview, he gave expression to many bizarre delusions. It was his opinion that he had been born with all his teeth, and that he remembered his first meal, which consisted of bubble and squeak, and that he took no nourishment until he was aged 49 months. He said that he was still closely attached to his twin brother, who visited him regularly. He was lucid and oriented, seemingly not hallucinated.

ADAM

For some years he was variously employed; he worked for a news agent, a market gardener, and as a manservant, but for the last 20 years he had been exclusively employed as a factory hand for the same firm. He had always worked to the complete satisfaction of his employers. When he was about 30, he married a woman of the same age. They had 3 children, 2 of whom had been placed for adoption.

He left home at the age of 17 and got employment in a neighboring town. He returned home on the death of his father in order to help his mother with the work on the farm, remaining there for a year or so. He then left home again and was variously employed.

Premorbidly he was said to have been open and friendly, although more ready to give in to other people than his twin brother had been. With the passing of puberty, he became more serious-minded and began to interest himself in religion. When he was about 22, he joined the Salvation Army, but resigned a couple of years later. He had, however, never ceased to take a close interest in the organization.

Psychotic episodes seemed to have been present ever since the age of 25–26 years. When he was 28, his fiancée became pregnant. They married a couple of years later, his wife being ignorant of his former psychotic episodes. These recurred some years later, usually at very infrequent intervals and lasting, as a rule, only a couple of days.

He had had permanent employment during the whole of his marriage, but the family's standard of living, socially as well as financially, had been reduced over the years by his psychotic episodes. These psychotic periods had been very similar, usually starting by his becoming increasingly religious, thinking that God spoke to him and that he "ought to do something for other people," with the result that, on many occasions, he gave large sums to the Salvation Army, which was a heavy drain on the family's resources.

Later a daughter was born, and after a further lapse of years, a son. Immediately prior to the birth of his son, the patient had been psychotic once more, and the family had been on the verge of bankruptcy, in consequence of which, among other things, his wife wanted a divorce and the baby was adopted.

As neither he nor his wife wished for more children, his wife wanted to be sterilized, but the family doctor advised the operation be done on Adam, "as it was easier to do on a man." Adam was, therefore, sterilized in 1951.

First admission, aged 46 years, diagnosis schizophreniform psychosis. Duration of stay in hospital, 2 months.

During his stay in hospital he had auditory hallucinations and religious delusions. He had quarreled with his wife because "there was something wrong with her relationship to God." His wife stated that the condition had lasted for about 10 months and had become gradually worse.

In hospital he was treated with electroshock, and in the course of a month he seemed to be his usual self again. On discharge he stated that he had no recollection of the religious problems that had led to his admission.

Second admission, aged 48 years, diagnosis schizophreniform psychosis. Duration of stay in hospital, 3 months.

FOLLOW-UP 1967

He seemed mentally unremarkable, there were no signs of delusions, hallucinations, or disordered thoughts, and his emotional and intellectual ability for establishing contact with others seemed normal. He appeared neat and orderly, was well dressed, and displayed no remarkable mannerisms; moreover, he seemed to have quite a good insight into his disease. He was able to account for how the psychotic periods began by his becoming increasingly occupied with religious subjects while, at the same time, feeling increasingly restless, beginning to smoke a great deal, and losing his appetite and his memory. Of the psychotic episodes themselves, he remembered nothing in particular. In the course of the interview, he complained of being so skinny, and in this connection made the only remarkable statement in the interview: "The government ought to do more for skinny people."

SUMMARY

Adam was born first, and it was unknown which twin was the bigger. There was no certain role distribution between the twins. Hjalmar fell ill when he was 22, starting with predominately depressive symptoms, continuing later with increasing hallucinations and delusions, disintegration of the personality, and association disturbances, together with autism. He had been almost uninterruptedly psychotic, at any rate since he was 23–24 years old.

Adam had had brief, apparently unprovoked psychotic periods, lasting from a couple of days to some months. During these psychotic periods, he had had auditory hallucinations and religious delusions, but he had not been described as autistic. In the intervals between the psychotic periods, he had been completely normal, fully capable of working and without residual symptoms. At the follow-up, he was found to be mentally unremarkable.

Author's diagnosis: Hjalmar, paranoid schizophrenia; Adam, episodic, schizophreniform psychosis.

PAIR #21

There is no information about the early development, but in the case records they are both described as mentally retarded, probably from birth. They grew up together in the countryside. Their father was a smallholder and unskilled laborer, lower social class. They both went to the ordinary village school, but had difficulties in learning. They started working as farmhands already in childhood. Twin B had rachitis at an early age and was stammering from childhood. Later on he was rejected from military service because of moderate deafness. There is no information about the health of twin A except that at 19 years old both ears were operated on for otitis media. He also was rejected from military service, reason unknown.

TWIN A

After school, he worked as a farmhand until a few months before his death. He was never married, and lived with his parents for many years. Later on he lived with his employer. When he was 68 years old, he came to an old peoples home a few months before he died. In the case notes he was described as mentally retarded but good-natured and easy to get on with, although he was easily hurt. He was a stable worker and stayed in his jobs for long periods.

From the age of 21, he had episodes when he became elated and excited, full of plans and energy. He did not want to work, but instead went into the nearby town, rambling and using his money extravagantly, and on several occasions he had to be brought home by the police. At the age of 21 and again at 30, he was admitted to the local hospital, where he calmed down in the course of some months (case notes not available).

At the age of 38, he was admitted to a psychiatric hospital because of a similar episode. On admission he was exalted but calmed down quickly. He appeared mildly elated, lively and effusive, a bit restless, and seemed to be mentally deficient. After 3 months, he was discharged as quiet and unremarkable. Hospital diagnosis: exaltatio in imbecilitate.

At age 40 he was committed to a psychiatric hospital because he suddenly had felt unsatisfied with his work and attacked his employer. On admission he was fatuously elated, with accelerated and curt speech, but otherwise he was unremarkable. After a month, he became excited, rummaged about in his bed, whispered by himself, made gestures, and was at times very talkative, yelling and erethetic toward the other patients. On sedatives he calmed down after some months, and at his discharge 6 months later he was quiet and unobtrusive. Hospital diagnosis: exaltatio in imbecilitate.

At age 41 and at age 59, he was again admitted to a psychiatric hospital. During the years, he had continued to have episodes of elation when he would be excited, singing and shouting; he might even undress himself in public. It seems that twin A later on managed his own affairs and his work until a few months before his death, and there is no further information about mood fluctuations.

TWIN B

After leaving school, he worked as a farmhand. He married at age 28 but had no children. In the case notes he was described as mentally retarded, a bit slow but good-natured, quiet, and well balanced. He was a good worker and stayed long in his jobs.

At age 33 he had an attack of confusion. During a very hot period of the summer, he left home and wandered on the road in his night shirt, apparently because he was afraid of something that he could not explain. He was admitted to the local hospital for a couple of weeks, after which he seemed to be well.

At age 34 he was admitted to a psychiatric hospital. One and a half months before the admission, he suddenly became psychotic, was excited, afraid of his wife, and had auditory hallucinations. He was first admitted to a somatic hospital, where he appeared slow and inhibited, was auditorily hallucinated, and would suddenly shout out answers. He replied to questions by repeating the last words of the question with a silly grin. Otherwise he appeared lucid and oriented. Gradually he became increasingly torpid, had to be helped with everything, and was at last transferred to a psychiatric hospital. On admission he was apathetic, with failing orientation. He disclosed persecutory delusions, said he was haunted by people from the village, that he wife had been unfaithful to him and that she and her brother wanted to kill him, and admitted to having both visual and auditory hallucinations. His mood seemed to be indifferent, and he appeared to be mentally retarded. At first he continued to be apathetic and stagnant, stayed mostly in bed underneath the blankets talking to himself. He mentioned that he did not have the right to be in the hospital or to talk or look at anybody, complained now and then that he was being destroyed by electricity from the power station. A few months later he became increasingly motoric excited, with peculiar theatrical gestures and attitudes, presumably according to hallucinatory orders. Now and then he sang and shouted, uttered obscenities, and exposed himself indecently. He gradually calmed down on sedatives, and 6 months after admission he was described as quiet and oriented, without any gestures. However, 3 months later he appeared to be elated, was gesticulating, called the nurse "the Queen," and became exalted and scolding when his wife visited. After a year in hospital he was described as being quieter, but it was difficult to establish rapport with him. Occasionally he made peculiar gestures, but mostly he was stagnant and apathetic. The following 1–2 years he was still apathetic, seemed unable to talk reasonably, appeared rather silly and dull. After almost 3 years in hospital, unremitting diarrhea and vomiting supervened, causing rapid loss of weight, and after one month he died at age 37. On autopsy tuberculosis intestini et miliares renuum was discovered. Hospital diagnosis: schizophrenia.

SUMMARY

Both twins became psychotic and appear from hospital diagnoses as a unique case of manic-depressive psychosis and schizophrenia in identical twins.

Twin A's symptoms support the diagnosis of manic-depressive disorder, with obvious manic elations and indisputable periodic course of illness with full remissions between episodes. In one episode, however, he also appeared slightly catatonic (rummaged about in the bed, made gestures and whispered to himself, was erethetic and shouted), but these atypical traits may be explained by his mental dificiency. He does not seem to have had any episodes of depression, and he is only proband with a pure manic disorder. As a differential diagnosis, episodic psychosis (exaltations in a person with mental retardation) might be considered, but there is no evidence of any psychotraumas. Schizophrenia seems unlikely.

In twin B the diagnosis is difficult to evaluate. Suspicion of schizophrenia arises partly from the symptoms, with auditory, visual, and tactile hallucinations, delusions of persecution, and the catatonic taint; and partly from the course of illness, with apparently persisting defect of rapport and of the integrity of personality. On the other hand, the course shows a periodicity with alternating periods of excitation, once with obvious elated mood, and periods with apathy, occasionally with self-deprecating ideas, which raises suspicion of an atypical manic-depressive psychosis in a mentally deficient person. Twin B did not live long enough for the clarification of the diagnosis, which then can only be evaluated as an atypical psychosis in a mentally retarded individual.

The twins are thus evaluated as partially concordant regarding diagnoses. They are concordant regarding hospitalization but not regarding hospital diagnoses.

Monozygosity assumed, it is most probable that twin A's and twin B's mental illness was a manifestation of the same genetic disposition. For twin A it has been possible to follow the course over a lifetime of 68 years, and the diagnosis of manic-depressive disorder seems quite reliable. If so, this twin pair demonstrates that manic-depressive disorder has a nosologic span including syndromes similar to catatonic schizophrenia.

CHAPTER 5

Clinical Typology of Bipolar Illness

J. Angst

MANIA

DEFINITION

The term "mania" used in this paper is identical with the term "manic syndrome," which is characterized by marked mood changes (elation, excitement, irritability), increase of speech and motor activity, flight of ideas, distracted attention (details are mentioned in A *Glossary of Mental disorders* [1968].

Manic syndromes can be observed in the course of many disorders (e.g., organic brain disorders), but most frequently in affective and schizoaffective disorders. This paper is concentrated on affective and schizoaffective disorders only.

PROBLEMS

There is an increasing interest in typology of affective and schizoaffective disorders as a consequence of the search for heterogeneity from a genetic point of view. Dunner et al. (1976) tried to distinguish two types of manic-depressive disorders, manic I (unipolar) and manic II (bipolar); the validity of this distinction is uncertain. Another open question is the occurrence of unipolar recurrent mania. Does it exist, is it a special nosological entity (ICD 296.1), or is unipolar mania only a product of a random process of bipolar manic-depressive disorders (Angst, 1978b)? In the search for heterogeneity of affective and schizoaffective disorders, we are looking for subtypes within the group of bipolar manic-depressive psychoses and schizoaffective psychoses. The hypothesis of a continuum based on a threshold model (Gershon et al., 1976) can probably be tested by a more detailed classification of bipolar illness based on the severity of the manifestation of manic episodes during the course of disorder. Such an attempt has been made (Angst, 1978a) with some surprising results.

This paper will describe the long-term course of subgroups of bipolar manic-depressive and schizoaffective patients and genetic aspects of these subtypes based on the investigation of first-degree relatives.

METHODOLOGY

The patient sample consists of all admissions to the Psychiatric University Clinic of Zurich during the years 1959 to 1963 with a diagnosis of depression or mania showing in the previous history or in the follow-up period until 1975, at least once a manic syndrome. Out of 254 patients with an affective disorder, 95 were found suffering also from mania (34.4%). The second group of the sample consists of 150 patients with a schizoaffective disorder, of which 97 had shown manic syndromes (64.7%).

The patients were examined at their admission to the hospital, and a follow-up was carried out at least every fifth year and at every additional readmission in the follow-up period until 1975. A longitudinal study of this kind must necessarily be performed both retrospectively and prospectively, because it has to cover the whole period of time of the natural course of the disorder. The follow-up is based on several types of information (from doctors, other informants, records of other institutions, by telephone calls or letters). The majority of the patients had been readmitted during the follow-up period. In all cases additional information was obtained, not only from the patients but from at least one other informant (relatives, doctors, social workers). The methodology is described in more detail in Angst (1978a) and Angst et al., (1978a). It has to be mentioned critically that there remain a lot of sources of errors: A follow-up of every fifth year may miss quite a few milder episodes because the patient or the informants may have forgotten them or, especially, because there may be an underreporting of mild, short mood-swings, e.g., hypomania. But such errors may be distributed by chance over the total sample so that they may be less important in an anlysis of subgroups. Anyhow, the reported figures may be minimal figures of morbidity.

The clinical findings were documented in a standarized way and computed using specially developed programs on IBM 370/155 at the computer center of our university in Zurich. The programs have been developed by P. Scheidegger.

PATIENT SAMPLES

The patient samples consist of two groups: manic-depressive disorders (N = 95) and schizoaffective disorders (N = 150). These two samples are split into five subgroups. The bipolar manic-depressive patients are classified into three subgroups that have been described in detail in another paper (Angst, 1978a):

Dm:* preponderantly depressed patients with hypomania (N = 43)
MD: severely manic and severely depressed patients (N = 36)
Md: preponderantly manic patients with mild depression (N = 16)

The schizoaffective sample was split into manic (N = 97) and nonmanic (N = 53) patients, corresponding to the bipolar and unipolar groups proposed by Cadoret et al., (1974). A schizoaffective patient was considered manic if at least once during his life a clear hypomanic or manic syndrome was observed (cross-sectionally together with schizophrenic symptoms or long-itudinally as a pure affective syndrome). The classification of schizoaffective patients based on the observed syndromes was published by Angst (1978a). In the same paper the course of schizoaffective disorders is described further without the dichotomy into manic or nonmanic patients.

Sex. In both samples (bipolar and schizoaffective patients), males are more prone to develop manic syndromes than females, and females are more prone to develop depression (Table 1). This trend can especially be demonstrated for the bipolar group, where the three subgroups show an increasing proportion of males correlated with the increasing preponderance of manic symptomatology: Dm 23% males, MD 47% males, Md 62% males(p < .001). In manic schizoaffective patients it is 34%; in nonmanic patients 15% males (p < .02).

Age. Table 1 shows that all five subgroups are similar in age (range of the arithmetic means between 57.7 and 62.7 years), and do not differ statistically. The figures characterising the course of the illness are therefore representative for a hospitalized patient group followed until the age of 60.

Length of Observation. In face of the same age of all subgroups at the last follow-up investigation, differences in the length of observation must be a consequence of differences in age at first episode. All subgroups were observed for 24 to 28 years on the average, and the prospective time period was 12 to 16 years. Table 1 shows also that the number of prospective episodes is slightly higher than the retrospective ones.

---

*D or M means that a depressed or manic syndrome required a treatment in a hospital; d or m means that an ambulatory treatment or no treatment was required for a mild depression or hypomania.

Table 1. Patient Samples, Descriptive Data

	Bipolar Disorder			Schizoaffective Disorder	
	Dm	MD	Md	Manic	Nonmanic
N	43	36	16	97	53
Males	10 (23)	17 (47)	10 (62)	33 (34)	8 (15)
Females	33	19	6	64	45
Age	62.7 ± 11.4	59.9 ± 14.1	58.8 ± 15.6	57.7 ± 13.2	61.2 ± 14.3
Years of observation	24.9 ± 11.2	28.3 ± 12.7	26.0 ± 12.1	28.4 ± 12.6	24.4 ± 12.8
Age at first episode	38.0 ± 14.6	31.6 ± 11.6	32.6 ± 15.3	29.2 ± 11.5	36.7 ± 13.9
Length of illness (years)	22.1 ± 11.5	26.4 ± 13.3	22.7 ± 13.1	24.1 ± 12.6	19.8 ± 12.6
Number of Episodes (median)					
total	7	10	8	9	5
retrospective	3	4	4	4	2
prospective	5	6	4	4	3
Episodes per year	.28	.35	.31	.32	.20
Last free interval N	34	23	12	81	42
Median	27.5	17	31	45	48.5
Length of cycles (median)	343.0	271.5	220.5	268.0	203.0
length of episodes (median)	3.4	5.4	4.4	3.9	4.7
Last free interval ≥ 5 years	8 (18.6%)	4 (11.1%)	4 (25%)	35 (36.1%)	20 (37.7%)

COURSE OF BIPOLAR AND MANIC SCHIZOAFFECTIVE DISORDERS

The course of the disorder will be described by different criteria, such as age at first episode, number of episodes, length of illness, length of episodes, length of cycles (time from the beginning of an episode until the beginning of the subsequent episode), and outcome. The course of bipolar and schizoaffective patients will not be described here because this has been done preliminarily elsewhere (Angst, 1978b; Angst et al., 1978b). This paper will concentrate on subgroups of bipolar and schizoaffective patients. A special emphasis will be given to the question of whether patients with a manic symptomatology or a more severe manic symptomatology than others have a more malignant course of the disorder. It is well known that unipolar depression takes a milder course than bipolar affective disorders (later onset, fewer episodes, higher proportion of five-year remission). Therefore, the *hypothesis* is justified that within bipolar patients, those with a preponderantly manic symptomatology should show a more malignant course of the disorder. The same should be true for manic versus nonmanic schizoaffective patients.

Age at First Episode

Within bipolar patients, the groups Md and MD have a mean age at first onset of 32.6 and 31.6 years. On the other hand, the preponderantly depressed group Dm has an age at first onset of 38 years, which is significantly higher ($p < .05$).

Another criterion of outcome is the duration of the last free interval at the follow-up. The last free interval was calculated as the time difference between the end of the last episode and the date of the follow-up examination. Table 1 gives only the frequency of patients who were free from relapses during five or more years. The figures for the three bipolar subgroups are rather small, and therefore the differences between the groups seem to be high (they vary between 11% and 25%), but they are statistically not significant. On the whole, 16 of 95 bipolar patients (17%) were relapse-free for five years or longer. This figure shows how active the process is still at an average age of 60 years.

In schizoaffective patients, the manic and nonmanic subgroups do not differ: of 36 respondants, 38% were relapse-free for five years or longer.

According to our hypothesis, the bipolar group Md should show a tendency to a lower age at first episode than the group MD, which is not found in the arithmetic means, but is true in the median (Md 26.5 years, MD 28 years).

In schizoaffective patients, the manic subgroups show a lower age at onset (29.2 years) than the nonmanic subgroups (36.7 years [$p < .001$]).

Our hypothesis that a pronounced manic symptomatology is correlated with an earlier age at onset is therefore confirmed by our findings.

Number of Episodes

Table 1 shows the median for the observed number of episodes, which has to be related to the length of observation in years. Within the *bipolar group,* the subgroup Dm shows only 7 episodes within 24.9 years, which means 0.28 episodes per year. Corresponding figures for the other two groups are MD, 35 episodes per year and Md, 31 episodes per year. Therefore, the course of the disorder was the most recurrent in the group MD and less recurrent in the two others.

As expected, manic *schizoaffective patients* show many more episodes (0.32 per year) than nonmanic patients (0.20 per year). In the latter subgroup, the time from one episode to the other was, on the average, 4.9 years. These arithmetic means do not give a respresentative picture because there is not a regular occurrence of episodes, but a well-known decrease in the length of the time from one episode to the next one (Angst et al., [1973]).

The hypothesis that mania is correlated with a higher relapse rate is partially confirmed for bipolar disorders, where the preponderantly depressed subgroup Dm shows the most benign course, whereas the nuclear group MD shows the highest recurrence. On the other hand, the hypothesis was not confirmed that the preponderantly manic group Md should show a more malignant course than the group MD. In schizoaffective disorders, the hypothesis is confirmed: Manic patients show a much higher recurrence than nonmanic patients.

Length of Illness

Table 1 gives the observed length of illness of all subgroups. These figures are more or less comparable because their average age is the same. The findings are again compatible with the hypothesis showing a longer length of illness for the group MD than for group Dm, and especially for manic versus nonmanic schizoaffective patients. Here again, the bipolar group Md does not confirm the hypothesis because the length of illness does not differ from the group Dm.

Length of Episodes

The length of episodes must not be correlated with the severity of a periodic course of a disorder, because we could also find that a more recurrent course could be correlated with a shorter duration of episodes. Therefore, no specific hypothesis can be derived in regard to the influence of mania.

The analysis was done as follows: For each patient the mean length of all episodes was calculated after logarithmic transformation, and at the end the median of all these intraindividual means and the logarithmic mean were given. Within bipolar patients, the preponderantly depressed group Dm shows the shortest length of episodes (3.4 months), followed by group Md (4.4 months) and MD (5.4 months). In schizoaffective patients, the manic subgroup shows a shorter length of episodes (3.9 months) than the nonmanic subgroup (4.7 months). This analysis does not go into details, because one could also compare the length of episodes with manic symptomatology versus episodes without manic symptomatology. This analysis was done elsewhere by a multiple regression analysis without a significant result.

Outcome

Outcome can be described in many respects. One criterion is the degree of remission given in Table 2. In bipolar disorder the preponderantly depressed

Table 2. Degree of Remission

	Bipolar Disorder			Schizoaffective Disorder	
	Dm	MD	Md	Manic	Nonmanic
1. Full	18	10	6	27	13
2. Incomplete	11	10	5	27	25
3. Unknown	—	—	—	1	1
4. Current episode	4	7	1	15	7
5. POS slight	1	1	—	7	1
6. POS severe	7	3	1	—	1
7. Death (illness)	2	2	3	14	3
8. Death (suicide)	—	3	—	3	2
9. ?	—	—	—	3	—

subgroup shows more or less the same amount of incomplete remission (62%) as the two other groups (50% n.s.). The same is true for schizoaffective patients; manic subgroup 50%, nonmanic subgroup 34% (n.s.).

Conclusion

The course of bipolar and schizoaffective patients was especially described, and studies took into account the severity of manic symptomatology in bipolar disorders and the presence or absence of manic symptoms in schizoaffective disorders. In this way manic symptoms were analyzed as an intervening variable. The hypothesis was derived from the differences between unipolar and bipolar affective patients where it is well known that the bipolar group shows a more malignant course of the disorder. Therefore, within bipolar subgroups the preponderantly manic patients should, compared to preponderantly depressed patients, show the same phenomenon. In schizoaffective disorders, the same hypothesis was raised, because both manic and nonmanic schizoaffective patients suffer from affective syndromes (manic or depressive syndromes).

The analysis shows that the hypothesis was supported for bipolar disorders and partly supported for schizoaffective patients. As an intervening variable, sex has to be considered, because in bipolar subgroups males are more frequent in severely manic subgroups compared to slightly manic subgroups. One could therefore raise the hypothesis for a further analysis that male bipolar patients should show a more malignant course of the disorder than female patients. As a criterion of severity, the age at first episode, the length of the illness, frequency and length of episodes, relapse-free time, and degree of remission at follow-up were used.

The results are the following: The preponderantly depressed subgroup of bipolar patients (Dm) differs considerably in the course of the disorder from the other two groups (severely manic and depressive patients MD and preponderantly manic patients Md). The group Dm has a later onset of the disorder, a lower frequency of episodes per years, a shorter length of episodes, and a trend to a higher frequency of full remission. Therefore, the group Dm has a better outcome than the other two subgroups of bipolar patients. The differences between the last two groups are rather small and not significant. This may also be due to the relatively small size of the group Md.

In schizoaffective patients, the hypothesis of a more malignant course in manic versus nonmanic patients was partially supported: The manic subgroup shows an earlier onset of the disorder and a higher frequency of episodes. On the other hand, the manic schizoaffective subgroup shows a shorter length of the episodes. Therefore, in this subgroup the manic symptomatology is only correlated with an earlier onset and a higher frequency of relapses, but that does not prolongate the length of episodes or worsen the outcome to a significant degree.

GENETICS OF BIPOLAR AND SCHIZOAFFECTIVE SUBGROUPS

Heterogeneity of Bipolar Probands

As mentioned in section 5.1., the three subgroups of bipolar probands differ in age at first episode, the depressed group (Dm) showing a higher age at first onset. On the other hand, it is known that the heredity loading of the relatives of late-onset probands is lower than that of early-onset probands. We should therefore expect a higher morbidity risk in the relatives of the subgroups MD and Md than in the subgroup Dm. Furthermore, the model of a continuum between recurrent depression and mania would assume the following: The lowest morbidity risk in relatives should be expected in the families of unipolar depressed patients, followed by the other groups (D < Dm < MD < Md < M), and the highest frequency should be found in recurrent mania.

Another hypothesis based on Leonhard (1957) would assume that monopolar patients (unipolar depression and unipolar mania) should show a lower morbidity risk in the families than bipolar patients. Therefore, the morbidity risk in families should show the following rank order: D < Dm < MD > Md > M (D = unipolar depression, M = unipolar mania).

Angst (1966), Perris (1966), and others have confirmed that unipolar depressive patients have a lower morbidity risk in their families than bipolar patients. There does not exist a study large enough to test the other hypothesis of Leonhard: whether recurrent mania has a low family loading too.

Our material contains only three recurrent manic patients, and they were added to the group Md (N = 16). Table 3 gives the morbidity risk of the first-degree relatives of the three subtypes of bipolar probands (Dm, MD, Md).

We are surprised to state that the highest morbidity risk for unipolar and bipolar disorders is to be found in group Dm, and the lowest group Md, whereas the group MD takes an intermediate position. Furthermore, it is remarkable that the rate of suicides is the highest in the relatives of group Dm, followed by MD. There were no suicides in the relatives of the group Md. Finally, schizoaffective and schizophrenic secondary cases were also frequently found in the relatives of group Dm.

These empirical data are unexpected and are not compatible with the two hypotheses mentioned above. The highest family loading of group Dm cannot be explained by one of the two hypotheses. The simple model of increasing severity of a pathological process from depression to mania would call for a lower morbidity risk in the group Dm than in the other two groups,

Table 3. Genetics of Bipolar Subtypes

	Bipolar Subtypes								Total	
	1 Dm		2 MD		3 Md				Total	
Probands N	43		36		16				296.3	
									95	
Relatives BZ*										
ICD 295 Schizophrenia	231.55		194.15		100.84				526.6	
ICD 296 Affective disorder	175.93		148.83		75.72				399.1	
ICD	N	%	N	%	N	%			N	%
1. 295 Schizophrenia	7	3.02	1	.52	2	2.0			10	1.9
2. 295.7 Schizoaffective disorders	6	2.59	1	.52	1	1.0			8	1.5
3. 296.2 Unipolar depressions	18	10.23	8	5.38	2	2.64			28	7.0
4. 296.3 Bipolar disorders	6	3.41	3	2.02	1	1.32			10	2.5
5. Suicides	8	4.55	5	3.36	—	—			13	3.3
6. 300 Neuroses	8	4.55	8	5.38	4	5.28			20	5.0
7. 301 Personality disorder	10	5.68	16	10.75	5	6.60			31	7.8
Total 1-5	45	23.80	18	11.80	6	6.96			69	16.2
1-7	63	34.03	42	27.93	15	18.84			120	29.0

*BZ (Bezugsziffer) Calculated by the method of Stroemgren and Slater.

MD and Md. On the other hand the monopolar-bipolar theory of Leonhard would give the expectation of a hereditary loading as follows: Dm < MD > Md. Therefore, both hypotheses are disproved by our findings. Of course it will be necessary to reconfirm this by a second sample (such a study is going on in our department).

The fact of a very high loading of the subgroup Dm is also of interest in another respect: Of course, most of the episodes have been treated by pharmaceutical drugs, and we have to consider the existence of a drug-induced hypomania in the group Dm. In this way we could put forward the hypothesis that we are dealing in this group with a large proportion of unipolar depressed patients manifesting a drug-induced hypomania. If this hypothesis was true, we should find a very low morbidity risk of the relatives, equal to that of unipolar depression. But the opposite is true. Therefore, also drug-induced hypomania does not explain the findings.

Another intervening variable may be sex. As mentioned in the description of the samples, we found a much higher proportion of females in group Dm (10m, 33f) than in group MD (17m, 19f) or in group Md (8m, 6f). Obviously, there is a systematic trend in the sex ratio among the three groups. If sex would explain the differences in morbidity risk of relatives of the three groups, we should expect that relatives of female probands would generally show a higher morbidity risk than relatives of male probands. It has to be mentioned that the morbidity risk of relatives of male versus female probands of both unipolar depression and bipolar disorder does not differ significantly (Angst et al. [1978c]).

In Table 4 the morbidity risk of female versus male probands is compared. If the difference among the three subgroups was due to the sex factor, the genetic differences among the stratified subsamples should disappear.

The results show that the subgroups are rather small in size, and, therefore, the interpretation has to be cautious. The morbidity risk of relatives for psychoses and suicides decreases as expected if we compare the group Dm with MD and Md.

This is more or less true for both sexes. The total morbidity risk, including neuroses and personality disorders, shows the same trend. The group Dm is characterized by an elevated risk for schizophrenia and schizoaffective disorders, and a certain heterogeneity can therefore not be excluded. The morbidity risk for affective disorders and suicide does not differ significantly among the female probands of the groups Dm and MD. This is not compatible with the hypothesis of a heterogeneity of bipolar manic-depressive disorder. But one has to consider that the schizoaffective cases may also belong to the bipolar entity and not to schizophrenia; in that case the group Dm shows a higher morbidity risk for relatives than does the group

Table 4. Genetics of Bipolar Subtypes by Sex

	Dm				MD				Md			
	M N	%	**F** N	%	**M** N	%	**F** N	%	**M** N	%	**F** N	%
Probands N	10		33		17		19		10		6	
Relatives BZ												
ICD 295 Schizophrenia	56.8		174.8		92.0		102.1		67.9		32.9	
ICD 296 Affective disorder	42.6		132.2		70.7		77.2		50.6		24.6	
ICD	N	%	N	%	N	%	N	%	N	%	N	%
1. 295 Schizophrenia	1		6	5.7	1	1.1	–		1	1.5	1	6.1
2. 295.7 Schizoaffective disorders	2		4		–		1	1.0	–		–	
3. 296.2 Unipolar depressions	5		13		1		7		1		1	
4. 296.3 Bipolar disorders	1	21.1	5	17.4	1	4.2	3	16.8	1	4.0	–	
5. Suicides	3		5		1		3		–		1	
6. 300 Neuroses	3		5		3		5		3		–	
7. 301 Personality disorders	1	9.4	9	10.6	10	18.4	6	14.2	5	15.8	1	4.1
Total 1–5	12	26.4	33	23.1	4	5.3	14	17.8	3	5.5	3	10.2
1–7	16	35.8	47	33.7	17	23.7	25	32.0	11	19.8	4	14.3

MD. Finally, there is no doubt that the morbidity risk of relatives of preponderantly manic probands Md is considerably lower than for group Dm. This is true for both sexes.

We may have to conclude that the hypothesis of a heterogeneity of bipolar disorder is still supported if we stratify the samples by the sex of the probands. But the figures are rather small and the conclusion cannot be definitive. We need a replication by a study of another proband sample.

Heterogeneity of Schizoaffective Disorders

The work of Angst (1966) and Perris (1966) has shown that there is a true genetic difference between unipolar depression and bipolar depressive disorders. The relatives of the former show a lower frequency of affective disorders, a lack of bipolar and unipolar manic disorders, and a higher morbidity of females. Based on these findings, one can raise the hypothesis that in schizoaffective families a similar trend should be present: Families of manic schizoaffective probands should show a higher incidence of affective disorders and a higher frequency of mania than those of the nonmanic group. On the other hand, we should expect a lower incidence of affective disorders in the families of nonmanic schizoaffective patients, and as secondary cases, mainly unipolar depression.

Table 5 gives the findings. The figures at risk have been calculated by the method of Stromgren and Slater. It is evident that there is no difference in

Table 5. Manic versus Nonmanic Schizoaffective Probands and Morbidity Risk of Relatives

		Proband Manic		Proband Nonmanic	
Probands N		97		53	
Relatives BZ					
ICD 295 Schizophrenia		538.6		336.4	
ICD 296 Affective disorder		404.3		252.3	
Diagnoses of Relatives		N	%	N	%
ICD					
295	Schizophrenia	32	5.94	14	4.16
295.7	Schizoaffective disorders	22	4.08	4	1.19
296.2	Unipolar depressions	24	5.94	13	5.15
296.3	Bipolar disorders	4	.99	3	1.19
299	Unspecified psychoses	2	.49	—	—
	Suicides	8	1.98	4	1.59
300	Neuroses	15	3.71	22	8.72
301	Personality disorders	28	6.93	20	7.93

morbidity for unipolar depression or bipolar affective disorders between the two groups. There is not even a trend in the expected direction. Schizophrenic secondary cases are also found in equal frequency in both groups. Only schizoaffective disorders seem to be more frequent in families of manic patients than in the others. In the families of non-manic patients there is a higher frequency of neuroses but this finding may be irrelevant because the morbidity risk is not elevated compared to the general population.

We have to conclude that from a genetic point of view manic and non-manic schizoaffective patients do not differ. Both show an elevated risk for schizophrenia and affective disorders in their families. There is no homo-typology in the sense that schizoaffective patients would show an especially high morbidity in their families for schizoaffective disorders. On the contrary, there is a relatively low morbidity for schizoaffective disorders. The attempt to show a heterogeneity of schizoaffective disorder by the criterion of mania has failed. The question of the heterogeneity of schizoaffective disorders has been dealt with in more details in ANGST et al. 1978b.

Conclusions

The search for a heterogeneity of bipolar manic-depressive and schizo-affectie disorders seems to be interesting. In schizoaffective disorders manic versus non-manic probands do not differ considerably from a genetic point of view: The morbidity risk of first degree relatives for schizophrenia, for unipolar and bipolar affective disorder is the same. Therefore mania does not seem to be a criterion to split schizoaffective probands successfully into two nosological subgroups.

It seems to be more interesting and promising to subdivide patients with affective disorders into subgroups. After the subdivision into unipolar and bipolar affective disorders, it is of interest to subdivide bipolar patients into further subgroups according to their preponderance of the symptomatology, prevailingly depressed (mildly manic) Dm, prevailingly manic (mildly depressed) Md, and severely both manic and depressed patients MD. The morbidity risk of the first-degree relatives of these three subgroups seems to differ. It is of great theoretical interest that the preponderantly depressed group Dm shows the highest morbidity, followed by group MD, and finally Md. These findings are certainly not expected, neither from Leonhard's hypothesis conerning monopolar and bipolar disorders nor from a simple theory suggesting a continuum between depression and mania with increasing severity of an underlying pathological process. Further studies will be necessary to unravel the influence of an unequal sex distribution within these subgroups.

It seems also of some interest that the preponderance of depression versus bipolar affective disorders is also found within subgroups of bipolar patients in the sense that the subgroup Dm is more frequent than the subgroup Md. That means that within bipolar disorders, mania is less frequent than depression.

We need certainly more comparative genetic investigations between bipolar subgroups and recurrent unipolar mania. The latter seems to be extremely rare, especially if the patients are followed up for many years. As long as we do not have any genetic evidence for differences between unipolar mania and bipolar affective disorders, we have to stick to the hypothesis of homogeneity.

SUMMARY

The study is devoted to the problem of heterogeneity of bipolar and schizoaffective disorders based on the presence or absence or on the severity of manic symptomatology. A certain heterogeneity can be shown in regard to the course of these two disorders and their genetic etiology (morbidity risk of first-degree relatives). The study is based on 95 bipolar and 150 schizo-affective patients and their first-degree relatives, broken down into three subgroups of bipolar disorders and two subgroups of schizoaffective disorders.

From a genetic point of view, it can be shown that subgroups of bipolar patients differ in a sense that is not compatible with current hypotheses. It will be of furture interest to replicte these findings. The attempt to subdivide schizoaffective patients into manic and nonmanic did not result in any genetic differences in their families.

The course of the subgroups of bipolar and schizoaffective disorders seems to be influenced by the presence and severity of manic symptomatology. Patients with mania generally show a more malignant course of the disorder: earlier age at onset, higher frequency of episodes. In the bipolar subgroup, the preponderantly manic symptomatology was correlated with longer episodes and lower frequency of full remission, whereas in schizoaffective patients the manic subgroup showed the contrary—a shorter length of the episodes and a higher frequency of full remission. In conclusion the search for heterogeneity of bipolar affective disorders seems paradoxically more promising than that for schizoaffective disorders.

REFERENCES

Angst, J., Zur Aetiologie und Nosologie endogener depressiver Psychosen. *Monogr. Gesamtgebiete Neurol. Psychiat. Heft* 112, Springer, Berlin, (1966).

Angst, J., The course of affective disorders. II. Typology of bipolar manic-depressive illness. *Arch. Psychiat. Nervenkr* 225 (1978a, in print).

Angst, J., The course of affective disorders. In *Handbook of Biological Psychiatry, H.M. van Praag, M.H. Lader, D.J. Rafaelsen, E.J. Sachar, eds. Marcel Dekker, New York, (1978b, in print).*

Angst, J., Baastrup, P., Grof, P., Hippius, H., Poeldinger, W., Weis, P. *The course of monopolar depression and bipolar psychoses. Psychiat. Neur. Neurochir.* 76, 489–500 (1973).

Angst, J., Felder, W., Frey, R. Bipolar disorders. Results of a genetic investigation I. (Manuscript in preparation).

Angst, J., Felder, W., Frey, P., Stassen, H.H. The course of affective disorders. I. Change of diagnosis of monopolar, unipolar and bipolar illness. *Arch. Psychiat. Nervenkr.* 225 (1978a in print).

Angst, J., Felder, W., Lohmeyer, B. Verlauf schizoaffektiver Psychosen. Ergebnisse katamnestischer Untersuchungen. In *Ziele, Methoden und Ergebnisse der Psychiatrischen Verlaufsforschung,* G.W. Schimmelpenning, ed. Huber, Bern (1978b, in print).

Cadoret, R.J., Fowler, R.C., McCabe, M.S., Winokur, G. Evidence for heterogeneity in a group of good-prognosis schizophrenics. *Comp. Psychiat.* 15, 443–450 (1974).

Dunner, D.L., Fleiss, J.L., Fieve, R.R. The course of development of mania in patients with recurrent depression. *Am. J. Psychiat.* 133, 905–908 (1976).

Gershon, E.S., Bunney, W.E., Leckmann, J.F., van Eerdewegh, M., DeBauche, B.A. The inheritance of affective disorders: A review of data and hypotheses. *Behav. Genet.* 6, 227–261 (1976).

Leonhard, K. Aufteilung der endogenen Psychosen. Akademia Verlag, Berlin (1957).

Perris, C. A study of bipolar (manic-depressive) and unipolar recurrent depressive psychoses. *Acta Psychiat. Scand. Suppl. 194* (1966).

A Glossary of Mental Disorder. Her Majesty's Stationery Office, London (1968).

CHAPTER 6

The Subjective Experience of Mania

Yakov Lerner

Modern psychiatry deals mainly with observable phenomena that can be described, measured, and verified. This holds true particularly in psychotic patients, whose statements are regarded as liable to distortion and fantasy. In textbooks of psychiatry, psychopathological phenomena are therefore described in a technical, objective, "scientific" way, avoiding subjective impressionistic or personal accounts. But precisely such authentic subjective reports can provide dramatic and rich material about the patient's experience from within and enable us to understand better these strange and baffling phenomena.

One should remember the initial enthusiasm that arose among psychiatrists who believed the psychedelic drugs to be able to elicit model psychoses, mimicking the symptoms of schizophrenia. Disillusionment came later, when important differences between schizophrenics and drug subjects were detected. What contributed much in pointing out these differences was the material gathered from self-accounts of schizophrenic patients. Moreover, schizophrenic patients who were given LSD experienced typical psychedelic manifestations but were nevertheless able to describe the difference between the drug's action and their own illness (Snyder, 1974). Thus clear and thorough subjective self-reports can help to clarify more delicate features of psychopathology, supplementing the observable behavioral manifestations.

Although there are many autobiographical books and articles written by schizophrenic patients (Freedman, 1974) during the onset and course or remission of psychotic episodes, such reports by manic-depressive patients are less known. In this chapter, published personal accounts of former manic patients will be reviewed. These descriptions will be compared with accounts from schizophrenic autobiographies and with personal accounts of psychedelic experiences in normal individuals. Several reviews were helpful, especially those of Landis (1964), Freedman (1974), and Kleinman et al. (1977). In Table 1, a list of known published personal accounts of manic patients is given.

**Table 1. Data on Publishing Personal Accounts
of Former Manic Patients**

Author	Date	Source of Report	Sex	Diagnosis
Anon	1858	Patient	Male	Affect. dis., manic type
Beers	1908	Patient	Male	Bipolar affect.
Reid	1910	Doctor	Female	Bipolar
MacCurdy	1925	Doctor	Male	Affect. dis., manic type
Anderson	1938	Doctor	Female	Affect. dis., manic type
Graves	1942	Patient	Male	Schizoaffective?
Custance	1952	Patient	Male	Affect. bipolar
Dahl	1959	Patient	Male	Affect. dis., manic type

One of the best formulations of the main features of the manic experience is given by Custance:

> They are...1) intense sense of well-being 2) heightened sense of reality 3) breach in the barriers of individuality 4) inhibition of the sense of repulsion 5) release of sexual and moral tension 6) delusions of grandeur and power 7) sense of ineffable revelation. [Custance, 1952, p. 55.]

In the following sections we will elaborate on some of these subjective symptoms, even if not all of them are mentioned in the other self-reports.

Elation does not mark the experience of every manic patient. But it is significant that practically the only state that is experienced by mental patients as being pleasant is that of mania.

> First and foremost comes a general sense of intense well-being. I know of course that this sense is illusory and transient...It is only when I have been free in the manic state that the ecstatic sensations accompanying it have their full effect...Although however the restrictions of confinement are apt at times to produce extreme irritation and even paroxysms of anger, the general sense of well-being, the pleasurable and sometimes ecstatic feeling tone remains as a sort of permanent backgroud of all experience during the manic period. [Custance, 1952, p. 30.]

Another patient remarked:

> I'm absolutely certain it's wrong when people say it's too good to be true, for the happier I am the more I'm conscious it's real...you just have a feeling you're part of the earth, not a person on your own, sort of melt into it. [Anderson, 1938, p. 83.]

Even when confronted with external restraint, the manic patient may not lose his high spirit.

> I have found myself happy, undisturbed, even while realising approaching conditions of physical discomfort and restraint, and have probed my consciousness wondering for reasons. [Graves, 1942, p. 673.]

Beers (1931) wrote that the manic period leaves, later on, mainly very pleasant impressions, and he cited a letter of Charles Lamb to Coleridge dated June 1796:

> I look back upon it at times with a gloomy kind of envy, for while it lasted, I had many, many hours of pure happiness. Dream not, Coleridge, of having tasted all the grandeur and wildness of Fancy till you have gone mad: All now seems to me vapid, comparatively so...[Beers, 1931, p. 91.]

This happy-feeling tone is accompanied by a sense of physical efficiency and well-being.

> The intense sense of well-being, which is physical as well as mental, is not wholly illusory. My digestive system functions particularly well, without the slightest trace of constipation or diarrhea, and I have an inordinate appetite. Metabolism is rapid. I can stand cold without difficulty or discomfort, an inner warmth seems to pervade me. I can, for example walk about naked out of doors on quite cold nights...[Custance, 1952, p. 59.]

In contrast to this general sense of well-being in the manic patient, some degree of depression was noted in 15 out of 16 schizophrenic personal accounts reviewed by Kleinman et al. (1977). The schizophrenic's mental suffering is often accompanied by pain and physical discomfort. Davidson described it vividly:

> That evening I felt the remarkably unpleasant sensation of a clamp around my head. I heard and felt the beating of what seemed like huge wings in my ears...At last for a few short moments in which I felt I must sink to the ground and die, I felt appalling agony, as of two horns being rammed down from above, through the front top part of my skull, right down into my very brain, while a rusty red light seemed to be closing in on me choking me. I was just able to keep from shouting out with pain...[Davidson, 1912, cited in Landis, P. 307.]

Fear is as commonly experienced by schizophrenic patients as depression (Kleinman et al., 1977). Usually it accompanies the beginning of the schizophrenic's mental breakdown. One of the examples we found in Peters' account:

> Fear comes suddenly, chilling and shocking. But in this there is no bold stroke, only the slow preparation of terror...With it come uncertainty and new shadows—shadows with movements and hidden life, the life of the small nighttime enemies: rodents, insects, marauders and...what? The sounds and movements of people are contained and stifled, the cry of alarm dies in the throat of the victim, the child looks quickly over a shoulder for what is not there, and the gesture is stealthy, ill. [Peters, 1949, p. 2.)

These excerpts of accounts by schizophrenic patients illustrate the protracted suffering, the immobility of terror, and the frightening feeling of unreality in contrast with the pleasurable, even ecstatic mood found in most manic self-reports. One cannot dismiss, of course, Carlson and Goodwin's findings (1973) on the frequency of dysphoric and depressive symptoms in the more severe progressive stages of untreated mania. But are the main features of depression, such as hopelessness, despair, and guilt feelings, really characteristic also of the dysphoric mood changes seen in manic patients, or are the latter secondary reactions to the inner turmoil and feelings of exhaustion experienced by the manic patient, presenting therefore, another quality of dysphoria? Comparing more self-reports about these different experiences would help to clarify this issue.

The feeling of well-being is often accompanied by a sense of enhanced sensory awareness. Sensory impressions seem clearer, brighter, more colorful. These sensations are not only more intense and vivid, but are also more pleasurable.

> The outer world makes a much more vivid and intense impression on me than usual...The first thing I note is the peculiar appearances of the lights—the ordinary electric lights in the ward. They are not exactly brighter, but deeper, more intense, perhaps a trifle more ruddy than usual. Moreover, if I relax the focussing of my eyes, which I can do very much more easily than in normal circumstances, a bright star-like phenomenon emanates from the lights, ultimately forming a maze of irridescent patterns of all colours of the rainbow...[Custance, 1952, p. 30.]

Visual stimuli appear so vivid that they may take on an illusory character.

> I had been accustomed to find surcease in absorbing sun rays, and had discovered odd and meaningless symbols apt to form behind eyelids in its light. I glanced at the orb, stood a minute in its light, and was pleased and surprised to find a renewal of the spectacle in elaborate form. A series of golden yellow bars flashed before my eyes, much like the rounded end strips which a medic uses to hold down a tongue in throat inspection...As I swung around to develop the display, one similar shape in green, and a fifth, in red, dropped over each other to form a kind of moon-track over the Parkway, the blend making a deep purple. [Graves, 1942, p. 283.]

The feeling of enhanced sensory awareness is often accompanied by a feeling of increased cognitive efficiency escalating to an almost incredible power of insight and wisdom. One of MacCurdy's patients states that

> during an exhilaration the mind penetrates infinitely more deeply into all things, and receives flashes of almost divine light and wisdom, which open to it, momentarily, regions of thought hitherto difficult or impossible of penetration. [MacCurdy, 1925, p. 301.]

Not always is the experience of increased mental activity a pleasurable one, especially when it reaches a state where the patient has the feeling that he has too many thoughts at once, a state like that described by Beers:

During the night, the floodgates of thought were wide open. So jealous of each other were the thoughts that they seemed to stumble over one another in their mad rush to present themselves to my re-enthroned ego. [Beers, 1931, p. 98.]

Sometimes the patients even complain that the thoughts were moving too quickly for them to follow each one.

The condition of my mind for many months is beyond all description. My thoughts ran with lightning-like rapidity from one subject to another. I had an exaggerated feeling of self-importance. All the problems of the universe came crowding into my mind, demanding instant discussion and solution—mental telepathy, hypnotism, wireless telegraphy, Christian Science, women's rights and all the problems of medical science, religion and politics. [Reid, 1910, p. 615.]

Sometimes the written account itself discloses the pressure of thoughts, the shift from one train of thought to the next. The following is from the diary of a patient who had experienced mania:

Often, I remember, have I lain on my sleepless bed, and strung one group of words together, as they thus occurred to me, and catching at some slight analogy in the last, would run off into another distinct series and thus, till the tongue fairly wearied, and the lips refused to move, have arranged the affairs and settled the disputes of generations past, present and yet to be: of princes and potentates, of injured queens, and defrauded heirs apparent—rummaging the legends of the Tower, and all the dark, romantic lore of Scottish feudal life; righting the wrong in every department or age of human existance, quarrelling most irreverently and partly with many characters which good people deem sacred, and elevating in my own imagination many of those luckless but interesting heroes who, with many dazzling and redeeming qualities, had yet the misfortune to be wicked. [Anon, 1858, cited in Landis, 1964, p. 149.]

Sometimes such descriptions of racing thoughts and enhanced sensory awareness can be found among schizophrenic accounts (Freedman, 1974). But usually the alternations in congnitive function as reported by these schizophrenic patients are more diverse and variable. Thoughts may be retarded or speeded, fragmented, confused, illogical, or bizarre. Instead of enhanced self-confidence, the schizophrenic patient often has a frightèning sense of loss of control of his thinking. Davidson described his distressing feeling:

I became aware, to my horror, that I had acted and thought in a cyclic manner... It seemed as if this self-centered sequence of thought had in itself a fearful compelling power over my body... I felt that the longer this went on, the stronger it would get, and I knew that it meant I should really go mad, tied by a cyclic chain of thought to a circular round of places. I broke into a sweat with fear, and prayed a short but fervent prayer for relief from certain appalling insanity and death. [Davidson, 1912, cited in Landis, 1964, p. 162.]

Often psychedelic experiences have been compared to those of schizophrenic patients, and the differences are pointed out (Kleinman et al., 1977). But many such hallucinogenic experiences are indeed similar to those reported above by manic patients, such as the vivid and colorful perceptions. Huxley, after taking mescaline, wrote:

> Half an hour after swallowing the drug I became aware of a slow dance of golden lights. A little later there were sumptuous red surfaces swelling and expanding from bright nodes of energy that vibrated with a continuously changing, patterned life. At another time the closing of my eyes revealed a complex of grey structures, within which pale blueish spheres kept emerging into intense solidity and having emerged would slide noiselessly upwards, out of sight. [Huxley, 1959, p. 16.]

A likewise effect was reported by Leary, after being administered dimethyltryptamine intramuscularly:

> Suddenly I opened my eyes and sat up...the room was celestial, glowing with radiant illumination...light, light light...Beneath the radiant surface I could see the delicate wondrous body machinery of each person, the network of muscle and vein and body—exquisitely beautiful... [Leary, 1966, p. 86, cited in Kleinman et al., 1977, p. 566]

The effects reported during the psychedelic experiences were predominantly of intense well-being (Kleinman et al., 1977), again more like those found in accounts of manic patients than those in the accounts of the schizophrenic patients.

In close relation to the two former characteristics of manic patients—the sense of well-being and heightened sensory awareness—manic patients often describe the feeling of breakdown of individuality, not in the negative sense of being intruded upon, but in reverse, a kind of self-expansion. Custance described it thus:

> It is actually a sense of communion, in the first place with God, and in the second place with all mankind...The sense of communion extends to all fellow-creatures with whom I come into contact; it is not merely ideal or imaginative but has a practical effect on my conduct. Thus when in the manic state, I have no objection to being more or less herded together—as is inevitable in public Mental Hospitals—with men of all classes and conditions. [Custance, 1952, pp. 37, 41.]

Feelings of communion may spill over to include all creation. Thus another patient reported:

> I seem to merge into everything...The whole being expands. If you are alone and you yield to it, the more it grows over you, and you feel you can't keep on the ground...You want to give yourself up to it because it seems as if something finally happened you would lose yourself... [Anderson, 1938, p. 85.]

Such ecstatic, pleasurable experiences seem to be unique to manic patients, and perhaps only in psychedelic experiences one can find similar descriptions. Watts, after using LSD, described his feelings:

> ...through the thin soles of my moccasins, I could feel the sound becoming alive under my feet, connecting me with the earth and the trees and the sky in such a way that I seemed to become one body with my whole surroundings. [Watts, 1960, p. 143.]

The feeling of exaltation, of increased cognitive efficiency and enhanced awareness, and the sense of communion with the universe lead to the delusions of the schizophrenics, which are aimed at evil and imaginary

> It seems to me that all my wishes are coming true, that all my ambitions, in work and in play, political, financial, personal, are going to be realised, that vital secrets of the Universe are being revealed to me and so on...I feel so close to God, so inspired by His spirit that in a sense I am God. I see the future, plan the Universe, save mankind; I am utterly and completely immortal; I am even male and female. The whole Universe, animate and inanimate, past, present and future, is within me. All nature and life, all spirits, are co-operating and connected with me; all things are possible. I am in a sense identical with all spirits from God to Satan. I reconcile Good and Evil and create light, darkness, worlds, universes. [Custance, 1952, pp. 51–52.]

Even if these are delusions, it seems that the manic patient may not be completely convinced of their truth.

> Of course it is all a dream, a vision, pure imagination if there is such a thing. I know perfectly well that in fact I have no power...and I can truthfully say that never in the midst of the wildest flights of grandiose ideas have I ever allowed myself to forget that. [Custance, 1952, p. 52.]

Beer's account gives the same message:

> After all, delusions of grandeur are the most entertaining of toys. The assortment which my imagination provided was a comprehensive one. I had tosses aside the blocks of childhood days. Instead of laboriously piling small squares of wood one upon another, in an endeavor to build the tiny semblance of a house, I now, in this second childhood of mine, projected against thin air phantom edifices, planned and completed in the twinkling of an eye. To be sure such houses of cards almost immediately superseded each other, but the vanishing of one could not disturb a mind which had ever another interesting bauble to take its place. [Beers, 1931, p. 188.]

Manic delusions are like wish-fulfilling dreams, full of self-confidence and self-pleasure. They differ, thus, from the common persecutory and hateful delusions of the schizophrenics, which are aimed at evil and imaginery enemies. Examples of such delusions are found in the following two schizophrenic self-reports:

> I am causing lots of people to become insane, accidentally, by reason of the power that leaves me and comes back—people are changing. This power causes railroad accidents, which is awful. My presence in the world is injurious to many people. I don't understand how; it is just an observation...People's voices change when talking; sometimes they appear pale and drowsy, again happy and full of life, and it seems to me that I am the medium of all that; it seems that I exercise some involuntary control over them...I imagine people losing their teeth, babies are dwarfed; people have nervous breakdowns, etc.,—all on my account. The blight seems to effect my two brothers; they, too, it seems are having physical and nervous trouble...I can't see how I could be such a freak of nature as to have these powers. [Karpman, 1953, p. 279.]

Another excerpt:

> During the paranoid period I thought I was being persecuted for my beliefs, that my enemies were actively trying to interfere with my activities, were trying to harm me, and at times even to kill me...In order to carry through the task which had been imposed upon me, and to defend myself against the terrifying and bewildering dangers of my external situation, I was endowed in my imagination with truly cosmic powers. The sense of power was not always purely defensive, but was also connected with a strong sense of valid inspiration. I felt I had power to determine the weather which responed to my inner moods, and even to control the movement of the sun in relation to other astronomical bodies. [Anon, 1955, p. 681.]

Delusions of power and grandeur sometimes give rise in some patients to ideas of divine revelation and beatitude.

> And now it is that as your goodness grows and your happiness increases, your eyes are unblinded more and more and your ears are undeafened more and more. As all resentments leave you, all hate, all angers and all contempts, how you grow to love yourself and your fellows and how now as this happens it also happens that you have eyes that see, and ears that hear, and more, so many things more, do these eyes see and hear, as in a revelation, than do the eyes and ears of your poor fellows.
>
>   How doth wisdom pour now into your soul, your psyche, your soulpsyche, your psyche-soul, your wholeness, your holiness. You see God in all around you and you can feel His Goodness outside you and in and now you speak. Or is it you speaking? Could it not be God speaking in you? [Dahl, 1959, p. 154.]

The sense of revelation is closely connected with the feeling of communion with God.

> Because I loved God, I felt He was in me, and I felt I wanted to go out and tell the world about it. I didn't actually see a Cross, but I was always conscious of the Cross and from it came the most amazing love and power. [Anderson, 1938, p. 83.]

Beers (1931) felt himself chosen for a mission:

I now interpreted the most trifling incidents as messages from God...Surely I
have been selected as the instrument wherewith great reforms shall be effected.
[Beers, 1931, p. 92.]

For Custance, revelation is an ecstatic experience:

In that peace I felt utterly and completely forgiven, relieved from all burden of
sin. The whole of infinity seemed to open up before me, and during the weeks and
months which followed I passed through experiences which are virtually
indescribable. The complete transformation of reality transported me as it were
into the Kingdom of Heaven. The ordinary beauties of nature particularly, I
remember, the skies at sunrise and sunset, took on a transcendental loveliness
beyond belief. Every morning, quite contrary to my usual sluggish habits, I
jumped up to look at them, and when possible went out to drink in, in a sort of
ecstasy, the freshness of the morning air...
A sense of ineffable revelation persists in varying degrees throughout the state
and seems intimately linked with the delusions of power. It seems to me as though
all truth, all the secrets of the Universe were being revealed, as though I had some
clue, some open-sesame to creation. [Custance, 1952, pp. 46, 52.]

Such ecstatic experiences can be found, perhaps, in psychedelic accounts.
Wasson, reporting his mescaline experience, gave the following description:

It permits you to see, more clearly than our perishing mortal eye can see, vistas
beyond the horizons of this life, to travel backwards and forwards in time, to
enter other planes of existence, even (as the Indians say) to know God. It is hardly
surprising that your emotions are profoundly affected, and you feel that an
indissoluble bond unites you with the others who have shared with you the sacred
agape. [Wasson, 1965, p. 35.]

The exaggerated elation, the delusions of grandeur and power, the feeling
of self-expansion, all these cannot be contained within the conventions of
society. As cultural inhibitons include many moral and sexual taboos, they
share the fate of other inhibitions in being disregarded by the manic patient.

There is a release of moral tension, particularly in the sexual sphere. The normal
inhibitions disappear, and sexual activity, instead of being placed, as in our
Western Christian civilization, in opposition to religion, becomes associated
with it...This was very clearly illustrated by the course of my first really intense
manic period, the first time my mind really slipped over the edge of the plateau of
reality and penetrated into the infinite regions beyond...One of the most
interesting features of this experience is the light it throws on the nature of the
sexual urge in mania. This urge is almost entirely impersonal. The question of
selecting an attractive girl, which normally plays a large part in sexual
adventures, did not trouble me in the least. I was quite content to leave it to
chance. Moreover it would be quite wrong to dismiss the whole episode as just a

matter of unbridled "lust." Lust is something very different. [Custance, 1952, pp. 44, 49.]

This loss of conventional inhibitions extends even to daily habits and customs.

I have no replusion to excreta, urine and so on. I have no distaste for dirt. I do not care in the least whether I am washed or not, whereas I am terrified of the slightest speck of dirt and continually wash my hands like Lady Macbeth when in a state of depression...[Custance, 1952, p. 421.]

The manic patient, free from inner inhibitions, does not concern himself much about the difference between a wish and its fulfillment. Whatever he is longing for becomes something that had already occurred without any sense of guilt.

...I could possibly, for example, aver ownership to real estate which I had in reality merely viewed and talked of buying, or assert a complete mastery of branches of learning whose merest rudiments I was perfectly well aware only to have examined superficially...And in this way I excuse myself to myself, by imagining that I am in somewhat the same category as the merchant or broker, who undertakes to deliver, at some future time, articles which he has not yet bought, or makes prices on things which do not belong to him. For, we both undoubtedly think that we can produce the goods when called upon to do so. [MacCurdy, 1925, p. 302.]

Although many of the excerpts included in this chapter emphasized the pleasurable affective tone accompanying many of the manic experiences, mania is not a period of complete happiness.

Sometimes the manic is overwhelmed by his intense emotions and senses, having the feeling that he is living in a kind of whirlwind, which may lead to exhaustion.

Graves pointed out this aspect of the manic experience:

In mania...the emotional flow is so irrationally fast (for reasons quite beyond my understanding), the change from extreme to extreme is so fluid, that any sort of definition of judgement about it is impossible...[Graves, 1942, p. 671.]

The manic's turmoil is therefore only partially recalled after the fading away of the acute phase. In Grave's words:

The state of waking from a dream isn't a very close comparison, because the memory after dreams is occasionally very good, while the memory of the manic conduct is absolutely cut off. [Graves, 1942, p. 668.]

Similarly:

But once I get out of a Mental Hospital all this changes. I find myself in a totally different atmosphere. I cannot, however hard I try, get even my most intimate relatives and friends to understand or take any interest in what may or may not have happened to me during my madness. Gradually the vividness of my memory fades; like my relatives, I try to put the whole experience out of my mind. [Custance, 1952, p. 115.]

Maybe this one of the reasons for the scarcity of manic self-reports.

One may well raise the question whether we can generalize from the content of a few personal accounts. Moreover, these patients who were able to relate their inner experinces probably possess exceptional introspective gifts and may not be representative of all patients. This is perhaps true, particularly in the case of Custance, on whose lucid descriptions I heavily draw. For all that, these personal accounts raise some interesting issues that deserve further discussion.

One of the important questions in psychiatric literature is how to distinguish mania from schizophrenia during the acute manifestations of psychosis, particularly if there are no previous psychotic episodes. Schizophreniform symptoms, such as paranoid delusions, bizarre behavior, even hallucinations and posturing, may occur in mania (Winokur et al., 1969; Lipkin et al., 1970; Carlson and Goodwin, 1973). Thus obervable phenomena are sometimes insufficient to help us differentiate the more psychotic mania from acute schizophrenia. Yet popular rating scales designed for assessing manic symptomatology, such as the Manic Scale (Beigel et al., 1971), deal mainly with behavioral phenomena. It would be worthwhile, therefore, to explore more extensively the subjective descriptions of the patients in the directions that are hinted at in the above-mentioned self-reports. If anger and irritability are predominant, we should carefully scrutinize the progressive unfolding of the present psychotic episode, and look for expressions such as enhanced sensory awareness, increased cognitive efficiency, symptoms with a pleasurable quality, or, perhaps, ecstatic and beatific experiences, all of which could precede the present atypical affective state.

Further instances of diagnostic difficulties in need of clarification are the delusional symptoms. By noting and analyzing the subjective descriptions, one may detect whether the delusions are more wish-fulfilling and less defensive and hateful, more oriented toward communion and less toward segregation. Hallucinations, which are on the whole rarer in manic patients, according to the self-reports, are more of the visual type and have an intense and vivid quality. The bright and colorful sensations mentioned, coupled sometimes with ecstatic, pleasurable feelings, seem to be much closer to the psychedelic experiences than to those of the schizophrenic.

Interestingly, there are no well-known studies on administering psychedelic drugs to manic patients in order to compare the psychedelic experience in these patients with the manic-proper experience. Biochemically, there may be some link between the action of LSD on the serotonergic system (Aghajanian and Wang, 1978) and the role the latter plays in affective disorder (Murphy et al., 1978). Moreover, the remitting course of the affective disorders, in contrast to the more typical protracted course of schizophrenia, is more similar to the transient, self-limited phenomena observed after psychedelic drug use.

Thus subjective first-hand information that we gain from manics' self-reports can be used in sharpening our diagnostic tools and can help us, perhaps, in adding supplementary clinical material to the study of bio-chemical models of affective disorders.

REFERENCES

Aghajanian, G.K., and Wang, R.Y. Physiology and pharmacology of central serotonergic neurons. In *Psychopharmacology, A Generation of Progress,* M.A. Lipton, A. DiMascio and K.F. Killom, eds. Raven, New York (1978).
Anderson, E.W. A clinical study of states of "ecstasy" occurring in affective disorders. *J. Neurol. Psych.* 4, 80–99 (1938).
Anon. An autobiography of a schizophrenic experience. *J. Ab. Soc. Psychol.* 51, 677–689 (1955).
Beers, C.W. *A Mind That Found Itself,* 5th ed. Doubleday, New York (1931).
Beigel, A., Murphy, D.L., and Bunney, W.E. The manic-state rating scale. *Arch. Gen. Psychiat.* 25, 256–261 (1971).
Carlson, G.A., and Goodwin, F.K. The stages of mania. *Arch. Gen. Psychiat.* 28, 221–228 (1973).
Custance, J. *Wisdom, Madness and Folly.* Pellegrini & Cudaby, New York (1952).
Dahl, R. *Breakdown.* Bobbs-Merrill, New York (1959).
Freedman, B.J. The subjective experience of perceptual and cognitive disturbances in schizophrenia. *Arch. Gen Psychiat.* 30, 333–340 (1974).
Graves, A. *The Eclipse of Mind.* Medical Journal, New York (1942).
Huxley, A. *The Doors of Perception.* Penguin, Middlesex, Eng. (1959).
Karpman, B. Dream life in a case of hebephrenia. *Psychiatr. Quart.* 27, 262–316 (1953).
Kleinman, J.E., Gillin, J.C., and Wyatt, R.J. A comparison of the phenomenology of hallucinogens and schizophrenia from some autobiographical accounts. *Schiz. Bull.* 3, 560–586 (1977).
Landis, C. *Varieties of Psychopathological Experience.* Holt, Rinehart & Winston, New York (1964).
Lipkin, K.M., Dykrud, J., and Meyer, G.G. The many faces of maia. *Arch. Gen. Psychiat.* 22, 262–267 (1970).
MacCurdy, J.T. *The Psychology of Emotion: Morbid and Normal.* Kegan Paul, London (1925).
Murphy, D.L., Campbell, I.C., and Costa, J.L. The brain serotonergic system in the affective disorders. *Prog. Neuropsychopharm.* 2, 1–31 (1978).
Peters, F. *The World Next Door.* Farrar Straus, New York (1949).
Reid, E.C. Autopsychology of the manic-depressive. J. Nerv. Ment. Dis. 37, 606–6d20 (1910).
Snyder, S.H. *Madness and the Brain.* McGraw-Hill, New York (1974).
Wasson, R.G. The hallucinogenic fungi of Mexico. In *The Psychedelic Reader,* G.M. Weil, R. Metzner and T. Leary, eds. University Books, New Hyde Park, New York (1965).
Watts, A. *This Is It.* Pantheon, New York (1960).
Winokur, G.W., Clayton, P.J., and Reich, T. *Manic-Depressive Illness.* C.V. Mosby, St. Louis (1969).

CHAPTER 7

X-Linkage of Bipolar Illness and the Question of Schizoaffective Illness

Julien Mendlewicz

Whether the affective disorders, and in particular mania, encompass different clinical and genetic syndromes is still an unresolved question. The issue of heterogeneity in affective illness has been much debated, and the affective disorders have recently been differentiated on the basis of genetic studies into bipolar and unipolar forms of illness (Angst and Perris, 1968). Bipolar patients present both manic and depressive episodes, and their genetic load is greater than unipolar patients, who suffer only from depression. Most twin studies show that the concordance rate for bipolar illness in monozygotic twins is significantly higher than the concordance rate for the disease in dizygotic twins (Winokur et al., 1969). This observation is taken as evidence in favor of a genetic factor in bipolar illness. The diagnostic criteria used in these twin studies were often vague, and no distinction was made between unipolar and bipolar psychosis. Furthermore, there are no twin studies on unipolar manic patients.

At the beginning of this century, the Munich school introduced the Weinberg proband method to estimate morbidity risks in relatives of affected probands. The morbidity risk for a disease is the probability of presentation of this disease during a lifetime. Many investigators have since used this method to conduct family studies in psychiatry and other fields. Most of the early studies on bipolar illness have shown that this illness tends to be familial. The lifetime risk for the disease in relatives of bipolar probands is significantly higher than the risk in the general population. Most of the early family studies were based on chronically hospitalized probands, and the information on relatives was often collected through charts or was provided by the probands. Theses studies may be subject to underdiagnosis, a hypothesis that would explain the relatively low risks (8%) reported for relatives of affectively ill probands.

Statistical and diagnostic criteria also vary among studies. Some investigators have used broader diagnostic criteria for bipolar illness, including cyclothymic cases, while others have limited their sample to patients who had been hospitalized for mania. The risks published by Kallman (1954) for parents of bipolar probands are 23.4%, and for sibs, 22.7%.

With regard to morbidity risks in the more distant relatives (second-degree relatives), the rates usually rnage from 1% to 4%. It is thus clear that the risks for the illness are decreased as the degree of consanguinity is lowered, as expected if there is a genetic component in the etiology of this disease.

Most of the early family studies have been influenced by Kraepelin's classification as far as nosology is concerned. As a result of this, the above-mentioned investigators have included among their probands patients suffering from mania and depression (bipolar) and patients presenting depression only (unipolar) without distinguishing between these. Thus, the samples investigated in the various studies are relatively heterogeneous. Leonhard (1959) in Berlin was one of the first investigators to make a clinical distinction between bipolar and unipolar forms of affective disorders on genetic grounds. The bipolar patients were shown to have greater genetic loading for affective disorder than the unipolar patients. They also had more relatives with hypomanic temperaments as compared to the unipolar patients, whose relatives had depressive temperaments. The concept of hypomanic termperament is related to individuals who experience mild manic behavior and is thus close to the concept of unipolar mania. It was also concluded that bipolar and unipolar disorders may have different genetic etiologies.

The risk for bipolar illness in the relatives of affected patients can be estimated at somewhere between 15% and 35%. There is, however, a large proportion of relatives of bipolar probands who exhibit unipolar illness only (of the depressive or manic type). When correction has been made for age, diagnoses, and statistical procedures, the morbidity risks for bipolar illness in different types of first-degree relatives (parents, sibs, children) are similar. This observation is consistent with a dominant mode or transmission in this disease.

Linkage results, originating from different laboratories, suggest that an X-linked dominant factor is involved in the transmission of the bipolar phenotype in at least some families (Reich et al., 1969; Mendlewicz et al., 1972; Winokur and Tanna, 1969; Mendlewicz and Fleiss, 1974). However, we were unable to measure linkage between unipolar depressive illness and either protanopia or the Xg blood group in 14 informative families, an observation ruling out X-linked inheritance as the mode of transmission of unipolar illness (Mendlewicz and Fleiss, 1979). The linkage studies conducted so far on manic-depressive illness are of great potential since they are able to discriminate between sex-linked and sex-influenced types of inheritance and they do provide an estimate of the significance of the results. They all point to the presence of an X-linked dominant factor in the transmission of bipolar illness.

The X-linked pattern of bipolar illness can not be evidenced in all pedigrees of bipolar psychosis (Mendlewicz and Fleiss, 1974) and X-linkage has also been found to be consistent with the transmission of varied psychoses, including schizoaffective psychosis, in some families (Belmaker and Wyatt, 1976; Barron, 1977). These observations may be consistent with a concept of broader genetic liability to affective illness (affective spectrum disorder), as we have postulated in our adoption study of bipolar illness (Mendlewicz and Rainer, 1977). This linkage approach is nevertheless of great interest and should be extended to the study of other psychiatric conditions, such as schizophrenia, unipolar mania, and schizoaffective illness, using other genetic markers located on different chromosomes, such as the HLA system for chromosome 6.

The above studies of families with affective disorders have shown that there are at least two different genetic subgroups in affective illness. As a result, most of the recent biological studies in this field differentiate between bipolar and unipolar psychosis. There are, however, a minority of affectively ill patients who seem to exhibit recurrent manic behavior without depressive episodes. This unipolar manic syndrome has been given little attention, probably because of its relative rarity and of the overall concept that relates manic behavior to bipolar illness.

Da Rocha, as early as 1921, had described isolated cases of chronic manic behavior, as did Cakeron in 1936, and these authors considered such patients to suffer from a specific psychopathological syndrome, different from manic-depression or schizophrenia. More recently, Perris (1966) found in a Swedish study of affective disorders that 4.5% of his bipolar manic-depressive patients reported only manic episodes without depressive ones, but it is not clear from Perris's data whether these unipolar manic patients had a different genetic background than bipolar patients.

Bratfos and Haug (1968) have studied the clinical course in a sample of affectively ill patients, including bipolar and unipolar depressive patients. Out of this mixed sample, 2% of the patients were characterized as having a unipolar manic course. In Winokur et al.'s population (1969) unipolar mania was found to be a rare entity. In our sample of 134 bipolar manic-depressive patients consecutively admitted to the New York State Psychiatric Institute between January 1971 and April 1973, there was not a single case diagnosed as suffering from a unipolar manic form of affective illness. Another study based on hospital cases from India was aimed at eliciting genetic and social differences that might exist between monopolar and bipolar manic patients

(Chopra, 1975). The factors investigated were the occurrence of psychiatric illness in first-degree relatives, parental death before the patient's fifteenth birthday, and socioeconomic status of the patients. Fifty-two cases were identified as unipolar manics (i.e., with recurrent attacks of mania only). There were no significant differences in familial psychiatric moribidity in the parents and sibs of unipolar manic patients as compared to bipolar manic-depressive patients. Nor was there any difference in early parental loss and social class between these patients.

Most studies described above indicate that unipolar mania is a rare syndrome, and one could question its very existence if there wasn't a report by Abrams and Taylor describing the incidence of unipolar mania in a group of 50 manic probands (1974). In this investigation, 14 subjects (i.e., 28%) were found to manifest mania alone, without depressive episodes.

When compared to the bipolar patients, the unipolar manic patients had a later onset for affective illness, and their genetic loading was lower than that observed in the bipolar population. The authors, however, attributed these differences to age of onset rather than to biological or behavioral parameters, and they considered unipolar mania to be a subgroup of bipolar mania.

It has indeed been shown that late-onset affective illness has a less severe course of illness with a lower degree of genetic loading (Mendlewicz et al., 1972). Thus a patient exhibiting a first manic episode late in life would be less likely to present an affective relapse (depressive or manic).

A more promising approach consists in looking at manic behavior from the clinical and genetic points of view. Most manic patients have a rather typical and even sterotyped behavior in their acute phase. They have a positive heredity for bipolar and unipolar affective illness, and tend to show a good therapeutic and prophylactic response to lithium salts. However, psychotic symptoms, such as hallucinations and paranoid delusions, may also be present in mania, and such *"atypical manics"* with schizophrenic-like symtoms raise some nosological and therapeutic questions. It is not clear whether these atypical manic-depressives belong to the group of major affective disorders or to the schizophrenias, or represent a separate entity. Nor is it well determined if they are good lithium responders. Sometimes, the atypical manic syndrome is followed by residual symptoms of the schizophrenic line. These patients have also been labeled "schizoaffective," and their therapeutic management remains problematic. Asano (1967), from Mitsuda's group in Japan, has studied atypical manic-depression patients, and the results of his genetic investigation show atypical manic-depression to be more frequent in their families. Clayton et al. (1968), from Winokur's group, have come to the same conslusions as Mitsuda's group.

Recently, Cohen et al. (1972) have investigated a large sample of twins hospitalized in the V.A. hospitals. The concordance rates in typical manic-depressive twins were comparable to the rates found in twins with atypical mania who were diagnosed as schizoaffective patients.

The data presented by Cohen et al. suggest that the heritability of schizoaffective illness is more comparable to the heritability of manic-depression than schizophrenia. It is thus highly probable that there is a genetic link between atypical mania or schizoaffective illness and the group of affective psychoses. However, it is clear that atypical mania is an hetero-geneous syndrome, both from the genetic and from the clinical point of view.

We have previously shown that schizoaffective patients belong to different disease states, some of which may be transmitted through an X-linked dominant heredity, whereas others show a polygenic pattern of inheritance (Mendlewicz, 1976; Suslak et al., 1976; Shopsin et al., 1976). These differences in the genetic determinants of atypical mania may be responsible for the differential response rate to lithium therapy of patients with atypical mania. Some of these patients may require additional medications, such as phenothiazines, in order to achieve satisfactory results in the acute phase of the illness and for long-term maintenance therapy. This clinical observation emphasizes the genetic heterogeneity of the schizoaffective syndrome.

To illustrate this point, we have compared the genetic backgrounds of patients with various psychiatric disorders who were part of an overall investigation of genetic factors in psychiatric illnesses (Mendlewicz, 1976). The probands were all from a population of 326 patients consecutively admitted from January 1971 to July 1973 in an outpatient (236 patients) and inpatient (90 patients) clinic that treated patients with affective disorders at the New York State Psychiatric Institute. The sample consisted of 70 unipolar depressive patients, 126 bipolar manic-depressive patients, 80 schizophrenic patients, and 50 patients with atypical mania, i.e., schizoaffective patients. All patients and relatives were investigated in a blind manner, using a structured questionnaire derived from the Current and Past Psychopathology Scales (C.A.P.P.S.). From this original sample, we were able to match for age and sex 45 patients in each diagnostic group.

The highest morbidity risks observed in relatives for all illnesses were for bipolar and schizoaffective illness. The risks for all affective illnesses in these relatives were also greater than in the relatives of schizophrenic and unipolar depressive patients. On the other hand, the risks for schizophrenia in the relatives of bipolar and unipolar patients were much lower than in the relatives of schizophrenics and schizoaffectives, whereas these risks were far from being negligible. The risks for schizoaffective illness in all groups were too low to be statistically evaluated.

The risks for bipolar and unipolar illness were comparable in the relatives of bipolar versus schizoaffective probands, although the risk for bipolar illness was slightly more elevated in the relatives of bipolar patients. The risks for unipolar illness in the relatives of schizophrenic patients were apparently higher than those expected in the general population. The above family-risk data indicate that both unipolar and bipolar depressive illnesses are as common in the relatives of bipolar patients as in those of schizoaffective patients. This may suggest some genetic overlap between the two psychoses.

Schizophrenia, however, was also present in a number of schizoaffective families, an observation indicating the presence of a possible genetic relationship between schizoaffective and schizophrenic psychoses. But, perhaps, the most striking finding was the rarity of schizoaffective illness in the relatives of schizoaffective probands.

From the gentic point of view, these observations make it very unlikely that schizoaffective illness represents a distinct genetic syndrome. More conceivable, however, is the hypothesis that some schizoaffective syndromes share common genes with affective disorders, while others may share genes with schizophrenia. At this point, we can say that there is no evidence that unipolar mania reprsents a separate biologic entity. Family and twin studies as well as linkage studies with chromosome markers are suggestive of a main genetic relationship between schizoaffective syndromes and affective psychoses.

It is thus conceivable that some atypical manic phenotype may express an allelic form of bipolar illness. Nevertheless, a higher than expected incidence of schizophrenia is also reported in the relatives of schizoaffective probands, indicating that at least one type of schizoaffective illness may be genetically related to schizophrenia. Schizoaffective illness including its atypical manic form is thus to be considered as an heterogeneous condition encompassing different genetic forms, some of which are related to the affective psychoses while others are related to schizophrenia. Further investigation on clinical, biological, and psychosocial parameters as they relate to therapeutic outcome in various manic syndromes may shed some light on this intriguing polymorphic entity.

The adoption method provides a unique opportunity to separate the respective roles of heredity and environment. Our investigation was carried out in Belgium because adoptive registers are available there, and the adoption agencies were willing to help us to obtain subjects. Our subjects were the adoptive and biological parents of manic-depressive adoptees. There were three sets of controls: (1) the parents of manic-depressives who were not adoptees; (2) the adoptive and biological parents of normal adoptees, and (3) the parents of individuals who had contracted poliomyelitis during childhood or adolescence. This last group was designed to control for the effect on parents of bringing up a disabled child.

The group of affected offspring (that is, manic-depressive adoptees) was ascertained by systematically examining the medical records of five outpatient clinics and five inpatient services in the vicinity of Brussels. All admissions during a 5-year period (1971–1976) were reviewed.

The major finding of this investigation is that psychopathology in the biological parents is in excess of that found in the adoptive parents of the same manic-depressive offspring (Table 1). If we focus on disorders which we may call the affective spectrum, namely, bipolar affective disease (episodes of mania and depression), unipolar affective disease (psychotic depressions without mania), schizoaffective psychosis (schizophrenic and affective episodes), and cyclothymia (cyclothymic personality), the difference is significant at the level of P<0.025.

Table 1. Diagnosis of the Parents

| | Normal Adoptees (N = 22) | | | | | | Poliomyelitis (N = 20) | | |
| | Adoptive Parents | | | Biological Parents | | | Biological Parents | | |
	H	F		H	F		H	F	
Bipolar	0	0	(0)	0	0	(0)	0	0	(0)
Unipolar	1	2	(3)	1	0	(1)	3	1	(4)
Schizoaffective	0	0	(0)	0	0	(0)	0	0	(0)
Cyclothymic	1	0	(1)	0	0	(0)	0	0	(0)
Affective Spectrum	2	2	(4)	1	0	(1)	3	1	(4)
Percentage	10	10	(10)	5	0	(2)	15	5	(10)
Schizophrenia	0	1	(1)	0	0	(0)	0	0	(0)
Alcoholism	0	0	(0)	1	2	(3)	1	0	(1)
Sociopathy	0	0	(0)	2	1	(3)	0	0	(0)
Other	0	0	(0)	0	1	(1)	0	0	(0)
All Psychopathology	2	3	(5)	4	4	(8)	4	1	(5)
Percentage	9	14	(11)	18	18	(18)	20	5	(12)

Another finding of interest is that no father-to-son transmission of manic-depressive illness was seen in our entire sample. This is consistent with a sex-linked model of bipolar illness, which has been suggested by previous genetic studies.

REFERENCES

Abrams, R., and Taylor, M.A. Unipolar mania: A preliminary report. *Arch. Gen. Psychiat.* 30, 441–443 (1974).

Angst, J., and Perris, C. Zur Nosologie endogener Depression: Vergleich der Ergebnisse der Untersuchungen. *Arch. Psychiat. Neurol.* 210, 373–386 (1968).

Asano, N. Clinico-genetic study of manic-depressive psychoses. In *Clinical Genetics in Psychiatry*, H. Mitsuda, ed. Osaka (1967).

Baron, M. Linkage between an X-chromosome marker (deutan color blindness) and bipolar affective illness. *Arch. Gen. Psychiat.* 34, 721–725 (1977).

Belmaker, R.H., and Wyatt, R.J. Possible X-linkage in a family with varied psychoses. *Israel Ann. Psychiat. Rev. Discip.* 14, 345–353 (1976).

Bratfos, O., and Haug, J.O. The course of manic-depressive psychosis. *Acta Psychiat. Scand.* 44, 90–112 (1968).

Cakeron, K. Chronic mania. *J. Ment. Sci.* 82, 592–594 (1936).

Chropra, H.D. Family psychiatric morbidity, parental deprivation and socio-economic status in cases of mania. *Brit. J. Psychiat.* 126, 191–192 (1957).

Clayton, P.J., Rodin, L., and Winokur, G. Family history studies. III. Schizoaffective disorders, clinical and genetic factors including a one to two year follow-up. *Compr. Psychiat.* 9, 31 (1968).

Cohen, S.M., Allen, M.G., Pollin, W., and Hrubec, Z. Relationship of schizoaffective psychosis to manic-depressive psychosis and schizophrenia. *Arch. Gen. Psychiat.* 26, 539 (1972).

Da Rocha, F. La manie chronique. *Ann. Méd. Psychol.* 11 412–422 (1921).

Kallmann, F.J. Genetic principles in manic-depressive psychoses. In *Depression*, P. Hoch and J. Zubin, eds. *Grune & Stratton, New York (1954), pp. 1–24.*

Leonhard, K. Aufteilung der endogenen Psychosen. Akademie-Verlag, Berlin (1959).

Mendlewicz, J. Genetic studies in schizoaffective illness. In *The Impact of Biology on Modern Psychiatry*, S. Gershon, R.H. Belmaker, S.S. Kety, nd M. Rosenbaum, eds. Plenum, New York (1976), pp. 229–240.

Mendlewicz, J., Fieve, R.R., Rainer, J.D., and Fleiss, J.L. Manic-depressive illness: A comparative study of patients with and without a family history. *Brit. J. Psychiat.* 120, 523–520 (1972).

Mendlewicz, J., and Fleiss, J.L. Linkage studies with X-chromosome markers in bipolar (manic-depressive) and unipolar (depressive) illnesses. *Biol. Psychiat.* 9, 261–294 (1974).

Mendlewicz, J., Fleiss, J.L., and Fieve, R.R. Evidence for X-linkage in the transmission of manic-depressive illness. *JAMA* 222, 1627 (1972).

Mendlewicz, J., and Rainer, J.D. Adoption study supporting genetic transmission in manic-depressive illness. *Nature* 268, 327–329 (1977).

Perris, C. A study of bipolar (manic-depressive) and unipolar recurrent depressive psychoses. *Acta Psychiat. Scand. Suppl. 194* 42 (1966).

Reich T., Clayton, P.J., and Winokur, G. Family history studies. V. The genetics of mania. *Am. J. Psychiat.* 125, 1358–1359 (1969).

Shopsin, B., Mendlewicz, J., Suslak, L., Silberg, E., Gershon, S. Genetics of affective disorders. II. Morbidity risk and genetic transmission. *Neuropsychobiology* 2, 28–36 (1976).

Suslak, L., Shopsin, B., Silberg, E., Mendlewicz, J., Gershon, S. Genetics of affective disorders. I. Familial incidence study of bipolar-unipolar and schizoaffective illness. *Neuropsychobiology* 2, 18–27 (1976).

Winokur, G., Clayton, P.J., and Reich, T. *Manic-depressive illness.* C.V. Mosby, St. Louis (1969).

Winokur, G., and Tanna, V.L. Possible role of X-linked dominant factor in manic-depressive diseases, *Dis. Nerv. Syst.* 30, 89–94 (1969).

CHAPTER 8

Are Mania and Schizophrenia Genetically Distinct?

Elliot S. Gershon and Ronald O. Rieder

Introduction

Accepting for the present discussion the evidence that schizophrenia and bipolar manic-depressive illness are genetically transmitted (Kety et al., 1975; Gershon et al., 1977), and that they often respond to the same psychotropic agents, could they be variants of the same disorder? That is, is there a shared genetic diathesis in some or all cases? Several types of evidence can be examined: clinical studies of patients and their relatives (including adoptees and twins), clinical-biological studies in these families, and studies of genetic linkage markers. Identification of pedigrees in which both mania and schizophrenia are linked to the same genetic marker would strongly suggest a shared single major gene for the two illnesses. However, even with this type of evidence there are other possible explanations. Such linkage could occur with genetically separate entities if they were allelic to each other or if they were themselves closely linked. Failure to find such linkage is not evidence against the hypothesis of a shared diathesis. There are similar problems with the clinical-biological approach. Finding a shared hereditary pathophysiologic mechanism would support the shared-gene hypothesis, but the lack of such a finding is not conclusive evidence against it.

Critical tests do exist that can reject at least certain forms of the shared-diathesis hypothesis. These tests can be applied to clinical studies of families and twins using analytical models recently developed for multifactorial and single major locus genetic transmission (Reich et al., 1972; Morton and McLean, 1974; Elston and Stuart, 1971). One of the models (Reich et al., 1972) hypothesizes different (diagnostic) manifestations of a single genetic diathesis according to the amount of liability to illness (genetic plus nongenetic) in each diagnostic entity, where the amount of liability can be estimated from the prevalences of the set of diagnoses in relatives. The other models have other mathematical formulations for the relation between genotype and clinical manifestations, and can be applied to pedigrees. In general, evidence against the shared-diathesis hypothesis consists of finding essentially no overlap between the two disorders within pedigrees. That is, shared genetic transmission in these models generally requires that an increased prevalence of one illness (i.e., bipolar) be found in the families of the other (i.e., schizophrenics), and vice versa. In the absence of this, findings of an overlap in the spectra of the two illnesses, such as increased alcoholism or schizoaffective disorder in the relatives of both types of patient, cannot be accepted as evidence of a shared specific diathesis, since numerous alternative explanations might be offered (see below).

We would emphasize that these models test the hypothesis that two (or more) illnesses are produced by qualitatively identical shared factors, and do not test whether a partially shared genetic diathesis is present. For example, if schizophrenia is hypthesized to represent a heterozygous condition, and bipolar illness a homozygous condition of the same genetic defect, the predictions on overlap in family studies must be satisfied or the hypothesis can be rejected. However, hypotheses that are more complex may prove untestable by these models. An example is the perhaps intuitive set of hypotheses of the genetic deficits A, B, and C, where A and B produce mania, B and C produce schizophrenia, A alone produces milder depressive disorders, and C alone produces milder schizophrenia-like disorders. This set of hypotheses is not testable from clinical data using currently explicated genetic models.

It is also necessary to note the influence that heterogeneity within a single disorder would have upon the ability of these models to recognize or reject a shared diathesis. In general, the models assume the illnesses under question to be genetically unitary, and the tests are only applicable given a genetically unitary illness or when a unitary illness comprises a preponderant proportion of the disorder being studied. Such tests cannot rule out a genetic relationship between small subgroups of two illnesses. For example, no familial overlap between anemia and schizophrenia might be found, but samples of vitamin B-12 deficient "schizophrenia" and B-12 deficient anemia might well show an overlap and thus a genetic relationship with each other if such samples were selectively studied.

In this paper, we shall discuss the available evidence on the shared-diathesis hypothesis, first looking for clinical overlap in family studies of mania, schizophrenia, and related disorders, and then looking at genetic, biological and linkage studies.

CLINICAL EVIDENCE ON GENETIC OVERLAP

The most immediately convincing clinical evidence of shared genetic factors might be offered by twin and adoption studies of mania and schizophrenia. Monozygotic twins are discordant for schizophrenia in about 50% of the informative pairs (Gottesman and Shields, 1972), and the discordance in affective illness (unipolar plus bipolar) is about 30%, if unipolar-bipolar pairs are considered concordant (Perris, 1974). Among the discordant MZ twins, no pair of MZ twins has been reported where one has schizophrenia and the other bipolar illness. The sharp division of the psychoses in these studies has been further supported by two recent twin studies that included probands with schizoaffective or schizophreniform psychosis (Cohen, 1972; Kringlen, 1967). Not only was there no instance of both schizophrenia and manic-depressive illness in one twin pair, but there was, in both studies, complete independence of all three categories of psychosis.

Adoption studies of schizophrenia (Kety et al., 1975; Rosenthal et al., 1975; Heston, 1966) have not shown any significant increase in the incidence of any of the major affective illnesses in the biological relatives of chronic schizophrenics, although there is an increase in some other disorders thought to represent the schizophrenia spectrum. None of the adoption studies employed the diagnostic category of schizoaffective disorder, and thus they do not shed a clear light on the relationship of this entity to either schizophrenia or bipolar illness. Biological relatives of adopted bipolar patients are reported to have increased affective illness as compared with relatives of suitable control adoptees (Mendlewicz and Rainer, 1977), but there was no increase in schizophrenia. Several cases of schizoaffective disorder in the biological relatives were noted.

In contrast to the consistent pattern that has emerged from the twin and adoption studies, the data from the early family studies seemed to indicate some overlap. Of five older studies reviewed by Rosenthal (Hoffman, 1921; Weinberg and Lobstein, 1936; Slater, 1938; Stenstedt, 1952), each, except for that of Weinberg, found an apparently elevated morbidity risk for schizophrenia in the children of affectively ill probands ranging from 2.0% to 3.1% as compared to an estimated population risk of 0.8%. A more recent study (Powell et al., 1973) suggested the same thing. However, neither this study nor the studies reviewed by Rosenthal were family studies in which a single investigator, using well-defined diagnostic criteria, examined the patients and relatives. There are some recent studies that meet this methodologic standard (Perris, 1966; Angst, 1966; James and Chapman, 1975; Mendlewicz and Ranier, 1974; Gershon et al., 1975), reporting a risk for schizophrenia in first-degree relatives of bipolar patients ranging from 0.3% to 2.0%. This range spans the population risk for schizophrenia and is much lower than the morbid risk of affective disorders in the same relatives in each study, thus supporting genetic independence of the two entities.

Some other family studies that have investigated the relationship between schizophrenia and affective illness are also subject to methodological criticisms. Among 322 offspring of 132 chronic schizophrenic mothers, Reisby (1967) found only two cases of affective psychosis, but the focus of this noncontrolled study was clearly on discovering schizophrenic psychopathology. Tsuang (1967) studied sibling pairs both hospitalized for a psychiatric disorder. Diagnoses were made blindly, by Slater, but without specified criteria. In 7 of 71 pairs, one sibling was diagnosed schizophrenic and the other as having major affective disorder. This compared with the nine pairs concordant for schizophrenia and 19 pairs concordant for major affective disorders. Shields (1968), in a review of a twin study by Slater (1953), noted that the 158 schizophrenics had nearly as many siblings with affective disorders as with schizophrenia, and there were 16 parents with affective psychosis compared to 12 with schizophrenia. Thus both these studies indicate a familial overlap between schizophrenia and affective illness. However, our own (unpublished ESG) review of the case summaries of Slater (1953) revealed a mixture of affective and thought disorder symptoms in several of the twin probands, leading us to believe that these such cases could have been diagnosed as schizoaffective psychosis had Tsuang or Slater and Shields used this diagnostic category. One reason that they may not have done so is that this term has lacked widespread acceptance and reliability.

A phenomenological description of schizoaffective (atypical, remitting) schizophrenia and the features distinguishing it from (chronic) schizophrenia and mania have been specified recently (Spitzer et al., 1975; Feighner et al., 1972), making such diagnoses more reliable now than at the time of the Slater study. The relationship of each of these disorders to the other can now be considered, using genetic models applied to family study data. Also, the two types of major affective disorder, unipolar and bipolar illness, which may be genetically distinct (Gershon et al., 1975; 1977), may now be considered independently in relation to the schizophrenic disorders. Unfortunately, no study has yet been done that determines, in both probands and relatives, all these categories of illness with defined diagnostic criteria. The design of such a study, to which genetic models could be applied and which would thus help establish the relationship of these entities, is shown in Figure 1.

Though such a complete family study has not been done, some data on the relationship of these entities has been collected, using systematic diagnostic criteria. Mendlewicz (1977) reported that the first-degree relatives of schizoaffective probands had risks for bipolar illness (13.7 ± 3.9%) and

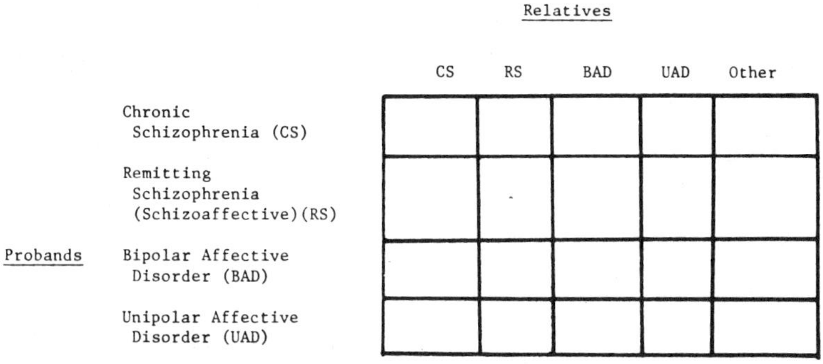

Fig. 1. Study Design for Determining the Relationship in Familial Transmission of the Schizophrenias to the Major Affective Disorders.

unipolar illness (22.6 $\pm$ 4.1%) that were similar to the risks he found for first-degree relatives of bipolar probands (18.6 $\pm$ 4.1% and 20.4 $\pm$ 2.8%, respectively). Unipolar probands had little bipolar or schizophrenic illness in their relatives, and the relatives of schizophrenic probands had little bipolar illness. However, the risk for unipolar illness in the first-degree relatives of schizophrenic patients was somewhat greater than in the general population (7.3 $\pm$ 3.3%). These results imply that there is a familial, possibly genetic relationship between bipolar and schizoaffective illness, and also a possible relationship between schizophrenia and unipolar illness. There are other studies that tend to support these connections. Perris (1966) reported 5.1% schizophrenia in the siblings of unipolar depressives, and he used strict criteria in diagnosing both the unipolar depression and the schizophrenia, such that schizoaffective (cycloid) psychoses were not included in either category. Tsuang (1976) found little schizophrenia in the relatives of unipolar depressives, but found that probands with atypical (remitting, schizo-affective) schizophrenia had a rate of both affective illness and schizophrenia in their relatives that was similar to bipolar disorder. This idea of a genetic link between atypical schizophrenia and affective illness was previously proposed by Mitsuda (1967) and supported by his studies.

Fowler (1978) reviewed the family studies of the Iowa and St. Louis groups (Winokur et al., 1969, 1971; McCabe et al., 1971). These studies found a higher morbidity risk of affective disorder in the relatives of bipolar patients than in the relatives of good-prognosis schizophrenics or unipolar de-pressives. The risk for schizophrenia in the relatives of good-prognosis schizophrenics was greater than the risk in the relatives of the other groups. He concluded that although "familial affective disorder is as common in good-prognosis schizophrenia as in unipolar depression, the higher fre-quency of familial schizophrenia in the former group precludes a conclusion that good-prognosis schizophrenia is simply a variant of affective disorder [1978, p. 72]"

We may summarize the evidence from family, twin, and adoption studies as not supporting overlap (cross-transmission) between bipolar illness and chronic schizophrenia. We would expect that genetic models in which one disorder is a variant of the other or is produced by greater amounts of a particular genetic and/or environmental liability than the other would no fit the available data. Different studies indicate overlap of remitting schizophrenia (acute schizophrenia, atypical schizophrenia, schizoaffective disorder, cycloid psychosis) with each of the other major psychoses. Numerous explanations of this overlap are possible, including that that patients with remitting schizophrenia include some persons with atypical bipolar illness and other with atypical chronic schizophrenia, or that there are some shared genetic elements among the three disorders (bipolar, acute schizophrenia, chronic schizophrenia). These explanations do not appear to offer testable hypotheses in the absence of biological or other nonclinicl genetic markers of any of the illnesses or of the hypothesized shared elements.

One caveat should be added to the above discussion and to the ideal study design proposed above. Studies of first-degree relatives must take selective mating into account. Some studies have shown that patients with affective illness and those with schizophrenia do not mate randomly (Gershon et al., 1973; Dunner et al., 1976; Fowler and Tsuang, 1975; Kirkegaard-Sorensen and Mednick, 1975; Rosenthal, 1975). Preferential mating between schizophrenics and manic-depressives would by itself elevate the joint occurrence of these two disorders in first-degree relatives. Such preferential mating has not been demonstrated, but studies of relationships among different disorders must evaluate mating patterns in the observed families.

We have focused the above discussion on the relationship among the four major psychoses (bipolar, unipolar, schizoaffective, schizophrenic), but mention should also be made of the overlap that these entities may have with disorders of lesser severity, and how these "spectra" may themselves overlap. As mentioned in the beginning of this chapter, such overlap cannot be regarded as evidence of a shared genetic diathesis between schizophrenia and mania, but this overlap indicates a common end result, if not causation. The question of a genetic spectrum of affective illnesses was recently reviewed (Gershon et al., 1977), with the conclusion that alcoholism, minor depression, and cyclothymic personality were associated with the major affective illnesses. The existence of a "schizophrenia spectrum" is a topic of current research and debate, with the leading candidate for inclusion in this spectrum being borderline schizophrenia (schizotypal personality in the proposed DSM-III [Rieder, in press]). "Borderline schizophrenia" sounds different from "minor depression" or "cyclothymic personality," but until the criteria for these diagnoses are developed, and until all these diagnoses are applied in studies of both types of probands, it must be left as an open question whether similar types of psychopathology have been given different titles depending on the investigator's focus. As evidence of this, in Heston's study (1966) of the adopted-away offspring of schizophrenics, a diagnosis of borderline schizophrenia was not used, and a significant ($p = .052$) increase of "neurotic personality disorder" was found. He described these individuals as complaining of anxiety or panic attacks, hyperirritability, and depression—in other words, of affective symptoms.

BIOLOGICAL MARKERS

One direct way of demonstrating a genetic link between any two disorders would be to discover a genetically controlled etiological factor shared by the disorders. There have been many studies of biological abnormalities in both schizophrenia and affective illness, and some specific abnormalities have been found in both disorders. These are (1) lowered platelet monoamine oxidase (MAO); (2) elevated serum creatinine phosphokinase (CPK); and (3) certain psychophysiological measures.

Platelet MAO was reported to be reduced in bipolar patients (Murphy and Weiss, 1972) and in chronic schizophrenics (Wyatt et al., 1973), but not in acute schizophrenics. These findings have been replicated by some but not all investigators, as reviewed elsewhere (Wyatt et al., in press; Wyatt and Murphy, 1975; Groshong et al., 1978). Platelet MAO activity is highly correlated between MZ twins and less highly correlated in DZ twins (Nies). It is reduced in unaffected MZ co-twins of schizophrenics (Wyatt et al., 1973) and in first-degree relatives of bipolar patients (Leckman et al., 1977). Conceivably, a genetically induced deficiency of platelet MAO produces and increased vulnerability to either chronic schizophrenia or bipolar illness, and this would provide direct evidence of a genetic link between the disorders. Before drawing this conclusion, however, it is necessary to demonstrate that lowered platelet MAO does indeed indicate a genetically increased vulnerability to these disorders, and the studies to date do not prove this. In Gershon et al.'s study (in press) of bipolar patients who themselves had low platelet MAO activity, low platelet MAO activity in the relatives was not associated with an increased risk for affective illness. (Such a study with schizophrenics and their relatives has not yet been completed.) Therefore, while low platelet MAO may be associated with both illnesses, it cannot now be considered a genetic risk factor linking schizophrenia and mania.

Serum CPK has been studied extensively by Meltzer and his colleagues (Meltzer, 1975, 1976), and they have found that there are elevated levels of this enzyme during the course of hospitalization in many patients with affective psychoses and in many with schizophrenic psychoses, but not in disturbed nonpsychotic psychiatric patients. They also found abnormal muscle biopsies and increased axonal branching of the motor neuron in a high percentage of patients with psychoses of either type. Each of these abnormalities was found to a greater extent among the first-degree relatives of the patients than among controls. Meltzer stated that "the excessive branching in the first-degree relatives has particular significance...It of course leaves unclarified why only some people vulnerable to develop psychosis, as indicated by the increased TIR's (terminal innervation ratio), become psychotic [1976, pp. 127–8]." Here Meltzer is concluding that there are some people who are "vulnerable to develop psychosis" and that the biological manifestation of this vulnerability is the same for schizophrenic and affective psychoses. Moreover, he indicates that it is a genetically induced vulnerability. Again, the increased psychiatric vulnerability of the relatives who have this neuromuscular abnormality or CPK elevation has not yet been demonstrated.

A final note can be made on psychophysiological similarities among the psychoses. In many ways, manics differ psychophysiologically from schizophrenics; for example, with evoked potentials schizophrenics tend to be reducers and bipolars tend to be augmenters (Buchsbaum, 1975). However, lower CNV (contingent negative variation) amplitude and prolonged slow-potential negativity have been found in all three groups of psychoses (Shagass, 1975). If genetic control of these measures was established, and if they were found to indicate increased vulnerability to psychosis then they, too, could provide a biologic-genetic link between the psychoses, but there is no evidence of this known to us.

LINKAGE MARKERS

As discussed above, linkage of two different disorders to the same marker locus in the same pedigrees would provide suggestive, though not conclusive, proof that the two disorders share a genetic vulnerability factor. No reports linking chronic schizophrenia and bipolar illness in this way have appeared to our knowledge. Schizoaffective disorder and bipolar illness have both been reported to be linked to red-green color blindness (an X-chromosome marker) in several, but not all, pedigrees of schizoaffective probands studied by Mendlewicz (1977) and Baron (1977). In these pedigrees, nearly all of the affected persons are bipolar or unipolar, and schizophrenia does not appear, suggesting that the schizoaffective disorder is a form of the color-blindness-linked bipolar affective disorder previously described by Mendlewicz and Fleiss (1974). However, the existence of bipolar illness closely linked to color blindness was not replicated in a recent series of informative pedigrees in which close linkage is clearly excluded between red-green color blindness and bipolar illness (Gershon et al., in press). It has been suggested that these results only appear to be incompatible with one another, and that there is genetic heterogeneity of BP illness, such that some cases are linked to color blindness and some are not. This explanation does not fit the data for the two reported series from the eastern United States (Gershon et al., in press; Mendlewicz and Fleiss, 1974), since *within* each series there is no heterogeneity among pedigrees; one series is homogeneous for no linkage, the other for close linkage (using the test of Morton, 1956). In a recent series (Mendlewicz and van Praag, unpublished data) in Brussels, there did appear to be heterogeneity, but the problem of conflicting results between the other series using virtually the same methodology remains unresolved. The question of linkage of BP illness to X-chromosome markers has been reviewed elsewhere, where it was concluded that existence of linkage is not established (Gershon and Bunney, 1976), and this remains true because of apparently contradictory evidence.

Studies of other marker loci have not consistently demonstrated their linkage or association with bipolar (or schizoaffective) illness. Linkage of Xg to bipolar illness was reported by Mendlewicz and Fleiss (1974), but not found by Leckman et al. (1978).

Human leukocyte antigen (HLA) associations with BP illness have been reported but not replicated (Targum et al., 1978; Beckman et al., 1978), and linkage of bipolar illness to HLA has been excluded by Targum et al. (1978). HLA associations with schizophrenia have been reported (Smeraldi et al., 1976; Ivanyi et al., 1976; McGuffin et al., 1978; Mercier et al., 1977; Eberhard et al., 1975), but as is the case in bipolar illness, the various reports have not replicated one another. Increased frequency in schizophrenics of HLA-A28 in Czechoslovakia (Ivanyi et al., 1976) and HLA-A9 in Sweden (Eberhard et al., 1975) satisfied statistically rigorous criteria for HLA association by taking into account the number of antigens tested. However, these two findings may be incompatible with each other. Pedigree-linkage studies of HLA in schizophrenia have not been reported.

The linkage approach offers great promise because of definitiveness of proof it offers. However, it should be noted that even with many (30) markers studied, thousands of sibships (of size 4) need to be studied to have a 30% prior probability of mapping a single allele with 50% penetrance (R. C. Elston, unpublished communication). That is, there could be a single allele responsible for a psychiatric disorder but not identifiable with currently available polymorphic genetic markers simply because the psychiatric allele is not within mapping distance of the markers.

CONCLUSIONS

Evidence from twin and family studies suggests that bipolar manic-depressive illness and chronic schizophrenia are distinct genetic entities. Schizoaffective and remitting schizophrenic patients have relatives with bipolar, unipolar, and schizophrenic illness, so there may be joint occurrence of a schizophrenic-like and bipolar disorder in some pedigrees. Evidence of a unipolar illness/schizophrenia overlap has also arisen (Mendlewicz, 1977; Perris, 1966), but has not been consistently demonstrated. There may still be a common genetic element leading to either bipolar or schizophrenic symptoms in some proportion of cases. Future biologic-genetic or chromosomal linkage studies may shed more light on this question.

REFERENCES

Baron, M. Linkage between an X-chromosome marker (deutan color blindness) and bipolar affective illness. *Arch. Gen. Psychiat.* 34, 721–725 (1977).

Beckman, L., Perris, D., Strandman, E., and Wahlby, L. HLA antigens and affective disorders. *Hum. Hered.* 28, 96–99 (1978).

Buchsbaum, M. Average evoked response augmenting/reducing in schizophrenia and affective disorders. In *Biology of the Major Psychoses: A Comparative Analysis,* D. Freedman, ed. Raven, New York (1975), pp. 129–142.

Cammer, L. Schizophrenic children of manic-depressive parents. *Dis. Nerv. Syst.* (March 1970), 177–180.

Cohen, S., Allen, M., Pollin, W., Hrubec, H. Relationship of schizo-affective psychosis to manic-depressive psychosis and schizophrenia in the schizophrenic patient. *Arch. Gen. Psychiat.* 26, 539–545 (1972).

Dunner, D.L., Fleiss, J.L., Addonizio, G., and Fieve, R.R. Assortative mating in primary affective disorder. *Biol. Psychiat.* 11, 43–51 (1976).

Eberhard, G., *Franzen, G., and Löw,* B. Schizophrenia susceptibility and HL-A antigen. *Neuropsychobiology* 1(4), 211–217 (1975).

Elston, R.C., and Stewart, J. A general model for the genetic analysis of pedigree data. *Hum. Hered.* 21, 523–542 (1971).

Feighner, J.P., Robins, E., and Guze, S.B. Diagnostic criteria for use in psychiatric research. *Arch. Gen. Psychiat.* 26, 57–63 (1972).

Fowler, R. Remitting schizophrenia as a variant of affective disorder. *Schiz. Bull.* 4(1), 68–77 (1978).

Fowler, R.C., and Tsuang, M.T. Spouses of schizophrenics: A blind comparative study. *Compr. Psychiat.* 16, 339–342 (1975).

Gershon, E.S., Belmaker, R.H., Ebstein, R., and Jonas, W.Z. Plasma monoamine oxidase activity unrelated to genetic vulnerability to primary affective illness. *Arch. Gen. Psychiat.* 34, 737–734 (1977).

Gershon, E.S., and Bunney, W.E., Jr. The question of X-linkage in bipolar manic-depressive illness. *J. Psychiatr. Res.* 13, 99–117 (1976).

Gershon, E.S., Dunner, D.L., Sturt, L., and Goodwin, F.K. Assortative mating in affective disorders. *Biol. Psychiat.* 7, 63–74 (1973).

Gershon, E.S., Targum, S.D., Kessler, L.R., Maxure, C.M., and Bunney W.E., Jr. Genetic studies and biologic strategies in the affective disorders. *Prog. Med. Genet., New Series,* 2, 101–164 (1977).

Gershon, E.S., Targum, S.D., Leckman, J., Guroff, J., and Murphy, D. Platelet monoamine oxidase (MAO) activity and genetic vulnerability to Bipolar (BP) affective illness. Presented at American College of Neuropsychopharmacology Meeting, San Juan, Puerto Rico, Dec. 14, 1977. *Psychopharmacol. Bull.* (In press).

Gershon, E.S., Targum, S.D., Matthysse, S., and Bunney, W.E., Jr. Color blindness linkage to bipolar illness not supported by new data. *Arch. Gen. Psychiat.* (In press).

Gottesman, I.I., and Shields, J. *Schizophrenia and Genetics: A Twin Study Vantage Point.* Academic, London (1972).

Groshong, R., Baldessarini, R.J., Gibson D.A., Lipinski, J.F., Axelrod, D., and Pope, A. Activities of types A and B MAO and Catechol-O-methyltransferase in blood cells and skin fibroblasts of normal and chronic schizophrenic patients. *Arch. Gen. Psychiat.* 35, 1198–1208 (1978).

Heston, L.L. Psychiatric disorders in foster home reared children of schizophrenic mothers. *Br. J. Psychiat.* 112, 819 (1966).

Hoffman, H. *Die Nachkommenschaft bei endogenen Psychosen,* Springer-Verlag, Berlin (1921).

Hoffman, H. *Studien uber Veregung Und Entstehung geistiger Storungen,* Springer-Verla, Berlin (1921b).

Ivanyi, D, Zemek, P., and Ivanyi, P. HLA antigens in schizophrenia. *Tissue Antigens* 8(3), 217–220 (1976).

Kety, S.S., Rosenthal, D., Wender, P.H., Schulsinger, F., and Jacobsen, B. Mental illness in the biological and adoptive families of adopted individuals who have become schizophrenic: A preliminary report based on psychiatric interviews. In *Genetic Research in Psychiatry,* R. Rieve, D. Rosenthal, and H. Brill, eds. Johns Hopkins Univ. Press, Baltimore (1975).

Kirkegaard-Sorensen, L., and Mednick, S.A. Registered criminality in families with children at high-risk for schizophrenia. *J. Abnorm. Psychol.* 84, 197–204 (1975).

Kringlen, E. *Heredity and Environment in the Functional Psychoses.* Norweigian Monographs on medical Science, Oslo (1967).

Leckman, J.F., Gershon, E.S., McGinniss, M., Targum, S.D., and Dibble, E. New data do not suggest linkage between the Xg blood group and bipolar illness. Presented at Society of Biological Psychiatry Annual Meeting, Atlanta, May 6, 1978.

Leckman, J.F., Gershon, E.S., Nichols, A.S., and Murphy, D.L. Reduced MAO activity in first-degree relatives of individuals with bipolar affective disorders. *Arch. Gen. Psychiat.* 34, 601–606 (1977).

McCabe, M.S., Fowler, R.C., Cadoret, R.J., and Winokur, G. Familial differences in schizophrenia with good and poor prognosis. *Psychol. Med.* 1, 326–332 (1971).

McGuffin, P., Farmer, A.E., and Rajah, S.M. Histocompatability antigens and schizophrenia. *Br. J. Psychiat.* 132, 149–151 (1978).

Meltzer, H. Neuromuscular abnormalities in the major mental illnesses. I. Serum enzyme studies. In *Biology of the Major Psychoses: A Comparative Analysis,* D. Freedman, ed. Raven, New York (1975), pp. 165–188. (Research Publications: Association for Research in Nervous and Mental Diseases, Vol. 54).

Meltzer, H. Neuromuscular dysfunction in schizophrenia. *Schizo. Bull.* 2(1), 106–135 (1976).

Mendlewicz, J. Genetic studies in schizoaffective illness. In *The Impact of Biology on Modern Psychiatry,* E.S. Gershon, R. Belmaker, S. Kety, and M. Rosenbaum, eds. Plenum, New York (1977), pp. 229–240.

Mendlewicz, J., and Fleiss, J.L. Linkage studies with X-chromosome markers in bipoolar (manic-depressive) and unipolar (depressive) illnesses. *Biol. Psychiat.* 9, 261 (1974).

Mendlewicz, J., Fleiss, J.L., and Fieve, R.R. Evidence for X-linkage in the transmission of manic-depressive illness. *JAMA* 222, 1624 (1972).

Mendlewicz, J., and Rainer, J.D. Adoption study supporting genetic transmission in manic-depressive illness. *Nature* 268, 327–329 (1977).

Mendlewicz, J., and van Praag, H. Colorblindness and bipolar illness. (In press, 1980).

Mercier, P., Sutter, J.M., Julien, R.A., and Kieffer, N. Schizophrenia: Association of the paranoid form and antigens HLA-A9 and B51. *Encephale* 3(1), 49–53 (1977).

Mitsuda, H. Clinical genetics in psychiatry. In *Clinical Gentics in Psychiatry*, H. Mitsuda, ed. Bunko-sha, Kyoto, Japan (1967), pp. 3–21.

Mitsuda, H. Clinico-gentic study of schizophrenia. In *Clinical Genetics in Psychiatry*, H. Mitsuda, ed. Bunko-sha, Kyoto, Japan (1967), pp. 49–90.

Morton, N.E. The detection and estimation of linkage between the genes for elliptocytosis and the Rh blood type. *Am. J. Hum. Genet.* 8, 80–96 (1956).

Morton, N.E., and Maclean, C.J. Analysis of family resemblance. III. Complex segregation of quantitative traits. *Am. J. Hum. Genet.* 26, 489–503 (1974).

Murphy, D.L., and Weiss, R. Reduced monoamine oxidase activity in blood platelets from bipolar depressed patients. *Am. J. Psychiat.* 128, 35–41 (1972).

Murphy, D.L., and Wyatt, R.J. Reduced MAO activity in blood platelets from schizophrenic patients. *Nature* 238, 225–226 (1972).

Odegaard, O. The psychiatric disease entities in the light of genetic investigation. *Acta Psychiat. Neurol. Scand.* 39, 94–104 (1963).

Perris, C. A study of bipolar manic-depressive and unipolar recurrent depressive psychoses. *Acta Psychiat. Scand. Suppl.* 194 (1966).

Perris, C. A study of cycloid psychoses. *Acta Psychiat. Scand. Suppl. 253* (1974).

Powell, A., Thomson, N., Hall, D.J., and Wilson, L. Parent-child concordance with respect to sex and diagnosis in schizophrenia and manic-depressive psychosis. *Br. J. Psychiat.* 123, 653–658 (1973).

Reich, T., James, J.W., and Morris, C.A. The use multiple thresholds in determining the mode of transmission of semi-continuous traits. *Ann. Hum. Genet.* 36, 163 (1972).

Reisby, N. Psychoses in children of schizophrenic mothers. *Acta Psychiat. Scand.* 43, 8–20 (1943).

Röll, A., and Entres, J.L. Zum Problem der Erbprognosebestimmung, *Z. Ges. Neurol. Psychiat.* 156, 169–202 (1936).

Rosenthal, D. *Genetic Theory and Abnormal Behavior*, McGraw-Hill, New York (1970).

Rosenthal, D., Wender, P.H., Kety, S.S., Welner, J., and Schylsinger, F. The adopted-away offspring of schizophrenics. *Am. J. Psychiat.* 128, 307–311 (1971).

Rosenthal, D. discussion: Subschizophrenic disorders. In *Genetic Research in Psychiatry*, R.R. Fieve, D. Rosenthal, and A. Brill, eds. Johns Hopkins, Baltimore (1975), pp. 199–208.

Rosenthal, D., Wender, P.H., Kety, S.S., Schulsinger, F., Welner, J., and Ostergaard, L. Schizophrenics' offspring reared in adoptive homes. In *The Transmission of Schizophrenia*, D. Rosenthal, and S. Kety, eds. Pergamon, New York (1968).

Shagass, C. EEG and evoked potentials in the psychoses. In *Biology of the Major Psychoses: A Comparative Analysis*, D. Freedman, Ed. Raven, New York (1975), pp. 101–128. (Research Publications: Association for Research in Nervous and Mental Disease, Vol. 54).

Shields, J. Summary of the genetic evidence. In *The Transmission of Schizophrenia*, D. Rosenthal and S.S. Kety, eds. Pergamon, London (1968), pp. 95–126.

Slater, E. *Psychotic and Neurotic Illnesses in Twins*. Her Majesty's Stationary Office, London (1953).

Slater, E. Erbpathologie des manisch-depressiven Irreseins, Die Eltern und Linder von Manisch-Depressiven, *Z. Ges. Neurol. Psychiat.* 163, 1–47 (1936).

Slater, E., and Cowie, V. *The Genetics of Mental Disorders,* Oxford Univ. Press, London (1971).

Smeraldi, E, Bellodi, L., and Cazzullo, C.L. Further studies on the major histocompatibility complex as a genetic marker for schizophrenia. *Biol. Psychiat.* 11(6), 655–661 (1976).

Smeraldi, E., Bellodi, L., Scorza-Smeraldi, R., Fabio, G., and Sacchetti, E. HLA-SD antigens and schizophrenia: Statistical and genetical considerations. *Tissue Antigens* 8(3), 191–196 (1976).

Spitzer, R.L., Endicott, J., and Robins, E. Research diagnostic criteria (RDC) for a selected group of functional disorders. *Biometrics Res.,* New York State Psychiatric Institute (1975).

Stenstedt, A. A study in manic-depressive psychosis: Clinical, social and genetic investigations. *Acta Psychiat. Neurol. Scand. Suppl.* 79 (1952).

Targum, S.D., Gershon, E.S., Van Eerdewegh, M., and Rogentine, N. Human leukocyte antigen (HLA) system not closely linked to or associated with bipolar manic-depressive illness. Presented at the Society for Biological Psychiatry Meeting, Atlanta, May 6, 1978.

Tsuang, M.T. A study of pairs of sibs both hospitalized for mental disorders. *Br. J. Psychiat.* 113, 283–300 (1967).

Tsuang, M.T., Dempsey, M., and Rauscher, F. A study of "atypical schizophrenia." *Arch. Gen. Psychiat.* 33, 1157–1160 (1976).

Weinberg, I., and Lobstein, J. Beitrag zur Vererbung des manisch-depressiven Irresins. *Psychiat. Neurol. Bull.* (Amsterdam) 1a(1), 339–372 (1936).

Winokur, G., Clayton, P.J., and Reich. T. *Manic Depressive Illness,* C.V. Mosby, St. Louis (1969).

Winokur, G., Cadoret, R.J., Dorzab, J., and Baker, M. Depressive disease. *Arch. Gen. Psychiat.* 24, 135–144 (1971).

Wyatt, R.J., Murphy, D.L., Belmaker, R., Cohen, S., Donnelly, C.H., and Pollin, W. Reduced monoamine oxidase in platelets: A possible genetic for vulnerability to schizophrenia. *Science* 179, 916–918 (1973).

Wyatt, R., Potkin, S.G., and Murphy, D.L. Platelet monoamine oxidase activity in schizophrenia: A review of the data. *Am. J. Psychiat.* (In press).

CHAPTER 9

Mania in Childhood and Adolescence

Thomas L. Lowe and Donald J. Cohen

The issue of affective disorders in childhood and adolescence has long been an area of controversy for psychiatrists, psychologists, and other mental health professionals. Although increasing evidence and clinicl impressions have led to a new attitude regarding the existence of depressive affective illness in children, mania and diagnostic manic symptomatology have yet to be widely recognized or accepted by professionals in the field. Diagnostic limitations, similarities between various behavioral disorders, and lack of definitive genetic or biochemical studies have all led to the continuing disagreement.

Studies of mania in childhood over the past fifty years have spoken to both sides of the issue of existence of the clinical entity. Although Kraepelin (1921) noted that 0.4% of his manic-depressive adult patients had clinical evidence of mania before age ten and cited a case of mania in a five-year-old male, clear cases of mania in childhood have rarely been documented. In their extensive 1960 review of the childhood literature, Anthony and Scott concluded that the "occurrence of manic-depression in early childhood *as a clinical phenomenon* has yet to be demonstrated." They did, however, develop "suggested criteria" for establishing the diagnosis of manic-depressive psychosis in prepubertal children, based primarily on adult criteria. The Anthony criteria include the following ten requirements:

1. Evidence of an abnormal psychiatric state at some time of the illness approximating the classical clinical description (Kraepelin, 1921)
2. Evidence of a "positive" family history suggesting a manic-depressive diathesis
3. Evidence of an early tendency to a manic-depressive type of reaction as manifested in (a) a cyclothymic tendency with gradually increasing amplitude and length of the oscillations, (b) delirious manic or depressive outbursts occurring during pyrexial illness
4. Evidence of a recurrent or periodic illness with at least two observed episodes
5. Evidence of a diphasic illness showing swings of pathological dimenison

6. Evidence of an endogenous illness indicating that the phases of the illness show minimal reference to environmental events

7. Evidence of a severe illness as indicated by the need for inpatient treatment, heavy sedation, electroconvulsive therapy

8. Evidence of an abnormal underlying personality of an extroverted type

9. Absence of features of schizophrenia or organic states

10. The evidence of current, not retrospective, assessments.

Anthony and Scott were able to find three cases in the literature that met five or six of their ten requirements. They further felt tht there is continuity between manic-depressive attacks in late childhood and attacks later in adult life. They stated their belief that the "manic-depressive tendency is latent in the susceptible individual" and that "it may be transiently manifested during childhood under strong physical or psychological pressure" (Anthony and Scott, 1960).

During the late 1960's and 1970's, repeated clinical case reviews of children exhibiting manic symptoms that closely resemble the adult manic criteria have been published. The best-described include juvenile versions of the manic-depressive illness, and recent cases include successful treatment with lithium carbonate (Feinstein and Wolpert, 1973; White and O'Shanick, 1977; Berg et al., 1974; Annell, 1969; Engstrom et al., 1978; Warneke, 1975).

Borrowing a term from the childhood mania literature of the early fifties, Thompson and Schindler (1976) reported a case of "embryonic mania" in a five-year-old boy. The child, who was originally diagnosed as hyperactive, led the authors to the conclusion that the case "supported the existence of the embryonic stage of mania in early childhood and illustrates the necessity for attempting to differentiate between hyperactivity and mania." Weinberg and Brumbach (1976) also discuss the occurrence of manic episodes in younger children and present a set of eight criteria for the diagnosis of childhood mania, developed and adapted from the adult criteria of Feighner et al. (1972). The Weinberg criteria for childhood mania are as follows:

A. The presence of either or both symptoms 1 and 2, and three or more of the remaining six symptoms (3–8)
    1. Euphoria
        (a) Denial of problems or illness
        (b) Inappropriate feelings of well-being, inappropriate cheerfulness, giddiness, or silliness
    2. Irritability and/or agitation (particularly belligerence, destructiveness, and antisocial behavior)
    3. Hyperactivity, "motor driven," intrusiveness
    4. Push of speech (may become unintelligible), garrulousness
    5. Flight of ideas
    6. Grandiosity (may be delusional)

7. Sleep disturbance (decreased sleep and unusual sleep pattern)
8. Distractibility (short attention span)

B. Each symptom must be a *discrete change* in the individual's usual behavior and must be present for longer than one month.

In all five of their case reports, Weinberg and Brumbach noted other family members with histories of affective disorders. They also found other case reports in the literature that met their criteria for childhood mania (Annell, 1969; McKnew et al., 1974; McHarg, 1954; Warneke, 1975).

The problem of diagnostic criteria for mania in childhood has long been a topic of discussion among clinicians. Harms (1952) captured the essence of the difficulty in his paper on differential patterns of manic-depressive disease in children. He asked: "How far can we use the symptoms we know as specific for the adult form to establish the existence of the juvenile form? And further, in what way is the juvenile form completely different in its symptoms from the adult, and what are the ways of identifying both which would justify our calling the juvenile form by the same name?

Although Anthony and Scott chose to diagnose based on ten strict adultlike criteria, others, such as Feinstein (1973), believe in a less rigorously defined process: "Rapidly shifting emotional states in children, which do not seem appropriate to the reality stress, should be carefully evaluated as the possible manifestation of a bipolar affective illness, especially if these states tend to remain prolonged and refractive to therapeutic contact. Attacks of manic behavior seem frequently not to obey the criteria of being 'well defined,' but can begin with a very subtle elevation of affect as a response to a reality situation, are not relieved by the shift in reality, and continue as an endogenously stimulated process."

The issue of diagnosis has been further complicated by the similarities between symptoms of mania and hyperactivity, leading some authors to hypothesize that hyperactivity may be one childhood form of manic-depressive disease. Studies of lithium treatment with hyperactive patients have led to the hypothesis that some of these patients and some manic-depressive adults may have variations of the same disease with a similar underlying metabolic etiology (Hava, 1973). Other studies, such as those of Stewart and Morrison (1973) warn against overemphasis of the relationship by showing that the prevalence of affective disorder in relatives of hyperactive children is no higher than among relatives of normal children.

The blurring of diagnosis between mania and hyperactivity (minimal brain dysfunction, MBD) is especially understandable in view of the lack of agreement in the diagnostic process in MBD. Recent discussion of childhood diagnosis has shown a clear overlap of some symptoms in the manic and MBD children. These common symptoms include distractibility, hyperactivity, irritability and agitation, and the lack of attention or concern for consequences of their actions, all items from the Weinberg criteria (Cohen, 1977; Cantwell, 1975; Wender, 1971).

To provide a clearer picture of childhood mania, we present a brief clinical vignette from the child psychiatric literature (Warneke, 1975):

CASE REPORT

The patient, a 14-year-old white male, was hospitalized after four days of grossly disturbed behavior. The onset was acute, without any apparent environmental stresses or psychological precipitants. He became very hyperactive and was described as full of energy, tearing around the community, not sleeping properly, full of grandiose ideas, and generally uncontrollable. Grandiose thoughts included talk about buying a ranch, borrowing "a trillion dollars," and buying race horses and a plane. He exhibited presure of speech and thought, and had not slept for 72 hours prior to admission. Two days prior to hospitalization, he had gone on a spending spree in town by himself and spent $200, as well as writing several bad checks. His parents were unable to control him, and he ran away from home twice, once being discovered agitated and exhausted after running several miles without stop. When he returned home, he was constantly making long-distance telephone calls to various people about land and investment deals. He was irritable and aggressive, and was once found struggling with two neighborhood children bigger than he. On the morning of admission, he had attacked his grandmother, toward whom he was normally very attached. During the three days prior to hospitalization, his appetite was increased, and he was eating voraciously and drinking a great deal of water. There was no weight change. Past history was remarkable in that there was a period of depressive symptoms, including elective mutism and refusal to eat at age 12. Family history was positive for depression (maternal uncle) as well as mood swings (maternal grandmother), which included periods of manic symptoms, including rapid speech, hyperactivity, and decreased sleep. After treatment with major tranquilizers, antidepressants, and ECT without prolonged improvement, the patient was treated with lithium (600 mg. tid), with dramatic improvement lasting through fourteen months of follow-up.

FAMILY STUDIES

Findings of a significant incidence of affective disorders in family members of manic children have led to an increasing literature describing children of diagnosed manic-depressive adults. The work of Winokur (1975), Mendlewicz and Rainer (1974), and others has shown that these children are at significant risk for developing affective illness. Evidence suggesting a genetically based theory of vulnerability and predisposition is compounded by the impact of environmental stresses inherent in growing up in the home of an affectively disordered parent. Indeed, the finding of an unexpectedly high morbidity risk for daughters of manic-depressive mothers speaks to this multiply determined effect (Mendlewicz and Rainer, 1974). Affective disturbances in children of bipolar parents often lean toward the depressive side of the affective spectrum (McKnew et al., in press; Robbins et al., 1977). However, several investigators report hyperactivity in the children of bipolar patients (Dyson and Barcai, 1970), lending support to the theory that a subgroup of "hyperactive" children actually represents early-onset manic-depressive illness (White and O'Shanick, 1977; Weinberg and Brumbach, 1976).

Careful retrospective studies of the childhood of adult manic-depressive patients are rare in the psychiatric literature. The most complete accounts of childhood symptoms are found in the psychoanalytic studies of M. Cohen and her coworkers (1954). Their intensive studies of 12 manic-depressive adults showed a "preponderance of normal infancies." Later childhood, however, revealed significant depressive symptoms with childhood memories of "extreme loneliness" and "extreme sensitivity to envy and competition." There was no evidence of manic or hyperactive symtoms in the group studied.

The use of lithium carbonate in the treatment of young children of bipolar parents has been attempted for numerous symptoms, including hyperactivity, childhood psychosis, temper outbursts, and depression. Although individual case reports indicate the existence of a lithium-responsive population of young children, a recent review concludes that in general, the lithium effects are "disappointingly non-specific" (Rapoport and Mikkelsen, 1978; Youngerman and Canino, 1978). In view of these differing findings, further careful clinical studies of lithium response seem warranted in symptomatic children of manic-depressive, lithium-responding parents.

OVERVIEW

It is perhaps most useful at this stage in the study of childhood mania to propose a classification describing a continuum of syndromes based on a genetic model, rather than to attempt to define a single specific clinical entity. This proposed classification would be made up of three groups: (1) a syndrome phenotypically similar to adult mania, with presumable genotypic similarity; (2) a syndrome of presumed genotypic similarity with dissimilarity in the phenotypic expression from the adult model; and (3) a syndrome of phenocopy that bears no genotypic similarity to the adult model and yet presents symptoms with the appearance of adult mania.

The first of these groups, with phenotypic and possible genotypic similarity, is represented by the case reports discussed earlier. These cases, although relatively infrequent, approach fulfillment of the strict criteria of Anthony and Scott (1960), and clearly fulfill the criteria of Weinberg and Brumbach (1976). These children may well represent the group most usefully studied clinically, biochemically, and pharmacologically during childhood.

The second group, lacking the complete phenotypic similarity, but perhaps having common genotypic basis, could well be represented by the subgroup of hyperactive children of lithium-responsive manic-depressive parents, whose symptoms many authors view as early indicators of later manic-depressive illness. Members of this group, especially those who are lithium-responders, would comprise a group to be carefully studied longitudinally for eventual signs of clinically diagnosable affective illness.

The third group is made up of patients exhibiting phenocopies of the adult manic state. High doses of corticosteroids have been associated with manic symtpoms in pediatric patients being treated for asthma and other disorders. In addition, two recent case reports have described phencyclidine (PCP, "angel dust") abuse in adolescents causing transient episodes of manic symtoms indistinguishabel from the naturally occurring affective disorder (Slavney et al., 1977).

We have also observed periods of time-limited manic symptoms in children who have recently been taken off of major tranquilizers, especially halo-peridol. This "rebound" effect, as it has often been called, clearly fulfills Weinberg's criteria, except for its brief duration (days rather than months). For example, during withdrawal from four milligrams of haloperidol in a ten-year-old white female child suffering from chronic multiple tics of Tourette's syndrome, the patient became increasingly silly, hyperactive, and grandiose for a period of three days. Following this, she became irritable and suspicious for 48 hours before returning to her normal prewithdrawal behavior. Possible alterations in noradrenergic, serotonergic, or other central neurotransmitter systems that correspond to the changes in drug levels and behavioral symptoms remain to be elucidated. Clinical and neurochemical study of these phenocopy patients may well provide important insight into the underlying mechanisms of mania in adults as well as children and adolescents.

In summary, that there is a symptom complex in children closely resembling adult mania becomes more undeniable with each clinical study. However, which of the many diagnostic criteria will prove most useful in research and care is not as yet clear. The conception of a continuum of childhood manic-depressive disease with varying degrees of severity and underlying similarities in neurochemical and neurophysiological mechanisms appears to best describe the current state of knowledge, and indicates useful directions for future clinical and basic science investigation.

REFERENCES

Annell, A.L. Lithium in the treatment of children and adolescents. *Acta Psychiat. Scan. Suppl.* 207, 19–30 (1969).
Anthony, E.J., and Scott, P. Manic-depressive psychosis in childhood. *J. Child Psychol. & Psychiat.* 1, 53–72 (1960).

Berg, I., Hullin, R., Allsopp, M., O'Brien, P., and McDonald, R. Bipolar manic-depressive psychosis in early adolescence: A case report. *British J. Psychiat.* 125, 416–417 (1974).

Cantwell, D.P., ed. *The Hyperactive Child: Diagnosis, Management, Current Research.* Halstead, New York (1975).

Cohen, D.J. Minimal brain dysfunction: Diagnosis and therapy. In *Current Psychiatric Therapies,* Vol. 17, J.H. Masserman, ed. Grune & Stratton, New York (1977), pp. 57–70.

Cohen, M.B., Baker, G., Cohen, R.A., Fromm-Reichmann, F., and Weigert, E.V. An intensive study of twelve cased of manic-depressive psychosis. *Psychiatry* 17, 103–137 (1954).

Dyson, L., and Barcai, A. Treatment of children of lithium responding parents. *Curr. Ther. Res.* 12, 286–290 (1970).

Engstrom, F.W., Robbins, D.R., and May, J.G. Manic-depressive disease in adolescence: A case report. *J. Am. Acad. Child Psychiat.* 17, 514–520 (1978).

Feighner, J.P., Robins, E., Guze, S.B., Woodruff, R.A., Jr., Winokur, G., and Munoz, R. Diagnostic criteria for use in psychiatric research. *Arch. Gen. Psychiat.* 26, 57–63 (1972).

Feinstein, S.C., and Wolpert, E.A. Juvenile manic-depressive illness: Clinical and therapeutic considerations. *J. Am. Acad. Child Psychiat.* 12, 123–136 (1973).

Harms, E. Differential pattern of manic-depressive disease in childhood. *Nerv. Child.* 9, 326–356 (1952).

Hava, F.A. Lithium, the hyperactive child, and manic-depressive illness. *J. Ark. Med. Soc.* 69, 299–300 (1973).

Kraepelin, E. *Manic-Depressive Insanity and Paranoia.* Livingstone, Edinburgh (1921).

McHarg, J.F. Mania in childhood: Report of a case. *AMA Arch. Neurol. & Psychiat.* 72, 531–539 (1954).

McKnew, D.H., Jr., Cytryn, L., and White, I. Clinical and biochemical correlates of hypomania in a child. *J. Amer. Acad Child Psychiat.* 13, 576–585 (1974).

McKnew, D.H., Jr., Cytryn, L., Efron, A.M., Gershon, E.S., and Bunney, W.E., Jr. Offspring of patients with affective disorders. (In press)

Mendlewicz, J., and Rainer, J.D. Morbidity risk and genetic transmission in manic-depressive illness. *AM. J. Hum. Genet.* 26, 692–701 (1974).

Rapoport, J.L., and Mikkelsen, E.J. Antimanic, antianxiety and miscellaneous drugs. In *Pediatric Psychopharmacology,* Werry, J., ed. Brunner-Mazel, New York (1978), pp. 316–355.

Robbins, D.R., Engstrom, F.W., Mrazek, D., and Swift, W. Psychological characteristics of children of manic-depressive mothers. Presented at the annual meeting of the American Academy of Child Psychiatry (1977).

Slavney, P.R., Rich, G.B., Pearlson, G.D., and McHugh, P.R. Phencyclidine abuse and symptomatic mania. *Biol. Psychiat.* 12, 697–700 (1977).

Stewart, M.A., and Morrison, J.R. Affective disorder among the relatives of hyperactive children. *J. Child Psychol. & Psychiat.* 14, 209–212 (1973).

Thompson, R.J., and Schindler, F.H. Embryonic mania. *Child Psychiat. & Hum. Dev.* 6, 149–154 (1976).

Warneke, L. A case of manic-depressive illness in childhood. *Can. Psychiatr. Assoc. J.* 20, 195–200 (1975).

Weinberg, W.A., and Brumbach, R.A. Mania in childhood. *Am. J. Dis. Child.* 130, 380–385 (1976).

Wender, P. *Minimal Brain Dysfunction in Children.* Wiley, New York (1971).

White, J.H., and O'Shanick, G. Juvenile manic-depressive illness. *Am. J. Psychiat.* 134, 1035–1036 (1977).

Winokur, G. Heredity in the affective disorders. In *Depression and Human Existence,* E.J. Anthony and T. Benedek, eds. Little, Brown Boston (1975), pp. 7–20.

Youngerman, J., and Canino, I.A. Lithium carbonate use in children and adolescents. *Arch. Gen. Psychiat.* 35, 216–224 (1978).

CHAPTER 10

Genetic Counseling for Affective Illness

Steven D. Targum and Elliot S. Gershon

There is widespread belief in a genetic predisposition to psychiatric illness in some families such that a realistic assessment of familial factors in risk of illness and treatment response would be of benefit to those persons who come for genetic counseling . Genetic counseling may be useful as an aid to family planning, to early ascertainment of illness, and to early entry into treatment. As support for genetic hypotheses for psychiatric disorders becomes more widespread, there will be increased requests for individual genetic consultation, as reflected in the recent literature (Kety et al., 1978; Tsuang, 1978).

Considerable evidence has been presented that there is a familial predisposition in the development of the major psychiatric disorders (schizophrenia and affective illness [Rosenthal, 1970; Zerbin-Rudin, 1972; Gershon et al., 1977]). Twin and adoption studies in both schizophrenia and affective illness suggest that there is a genetic basis to the familiality of these disorders. Although the relative contribution of genetic factors is not precisely known, it is possible to determine an empirical morbidity risk for the development of illness in relatives of ill persons. This risk is greater than 10% for first-degree relatives (siblings, offspring) of either schizophrenic or affectively ill individuals. In some circumstances, the morbidity risk is extremely high. The concordance rate for affective illness in monozygotic twins has been reported to be 69% (Gershon et al., 1977), and the offspring of two affectively ill parents have a greater than 40% morbid risk of becoming ill (Winokur and Clayton, 1967).

The estimate of risk and prognostic speculations may be improved by the subclassification of the affective disorders. Unipolar and bipolar subforms of affective illness may be distinct genetic disorders, although not all investigators agree (Gershon et al., 1977). From a clinical standpoint, it is notable that the probability of affective illness in a first-degree relative is about 15% if the proband is bipolar and 6% if the proband is unipolar (Gershon et al., 1977). Other variables, such as age of onset or sex of the proband, may also be of predictive value. An early age of onset for affective illness in the proband is

predictive of greater morbid risk in relatives. An X-chromosome transmission of bipolar illness has been hypothesized for some families, but
remains a controversial issue (Gershon and Bunney, 1976). If it were true,
there would be no risk of father-to-son transmission in those specific families
and a very high risk of father-to-daughter transmission of the disorder.

Specific genetic markers of the physiological or biological vunerability to
developing psychiatric illness have been sought, as reviewed elsewhere
(Gershon et al., 1977). Two types of markers have been sought, the first type
based on the presumed pathophysiologic defect in the psychiatric illness and
the second type based on linkage of the disorder to known genetic markers at
specific loci on known chromosomes. While very provocative, these studies
have as yet revealed no replicable markers and are therefore of no utility to
genetic counseling presently.

The controversiality of genetic factors in human behavior, and the
stigma and fear of mental illness in oneself or in one's family, lends a
particular delicacy to genetic consultations in psychiatry. For many people,
there is also a narcissistic investment in their ability to consciously determine
their own mental lives, which makes genetic determination a psychological
threat, especially when one's mental life has been undisturbed through the
formative years of childhood. We consider psychiatric genetic counseling as
dealing with these three basic concerns: (a) possibly emergent psychiatric
illness in the consultand or a relative; (b) marriage and reproductive
planning; and (c) the psychological effect that this counsel will have on those
who receive it.

Kallman (1962) believed that the genetic counselor should provide
scientifically valid yet psychologically undamaging advice, and he suggested
that the sessions would be most effective if conducted along the lines of short-
term psychotherapy aimed at reducing anxiety and tension. It is the role of the
counselor to help the consultand understand and cope with the reality of the
probability of a psychiatric diagnosis and the current lack of knowledge on
how to alter this probability. The emotional facets of an affective illness can
become compounded by the additional anxieties and misconceptions con-
strued by a genetic diagnosis. A resolution of the emotional sequelae of a
genetic diagnosis will facilitate achievement of other goals: comprehension of
medical facts, and appreciation of the risk of occurrence of the illness, and a
willingness to consider whether there is a need for adjusted personal plans
related to marriage and child rearing.

A rational, standardized approach to genetic counseling for psychiatric
disorders is essential in order to assure satisfactory service and accurate
assessment of methodology and outcome. We believe that an optimum
approach to genetic counseling includes the following steps:

1. Establishment of a therapeutic relationship
2. Assessment of the motive for the consultation

3. Establishment of an accurate diagnosis of the consultand and of family members, and determination of the risk of occurrence of the illness
4. Assessment of the consultand's concept of burden of illness, capacity to comprehend the genetic information, and competence to make appropriate decisions
5. Communication of the genetic information (i.e., estimate of morbid risk, and nature and burden of the illness)
6. Helping to alleviate anxiety and the emotional sequelae of a genetic diagnosis
7. Assissting but not directing, individuals to reconsider personal plans in light of genetic information
8. Periodic monitoring through follow-up visits to assess the outcome of the counsel and the psychiatric status of family members

The obstacles to a satisfactory outcome begin prior to the initial interview and exist throughout all phases of the counseling procedure, due, in part, to misinterpretation and subjective interpretation. A reappraisal of the consultand's original objectives and conceptions should be made following the communication of the genetic information and the description of the illness. The acomplishment of procedural tasks will have been pointless if the consultand's needs have gone unmet, and if the anxiety that triggered the consultation still remains.

THE ASSESSMENT OF MOTIVE

The counselor should not presume to know the motive for consultation. Factors such as apprehension, guilt, anxiety, curiosity, coercion, manipulation, or mere compliance with a referring physician's recommendation may be involved. The consultand may fear illness within himself as well as in future offspring or children entering the age of risk. A spouse may be consulting about the other spouse out of general concern or because of fears engendered by their relationships. Alternatively, a spouse may be seeking to direct responsibility for mental illness to the other side of the family. Shame about family secrets or past history, or guilt about child rearing, may stimulate an individual to seek exoneration for responsibility by attributing the illness to genetics (much as the person prone to mania may use his illness as an excuse for periods of irresponsibility).

The meaning of the consultation may reside more in the dynamics of the motivation than in any specific interest in the risk for illness or in rational family planning based upon genetic information. The counselor must know what he is being asked to provide. Highly intelligent individuals may regress when confronted with genetic risks. The information may be overwhelming to some individuals if the counselor fails to understand the original objectives that triggered the consultation.

DIAGNOSIS OF THE DISEASE IN QUESTION

An accurate diagnosis is critical in all genetic evaluations. The application of objective clinical criteria for psychiatric disorders has become possible (Spitzer et al., 1978). Wherever possible, corroborative interviews with other family members may help to establish the extent of illness in a particular pedigree and to improve the meaning of the empirical risk figure. In our experience, interviews with other family members have not been difficult to obtain. The willingness and accessibility of family members to participate in such an evaluation will obviously vary and must be assessed by the counselor. Their perception of illness within the family, and their belief in the hereditary nature of that illness, will influence their involvement and affect the impact and meaning of their participation. The denial of illness is not uncommon, and the true extent of illness in a particular family may be revealed only through multiple sources.

THE DETERMINATION OF RISK IN A PARTICULAR PEDIGREE

The lack of a well-demonstrated mode of inheritance or genetic marker in the major psychiatric illnesses is an impediment to efficient use of pedigree information. The best estimate for persons without a large pedigree is the empirical risk figure for family studies. In offering these figures, we undoubtedly overestimate risks for some individuals and underestimate them for others. By adding information on the consultand's pedigree, we can possibly improve our risk estimates, at least in larger pedigrees. The use of computer programs to calculate maximum likelihood of different modes of inheritance, and of genotype of the consultand under any particular mode of inheritance, may prove most useful (Kety et al., 1978). A conspiciously loaded family history of homotypic mental illness indicates that the consultand has a greater risk and that a more guarded prognosis is advisable, and a completely negative family history in a large family offers grounds for a more favorable prognosis.

There may be heterogeneity such that all forms of the disease that we can recognize do not have the same pattern. A spectrum of disorders, including minor depressive illness (neurotic depression), cyclothymic personality, and acute psychosis, have been reported in the families of patients with affective illness (Gershon et al., 1975). These findings suggest that the underlying diathesis for affective illness may have variable clinical manifestations. Consequently, it would be spurious to convey certainty when quoting empirical risks for psychiatric disorders, although the empirical risks are the best estimates we can offer.

THE PERCEPTION OF BURDEN AND RISK

The estimation of burden and risk depends on the variable subjective reckoning of the consultand. Some determining factors include intelligence, educational background, personal experience, tolerance threshold, personality type and defensive style (i.e., denial, rationalization), as well as religious and cultural dictates. An individual must perceive himself, or his family, as susceptible to a particular illness that he sees might cause serious personal consequences before he will take an active role in preventive health measures. Rosenstock (1966) has termed this prerequisite "psychological readiness."

The concept of affective illness and the perception of its burden and risk by family members may be at considerable variance with the informed opinion of the medical counselor. The perception is complicated by the variable clinical manifestations that can be present even within the same pedigree. A consultand's concept of disease is formed by personal exposure to ill family members, and will be influenced by the extent of disruption caused by the illness. Some families may discount the burdensome aspects of psychiatric illness in light of positive aspects they attribute to the condition. Family members may emphasize the increased capacity and energy noted in bipolar illness, and deny the more burdensome aspects of the illness. The possibility of personal failure, chronic illness, incapacity, or suicide will be weighed in accordance with the consultand's experience and the family history. When affective illness has been particularly disruptive, a higher estimate of burden may be assumed than in those families where the illness has had little impact. These variable estimates are useful, since psychiatric entities are presumably due to multiple genotypes and are affected by environmental variance.

Affective illness may create a burden both during acute phases and between episodes. When he or she is acutely ill, the manic patient may be intrusive, irrational, pressured, and violent. The acutely depressed patient may be withdrawn, helpless, and suicidal. The family may perceive the affectively ill patient's behavior differently than the patient. Janowsky et al. (1970) reported that the well spouse often felt that the manic phase was a willful, spiteful act, whereas the patient felt unfairly victimized and blamed for things beyond his or her control. There is also a chronic burden associated with affective illness. Follow-up studies (Winokur et al., 1972; Carlson et al., 1974) report that over one third of bipolar individuals remained functionally impaired with affective symtoms, which interfered with their careers and interpersonal relations. Descriptive case studies (Ablon et al., 1975; Cohen et al., 1954) have portrayed the manic-depressive as an individual who forms markedly dependent relationships, with demands for attention and love that are never reciprocated, a low frustration tolerance, and a reliance upon manipulation, coercion, pity, and submission to attain insatiable needs. Targum et al., (unpublished data) have documented the regrets about marriage and chidbearing that the well spouses of bipolar patients have expressed, and the relative denial by the patients themselves. In a sample of 19 couples, 53% of well spouses, compared to only 5% of bipolar patients (p < .05), stated that they would not have married had they known more about the existence of illness in their spouse prior to marriage. Similarly, 47% of well spouses compared to only 6% of bipolar patients (p < .05), stated that they would not have had children had they known more about the illness prior to making this decision. Hirschfeld and Klerman (1979) have noted that unipolar depressives appear to be more likely to break down under stress, have less energy, are more insecure and sensitive, more obsessional, and less socially adroit than normal individuals. Thus, the data reflect a high degree of chronic burden associated with the major affective illnesses.

As described above, the consultand's perception of burden will be largely determined by his or her peronal exposure to illness. The risk figure is also subject to personal interpretation. Some degree of mathematical sophistication is required in order to use numbers to reflect the perception of odds. The counselor must be prepared to educate the consultand, probe the reactions of all parties involved, provide the opportunity to voice apprehension or clarify misunderstanding, and expect a reemergence of old conflicts when issues of genetics and psychiatric illness are brought up. Aspects of denial, guilt, and projection, as well as the impact of a liability for mental illness on the family system, must be explored in order to allow a clearer conception of burden and risk. Consultands advised of the nature and risk of a genetic diagnosis may initially deny the implications and block out much of the counsel.

THE COMMUNICATION OF GENETIC INFORMATION

A description of the nature and course of affective illness, and a recitation of empirical morbid risks, must be given in association with an understanding of the consultand's perception of burden. There is little concrete advice that can be given to parents regarding minimizing the risk for the development of psychiatric illness. Adoption studies have shown that parental environment has little impact on the eventual development of psychiatric illness in those who are biologically predisposed (Kety et al., 1976). The genetic counselor should not use coercion to force a consultand to make decisons about future family planning. In most instances, the risk to offspring is not extremely high. However, we would discourage dual matings between individuals who have both had psychotic illnesses. In addition, we would suggest a delay in childbearing for rapidly cycling bipolar patients, frequently rehospitalized patients, and those individuals who have made multiple suicide attempts. The likelihood for divorce is high, as is the probability for social impairment.

DISCUSSION

Increased requests for psychiatric genetic counseling have been generated by increased acceptance of genetic hypo.heses for psychiatric disorders and the widespread belief by families in a genetic predisposition to psychiatric illness. We believe that persons who come for counseling require a realistic assessment of familial factors in risk of illness. Genetic counseling can be an informative and supportive therapeutic technique for patients with major psyschiatric disorders, their spouses, and concerned relatives, and an aid to life plans regarding marriage and childbearing. In the past generation, hospitalization time for the major psychiatric disorders has been reduced, and medication (particularly phenothiazines for schizophrenia, and lithium carbonate for affective illness) has raised the potential for substantial interpersonal relationships. Whereas formerly it was believed that the reproductive and marriage rates for patients who have had psychotic illness were considerably lower than those of the general population, recent studies (Odegaard, 1960; Erelenmeyer-Kimling, 1976) have noted an increasing rate, and in particular an increase in dual matings (marriages between two patients who have had psychotic illnesses). A high incidence of assortative mating for affective illness has been noted as well (Gershon et al., 1973; Dunner et al., 1976). Consequently, the need for psychiatric genetic counseling is growing.

We believe that most self-referred consultands will be competent to make their own moral decision regarding marriage and childbearing, given the appropriate information and the unbiased support of the genetic psychiatric counselor. Perhaps those who most need this type of counsel will be too defensive or too incompetent to accept the information.

Our present social policy does not openly advocate reproductive limitation to avert psychiatric illness or mental retardation. This offers an ethical and moral challenge to the psychiatric profession, which must consider the appropriateness and desirability of coercive methods in genetic counseling for persons incompetent to make their own judgment (i.e., mentally retarded individuals), and the extent of our obligation to society.

REFERENCES

Ablon, S.L., Davenport, Y.B., Gershon, E.S., and Adland, M.L. The married manic. *Am. J. Orthopsychiat.* 45(5), 854–866, 1975.

Carlson, G.A., Kotin, J., Davenport, Y.B., and Adland, M. Follow-up of 53 bipolar manic-depressive patients. *Brit. J. Psychiat.* 124, 134–139, 1974.

Cohen, M.D., Baker, C., Cohen, R.A., et al. An intensive study of twelve cases of manic-depressive psychosis. *Psychiatry* 17, 103–137, 1954.

Dunner, D.L., Fleiss, J.L., Addanizio, G., and Fieve, R.R. Assortative mating in primary affective disorder. *Biol. Psychiat.* 11, 43–51, 1976.

Erlenmeyer-Kimling, L. Schizophrenia: A bag of dilemmas. *Soc. Biol.* 23, 123–134, 1976.

Gershon, E.S., Dunner, D.L., Sturt, L., and Goodwin, F.K. Assortative mating in the affective disorders: A preliminary report. *Biol. Psychiat.* 7, 63–74, 1973.

Gershon, E.S., Mark, A., Cohen N., et al. Transmitted factors in the morbid risk of affective disorders: A controlled study. *J. Psychiatr. Res.* 12, 238–299, 1975.

Gershon, E.S., and Bunney, W.E., Jr. The question of X-linkage in bipolar manic-depressive illness. *J. Psychiatr. Res.* 13, 99–117, 1976.

Gershon, E.S., targum, S.D., Kessler, L.R., et al. Genetic studies and biologic strategies in the affective disorders. *Prog. Med. Genet.* 11, 101–164, 1977.

Hirschfeld, R.M.A. and Klerman, G.L. Personality attributes and affective disorders. *Am. J. Psychiat.* 136, 67–70, 1979.

Janowsky, D.S., Leff, M. and Epstein, R.S. Playing the manic game. *Arch. Gen. Psychiat.* 22, 252–261, 1970.

Kallman, F.J. Genetic research and counseling in the mental health field. In *Expanding Goals of Genetics in Psychiatry,* F.J. Kallman, ed. Grune & Stratton, New York (1962), pp. 250–255.

Kety, S.S., Rosenthal, D., Wender, P.H., Schulsinger, F., and Jacobsen, B. Mental illness in the biological and adoptive families of adopted individuals who have become schizophrenic. *Behav. Genet.,* 6, 219–225, 1976.

Kety, S.S., Matthysse, S., and Kidd, K.K. Genetic counseling for schizophrenic patients and their families. In *Controversy in Psychiatry,* J.P. Brady and H.K.H. Brodie, eds. W.B. Saunders, Philadelphia (1978), pp. 776–784.

Odegaard, O. Marriage rate and fertility in psychotic patients before admission and after discharge. *Int. J. Soc. Psychiat.* 6, 25–33, 1960.

Rosenstock I.M. Why people use health services. *Milband Mem. Fund Quart.* 44 (No. 3, Part 2), 94–1966.

Rosenthal, D. *Genetic Theory and Abnormal Behavior.* McGraw-Hill, New York (1970).

Spitzer, R.L., Endicott, J., and Robins, E. Research Diagnostic Criteria: Rationale and reliability. *Arch. Gen. Psychiat.* 35, 773–782, 1978.

Targum, S.D., Dibble, E.D., Davenport, Y.B., and Gershon, E.S. Etiology, familial risk, and chronic burden of bipolar illness: Contrasting perceptions of the patient and spouse. (Submitted for publication.)

Tsuang, M. Genetic counseling for psychiatric patients and their families. *Am. J. Psychiat.* 135, 1465–1475, 1978.

Winokur, G., and Clayton, P. Family history studies. I. Two types of affective disorders separated according to genetic and clinical factors. In *Recent Advances in Biological Psychiatry,* Vol. 9. Plenum, New York (1967).

Winokur, G., Morrison, J., Clancy, J. and Crowe, R.R. The Iowa 500. *Arch. Gen. Psychiat.* 27, 462–464, 1972.

Zerbin-Rudin, E. Genetic research and the theory of schizophrenia. *Int. J. Ment. Health* 1, 42–62, 1972.

CHAPTER 11

The Lithium Ion:
Is It Specific for Mania?

William Annitto, Robert Prien, and Samuel Gershon

INTRODUCTION

The issue we raise here is more than semantic. The psychotherapeutic use of lithium for all sorts of human psychopathology has increased geometrically, it seems, while the scientific rationale for this plods along, at best, arithmetically. Many authors, caught in the dilemma of American psychiatry's unworkable nosology, accept a positive response to lithium as prima facie evidence that affective disorder is the "cause" of the treated psychopathology.

For this group, lithium remains disease specific. Alternatively, many recognize a positive response to lithium as perhaps fortuitous. For this group, nosology has become another example of the foibles of man. Whatever the stance, it is clear that conditions other than typical manic-depressive disorder respond to treatment with lithium. In this sense, then, lithium may no longer be considered "specific" for mania. However, we continue to feel that it remains the mainstay in the long-term treatment of manic-depressive disorder (Annitto and Gershon, 1978).

The major dilemma in this concundrum is that of diagnosis. As we have pointed out elsewhere (Annitto et al., 1978), many authors would permit the psychopathology of disordered thought to be included under the rubric of mania so long as this pathology "cleared" with lithium treatment. We would rather hypothesize that there exists in the range of human psychopathology that type which is cyclic, episodic, fully remitting, with healthy interphases, which is indeed not mania, but rather a phasic disruption of the patient's psychic state. Hence this would be neither schizophrenia, schizoaffective type, bipolar disease, manic type, nor cycloid psychosis. We literally have no category!

Purists will question our strength of conviction and our apparent lack of research diligence, while, unfortunately, the adventurous could abuse this hypothesis and administer lithium to anyone who occasionally expresses his or her personal ennui with daily living in any but the most demure manner.

Our only option is to examine some of the voluminous data on the treatment of psychopathology with lithium salts. Here we can look at this piece of fruit, sniff at its fragrance, sense its texture. Alas, the essence of the fruit will not be ours to savor. To have sought for clues, developed leads, and followed various paths will not, we hope, be judged as sloth by future researchers to whom we are leaving this mystery to be solved. Rather, they will understand our studied ingnorance as that quantum of knowledge that had yet to exist in our time.

LITHIUM IN MANIA

This literature has been reviewed (Annitto and Gershon, 1978; Prien, 1975; Gerbino et al., 1978; Gershon, 1975) rather extensively. Methodologic difficulties certainly remain in many of the earlier works. However, general consensus of researchers and clinicians alike is that lithium, when compared to placebo, is an effective treatment for mania (Gerbino et al., 1978). The major difference of opinion had arisen concerning the issue of the use of neuroleptics vs. lithium in the treatment of mania. Prien et al. (1972) found that highly active patients responded less satisfactorily to lithium than did mildly active patients. Moreover, they found that CPZ was more effective in that highly active population. This was in contrast to Johnson et al. (1971), who found that lithium produced a controlled remission in the majority of patients with acute mania.

Shopsin and Gershon (1975) found that neither haloperidol nor chlorpromazine produced better results than lithium alone in acute manics. They added that CPZ's success in highly active patients (Prien, 1975) may only be the clinician's recognition that lithium has a slower, more even onset of action. Sedation and decreased motor activity should not be accepted as dissolution of mania. Shopsin and Gershon continued to believe that lithium differed qualitatively from the neuroleptics in the treatment of mania. They postulated that more efficient rating scales for manic symptoms would confirm their position.

Takahashi et al. (1975) attempted to respond to this controversy. They found in a series of 80 cases of "endogenous manic psychosis" that lithium was significantly superior CPZ in efficacy. However, their CPZ group was treated with only 400 mg. One could easily state that from an American psychopharmacological point of view, this group was undertreated with neuroleptics. They respond to this by stating in the body of their paper that cultural differences account for this increased Japanese sensitivity to CPZ.

Of course another treatment issue arises here that is, as yet, unanswered. Would the combination of neuroleptics plus lithium be more efficacious than either alone in mania? Most clinicians would now agree that neuroleptics should be used initially in the agitated, dangerously hyperactive patient as a means of gaining rapid motor control. Lithium would be the drug of choice for the more cooperative, less disturbed patient. This neatly avoids the nosological dilemma, i.e., is the "more disturbed" patient an acutely excited schizophrenic?

In summary, the conflict over whether to treat acute mania with lithium or neuroleptics (or both), is more apparent than real. Prien reviewed his own work in Johnson's textbook, *Lithium Research and Therapy* (1975). Here he states that "control" of excited behavior is not as critical with mildly active (manic) patients and lithium [alone] does well with this subgroup." He also points out that impressionistic data—that alone which is available at this time—suggests that neuroleptics plus lithium are the treatment of choice for the dangerously excited hyperactive patient. This most active subgroup seems to do less well without neuroleptics. We all agree that there are no controlled studies to refute these clinical impressions. Moreover, we have no scientific basis for denying neuroleptic medication to a severely excited psychotic patient. The diagnosis must not be defined by response to treatment.

LITHIUM AS PROPHYLAXIS IN MANIA

Prien (1975) and Gerbino et al. (1978) have extensively reviewed this literature in recent years. It would be excessive to repeat their work. Gerbino et al. (1978) described the criteria for positive prophylaxis as (1) decrease in the number of manic episodes; (2) decrease in the severity of individual episodes; (3) decrease in duration of illness; (4) increased duration of healthy interphase; (5) increased level of social functioning. Both agree that available studies essentially satisfy these criteria.

Prien (1975), moreover, adds that lithium has effective prophylaxis in both bipolar and unipolar illness. Significantly, he found that imipramine prophylaxis was poorly tolerated in bipolar disease, with an excessive number of manic attacks. In unipolar disease, lithium and imipramine were equally effective.

It must be stressed that neuroleptics have not been used as prophylactic agents in recurrent mania. Their efficacy cannot be compared with lithium. However, with the recent concern among clinicians regarding long-term neuroleptic use and development of tardive dyskinesia, this may be a felicitous lacuna in psychopharmacologic research.

ECT AND MANIA

Little controlled work has been published concernig the efficacy of ECT vs. lithium in mania. Perhaps this is due to the poor public image of electroconvulsive therapy. More likely it is due to the widely known efficacy of lithium. McCabe and Norris (1977) did a retrospective analysis of 56 patients (half treated with ECT, half with CPZ) who satisfied "research diagnosis criteria of mania." These groups were compared with 28 controls who had been hospitalized for mania before any treatment was available. They found no difference between the ECT and CPZ groups in terms of outcome after 5.2 and 3.1 years respectively. Both groups did equally better than the patients from the pre-somatotherapy era.

In a second paper, McCabe (1976) makes the point that a prospective study comparing the various treatment modalities—ECT, lithium carbonate, and neuroleptics—in mania is needed. He adds that since 96% of the ECT group was sufficiently improved to be discharged home, ECT may be a valuable therapeutic tool in mania.

Aden (1976) describes the clinical course of identical twins with manic illness. Both were treated with lithium, but one received ECT plus phenothiazine and the other only phenothiazine. He found that ECT may improve occupational adjustment and shorten the duration of hospitalization for the manic episode. However, we must accept this case report with some reservations. Both twins had been diagnosed previously on multiple hospitalizations as paranoid schizophrenics; moreover, both had symptoms of peculiar religious delusions and active thought disorder. Again we are confronted with the illogical thinking that since lithium therapy yields a positive response, then the disease must be affective disorder.

LITHIUM IN THE GROUP OF SCHIZOPHRENIAS

Introduction

We are here occupied with the crucial issue. If lithium creates a positive therapeutic response in a patient with schizophrenic symptoms, does that patient then become an "atypical" manic (Taylor and Abrams, 1973)? Or does lithium have some additive central effect that is therapeutic in this condition?

Schizophrenia or Mania?

Taylor and Abrams (1973) contend that clinicians overdiagnose schizophrenia. They found 52 patients who satisfied "research criteria" of mania, with hyperactivity, pressured speech, and euphoric, expansive, or irritable mood. Of these, 26.9% had autochthonous ideas and visual hallucinations; 13.5% had catatonic motor disturbances; 11.5% had first-rank symtoms of Schneider; 58.6% had grandiose delusions; 48.1% were assaultive; 48.1% had incomplete auditory hallucinations; 42.3% had persecutory delusions; 28.8% had a labile, depressive mood. Ten of 17 patients on lithium alone showed "full remission."

In another study (Abrams et al., 1974), this same group found 41 patients "misdiagnosed." Of these, 81% had thought disorder, 90.5% had apopharnous phenomena; 42.9% had auditory hallucinations; 14.3% had first-rank symptoms. Thirteen patients of this group on lithium alone showed marked improvement or "remission."

Again (Abrams and Taylor, 1976), this group describes the misdiagnosis of catatonia where their mania exists. The list of accepted schizophrenia symtoms included is large. Again, 8 patients (of 56) either remit or show marked improvement on lithium alone.

What has happened, then, in this group of "studies" is that treatment outcome has been used to dictate diagnosis. Nosology has been disregarded, if not subverted. Moreover, therapeutics have not been properly served, either, since they add no clear means to decide which of these "atypical" manic patiens would be the lithium responder. None of their work was controlled.

Welner et al. (1972) recently reported on the follow-up of 114 patients diagnosed as schizoaffectives and "related psychoses." They used cyclic recurrence to evaluate the nature or type of illness (i.e., episodic vs. chronic) and quality of three life variables (marital, occupational, and social successes) to evaluate course of illness. Seventy-one percent had a chronic, nonepisodic type of illness, while 10% were episodic in nature. Eighty-one percent of the chronic patient group manifested deterioration as their course of illness. More importantly, 90 of the 114 met "diagnostic criteria" for unipolar (N = 64) or bipolar (N = 24) disease, plus thought disorder and/or behavior disorder. Yet neither episodic type of illness nor deteriorative course could be used to differentiate statistically these "affectively loaded" groups from their more affectively blunted schizophrenic counterparts. They concluded that the presence or absence of affective symptoms had no predictive value on cyclicity of illness or course of illness. They added that their group of schizoaffectives more closely resembled schizophrenics than affective disorder patients. Perhaps, then, illness outcome and quality of life are more valid diagnostically than quantity or type of affect during any episode.

Strauss and Carpenter (1978), in their most recent review of just this area, lean toward this hypothesis. In fact, they state that longitudinal variables of prognostic, and for our argument, diagnostic value are important in both schizophrenic and nonschizophrenic disorders. The latter group were, in fact, only slightly better in having less hospitalization (and, we can hypothesize, a better quality of life) at two years of follow-up. Moreover, they found only 8% of first admissions who did not show major affective symptoms and signs. Thus, presence of affective components does not alone dictate diagnostic category, since 92% of first admissions to any hospital are not manic-depressives.

Lithium and Neuroleptics in Schizophrenia

Shopsin et al. (1971) described a controlled blind study in which 21 acute schizophrenics were treated with either lithium or CPZ. They found "unequivocally" that CPZ was superior to lithium in terms of reducing symptoms and producing clinical remission. They admit, however, that the notion lithium could be useful for some schizophrenics could not be ruled out.

Prien et al. (1972) reported on 83 newly admitted excited schizoaffectives. They found that lithium was less effective than CPZ in treating the highly active group, while there were no differences among the treatments in the mildly active group. Fortunately, this group did not decide to rearrange nosology, but rather, they postulated that lithium may have some neuroleptic properties that would explain its beneficial effects in schizoaffectives. They raised the issue that perhaps lithium should not be considered specifically antimanic.

Earlier, Angst et al. (1970) found that schizoaffectives on lithium therapy had significantly fewer psychotic episodes and hospital admissions. They had no placebo control group. Smulevitch et al. (1974) studied 100 patients (50 manic-depressives, 49 schizoaffectives, 1 organic) with a 100-patient "control group." They had varying lengths of follow-up and maintained plasma lithium levels between 0.6 and 0.8 meq/L. Generally, they found that lithium treatment reduced the severity of illness, reduced the number of days of illness, and decreased the number of episodes. Forty-one of the 49 schizophrenics showed "complete disappearance of phases, reduction in their number, or a shortened duration of phases with 'reduced affective signs.'" They had eight schizophrenics who "displayed no changes" in their illness. Thus, of three gross categories for improvement—from complete remission to shortened duration of episode—the vast majority of patients benefited from lithium treatment.

Steinbrook and Chapman (1970) studied 29 psychotic patients using various psychometric test measures. Preadmission diagnosis favored schizophrenia, discharge diagnosis favored mania. Fifteen patients in this group responded positively to lithium treatment, either alone or in combination with neuroleptics. They found that all 15 positive responders had scored highly on the Acquiesence Scale. Interestingly, there was no statistical correlation between positive response to lithium and either pre- or post-admission diagnoses. They hypothesized that these high Ac, positive lithium responders suffered a common "Activation Disorder" unrelated to their diagnostic category. Again, these data favor our hypothesis that positive response to lithium is cross-diagnostic and not specific to manics. As noted, however, this group tended to allow lithium response to dictate final diagnosis.

Small et al. (1975) studied 22 chronic schizophrenics. They were receiving continuous neuroleptic therapy, and in crossover design received either lithium or placebo for alternating 4-week periods. They found significantly less pathology during lithium periods. Moreover, there was no increased incidence of neurotoxicity or impairment of congnitive functioning. Admittedly, they had few patients. However, we are here confronted with the additive beneficial effects of lithium in patients with *no* affective components. These were chronic schizophrenics clearly delimited from acute psychotics of any genera!

More recently Biederman et al. (1979) studied 36 excited schizoaffectives. Eighteen received lithium plus haloperidol, and 18 received placebo plus haloperidol. They found "modest" but statistically significant differences in favor of lithium plus haloperidol (by 5 weeks). Interestingly, the improvement was not limited to affective symptoms: "We could demonstrate no specificity of lithium for manic symptoms." They also found, in the lithium plus haloperidol group, that their "affective" schizoaffectives improved more than their "schizophrenic" schizoaffectives. As noted, both did better than either subdivision on haloperidol plus placebo. It should be noted that here, as in the Small study, there is no question of diagnostic category. It would have been ideal if they had had a group of patients on lithium plus placebo.

In summary, the use of lithium in schizophrenics (either alone or in combination with neuroleptics) is clearly a new and significant issue. Clinical research, as well as case reports, abounds. The data presented here (admittedly the highlights) demonstrate that lithium appears to have a beneficial effect on the course of certain schizophrenics. That the combination of neuroleptics and lithium appears statistically better in these studies than neuroleptics alone is all the more interesting given the recent work of Rivera-Calimlim et al. (1977). They have found that administering chlorpromazine together with lithium lowered CPZ plasma levels by 40.3%. There is, then, no simple explanation as to how lithium improves schizophrenic psychopathology while simultaneously decreasing plasma neuroleptic level. Given the most recent work of Biederman et al., it is difficult to argue that the improvement noted is due to neuroleptics alone. Moreover, with improvement noted in chronic patients, the need to search for "atypical manics" among groups of bona fide schizophrenics is also thwarted.

CYCLOID PSYCHOSIS AND LITHIUM

Carlo Perris (1974) has studied patients in the European category of cycloid psychosis for years. He defines the psychoses as "syndromes characterized by affective symptoms...and two or more of the following": confusion with agitation or retardation, paranoia or hallucinations *not* syntonic with levels of mood; motility disturbances; episodes of ecstasy; pananxiety (not bound to objects or situation [Perris, 1978]).

Clearly, in American nosology some of these patients would be schizoaffectives, excited. Be that as it may, Perris has found that "well-conducted lithium maintenance treatment has a favorable morbidity suppressive effect in...cycloid" patients (1978). He also found a statistically significant decrease in time spent in the hospital in that group of patients taking lithium regularly. This work deals with only 30 patients and lacks a placebo control group. However, the patients were followed for 1 to 8.5 years, and clinically, the results are certainly valid. Those patients who ingested lithium on a regular basis spent less time in hospital (and presumably more time well) than those who did not faithfully ingest the salt.

Perris' work, then, supplements our hypothesis that there exists a fully remitting, episodic psychic disturbance that apparently is quieted by lithium.

NEUROTOXICITY OF LITHIUM AND SPECIFICITY

We do not intend to review the physical signs and subjective symptoms of lithium-induced neurotoxicity here. This has been amply presented elsewhere (Annitto and Gershon, 1978; Reisberg and Gershon, 1978; Vacaflor, 1975). Nor are we to focus on the specific EEG changes most commonly encountered with lithium use. These include (1) diffuse slowing and increased amplitude; (2) changes in average evoked responses; (3) decreased alpha activity, with increased theta and delta waves; and (4) increased synchronization (Reisberg and Gershon, 1978; Vacaflor, 1975). Rather, we would clarify the hypothesis that certain patients—i.e., schizophrenics—are more prone to the central toxic effects induced by lithium than other patients (Shopsin et al., 1971).

Dimitrakoudi and Jenner (1975) reviewed the literature concerning the electroencephalographic effects of lithium. They found that, generally, EEG effects correlated to some degree with serum lithium level. This was earlier refuted by Johnson et al. (1970), who found that although there was "some relationship" between serum levels and EEG changes, the most important variables were patient-specific responses to lithium and preexisting cerebral organic disease. Complimenting this, Jus et al. (1973) found that in 5 of 8 temporal lobe epileptics, the chronic administration of lithium exacerbated EEG abnormalities and increased seizure frequency. Reilly et al. (1973) suggested that lithium accentuates existing underlying EEG abnormalities. They found that 2 of 12 normal volunteers developed abnormal EEG's while receiving lithium. Moreover, 4 of the 12 had accentuation of preexisting abnormalities during the drug period.

We should add to this the negative data from studies described elsewhere in this chapter (Prien et al., 1972; Angst et al., 1970; Smulevitch et al., 1974; Steinbrook and Chapman, 1970; Small et al., 1975; Rivera-Calimlin et al., 1977; Reilly et al., 1973; Kline and Simpson, 1975; Rifkin et al., 1972; Müllerova et al., 1974). None of these authors studying lithium in various schizophrenia, schizoaffective, cycloid, or aggressive disorders reported undue neurotoxic side effects in any diagnostic category. Small et al. (1975) in fact take pains to point out that their use of lithium, in combination with neuroleptics, caused no increase in neurotoxicity.

Most recently, Heninger (1978) has studied the effects of lithium on the EEG of 18 patients (15 manic-depressives; 3 schizoaffectives). He found that somatosensory (SER) cerebral-evoked-response (CER) changes in the EEG preceded the side effects of lethargy, muscular tremor, nausea, and polyuria. He added that the observed changes in CER and EEG did not solely represent "neurotoxic" effects.

In summary, then, it appears that the neurotoxicity induced by lithium salts is not related to diagnostic category. Rather, it is apparently more clearly related to the electrical and physiologic status of the central nervous system before the addition of this ion. Clinically, one could say that lithium should be used with extreme caution (if at all) with careful attention to toxic-symptomatic response in that patient who already has an aberrant EEG.

LITHIUM AND "OTHER" CYCLIC DISORDERS

Kline and Simpson (1975), and more recently Gerbino et al. (1978), have reviewed this topic. We will give a brief summary of their findings and add six papers under the appropriate headings.

Epilepsy

Lithium has been used as an anticonvulsive for nearly a century (Kline and Simpson, 1975). Kline and Simpson cautiously suggest that the weight of study data purportedly shows lithium to have beneficial effects on some epileptics. Conversely, they warn that induction of seizures and status epilepticus remain serious toxic effects of lithium, having occurred even in the "therapeutic dose range."

Emotionally Unstable Character Disorder

Gerbino et al. (1978) define this as chronic maladaptive behavior patterns with nonobject-related mood swings of short duration. Both reviewers describe the study by Rifkin et al. (1972), in which lithium (vs. placebo) significantly diminished the intensity of the mood changes without effecting amelioration of the characterological difficulties.

Recurring Aggression

This area is one of society's continuing dilemmas. On the one hand, the civil libertarians decry the "Clockwork Orange" aura of anyone "experimenting" on prisoners, minors, or subnormals. Conversely, the researcher can point with humane self-righteousness to the clear evidence (Gerbino et al., 1978; Kline and Simpson, 1975) that lithium has had a positive effect in reducing inappropriate aggression. Controlled studies have shown that during lithium treatment periods there has been a decrease in total number of infractions, reprimands, and "disciplinary actions," with a concomitant increase in feelings of self-control (and presumably in well-being and self-esteem) in the prisoner-subjects.

In reviewing the literature on subnormals with aggressive behavior treated with lithium, Kline and Simpson (1975) note generally positive effects. They mention that although most studies are uncontrolled, there is data suggesting that hyperkinesis, inappropriate outward and self-directed aggression, explosive anger, and low frustration tolerance have responded positively to lithium. Treatment reduced the duration of episodes in one study. Mullerova et al. (1974) studied 20 "oligophrenics" or behaviorally disturbed mental retardates. They found that lithium "improved significantly" sociability and adaptability, and in 4 patients induced [positive] changes in "emotivity."

More recently, Goetzl et al. (1972) reviewed the literature and added three more cases on lithium in aggressive retardates. They report a positive response with decreases in "cyclical overactivity," self-mutilation, irritability, inappropriate aggressiveness, and mood swings. However, they theorize that lithium may be effective because manic-depressive illness is possibly masked by the more obvious, socially troubling symptoms. We would hesitate to agree with this posture, but would concur that lithium clearly has a place in the treatment of this generally unresponsive and prognostically pessimistic subgroup, whatever its diagnostic label.

Whatever one's sociopolitical orientation, it seems that denying any "class" of patient the opportunity for beneficial treatment on humanitarian grounds is at best illogical and at worst Orwellian "double speak." We strongly maintain, however, that research and treatment should be undertaken only with proper informed consent and where the benefits satisfactorily outweigh the "costs."

Periodic Catatonia

There are admittedly few data on this entity. Kline and Simpson (1975) report two studies on few patients, only one showing any indication of positive response to lithium. Sovner and McHugh (1974) report on one case they followed extensively on lithium treatment. Interestingly, lithium "did dissociate" the periodic psychopathology from the concomitant metabolic changes. Before the addition of lithium, they noted, the BUN, pulse rate, and blood pressure would rise simultaneously with the aberrant behavior, while on lithium these "metabolic" parameters remained normal as the catatonic motor disorder continued. They theorize that lithium may act in the central nervous system "perhaps in the limbic hypothalamic" areas; or it could depress a more peripheral "adrenergic shift."

Alcoholism

There is general consensus that within the group of alcoholics there exists a subgroup that suffers depression (Gerbino et al., 1978). It is hypothesized that their excessive ingestion of alcohol is a response to the affective disorder. In the few controlled studies available (Gerbino et al, 1978; Reilly et al., 1973; Reynolds et al., 1977), it has been consistently shown that those alcoholics who score in the depressed range on the Beck Scale will have fewer "days drinking" and will subjectively admit to feeling less depressed when treated with lithium.

These should be heartening data for those clinicians who regularly treat this extremely refractory population. It would certainly mitigate against a blanket pessimistic view concerning alcoholism.

Premenstrual Tension

Again we are confronted with a common human problem for which there is as yet no satisfactory treatment. Both reviewers report anecdotal studies showing positive response to lithium, while the two controlled studies noted failed to confirm lithium's benefit. This, too, remains an equivocal area.

Chronic Cluster Headache

Cluster headaches, or Horton's Cephalgia, occur in clusters, are usually of short duration, with months between the clusters. They are characterized as being unilateral, with tearing of the homolateral eye and nasal congestion. Ekbom (1977) describes the positive response to lithium in 5 male patients suffering from cluster headaches (3 chronic, 2 periodic). He notes that all suffered recurrence upon withdrawal of the salt. He then reviews earlier work by Kudrow (1976). Here 25 of 32 patients (6 were dropped for "intolerable side effects") obtained "marked improvement." Moreover, Kudrow found lithium significantly superior to prednisone or methysergide. Clearly, the data are limited, but they certainly warrant more extensive and controlled study.

Summarizing, we have here briefly considered seven episodic "disorders" and their "treatment" with lithium. We agree that some of the data is uncontrolled and much of it needs more careful elucidation and expansion. However, we are impressed with the beneficial effects lithium seems to engender in that broad segment of patients whose main psychic state can be characterized by its cyclic, remitting bursts of ineffective and frequently personally harmful, aggressive behavior. It would be unwise at this nascent juncture to advocate any uncontrolled ingestion of lithium. However, it is imperative that the research necessary to clearly delineate lithium's therapeutic profile be carried out. The public sector must be made aware that the therapeutic advances of this explosive era in psychopharmacology are not self-propelling. Adequate funding and rational criticisms together should lead to continued advances.

CONCLUSIONS, CONUNDRUMS, AND "PROLOGUES"

We set about to present intelligently the case for and against the specificity of the lithium ion in mania. We have derived that lithium most certainly is a satisfactory treatment of this disease. With the addition of neuroleptics, even the most disturbed and disturbing manic patient can be treated. Moreover, lithium's long-term beneficial effects for the treatment of recurrent mania is also augured.

At this point in the history of psychopharmacologic research and therapy, it should no longer be baffling that some schizophrenics can respond to lithium with a reduction in psychopathology. At present, the scientific demand is to discover the neuropharmacologic mechanisms underlying this apparent dichotomy; not, as some have advocated, to reorder the basic meaning of the mental status examination.

We would be overly vain if we were to gratuitously offer still another category under which to subsume that group of patients who, suffering a cyclic, remitting, nondeteriorative illness, respond with return to previous levels of functioning after ingesting lithium. We will leave that for the psychiatric taxonomists. We would admonish those who follow, however, that what is needed are placebo-controlled, double-blind, symptomatically specific studies of groups of patients. We do not need to know how many angels can dance on the head of a pin; rather, we should set about learning more about the angel.

REFERENCES

Abrams, R., and Taylor, M. Catatonia. *Arch. Gen. Psychiat.* 33, 379-281 (1976).

Abrams, R., Taylor, M., and Gaztanaga, P. Manic-depressive illness and paranoid schizophrenia. *Arch. Gen. Psychiat.* 31, 640-642 (1974).

Aden, G. Lithium carbonate versus E.C.T. in the treatment of the manic state of identical twins with bipolar affective disease. *Dis. Nerv. Syst.* 393-397 (1976).

Angst, J., Weis, P., Grof, P., Baastrup, P., and Schou, M. Lithium prophylaxis in recurrent affective disorders. *Brit. J. Psychiat.* 116, 604-614 (1970).

Annitto, W., and Gershon, S. Antimanic agents, lithium and mania, plasma levels and clinical response. In *Plasma Level Measurement of Psychotropic Drugs and Clinical Response,* G. Burrows, ed. M. Dekker, New York (1978, in press).

Annitto, W., Shopsin, B., and Gershon, S. The neuropharmacology of mania. In *Manic Illness: A Profile in Psychobiological Research,* B. Shopsin, ed. Raven, New York (1978).

Biederman, J., Lerner, Y., Belmaker, R. Combination of lithium plus haloperidol in schizoaffective disorders: A controlled study. *Arch. Gen. Psychiat.* 36, 327-333 (1979).

Dimitrakoudi, M., and Jenner, F. Electroencephalographic effects of lithium. In *Lithium Research and Therapy,* F.N. Johnson, ed. Academic Press, New York (1975).

Ekbom, K. Lithium in the treatment of chronic cluster headaches. *Headache* 17, 39-40 (1977).

Gerbino, L., Oleshansky, M., and Gershon, S. Clinical use and mode of action of lithium. In *Psychopharmacology: A Generation of Progress,* A. DiMascio and K.F. Killam, eds. Raven, New York (1978).

Gershon, S. Lithium. In *American Handbook of Psychiatry,* Silvano Arieti, ed. Basic, New York (1975).

Goetzl, U., Grunberg, F., and Berkowitz, B. Lithium carbonate in the management of hyperactive aggressive behavior of the mentally retarded. *Compr. Psychiat.* 18, 599-606 (1972).

Heninger, G.R. Lithium carbonate and brain function. *Arch. Gen. Psychiat.* 35, 228-233 (1978).

Johnson, F., Maccario, M., Gershon, S., and Korein, J. The effects of lithium on electro-encephalogram, behavior and serum electrolytes. *J. Nerv. Ment. Dis.* 151, 273-289 (1970).

Johnson, G., Gershon, S., Burdock, E., Floyd, A., and Hekimian, L. Comparative effects of lithium and chlorpromazine in the treatment of acute manic states. *Brit. J. Psychiat.* 119, 267-276 (1971).

Jus, A., Villeneuve, A., Gautier, J., Pires, A., Cote, M., Jus, K., Villeneuve, R., and Perron, D. Some remarks on the influence of lithium carbonate on patients with temporal lobe epilepsy. *Int. J. Clin. Pharmacol. Ther. Toxicol.* 7, 67-74 (1973).

Kline, N., and Simpson, G. Lithium in the treatment of conditions other than the affective disorders. In *Lithium Research and Therapy*, F.N. Johnson, ed. Academic Press, New York (1975).

Kudrow, L. Prophylactic lithium in treatment of chronic cluster headache. *Headache* 16, 81-82 (1976).

McCabe, M. ECT in the treatment of mania: A controlled study. *Am. J. Psychiat.* 133, 688-891 (1976).

McCabe, M., and Norris, B., ECT versus chlorpromazine in mania. *Biol. Psychiat.* 12, 245-254 (1977).

Mullerova, S., Novotna, J., Rehan, V., and Skula, E. Lithium treatment of behavioral disturbances in patients with defective intellect. *Activ. Nerv. Suppl. (Praha) 16* 196 (1974).

Perris, C. A study of cycloid psychoses. *Acta Psychiatr. Scand. Suppl. 253* 1-77 (1974).

Perris, C. Morbidity suppressive effect of lithium carbonate in cycloid psychosis. *Arch. Gen. Psych.* 35, 328-331 (1978).

Prien, R., McCaffey, E., and Klett, C.J. A comparison of lithium carbonate and chlorpromazine in the treatment of excited schizo-affectives. *Arch. Gen. Psychiat.* 27, 182-189 (1972).

Prien, R.F., McCaffey, E.M., and Klett, C.J. Relationship between serum lithium level and clinical response in acute mania treated with lithium. *Brit. J. Psychiat.* 120, 409-414 (1972).

Prien, R.F. The clinical effectiveness of lithium: comparisons with other drugs. In *Lithium Research and Therapy*, F.N. Johnson, ed. Academic Press, New York (1975).

Reilly, E., Halmi, K., and Noyes, R. Electroencephalographic responses to lithium. *Int. Pharmacopsychiat.* 8, 208-213 (1973).

Reisberg, B., and Gershon, S. Toxicology and side effects of lithium therapy. *Amer. J. Psychiat.* (1978, in press).

Reynolds, C.M., Merry, J., and Coppen, A. Prophylactic treatment of alcoholism by lithium carbonate: An initial report. *Alcoholism* 1, 109-111 (1977).

Rifkin, A., Quitkin, F., Carillo, C., Blumberg, A., and Klein, D.F. Lithim carbonate in emotionally unstable character disorder *Arch. Gen. Psychiat.* 27, 519-523 (1972).

Rivera-Calimlin, L., Kerzener, B., and Karch, F. Effect of lithium on plasma chlorpromazine levels. *Clin. Pharmacol. Therap.* 23, 451-455 (1977).

Shopsin, B., and Gershon, S. Psychoactive drugs in mania. *Arch. Gen. Psychiat.* 32, 34-42 (1975).

Shopsin, B., Kim, S., and Gershon, S. A controlled study of lithium versus chlorpromazine in acute schizophrenics. *Brit. J. Psychiat.* 119, 435-440 (1971).

Small, J., Kellams, J., Milstein, V., and Moore, J. A placebo-controlled study of lithium combined with neuroleptics in chronic schizophrenic patients. *Am. J. Psychiat.* 132, 1315-1317 (1975).

Smulevitch, A., Zavidovskaya, G., Igonin, A., and Mikhailova, N. The effectiveness of lithium in affective and schizo-affective psychoses. *Brit. J. Psychiat.* 125, 65-72 (1974).

Sovner, R., and McHugh, P. Lithium in the treatment of periodic catatonia: A case report. *J. Nerv. Ment. Dis.* 15B, 214-221 (1974).

Steinbrook, R.M., and Chapman, A.B. Lithium responses: An evaluation of psychological test characteristics. *Compr. Psychiat.* 11, 524-530 (1970).

Strauss, J.S., and Carpenter, W.T. The prognosis of schizophrenia: Rationale for a multi-dimensional concept. *Schiz. Bull.* 4, 56-67 (1978).

Takahashi, R., Sakuma, A., Itoh, K., Itoh, H., Kurihara, M., Saito, M., and Watanabe, M. Comparison of efficacy of lithium carbonate and chlorpromazine in mania. *Arch. Gen. Psychiat.* 32, 1310-1318 (1975).

Taylor, M., and Abrams, R. The phenomenology of mania. *Arch. Gen. Psychiat.* 29, 520-522 (1973).

Vacaflor, L. Lithium side effects and toxicity: The clinical picture. In *Lithium Research and Therapy,* F.N. Johnson, ed. Academic Press, New York (1975).

Welner, A., Croughan, J., Fishman, R., and Robins, E. The group of schizoaffective and related psychoses: A follow-up study. *Compr. Psychiat.* 18, 413-422 (1972).

CHAPTER 12

Animal Models of Mania

T.W. Robbins and B.J. Sahakian

"Animal models of the endogenous psychoses do not exist."
—M. Schou, 1976

One of the necessary prerequisites for modeling human psychopathology is to have an accurate description of the behavioral disturbance under study. Psychiatric diagnoses of mania are apparently well defined, and yet comparison of different descriptions sometimes brings to light an ommission or inconsistency that completely alters the weightings attributed to the various features of the model.

For example, a recent set of diagnostic criteria suggests that the essential feature of a manic episode is one of elevated mood or irritability, and that this symptom may be associated with others, including hyperactivity, increased talking, a flight of ideas, a decreased need for sleep, and ease of distractability (APA Diagnostic and Statistical Manual of Mental Disorders, 1977). However, there are isolated reports of occurrences of perserverative or stereotyped behavior in mania (Medical Research Council Brain Metabolism Unit, 1972; Randrup et al., 1975), which are not numbered among its traditional diagnostic criteria. Further, even the "essential features" of the manic episode have been challenged. Murphy and Beigel (1974) have provided phenomenological analyses of mania by means of a behavioral rating scale which failed to support the assumption that disturbance in mood in the direction of euphoria or elated affect is a "core" symptom. Rather, these effects only occurred in a subgroup of manic patients, whereas the rest of the population exhibited a tendency toward depressed thoughts and behavior, which apparently was correlated positively with the increasing severity of the mania. Mood is a crucial criterion for differentiating mania from other forms of psychosis, including schizophrenia. Nevertheless, the division is not sufficiently sharp as to exclude the controversial classification of schizo-affective psychosis, which appears to span the gray areas between mania and schizophrenia. The broad category of mania has been subdivided, for example, into hypomania, acute mania, delirious mania, or chronic mania, but likewise, there seem to be few clear boundaries among these subdivisions that might be of assistance in model-building. Delirious mania as distinct from the other forms generally involves perceptual disorientation as a major symptom. The onset of chronic mania generally occurs only after 40 years of age, but this exception apart, developmental considerations appear unimportant. The other distinctions are based primarily on the degree of recurrence of the manic symptoms, their duration, and severity (Batchelor, 1969). An added complication is the close link of mania with depression. Most manic episodes have brief periods of depression following them. If these depressive episodes become more frequent or marked, the condition is termed manic-depressive psychosis, or bipolar depression.

If the behavioral descriptions of mania lack the detail that is necessary to discriminate among different models, further attempts at validation can be made by considering other factors, such as the etiology and chemotherapy of mania. Unfortunately, the etiology of mania is obscure. Although there is evidence of genetic predisposition, there appear to be no precipitating factors that are necessary or sufficient for inducing manic episodes. At first glance, the variety of pharmacological strategies used for treating mania (including the use of neuroleptic drugs, α-methyl-p-tyrosine, tryptophan, and physostigmine) also supports the view that we are dealing with a polymorphous entity. However, recent evidence suggests that lithium treatment may have a relatively selective therapeutic effect for mania that is not, in general, shared by the other compounds. Goodwin and Ebert (1973) reached this tentative conclusion after reviewing evidence that lithium produces a relatively specific therapeutic action on mania while producing limited or no improvement in related syndromes, such as schizoaffective psychosis. While this conclusion may still be tentative and is certainly disputed in part, if not in whole, (Quitkin et al., 1973), the criterion of a selective therapeutic effect promises to be a valuable tool for analyzing and discarding putative animal models.

RATIONALE FOR THE USE OF ANIMAL MODELS TO INVESTIGATE MANIA

General Points

Definition of Animal Model

In developing an animal model, one applies treatments to animals which make them mimic in a variety of ways the behavior of human subjects with a certain disorder. There are three criteria for a good animal model of a human disorder:

(i) strong behavioral similarities, (ii) common etiology, and (iii) common treatment.

i. An animal model of a particular human disorder or syndrome must, first of all, resemble behaviorally the human disorder. Hence an animal showing repetitive perseverative movements, such as the stereotyped behavior of rats treated with psychomotor stimulant drugs, would remind an observer of the stereotyped behavior of autistic children. Conversely, a rat that is placid and inactive would not readily call to mind a patient with mania. The ability of an animal model to 'look like' a human disorder gives the model *face validity*. However, a superficial face validity is only a first step in establishing a model; a stringent behavioral analysis is necessary to determine in which ways the behavior is similar and in which ways it differs.

ii. For certain human disorders, the etiology of the disorder is known. Therefore one might try to produce an animal model by subjecting animals to the same causal factor that had produced the disorder in humans. For example, it is known that striatal dopamine is depleted in patients with Parkinson's disease. When rats are given lesions of the nigrostriatal dopamine system with the neurotoxin 6-hydroxydopamine, these rats become akinetic and rigid, two of the primary symptoms of Parkinson's disease.

iii. The third criterion for a good animal model is whether the known therapeutic agents for the treatment of the human disorder can also be used to 'treat' the animal model. As previously mentioned, a possible animal model for autistic behavior in the child is stereotyped behavior induced by psychomotor stimulant drugs in the rat. The class of drugs known as neuroleptics are the most commonly used drugs in the treatment of autism, and neuroleptics are effective in suppressing stereotypy induced by stimulant drugs.

Advantages of animal models

Animal models are useful for a number of reasons:

i. Experimental animals are available for research in large quantities, and they can be manipulated in a variety of ways that would be considered unethical if one was experimenting with human subjects.

ii. Animal models permit an experimental analysis of a simplified system. For example, it is relatively easier to examine environmental effects on stereotyped behavior in the rat after treatment with psychomotor stimulant drugs than to look at these effects in autistic children. The experimenter is in control of the environment, the drug dose, and possibly even the past history of the animal. The experimenter can focus on the stereotyped behavior without considering other complicating factors, such as language. This type of simplified system may be difficult or even impossible to obtain when working with autistic children. Using a simplified paradigm such as this might provide insights into the etiology or mechanisms involved in mediating stereotypy that would otherwise have been obscured by the more complicated analysis of behavior of the autistic child.

iii. Finally, in determining the best treatment for a human disorder, animal models can prove useful. Again, the necessity for a large number of subjects and the capacity to manipulate precisely various parameters may make this kind of evaluation in clinical trials difficult or impossible. Also, in terms of developing and assessing the therapeutic efficacy of new agents for a human disorder, it is preferable to screen novel drugs using an animal model of the disorder before attempting to use them in clinical experiments.

Disadvantages of animal models

Obviously, there are some disadvantages in using animal models, such as the danger of oversimplification or the difficulty of extrapolating from one species to another. Hyperactivity is merely one major component of the syndrome known as mania. Another major symptom of that syndrome is exaggeration of mood. However, while hyperactive behavior induced by various pharmacological agents in the rat may provide a great deal of insight into the increased motor behavior of manic patients, it may or may not be able to provide insight into this inability to display appropriate emotions and social interaction.

Finally, it is clear that just as there are similarities in behavior among species, there are also species-specific differences, as the literature on constraints on learning has emphasized (Hinde and Stevenson-Hinde, 1973). When one is dealing with the complexity of man, it is necessary to apply caution in cross-species comparisons (Hinde, 1976).

However, with these reservations in mind, it seems that the advantages of using an animal model far outweigh the disadvantages.

CRITERIA FOR ANIMAL MODELS

Our search is for models that exaggerate the similarities, rather than the differences, between human and animal psychopathology. While the study of differences can be useful in certain cases, as Hinde (1976), for example, has argued, this is only generally true when a basic corpus of information has accrued and differences can be used to analyze the finer issues. This state of affairs may be found in studying the comparative effects of social isolation and early experience on behavior (Hinde, 1976); we do not believe, however, that it holds for animal models of mania where analysis is currently on a far more primitive level.

Behavioral Criteria for Animal Models of Mania

We suggest that there are four behavioral aspects of mania that have to be modeled. The first of these, "hyperactivity," refers to the general increases in behavioral activity characteristic of mania. The next two elements, "elation" and heightened "irritability", reflect the affective components of mania. The final aspect is the swing or switch to a depressed state, which occurs to varying extents in many manic episodes. Our choice of these aspects depends upon our own reading of the clinical literature; we have not endeavored to extract core symtoms from phenomenological analyses of mania using factor analysis. It seems possible that many of the clinical features of mania—for example, overtalkativeness—could be considered as a manifestation of hyperactivity, or even of "elation." The relationships among hyperactivity, "elation" and "irritability" are also unclear. For example, "elation" could be considered as an increased *reactivity* shown towards sensory stimuli of a positive ("rewarding") nature, whereas "irritability" could be considered as an increased reactivity to stimuli of a negative nature. In addition, it seems that hyperactivity is often correlated with positive affect, and that the relationships between mood and movement are not always easy to disentangle. Notwithstanding these conceptual problems, we shall first consider three of the major features of mania that might be modeled in animal studies:

1. Hyperactivity
2. "Elation"
3. "Irritability"

And we will comment on a fourth feature;

4. Depression

Hyperactivity. In behavioral pharmacology and physiological psychology, this term generally implies increases in walking or running. However, some definitions encompass any increment in motor activity, including, for example, tremor of the limbs or repetitive head movements. In considering human mania, we have to decide whether the increased volubility, distractability, and flight of ideas are manifestations of hyperactive behavior. The position taken here is that they are. However, this does not mean necessarily that we should be content in measuring whole body movements or repetitive head movements in animals as models of mania. The nature of hyperactive behavior should be analyzed, and its possible underlying behavioral mechanisms identified. In a particular case, hyperactivity might be seen as selective increases in some patterns of behavior or as rapid transitions from one type of activity to another. It is not clear to us which of these forms of hyperactivity is most prevalent in the manic condition. Nor is it clear whether both forms exist within different populations of manic subjects or even within the same manic individual. In addition, we are unsure if manic hyperactivity is dependent primarily on derangements in sensory attentional processes, or is a form of hyperkinesis, or, again, is a mixture of both of these. When the hyperactivity depends on the nature of sensory stimulation impinging on the organism, the increased response is often called hyperreactivity. Distinctions between hyperactive and hyperreactive behavior have been made previously in connection with the effects of various brain lesions (Gross, 1968), which we shall discuss in section C. 6. As noted before, "elation" and "irritability" could be considered forms of hyperreactivity. One form of reactivity that is difficult to describe as having affective correlates such as "elation" or "irritability" is exploratory behavior. A potent determinant of exploration is a novel stimulus change. Exploration of such stimuli may require responses different from locomotion, including (in the rat) orientation, observing responses, sniffing, and manipulation of the stimulus. To say that an organism is hyperactive does not necessarily imply that it is also hyperexploratory. This distinction has sometimes been overlooked in studies purporting to measure exploration.

Hyperactivity can be measured by many different devices. The motor behavior of animals can be quantified, for example, in open-field situations, in photocell cages, in running wheels, in stabilimeters, and in devices utilizing changes in electrocapacitance (Finger, 1972; Robbins, 1977). In clinical psychopharmacology, the means of measurement are also diverse, including, for exmple, open fields, stabilimetric cushions, actophotometers, and clinical rating scales. The nature of the behavior measured probably differs markedly in these cases. In addition, the search for objective measurement of activity has sometimes ignored an analysis of the nature of the behavior being measured. It seems possible that future progress in the development of animal models of mania will have to depend on greater refinement in analyzing hyperactive behavior in both animal and man.

Finally, as mania has no obvious consistent precipitating factors, it seems justifiable to employ models of hyperactivity that are generated by a variety of factors, including drugs, brain lesions, and behavioral procedures. Recognizing that hyperactivity can be modulated by many internal and external factors (for example, genetic strain, age, nutritional and hormonal state, and previous experience, [see Robbins, 1977, for a brief review]), we might also be able to determine the conditions producing forms of hyperactive behavior that are most comparable to those of mania. If the patterns of behavior produced by one set of manipulations are more similar to manic patterns than to those produced by other manipulations, then it is possible that the former manipulations impinge on a mechanism involved in the etiology of mania.

Elation. Mania is held to be an affective disorder involving upward swings in mood ("elation," "euphoria," etc.) and, occasionally, downward swings ("depression," "disappointment," "irritability," etc.). Although there is some doubt as to the precise nature of mood changes in mania (Murphy and Beigel, 1974), there seems to be a need for an objective model of "changes in mood" in animals. Subjective measurement of elation is impossible in animals and can be misleading in man. As a necessary compromise we suggest an operational approach, that "elation" is correlated with a reduction in threshold for reinforcement or reward. There are several ways in which such reductions might be assessed. Two of the more obvious examples are in the maintenance of behavior resulting in the self-administration of drugs, or of electrical current to the brain (intracranial self-stimulation, or ICSS). For example, in both cases, the smallest possible dose of drug or level or electrical current required to maintain the behavior can be used as an index or reinforcement threshold. A reduction in threshold by a particular treatment can be said to correspond to increased "elation." Stein and Ray (1960) developed an interesting method for titrating self-stimulation thresholds in rats. The method involved a two-lever Skinner box in which one of the levers provided a burst of brain stimulation upon each press but at the same time caused the current level to be set at a lower level for the next response. Pressing the second lever reset the current delivered on the first lever to its maximum level but had no other consequences for the rat. This situation generated a pattern of responding between the two levers that titrated a fairly constant level of current, called the threshold. Various drugs altered the reinforcement threshold in an upward or downward fashion.

A second, related procedure for determining changes in threshold with intracranial self-stimulation is to generate the rate-intensity function (Valenstein, 1964; Goodall and Carey, 1975), which relates the rate of responding of ICSS to the current level employed. Different neuroanatomical loci often yield rate-intensity functions of different shape and slope (Goodall and Carey, 1975). However, functions are often sigmoid in nature and are shifted to the right or left following various treatments in a way suggestive of changes in reinforcement value (Steiner and Stokely, 1973). Other, perhaps more indirect means of assessing changes in reinforcement value in animals depend on the establishment of conditioned reinforcers, or on the study of "contrast" phenomena. Conditioned reinforcers are stimuli, often of previously neutral motivational significance, that can acquire reinforcing properties of their own by being associated with primary rewards (Wike, 1966; Mackintosh, 1974). It might be expected that the capacity of these stimuli to control behavior would be enhanced in an "elated" state. Some examples of an exaggerated control over behavior by conditioned reinforcers will be discussed in section C.

"Elation" and "depression" analogues in animals have been studied in procedures that suddenly shift the density or quality of reinforcement from one level to another. These phenomena are sometimes called "contrast" effects, where the behavioral performance depends not upon the absolute level of reinforcement, but on the comparison of present levels of reinforcement with previous levels.

Early work by Crespi (1942) and Zeaman (1949) showed, in a situation where rats ran for food, that those animals given an upward shift in the amount of food presented for each run came to increase their running speed, whereas rats subjected to a downward shift came to decrease their running speed on subsequent trials. These increases overshot and undershot control running speeds obtained with constant high or constant low levels of reinforcement, and were called "elation" and "depression" effects, respectively. A naïve extrapolation would suggest that manic-depressive behavior might represent exaggerations of these phenomena, being modulated by enhanced sensitivity to changes in reinforcement density. However, this interpretation is doubtless far too simple. Contrast effects are often transient, whereas manic episodes are generally prolonged. In addition, a variety of different effects, labeled "behavioral contrast," have been discovered using different procedures, and many of these effects may be unrelated and explained in differnt terms (Mackintosh, 1974). One enduring problem has been that positive contrast ("elation") effects have proven less reliable than negative ones after the appropriate control precautions have been observed. However, several viable demonstrations of positive contrast have now been reported (Marx, 1969; Baltzer and Weiskrantz, 1970; Mellgren, 1971; Weiskrantz and Baltzer, 1975), and two recent studies have demonstrated positive contrast effects using brain stimulation as the reinforcer (Koob, 1977; Atrens et al., 1973). In the former of these, positive contrast effects were more easily obtained than negative contrast effects.

As mentioned previously, the idea that contrast effects reflect an expression of changes in emotional state is controversial and probably not applicable to all cases. However, Weiskrantz and Baltzer (1975) cite some interesting unpublished data suggesting that their "undershoot" and "overshoot" effects can be related to emotional changes. They found that the overshooting effect was enhanced by maprotiline, a new antidepressant drug. Although it would seem decidedly premature to ascribe the complicated behavioral changes in mania to an enhanced sensitivity to changes in reinforcement density, it is possible that contrast effects have been overlooked in the analysis of manic-depressive behavior and may contribute to the development of new animal models.

Irritability. A person exhibiting manic behavior does not react in an "elated" fashion to all stimuli. There are frequent reports of increased "irritability," often combined with a tendency toward increased aggression in social situations. "Irritability" is perhaps the least well-defined category that we deal with here, but is considered as an enhanced behavioral response or reactivity to an aversive stimulus. A simple way of assessing "reactivity" is the method of Marshall (1975), which involved the presentation of various stimuli (olfactory, tactile, and visual) to rats and the measurement of the latency and accuracy of an orientation response of the head directed toward the stimuli. Other methods of assessing reactivity include measurement of the startle response produced by an intense (usually auditory) stimulus (Brown et al., 1951) and measurement of the flinch or jump threshold in response to foot shock (Miczek and Barry, 1976). Irritability in the human manic case is often directed toward another individual, and so aggressive behavior elicited in a social context or in response to noxious stimuli might similarly provide an appropriate bahavioral model. Many studies have shown that the delivery of a noxious stimulus will produce, in several species, contact with and perhaps destruction of other objects in the environment, including other organisms (Miczek and Barry, 1976; Hutchinson, 1977). In squirrel monkeys, for example, these responses often take the form of biting attacks, which both precede and follow the occurrence of regularly presented noxious stimuli, such as electric shocks to the tail (Ulrich and Azrin, 1962). It is interesting that attack can also be induced in situations in which small amounts of food are presented at periodic intervals to hungry animals (Staddon, 1977). This form of "adjunctive behavior" might be induced by the aversive properties of schedules of reinforcement involving temporal delay, and even be related to the familiar "displacement activities" studied by ethologists (Falk, 1977).

The precise relevance of these phenomena to mania of course remains unclear. However, it would seem that a viable model of manic behavior has to include not only hyperactive behavior but also the potential for increased reactivity to particular environmental stimuli in the ways outlined above.

Depression. In most cases of mania, except for the chronic condition, the bouts of manic behavior are interrupted by brief depressed phases. Thus, we might expect an ideal model of mania to include short periods of inactivity interspersed within the manic phase. However, this behavioral condition at present seems to be the most difficult for which to find even the most superficial analogy.

Pharmacological Criteria for Animal Models of Mania

Biochemical studies

Since human manic behavior has been associated with complex bio-chemical changes occurring in the central nervous system (Schildkraut and Kety, 1967; van Praag, 1978), the better behavioral models of mania in animals might also be expected to exhibit these changes. No directionality is implied in a causal relationship between behavioral and biochemical states; the causality could operate in either direction. However, the network of interrelationships between human mania and animal models would clearly be strengthened if a similar pattern of biochemical changes could be discerned in both. Unfortunately, there seems to be a lack of consensus regarding biochemical changes in human mania, probably resulting from any of a number of factors that contribute to discrepancies in this field (see Randrup et al., 1975). Changes have been described that involve both the catecholamine neurotransmitters and serotonin (or 5HT). Evidence initially pointed toward increases in noradrenaline metabolism (Schildkraut and Kety, 1967).

More recently, Randrup et al., (1975) have reviewed evidence suggesting that manic patients had significantly different baseline levels of HVA (a metabolite of dopamine) in CSF compared to those of controls. For example, Sjöstrom and Roos (1972) found significantly higher levels of HVA in CSF in manics than in controls, but the M.R.C. Brain Metabolism Unit (1972) apparently did not repeat these results. Similarly, the evidence that there are changes in serotoninergic neurones in mania is weak. Coppen (1973) found reduced 5HIAA (a metabolite of serotonin) levels in CSF in groups of both depressed and manic patients. However, other work (e.g., Bowers et al., 1969), found normal levels of 5HIAA in the CSF of manic patients. Green and Grahame-Smith (1975) have listed the several constraints of interpreting results with CSF-5HIAA measurements before they can "find their proper place in psychiatric practice [p. 215]."

Treatment

Another, possibly more illuminating criterion, involves the chemotherapy of mania. Several drugs have been used for this purpose. Lithium is now the preferred treatment for mania (Cade, 1949; Schou, 1968; Goodwin and Ebert, 1973) although the specificity of the treatment is currently under debate (Quitkin et al., 1973; Shopsin and Gershon, 1978). The problem of specificity may be considered in two ways: (1) Do other forms of chemotherapy have a therapeutic effect in mania? (2) How specific is the therapeutic effect of lithium for mania relative to other psychiatric disorders? The answers to both of these questions suggest that lithium exerts a relatively specific antimanic effect. First, several other drugs have been used to treat mania with varying degrees of success, but have almost been found to be less effective than lithium in controlled clinical studies (Goodwin and Ebert, 1973). The list of compounds nevertheless having some therapeutic success is challenging in its diversity:

1. Neuroleptic drugs, such as chlorpromazine and haloperidol, which are relatively specific dopamine-receptor antagonists (Shopsin et al., 1975)
2. α-methyl-para-tyrosine, an inhibitor of the enzyme tyrosine hydroxylase, the rate limiting step in the biosynthesis of dopamine and noradrenaline (Bunney et al., 1971)
3. Tryptophan, the amino-acid precursor of serotonin (Prange et al., 1974)
4. Physostigmine, an anticholinesterase that increases cholinergic activity (Davis et al., 1978)
5. Finally, there have also been claims of therapeutic effects of other agents, including the serotoninergic antagonist cinanserin (Kane, 1970) and the dopaminergic agonist piribedil (Post et al., 1976)

It is probably impossible to reduce the therapeutic action of these varied compounds and lithium salts to a common neuropharmacological denominator. Neuroleptics and α-methyl-para-tyrosine presumably act by reducing catecholaminergic activity. Tryptophan treatment increases 5HT levels. It is possible that the anticholinesterase physostigmine, by increasing cholinergic activity, will exert an indirect inhibitory effect on certain catecholamine projections: For example, it is well known that a DA-cholinergic (ACh) interaction occurs in the striatum (Stadler et al., 1973). Lithium itself has a range of effects on the monoamines, none of which have been definitely linked with its therapeutic action. For example, Schildkraut, in a 1973 review, writes: "The findings reviewed in this chapter suggest that under some conditions of administration, lithium produces alterations in the turnover and metabolism of the biogenic amines norepinephrine, serotonin, and possibly dopamine (p. 70)."

Some of the clearer findings are that short-term administration of lithium increases noradrenaline turnover in rats (Corrodi et al., 1967) although longer-term administration does not have this effect (Corrodi et al. 1969). Limited clinical data tend to endorse these conclusions (Schildkraut, 1973). These findings are apparently difficult to reconcile with a theory that an excess of noradrenaline accompanies mania. However, other work suggests that the rate of uptake of noradrenaline into synaptosomes is increased by lithium pretreatment in rats (Colburn et al., 1967), an action that would presumably tend to counteract increased noradrenergic functioning. But even the importance of this finding is questionable (Schildkraut, 1973).

The effect of lithium on serotoninergic functioning seemed at the time of Schildkraut's review to be inconsistent, and this conclusion was confirmed by Green and Grahame-Smith (1975). However, a recent set of experiments has tried to link the therapeutic effect of lithium to a number of parameters of serotoninergic function (Mandell and Knapp, 1976). In considering all of these findings, it is remarkable that lithium, in view of its varied biochemical action, has any specific behavioral effect at all.

Although treatment with lithium salts is known to produce a dramatic antimanic response, investigations have tried to extend its therapeutic action to other psychiatric disorders, including depression (Fieve et al., 1968), schizophrenia, schizoaffective states, neurosis, personality disorders, epilepsy, childhood disorders including hyperactivity, and premenstrual tension (Quitkin et al., 1973). In general, the evidence that lithium has a therapeutic advantage for syndromes without an affective component is slim. However, Rifkin et al. (1972) have claimed a therapeutic effect in the treatment of a syndrome called "emotionally unstable character disorder." The symptoms of this neurotic disorder, although not primarily affective in nature, seem to us very reminiscent of manic-depression. In another report of a therapeutic effect in a nonpsychotic population, Tupin (1971) has shown that lithium may control violence and aggression in prisoners.

Perhaps the most important therapeutic comparisons with mania are those of depression, schizoaffective disorders, and schizophrenia. Only mild antidepressant effects of lithium are evident in depressed patients (Fieve et al., 1968), and these are probably restricted to patients with manic-depressive illness (Goodwin et al., 1969).

Johnson et al., (1971) compared the efficacy of chlorpromazine and lithium in treating schizoaffective psychosis, and concluded that although lithium was superior to chlorpromazine in the treatment of mania, it was inferior in treating schizoaffective states. Quitkin et al. (1973), however, have criticized this latter conclusion of a "double-dissociation" of drug effects on statistical grounds. Moreover, Prien et al. (1971) found that although chlorpromazine was superior for "highly active" schizoaffectives, neither treatment was superior for less active ones. Incidentally, some of the schizoaffectives who improved with lithium showed improvements in cognitive deficits as well as in manic symptoms. However, as Quitkin et al. (1973) suggest, this unexpected improvement might have been secondary to the effect of lithium on mood.

The comparative effects of lithium and chlorpromazine on schizophrenics seem to be better dissociated. For example, Shopsin et al. (1971) found that lithium was inferior to chlorpromazine for a mixed group of schizophrenics. Indeed, lithium produced neurotoxic effects in some of the patients.

A final question of specificity revolves around the effect of lithium on "normal" subjects. Effective clinical doses for mania seem to have little effect on "normal" human subjects (Schou, 1968). In one study where Schou and his collaborators took lithium themselves, only slight effects, of muscular weakness and tremor, were noted during 3 to 6 weeks of taking 25 mEq/day. When the dose was increased to 50 mEq/day (a typical therapeutic dose), effects of nausea, hand tremor, and muscular weakness and a variety of subtle psychological effects were noted. Some investigations have reported that short-term lithium administration in reasonably low doses can produce decremental effects upon various indices of activity in rats exposes to situations such as the open field, jiggle cage, lever pressing in an operant chamber (Smith and Smith, 1973), and in a box measuring rearing (Johnson and Wormington, 1972). These effects on activity were possibly not due simply to muscular weakness, since the lithium-pretreated animals showed a similar capacity to swim to exhaustion as controls (Smith and Smith, 1973). However, we shall put aside the question of whether lithium specifically reduces manic-hyperactivity or acts as a general depressant. Perhaps it should be noted, however, that the effects of many drugs depend on baseline; they rarely add or subtract a constant parameter from behavior. Neuroleptics are another class of drugs where small doses may have no apparent effect upon normal human subjects or animals, but will be effective in counteracting schizophrenia or, for example, amphetamine-induced hyperactivity. In considering the question of the specificity of effect of lithium, a viable animal model will have to demonstrate effects of lithium that are greater than the other commonly used antimanic agents, such as the neuroleptics, at any dosage. Therefore, any valid comparison between the two agents has to consider a wide dose-response range, particularly when considering the narrow limits within which lithium is clinically effective (approximately 1.0–1.5 mEq/l plasma [see Davis et al., 1973]). This comparison is complicated by three factors: First, lithium often has to be administered for several days before attaining steady-state plasma levels and becoming clinically effective (Schou, 1968). Thus a comparison is generally being made between a chronic treatment and an acute one, and the relevant parameter of dosage for lithium may not simply be its level in plasma. Second, some consideration has to be made of what constitutes a level of chronic treatment of lithium in animals comparable to that used in the clinical setting. Third, lithium is often not effective in treating mania initially, and neuroleptics are often used to control acute manic episodes (Schou, 1968).

A second problem for the animal model is to demonstrate specificity of action for a particular syndrome. For example, it could be shown that whereas lithium is effective in reducing one form of hyperactivity, it is ineffective in reducing another form produced by a different agent. This dissociation would show that lithium was not simply producing general reductions in activity but was exerting a specific effect. Hopefully, too, lithium might even be shown to exacerbate some syndromes, particularly in view of the neurotoxic effects it can have in schizophrenics. Finally, given the "prophylactic" action that lithium might have for manic-depressive illness, when chronic treatment prevents recurrent episodes (Schou, 1968), it would be valuable to demonstrate an analogous "prophylactic" effect in the induction of certain syndromes in animals.

Lithium is not the only key to evaluating animal models. One of the most successful techniques in biological psychiatry has been to rank-order the clinical potency of a range of structurally related compounds and correlate them with some other aspect of their action. A good recent example concerns the high correlations shown between the clinical potency of neuroleptic drugs and their affinity for haloperidol receptors and for blocking amphetamine-induced sterotypy (Creese et al., 1976). This technique could easily be adapted for our use. There are in fact tentative rankings of the neuroleptics along several dimensions of therapeutic action, including a distinct antimanic dimension (Bobon et al., 1972). However, before hopes are raised too high, Wyatt and Torgow (1976) could find no real differences in the capacity of neuroleptics for treating mania and schizophrenia, and it seems that this report might actually cast doubt on the idea that different neuroleptics can have optimal "profiles" for different forms of psychosis.

ANIMAL MODELS OF MANIA: EXAMPLES

It is highly doubtful whether any of the existing models of mania could meet up to the behavioral and pharmacological criteria that we have stipulated. However, as we shall see, investigation guided by many of these criteria is incomplete, and probably deserving of further attention.

The models reviewed in this section will include not only examples which have been explicitly advanced as animal models of mania, but also other syndromes which might potentially be used as models. Most of the models previously proposed involve the study of hyperactive behavior, which, however, is only one of the behavioral criteria that we have discussed. Several of the models have been developed from speculations regarding the neurochemical correlates of mania, and so drug-induced hyperactivity has been a prominent source of study. However, the etiology of mania remains uncertain, and associated behavior can be induced by other than pharmacological means, including brain damage and behavioral experience. Of course, it is likely that these latter factors might also be correlated with pharmacological changes.

We review the main models under three main headings:

Drug models
Lesion models
Behavioral models

We recognize that there will be occasional overlap among these categories.

Drug Models

Catecholamine hypothesis

Since noradrenergic (Schildkraut and Kety, 1967) and dopaminergic overactivity (Randrup et al., 1975) have been implicated in mania, drugs that modulate the action of these neurotransmitters have proven to be popular areas of study in animals.

Amphetamine and related drugs. Amphetamine has several actions upon the catecholamines NA and DA, including release from presynaptic terminals, blockade of reuptake following release, and, at higher doses, inhibition of the intraneuronal MAO (Moore, 1978, for review). This drug has been the cornerstone of behavioral pharmacology because of its variety of behavioral effects (Grossman and Sclafani, 1971; Lyon and Robbins, 1975). In man, the drug can produce euphoria (Smith and Davis, 1977). However, repeated use leads to a dissipation of the euphoria, and in some cases to the induction of an amphetamine psychosis, which has similarities to paranoid schizophrenia (Connell, 1958). The amphetamine psychosis is often accompanied by the occurrence of repetitive patterns of behavior, called "punding" in Scandinavian circles (Rylander, 1971).

In animals, amphetamine has two predominant effects. At low doses it generally produces an increase in locomotor activity, and at higher doses it induces stereotyped behavior, which can be defined as the performance of an invariant sequence of movements in a repetitive manner. These stereotyped effects of amphetamine have been observed in all mammals studied (Randrup and Munkvad, 1967) and are almost certainly related to the human "punding" phenomena described by Rylander (1971). Chronic administration of amphetamine in animals leads to a variety of changes, including "fragmentation" of the stereotypies and a "hypervigilance," which collectively have been used as models of schizophrenia (Ellinwood et al., 1972). Perhaps for these reasons the use of amphetamines as a model for mania has not received particular attention. This is surprising, because amphetamine produces several effects that are manic in nature.

Hyperactivity. d-Amphetamine produces dose-related increases in locomotor activity in most mammals studied in defined situations (Grossman and Sclafani, 1971). There have been several analyses of the nature of the hyperactivity. Norton (1973), using a time lapse cinematography method, classified the behavior of rats into a number of "acts" and observed the effects of 0.25, 0.5, and 1.0 mg/kg. The drug caused dose-related changes in frequency of certain behavioral acts such as rearing and walking, and reductions in others such as eating and forms of grooming. There was also a reduction in the average duration of particular acts and a general tendency towards increased randomization of behavioral sequences. These results are interesting and can be related to Schirring's findings (1971) of "selective stimulation" of certain items of behavior observed in rats following 5 mg/kg d-amphetamine. He found that the drug initially increased locomotion and rearing while reducing forms of grooming behavior. Eventually, locomotion and rearing themselves were reduced as the rats entered an intense stereo-typed phase of repetitive sniffing and head movements. It is interesting however, that the locomotor activity itself had a stereotyped quality in that the rats tended to move along somewhat restricted routes. Similar effects at much lower doses have been noted by Segal (1975) in rats, and Willner et al. (1970) have observed stereotyped running in dogs.

Therefore, a reasonable characterization of amphetamine-induced hyper-activity would be that it causes in rats rather selective increases of certain types of response. The behavioral mechanisms by which this occurs are uncertain; for example, it is unclear whether there is a selective inhibition of certain items (Schirring, 1971), or whether this inhibition arises from behavioral competition between the variously stimulated response categories (Lyon and Robbins, 1975). The relationship between amphetamine hyper-activity and stereotypy is also unclear. It is possible that these features of the amphetamine response are mediated by separate neurochemical systems. For example, there is a good deal of evidence that amphetamine-induced stereotypies of the sniffing and licking variety are mediated by the striatum (Creese and Iversen, 1975; Kelly et al., 1975), whereas amphetamine-induced hyperactivity is mediated by another forebrain DA projection to the nucleus accumbens and olfactory tubercle (Kelly et al., 1975; Pijenburg et al., 1976). In behavioral terms the relationship has been described as an increasing rate of responding within a decreasing number of response categories (Lyon and Robbins, 1975). This characterization has emphasized the continuum of "psychomotor stimulation" produced by amphetamine, which culminates in stereotyped behavior. Some recent evidence in support of this idea is that doses of 2–16 mg/kg d-amphetamine given to rats produce dose-related increases in head-dipping in a 16-hole board device, but that with increasing dose, the animals tended to make repeated dips into the same hole (Makanjuola et al., 1977). The authors considered head-dipping as a form of exploratory behavior. It is worth noting that several articles have shown that ampheta-mine often produces larger increases in activity in familiar rather than novel situations (e.g., Marriot, 1968). It is possible that amphetamine-like drugs actually reduce preferences for exploring novel stimuli (e.g., Dyne and Hughes, 1970). However, it seems probable that amphetamine reduces the duration of certain forms of exploratory behavior as an indirect effect of competition with increased locomotor activity (Robbins and Iversen, 1973; Hughes and Grieg, 1976).

One aspect of the relationship between locomotor activity and more focused stereotypies produced by amphetamine is the competitive relationship that can be seen between these two activities. Stereotypy is often accompanied by a reduction of whole-body activity (Segal, 1975). Lesions to the nigrostriatal pathway, which reduce stereotypy produced by d-amphetamine, generally cause increases in locomotor activity with the drug (Creese and Iversen, 1975), also indicative of a competitive relationship between the two.

Elation. d-Amphetamine increases rates of responding in rats with brain stimulation as the reinforcer (Stein, 1964). However, this fact hardly indicates that the drug increases "elation." d-Amphetamine can produce increases in the rate of responding in many situations that may simply be the result of a rate dependency whereby the drug increases low, but not high, rates of control responding (Dews, 1958).

Nevertheless, Stein (1964), using the titration techniques described earlier, showed that 1 mg/kg of methamphetamine reduced the preferred intensity of electrical stimulation in rats responding for ICSS. (This interpretation may be criticized, however; see Valenstein, 1964). There are other reasons for suspecting that the psychomotor stimulants have some enhancing effect on the reinforcing properties of brain stimulation. Steiner and Stokeley (1973) shifted the rate-intensity function to the left after doses of 0.5 mg/kg methamphetamine. Thus, lower currents then produced higher response rates. Atrens et al. (1974), using a preference procedure that did not involve the measurement of rate, found that 0.5 mg/kg of amphetamine reduced the time taken for rats to initiate intracranial stimulation turned on at one end of the box, and increased the time taken for the animals to move from that end of the box to terminate the intracranial stimulations. Again, while these findings can be interpreted in other ways (Lyon and Robbins, 1975, pp. 134–135), they provide evidence that the drug enhances the reinforcing properties of brain stimulation.

In an extension of Stein's hypothesis, Hill (1970) suggested that the psychomotor stimulants also enhanced the reinforcing or rewarding effects of stimuli associated with rewards (conditioned rewards or reinforcers). In a remarkable experiment, he showed that rats treated with 10 mg/kg of pipradrol exhibited increases in responding in extinction when responding produced an auditory stimulus that had previously been correlated with the presentation of food. If no stimulus was presented following responding, however, the drugged animals showed *less* responding than controls, exhibiting instead an obvious stereotyped behavior. These results indicate a clear interaction of the drug with the conditioned reinforcing stimulus. Hill (1972) later presented these results as a model for the euphorigenic action of amphetamine-like drugs.

These results have largely been confirmed by others (Robbins, 1975; 1976; 1978; Robbins and Koob, 1978). In some of these experiments it was shown that animals treated with pipradrol showed a dose-related facilitation of acquisition of a new response reinforced merely by a stimulus formerly correlated with water (Robbins, 1976; 1978) or with brain stimulation delivered to the lateral hypothalamus (Robbins and Koob, 1978). Control experiments ruled out the possibility that the increases in responding were due to nonspecific influences. For example, there was no increase in responding for the same stimulus when it had been only randomly correlated with reinforcement (Robbins, 1976). These results are interesting because, once again, they demonstrate a selective increase in certain types of behavior produced by an amphetamine-like drug, in this case where the behavior is clearly selected by a contingency that produces reward-related stimuli and is associated with previous experience of the organism.

Unresolved problems for this model are, first, that the responding for the reward-related stimulus can be perserverative in nature (Robbins, 1976); it is not clear what implications this has for the hypothesis that the drug is enhancing the effects of reinforcement. Second, the effects are obtained far more readily with pipradrol and methylphenidate than with d-amphetamine (Robbins, 1978). The reasons for this dichotomy are not known, but may be related to subtle differences in action in the catecholamine neurons existing between these two classes of drug (Scheel-Krüger, 1971).

So far, none of these studies take into account the fact that manic episodes may be interspersed with depressed ones. There is really no adequate animal model of this pattern, although recent evidence has accrued that an analog of "post-amphetamine depression" in man (Watson et al., 1972) may occur in rats given chronic amphetamine for a period of days during testing for intracranial self-stimulation (Leith and Barrett, 1976). These authors found that 0.25 mg/kg of d-amphetamine initially increased rates of self-stimulation. However, following chronic treatment with doses of the drug ascending from 1 to 12 mg/kg over few days, this increase was no longer evident. In a second experiment, similar results were found with 0.5 mg/kg, but the response to saline was reduced below baseline following chronic treatment, in addition. The chronic treatment was given while the rats were not being tested for ICSS, and so the subsequent "depression" of responding cannot be linked to a behavioral tolerance produced by the drug or a "contrast" effect. However, although the reduction in response may correspond to the "post-amphetamine depression" seen in man, and may provide an interesting example of how a treatment can cause responding to fluctuate both above and below a baseline, the results would have been yet more impressive for our purposes had a postdrug depression been by the same dose that was capable of producing an increase in rate.

Irritability. There have been a few studies that indicate that amphetamine can enhance responding to external stimuli in a nonspecific way. For example, Kirkby et al. (1972) found that 0.5 mg/kg methamphetamine produced no serious effect on the orientation response of rats towards auditory stimuli, although 5 mg/kg impaired the "accuracy" of this response, and in another situation markedly increased the amplitude of the "startle" response. Other studies confirm that rather high doses of d- or l-amphetamine can increase the amplitude of the startle response exhibited to an intense auditory stimulus (Davis et al., 1975). The effects of amphetamine on "aggressive" behavior are diverse, depending on dose, species, and method employed to measure aggression. One of the best studies (Miczek, 1974) measured several components of intraspecies aggression in rats and found that low doses (0.05, 0.1 mg/kg, i.m.) given to the "dominant" rat increased the number of attack bites and display of aggressive postures, whereas higher doses suppressed attacks and threats. These biphasic effects of doses were also shown by Crowley (1972), employing foot shock to induce aggression in rats. There are indications, however, that elements of aggressive behavior can still be observed in rats treated with high doses of amphetamine, particularly in animals pretreated with monoamine oxidase inhibitors (Randrup and Munkvad, 1969).

Effects of lithium on amphetamine response. There have been at least eight studies of the effects of lithium on the response to amphetamine in rat or mouse. These studies can loosely be divided into those that have considered amphetamine-induced locomotor activity induced by relatively low doses, and those that have considered amphetamine-induced stereotypy induced by rather higher doses. Only a few of those papers have made measurements of both types of behavior, and in none of them has the possible interaction or competition between locomotor activity and stereotypy been considered. The results of the studies have been summarized in Table 1. To these findings can be added recent unpublished observations by Lewis and Robbins suggesting that high doses of d-amphetamine ($\sim$ 10 mg/kg) enhance lithium toxicity. These investigators treated hooded male rats (n = 10) weighing approximately 350 g with 3.0 mEq/kg lithium (or an equivalent dose of sodium) followed 12 h later by an intraperitoneal injection of 10 mg/kg d-amphetamine. The behavioral results following lithium pretreatment were dramatic. At variable times (approximately 10–40 minutes) postinjection, the lithium-pretreated animals began to show uncoordinated jumping at the walls of the cage, followed by an assumption of a splayed, ataxic posture, while the animals were still exhibiting violent head-jerking or head-movement stereotypies. Some of the animals initially showed increased rearing and tremors of the forepaws as well as erection of the tail. Seizures occurred in some rats. The animals were not cataleptic; they would not stay on a vertical wire netting. However, they would stay in abnormally imposed postures. The animals remained quite reactive to external stimuli and retained control of basic reflexes such as the righting reflex. The neurochemical basis of this effect is at present unknown, but is being investigated.

Taken together, these results suggest that although lithium can antagonize amphetamine-induced locomotor activity, it does not antagonize amphetamine-induced stereotypy. If anything, a tendency toward enhanced stereotyped responses is found, together with what appears to be an enhanced susceptibility to lithium toxicity. These results are crucially important. First, it seems that amphetamine locomotor activity and stereotypy may respond differently to lithium pretreatment. This result suggests that amphetamine activity might be a reasonable model for mania, but that certain forms of stereotyped behavior might not. To this conclusion is attached several qualifications: As mentioned above, no experiment with lithium has measured; amphetamine activity and stereotypy in the same design, and so the possible interaction between locomotor activity and stereotypy remains uncertain. In addition, the reductions in activity are often evident with acute, as well as chronic, pretreatment with lithium; this result would not be expected in view of the relative inefficacy of short-term lithium therapy in man. A second important implication is that the amphetamine stereotypies might be related to other forms of psychotic disorder. We noted previously that lithium can even have neurotoxic effects in human schizophrenics. Lewis and Robbins may have found an analogous effect of lithium on animals given high doses of amphetamine.

What are the neurochemical correlates of the antagonism of amphetamine response by lithium? Several interesting connections have been discussed to which we can but briefly refer here. Segal et al. (1975) link the relative failure of chronic lithium treatment to reduce amphetamine activity with compensatory increases in tyrosine hydroxylase activity in the substantia nigra and striatum. Conversely, Furukawa et al. (1975) speculate that an interaction with noradrenaline is important. Perhaps the most interesting idea, however, is that of Mandell and Knapp (1975). They found that 100 mg/kg of cocaine reduced the conversion of tryptophan to serotonin in striate synaptosomes and induced a compensatory increase in tryptophan hydroxylase solubilized from striate synaptosomes. Lithium had opposite effects. When rats were pretreated with 10 mEq/kg of lithium for 3 days and then injected with 100 mg/kg of cocaine, there was no effect of cocaine on either tryptophan or the enzyme activity. Analogous results have apparently been found for amphetamine. Thus, Mandell and Knapp consider the antagonism of effects of amphetamine and cocaine by lithium to depend on the action of the latter in "buffering" the serotoninergic system against drug-induced changes.

Surprisingly, there has been little study of the effects of lithium on other aspects of behavior influenced by amphetamine. Cassens and Mills (1973) found that lithium (1 mEq/kg) tended to increase the threshold of reinforcement in rats that had been trained with intracranial stimulation. D-amphetamine was shown to have the reverse effect, but combinations of the two drugs were not tried. A more recent study by Liebman and Segal (1976) showed that chronic treatment with lithium failed to reduce the rate-increasing effect of d-amphetamine upon self-stimulation at sites in the substantia nigra. This result is interesting for two reasons: First, there was a reduction in rate of the increases produced by morphine (see section C(a) III.), suggesting a specificity in the latter action and also ruling out pharmacological tolerance to lithium as a possible explanation. Second, the results suggest that the "elation" induced by amphetamine is not antagonized by lithium. This important result requires further research.

Effects of Other Antimanic Agents on the Response to Amphetamine. The behavioral effects of amphetamine can be antagonized by α-methl-p-tyrosine and neuroleptics (Moore, 1978). These drugs, unlike lithium, are effective in antagonizing not only the stereotyped behavior but also the locomotor activity induced by amphetamine. There is currently little systematic evidence that the different neuroleptics can selectively reduce locomotor activity with little or no effect upon stereotypy, although it has been pointed out that clozapine and thioridazine are relatively ineffective in antagonizing amphetamine stereotypy (Mattysse and Sugerman, 1978). Interestingly, Bobon et al. (1972) claim that the neuroleptic droperidol has a pronounced antimanic action, but has little effect upon autistic or delusional symptoms. If this claim is substantiated, it would be interesting to determine the effects of droperidol on amphetamine-induced activity and stereotypy.

Cholinergic drugs such as pilocarpine can antagonize amphetamine-induced activity (Fibiger et al., 1970), and other cholinergic drugs such as physostigmine have been found to antagonize stereotyped behavior (Arnfred and Randrup, 1968; Sahakian et al., 1978a). Neither of these effects is particularly striking. Sahakian et al.(1978a) recently produced elevations in brain acetyl choline by administration of the amino-acid precursor choline. There were, however, only small decremental effects upon stereotypy induced by apomorphine. On the other hand, the evidence that cholinergic antagonists such as scopolamine can enhance the effects of amphetamine is strong (Fibiger et al., 1970; Carlton, 1963). This potentiation has been used as evidence for a mutual cholinergic-adrenergic antagonism (Carlton, 1963). (These results, however, seem also to be explicable in terms of a cholinergic-DA interaction at least as well as a cholinergic-NA one.) These considerations

Table 1. Effects of Lithium on Amphetamine-Induced Behaviors

Study	Lithium Dose and Regimen	Amphetamine Dose	Species	Measurements	Effects of Lithium on Amphetamine-Induced Activity or Stereotypy
1. Matussek and Linsmayer, 1968	4 x 2.36 mEq/kg chronic	6mg/kg amphetamine	rat	Activity Stereotypy	"Excitation" not reduced Prolongation of stereotypy
2. Cox et al., 1971	1 x 2 mEq/kg acute	1.18 mg/kg d-amphetamine	rat	Y-maze activity	No effect on activity
3. Lal and Sourkes, 1972	10 x 2.5 – 7.5 mEq/kg chronic	10 mg/kg amphetamine	rat	Latency, duration of stereotypy	No effect
4. Davies et al., 1974	3 mEq/kg acute	1.18 or 2.36 mg/kg d-amphetamine	rat	1. Hole board; head dips 2. Photocell cage: activity	1. reduction at 1.18 mg/kg 2. No effect

5. Flemembaum, 1975	3 mEq/kg chronic	2.5 mg/kg d-amphetamine	rat	1. Running wheel activity 2. Observation of stereotypy	1. Reduction in activity 2. No effect
6. Segal et al., 1975	a. 8 x 1.5 mEq/kg chronic b. 1.5 mEq/kg, 24 h prior acute c. 1.5 mEq/kg, 1 h prior acute	0.5 mg/kg d-amphetamine	rat	Activity cages Locomotor activity	a., b., and c. all reduced activity. Chronic treatment (a) had least effect.
7. Furukawa et al., 1975	0.52 – 4.72 mEq/kg acute and chronic	5 or 2 mg/kg methamphetamine	mouse	Open-field activity	Reductions in activity greater with increasing dose or duration of Li treatment
8. Ozawa and Miyauchi, 1977	2.36 or 4.72 mEq/kg acute	5–7 mg/kg methamphetamine	mouse	Stereotypy	1. Increased gnawing 2. Increased stereotypy

are particularly relevant in view of the recent use of physostigmine in treating mania (Davis et al., 1978).

Manipulations of central serotoninergic systems also affect the behavioral response to amphetamine. Mabry and Campbell (1973) reported that parachlorophenylalanine (PCPA), an inhibitor of serotonin synthesis, potentiated the locomotor response to amphetamine. PCPA lacks specificity in its neurochemial actions (Miller et al., 1970; Koe and Weissman, 1966). But treatment with intracisternal 5,6-dihydroxytryptamine, a neurotoxic agent that destroys serotoninergic neurones, also potentiates the response to amphetamine (Breese et al., 1974). In the Breese et al. study, PCPA was reported not to alter amphetamine-induced stereotyped behavior, although there was a greater frequency of rearing responses. Segal (1975) showed that the greater activity induced by PCPA in combination with d-amphetamine actually occluded the more "focussed" sterotypies and also reduced their duration. In support of this finding, Sahakian et al. (1978b) have shown that rats maintained on low-tryptophan diets also exhibit shorter durations of stereotypy than normal. Moreover, these effects can be abolished prior to treatment with quipazine or MK-212, both being serotonin agonists. However, results with serotonin-receptor agonists and antagonists produce seemingly contradictory effects (Wallach, 1974). For example, methergoline may increase stereotyped sniffing (Scheel-Krüger and Mogilnicka, 1975).

In general, both cholinergic and serotoninergic drugs appear to modulate the behavioral response to amphetamine, and as yet there is no clear-cut distinction between their effects on locomotion and stereotypy.

Amphetamine and chlordiazepoxide mixtures. Steinberg and her colleagues have employed mixtures of amphetamine and chlordiazepoxide in rats or mice to induce large increases in activity, greater than can be obtained with either agent alone. These increaes have been measured in the Y maze, in a hole-board situation, and in photocell cages.

If the dose combinations are approximately adjusted, this hyperactivity consists of "fast and co-ordinated but characteristically repetitive and apparently compulsive walking, as well as other activities, depending on the species of the animal and on the kind of test environment used" (Davies et al., 1974, p. 264). The authors go on to differentiate this syndrome from that of the stereotyped head-shaking and sniffing produced by large doses of amphetamine alone, and to stress that the syndrome can only be elicited by mixtures of the two drugs. Although the distinction from amphetamine stereotypy is empirically valid, it seems that the activity described above definitely could be considered as stereotyped. There is no reason to restrict this description merely to the repetitive head movements with sniffing seen frequently with amphetamine. The behavior the authors describe may very well be another manifestation of stereotypy, just as other investigators have seen stereotyped locomotor patterns (e.g., Lal, 1975; Segal, 1975).

Cox et al. (1971) found that acute pretreatment with 2 mEq/kg of lithium roughly halved the hyperactivity in an unfamiliar Y maze induced by a mixture of d-amphetamine (1.18 mg/kg) and chlordizaepoxide (12.5 mg/kg) in rats. The smaller increases in activity produced by the two drugs separately were not affected by the lithium pretreatment. It should also be noted that plasma lithium levels were increased in the rats tested with the mixture (mixture 0.67 ± 0.20: saline 0.49 ± 0.09 mEq/1, mean ± s.d.), but not in those rats tested with the separate drugs (d-amphetamine 0.52 ± 0.14; chlordiazepoxide 0.52 ± 0.18). In other experiments, chronic pretreatment with lithium (3 mEq/kg) for 15 days had no effect on activity produced by the drug mixture, although a single acute administration of 3 mEq/kg given 3 h prior to treatment with the drug mixture attenuated the induced hyperactivity. The authors also note that the drug mixture produced ataxic effects, but that these were not exacerbated by lithium. The chronic lithium regimen of 3 mEq/day produced plasma lithium levels of 0.69 ± 0.17 and 0.84 ± 0.11 mEq/1 (mean ± s.d.), compared with the acute effect of 3 mEq/kg, 1.06 ± 0.26 and 0.83 ± 0.10 for the rats treated with the drug mixture and saline respectively. Thus it appears that the reduction in hyperactivity produced by lithium does not depend merely on its plasma level; the regimen of adminstration is also important, with tolerance developing to chronic adminstration.

In a later experiment (Davies et al., 1974), these results were extended in several ways: First, rats treated with chlordiazepoxide (12.5 mg/kg) alone could be made hyperactive in the Y maze by previous experience of being placed into a separate open field on each of 8 days. It is not clear if this hyperactivity resembled that produced by the drug mixture, but lithium in a dose of 2 mEq/kg reduced this activity while not affecting activity in naïve rats treated with chlordiazepoxide or the activity of other control groups.

Second, activity in mice was measured in two different procedures: as head dips in a 16 hole-board apparatus, and in photocell activity cages. The behavior shown in the hole-board situation is particularly interesting: "Mixture-treated mice showed 'repeated dips' i.e. they successively dipped their heads into the same hole or over the edge of the board while standing in the same place" (p. 266). Lithium pretreatment (3 mEq/kg) blocked head-dipping observed with the drug mixture (d-amphetamine 1.18 mg/kg plus chlordiazepoxide 12.5 mg/kg or 2.36 ± 25.0 mg/kg), although, again, head-dipping produced by the two drugs separately, or by saline alone, was relatively unaffected. (There was, however, a significant reduction with 1.18 mg/kg d-amphetamine).

In the photocell cages, activity only increased following the larger doses of the mixture and with 2.36 mg/kg d-amphetamine. However, lithium pretreatment had no effect on these increases. The authors argue that the "familiarity" of the environment may have been a significant factor, that hyperactivity is more prevalent in the novel hole-board than in a photocell cage resembling the home cage. This conclusion, however, seems premature. No data are provided for the effects of the drugs in the photocell cages. Therefore, it is quite possible that the smaller effects observed were less susceptible to reductions after lithium than were the higher levels of activity seen in the hole board. This consideration of baseline may in itself be an explanation for why lithium has an effect with the drug mixture but not with the drugs separately. There are, in fact, hints that the lithium reductions are not restricted to activity produced by the mixture.

The attenuation of the hyperactivity caused by the drug mixture was not confined, however, to lithium. Mice receiving α-methyl-p-tyrosine (300 mg/kg) showed a similar reduction. Moreover, this pretreatment had little effect on control animals. These results indicate that the hyperactivity can be attentuated about as effectively by antimanic agents other than lithium.

Finally, the attenuating effects of α-methyl-p-tyrosine and lithium were not restricted merely to hyperactivity produced by a drug mixture of d-amphetamine and chlordiazepoxide. The increased Y-maze activity induced in rats by 1 mg/kg of the anitcholinergic drug scopolamine was attentuated either by a pretreatment of 2 mEq/kg of lithium or by 3 x 60 mg/kg pretreatments with α-methyl-p-tyrosine (Sanger and Steinberg, 1974). These results show that hyperactivity produced by a variety of agents may be blocked by these two antimanic drugs. It would be interesting to know if there is some critical upper level of activity that would be susceptible to the effects of lithium regardless of how this level was produced.

Miscellaneous catecholamine models. One of the earliest "models of mania" was reported by Matussek and Linsmayer (1968). They induced a hyperactive syndrome in rats by treatment with 20 mg/kg desmethyl-imipramine (DMI) and the benzoquinolizine RO 4-1284. This syndrome has previously been graphically described by Sulser et al. (1964). These authors emphasize the "automatic" type of activity observed, its lack of dependence on external stimuli, and the apparent lack of social interaction among the treated rats. Also, "Placed in an elevated platform the rats given DMI and RO4-1284 move around and keep poking their heads over the edge, each stretching outwards and a little more until finally they topple down. They will repeat the performance regardless of a hard fall [p. 322]." And, "In a treadmill, rats treated with the combination of drugs are ceaselessly on the go, turning the wheel almost continuously [p. 322]." In both cases, this form of hyperactivity is compared with the more transitory behavior induced by amphetamine. A final item of interest is that the hyperactivity is not induced in relatively immature rats ($<$ 5 weeks old).

Matussek and Linsmayer (1968) found that lithium (in doses of approximately 2.36 and 4.72 mEq/kg) administered acutely at varying times before the DMI RO 4-1284 combination had a strong antagonistic effect on the hyperactivity induced by the combination. Even stronger antagonism was found after chronic dosing with lithium.

These results were interesting when compared to those in which pretreatment of various doses of amphetamine (0.1–3.0 mg/kg) actually also reduced the DMI RO 4-1284 hyperactivity. The results with amphetamine were paradoxical since DMI by itself often potentiates the behavioral effects of this drug (Stein, 1962). It is pity that a more complete behavioral description of the effects of amphetamine on the DMI RO 4-1284 syndrome was not given so that the behavior might have been compared more closely with normal or after-lithium pretreatment. Amphetamine, of course, is often used in treatment of the hyperactive child, where it produces a "paradoxical" calming action (e.g., Millichap, 1968). There have been few indications that amphetamine has been used in the treatment of mania, although the MRC Brain Metabolism Unit, (1972) mentions a case in which an improvement was actually seen using such therapy. For the moment, however, the relationship between child hyperactivity and mania remains unclear.

The neurochemical basis of the effects observed by Matussek and Linsmayer also remains obscure. In Table 2 we summarize results quoted by Sulser et al. (1964) that seem to indicate that DMI may produce hyperactivity in combination with other drugs by a rapid release of catecholamines, particularly noradrenaline.

More recently, Furukawa et al. (1975) have shown that a hyperactivity syndrome can be induced in the mouse in the open field by combining doses of 5 mg/kg of tetrabenazine (a reserpinelike compound) and a monoamine oxidase inhibitor, nialamide (10 mg/kg, 24 h prior). Most interestingly, this hyperactivity was *not* significantly reduced by lithium pretreatment, in contrast to that induced by methamphetamine (see Table 1). This result is important since it demonstrates that lithium does not necessarily antagonize all forms of hyperactivity. The levels of activity induced by the tetrabenazine and nialamide combinations were comparable to those produced by methamphetamine. This finding requires further study and confirmation. A final result of interest noted in this paper is that lithium actually produced short-lived increases in ambulation in mice whose activity was reduced by tetrabenazine given alone, and also produced unusual "jumping behaior." Again, the precise neurochemical mechanisms underlying these effects remain unclear.

Smith (1976) used another means of inducing hyperactivity, by combining a dose of L-dopa (150 mg/kg) with a low dose of a peripheral decarboxylase inhibitor, RO 4-4602. Lithium pretreatment (1.5 mEq/kg) twice per day for 5 days, producing plasma levels of 0.86 ± mEq/1 at the time of testing, was effective in reducing the hyperactivity to control levels. The pharmacological manipulations used by Smith are known to cause increases in brain catecholamine levels, particularly of dopamine (Bartholini et al., 1969). However, the hyperactivity cannot be unequivocally attributed to dopamine. L-dopa in large doses can also produce aggression and fighting in rats and cats and increases in locomotor activity in the squirrel monkey, mouse, and dog (Scheckel et al., 1969). These results with L-dopa are particularly interesting because of the linkage of this drug to manic states in human subjects. For example, L-dopa administered to depressed subjects can produce hypomanic episodes (Murphy, 1972).

Table 2. Effect of DMI on Behavior after Various Pretreatments (based on Sulser et al., 1964)

Drug	Dose	Rate of NA Release	Effect without DMI	Effect with DMI
Reserpine	5 mg/kg i.p.	fast	sedation	hyperactivity
RO 4-1284	15 mg/kg/ i.p.	fast	sedation	hyperactiviy
Tetrabenazine	20 mg/kg i.p.	fast	sedation	hyperactivity
α-Methyl-meta-tyrosine	500 mg/kg i.p.	slow	no sedation	no hyperactivity
Reserpine	5 x 7 mg/kg i.p.	slow	sedation	no hyperactivity

A final study to be described in this section concerns the hyperactivity associated with neonatal hyperthyroidism in rats induced by daily postnatal administration of l-tri-iodothyronine for 30 days (Rastogi and Singhal, 1977). This treatment also results in significant increases in turnover of brain noradrenaline and dopamine. Repeated administration of lithium (60 mg/kg Li_2CO_3; approx. 1.67 mEq/kg Li) for a period of 6 days reduced the hyperactivity produced by the hormone treatment. This effect was paralleled by an antagonism of the neurochemical changes caused by l-tri-iodothyronine. By itself, the hormone produced several effects in particular on several dopaminergic parameters: (1) elevated DA levels in the hypothalamus, midbrain, striatum, and cerebral cortex; (2) increased levels of the DA metabolites, HVA and DOPAC; and (3) elevated striatal tyrosine hydroxylase activity. Lithium attenuated most of these effects.

In summarizing the studies in this section, it is clear that pharmacological manipulation of the catecholamine systems can lead to hyperactivity, which in some cases can be antagonized with lithium. However, the neurochemical correlates of these behavioral effects are not absolutely clear in all cases. Some evidence (Smith, 1976; Rastogi and Singhal, 1977) links the hyperactivity with dopaminergic changes. In the next section a brief review of the separate roles of the catecholamine systems in motor activity will be made in the hope that it might provoke further research into the implications for manic syndromes.

Dopaminergic hyperactivity. If the dopaminergic terminals within the nucleus accumbens septi are destroyed with the neurotoxin 6-hydroxydopamine, the heightened locomotor activity produced by d-amphetamine is attenuated. Interestingly, the locomotor response to apomorphine (1.0 mg/kg, i.p.), a direct DA agonist, is markedly increased. This enhanced response may be due to denervation supersensitivity (Kelly et al., 1975). Rats with 6-OHDA lesions of the nucleus accumbens also show heightened locomotor responses to other drugs that might act as dopamine agonists—for example, to the ergot alkaloids such as ergometrine; to apomorphine alkaloids such as (± -N-n-propylnorapomorphine), and to LSD (Kelly, 1977). There are a few reports that 6-hydroxydopamine itself can induce spontaneous increases in locomotor activity. Shaywitz et al. (1976) found that rat pups treated with 6-OHDA at 5 days of age develop transient increases in motor activity between 2 and 4 weeks of age. Those authors, noting the dependence of the hyperactivity on the age of the animals, have used this as an experimental model of the hyperactive child. The increased activity presumably depends on a supersensitivity of catecholamine receptors.

There is some evidence that an analogous supersensitivity may develop in response to chronic treatment with neuroleptic drugs. Sahakian et al., (1976) showed that treatment of young rats with 0.2 mg/kg of the DA antagonist α-flupenthixol over 10 days and produced heightened spontaneous activity, measured in photocell cages. This result could, however, have been due to a transient compensatory increase in DA turnover.

Whether receptor supersensitivity is a plausible neurochemical correlate of mania is unknown. However, results reviewed in this section suggest that the idea is worthy of consideration.

Noradrenergic hyperactivity. Almost the only piece of convincing evidence that noradrenergic systems are involved in controlling activity is the experiment of Geyer et al. (1972) in which noradrenaline and dopamine were infused intraventricularly into rats. Locomotor activity was increased by both neuroransmitter substances, but the activity due to dopamine could be blocked by treatment with imipramine, suggesting that the effect of dopamine was mediated via its uptake into noradrenergic neurones and subsequent conversion to noradrenaline (Geyer and Segal, 1973). None of the specific manipulations described in sections IV and V have been used as tools for analyzing mania. It is not necessarily clear that any of these hyperactive syndromes are appropriate for the mood change in mania. However, there are several indications that both the noradrenergic and dopaminergic systems are involved in mediating the effects of intracranial self-stimulation, with the weight of the evidence in favor of dopamine. (A brief review of this work is made in the section on Animal Models of Mania; Behavioral models.

It is important to note also the possible role of serotoninergic systems in hyperactive behavior. Green and Grahame-Smith (1975) have described a hyperactive syndrome caused by increased serotonin levels, which is, however, very different from the ones we have described, as we shall see in the next section.

Indoleamine hypothesis

A reduction in serotoninergic neurotransmission has been postulated by Kety (1971) as a factor that is involved in the induction of both depression and mania. However, the expression of mania or depression was held to be also dependent on catecholaminergic neurotransmission, with increased activity underlying mania. Consequently, there has been much interest, not only in serotoninergic hyperactivity syndromes per se, but also in their interaction with catecholamine systems. In this somewhat bewildering field, hyperactive syndromes have been discovered that depend on both increased synthesis of serotonin and depletion of serotonin. We deal with these syndromes separately.

Hyperactivity produced by l-tryptophan-MAO-inhibitor combinations. Grahame-Smith (1971a) found that treating rats with a combination of the monoamine oxidase inhibitor tranylcypromine and the amino-acid precursor of serotonin, l-tryptophan, produced a marked increase in activity as measured in an Animex meter. The changes in activity were accompanied by many other behavioral and physiological effects, described in detail by Grahame-Smith. Initially, the treated rats showed signs of salivation and defecation, increased vocalization when handled, piloerection, proptosis, penile erection, and a tendency to exhibit somewhat steryotyped "head-weaving." This stage was followed by a period of "compulsive" movement, including circling, "padding" of the forepaws, ataxia of the hind limbs, a lack of responsivity to visual stimuli such as the edge of the table, and the induction of opisthotonous, and short clonic fits. The animals were also hyperpyrexic and exhibited shivering responses. The degree of hyperactivity was directly related to the increase in rate of 5HT-synthesis. It is important to note that this syndromes depends on the joint administration of these two compounds; injection of either one alone has no appreciable behavioral effect. The syndrome can also be induced by injection of either l-tryptophan, or L-dopa in conjunction with other monoamine oxidase inhibitors, such as pargyline (Jacobs, 1974).

There is considerable doubt that this syndrome represents simply a "psychomotor stimulation" of behavior, such as that produced by amphetamine. For example, Herberg and Franklin (1976) found that a combination of l-tryptophan and pargyline, while producing a considerable increase in activity, actually produced a dose-dependent suppression of rates of self-stimulation in rats. These authors suggest that the self-stimulation behavior is reduced because of an increased susceptibility to seizures induced by the drug combination. This finding provides evidence against the use of this syndrome as an animal model of mania. However, more conclusive evidence would be provided if a wider range of self-stimulation sites in the brain was explored.

Other pharmacological aspects of this hyperactivity syndrome are of considerable interest, however: First, the syndrome can be antagonized with doses of chlorpromazine, which apparently do not alter 5-HT synthesis (Grahame-Smith, 1971b). This result suggests a mediation of the hyperactivity through a catecholaminergic mechanism. Other evidence (Green and Grahame-Smith, 1974, 1976), which shows that the hyperactivity can be blocked by other neuroleptics such as haloperidol, spiroperidol, and α-flupenthixol, and by depletion of brain dopamine, suggests that the hyperactivity depends upon a dopaminergic mechanism. Both Marsden and Curzon (1976) and Jacobs (1974), however, failed to produce a significant blockade with the potent DA antagonist pimozide, and so this conclusion remains for the moment controversial. Consideration of Figure 7 of Marsden and Curzon suggests, in fact, that there was a mild antagonism of the effects of monoamine oxidase inhibition and tryptophan, which might have reached significance with a larger number of subjects. It is clear, however, that the antagonism is much less potent than the effects of d-amphetamine.

Second, 2 or 3 days of lithium administration to rats, preceding MAO inhibition, produces a syndrome indistinguishable from that produced by tryptophan (Grahame-Smith and Green, 1974). This finding provides strong evidence that lithium acts by increasing 5-HT synthesis, especially since the effect can be antagonised by treatment with PCPA, an inhibitor of serotonin synthesis (Grahame-Smith, 1974). A putative hallucinogen of the indolealkylamine type, 5-methoxy-N, N-dimethyltryptamine (5MeODMT), also produces hyperactivity similar to that seen after l-tryptophan. This hyperactivity, however, is not increased by lithium, which suggests, since 5MeODMT is a probable postsynaptic 5HT receptor agonist, that lithium is altering the amount of serotonin available for release presynaptically.

Nialamide-induced hyperactivity. Large doses of the monoamine oxidase inhibitor nialamide also produce increased locomotion, head movements, and tremor in mice, perhaps due to increases in brain 5-HT. In addition, the syndrome can be potentiated by 5-HT reuptake inhibitors such as chlorimipramine (Modigh and Svensson, 1972; Buus Lassen and Squires, 1976). Lithium pretreatment produced a strong potentiation of the "hyper-motility" response (Buus Lassen and Squires, 1976). All of these facts point to a clear affinity of this syndrome with that produced by monoamine oxidase inhibition and tryptophan in rats.

In summary, it seems that the serotoninergic hyperactivity syndromes may not be a viable model of mania in view of the associated reduction in self-stimulation, and the effects of lithium. Nevertheless, they remain a valuable way of elucidating further the action of lithium and of exploring possible catecholaminergic-serotoninergic interactions.

Hyperactivity induced by LSD. Jacobs et al. (1976) have described a bizarre pattern of behavior induced by various doses of LSD (10–100 μg/kg) in cats. Rather than measuring activity in automatic apparatus, they have identified various behavioral elements that seem to be either normal elements increased by LSD, such as investigatory behavior, or "abnormal" responses produced by the drug, such as "abortive grooming" or "limb-flicking." In terms of models of mania, the authors' descriptions of the behavior of the cats are most interesting: "Our impression was that the emergence of abortive grooming was reflective of the fragmentary or disjunctive nature of all behavior in these animals. They would rarely sustain any active behavior continuously for more than several seconds. It appeared as though the attention was constantly being diverted, and as a result, their ongoing behavior was frequently interrupted and changed or even aborted prior to consummation, as in the case of grooming. They would, for example, change from play behavior to grooming and back agin with a period of a few seconds" [p. 742].

From behavioral considerations, these actions of LSD are interesting, but their uses as models of mania should perhaps be tempered by the lack of a facilitatory effect upon self-stimulation and by the apparent failure to find reliable self-administration of the drug by animals. Both of these latter actions obscure assessment of the affective correlates of LSD.

In pharmacological terms, Jacobs et al. (1976) consider the effects of LSD to depend on an antagonistic action at serotoninergic receptors, a view supported by their findings that similar effects can be found with high doses of methysergide and that the effects of LSD can be potentiated by PCPA (Trulson and Jacobs, 1976). However, it must not be overlooked that LSD may have agonist effects on DA receptors in mesolimbic areas (Kelly and Iversen, 1975).

Hyperactivity induced by serotonin depletion.

Parachlorophenylalanine (PCPA). Any interpretation of the effects of PCPA has to be tempered by a recognition of its nonspecific action. Although this drug produces a relatively long-lasting depletion of serotonin, it also has effects on other neurotransmitter systems (Miller et al., 1970).

PCPA induces hyperactivity (Fibiger and Campbell, 1971), but this activity is affected by several factors. Marsden and Curzon (1976) have performed a most detailed analysis. They found that there was a circadian modulation of the hyperactivity induced by PCPA. For example, the drug greatly increased the somewhat low levels of activity shown by rats in the light, but did not increase the already high levels shown during the dark period. The pattern of activity in darkness, however, was changed by the drug, with activity becoming more continuous, and with fewer bursts of activity and fewer periods of inactivity than in undrugged rats. PCPA also reduced activity in the open field, indicating a probable increase in reactivity produced by the drug. This interpretation is supported by evidence that PCPA-treated rats exhibit higher levels of activity than controls in response to a sudden change in stimulus conditions within the open field (Ellison and Bresler, 1974). Eventually, the heightened reactivity gives way to increased locomotor activity after a 30 min period of exposure (Fibiger and Campbell, 1971).

Marsden and Curzon (1976) point out that the hyperactivity induced by PCPA is dissimilar to that produced by monoamine oxidase inhibition and l-tryptophan. There is, for example, no lack of social interaction and frequent "aggressive/playful" contacts are made. The hyperactivity induced by PCPA depends on serotonin, since it can be reversed either by 5HTP or by tryptophan. However, Marsden and Curzon (1976) could find no significant blockade of the PCPA-induced hyperactivity by pimozide in a dose (0.3 mg/kg) that blocked amphetamine-induced activity. At higher doses of pimozide, the PCPA-induced activity was attenuated. PCPA also blocks the suppressant effect of lithium upon activity in the open field (Smith, 1975).

Early work showed that PCPA increased rates of self-stimulation behavior in rats (Poschel and Ninteman, 1971). However, this generalization is now known to be invalid because of the recent work of Phillips and colleagues. Self-stimulation rates at both caudate and hippocampal sites were shown to be *reduced* after PCPA, whereas rates of lateral hypothalamic self-stimulation, as reported previously, were *increased* by the drug (Phillips et al., 1976; van der Kooy et al., 1977). These results, of course, make difficult generalizations about the role of monoamines in reinforcement processes, since it appears that serotonin depletion can result in either increases or decreases in rate of presumed catecholaminergic sites.

Miliaressis et al. (1975) have also reported self-stimulation sites in the median raphe nucleus, which probably depend on serotonin since PCPA produces reductions in rates of responding.

In summary, the effects of PCPA are most interesting since this drug produces, predominantly, increases in reactivity, as well as hyperactivity in certain situations. It is perhaps unsurprising that the drug also causes increased aggression, and the these effects can be antagonized by lithium (Sheard, 1970).

5,6 and 5,7-dihydroxytryptamine (5,6 or 5,7 -DHT). These neurotoxins, when administered centrally, can cause relatively specific destruction of serotoninergic neurones (Green and Grahame-Smith, 1975). Diaz et al. (1974) used multiple intraventricular injections of 5,6-DHT according to two dosing schedules: three or six repeated adminstrations. The rats with the more extensive 5-HT lesions, produced by six injections, showed decreased loco-motion but increased rearing in an open field, whereas the animals with smaller lesions produced by three injections showed increased locomotion but reduced rearing. The pattern of activity shown by the rats with larger lesions was similar to that observed after PCPA (Ellison and Bresler, 1974). Diaz et al. hypothesize that the rats with smaller 5-HT lesions are exhibiting recovery, with heightened responses due to stimulation of supersensitive 5-HT receptors, whereas the rats with larger lesions are displaying the hyperreactive syndrome characteristic of 5-HT depletion following PCPA. However, regional deple-tion of serotonin by injection of 5,7-DHT into the midline raphe nucleus, where several 5HT projections arise, did not alter locomotor activity in the open field, although rearing failed to habituate as rapidly as in controls (Lorens et al., 1976). Hence, the precise correlates of hyperactivity produced by serotonin depletion remain unclear.

The effects of serotonin depletion by 5,6- or 5,7-DHT on self-stimulation behavior have not been extensively studied. Poschel et al. (1974) reported increases in rate of responding following treatment with 5,6-DHT, but, expecially in considering the results of van der Kooy et al. (1977), care has to be made in generalizing from these results.

Summary. Increasing or decreasing serotoninergic activity in the brain produces hyperactivity syndromes of two distinct sorts, neither of which are compelling models of mania. A possible role for serotonin in mania, however, seems likely in view of the actions of lithium (cf. Knapp and Mandell, 1976). It is probable that changes in the serotoninergic system are best understood within the context of other neurotransmitter systems, particularly noradren-aline and dopamine. For example, the potentiation of the locomotor effects of amphetamine by serotonin depletion (Breese et al., 1974; Segal, 1975) suggests that serotonin modulates DA functioning within mesolimbic areas. Moreover, the increased activity produced by electrolytic lesion to 5-HT cell bodies in the median raphe are not only negatively correlated with tryptophan hydroxylase activity in the hippocampus, but are also positively correlated with tyrosine hydroxylase activity in the striatum, suggesting an enhancement of dopa-minergic function (Geyer et al., 1976). These interactions are not incompatible with the general scheme advanced by Kety (1971) and others; further work must be aimed at specifying more clearly the nature of monaminergic interactions.

Morphine

When administered acutely, morphine can produce a hyperactive response in the cat, rabbit, rat, and mouse. Wikler (1944) described the effects of 10–15 mg/kg of morphine in cats as producing a restless, frightened state in which the animals resisted handling and showed enhanced startle responses to external stimuli. Dhasmana et al. (1972) found similar results. Whereas low doses (7 mg/kg) of morphine had little effect, cats receiving 5.0 mg/kg of morphine showed effects of sedation mixed with "mild excitement," including pilo-erection and clawing and biting of the cage bars. These effects were seen in all of the cats tested with 20 mg/kg. Morphine also increases locomotor activity in rats and mice, although the dose-response parameters differ. A wide range of doses (e.g., 5–225 mg/kg) induces hyperactivity in mice (Rethy et al., 1971; Carrol and Sharp, 1972). In rats, however, only lower doses (1.5–5.0 mg/kg) are effective, although higher doses produce hyperactivity after a period of sedation (Babbini and Davis, 1972). There are marked increases in activity of rats also following chronic morphine treatment sufficient to induce tolerance. However, this activity is interrupted by long periods of steretyped sniffing, licking, and biting (Fog, 1970).

A more detailed analysis of the hyperactive syndrome reveals some interesting comparisons to that produced by amphetamine. Ayhan and Randrup (1973) showed that acute doses of morphine (1–5 mg/kg) produced a dose-dependent hyperactivity in the rat characterized by sudden bursts of locomotion or rearing, which alternated with periods of sedation. Other behavioral activities such as scratching with the hind-limb and licking of the hindpaws, as well as eating and drinking, were also increased by morphine. Schirring and Hecht (1974) reported an augmentation of forms of social interaction. Morphine-treated rats (2 mg/kg) showed increased sniffing of one another, increased bodily contact in terms of crawling over and under one another, and an enhanced tendency to follow other rats. In general, it is safe to conclude that the hyperactivity produced by morphine, unlike that of amphetamine, in the rat is characterized by rapid transitions from one form of behavior to another in a rather nonspecific manner.

The greater persistence seen in amphetamine-treated rats as behavioral stereotypy can be observed in morphine-treated rats under special conditions. Rats made tolerant to morphine with large doses (about 200 mg/kg/day) show enhanced snifing, biting, and licking as mentioned above. In this case, however, instead of representing a transition from hyperactivity, as in the case of amphetamine, the stereotypy actually appears to be in behavioral competition with the more erratic bursts of activity produced by morphine. In the mouse, morphine apparently produces a rather different form of activity. Carroll and Sharp (1972) describe it as follows: "The rate of running is regular and the behavior has a driven, stereotyped quality; it does not resemble exploratory or escape behavior. The mice do not display aggression and they are easily handled" [p. 127]. These authors again contrast morphine hyperactivity with that induced by amphetamine, which for the mouse consists of more "episodic" running at high doses and enhanced aggression. The morphine hyperactivity in mice depends on both genetic and experiential factors (Oliveiro and Castellano, 1974a, b). Interestingly, the activity is enhanced by environmental change or sensory stimulation. In fact, previous experience of the test cage blocks the activation induced by 20 mg/kg of morphine (Oliveiro and Castellano, 1974b). This pattern is again different from that of amphetamine, which in the rat, at least, is enhanced by familiar environments (Marriot, 1968). Morphine hyperactivity seems to be of a more reactive type. Nevertheless, stereotypy is produced by both drugs. Mice show stereotyped sniffing, gnawing, and "digging" into sawdust or straw during the second hour after treatment with morphine as the running response diminishes. As we shall discuss briefly later, the apparent discrepancies in form of morphine hyperactivity in rat and mouse may depend in part on neuropharmacological differences.

Is the hyperactivity, and apparently increased "irritability", produced by morphine accompanied by changes in reinforcement threshold? Lorens and Mitchell (1973) supplied evidence for this suggestion by showing that 5–20 mg/kg of morphine first suppressed and then elevated rates of responding in rats with electrical stimulation of the lateral hypothalamus as the reinforcer. The excitatory effects initially appeared only several hours after administration, although with repeated treatment they became apparent at an earlier time. Tolerance developed to the suppressant effect, but not to the facilitatory effect. Activity measures in running wheels made in parallel with the brain stimulation studies failed to demonstrate any correlations between activity levels and rates of responding with brain stimulation.

A more recent study has confirmed and extended these results by making direct measurements of morphine effects upon reinforcement threshold using titration of the electrical current necessary to maintain self-stimulation behavior in rats (Esposito and Kornetsky, 1977). No tolerance developed to threshold-reducing effects of morphine. These reductions were accompanied by increases in locomotor activity, but the authors argue, again, that these increases are insufficient in themselves to account for the reductions in threshold observed.

Effects of lithium and other antimanic agents on morphine response.
Surprisingly, there have been few studies of the effects of lithium on morphine
hyperactivity. Carroll and Sharp (1971) induced a "stereotyped hyperactivity" of a form described above in mice with 25 mg/kg of morphine.
Lithium was administered in a dose of 5 mEq/kg for 4 days prior to
morphine, with an additional dose of lithium 30 min prior to treatment. There
was an attenuation of the hyperactive response, but no data are reported for
activity of mice receiving neither morphine nor lithium, so it is difficult to
ascertain whether the activity was reduced close to levels shown by undrugged
mice.

There are some intriguing data on the effects of lithium on self-stimulation
after morphine and on self-administration of the drug, which may both reflect
the affective correlates of morphine action. Liebman and Segal (1976) found
that 1.5 and 2.0 mEq/kg of lithium antagonized the facilitatory effect of
morphine on self-stimulation in rats at sites in the substantia nigra. The
important points of this paper, however, were (1) that no tolerance developed
to these effects after chronic lithium treatment, and (2) that this lack of
tolerance was *not* evident for the effects of lithium on amphetamine-induced
increases in responding. This dissociation may have striking implications for
animal models of mania that suggest that morphine-induced hyperactivity
and "elation" are more viable models for mania than analogous effects of
amphetamine. In further apparent support for this view, Tomkiewicz and
Steinberg (1974) found that treatment with chronic lithium (2 mmol/kg)
reduced the oral self-administration of morphine in sucrose solutions as
measured in a choice situation. Control experiments ruled out the possibilites
that morphine was producing these effects by causing taste aversion. The
effects of lithium on self-administration of amphetamine have not been
studied, to our knowledge, but would obviously provide an interesting
comparison.

In a later paper, Carroll and Sharp (1972) studied the effects of a range of
other compounds on morphine hyperactivity in mice. It was shown that the
morphine response could also be antagonized by α-methyl-p-tyrosine,
PCPA, haloperidol, chlorpromazine, the noradrenergic antagonists phenoxybenzamine and phentolamine, and the serotoninergic antagonists cinanserin and methysergide. The hyperactive response was enhanced by L-dopa,
pargyline, or imipramine. No effects were found with the antimuscarinic
agent atropine or the serotonin precursor tryptophan.

Several other studies have confirmed many of the conclusions of the
Carroll and Sharp article in other speices, including the cat (Dhasmana et al.
1972; Loewe, 1956; Sturtevant and Drill, 1957) and the rat (Ayhan and
Randrup, 1973). For example, Ayhan and Randrup reported that the
morphine-induced hyperactivity could be blocked by inhibition of catechol-

amine synthesis with α-methyl-p-tyrosine; by blockade of synthesis of noradrenaline with FLA-63; by blockade of NA receptors (acerperone and phenoxybenzamine) or DA receptors (pimozide or spiramide). There did not seem to be any dramatic differences among these agents in their effects upon different elements of the morphine hyperactivity. Interestingly, a similar pattern of antagonism was also found for these agents upon hyperactivity induced by amphetamine (1 mg/kg).

An equivalence of effect of NA and DA receptor antagonists was not found, however, by Dhasmana et al. (1972) for the cat. They found that whereas haloperidol and chlorpromazine could antagonize "morphine mania," phenozybenzamine and propanolol could not. Carroll and Sharp (1972) found with mice that haloperidol was far more effective in antagonizing the hyperactivity than either NA antagonists or chlorpromazine, with which it shares similar potencies for blockade of NA receptors. Taken together, these results suggest a significant role for DA in the mediation of morphine hyperactivity, although clearly the noradrenergic and serotoninergic systems also modulate this behavior.

Recently, Iversen and Joyce (1978) have found furher indirect evidence that DA receptors at mesolimbic sites mediate morphine hyperactivity. They administered morphine chronically to rats following 6-OHDA lesions of the DA terminals in the caudate nucleus. A dose of 0.1 mg/kg (s.c.) apomorphine subsequently produced the usual enhancement of sterotyped licking and biting in this preparation, perhaps due to supersensitive DA receptors (see section C[1] iv.). However, this stereotypy was interspersed with rapid bursts of locomotion of the type normally seen with apomorphine following 6-OHDA lesions of the DA terminals of the nucleus accumbens. The implication is that chronic morphine treatment in some way induces supersensitivity of DA receptors in the nucleus accumbens. In further support of this claim, it was also found that chronic morphine treatment by itself induced an enhanced running response to 0.1 mg/kg (s.c.) of apomorphine.

The differing forms of hyperactivity produced by morphine across species and their dependence on particular doses and time-course of effect make difficult firm conclusions about the neuropharmacology of morphine-induced "mania." There are recent indications that morphine hyperactivity in the rat and mouse may even depend on partly different neuropharmacologicalsubstrates (Oka and Hosoya, 1977). Furthermore, the realization that some of the behavioral effects of morphine might depend on interactions with central opiate receptors (Snyder, 1977) also suspends theoretical speculation. Facts relevant to this latter discovery are that the opiate antagonist nalorphine can block morphine hyperactivity at low doses in the mouse (Carroll and Sharp, 1972) and morphine stereotypy in the rat (Fog, 1970). Naloxone, another antagonist, has also been used to block morphine hyperactivity in the mouse (Rethy et al., 1971) and rat (Joyce, unpublished observations).

The implications of studies of morphine hyperactivity for mania are unclear. Although morphine hyperactivity is antagonized by lithium and neuroleptics, as well as by other putative antimanic agents such as the serotonin antagonist cinanserin, there are plenty of indications that this response can also be at least modulated by drugs not thought to have much therapeutic benefit for mania, such as PCPA and nalorphine. However, it is interesting to note that although both amphetamine hyperactivity and morphine hyperactivity may be mediated in part by dopaminergic mechanisms, the pattern of results obtained with morphine in combination with other drugs, affecting serotinergic and cholinergic systems, for example, suggests that the model of morphine hyperactivity provides an interesting alternative to that of amphetamine hyperactivity, worthy of further study.

Hyperactivity as a form of behavioral toxicity

Hyperactivity can be induced by toxic agents, and in the case of lead poisoning with hyperactive children (David et al., 1972), such effects have been shown to have clinical relevance. There is no evidence that mania is induced by an analogous form of toxicity. However, perhaps our ignorance of the etiology of mania should not preclude a brief survey of this area.

An animal model of lead poisoning has been developed by Silbergeld and Goldberg (1974), in which suckling mice were exposed to lead acetate first through their mothers and then directly after weaning. At between 40 and 60 days of age, the mice exposed to lead are three times as active as controls, more aggressive, and show "stereotyped repetitive behavior as manifested by excessive self-grooming" [Sauerhoff and Michaelson, 1973]. Silbergeld and Goldberg found that d-amphetamine and methylphenidate suppressed the activity of these animals, and phenobarbital increased activity, all in ways reminiscent of the "paradoxical" effects on hyperactive children. The hyperactivity might be correlated with changes in catecholamine metabolism (Sauerhoff and Michaelson, 1973).

Another form of heavy metal poisoning by cadmium also appears to induce hyperactivity in rats, perhaps by increasing turnover of the monoamines (Rastogi et al., 1977). Perhaps more salient to the problem of mania is hyperactivity induced by rubidium, which is an alkaline earth metal of the same series as lithium. Carroll and Sharp (1971) contrasted its behavioral actions with those of lithium. Rubidium causes increased activity, aggression and EEG arousal in monkeys (Meltzer et al., 1969). Rubidium ion adminstered to mice (3 mEq/kg chronically and 30 minutes before test) produced a potentiation of the same hyperactivity response to morphine that was attenuated by pretreatment with lithium (Carroll and Sharp, 1971). The latter authors point out that antidepressant drugs such as the tricyclics (e.g., imipramine) and monoamine oxidase inhibitors (e.g., pargyline) potentiate the morphine response in a manner similar to that of rubidium. However, little appears to be known of the neuropharmacological action of rubidium except that it tends to increase noradrenaline metabolism, an effect again contrary to that of lithium (Stolk et al., 1970). Probably the most detailed behavioral study performed in the realm of hyperactivity induced by toxic agents is that by Norton et al. (1976). They compared the behavioral structure of the hyperactive syndromes produced in rats by three different agents:

1. X-irradiation at gestational day 14 or 15
2. Exposure to carbon monoxide on the fifth day of postnatal life
3. Bilateral electrolytic lesions of the globus pallidus

These agents presumably produce very different, but possibly overlapping, areas of brain damage, and so a behavioral comparison of the different forms of hyperactivity is particularly interesting.

The behavior of the brain-damaged rats was analyzed by means similar to those used for amphetamine in an earlier study (Norton, 1973). The brain-damaged rats and their controls were photographed at 1 frame/sec during their first exposure to a cage. The frequency of 15 motor acts, with the duration of their occurrence, and temporal sequence were analyzed. The fifteen acts were divided into clusters labeled "grooming," "exploratory," and "attention" behaviors. In all three cases, hyperactivity was associated also with an increased frequency and shortened duration of "exploratory" acts, whereas "grooming" and "attention" behavior generally decreased both in duration and frequency, and there was a general increase in "randomness" of structure.

The interesting implication of these findings, which parallel those found with d-amphetamine (Norton, 1973), is that hyperactivity has the same basic structure and description, whatever its causes. This conclusion would run somewhat counter to the idea that morphine hyperactivity and amphetamine hyperactivity are qualitatively different, but morphine hyperactivity has not been subjected to the same detailed study as the forms described above. The conclusion would also not be invalidated by the fact that hyperactive syndromes in animals can be markedly influenced by the environment in which they are tested. The complexity and sublety of environmental control over hyperactivity would not in itself contribute to the *form* of the hyperactivity, only to its *occurrence*. These considerations lead us to discuss the effects of different brain lesions where hyperactivity is frequently modulated by widely varying environmental determinants.

Lesion Models

It would take a madman or a genius to attempt to summarize succinctly the literature the hyperactivity and hyperreactivity syndromes produced by various brain lesions. However, although their relevance to human mania may be questioned by the apparent lack of evidence for brain damage in mania, they command our attention for at least two reasons: First, these syndromes contribute to a study of the behavioral nature of hyperactivity and to the environmental stimuli that may modulate it. Second, the lesions often produce neurochemical changes that are significant in analyzing the neuropharmacological substrates of behavior.

Hyperactivity is a common consequence of brain lesions, and several different anatomical locations have been implicated. For example, hyperactivity in some form has been seen following lesions to the septal area, to the hippocampus, frontal cortex, caudate nucleus, accumbens, globus pallidus, ventral tegmentum, and raphe nucleus. Whether these structures are elements in a large system controlling locomotor activity or whether they control different forms of activity is unknown. We now consider the syndrome produced by some of these areas in turn, attempting to assess in particular possible implications for human mania.

Septum

The best-known effect of septal damage is "septal rage" or hyperreactivity, first reported by Brady and Nauta (1953). These animals, besides being difficult to handle, also display greatly heightened startle responses. Septal rats also show activity changes that may or may not be related to their hyperreactivity. The lesion produces hyperactivity when measured in maze-type situations and when a stimulus change is introduced into a familiar environment (Corman et al., 1967). On the other hand, septal rats may be no more active than sham-lesioned rats in familiar situations such as the home cage (Thomas et al., 1959), and are also less active in running wheels (Douglas and Raphelson, 1966). In order to reconcile these findings, it is necessary to hypothesize that septal lesions increase reactivity to novel stimulus change, perhaps by enhancing exploration. However, it is clear that hyperreactivity does not inevitably result in heightened activity levels. The heightened reactivity might also be correlated with an enhanced response to foot shock in terms of fighting or jumping (Wetzel et al., 1967; Lints and Harvey, 1969). There may also be changes in appetitive reinforcement threshold. For example, rats with septal lesions show increased rates of self-stimulation behavior with electrodes in the lateral hypothalamus (Lorens, 1966) and enhanced acquisition of saccharin drinking and enhanced intake of sucrose

(Beatty and Schwartzbaum, 1967, 1968). Perhaps the septal rats show an increased reactivity to stimulus change, particularly those tied to motivational states. However, it should be noted that septal lesions have several other effects on behavior that are dissociable from those described. The lack of a unitary function might be expected from the many anatomical connections of the septal area (Fried, 1972).

In terms of mania, the effects of septal lesions are interesting in that these animals appear to exhibit many of the "affective" signs of mania, or the "elation" and "irritability" of our own designation, without a persistent accompanying hyperkinesia. It would be interesting to explore this model for assessing the effects of antimanic agents thought to attenuate "affective" rather than "hyperkinetic" aspects of mania. Indeed, some preliminary work by Mukherjee and Pradhan (1976) suggests that lithium antagonizes the hyperexcitability produced by septal lesions.

Hippocampus

Hippocampal rats have been reported as hyperactive in strange cages (Teitelbaum and Milner, 1963) and also in the open field (Jarrard, 1968). However, these animals are also more active than controls in the dark part of the light/dark cycle (Jarrard, 1968), unlike septal-lesioned animals (see above). In addition, the movements of hippocampal rats have been described as "sterotyped" (Nadel and O'Keefe, 1974), and in the case of the gerbil, appear to lack exploratory or manipulative characteristics (Glickman et al., 1970), again in contrast to the septal-lesioned rat. Of course, hippocampal lesions have other profound effects upon behavior, but the gross motivational changes to be expected of mania do not number among them.

Frontal Cortex

Extensive bilateral frontal pole lesions in the rat can produce hyperactivity (Iversen, 1971; Lynch, 1970), although Lynch (1970) only found the hyperactivity in running wheels and not in stabilimeters. Similar lesions to the monkey frontal cortex also produce hyperactivity often characterized by "stereotyped pacing" (Ruch and Shenkin, 1943). The frontal-lesioned monkeys are probably hyperreactive also. Isaac and de Vito (1958) found that their activity was greatly increased by illumination, whereas it was close to control levels in dark conditions.

It is interesting that frontal lesions in man can produce changes in mood that vary from "euphoria" and "irritability" to "emotional indifference." However, these subjects often lack planning ability and initiative, deficits perhaps antithetical to the behavior of the manic subject! Nauta (1971) has reviewed these and other complex effects of frontal lobe damage in animals and man.

Caudate Nucleus, Globus Pallidus, and Nucleus Accumbens

These structures are considered together, following Heimer and Wilson (1975), as constituent parts of the striatum, although there may be neuro-anatomical grounds for considering the nucleus accumbens as part of the limbic system (e.g., Swanson and Cowan, 1975). Electrolytic lesions to the caudate nucleus and globus pallidus in the rat produce hyperactive syndromes that, however, are situation dependent. For example, Costall et al. (1972) found hyperactivity in caudate-lesioned rats only during the dark cycle. Similarly, Norton (1976) found that lesions of the globus pallidus produced hyperactivity in the rat mainly during the dark period. Neill et al. (1974a) found a functional differentiation, since although electrolytic lesions to the dorsal portion of the anterior striatum produced increased wheelrunning, comparable lesions to the ventral striatum actually reduced the wheel-running response. The striatal syndrome seems quite different from that produced in septal animals. Neill et al. (1974b) found that in contrast to septal rats, lesions to the striatum did not enhance acquisition of saccharine drinking, possibly suggesting that this syndrome is not accompanied by a reduction in reinforcement threshold. The distinction between the effects of these two lesions again points to a functional differentiation between affective and hyperkinetic components in behavior.

Lesions of the nucleus accumbens have been less studied. Lorens et al. (1970) found that electrolytic lesions to this area increased locomotor activity. In contrast, 6-hydroxydopamine lesions of the same structure produced hypoactivity (Koob et al., 1978). It is interesting to note that the neurochemical lesion produces opposite effects to those of the electrolytic lesion.

Ventral Mesencephalic Tegmental (VMT) Syndrome

Although it is apparent that lesions of many areas of the forebrain produce hyperactive behavior, the brain stem structures contributing to these syndromes have not always been identified. Most of the pathways connecting the forebrain and the so-called limbic midbrain area pass through the ventral mesencephalic tegmentum. Many of these pathways involve the ascending tracts of the monoamine neurotransmitters: the DA A10 cell bodies contributing to the mesolimbic projection arise at this level.

Radio-frequency lesions of the VMT produce increases in activity in rats in both portions of the light/dark cycle in a cylindrical corridor supplied with photocell beams. The animals were also hyperreactive in that their activity levels were further augmented by the provision of illumination and sound (Le Moal et al., 1976). This syndrome can be reproduced by small injections of 6-hydroxydopamine into the VMT, and the resulting hyperactivity is highly correlated with the reduction in DA levels in the frontal cortex. (Le Moal et al., 1976).

In later extensions to this work, it has been shown that the rats with lesions show a disruption in feeding activities and hoarding behavior. Typically, the behavior is more fragmented and transitory (Stinus et al., 1978a). Finally, it is interesting that small doses of apomorphine (30 and 60 μg/kg) reduce the locomotor activity of VMT lesioned rats. Stinus et al. (1978b) suggest that the syndrome might be an appropriate model for hyperactive children or mania. The suggestion is interesting in view of the report that piribedil has a therapeutic effect in mania (Post et al., 1976). The effects of other antimanic agents, in particular lithium, would also be interesting to know.

Raphe Nucleus

Among the most important structures innervating the forebrain is the raphe nucleus, which is also the origin of ascending serotoninergic projections. Electrolytic lesions of the midbrain raphe nucleus produce increases in locomotor activity, though not in rearing or in "exploratory head dipping." These animals also exhibit defics in avoidance behavior (Lorens et al., 1976). A more detailed analysis (Srebro and Lorens, 1975) revealed that median raphe lesions increased running-wheel activity and open-field activity but produced no change in home-cage activity. There were also changes in responsiveness to novel stimuli that were suggestive of altered reactivity. Geyer et al. (1976), using electrolytic lesions of the median raphe aimed at the B8 group of 5HT cell bodies, found increased activity and heightened responsiveness to "air-puffs." In contrast to these behavioral changes, lesions of the dorsal raphe had few behavioral effects (Lorens et al., 1976; Geyer et al., 1976).

Despite the depletion in forebrain serotonin produced by these electrolytic lesions, more severe depletions using the neurotoxin 5,7 dihydroxytryptamine did not produce similar behavioral effects (Lorens et al., 1976). In another paper, Lorens et al. (1975) suggest that many of the behavioral and biochemical changes produced by raphe lesions can be duplicated by electrolytic lesions of Gudden's tegmental nuclei. The relationship of the behavioral changes produced by raphe lesions to serotonin depletion is therefore controversial. It is possible that a nonserotoninergic substrate might be mediating some of the effects.

The behavioral syndrome produced by electrolytic lesions of the median raphe is interesting because of its similarity to syndromes produced by limbic lesions, suggesting possibly common neuronal circuitry. This connection is strengthened by the finding that hippocampal lesions block increases in locomotion produced by lesions to the raphe or PCPA (Jacobs et al., 1974). The implication is that the changes are due to destruction of the B8 serotonin projection to the hippocampus. However, Srebro and Lorens (1975) have documented the several differences between the forms of activity produced by septal, hippocampal and raphe lesions, and so attempts at parsimony at this juncture seem premature.

Behavioral Models

Hyperactivity in different forms can be induced by several behavioral manipulations. We have already described how the mere presentation of small amounts of food at periodic delays can lead to marked increases in certain types of adjunctive behavior, including drinking, running, as well as aggression (Staddon, 1977). The importance of these findings should not be underestimated in striving to find agents capable of inducing mania. Such activity may depend in subtle ways upon the previous history of the individual and on his present environmental circumstances. In this section we describe the effects of two radically different procedures that can induce hyperactivity in animals, brain stimulation and social isolation.

Brain Stimulation

Behavioral characteristics. Human patients have received electrical stimulation of the brain either to explore functional localization prior to brain surgery or to treat intractable pain, or for therapy of disabilities such as epileptic fits. In Delgado's review (1976) of brain stimulation in man, it is reported that coinciding with the electrical stimulation of a cerebral point is a positive change in the mood of the patient. There is an increase in the amount of talking and "positive expressions." However, the subject matter is not necessarily related, nor is it connected with a particular environmental stimulus. In one patient in which the increase in rate of speech was quantified, it was found that the frequency of words per minute was fivefold that during nonstimulation periods. Some of the positive mood changes are so intense as to qualify for descriptions of euphoria, referred to as the "Positive II" category by Sem-Jacobsen (1976). In addition to this euphoria, there may also be sexual thoughts induced by the electrical brain stimulation. Stimulation in the right temporal lobe, the fronto-temporal region, or the septal area in human patients may produce giggling, funny comments, sexual thoughts, and even direct sexual overtures. Since electrical stimulation of the brain in man can produce elation, flight of thoughts, rapid speech, and increased sexual thoughts and overtures, its study in animals should perhaps be regarded as a potentially useful model of mania.

In animals, brain stimulation applied to different sites can elicit in diverse species a variety of different responses, including locomotion, eating, drinking, and aggression (for a review, see Valenstein, 1976). Interestingly, the nature of the response performed appears to depend to some extent on the prior experience of the animal and upon stimuli present in the environment. Thus, Valenstein (1976) describes earlier work indicating how different behavioral responses could be obtained using the same parameters of electrical stimulation delivered to the same neuronanatomical locus. The response displayed often depended on the presence of an appropriate goal-object. In the presence of food, a rat might eat when stimulated. In the presence of water, it might drink. In the absence of goal-objects, increased locomotor activity was predominant. A further interesting feature of these results was that the elicited behavior often emerged only gradually with repeated testing. Valenstein (1976) pointed to the nonspecific consequences of the stimulation as producing activation or arousal, which could be channeled into different responses, depending on the animal's previous history and present circumstance. Once the response was performed initially, it was strengthened on subsequent trials, perhaps by a learning proces, until that response occupied the whole of the stimulation period from beginning to end. In his excellent review, Valenstein (1976) has also emphasised the rigid and inflexible forms of behavior observed when electrical stimulation of the brain is used to elicit eating (Hess, 1957) and drinking (Greer, 1955). It is interesting that there appears to be a superficial similarity between these elicited behaviors and the stereotypies elicited by amphetamine. In both cases it seems that the increased activation produced by the stimulation or by amphetamine is focused into the performance of certain responses, often related to the previous history of the animal.

Valenstein's argument that the behavioral effects of electrical stimulation depend on nonspecific activiation has been criticized because of the lack of neuroanatomical specificity of the stimulation itself. However, recent evidence has strongly supported his position, albeit in an indirect manner. Antelman and Szechtman (1975) found that merely pinching a rat's tail can be sufficient to elicit a variety of responses in a way similar to that of brain stimulation. The nature of the response exhibited depends on the presence of appropriate goal-objects and on previous experience (Koob, 1977; Sahakian and Robbins, 1977). Again, in the absence of suitable stimuli, or goal-objects, hyperactivity is generally observed (Valenstein, 1976).

The classical finding that linked the effects of brain stimulation to those of reward or reinforcement was, of course, that rats would learn a new response with brain stimulation as the reinforcer (Olds and Milner, 1954). The effect has been confirmed in a variety of vertebrate species. We have already described the use of this phenomenon in determining a "reinforcement threshold" suitable as an objective measure of "elation." Of crucial importance is the possible separation of these "affective" aspects of the stimulation from its response-eliciting properties. Such a distinction might have implications for hypotheses equating mood with activity level or for hypotheses attempting to dissociate these aspects of mania. Many of the behavioral measurements of ICSS fail to separate these entities; it is possible that a dissociation might have to depend on neuronanatomical or neuropharmacological considerations.

Neuropharmacological characteristics. We cannot attempt a detailed review of this complex topic, but must confine ourselves to demonstrating possible relationships of ICSS to mania and hyperactivity.

Early mapping of the neuroanatomical loci that supported ICSS revealed that high rates of responding were obtained from sites in the medial forebrain bundle, which are now known to correspond to the course of the ascending monoamine neurotransmitter systems (German and Bowden, 1974). A catecholaminergic hypothesis of ICSS is supported by the facilitatory effects of amphetamine-like drugs. However, these effects fail to differentiate between NA or DA mediation. The neuroleptic drugs haloperidol and pimozide, which block DA receptors rather specifically, also drastically reduce rates of responding with ICSS (Wauquier, 1976). A suggestion of DA involvement in ICSS is highly interesting in view of the connection of DA with amphetamine-induced locomotor activity and stereotyped behavior (Kelly et al., 1975). Further suggestive data are provided by the demonstration that dose-related increases in rates of responding with ICSS are paralleled by increases in stereotyped behavior (but not locomotor activity) with the psychomotor stimulant pipradrol (Sahakian and Koob, 1978). These findings tend to support the notion that the performance of motor acts may itself have affective correlates or consequences. It is interesting in this regard that depletion of striatal dopamine produced by injecting 6-hydroxydopamine centrally disrupts not only ICSS, but also behavior elicited by brain stimulation and tail pinch (Phillips and Fibiger, 1976; Antelman et al., 1975). Many of the neuropharmacological studies of the reinforcing correlates of ICSS have relied exclusively upon rate of responding as the dependent variable. This has made it difficult to dissociate the effect of various manipulations upon reinforcement from effects upon the performance of motor responses that express the rewarding properties of the stimulation. Phillips et al. (1976) tried to dissociate these two possible actions by utilizing a special preparation in which electrodes were implanted in the caudate nucleus (which supports quite high rates of ICSS). Lesions were made with 6-hydroxydopamine, either contralateral or ipsilateral to the electrode, in the region of the A9 DA cell bodies of the substantia nigra, pars compacta. These lesions produced a profound and rather selective depletion of striatal DA. Reduction in rates of responding with both types of lesion was initially observed. However, the response rate of the ipsilateral group fell almost to operant levels, whereas the response rate of the contralateral group recovered to prelesion levels. These results were interpreted as showing that the DA system was involved in both motor and reward functions. A motor deficit was expressed as the initial general reduction in responding, regardless of lesion site. The attenuation of reinforcement or reward was exhibited by the prolonged reduction in responding in the ipsilateral group alone, since it was argued that a motor impairment should have affected the ipsilateral and contralateral groups equally. An analogous result has recently been found by Koob et al. (1978), where ipsilateral lesions of DA cell bodies in the ventral tegmental area produced long-lasting reductions in responding either in the ipsilateral lateral hypothalamus or in the ipsilateral locus coeruleus. It is interesting to note that the locus coeruleus is the origin of cell bodies of the dorsal NA bundle; hence it would apper that "noradrenergic" self-stimulation might have to depend on dopamine systems for its expression. It would perhaps be reasonable to inject an antimanic agent, such as lithium, in small doses either ipsilateral or contralateral to a stimulating electrode to explore the possibilities of a similar dissociation in the effects of this drug.

There have, in fact, been comparatively few studies of the effects of lithium on ICSS. We have already mentioned the study of Cassens and Mills, which showed that an acute dose of lithium (1 mEq/kg) produced elevations in threshold 0–2 hrs and 24–26 hrs following injection, with the later testing period providing larger effects. Other studies (Ramsey et al., 1972; Liebman and Segal, 1976; Edelson et al., 1976) have also found initial transient reductions in the effects of lithium upon rate of responding with ICSS. In the last case, greater decremental effects were found in rats with the higher rates. Interestingly, there was a tolerance effect with chronic lithium in the studies of Liebman and Segal (1976) and Edelson et al. (1976). It is unclear whether this tolerance was of a simple pharmacological type or due to behavioral adaptation. These findings, however, have obvious implications for ICSS as a model of the "elation" aspects of mania, since mania itself responds to chronic, rather than acute, lithium treatment. There are several ways in which this work can be extended. For example, would tolerance to the effects of lithium be seen with a "threshold" measure of ICSS raher than with a rate measure? By our own criterion, the former measure is a more valid index of "elation." In addition, would the "tolerance" effects be seen at all neuro-anatomical loci supporting ICSS? The studies reviewed have utilized placements in or around the medial forebrain bundle, including sites in the substantia nigra (Liebman and Segal, 1976).

Several other antimanic agents affect ICSS in a manner generally similar to their effects upon hyperactivity. For example, cholinergic muscarinic agents such as pilocarpine and the cholinesterase inhibitor physostigmine have a depressant effect upon ICSS in rats (Wauquier, 1976). These results serve to emphasize the interactive relationships among the various neurotransmitters in control of ICSS. It is hardly surprising, in addition, that ICSS can produce changes in activity in several neurotransmitter systems, including acetylcholine, as well as in noradrenaline and dopamine projections (Pradhan, 1976).

Recent work has even suggested the possibility of a serotoninergic self-stimlation site in the raphe nucleus (Miliaressis et al., 1975).

Social Isolation

The rearing of rats and other species in social isolation produces a syndrome in which hyperactivity is a major component, whether measured in the open field or in photocell cages (Morgan, 1973; Syme, 1973; Valzelli, 1973; Sahakian et al., 1975; Konrad and Melzack, 1975). Rats reared in isolation are initially more active when placed in a novel environment and also take longer to habituate to that environment than rats reared in social groups (Sahakian et al., 1975; Einon et al., 1975). The behavioral mechanisms underlying the hyperactivity have not been determined. It may be related to a heightened reactivity to novel stimuli (Konrad and Melzack, 1975; Sahakian et al., 1977) or to an inability to inhibit responding (Morgan et al., 1975). Although the question of whether isolation-rearing enhances or reduces exploration is unresolved (Luchins and Forgus, 1955; Lore and Levowitz, 1966; Sahakian et al., 1977; Einon and Morgan, 1976) there is some evidence that isolated rats may explore novel stimuli for as long as group-reared rats, but exhibit many more exploratory episodes, perhaps due to competing hyperactivity (Sahakian et al., 1977). The combination of hyperactivity and an inability to complete responses makes the isolation-reared rat a potential model of mania.

As we have seen with so many of the hyperactivity syndromes that we have discussed, isolates often exhibit stereotyped forms of behavior (Bronfenbrenner, 1968), which may also be reflected in a greater persistence or perseveration seen in operant tasks (Morgan et al., 1975). Interestingly, Sahakian et al. (1975) showed that isolated rats also exhibit enhanced sniffing stereotypies induced by low doses of amphetamine-like drugs, suggesting a possible increase in the functional activity of the dopaminergic system. This hypothesis is supported by both behavioral and neurochemical evidence. For example, isolation-reared rats exhibited shorter latencies to initiate licking or gnawing of food or woodchips with tail-pinch stimulation (Sahakian and Robbins, 1977), a form of behavior believed to be dependent on the nigrostriatal DA projection (Antelman et al., 1975). The isolated rats were also less susceptible to the antagonistic effects of the dopamine antagonist α-flupenthixol. Kostowski and Czonkowski (1973) also showed that isolation-housed rats were less susceptible to the cataleptic effects of haloperidol and chlorpromazine. Considering studies that have actually made direct measurements of DA changes, Segal et al. (1973) found evidence for an increase in tyrosine hydroxylase activity in the neostriatum, which is highly suggestive of increases in DA activity, and Thoa et al. (1977) have detected increased DA turnover in the olfactory tubercle of isolated rats.

On the other hand, Weinstock et al. (1978) found no differences in DA turnover after inhibition of catecholamine synthesis with α-methyl-p-tyrosine in isolates that had just been exposed to an open field, compared with socially reared rats that had been similarly exposed. Interestingly, the α-methyl-p-tyrosine pretreatment produced a selective reduction in activity of the isolates. These authors have linked the increased open-field activity of isolates with changes in noradrenaline turnover. In isolates kept in their home cages, there was a reduction in both forebrain and hindbrain NA turnover, compared with controls. For isolates exposed to the open-field situation, however, noradrenaline turnover in the forebrain was greatly increased, compared with the socially reared controls. Stolk et al. (1974) similarly found increased NA turnover in the brain stem after isolation of rats, but Thoa et al. found reductions in NA turnover in 6 out of 23 brain regions studied. The reasons for some of these discrepancies are not clear. It is interesting that isolation was imposed at different developmental stages in the studies of Thoa et al. and Stolk et al. (24 days and 70 days of age, respectively).

If socially deprived rats do show chronic reduction in NA turnover in normal living conditions, it is possible that a supersensitivity of NA receptors develops (Weinstock et al., 1978). In support of this hypothesis, Speiser and Weinstock (1974) found that isolates were more sensitive to the stimulant effects of isoprenaline on peripheral β adrenoreceptors. The increased activity of isolates can also be antagonized by intraventricular 6-hydroxydopamine and by the noradrenaline receptor antagonists propanolol and phenoxybenzamine (Weinstock et al., 1976). Finally, Weinstock et al. (1978) used chronic amphetamine administration in an attempt to "desensitize" supersensitive receptors in isolates. As predicted, the chronic amphetamine treatment selectively reduced the activity of the isolates, although it is not certain to what extent this effect depended on NA receptors. Presumably, DA receptors would also be affected by this treatment. The findings of changes in noradrenaline turnover in isolates may at first sight be difficult to reconcile with other work suggesting that the functional activity of the DA may be altered by social deprivation. However, the possibility of DA-NA interaction should not be ignored. There is a precedent of another form of behavior—the activation of eating by tail-pinch stimulation, producing changes in NA rather than DA turnover, and yet still being dependent on the functioning of the DA nigrostriatal projection (Antelman et al., 1975).

In addition to producing changes in reactivity, isolation in several species produces increases in aggressive behavior. This aggression in rats may also be somewhat repetitive and "compulsive" in nature (Valzelli, 1977). These traits are interesting in view of the heightened irritability and stereotypy of manic individuals. It is possible that the aggression is related to the increased reactivity of the isolate and depends on changes in NA turnover, as described above. However, decreased serotonin turnover has been found both in mice made aggressive by social isolation and in rats that display muricide, or mouse-killing (Garattini et al., 1969; Valzelli and Garattini, 1972). In addition, Segal et al. (1973) have found decreases in septal tyryptophan hydrozylase activity.

Some of the features of the isolation "syndrome" described do not make it a compelling model for mania. For example, the induction of hyperactivity is critically tied to housing and developmental variables. The heightened activity develops after a week and persists into adulthood in rats isolated during their third week of age (Sahakian, 1976; Einon and Morgan, 1977), but is not apparent in rats housed in isolation for the first time when adult for comparable periods of time (Einon and Morgan, 1977). Nevertheless, some of the features of the isolation "syndrome" can be precipitated by housing mature animals in isolation. This is true for the great increase in latency shown by isolates in emerging from a small enclosure into an adjacent open field (Einon and Morgan, 1977), and also for the increased irritability and aggression exhibited. It is possible, therefore, that the increased hyperactivity and irritability of the isolate may be dissociable behavioral effects.

Is is not known if isolates show reductions in reinforcement threshold, although it is interesting that isolation-reared rats tend to respond more in operant situations, exhibit increases in "anticipatory" responding (Morgan and Einon, 1975), and also gain weight and eat more than socially reared animals (Morgan, 1973). For our purposes it is also unfortunate that there seem to have been no systematic comparative studies of the effects of lithium and neuroleptics in isolates. The isolation-rearing model remains interesting because of the fact that variation in early social experience in animals can apparently induce an enduring hyperactivity syndrome in the mature organism. Moreover, this hyperactivity persists even when isolates are rehoused with socially reared rats (Einon and Morgan, 1977).

Discussion

Perhaps Schou is right, and there are no compelling animal models of mania. We have subjected the patient reader to descriptions mainly of highly active rodents indulging in diverse forms of behavior, including running, sniffing, head dipping, fighting, jumping in response to shock or loud noise, intracranial self-stimulation, and all manner of stereotyped activities. This plethora of hyperactivity syndromes has resulted from treatment with drugs and brain lesions, and from variations in past experience and present contingencies of reinforcement. Many of the syndromes reviewed share features that might be said to characterize human mania, but few of them meet the criteria we stipulated to define an adequate model. This discussion will deal with the issues arising from comparison and evaluation of these models, and with their implications for psychotic behavior in general.

Comparison of different models. It became clear to us when reviewing the different hyperactive syndromes that this discussion should not become a vague sifting process by which some models were discarded as irrelevant and others, by default, were acclaimed as authentic and deserving of further study. We could select positive features of many models, for example, of amphetamine and morphine as possibly representing different forms of hyperactivity, of electrical stimulation of the brain because of the types of response it can elicit in human subjects, and of septal lesions that seem to enhance the "affective" responses of the organism without necessarily producing an accompanying hyperkinesis. At this early stage or research, however, it seems more prudent to discuss the issues arising from collective consideration of the models and to try to devise general principles for conducting further research.

Behavioral analysis of the different hyperactivity syndromes has not proceded in a particularly systematic fashion. The effects of certain drugs and of various limbic lesions have been most thoroughly analyzed, but the lack of uniformity of analysis with respect to other models renders comparison difficult. There are three main problems that impinge on human mania:

1. The behavioral nature of hyperactivty
2. The significance of stereotyped behavior
3. The relationships of hyperactivity with "elation," "irritability," and reactivity in general

Hyperactivity. One standpoint from which to examine hyperactivity is to consider the complete repertoire of response types that the organism can perform. In the two simplest cases, hyperactivity can be conceived as increasing rates of responding in any one type of response, or as rapid transitions from one response to another. These simplifications depend on the breadth of meaning encompassed in "response type." There is no difficulty when considering topographically dissimilar responses, such as running and grooming for the rat. Then, the hyperactivity produced by increasing doses of amphetamine might reasonably be distinguished from the hyperactivity produced by morphine. Amphetamine tends to increase the frequency of some response types, but not others (Norton, 1973), whereas morphine has been said to increase the frequency of many types of response (Ayhan and Randrup, 1973).

A problem occurs, however, when one begins to "split the response" into its constituent motor elements. Considering a respone such as locomotion, an organism displaying continuous running may be said to be performing a restricted class of motor outputs unrelated to changing exteroceptive conditions. This form of response is exemplified by the several cases of "automatic" locomotion mentioned in this review. On the other hand, locomotor activity might be elicited by diverse stimuli impinging on the organism that cause shifts in the vector of movement. This continual shifting is presumably at the core of the notion of "distractability," a manic characteristic. Between these two extremes is the case of "stimulus tracking," in which the organism is involved in following a mobile but constant stimulus, which may itself move in a continuous or discontinuous manner. These two examples seem to contain elements of hyperactivity and of "stereotypy." The stereotypy may be seen, however, as a more cognitive form than the repetition of individual motor elements.

Separation of these possibilities has to depend on the controlled variation of the exteroceptive environment of the organism, and on consideration of its past experience of such changes. Unfortunately, analysis at this level has not been carried very far in animal studies of "mania" nor in clinical accounts of human mania. Interest has focused instead on the use of rating scales of mood and activity levels as means of measuring the severity of mania. While such scales provide very interesting and worthwhile information, we feel that some benefit might also accrue by analyzing the external structure of manic behavior. Such an analysis, although obviously complex and difficult, would facilitate comparison with animal models, if these were treated in the same way.

Stereotypy. Stereotypy is a description of behavior emphasizing repetition of invariant sequences of responding. The term is often used to denote the repetition of simple motor responses, but as noted above and elsewhere (Mattysse and Silverman, 1978), it can also be used to refer to more complex response sequences in both animals and man.

Review of the hyperactivity syndromes described suggests that the majority show clear evidence of a selective enhancement of certain responses. We would like to argue that this selective increase is the first step on the path to behavioral stereotypy. Lyon and Robbins (1975) have suggested that amphetamine stereotypy is the culmination of a process of an increasing rate of responding within a decreasing number of types of response.

It is remarkable that many of the hyperactive syndromes we have described show signs of stereotypy. The amphetamine stereotypy is well known, but the repetitive head dipping induced by mixtures of amphetamine and chlordiazepoxide, the "rigid" or persistent behavior sometimes induced by brain stimulation or social isolation, the behavior of rats treated with MAO inhibitors and tryptophan, and the "automatic" locomotion of hippocampal rats may similarly be described as stereotyped. Even drugs such as morphine and scopolamine, which produce increases in locomotor activity but are not noted for producing behavioral stereotypy, may induce such behavior under certain doses and conditions (Fog, 1970; Sahakian, 1976).

Given that stereotypy occurs in so many animal hyperactivity syndromes, it seems unsurprising that it should occur in mania, albeit in complex fashion: "The movements may then in certain circumstances be very monotonous and senseless and may occasionally give quite the impression of compulsion." [Kraepelin, 1921, p. 55.] It seems significant that stereotypy generally follows temporally the more obvious forms of hyperactivity. Fentress (1976) has suggested, in an ethological context, that repetition of responding requires less stimulus processing and may serve an adaptive function to reduce a barrage of input from very many sensory channels. Another, perhaps related, notion (Lyon and Robbins, 1975) is that stereotypy results from a competition among responses as the time for their execution via the motor system becomes progressively constrained. It is therefore easier to repeat the same response than to shift to another one. Thus, once the motor system "locks on" to the performance of a response, it is repeated at a high rate to the exclusion of other competing behavior. What, then, determines which programmed responses gain access to the motor system? Two major determinants would seem to be, first, that responses of small amplitude and short duration will tend to survive more readily than complicated sequences of behavior, and second, that responses that have some special significance to the organism, perhaps due to previous training and experience, may obtain preferential access. It is this latter feature that allows some of the stereotyped behavior of rats treated with stimulants to have been part of an apparently motivated sequence of behavior (e.g., Robbins, 1976), and perhaps stereotypy in the manic subject is similarly determined.

Summary of hyperactivity models. According to the theoretical views described above, it may also be possible to reconcile the two different models of hyperactivity represented by morphine and amphetamine—rapid transitions between responses or selective increases in certain responses, respectively. Perhaps these two forms of activation differ mainly in the quantitative sense and can be represented along a single continuum of "activation." A tendency to switch rapidly and randomly between responses at low to intermediate levels of activation may give way to selective increases and stereotypy at higher levels. Fentress (1976) has noted that when one is instructed to make random finger movements at an accelerating rate, repetitions of movement of a single finger become prevalent.

A parsimonious view of activation at least has some advantages when trying to account for the results of Norton et al. (1976), which show that the structure of hyperactivity is similar across a range of treatments, causing widely differing brain damage. It seems possible that the common structure of the hyperactivity syndromes is expressed through a single mechanism, regardless of etiology. This possibility has implications for therapy in mania, as we shall discuss below.

Relationships of hyperactivity to affective states. To what extent is mood dependent on movement? This fundamental question is difficult to begin to answer. Some theorists have believed that there is a definite relationship between the two. For example, "The low tone of the muscle in sadness as contrasted with the high muscle tone in joy appears to play an important role in the production of these psychic states" [Gellhorn, 1970, p. 62].

Recent evidence has cast doubt on an intrinsic association of "elation" with manic behavior (Murphy and Beigel, 1974). From our survey of the animal literature, however, we could find few examples in which treatments that produced hyperactivity were not accompanied by reductions in reinforcement threshold. Rather, in the cases of amphetamine, morphine, and septal lesions, there seemed to be reduction in this threshold, although in the case of the serotoninergic hyperactivity syndrome (Herberg and Franklin, 1976), there may have been a dissociation. It is also remarkable that many of the central structures implicated in mediating reinforcement, such as the catecholaminergic neurotransmitter pathways, are the same pathways that seem also to mediate "activiation" or "arousal."

These considerations lead to the notion that affect is not a cause of motor behavior, but a consequence or correlate of it. The former possibility would suggest that affect is tied more closely to the performance of motor responses, the latter that affective responses are determined more or less in parallel with motor ones. We find some support for these speculations from Sack's observations (1973) of postencephalitic Parkinsonian patients treated with L-dopa, when remarkable improvements in motor performance were accompanied by equally astounding changes in affect, and also from Rylander's observations (1971) of the apparently "pleasant" hedonic correlations of the punding activities of amphetamine addicts. We note also that stereotyped behavior in animals may have "affective" correlates in that its performance may be tied to previous contingencies of reinforcement (Robbins, 1976).

Whereas "elation" often seems connected with repetition of responding, "irritability" seems to be associated with interruptions of behavior, involving switching between ongoing responses. Therefore, the threshold of exteroceptive stimulation required to elicit a response may be reduced by low levels of "activation," which cause the organism to switch from its ongoing response. At higher levels of "activation," a stimulus may not elicit a response so readily because of competing stereotyped behavior. If the stimulus is sufficiently intense or salient, however, it may interrupt the stereotypy and elicit an even stronger response than that seen at lower levels of activation. The huge increase in startle amplitude caused by large doses of amphetamine sufficient to cause intense stereotypy (Davis et al., 1975) can be explained in these terms.

Although these ideas are probably too simple to apply in the clinical situation, they may suggest that an empirical analysis of manic behavior would be an important supplement to the usual ratings of activity and mood.

Some of the most severe objections to a relatively unitary hypothesis of activation that we have discussed perhaps derive from studies that attempt to dissociate different aspects of activation, or "affective" changes from motor ones, by manipulation of the central nervous system. We now deal with these and their implications for therapy in mania.

Neural mechanisms and implications for treatment of mania. The behavioral account of activation that we have described of course depends upon the concerted action of several mechanisms or neurotransmitters. In general, as we should expect, many of the hyperactivity syndromes depend on dopamine. Even the serotoninergic hyperactivity syndrome of Green and Grahame-Smith (1974) can be antagonized by chlorpromazine, indicating a possible DA involvement. However, recent work (Marsden and Curzon, 1976) seems to show that a patent DA antagonist, pimozide, cannot block this syndrome. This anomaly is of great importance, since Norton's formulation (1976) of a general hyperactivity model suggests that there is a "final common pathway" involved in the expression of hyperactivity induced by diverse means, and we should expect this "final common pathway" to be crucially dependent on dopaminergic neurotransmission. It is, of course, a truism that no behavior is "coded" by a single neurotransmitter. It is a balance of activity between them that is crucial. There are several modulating influences on dopamine systems, including gabaminergic, cholinergic, and, probably, noradrenergic and serotoninergic contributions (Stadler et al., 1973; Bartholini and Stadler, 1977; Iversen, 1977; Kelly, 1977). In general, the modulatory influences are antagonistic, but doubtless there are exceptions, and the nature of DA-NA interactions remains controversial (Antelman and Caggiula, 1977). The major role of these other pathways might be to regulate a flow of sensory information to the dopamine pathways, which determine response repetition or response switching. The increasing activity in dopamine pathways might also cause "rebound" activity in the other systems, which thus produce the "affective correlates" or consequences of responding. Again, these are obviously vague and unsubstantiated speculations, but the fact remains that investigators have frequently tried to dissociate the actions of various drugs on manic symptoms. It is often implied, for example, that lithium acts rather specifically on mood, whereas the neuroleptics produce a general sedation or hypokinetic effect (Schou, 1968). In the studies we reviewed, however, it was somewhat surprising to find that lithium generally reduced all forms of hyperactivity, no matter how they were generated. The main exception was that of Furukawa et al. (1975), who found that lithium did not apparently antagonize hyperactivity induced by tetrabenazine following MAO inhibition, although comparable levels of activity induced by methamphetamine were reduced. This exception to the rule is most interesting; is it possible, for example, that the treatment with tetrabenazine does not produce "affective" changes by reducing the reinforcement threshold? Another issue raised by this study is the effect of lithium upon low levels of activity. Lithium produced some increases in activity reduced by tetra-benazine, an interesting finding in view of the "anti-depressant" action of lithium (Schou, 1968). It is known that many drug effects depend on the control rate of responding (Dews, 1958). Perhaps some of the effects of lithium are rate-dependent, producing rate-reducing effects upon high control rates of responding and rate-increasing effects upon low control rates. It seems surprising that no one appears to have measured the effects of lithium upon performance engendered by a fixed-interval schedule of reinforcement, which generates both high and low levels of responding.

There are two reasons, however, for believing that lithium might have some specific actions in animals. First, although it reduces hyperactivity induced by many treatments, its effect upon stereotyped behavior, at least of certain forms, is less certain. For example, lithium reduces the "repetitive head dipping" produced by mixtures of amphetamine and chlordiazepoxide and the "stereotyped hyperactivity" in mice induced by morphine. However, lithium has been reported to have no effect on, or to exacerbate, stereotypy induced by amphetamine (see Table 1). If this is confirmed, lithium is one of the few drugs studied that seem to exert differential effects upon locomotor activity and stereotypy induced by amphetamine. This dissocation may have important implications for the use of amphetamine-induced activity and stereotypy as models for mania and schizophrenia, respectively. It also seems important in this regard that lithium in conjunction with monoamine oxidase inhibition actually mimics the serotoninergic "hyperactivity" syndrome (Grahame-Smith and Green, 1974). A second finding that points to a specific action of lithium is the discovery that a low dose of lithium can potentiate the effects of a low dose of neuroleptic in producing reductions in responding in rats under a shock-avoidance schedule (Ahlenius and Engel, 1974). This potentiation suggests that lithium does not reduce hyperactivity in the same manner as neuroleptics, and supports the view that these drugs act differently in the control of mania (Schou, 1968). What is the nature of the different effect? It is interesting that another drug having a somewhat complementary effect upon amphetamine-induced locomotor activity and stereotypy is PCPA, an inhibitor of serotonin synthesis. Lithium antagonizes the increases in activity in an open field produced by PCPA (Smith, 1975), and so perhaps the actions of lithium can be linked to its effects upon serotoninergic neurotransmission, as Knapp and Mandell (1975) have suggested. These authors have argued strongly that lithium antagonizes the effects upon serotoninergic neurones of three agents (cocaine, morphine, and ethanol) that induce hyperactivity.

Before leaving the important topic of lithium, we are bound to report that many of the effects of lithium we have described in animals are obtained with acute, rather than chronic, administration. It would seem most useful to develop an animal model that responded to chronic, but not acute, lithium treatment in view of the clinical dichotomy between these forms of treatment for mania.

Other agents such as physostigmine have now been reported to have "selective" effects upon features of mania. Davis et al. (1977) have suggested that this drug produces a selective "rate-reducing" effect without particularly influencing the affective features of mania. It would be most interesting to see if lithium and physostigmine produce a potentiation of effect in antagonizing animal hyperactivity syndromes.

There have been few animal studies that have attempted to dissociate different aspects of activation, or of activation and reinforcement, by pharmacological means. Two of the most important dissociations involved have both involved dopamine. Kelly et al. (1975) showed tht amphetamine hyperactivity and stereotypy were mediated by mesolimbic and striatal DA mechanisms respectively. It remains possible that postmortem biochemical investigation of mania will find DA changes within the mesolimbic areas. However, the true significance of the animal findings will not become clear until the nature of the interaction between these two forebrain DA mechanisms is elucidated. Two possibilities, at least, can be envisaged: The first possibility is that these two DA systems control the execution of different responses—for example, the mesolimbic A10 projection controls locomotion, whereas the nigrostriatal projection controls sniffing, head movements, licking, and gnawing. A second possibility is that the two systems are activated in a sequential manner, with the mesolimbic activation preceding the striatal activation. Neither of these possibilities necessarily contradicts the model for behavioral activation advanced earlier.

A second interesting dissociation concerns the role of the dopamine system in mediating "motor" or "motivational" effects of brain stimulation. Ingenious experiments involving unilateral stimulation and unilateral 6-OHDA lesions of the dopamine systems seem to implicate the dopaminergic projections in both motor control and reinforcement (Koob et., 1978; Phillips et al., 1976). However, no functional distinction was made between the two DA projections (A9 and A10) in these studies, and it seems more fascinating that DA should be mediating *both* motor and motivational effects than that there is a dissociation between these two behavioral mechanisms.

Manic-depression and schizophrenia. We are already overdrawn on our credit for speculation, and so we remain content to make a few general points about how the relationships between mania, depression, and schizophrenia can even begin to be analyzed with animal models. While hyperactivity in animals has good "face" validity as a model of mania, it is unclear what an animal model of schizophrenia should entail. Bleuler (1950) stated that stereotypy is one of the most striking external manifestations of schizophrenia, and it seems that if this term is used in a broad sense to cover cognitive phenomena as well as motor ones, then a review of the classical schizophrenic symptoms, such as thought disorder, in these terms might be interesting. It seems appropriate, given that schizophrenia is probably a more debilitating disorder than manic-depression, that stereotypy also represents a higher level of activation than does heightened levels of locomotor activity, being caused, for example, by higher doses of drugs.

What seems to have been ignored, however, is the progression and modification of hyperactivity and stereotypy over time. Chronic amphetamine treatment produces behavior in animals that progressively loses contact with the original conditions or contingencies that established it. The behavior may also become increasingly "fragmented" (Ellinwood et al., 1972). In this sense it resembles the progressive deterioration of chronic schizophrenia.

Mania also shows a course of progressive deterioration. Thus, the initial grandiosity and elation may give way eventually to increased hostility and paranoid delusions (Carlson and Goodwin, 1973). By resorting to chronic regimens and maintaining hyperactive behavior for long periods in animals, it is possible that a similar deterioration will be observed that also contains "depressed" episodes. We have alluded already to the "post-amphetamine depression" found in rats (Leith and Barrett, 1975). In neurochemical terms, this depression could be correlated with reductions in monoaminergic activity caused by the prolonged release and subsequent depletion of these neurotransmitters. This depletion could lead to the development of "supersensitive" receptors (cf. MRC Brain Metabolism Unit, 1972; Weinstock et al., 1978), which may intermittently be stimulated by the release of the newly synthesised neurotransmitter. When is the neurotransmitter released? As Antelman and Caggiula (1977) have suggested, it is plausible that the release occurs under conditions of stress or "activation." In this case, a manic episode is observed that is correlated with the stimulation of supersensitive receptors. Precisely which neurotransmitter systems are involved is difficult to specify. Antelman and Caggiula themselves talk in terms of NA-DA interactions, with NA regulating the activity of the DA system. They predict a swing from suppressed to potentiated behavior when animals depleted of noradrenaline are exposed to an activating environment. It is possible that the data of Weinstock et al. (1978) suggesting the existence of supersensitive NA receptors in isolated rats might also be reconciled with this type of approach. It is also possible, of course, that the hypothesis of Kety (1971) concernig serotonin-DA interactions is to be explained in a similar way. Neither of these schemes severely contradict the hypothesis that the major role of NA or serotonin might be to regulate the flow of sensory information to the DA pathways that initiate behavior.

In a more behavioral vein, the depressed phase of bipolar depression might be caused by "behavioral contrast" from the elation of the manic episode. The therapeutic effect of lithium on depressive episodes in manic-depression may then be expected to work indirectly on depression by the blockade of the manic episode. The "contrast" effect in turn could be due to lack of synchronization between supply and demand for synthesized neurotrans- mitter.

In this chapter on mania, we have at times been discursive ourselves in describing its animal models. This is not surprising in view of our present paucity of knowledge. The models have failed in their most ambitious aim, that of specifying causation. This finding itself is significant, since mania probably has a diverse etiology. The models offer far more in contributing to the development of new pharmacological therapy for mania. They also supply the clinician with new ideas, enabling him to cut the "apple" that is psychosis in different ways, and to divide it into more palatable portions.

ACKNOWLEDGMENTS

We would like to thank Dr. A.V.P. MacKay for providing salient references, and Dr. M. E. Lewis for similar help and for his critical comments about the manuscript.

REFERENCES

Ahlenius, S., and Engel, J. Potentiation by lithium of the haloperidol-induced behavioral suppression. *J. Neural Trans.* 35, 83–86 (1974).

Antelman, S.M., and Caggiula, A.R. Norepinerphrine-dopamine interactions and behavior. *Science* 195, 646–653 (1977).

Antelman, S.M., and Szechtman, H. Tail pinch induces eating in sated rats which appears to depend on nigrostriatal dopamine. *Science* 189, 731–733 91975).

Antelman, S.M., Szechtman, H., Chin, P., and Fisher, A.E. Tail pinch-induced eating, gnawing and licking behavior: Dependence on the nigro-striatal dopamine system. *Brain Res.* 99, 319–337 (1975).

A.P.A. Diagnostic and Statistical Manual of Mental Disorders, 3rd ed. Draft published by the American Psychiatric Assoication, Washington, D.C. (April 15, 1977).

Arnfred, T., and Randrup, A. Cholinergic mechanism in brain inhibiting amphetamine-induced stereotyped behaviour. *Acta. Pharmacol. Toxicol.* 26, 384–394 (1968).

Atrens, D.M., von Vietinghoff-Riesch, F., and Der Darabetian, A. Reinforcement contrast effects on the rewarding and aversive components of intracranial stimulation. *Learn. & Motivat.* 4, 397–404 (1973).

Atrens, D.M. von Vietinghoff-Riesch, F., Der Karabetian, A., and Masliyah, E. Modulation of reward and aversion process in the rat diencephalon by amphetamine. *Amer. J. Physiol.* 226, 874–880 (1974).

Ayhan, I., and Randrup, A. Behavioral and pharmacological studies on morphine-induced excitation of rats: Possible relation to brain catecholamines. *Psychopharmacologia (Berlin)* 29, 317–328 (1973).

Babbini, M., and Davis, W. M. Time-dose relationships for locomotor activity effects of morphine after acute or repeated treatment. *Br. J. Pharmacol.* 46 213–224 (1972).

Baltzer, V., and Weiskrantz, L. Negative and positive behavioural contrast in the same animals. *Nature (Longon)* 228, 581–582 (1970).

Bartholini, G., and Stadler, H. Evidence for an intrastriatal GABA-ergic influence on dopamine neurones of the cat. *Neuropharmacology* 16, 343–347 (1977).

Bartholini, G., Blum, J.E., and Pletscher, A. Dopa-induced locomotor stimulation after inhibition of extracerebral decarboxylase. *J. Pharm. Pharmacol.* 21, 297–300 (1969).

Batchelor, I.R.C. *Henderson and Gillespie's Textbook of Psychiatry.* 10th ed., Oxford Univ. Press, London (1969), pp. 210–245.

Beatty, W.W., and Schwartzbaum, J.S. Enhanced reactivity to quinine and saccharine solutions following septal lesions in the rat. *Psychon. Sci.* 8, 483–484 (1967).

Beatty, W.W., and Schwarzbaum, J.S. Consummatory behavior for sucrose following septal lesions in the rat. *J. Compr. Physiol. Psychol.* 65, 93–102 (1968).

Bleuler, E. *Dementia Praecox.* International Universities Press, New York (1950).

Bobon, J., Pinchard, A., Collard, J., and Bobon, D.P. Clinical classification of neuroleptics with special reference to their anti-manic, anti-autistic and ataraxic properties. *Compr. Psychiat.* 13, 123–131 (1972).

Bowers, M.B. Jr., Heninger, G.R., and Gerbode, F.A. Cerebrospinal fluid 5-hydroxyindoleacetic acid and homovanillic acid in psychiatric patients. *Int. J. Neurophramacol.* 8, 255–262 (1969).

Brady, J.V., and Nauta, W.J.H. Subcortical mechanisms in emotional behavior: affective changes following septal forebrain lesions in the albino rat. *J. Compr. Physiol. Psychol.* 46, 339–346 (1953).

Breese, G.R., Cooper, B.R., and Mueller, R.A. Evidence for involvement of 5-hydroxytryptamine in the actions of amphetamine. *Br. J. Pharmacol.* 52, 307–414 (1974).

Bronfenbrenner, U. Early deprivation in a cross-species analysis. In *Early Experience and Behavior.* G. Newton and S. Levine, eds, Charles C. Thomas, Springfield, Illinois (1968), pp. 627–724.

Brown, J.S., Kalish, H.I., Farber, I.E. Conditioned fear as revealed by magnitude of a startle response to an auditory stimulus. *J. Exp. Psychol.* 41, 317–328 (1951).

Bunney, W.E., Brodie, K.H., Murphy, D.L., and Goodwin, F.K. Studies of alpha-methyl-para-tyrosine, L-dopa and L-tryptophan in depression and mania. *Am. J. Psychiat.* 127, 872–881 (1971).

Buus Lassen, J., and Squires, R.F. Potentiation of nialamide-induced hypermotility in mice by lithium and the 5-HT uptake inhibitors chlorimipramine and FG 4963. *Neuropharmacology* 15, 665–668 (1976).

Cade, J.F. Lithium salts in the treatment of manic excitement. *Med. J. Australia* 36, 349–352 (1949).

Carlson, G., and Goodwin, F.K. The stages of mania: A longitudinal analysis of the manic episode. *Arch. Gen. Psychiat.* 28, 221–228 (1973).

Carroll, B.J., and Sharp, P.T. Rubidium and lithium: Opposite effects on amine-mediated excitement. *Science* 172, 1355–1357 (1971).

Carroll, B.J., and Sharp, P.T. Monoamine mediation of the morphine-induced activation of mice. *Br. J. Pharmacol.* 46, 124–139 (1972).

Carlton, P. Cholinergic mechanisms in the control of behavior by the brain. *Psychiatr. Review.* 70, 19–39 (1963).

Cassens, G.P., and Mills, A.W. Lithium and amphetamine: Opposite effects on threshold of intracranial reinforcement. *Psychopharmacologia (Berlin)* 30, 283–290 (1973).

Colburn, R.W., Goodwin, F.K., Bunney, W.E., and Davis, J.M. Effect of lithium on the uptake of noradrenaline by synaptosomes. *Nature (London)* 215, 1395–1397 (1967).

Connell, P.H. *Amphetamine Psychosis.* Maudsley Monographs No. 5. Chapman & Hall, London (1958).

Coppen, A. Role of serotonin in affective disorders. In *Serotonin and Behavior,* J. Barchas and E. Usdin, eds. Academic Press, New York (1973) pp. 523–527.

Corman, C.D., Meyer, P.M., and Meyer, D.R. Open field activity and exploration in rats with septal and amygdaloid lesions. *Brain Res.* 5, 469–476 (1967).

Corrodi, H., Fuxe, K., and Schou, M. The effects of prolonged lithium administration on cerebral monoamine neurons in the rat. *Life Sci.* 8, 643–651 (1969).

Corrodi, H., Fuxe, K., Hokfelt, T., and Schou, M. Effect of lithium on cerebral monoamine neurons. *Psychopharmacologia (Berlin),* 11, 345–353 (1967).

Costall, B., Naylor, R.J., and Olley, J.E. On the involvement of the caudate-putamen, globus pallidus and substantia nigra with neuroleptic and cholinergic modification of locomotor activity. *Neuropharmacology* 11, 317–330 (1972).

Cox, C., Harrison-Read, P.E., Steinberg, H. and, Tomkiewicz, M. Lithium attenuates drug-induced hyperactivity in rats. *Nature (London)* 232, 336–338 (1971).

Creese, I., and Iversen, S.D. The pharmacological and anatomical substrates of the amphetamine response in the rat. *Brain Res.* 83, 419–436, (1975).

Creese, I., Burt, D.R., and Snyder, S.H. Dopamine receptor binding predicts clinical and pharmacological potencies of anit-schizophrenic drugs. *Science,* 192, 481–483 (1976).

Crespi, L.P. Quantitative variation of incentive and reinforcement in the white rat. *Am. J. Psychol.* 55, 467–517 (1942).

Crowley, T.J. Dose-dependent faciliation or suppression of rat fighting by methamphetamine, phenobarbital, or imipramine. *Psychopharmacologia (Berlin)* 27, 213–222 (1972).

David, O., Clark, J., and Voeller, K. Lead and hyperactivity. *Lancet* II, 900–903 (1972).

Davies, C., Sanger, D.J., Steinberg, H., Tomkiewicz, M., and U'Pritchard, D.C. Lithium and α-methyl-p-tyrosine prevent "manic" activity in rodents. *Psychopharmacologia,* 36, 263–274 (1974).

Davis, J.M., Janowsky, D.S., and El-Yousef, K. Pharmacology—the biology of lithium. In *Lithium: Its role in psychiatric research and treatment,* S. Gershon and B. Shopsin, eds. Plenum, New York (1973) pp. 167–181.

ANIMAL MODELS 205

Davis, J.M., Janowsky, D.S., Tamminga, C., and Smith, R.C. Cholinergic mechanisms in schizophrenia, mania and depression. In *Cholinergic mechanisms and psychopharmacology*, D.J. Jenden, ed. Plenum, New York (1977) pp. 805–813.

Davis, K.L., Berger, P.A., Hollister, L.E., and Barchas, J.D. Cholinergic involvement in mental disorders. *Life Sci.* (In press, 1978).

Davis, M., Svennson, T.H., and Aghajanian, G.K. Effects of d- and l-amphetamine on habituation and sensitization of the acoustic startle response in rats. *Psychopharmacologia (Berlin)* 43, 1–11 (1975).

Delgado, J.M.R. New orientations in brain stimulation in man. In *Brain-Stimulation Reward*. A. Wauquier, E.T. Rolls, eds. North-Holland/American Elsevier, New York, (1976), pp. 481–503.

Dews, P.B. Studies on behavior. IV. Stimulant actions of methamphetamine. *J. Pharmacol. Exp. Ther.* 122, 137–147 (1958).

Dhasmana, K.M., Dixit, K.S., Jaju, B.P., and Gupta, M-L. Antagonism of morphine mania in cat. *Psychopharmacologia (Berlin)* 24, 380–383 (1972).

Diaz, J., Ellison, G., and Masouka, D. Opposed behavioral syndromes in rats with partial and more complete central serotonergic lesions made with 5,6-dihydroxytryptamine. *Psychopharmacologia (Berlin)* 37, 67–79 (1974).

Douglas, R.J., and Raphelson, A.C. Septal lesions and activity. *J. Compr. Physiol. Psychol.* 62, 465–467 (1966).

Dyne, L.J., and Hughes, R.N. Effects of mehtylphenidate on activity and reactions of novelty in rats. *Psychon. Sci.* 19, 267–268 (1970).

Edelson, A., Gottesfeld, Z, Samuel, D., and Yuwiler, A. Effects of lithium and other alkali metals on brain chemistry and behavior. II. Intracranial self-stimulation behavior. *Psychopharmacologia (Berlin)* 45, 233–237 (1976).

Einon, D.F., and Morgan, M.J. A critical period for social isolation in the rat. *Develop. Psychobio.* 10, 123–132 (1977).

Einon, D.F., and Morgan, M.J. Habituation of object contact in socially reared and isolated rats (Rattus norvegicus). Animal Behav. 24, 415–420 (1976).

Einon, D.F., Morgan, M.J., and Sahakian, B.J. The development of intersession habituation and emergence in socially-reared and isolated rats. *Develop. Psychobio.* 8, 553–559 (1975).

Ellinwood, E.H., Sudilovsky, A., and Nelson, L. Behavioral analysis of chronic amphetamine intoxication. *Biol. Psychiat.* 4, 215–230 (1972).

Ellison, G., and Bresler, O. Tests of emotional behavior in rats following depletion of norepinephrine, of serotonin, or of both. *Psychopharmacologia (Berlin)* 34, 275–288 (1974).

Esposito, R., and Kornetsky, C. Morphine lowering of self-stimulation thresholds: Lack of tolerance with long-term administration. *Science* 195, 189–191 (1977).

Falk, J.L. The origin and functions of adjunctive behavior. *Anim. Learn. Behav.* 5, 325–335 (1977).

Fentress, J.C. Dynamic boundaries of patterned behaviour—interaction and self-organization. In *Growing Points in Ethology*, P. Bateson and R.A. Hinde, eds. Cambridge Univ. Press, Cambridge (1976), pp. 135–169.

Fibiger, H.C., and Campbell, B.A., The effect of parachloropheylalamine on spontaneous locomotor activity in the rat. *Neuropharmacol.* 10, 25–32 (1971).

Fibiger, H.C., Lytle, L.D., and Campbell, B.A. Cholinergic modulation of adrenergic arousal in the developing rat. *J. Comp. Physiol. Psychol.* 72, 384–389 (1970).

Fieve, R.R., Platman, S.R., and Plutchik, R.R. The use of lithium in affective disorders. I. Acute endogenous depression. *Am. J. Psychiat.* 125, 487–491 (1968).

Finger, F.W. Measuring behavioral activity. In *Methods in Psychobiology*, Vol. 2. R.D. Myers, ed. Academic Press, London (1972), chap. 1, pp. 1–19.

Flemenbaum, A. Lithium and amphetamine hyperactivity in rats. *Neuropsychobiology,* 1, 325–334 (1975).

Fog, R. Behavioral effects in rats of morphine and amphetamine and of a combination of the two drugs. *Psychopharmacologia (Berlin)* 16, 305–312 (1970).

Fried, P.A. Septum and behavior: A review. *Psychol. Bull.* 78, 292–310, (1972).

Furukawa, T., Ushizima, I., and Ono, N. Modification by lithim of behavioral responses to methamphetamine and tetrabenazine. *Psychopharmacolgia (Berlin)* 42, 243–248 (1975).

Garattini, S.; Giacalone, E., and Valzelli, L. Biochemical changes during isolation-induced aggressiveness in mice. In *Aggressive Behavior,* S. Garattini, and E.B. Sigg, eds. Excerpta Medica, AMsterdam (1969) pp. 179–187.

Gellhorn, E. The emotions and the ergotrophic and tryphotropic systems. *Psychol. Forsch.* 34, 48–94 (1970).

German, D.C., and Bowden, D.M. Catecholamine systems as the neural substrate for intracranial self-stimulation: hypothesis. *Brain Res.* 73, 381–419 (1974).

Geyer, M.A., and Segal, D.S. Differential effects of reserpine and alpha-methyl-p-tyrosine on norepinephrine and dopamine induced behavioral activity. *Psychopharmacologia (Berl.)* 29, 131–140 (1973).

Geyer, M.A., Segal, D.S., and Mandell, A.J. Effect of intraventricular infusion of dopamine and norepinephrine in motor activity. *Psyiol. Behav.* 8, 652–658. (1972).

Geyer, M.A., Puerto, A., Menkes, D.B., Segal, D.S., and Mandell, A.J. Behavioral studies following lesions of the mesolimbic and mesostriatal serotonergic pathways. *Brain Res.* 106, 257–270 (1976).

Glickman, S.E., Higgins, T.J., and Isaacson, R.L. Some effects of hippocampal lesions on the behavior of mongolian gerbils. *Physiol. Behav.* 5, 931–938 (1970).

Goodall, E.B., and Carey, R.J. Effects of d- versus l-amphetamine, food deprivation, and current intensity on self-stimulation of the lateral hypothalamus, substantia nigra and medial frontal cortex of the rat. *J. Comp. Physiol. Psychol.* 89, 1029–1045 (1975).

Goodwin, F.K., and Ebert, M.H. Lithium in mania: Clinical trials and controlled studies. In *Lithium: its role in psychiatric research and treatment,* S. Gershon and B. Shopsin, eds. Plenum, New York. (1973), Chap. 12, pp. 237–252.

Goodwin, F.K., Murphy, D.L., and Bunney, W.E. Jr. Lithium carbonate treatment in depression and mania. *Arch. Gen. Psychiat.* 21, 486–496 (1969).

Grahame-Smith, D.G. Studies *in vivio* on the relationships between brain tryptophan, brain 5HT synthesis and hyperactivity in rats treated with a MAO inhibitor and l-tryptophan. *J. Neurochem.* 18, 1053–1066 (1971a).

Grahame-Smith, D.G. Inhibitory effect of chlorpromazine on the syndrome of hyperactivity produced by l-tryptophan or 5 methoxy-N,N-dimethyltryptamine in rats treated with a monoamine oxidase inhibitor. *Br. J. Pharmacol.* 43, 856–864 (1971b).

Grahame-Smith, D.G., and Green, A.R. The role of brain 5-hydroxytryptamine in the hyperactivity produced in rat by lithium and monoamine oxidase inhibition. *Br. J. Pharmacol.* 52, 19–26 (1974).

Green, A.R., and Grahame-Smith, D.G. The role of brain dopamine in the hyperactivity syndrome produced by increased 5-hydroxytryptamine synthesis in rats. *Neuropharmacology* 13, 949–959 (1974).

Green, A.R., nd Grahame-SMith, D.G. 5-hydroxytryptamine and other indoles in the central nervous system. In *Handbook of Psychopharmacology.* Vol. 3, L.L. Iversen, S.D. Iversen, and S.H. Synder, eds. Plenum, New York (1975), Chap 4, pp. 169–245.

Green, A.R., and Grahame-Smith, D.G. Effects of drugs on the processes regulating the functional activity of brain 5-hydroxytryptamine. *Nature (Lond.)* 260, 487–491 (1976).

Greer, M.A. Suggested evidence of a primary 'drinking center' in the hypothalamus of the rat. *Proc. Soc. Expt. Biol. (N.Y.)* 89, 59–62 (1955).

Gross, C.G. General activity. In *Analysis of Behavioral Change*, Chap. 5. L. Weiskrantz, ed. Harper & Row, New York (1968) pp. 91–106.

Grossman, S.D., and Sclafani, A. Sympathomimetic amines. Chap. 6. E. Furchgott, ed. Academic Press London (1971) pp. 269–344.

Heimer, L., and Wilson, R.D. The subcortical projections of the allocortex: Similarities in the neural associations of the hippocampus, the piriform cortex, and the neocortex. In *The Golgi Centennial Symposium: Perspectives in Neurobiology*, M.M. Santini, ed. Raven, New York (1975).

Herberg, L.J., and Franklin, K.B.J. The 'stimulant' action of tryptophan monoamine oxidase inhibitor combinations: suppression of self-stimulation. *Neuropharmacology* 15, 349–351 (1976).

Hess, W.R. *The Functional Organization of the Diencephalon*. Grune & Stratton (1957).

Hill, R.T. Facilitation of conditioned reinforcement as a mechanism for psychomotor stimulation. In *Amphetamines and related compounds*, E. Costa and S. Garattini, eds. Raven, New York (1970) pp. 791–795.

Hill, R.T. Animal models of the euphorigenic action of amphetamine-like stimulant drugs. Talk presented to APA (Div. 28), Honolulu, Sept. 4, 1972.

Hinde, R.A. The use of differences and similarities in comparative psychopathology. In *Animal Models in Human Psychobiology*, G. Serban and A. Kling, eds. Plenum, New York (1976), pp. 187–202.

Hinde, R.A., and Stevenson-Hinde, J., eds. *Constraints on Learning: Limitations and Predispositions*. Academic Press, London (1973).

Hughes, R.N., and Grieg, A. Effects of caffeine, methamphetamine and methylphenidate on reactions on novelty in rats. *Neuropharmacology* 15, 673–676 (1976).

Hutchinson, R.R. By-products of aversive control. In *Handbook of Operant Behavior*, W. Honig and J.E.R. Staddon, eds. Prentice-Hall, New Jersey (1977), Chap. 14, pp. 415–431.

Isaac, W., and de Vito, J.L. Effect of sensory stimulation on the activity of normal and prefrontal lobectomised monkeys. *J. Compr. Physiol. Psychol.* 51, 172–174 (1958).

Iversen, S.D. The effect of surgical lesions to frontal cortex and substantia nigra on amphetamine responses in rats. *Brain Res.* 31, 295–311 (1971).

Iversen, S.D. Striatal function and stereotyped behaviour. In *The Psychobiology of the Striatum*, A.R. Cools, A.H.M. Lohman, and J.H.L. van der Bercken, eds. North-Holland, Amsterdam (1977), pp. 99–118.

Iversen, S.D., and Joyce, E.M. Effect in the rat of chronic morphine treatment in the behavioural response to apomorphine. *Br. J. Pharmacol.* 62, 390 (1978).

Jacobs, B.L. Evidence for functional interaction of two central neurotransmitters. *Psychopharmacologia (Berlin)* 39, 81–86 (1974).

Jacobs, B.L., Trulson, M.E., and Stern, W.C. An animal behavior model for studying the actions of LSD and related hallucinogens. *Science* 194, 741–743 (1976).

Jacobs, B.L. Trimbach, C. Eubanks, E.E., and Trulson, M.E. Hippocampal mediation of raphe lesion and PCPA-induced hyperactivity in the rat. *Brain Res.* 94, 253–261 (1975).

Jarrard, L.E. Behavior of hippocampal lesioned rats in home cage and novel situations. *Pysiol. Behav.* 3, 65–70 (1968).

Johnson, F.N., and Wormington, S. Effect of lithium on rearing activity in rats. *Nature (New Biol.) (London)* 235, 159–160 (1972).

Johnson, G., Gershon, S., Burdock, E, I., Floyd, A., and Hekimian, L. Comparative effects of lithium and chlorpromazine in the treatment of acute manic states. *Br. J. Psychiat.* 119, 267–276 (1971).

Kane, F.J. Treatment of mania with cinanserin, an anti-serotonin agent. *Amer. J. Psychiat.* 126, 1020–1023 (1970).

Kelly, P.H. Drug-induced motor behavior. In *Handbook of Psychopharmacology*, Vol. 8, L.L.

Iversen, S.D. Iversen, S.H. Snyder, eds. Plenum Press, New York (1977), Chap. 7 pp. 295–331.

Kelly, P.H., and Ivsen, L.L. LSD as an agonist at mesolimbic dopamine receptors. *Psychopharmacologia (Berlin)* 45, 221–224 (1975).

Kelly, P.H., Seviour, P.W., and Iversen, S.D. Amphetamine and apomorphine responses in the rat following 6-OHDA lesions of the nucleus accumbens septi and corpus striatum. *Brain REs.* 94, 507–522 (1975).

Kety, S.S. Brain amines and affective disorders. In *Brain Biochemistry and Mental Disease*, B.T. Ho and W.M. McIsaac, eds. Plenum, New York (1971), pp. 237–263.

Kirkby, R.J., Bell, D.S., and Preston, A.C. The effects of methyl-amphetamine on stereotyped behavior, activity, startle, and orienting responses. *Psychopharmacologia (Berlin)* 25, 41–48 (1972).

Koe, B.C., and Weissman, A. P-chlorophenylalanine: A specific depletor of brain serotonin. *J. Pharmacol. Exp. Ther.* 154, 499–516 (1966).

Konrad, K., and Melzack, R. Novelty-enhancement effects associated with early sensory-social isolation. In *The Developmental Neuropsychology of Sensory Deprivation*, A. Riesen, ed. London, Academic Press (1975), pp. 253–276.

Koob, G.F. Incentive shifts in intracranial self-stimulation produced by different series of stimulus intensity presentations. *Physiol. Behav.* 18, 131–135 (1977).

Koob, G.F., Fray, P.J., and Iversen, S.D. Tail-pinch stimulation: Sufficient motivation for learning. *Science,* 194, 637–639 (1976).

Koob, G.F., Fray, P.J., and Iversen, S.D. Self-stimulation at the lateral hypothalamus and locus coeruleus after specific unilateral lesions of the dopaminergic system. *Brain Res.* 146, 123–140 (1978a).

Koob, G.F., Riley, S.J., Smith, C.S., and Robbins, T.W. Effects of 6-hydroxydopamine lesions of the nucleus accumbens septi and olfactory tubercle on feeding, locomotor activity and amphetamine anorexia in the rat. *J. Compr. Physiol. Psychol.* (1978b) In press.

Kostowski, W., and Czlonkowski, A. The activity of some neuroleptic drugs and amphetamine in normal and isolated rats. *Pharmacology* 10, 82–87 (1973).

Kraepelin, E. Manic-depressive insanity. In *Manic-Depressive Illness* E. Wolpert, ed. International Universities Press, New York (1977), pp. 33–111. Reprinted from *Manic-Depressive Insanity and Paranoia.* E. & S. Livingstone (1921), pp. 1–52, 165–201.

Lal, S., and Sourkes, T.L. Potentiation and inhibition of the amphetamine stereotypy in rats by neuroleptics and other agents. *Arch. Int. Pharmacodyn. Ther.* 199, 289–301 (1972).

Lat, J. The spontaneous exploratory reactions as a tool for psychopharmacological studies. In *Pharmacology of Conditioning, Learning and Retention.* Pergamon, Czechoslovak Medical Press, Praha (1965), pp. 47–63.

Leith, N.J., and Barrett, R.J. Amphetamine and the reward system: Evidence for tolerance and post-drug depression. Psychopharmacology 46 19–45 (1976).

Le Moal, M., Stinus, L., and Galey, D. Radiofrequency lesion of the ventral mesencephalic tegmentum: Neurological and behavioral considerations. *Exp. Neurol.* 50, 521–535 (1976).

Le Moal, M., Stinus, L., Simon, H., Tassin, J.P., Thierry, A.M., Blanc, G., Glowinski, J., and Cardo, B. Behavioral effects of a lesion in the ventral mesencephalic tegmentum: Evidence for involvement of A10 dopaminergic neurons. In *Advances in Biochemical Psychopharmacology,* Vol. 16, E. Costa and G.L. Gessa, Eds. Raven, New York (1977), pp. 237–245.

Liebman, J.M., and Segal, D.S. Lithium differentially antagonises self-stimulation facilitated by morphine and (+)-amphetamine. *Nature (London)* 260, 161–163 (1976).

Lints, C.E., and Harvey, J.A. Altered sensitivity to footshock and decreased brain content of serotonin following brain lesions in the rat. *J. Compr. Physiol. Psychol.* 67, 23–31 (1969).

Loewe, S. Influence of chlorpromazine, dibenzyline and desoxy-corticosterone upon morphine-induced feline mania. *Arch. Int. Pharmacodyn.* 108, 453–456 (1956).

Lore, R.K., and Levowitz, A. Differential rearing and free versus forced exploration. *Psychon. Sci.* 5, 421–422 (1966).

Lorens, S.A. Effect of lesions in the central nervous system on lateral hypothalamic self-stimulation in the rat. *J. Compr. Physiol. Psychol.* 62, 256–262 (1966).

Lorens, S.A., Sorensen, J.P., and Harvey, J.A. Lesions in the nuclei accumbens septi of the rat: Behavioral and neurochemical effects. *J. Compr. Physiol. Psychol.* 73, 284–290 (1970).

Lorens, S.A., and Mitchell, C.L. Influence of morphine on lateral hypothalamic self-stimulation in the rat. *Psychopharmacologia (Berlin)* 32, 271–277 (1973).

Lorens, S.A., Køhler, C., and Goldberg, H.C. Lesions in Gudden's tegmental nuclei produce behavioral and 5-HT effects similar to those after raphe lesions. *Pharmacol. Biochem. Behav.* 3, 653–659 (1975).

Lorens, S.A., Guldberg, H.C., Hole, K., Køhler, C., and Srebro, B. Activity, avoidance learning and regional 5-hydroxytryptamine following intrabrain stem 5,7-dihydroxytryptamine and electrolytic midbrain raphe lesions in the rat. *Brain Res.* 108, 97–113 (1976).

Luchins, A.S., and Forgus, R.H. The effects of differential post-weaning environment on the rigidity of an animal's behavior. *J. Genet. Psychol.* 86, 51–58 (1955).

Lynch, G. Separable forebrain systems controlling different manifestations of spontaneous activity. *J. Compr. Physiol. Psychol.* 70, 48–59 (1970).

Lyon, M., and Robbins, T.W. The action of central nervous system stimulant drugs: A general theory concerning amphetamine effects. In *Current Developments in Psychopharmacology,* Vol. 2., W.B. Essman and L. Valzelli, eds. Spectrum, New York (1975) Chap. 4. pp. 79–163.

Mabry, P.D., and Campbell, B.A. Serotonergic inhibition of catecholamine-induced behavioral arousal. *Brain Res.* 49, 381–391 (1973).

Mackintosh, N. *The Psychology of Animal Learning.* Academic Press, London (1974).

Makanjuola, R.O.A., Hill, G., Maben, I., Dow, R.C., and Ashcroft, G.W. An automated method for studying exploratory behavior in rat. *Psychopharmacology* 52, 271–277 (1977).

Mandell, A.J., and Knapp, S. Current research in the indoleamine hypothesis of affective didorders. *Comm. Psychopharmacol.* 1, 587–597 (1975).

Mandell, A.J., and Knapp, S. A neurobiological model for the symmetrical prophylactic action of lithium in bipolar affective illness. *Pharmako-Psychiat. Neuropsychopharmacol.* 9, 116–126 (1976).

Marriott, A.S. The effects of amphetamine, caffeine and methylphenidate on the locomotor activity of rats in an unfamiliar environment. *Int. J. Neuropharmacol.,* 7, 487–491 (1968).

Marsden, C.A., and Curzon, G. Studies on the behavioural effects of tryptophan and P-chlorophenylalanine. *Neuropharmacology* 15, 165–171 (1976).

Marshall, J.F. Increased orientation to sensory stimuli following medial hypothalamic damage in rats. *Brain Res.* 86, 373–387.

Marx, M.H. Positive contrast in instrumental learning from qualitative shift in incentive. *Psychon. Sci.* 16, 254–255 (1969).

Mattysse, S., and Sugerman, J. Neurotransmitter theories of schizophrenia. In *Handbook of Psychopharmacology,* Vol. 10, L.L. Iversen, S.D. Iversen, S.H. Snyder, eds. Plenum, New York (1978), Chap. 7, pp. 217–238.

Matussek, N., and Linsmayer, M. The effect of lithium and amphetamine on demethylimi-pramine-RO-4 1284 induced motor hyperactivity. *Life Sci.* 7, 371–375 (1968).

Medical Research Council Brain Metabolism Unit. Modified amine hypothesis for the aetiology of affective illness. *Lancet* II 573–577 (1972).

Mellgren, R.L. Positive contrast in the rat as a function of number of pre-shift trials in the runway. *J. Compr. Physiol. Psychol.* 77, 329–336 (1971).

Meltzer, H.L., Taylor, R.M., Platman, S.R., and Fieve, R.R. Rubidium: A potential modifier of affect and behaviour. *Nature* 223, 321–322 (1969).

Miczek, K.A. Intraspecies aggression in rats: Effects of d-amphetamine and chlordiazepoxide. *Psychopharmacologia (Berlin)* 39, 275–301 (1974).

Miczek, K.A., and Barry, H., III. Pharmacology of sex and aggression. In *Behavioral pharmacology,* S.D. Glick and J. Glick and J. Goldforb, eds. C.V. Mosby, St. Louis (1976) Chap. 6, pp. 176–257.

Miliaressis, E., Bouchrd, A., and Jacobowitz, D.M. Strong positive reward in median raphe: Specific inhibition by para-chlorophenylalanine. *Brain Res.* 98, 194–201 (1975).

Miller, F.P., Cox, R.H., Snodgrass, W.R., and Maikel, R.P. Comparative effects of p-chlorophenylalanine, p-chloroamphetamine, and p-chloro-N methylamphetamine on rat brain norepinephrine, serotonin and 5-hydroxyindole-3-acetic acid. *Biochem. Pharmacol.* 19, 435–442 (1970).

Millichap, J.G. Drugs in management of hyperkinetic and perceptually handicapped children. *JAMA,* 206, 1527–1530 (1968).

Modigh, K., and Svennson, T.H. On the role of central nervous system catecholamines and 5-hydroxytryptamine in the nialamide-induced behavioral syndrome. *Br. J. Pharmacol.* 46, 32–45 (1972).

Moore, K.E. Amphetamine: Biochemical and behavioral actions in animals. In *Handbook of Psychopharmacology,* Vol. 11, L.L. Iversen, S.D. Iversen, and S.H. Snyder, eds. Plenum, New York (1978), Chap. 2, pp. 41–98.

Morgan, M.J. Effects of post-weaning environment on learning in the rat. *Animal Behav.* 21, 429–442 (1973).

Morgan, M.J., and Einon, D.F. Incentive motivation and behavioral inhibition in socially-isolated rats. *Physiol. Behav.* 15, 405–409 (1975).

Morgan, M.J., Einon, D.F., and Nicholas, D. The effects of isolation rearing on behavioural inhibition in the rat. *Quart. J. Exp. Psychol.* 27, 615–634 (1975).

Mukherjee, B.P., and Pradhan S.N. Effects of lithium on septal hyperexcitability and muricidial behavior. *Res. Comm. Chem. Pathol. Pharmacol.* (1976 in press).

Murphy, D.L. L-dopa, behavioral activation and psychopathology. In *Neurotransmitters, Res. Publ. A.R.N.M.D.,* Vol. 50 (1972), Chap. 23, pp. 472–493.

Murphy, D.L., and Beigel, A. Depression, elation and lithium carbonate responses in mania patient subgroups. *Arch. Gen. Psychiat.* 31, 643–648 (1974).

Nadel, L., and O'Keefe, J. The hippocampus in pieces and patches: An essay on modes of exploration in physiological psychology. *Essays on the Nervous System: A Festschrift for Professor J.Z. Young,* R. Bellairs and E.G. Gray, eds. Oxford Univ. Press, London (1974), Chap. 15, pp. 367–390.

Nauta, W. The problem of the frontal lobe: A re-interpretation. *J. Psychiat. Res.* 8, 167–187 (1971).

Neill, D.B., Ross, J.F., and Grossman, S.P. Effects of lesions in the dorsal or ventral striatum on locomotor activity and on locomotor effects of amphetamine. *Pharmacol. Biochem. Behav.* 2, 697–702 (1974a).

Neill, D.B., Ross, J.F., and Grossman, S. Comparison of the effects of frontal, striatal and septal lesions in paradigms thought to measure incentive motivation or behavioral inhibition. *Physiol. Behav.* 13, 297–305 (1974b).

Norton, S. Amphetamine as a model for hyperactivity in the rat. *Physiol. Behav.* 11, 181–186 (1973).

Norton, S. Hyperactive behavior in rats after lesions of the globus pallidus. *Brain Res. Bull* 1, 193–202 (1976).

Norton, S., Mullenix, P., and Culver, B. Comparison of the structure of hyperactive behavior in rats after brain damage from X-irradiation, carbon monoxide and pallidal lesions. *Brain Res.* 116, 49–67 (1976).

Oka, T., and Hosoya, E. The different effect of humoral modulators on the morphine- and central nervous system stimulant-induced hyperactivity in rats. *Neuropharmacology* 16, 115-119 (1977).

Olds, J., and Milner, P. Positive reinforcement produced by electrical stimulation of septal area and other regions of rat brain. *J. Compr. Physiol. Psychol.* 47, 419-427 (1954).

Oliveiro, A., and Castellano, C. Experience modifies morphine-induced behavioural excitation in mice. *Nature (London)* 252, 229-230 (1974a).

Oliveiro, A., and Castellano, C. Genotype-dependent sensitivity and tolerance to morphine and heroin: Dissociation between opiate-induced running and analgesia in the mouse. *Psychopharmacologia (Berlin)* 39, 13-22 (1974b).

Ozawa, H., and Miyauchi, T. Potentiating effect of lithium chloride on methamphetamine-induced stereotypy in mice. *Europ. J. Pharmacol.* 41, 213-216 (1977).

Phillips, A.G., and Fibiger, H.C. Deficits in stimulation-induced feeding and self-stimulation after 6-hydroxydopamine administration in rats. *Behav. Biol.* 16, 127-143 (1976).

Phillips, A.G., Carter, D.A., and Fibiger, H.C. Differential effects of para-chlorophenylalanine on self-stimulation in caudate-putamen and lateral hypothalamus. *Psychopharmacology*, 49, 23-27 (1976a).

Phillips, A.G., Carter, D.A., and Fibiger, H.. Dopaminergic substrates of intracranial self-stimulation in the caudate-putamen. *Brain Res.* 104, 221-232 (1976b).

Phillips, A.G., van der Kooy, D., and Fibiger, H.C. Maintenance of intracranial self-stimulation in hippocampus and olfactory bulb following regional depletion of noradrenaline. *Neurosci. Letters,* 4, 77-84 (1977).

Pijnenburg, A.J.J., Honig, W.M.M., van der Heyden, J.A.M., and van Rossum, J.M. Effects of chemical stimulation of the mesolimbic dopamine system upon locomotor activity. *Eur. J. Pharmacol.* 35, 45-58 (1976).

Poschel, B.P.H., and Ninteman, F.W. Intracranial reward and the forebrain's serotonergic mechanism: Studies employing para-chlorophenylalanine and para-chloroamphetamine. *Physiol. Behav.* 7, 39-66 (1971).

Poschel, B.P.H., Nineteman, F.W., McLean, J.R., and Potoczack, D. Intracranial reward after 5,6-dihydroxytryptamine: Further evidence for serotonin's inhibitory role. *Life Sci.* 15, 1515-1522 (1974).

Post, R.M., Gerner, R.H., Carman, J.S., and Bunney, W.E. Effects of low doses of a dopamine receptor stimulator in mania. *Lancet* I, 203-204 (1976).

Pradhan, S.N. Balance of various neurotransmitter actions in self-stimulation behavior. In *Brain-Stimulation Reward.* A. Wauquier, E.T. Rols, eds. North-Holland/American Elsevier, New York (1976), pp. 171-185.

Prange, A.J., Wilson, I.C., Lynn, C.W., L.B., Stikeleather, R.A., and Raleigh, N.C. L-tryptophan in mania. *Arch. Gen. Psychiat.* 30, 52-62 (1974).

Prien, R.F., Caffey, E.M., and Klett, C.J. A comparison of lithium carbonate and chlorpromazine in the treatment of excited schizo-affectives. *Co-operative Studies in Psychiatry,* Report No. 89, Vol. 86. VA-NIMH Collaborative Study Group, Perry Point, Maryland (1971).

Quitkin, F.M., Rifkin, A., and Klein, D.F. Lithium in other psychiatric disorders. In *Lithium: Its Role in Psychiatric Research and Treatment,* S. Gershon and B. Shopsin, eds. Plenum, New York (1973), Chap. 15, 295-315.

Ramsey, T.A., Mendels, J., Hamilton, C., and Frazer, A. The effect of lithium carbonate in self-stimulating behavior in the rat. *Life Sci.* 11 (i), 773-779 (1972).

Randrup, A., and Munkvad, I. Stereotyped activities produced by amphetamine in several animal species and Man. *Psychopharmacologia (Berlin)* 11, 30-310 (1967).

Randrup, A., and Munkvad, I. Relation of brain catecholamines to aggressiveness and other form of behavioural excitation. In *Aggressive Behavior,* S. Garattini and E.B. Sigg, Eds. Excerpta Medica Foundation, Amsterdam (1969) pp. 228–235.

Randrup, A., and Munkvad, I. Biochemical, anatomical and psychological investigations of stereotyped behaviour induced by amphetamine. In *Amphetamine and Related Compounds.* E. Costa and S. Garattini, eds. Raven, New York (1970), pp. 695–713.

Randrup, A., Munkvad, I., Fog, R., Gerlach, J., Molander, L., Kjellberg, B., and Scheel-Krüger J, Mania, depression and brain dopamine. In *Current Developments in Psychopharmacology,* Vol. 2, W.B. Essman and L. Valzelli, eds. Spectrum, New York (1975), pp. 207–248.

Rastogi, R.M., and Singhal, R.L. Lithium suppresses elevated behavioural activity and brain catecholamines in developing hyperthyroid rats. *Can. J. Physiol. Pharmacol.* 55, 490–495 (1977).

Rastogi, R.B., Merali, Z., and R.L. Singhal. Cadmium alters behaviour and biosynthetic capacity for catecholamine and serotonin in neonatal rat brain. *J. Neurochem.* 28, 789–794 (1977).

Rethy, C.R., Smith, C.B., and Villarreal, J.E. Effects of narcotic analgesics upon the locomotor activity and brain catecholamine content of the mouse. *J. Pharmacol. Exp. Ther.* 176, 472–479 (1971).

Rifkin, A., Quitkin, F. Carrillo, C., Blumberg, A., and Klein, D.F. Lithium in emotionally unstable character disorder. *Arch. Gen. Psychiat.* 27, 519–522 (1972).

Robbins, T.W. The potentiation of conditioned reinforcement by psychomotor stimulant drugs: A test of Hill's hypothesis. *Psychopharmacologia (Berlin)* 45, 103–112 (1975).

Robbins, T.W. Relationship between reward-enhancing and stereotypical effects of psychomotor stimulant drugs. *Nature (London)* 264, 57–59 (1976).

Robbins, T.W. A critique of the methods available for the measurement of spontaneous motor activity. In *Handbook of Psychopharmacology,* Vol. 7, L.L. Iversen, S.D. Iversen and S.H. Snyder, eds. Plenum, New York (1977), Chap. 2, pp. 37–82.

Robbins, T.W. Acquisition of responding with conditioned reinforcement: Effects of pipradrol, methylphenidate, d-amphetamine and nomifensine. *Psychopharmacology* (1978, in press).

Robbins, T. and Iversen, S.D. A dissociation of the effects of d-amphetamine on locomotor activity and exploration in rats. *Psychopharmacologia (Berlin)* 28, 155–164 (1973).

Robbins, T.W., and Koob, G.F. Pipradol enhances reinforcing properties of stimuli paired with brain stimulation. *Pharmacol. Biochem. Behav.* 8, 219–222 (1978).

Ruch, T.C., and Shenkin, H.A. The relation of area 13 on orbital surface of frontal lobes to hyperactivity and hyperphagia in monkeys. *J. Neurophysiol.* 6, 349–360 (1943).

Rylander, G. Stereotype behaviour in man following amphetamine abuse. In *The Correlation of Adverse Effects in Man with Observations in Animals.* S.B. de C. Baker, Ed. Excerpta Medica, Amsterdam (1971), pp. 28–31.

Sacks, O. *Awakenings.* Duckworth, London, 1973.

Sahakian, B.J. Effects of isolation on unconditioned behaviour and response to drugs in rats. Unpublished Ph.D. Thesis, Univ. of Cambridge, 1976.

Sahakian, B.J., and Koob, G.F. The relationship between pipradol-induced responding for electrical brain stimulation, stereotyped behaviour, and locomotor activity. *Neuropharmacology* (1978, in press).

Sahakian, B.J., and Robbins, T.W. Isolation-rearing enhances tail pinch-induced oral behavior in rats. *Physiol. Behav.* 18, 53–58 (1977).

Sahakian, B.J., Robbins, T.W., and Iversen, S.D. α-flupenthixol-induced hyperactivity by chronic dosing in rats. *Eur. J. Pharmacol.* 37, 169–178 (1976).

Sahakian, B.J., Robbins, T.W., and Iversen, S.D. The effects of isolation rearing on exploration in the rat. *Animal Learn. Behav.* 5, 193–198 (1977).

Sahakian, B.J., Robbins, T.W., Morgan, M.J., and Iversen, S.D. The effects of psychomotor stimulants on stereotypy and locomotor activity in socially deprived and control rats. *Brain Res.* 84, 195–205 (1975).

Sahakian, B.J., Growdon, J.H., Millington, W.R., Barr, J.K., and Wurtman, R.J. The effects of cholinergic agonists on apomorphine-induced stereotyped behavior in the rat. *Comm. Psychopharm.* (1978a, in press).

Sahakian, B.J., Wurtman, R.J., Barr, J.K., and Millington, W.R. The effects of a low-tryptophan diet on apomorphine-induced stereotyped behavior in rats. *Society for Neuro-science Abstracts.* (1978b, in press).

Sanger, D.J., and Steinberg, H. Inhibition of scopolamine-induced stimulation of Y maze activity by α-methyl-p-tyrosine and by lithium. *Europ. J. Pharmacol.* 28, 344–349 (1974).

Sauerhoff, M.W., and Michaelson, I.A. Hyperactivity and brain catecholamines in lead-exposed developing rats. *Science* 182, 1022–1024 (1973).

Scheckel, C.L., Boff, E., and Pazery, L.M. Hyperactive states related to the metabolism of norepinephrine and similar biochemicals. *Ann. N.Y. Acad. Sci.* 159, 939–958 (1969).

Scheel-Krüger, J. Comparative studies of various amphetamine analogues demonstrating different interactions with the metabolism of the catecholamines in the brain. *Eur. J. Pharmacol.* 14, 47–59 (1971).

Scheel-Krüger, J., and Mogilnicka, E. Evidence for the involvement of serotonergic mechanisms on stereotypy induced by dopaminergic stimulating drugs in the rat. *Fifth Congress of the Polish Pharmacological Society.* Szeczecin, Poland (1975).

Schildkraut, J. Pharmacology—the effects of lithium on biogenic amines. In *Lithium: Its Role in Psychiatric Research and Treatment.* S. Gershon and B. Shopsin, eds. Plenum, New York (1973), pp. 57–73.

Schildkraut, J.J., and Kety, S.S. Biogenic amines and emotion. *Science* 156, 21–30 (1967).

Schiørring, E. Amphetamine-induced selective stimulation of certain behaviour items with concurrent inhibition of others in an open-field test with rats. *Behavior* 39, 1–17 (1971).

Schiørring, E., and Hecht, A. Behavioural responses of non-tolerant rat groups to the administration of 2 mg/kg morphine in an open field test. (In preparation).

Schou, M. Pharmacology and toxicology of lithium. *Ann. Rev. Pharm. Tox.* 16, 231–243 (1976).

Schou, M. Special review: Lithium in psychotic therapy and prophylaxis. *J. Psychiat. Res.* 6, 67–95 (1968).

Segal, D.S. Behavioral characterization of d- and l-amphetamine: neurochemical implications. *Science* 190, 475–477 (1975).

Segal, D.S. Differential effects of para-chlorophenylalanine on amphetamine-induced loco-motion and stereoypy. *Brain Res.* 116, 267–276 (1976).

Segal, D.S., Callaghan, M., and Mandell, A.J. Alterations in behavior and catecholamine biosynthesis induced by lithium. *Nature (London)* 254, 58–59 (1975).

Segal, D.S., Knapp, S., Kuczenski, R., and Mandell, A.J. The effects of environmental isolation on behavior and regional rat brain tyrosine hydroxylase and tryptophan hydroxylase activities. *Behav. Biol.* 8, 47–53 (1973).

Sem-Jacobsen, C.W. Electrical stimulation and self-stimulation in man with chronic implanted electrodes. Interpretation and pitfalls of results. In *Brain-Stimulation Reward,* A. Wauquier, E.T. Rolls, eds. North-Holland/American Elsevier, New York (1976), pp. 508–520.

Shaywitz, B.A., Yager, R.D., and Klopper, J.H. Selective brain dopamine depletion in developing rats: An experimental model of minimal brain dysfunction. *Science* 191, 305–307 (1976).

Sheard, M.H. Behavioral effects of p-chlorophenylalanine, inhibition by lithium. *Comm. Behav. Biol.* 5, part A, 71–74 (1970).

Shopsin, B., and Gershon, S. Lithium: Clinical considerations. In *Handbook of Psychopharm-acology,* Vol. 14, L.L. Iversen, S.D. Iversen, S.H. Snyder, eds. Plenum, New York (1978), Chap. 7, pp. 273–323.

Shopsin, B., Kim, S.S. and Gershon, S.S. A controlled study of lithium vs. chlorpromazine in acute schizophrenics. *Brit. J. Psychiat.* 119, 435–440, (1971).

Shopsin, B., Gershon, S., Thompson, H., and Collins, P. Psychoactive drugs in mania: A controlled comparison of lithium carbonate, chlorpromazine and haloperidol. *Arch. Gen. Psychiat.* 32, 34–42 (1975).

Silbergeld, E.K., and Goldberg, A.M. Lead-induced behavioral dysfunction: An animal model of hyperactivity. *Expt. Neurol.* 42, 146–157 (1974).

Sjöstrom, R., and Roos, B-E. 5-hydroxyindoleacetic acid and homovanillic acid in cerebrospinal fluid in manic-depressive psychosis. *Europ. J. Clin. Pharmacol.* 4, 170–176 (1972).

Smith, D.F. Biogenic amines and the effect of short-term lithium administration on open-field activity in rats. *Psychopharmacologia (Berlin)* 41, 295–300 (1975).

Smith, D.F. Antagonistic effect of lithium chloride on L-dopa induced locomotor activity in rats. *Pharmacological Res. Comm.* 8, 575–579 (1976).

Smith, D.F., and Smith, H.B. The effect of prolonged lithium administration on activity, reactivity and endurance in the rat. *Psychopharmacologia (Berlin)* 30, 83–88 (1973).

Smith, R.C., and Davis, J.M., Comparative effect of d-amphetamine, l-amphetamine and methylphenidate on mood in man. *Psychopharmacology* 53, 1–12 (1977).

Snyder, S.H. Opiate receptors and internal opiates. *Scientific American* 236, 44–56 (1977).

Speiser, Z. and Weinstock, M. Supersensitivity to isoprenaline induced in rats by prolonged isolation. *Br. J. Pharmacol.* 52, 605–609 (1974).

Srebro, B., and Lorens, S.A. Behavioral effects of selective midbrain raphe lesions in the rat. *Brain Res.* 89, 303–325 (1975).

Staddon, J.E.R. Schedule-induced behavior. In *Handbook of Operant Behavior*, W.K. Honig and J.E.R. Staddon, eds. Prentice-Hall, New Jersey (1977), Chap. 5, pp. 125–152.

Stadler, H., Lloyd, K.G., Gadea-Ceria, M., and Bartholini, G. Enhanced striatal acetylcholine release by chlorpromazine and its reversal by apomorphine. *Brain Res.* 55, 476–480 (1973).

Stein, L. Effects and interactions of imipramine, chlorpromazine, reserpine and amphetamine on self-stimulation. Possible neurophysiological basis of depression. *Recent Advances in Biological Psychiatry* 4, 288–308 (1962).

Stein, L. Amphetamine and neural reward mechanisms. In *Animal Behaviour and Drug Action*, H. Steinberg, A. de Reuck and J. Knight, eds. Churchill, London (1964) pp. 91–118.

Stein, L., and Ray, O.S. Brain stimulation reward 'thresholds' self-determined in the rat. *Psychopharmacologia (Berlin)* 1, 251–256 (1960).

Steiner, S.S., and Stokely, S.N. Methamphetamine lowers self-stimulation thresholds. *Physiol. Psychol.* 1, 161–164 (1973).

Stinus, L., Simon, H., and Le Moal, M. Disappearance of hoarding and disorganization of eating behavior after ventral mesencephalic tegmentum lesion in rats. *J. Compr. Physiol. Psychol.* (1978a, in press).

Stinus, L., Gaffori, O., Simon, H., and Le Moal, M. Small doses of apomorphine and chronic administration of d-amphetamine reduce locomotor hyperactivity produced by radiofrequency lesions of dopaminergic A10 neurons area. *Biol. Psychiat.* (1978b, in press).

Stolk, J.M., Nowack, W.J., Barchas, J.D., and Platman, S.R. Brain-norepinephrine enhanced turnover after rubidium treatment, *Science* 168, 501–503 (1970).

Stolk, J.M., Conner, R.L., and Barchas, J.D. Social environment and brain biogenic amine metabolism in rats. *J. Compr. Physiol. Psychol.* 87, 203–207 (1974).

Sturtrevant, F.M., and Drill, V.A. Tranquilizing drugs and morphine-mania in cats. *Nature (London)* 179, 1253 (1957).

Sulser, F., Bickel, M.H., and Brodie, B.B. The action of desmethylimipramine in counteracting sedation and cholinergic effects of reserpine-like drugs. *J. Pharmacol. Exp. Ther.* 144, 321–330 (1964).

Swanson, L.W., and Cowan, W.M. A note on the connections and development of the nucleus accumbens. *Brain Res.* 92, 324–330 (1975).

Syme, L.A. Social isolation at weaning: Some effects on two measures of activity. *Animal Learn. Behav.* 1, 161–163 (1973).

Teitelbaum, H., and Milner, P.M. Activity changes following partial hippocampal lesions in rats. *J. Compr. Physiol. Psychol.* 56, 284–289 (1963).

Thoa, N.B., Tizabi, Y., and Jacobowitz, D.M. The effect of isolation on catecholamine concentration and turnover in discrete in rat brain. *Brain Res.* 131, 259–269 (1977).

Thomas, G.J., Moore, R.Y., Harvey, J.A., and Hunt, H.F. Relations between the behavioral syndrome produced by lesions in the septal region of the forebrain and maze learning of the rat. *J. Compr. Physiol. Psychol.* 52, 527–532 (1959).

Tomkiewicz, M., and Steinberg, H. Lithium treatment reduces morphine self-administration in addict rats. *Nature (London)* 252, 227–229 (1974).

Trulson, M.E., and Jacobs, B.L. LSD acts synergistically with serotonin depletion: Evidence from behavioral studies in cats. *Pharmacol. Biochem. Behav.* 43, 231–234 (1976).

Tupin, J. (1971), cited in Quitkin et al. (1973).

Ulrich, R.E., and Azrin, N.H. Reflexive fighting in response to aversive stimulation. *J. Exp. Anal. Behav.* 5, 511–520 (1962).

Valenstein, E. Problems of measurement and interpretation with reinforcing brain stimulation. *Psych. Rev.* 71, 415–437 (1964).

Valenstein, E. The interpretation of behavior evoked by brain stimulation. In *Brain-Stimulation Reward.* A. Wauquier and E. Rolls, eds. North-Holland/American Elsevier, New York (1976), pp. 557–575.

Valzelli, L. The "isolation syndrome" in mice. Psychopharmacologia (Berlin) 31, 305–320 (1973).

Valzelli, L. Social experience as a determinant of normal behavior and drug effect. In *Handbook of Psychopharmacology,* Vol. 7, L.L. Iversen, S.D. Iversen, S.H. Snyder, eds. Plenum, New York (1977), Chap. 11, pp. 369–382.

Valzelli, L., and Garattini, S. Biochemical and behavioral changes induced by isolation in rats. *Neuropharmacology,* 11, 17–22 (1972).

van der Kooy, D., Fibiger, H.C., and Phillips. A.G. Monoamine involvement in hippocampal self-stimulation. *Brain Res.* 136, 119–130 (1977).

van Praag, H.M. Amine hypothesis of affective disorders. In *Handbook of Psychopharmacology,* Vol. 13, L.L. Iversen, S.D. Iversen, S.H. Snyder, eds. Plenum, New York (1978), Chap. 4, 877–297.

Wallach, M.B. Drug-induced stereotyped behavior: Similarities and differences. In *Neuropsychopharmacology of Monoamines and Their Regulatory Enzymes.* E. Usdin, ed. Raven, New York (1974), pp. 241–258.

Watson, R., Hartman, E., and Schildkraut, J. Amphetamine withdrawal, affective state, sleep patterns and MHPG excretion. *Am. J. Psychiat.* 129, 263–269 (1972).

Wauquier, A. The influence of psychoactive drugs on brain self-stimulation in rats: A review. In *Brain-Stimulation Reward,* A. Wauquier, E.T. Rolls, eds. North-Holland/American Elsevier, New York (1976), pp. 123–170.

Winstock, M., Speiser, Z., and Ashbenazi, R. Biochemical and pharmacological studies on an animal model of hyperactivity states. In *The Impact of Biology on Modern Psychiatry.* E.S. Gershon, R.H. Belmaker, S.S. Kety, and M. Rosenbaum, eds. Plenum, New York (1977), pp. 149–161.

Weinstock, M., Speizer, Z., and Ashkenazi, R. Changes in brain catecholamine turnover and receptor sensitivity induced by social deprivation in rats. *Psychopharmacology,* 56, 205–209 (1978).

Wieskrantz, L., and Baltzer, V. Body weight, short-term satiation and the response to reward magnitude shifts. *Quart. J. Exp. Psychol.* 27, 73–91 (1975).

Wetzel, A.B., Conner, R.L., and Levine, S. Shock-induced fighting in septal-lesioned rats. *Psychon. Sci.* 9, 133–134 (1967).

Wike, E.L. *Secondary Reinforcement.* Harper & Row, New York (1966).

Wikler, A. Studies on the action of morphine on the central nervous system of cat. *J. Pharmacol. Exp. Ther.* 80, 176–187 (1944).

Willner, J.H., Samach, M., Angrist, B.M., Wallach, M.B., and Gershon, S. Drug-induced stereotyped behavior and its antagonism in dogs. *Comm. Behav. Biol.* 5, 135–141 (1970).

Wyatt, R.J., and Torgow, J.S. A comparison of equivalent clinical potencies of neuroleptics as used to treat schizophrenia and affective disorders. *J. Psychiat. Res.* 13, 91–98 (1976).

Zeaman, D. Response latency as a function of amount of reinforcement. *J. Exp. Psychol.* 39, 466–483 (1949).

CHAPTER 13

Biochemical Theories of Mania

Robert M. Post

INTRODUCTION

Many of the biochemical theories of mania have evolved from initial formulations of a bipolar model of mania and depression inherent in the catecholamine hypothesis. In turn, this hypothesis was generated largely from indirect pharmacological data. Current biochemical approaches to mania may be conceptualized more broadly, however. There has been increasing recognition that dopaminergic mechanisms may be involved in some aspects of manic illness. This approach is derived not only from a reassessment of the original catecholamine hypothesis, but from the newer evidence of the relatively specific effects of some neuroleptics in blocking dopamine receptor sites and their clinical utility in mania. The empirical and theoretical work involved in the exploration of the role of dopamine in the schizophreniform psychoses has been particularly useful in this regard: that is, the psychopharmacology of schizophrenia and mania overlap considerably. We will also address the question of whether other treatment approaches to the excited psychotic states are useful in mania and whether they provide indirect neuropharmacological evidence for neurotransmitter alterations in mania. These might include low-dose dopamine agonist treatment, tryptophan or 5-hydroxytryptophan (5HTP) to increase serotonergic tone, α- and β-noradrenergic manipulations, and use of anticonvulsant agents such as carbamazepine.

Similarly, newer theories about the mechanisms of action of lithium carbonate in depression and mania may provide important conceptual approaches to the study of biochemical alterations in manic illness. In particular, lithium not only affects a variety of neurotransmitter systems at different sites in the central nervous system, but also appears to have direct effects at dopaminergic and adrenergic receptor sites. Do the receptor active effects of lithium give us important hints into the biophysiology of mania? At the same time, lithium's therapeutic effects in mania lead to a direct exploration of a possible role of electrolyte alterations in manic illness.

Several other pharmacological models for mania will be explored. Repeated administration of a variety of psychomotor stimulants and direct- and indirect-acting dopamine agonists produce marked effects on locomotor activity and stereotypy in several animal species. In some instances, repeated dopamine agonist treatment leads to behavioral sensitization or a pharmacological kindling effect, which may have implications for biochemical theories of mania. What dopaminergic mechanisms may be involved in the behavioral sensitization to the activating effects of these agonist compounds?

Morphine may also produce major effects on mood and behavior reminiscent of similar alterations associated with the manic state. A morphine model may lead to new conceptual approaches to the illness. Of particular interest is the relation of the newly defined endogenous opiate system to manic illness. Are endorphins and enkephalins involved in a modulatory role in some aspects of the illness? Do other nervous system peptides play a role?

The rhythmicity of manic-depressive illness may be of particular biochemical importance. Mania is often characterized by a recurrence of episodes, which may increase in frequency over time. Many workers have conceptualized separate biochemical mechanisms for the underlying alteration in rhythmic phenomena independent of the qualitative characteristics of the manic illness itself. We will briefly review several aspects of the chemical findings in mania that bear on the relationship of rhythmic alterations and their underlying neurosubstrate, as opposed to the phenomenology of manic illness itself.

Consideration of the anatomical locus of action of each of the compounds discussed should be critically reviewed in any biochemical theory of mania, as there may be regional specificities to the neurotransmitter alterations and pharmacological effects. For example, considerable evidence suggests that mesolimbic dopaminergic terminals in the nucleus accumbens may be associated with modulation of locomotor activity to a greater extent than striatal dopaminergic terminals, which may be more closely linked to stereotyped behavior. This regional dissection of dopaminergic mechanisms may be relevant to conceptual approaches to the biochemistry of mania.

Although we will discuss single neurotransmitter systems for convenience and ease of presentation, a major theme stressed throughout the chapter is the critical nature of neurotransmitter effects in relation to each other, their balance, and interregulation. For example, most investigators would agree that the primary deficit in Parkinson's disease is in dopaminergic neurons, but a variety of manipulations in both the dopaminergic and cholinergic systems produce either therapeutic effects or exacerbations of the illness. Our modern wiring diagrams of the substantia nigra dopaminergic neuron might also include an inhibitory feedback of γ-aminobutyric acid (GABA) and substance P neurons on these calls as well as an acetylcholinergic interneuron. These dopaminergic cells may also receive input from enkephalinergic, noradrenergic, and serotonergic systems. Thus, it may be important to consider a variety of neurotransmitter effects in relation to each other as they might influence behavior.

NOREPINEPHRINE

Indirect and direct evidence of alterations in norepinephrine metabolism has been reviewed by a variety of investigators (Schildkraut, 1965, 1978; Bunney and Davis, 1965; Schildkraut and Kety, 1967; Akiskal and McKinney, 1973, 1975; Baldessarini, 1975; Shopsin et al., 1973; Goodwin and Post, 1975). Indirect pharmacological data suggest that decreases in noradrenergic function, such as those produced by reserpine and the neuroleptics, might be associated with an increased incidence of depression as well as therapeutic effects in mania. Conversely, agents that potentiate the noradrenergic system might be associated with antidepressant effects and with an increased incidence of mania. Treatment with tricyclic antidepressants or the monoamine oxidase inhibitors has been associated with an increased incidence of manic episodes when these treatments have been used in acute or prophylactic treatment of depression (Prien et al., 1974; Bunney, 1977).

Several approaches have been used in man in an attempt to directly assess these postulated alterations in noradrenergic metabolism. One approch is the study of urinary MHPG, a breakdown product of norepinephrine thought to be derived at least in part from sources in the central nervous sytem (Ebert and Kopin, 1975; Maas et al., 1977). Details and limitations of the various techniques described in this chapter cannot be discussed in detail because of limitations of space, and the interested reader is referred to several methodological reviews in the literature, as well as to the primary sources (see Post and Goodwin, 1978).

As summarized in Table 1a, longitudinal studies of individual patients during manic and depressed episodes consistently demonstrate higher urinary MHPG in mania as compared to depression (Jenner and Sampson, 1972; Bond et al., 1972; DeLeon-Jones et al., 1973; Post et al., 1976; Wehr, 1977; but not Bunney et al., 1972). Although there is more variability in the interindividual data, manic patients as a group tend to have higher urinary MHPG levels than depressed patients, although values are not always significantly higher than those observed in normal controls (Greenspan et al., 1970;

Table 1a. Norepinephrine Metaboism in Mania:
Urinary 3-Methoxy-4-hydroxyphenyl Glycol (MHPG)
in Mania Compared to Depression

MHPG Finding	Comparison	Significance	Reference
Higher MHPG in mania	Depression	$p < 0.01$	Greenspan et al., 1970
No significant elevation	End of depression	NS*	Bunney et al., 1972
of MHPG in mania	Controls	NS*	Casper et al., 1977
Higher MHPG in mania†	Depression	$p < 0.001$	Jenner and Sampson, 1972
Higher MHPG in mania†	Depression	$p < 0.01$ (estimate)	DeLeon-Jones et al., 1973
Higher MHPG in mania	Bipolar depressed	$p < 0.05$	Goodwin and Beckmann, 1975
Higher MHPG in mania†	Mania	$p < 0.001$	Post et al., 1977b
Higher MHPG in mania†	Mania	$p < 0.001$	Wehr, 1977

*NS = not significant.
†Detailed longitudinal case studies through several mood switches.

Schildkraut et al., 1973; Goodwin and Post, 1975; DeLeon-Jones et al., 1973; Post et al., 1977b; Casper et al., 1977).

Motor Activity and Stress

Kupfer et al. (1972, 1974) and Weiss et al. (1974a, b) have documented large increases in motor activity in the manic phase of the illness, and the possible relationship of these increased levels of activity to urinary MHPG remains problematic (Post and Goodwin, 1973, 1978). Initial studies in our laboratroy (Post et al., 1973a; Ebert et al., 1972) suggested that a 4-hour program of increased motor activity elevates urinary and CSF MHPG (Figure 1). However, in several studies of normal volunteers Goode and collaborators (1973) have not been able to duplicate these findings. Muscettola et al. (1976) reported increases in urinary MHPG following exercise in depressed patients but not in normal volunteers, a finding that may resolve some of the discrepancies in the literature. Sweeney and collaborators (1977) have suggested that levels of rated anxiety correlate better than does motor activity with the increases in urinary MHPG observed during exercise. In any event, secondary alterations in either motor activity or the stress associated with an activity procedure do appear capable of spuriously increasing urinary or cerebrospinal fluid MHPG. One patient studied on 52 manic and 84 depressed days with urinary MHPG and daily monitoring of activity showed no point-to-point correlation of activity and urinary MHPG, although both motor activity and urinary MHPG were higher in mania than in depression (Post et al., 1977b [Figure 2]).

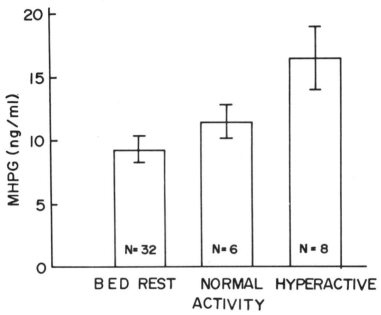

EFFECT OF ACTIVITY ON SPINAL FLUID MHPG IN DEPRESSED PATIENTS

Fig. 1. Significant (p < .05) increases in CSF MHPG are noted following 4 hours of activity prior to lumbar puncture compared to patients studied at bed rest (data from Post et al., 1973a).

Cerebrospinal Fluid MHPG

Another appraoch to the study of central nervous system norepinephrine metabolism is the assessment of its metabolites in cerebrospinal fluid. Initial studies with gas chromatographic techniques and now more recent studies of MHPG and VMA with mass fragmentographic assays allow a reliable assessment of small quantities of these metabolites in cerebrospinal fluid. Initial gas chromatographic studies in our laboratory (Gordon and Oliver, 1971) revealed lower CSF MHPG in depressed patients compared to a variety of neurological and psychiatric comparison groups. A larger replication (Post et al., 1973b) and subsequent work continued to document higher levels in

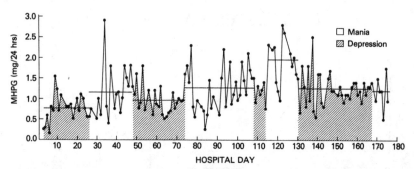

Fig. 2. Urinary MHPG was significantly higher in manic compared to depressed phases of the illness in one rapidly cycling patient. Substantial increases in MHPG did not precede the switch. Telemetrically measured 24-hour motor activity was higher in mania than depression, but day-to-day activity counts did not correlate with urinary MHPG (data from Post et al., 1977b).

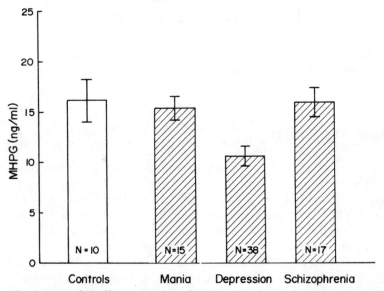

Fig. 3. Lack of significant elevation of CSF MHPG in mania compared to normal or schizophrenic comparison groups. Values were higher in manics compared to depressives (from Post et al., and Goodwin, 1975).

Table 1b. Noradrenergic Mechanisms in Mania: MHPG and VMA in CSF

Investigators	Controls	Depressed	Manic
Baseline CSF MHPG			
Wilk et al., 1972	16 ± 4.2 (24)	17.6 ± 1.2 (8)	31.6 ± 5.8 (11)
Post et al., 1973b	15.1 ± 3.6 (44)	10.2 ± 2.4 (55)	15.4 ± 5.5 (26)
Ashcroft et al., 1976	13 ± 8* (11)	12 ± 6† (7) / 24 ± 13‡ (8)	29 ± 18*
Goodwin and Post, 1977†		10.50 ± 5.15* (36)	11.15 ± 6.83* (13)
Baseline CSF VMA			
Jimerson et al., 1977	1.94 ± 0.25 (16)	1.46 ± 1.51 (32)	1.264 ± 0.65 (12)
Probenecid CSF MHPG			
Goodwin and Post, 1977†		10.50 ± 5.15* (36)	17.06 ± 10.42* (16)
Probenecid CSF VMA			
Jimerson et al., 1977†	2.55 ± 0.46 (13)	1.996 ± 1.159 (35)	2.745 ± 1.56 (15)

*Standard deviation.
†Determinations by Mass Fragmentographic Techniques in Collaboration with E. Gordon.
‡Retarded.
††Agitated.

mania compared to depression, but not compared to normal and neurological controls (Figure 3). Recent studies (Gerner, Gordon, Goodwin, and Post, unpublished data) using mass fragmentographic techniques have also shown nonsignificant alterations in manics compared to normal controls (Table 1b). Wilk et al. (1972) and Shopsin et al. (1973) reported increases in CSF MHPG in manic patients compared to depressed patients and controls, although time of lumbar punctures and degree of bed rest were not clear. Ashcroft et al. (1976) found higher MHPG in manics compared to retarded but not agitated depressed patients. Cerebrospinal fluid values of vanillylmandelic acid (VMA) [Jimerson et al., 1975] did not reveal increased levels in manic patients compared to nondepressed psychiatric and neurological control populations (Figure 4).

Cerebrospinal Fluid Norepinephrine

In contrast to the inconsistent findings of elevated CSF, MHPG, or VMA in manic patients compared to depressed or control populations, we have

VMA IN CSF OF PSYCHIATRIC PATIENTS : EFFECT OF PROBENECID

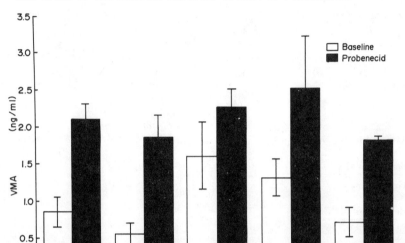

Fig. 4. Baseline VMA and probenecid values were not significantly elevated in manics compared to nondepressed comparison populations (from Jimerson et al., 1975).

observed notable increases in CSF norepinephrine itself measured by sensitive radio enzymatic assay (Post et al., 1978c). As illustrated in Figures 5a and b, both baseline levels of norepinephrine and accumulations following probenecid administration were higher in manic patients compared to depressed or neurological control groups. A variety of indirect data support the concept that cerebrospinal fluid norepinephrine levels originate in part from central nervous system metabolism and are independent of peripheral levels. For example, Ziegler and collaborators (1977) studied one patient with pheochromocytoma who had a markedly elevated norepinephrine level in blood (9,680 picograms/ml) and a normal level (200 picograms/ml) in the cerebrospinal fluid.

Although we attempted to study all patients and controls while at bed rest, several manics were unable to cooperate with this manipulation. It is possible that the elevated CSF norepinephrine levels were related to either postural changes or the increased psychomotor activity itself. However, this does not appear to be a sufficient explanation, since several manics were studied following complete bed rest and their levels were as high as or higher than the

BASELINE CSF NOREPINEPHRINE IN DEPRESSION AND MANIA

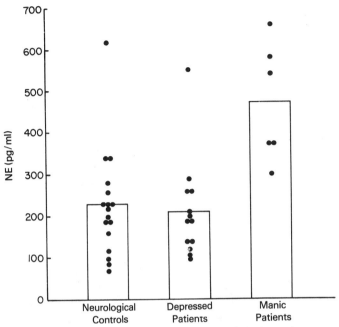

Fig. 5a. Baseline CSF norepinephrine values were higher in manics compared to depressives (p < .001) or neurological controls (p < .001).

rest of the manic group. In addition, one nonmanic patient was studied following four hours of moderately intense physical activity. Her CSF norepinephrine increased from 116 to 201 pg/ml following an increase in monitored activity from 55 counts/ to 373 counts/hr. In addition, earlier in this patient's hospitalization when she was in a profoundly anxious state, her cerebrospinal fluid norepinephrine levels were 500 pg/ml. This suggests that anxiety and the affective state of the patiet can be a more important determinant of CSF norepinephrine levels than four hours of acute motor activity. A number of questions about both the severity and the time course of the psychomotor manipulation in relation to the norepinephrine values remain to be elucidated, however. While both the baseline and probenecid data in mania are highly suggestive, they should be viewed tentatively in relation to etiological assumptions regarding norepinephrine in mania.

Nonetheless, these high levels of CSF norepinephrine in manic patients are interesting in light of the observations of Segal and Mandell (1970) and Geyer et al. (1972) that slow infusions of norepinephrine directly into the ventricular

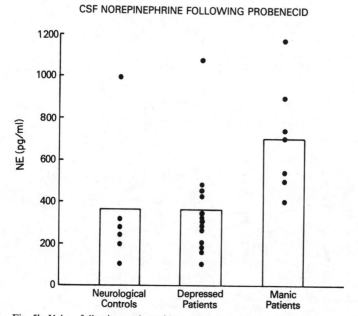

CSF NOREPINEPHRINE FOLLOWING PROBENECID

Fig. 5b. Values following probenecid revealed the same pattern of elevated norepinephrine in mania compared to depressives ($p < .05$) or controls ($p < .10$, two tailed students t-test, from Post et al., 1978b).

CSF of animals produce increases in motor activity. It is more possible that the linkage of noradrenergic activity to psychomotor activation is a direct one than that motor activity during mania would alter CSF norepinephrine levels in an artifactual or epiphenomenal sense. The studies of Segal and collaborators (1972) also suggest that increases in motor activity may be enhanced by pretreatment with reserpine or alpha-methylparatyrosine (AMPT), which have been documented to lead to the development of receptor supersensitivity in response to catecholamine challenges. It is noteworthy that infusions of norepinephrine, but not dopamine, in these pretreated animals produced the enhanced elevations in motor activity.

Dopamine β-hydroxylase, the enzyme which converts dopamine to norepinephrine, has been measured in CSF and may be an alternate marker of CNS noradrenergic function. Initial studies reported low DBH in a small group of manic patients (Lerner et al., 1978), but recent longitudinal data do not support this finding (P. Lerner, personal communication, 1978).

The norepinephrine findings, although highly preliminary, are of particular interest in light of recent data suggesting that the cerebrospinal fluid system may be the pathway for neuroendocrinological as well as behavioral integration (Knigge et al., 1975; Rodriguez, 1976). As such, it is possible that substances in cerebrospinal fluid may not be only markers of important central nervous systems events, but also more direct links in a neurotransmitter or neuromodulatory role in relation to behavior.

Indirect Approaches to Norepinephrine in Mania

Sack and Goodwin (1974) showed that inhibition of dopamine β-hydroxylase with the use of fusaric acid did not produce an overall improvement in manic symptomatology and worsened psychosis. This is at partial variance with the data implicating increased levels of norepinephrine in the cerebrospinal fluid of manic patients. Disulfiram, another DBH inhibitor, has also been associated with the precipitation of manic and other affective syndromes.

Clonidine, an alpha-adrenergic agonist (which probably acts preferentially at presynaptic autoreceptors) decreases firing of the noradrenergic cells of the locus coeruleus (Svensson et al., 1975; Aghajanian et al., 1977). This drug would provide a relative specific test of the noradrenergic hypothesis of mania but has not yet been extensively studied. Jimerson, Post, and Bunney (unpublished observations, 1977) have noted an increase in manic psychosis in one patient during the period of placebo substitution for clonidine, a period associated with increased noradrenergic activity (Svensson and Strombom, 1977).

In another manic patient (#022), switches into mania that occurred during the night were noted to be consistently associated with the end of a rapid-eye-movement sleep episode (Gillin et al., 1977). Since the termination of REM sleep has been associated with increased firing of the locus coeruleus (McCarley and Hobson, 1975), these indirect data are at least consistent with a greater proclivity to the manic switch during times of presumptive increased noradrenergic activity in this patient. Studies of the alpha and beta antagonists (phenoxybenzamine and propanolol) in mania should also provide useful tests of adrenergic hypotheses of mania. Preliminary data of Zerssen (1976) and Moller et al. (1978) indicate that some manic patients improve during treatment with d-propranolol.

It is noteworthy that carbamazepine has been reported not only to block reuptake of norepinephrine into brain synaptosomes, but to decrease stimulated induced release of norepinephrine from rabbit ear arteries (Purdy et al., 1977). Carbamazepine, which appears to be a novel antimanic agent (Okuma et al., 1973; Ballenger and Post, 1978), decreased CSF norepinephrine in four manic patients (Post et al., 1978b).

Table 2. Dopamine Metabolism in Mania: Homovanillic Acid (HVA) in CSF

Investigator	Comparison Groups Controls*	Depressed*	Manic*	Significance Compared to Controls
Baseline Values				
Roos and Sjostrom, 1969	44 ± 31 (7)	29 ± 7 (6)	41 ± 23 (7)	NS
Bowers et al., 1969		22.7 ± 14.1† (8)	22.2 ± 16.3† (7)	
Sjostrom and Roos, 1972	36 ± 4 (23)	34 ± 4 (27)	59 ± 6 (36)	↑
Mendels et al., 1972		27.1 ± 22 (12)	44.2 ± 8.5 (2)	—
Goodwin et al., 1973	22.4 ± 2.4 (28)	15.2 ± 2.1 (49)	25.7 ± 4.3 (16)	NS
Sjostrom, 1973	34 ± 3 (38)	24 ± 3 (16)	59 ± 10 (11)	↑
Ashcroft and Glen, 1974	41 ± 23† (31)	34 ± 16† (9)	35 ± 15† (11)	(NS, but low HVA in recovered manics
Banki, 1977	33.4 ± 1.0 (32)	24 ± 1.5 unipolar (55) 15.9 ± 2.0 bipolar (16)	44.4 ± 3.8	↑
Probenecid Induced Accumulations				
Roos and Sjostrom, 1969	86 ± 43† (7)	48 ± 19† (6)	94 ± 57† (7)	NS
Sjostrom and Roos, 1972	(240% increase)	(83% increase)	(73% increase)	↓
Sjostrom, 1973	76 ± 14 (12)	44 ± 8 (7)	75 ± 15 (9)	NS
Goodwin et al., 1973		204 ± 17 (26)	226 ± 35 (8)	NS
Bowers, 1976		116 ± 11 (12)	169 ± 13 (10)	↑ vs. depressives
Goodwin and Post, 1977		215.8 ± 68.6† (41)	234.0 ± 87.0† (16)	NS

*Number of patients in parentheses.
†Standard deviation.
 Values = mean ± SEM in ng/ml.

EVIDENCE FOR DOPAMINE ALTERATIONS IN MANIC PATIENTS

Direct Measurements in Mania

As illustrated in Table 2, studies of baseline levels of HVA in the cerebrospinal fluid of manic patients do not note consistent alterations when compared to controls. Accumulations of homovanillic acid following probenecid administration are thought to represent a better measure of turnover of dopamine in the central nervous system than baseline levels (Goodwin et al., 1973). These accumulations following probenecid also indicate that HVA is not elevated in manic compared to psychiatric or normal control populations (Sjostrom and Roos, 1972; Sjostrom, 1972, 1973a, b; Goodwin et

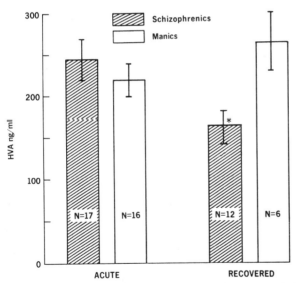

DIFFERENCES IN HVA ACCUMULATION IN
RECOVERED SCHIZOPHRENICS AND MANICS

Fig. 6. HVA accumulations following probenecid were not significantly higher in manic compared to acute schizophrenic patients. Manic patients restudied during a recovered period medication-free did not have decreased CSF HVA as did recovered schizophrenics (from Post et al., 1975).

al., 1973; Post et al., 1975; Post and Goodwin, 1975), although Bowers (1976) reported higher HVA accumulation in manics compared to depressives. In fact, the studies of Sjostrom and Roos suggest that, if anything, HVA levels may be *lower* than those in other comparison groups. As illustrated in Figure 6, HVA accumulations were also not significantly reduced when manic

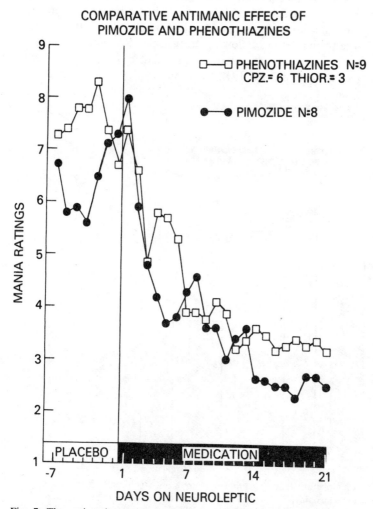

Fig. 7. The antimanic response to pimozide, a relatively specific blocker of dopamine receptors, is similar to that of chlorpromazine or thioridazine. These data indirectly implicate dopaminergic mechanisms in the manic syndrome. Note one to two day lag in onset of therapeutic efficacy (unpublished data with D. Jimerson, F.K. Goodwin, and W.E. Bunney, Jr.).

patients were restudied during a recovered period off medication, as were HVA's in restudied, improved schizophrenics (Post et al., 1975). There are no published data on the levels of dopamine itself in cerebrospinal fluid of manic patients. Increased excretion of urinary dopamine has been reported in manic patients (Sloane et al., 1966; Strom-Olsen and Weil-Malherbe, 1958; Messiha et al., 1970), although the relationship of urinary dopamine to CNS function remains problematic.

Indirect Pharmacological Data

The generally consistent negative finding of normal or below normal accumulations of HVA in cerebrospinal fluid contrasts with a large body of pharmacological evidence indicating a role for dopamine in the manic syndrome. Many neuroleptics, including the relatively specific dopamine receptor antagonist pimozide, are effective in treating the manic syndrome (as reviewed by Randrup et al., 1975; Post, unpublished manuscript, 1978) [Figures 7 and 8]. Lithium also has effects on dopaminergic mechanisms and

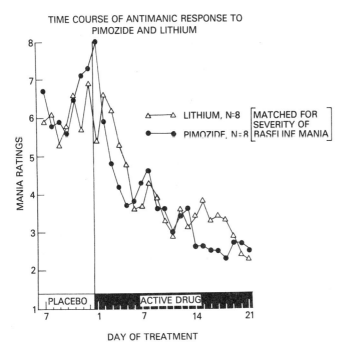

Fig. 8. The antimanic response to pimozide also compares favorably with that of lithium in a separate group of manic patients. Again, note the several day lag before onset of therapeutic effects in the lithium-treated patients (data from Post et al., unpublished manuscript, 1978).

has recently been shown to block the behavioral and dopaminergic receptor supersensitivity phase that usually follows neuroleptic administration (Pert et al., 1978). Carbamazepine significantly reduced HVA accumulations in five manic patients (Post et al., 1978b), an effect opposite to that of the antimanic neuroleptics, which block dopamine receptors and produce a compensatory increase in presynaptic dopamine synthesis. The mechanism of carbamazepine's effect on dopamine metabolism and the relationship to its antimanic properties are unknown.

Moreover, there are reports of the precipitation of mania following treatment with levodopa in a high proportion of bipolar depressed patients (Goodwin et al., 1978; Bunney, 1978; Murphy, 1972). In a single patient (Figure 9), we observed the consistent precipitation of mania following administration of either amphetamine or the direct dopamine agonist piribedil (Gerner et al., 1976). It is particularly noteworthy, however, that in more than 15 other patients studied with intravenous infusions of d-amphetamine (Jimerson et al., 1976; Reus et al., 1978) and/or given antidepressant clinical trials with the agonist piribedil (Post et al., 1978d), manic episodes were not observed. This patient may have had a particularly increased susceptibility to dopamine active compounds. In contrast, another manic patient was particularly unresponsive to several manipulations of the dopaminergic system (including pimozide, chlorpromazine, and low-dose

RELATIONSHIP OF MANIA TO DOPAMINE AGONISTS AND ANTAGONIST

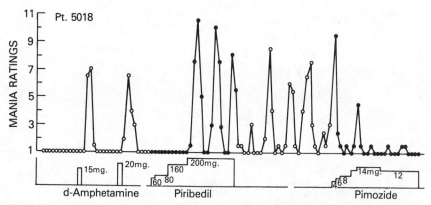

Fig. 9. The patient received amphetamine and piribedil during a depressive phase. Each was associated with the delayed onset of brief manic episodes lasting three to four days. These persisted following discontinuation of piribedil and were partially suppressed by the relatively specific dopamine receptor antagonist pimozide (from Gerner et al., 1977).

piribedil) and yet was exquisitely sensitive to lithium, both acutely and prophylactically. These data are suggestive of the presence of biochemical heterogeneity in the manic syndrome and that different patients may have dopamine sensitive or insensitive processes.

The increased frequency of manic episodes during long-term prophylactic treatment of depression with the tricyclic antidepressants is of interest in relation to effects on norepinephrine and serotonin, but also because of the recent suggestion that these compounds may have biochemically and behaviorally relevant effects on dopamine metabolism (Halaris and Freedman, 1975; Randrup and Braestrup, 1977). Possible explanations that might help reconcile the strong indirect pharmacological evidence for a role of dopamine in mania with the lack of direct biochemical evidence will be discussed later in the paper (section 9).

EVIDENCE OF SEROTONERGIC INVOLVEMENT IN MANIA

The major metabolite of serotonin 5-hydroxyindoleacetic acid (5-HIAA), like the dopamine metabolite HVA, is either unaltered or low in most studies of manic patients compared to controls (see Table 3). These data are of interest from several perspectives. L-tryptophan and 5-hydroxytryptophan (5-HTP) have been reported to have either antimanic or prophylactic effects in affective illness (Prange et al., 1974; van Praag, 1977, 1978). Moreover, a host of clinical and laboratory data implicate low serotonergic function in a variety of behavioral states that could be viewed as "release" from inhibitory control.

Many laboratory results indicate that decreased serotonergic function may increase not only spontaneous aggressive behaviors but also psychomotor activity and stereotypy following challenges with psychomotor stimulants. In animals, alterations in dopaminergic/serotonergic balance in favor of dopamine have been associated with increases in activation, exploration, hyperactivity, appetite, sexuality, and other symptoms commonly associated with the manic syndrome (Maj, 1976).

Consistent with these findings are the observations in man of a substantial negative correlation of CSF 5-HIAA with levels of aggression in patients with personality disorder (Brown et al., 1978). In schizophrenic patients, lower cerebrospinal fluid 5-HIAA was associated with increased Schneiderian positive symptoms and visual or auditory hallucinations (Post et al., 1975). Kirstein et al. (1976) reported higher levels of agitation and motor activity in schizophrenics with lower CSF 5-HIAA levels. Serotonin or its metabolite 5-HIAA have also been reported lower in brain autopsy specimens of Parkinsonian patients who became psychotic during levodopa administration

Table 3. Serotonin Metabolism in Mania:
5-Hydroxyindoleacetic Acid (5-HIAA) in CSF

Investigator	Comparison Groups			Significance Compared to Controls
	Controls*	Depressed*	Manic*	
Baseline Values				
Dencker et al., 1966			Low (6)	↓
Ashcroft et al., 1966	19.1 ± 4.4† (21)	11.1 ± 3.9† (24)	18.7 ± 5.4† (4)	NS
Bowers et al., 1969	39.5 ± 13.1† (8)	34.0 ± 11.5† (8)	32.0 ± 10.3† (8)	NS
Coppen et al., 1972	42.3 ± 14† (20)	19.8 ± 8.5† (31)	19.7 ± 6.8† (18)	↓
Roos, 1972	29 ± 7† (26)	31 ± 8† (17)	36 ± 9† (19)	↑
Mendels et al., 1972		12.9 ± 6.0 (2)	17.1 ± 14.6 (4)	NS
Goodwin et al., 1973	27.3 ± 1.6 (29)	25.5 ± 1.3 (58)	28.7 ± 2.5 (16)	NS
Sjostrom, 1973	29 ± 1 (39)	30 ± 1 (23)	33 ± 2 (15)	NS
Ashcroft and Glen, 1974	16 ± 8† (30)	18 ± 8† (9)	15 ± 6† (11)	NS, but low after treatment
Goodwin and Post, 1977		24.27 ± 9.79† (104)	29.00 ± 12.72† (28)	NS
Banki, 1977	27.5 ± 1.2 (32)	14.6 ± 1.7 (16)	13.9 ± 2.9 (10)	↓
Probenecid Induced Accumulations				
Roos and Sjostrom, 1969	46 ± 13† (11)	38 ± 11† (17)	43 ± 13† (19)	NS
Sjostrom and Roos, 1972	(66% increase) (13)	(27% increase) (24)	(20% increase) (21)	↓↓
Sjostrom, 1973	52 ± 4 (21)	37 ± 4 (11)	40 ± 4 (10)	NS
Goodwin et al., 1973		132 ± 7 (26)	133 ± 12 (8)	—
Bowers, 1976		106 ± 14 (12)	120 ± 11 (10)	—
Goodwin and Post, 1977		143 ± 54.0† (70)	164.6 ± 57.7† (24)	—

*Number of patients in parentheses.
†Standard deviation.
Values = means ± SEM in ng/ml.

compared to those who did not (Birkmayer et al., 1974). Low 5-HIAA in depressed patients was associated with an increased degree of amphetamine-induced dysphoria (Jimerson et al., 1977), and low 5-HIAA was associated with increased severity of Gilles de la Tourette's disease (Cohen et al., 1978). While complicated, the bulk of the evidence supports an inhibitory role for serotonin in the modulation of some symptoms in a variety of excited and/or psychotic states; its role in mania remains to be defined.

Counterbalancing this view of a serotonin deficiency "releasing"behavior from inhibitory control and an excess "damping" of a variety of states are the findings of increased motor activity when serotoninergic agents are given in combination with a monoamine oxidase inhibitor. Moreover, different areas of the serotonergic raphe system may differentially affect behavior (Geyer et al., 1976), also making a simple serotonin hypothesis difficult.

An inhibitory role for serotonin is difficult to reconcile with the recent finding of de Montigny and Aghajanian (1977) that chronic tricyclic administration leads to an increase in serotonergic receptor sensitivity as measured by firing of nerves in the lateral geniculate area following iontophoresis of 5-HT. An increased serotonergic receptor sensitivity might be expected to decrease rather than increase the incidence of mania during chronic tricyclic administration. Repeated ECT also has been reported to increase 5-HT (as well as NE and DA) receptor sensitivity (Grahame-Smith et al., 1978; Green et al., 1977).

γ-AMINOBUTYRIC ACID (GABA)

An inhibitory role for GABA on dopaminergic neurons has been postulated, leading to the suggestion that deficiency in GABA might be associated with hyperdopaminergic function in various psychotic states, such as mania and schizophrenia (Roberts, 1976; van Kammen, 1977). Few direct data are available in man, although one rapidly cycling schizoaffective patient (Table 4) had statistically significantly higher levels of GABA during manic phases of

Table 4. Evidence of Increased CSF Norepinephrine and GABA in Mania in a Rapidly Cycling Patient[1]

	Baseline		Probenecid	
	Depressed (n = 3)	Manic (n = 4)	Depressed (n = 5)	Manic (n = 1)
HVA2	64.3 ± 7.7	84.8 ± 2.2	267.0 ± 11.2	255
5-HIAA[2]	38 ± 12 (2)	34.3 ± 2.6	138 ± 11.8	110
NE[3]	205 (1)	390.0 ± 11.0	252.0 ± 60.5	433
GABA[4]	176.7 ± 12.0	250.0 ± 4.1	218.0 ± 16.9	260

[1]Patients cycles illustrated in Figure 10 (patient #33 in collaboration with A. Rey).
[2]Values = ng/ml ± SEM, number of values in parentheses (with Drs. Goodwin, Jimerson, Gordon).
[3]Values = pg/ml (in collaboration with R. Lake).
[4]Values = picomoles/ml (in collaboration with T. Hare).

his illness than when depressed (Post, Jimerson, Rey, Bunney, and Hare, unpublished data). An inverse relationship with postulated dopaminergic hyperactivity would also be consistent with data that levodopa increases and neuroleptics decrease GABA levels in rat substantia nigra acutely but not chronically as tolerance develops (Lloyd and Hornykiewicz, 1978).

CEREBROSPINAL FLUID ELECTROLYTES AND CYCLIC NUCLEOTIDES IN MANIA

Weston and Howard (1922) observed irritability and "maniacal attacks" following perfusion with low calcium solutions and suggested that "the maniacal activity of patients with manic depressive insanity...might be associated with a deficiency of calcium in the blood or spinal fluid or both." In studies originated by John Carman in our laboratory, we have been unable to document a significant decrease in serum calcium in spinal fluid of manic patients compared to controls. However, as illustrated in Figure 10, when individual patients are studied during different mood phases, levels of CSF

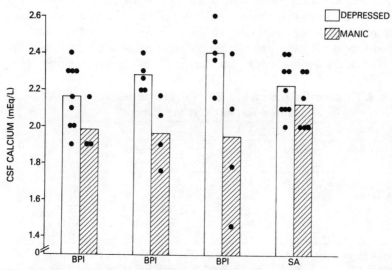

Fig. 10. Lower values of total CSF calcium were observed in the manic compared to depressed phases of rapidly cycling patients (from Jimerson et al., 1978).

calcium are significantly lower during the manic phase compared to the depressed phase (Jimerson et al., 1978). Carman and Wyatt (1977) have reported similar decreases in CSF calcium in cycling schizoaffective and schizophrenic patients, with low levels during the excited phase compared to the depressed phase. Interestingly, levels of cerebrospinal fluid calcium were lower in acutely psychotic schizophrenic patients compared to when they were restudied during recovery (Jimerson et al., 1978). In the future, measures of ionized calcium, which may represent a more sensitive index of altered calcium metabolism than total CSF calcium, should be studied and may resolve some of the controversy in the literature regarding the relationship between CSF calcium and psychiatric pathology.

Physiological and behavioral findings in animals are consistent with the notion of a general inverse relationship between brain calcium and neuronal excitability or psychomotor activation. In man, severe hypocalcemia associated with hyperparathyroidism may lead to seizures and excited states. Artificially lowered CSF calcium produces behavioral arousal in goats (Pappenheimer et al., 1962), while increases in calcium are anticonvulsant (Zuckerman and Glaser, 1973) or sedative (Felberg and Sherwood, 1957; Veal and Myers, 1971). Thus, the preliminary clinical data are provocative and require follow-up, not only because of the suggestive role of calcium itself in behavioral alterations, but also in light of the antimanic effects of lithium carbonate. Lithium carbonate alters a variety of neurochemical or electrolyte systems in the central nervous system, including that of the divalent cation calcium. Data supporting alterations in other electrolytes during mania have been reviewed elsewhere (Murphy et al., 1972).

The cyclic nucleotide adenosine 3' 5'-monophosphate (cyclic AMP) may serve as a second messenger in several neurotransmitter systems (Greengard, 1976; Nathanson and Greengard, 1977). Urinary cyclic AMP has been reported to be increased during the switch into mania in one study (Paul et al., 1971) and not another (Hullin et al., 1974). Jenner et al. (1972) and Brown et al. (1972) also failed to find significant increases in urninary cyclic AMP in mania compared to depression.

Preliminary CSF data in a small number of manic patients do not support the notion that there are major alterations in cerebrospinal fluid levels of either cyclic AMP or cyclic GMP (Cramer et al., 1972; Smith et al., 1976; Post et al., 1977a [Figure 11]).

The origin of cyclic nucleotides in CSF and their relationship to central nervous sytem function remain obscure, however. A variety of pharmacological agents do not appear to produce major alterations in cyclic AMP in CSF, and more sensitive indicators of alterations in neurotransmitter function a receptor level in man are needed before drawing conclusions about altered cyclic AMP or receptor function in mania.

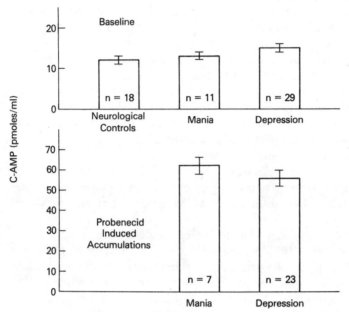

CYCLIC AMP IN CSF OF MANIC AND DEPRESSED PATIENTS

Fig. 11. Baseline or probenecid-induced accumulations of cyclic AMP were not significantly different in manic compared to depressed or neurological patients (Post et al., 1977a).

NEUROENDOCRINE AND PEPTIDE APPROACHES TO MANIA

Clinicians have long been aware of the potential euphoriant actions of adrenocorticotropic hormone (ACTH) and glucocorticoid administration. Few data are available that demonstrate alterations in the pituitary adrenal axis in manic patients, however (Murphy et al., 1975). Carroll (1978) has recently reported lower levels of urinary-free cortisol and a better response to dexamethazone suppression in the manic state compared to the depressed phase of the illness, although an overall change in manic patients compared to controls remains to be documented. The concept of limbic-hypothalamic dysregulation of ACTH and glucocorticoids in affective illness (Carroll, 1976) remains attractive and deserves future exploration.

A decreased growth-hormone responsiveness to dopamine agonist or insulin challenge has also been reported in several studies of small numbers of manic patients (Gold et al., 1976; Casper et al., 1977; Rotrosen, 1978). An increased excretion of urinary melatonin was found in four manic patients compared to a depressed patient comparison group (Lewy et al., 1978). These findings are provocative not only in relation to the possible effects of melatonin on mood (Carman et al., 1976), but as they may provide an index of central β-adrenergic receptor activity in the CNS of man.

The recent reports on behaviorally active ACTH fragments devoid of glucocorticoid effects (DeWeid, 1977) also suggest a new avenue of investigation in mania. TRH and MIF-I are both behaviorally active in animal studies and have been reported to have antidepressant effects (Prange et al., 1978; Ehrensing and Kastin, 1978). These and many other peptide compounds, including vasopressin (Gold et al., 1978; Raskind et al., 1978), have not been documented as altered in mania, but provide new possible approaches to the illness. They also have a time course of onset of action and duration that make them particularly relevant in light of the temporal charactistics of many psychiatric syndromes and their slow response to acute pharmacological treatments.

The newly discovered endogenous opiate systems, involving enkephalins and β-endorphin, have also become candidates for postulated alterations in mania in light of their prominent effects on mood and psychomotor activity. Judd and collaborators (1978) reported antimanic responses in several patients following the administration of intravenous doses of naloxone, a blocker of endogenous opiate receptors. No clinically relevant antimanic effects have been observed in the studies of Davis et al. (1977, 1978) although one manic patient showed decreases in pressure of speech during repeated injections of naloxone compared to placebo. Lindstrom and collaborators (1978) have also reported increases in endogenous opiate activity (Fraction I) measured in cerebrospinal fluid in manic patients.

Again, these highly preliminary data are particularly intriguing both in their own right and also for the new conceptual framework they present for biochemical studies in manic illness. In may biochemical systems, acute biochemical or environmental stressors are capable of producing long-lasting changes in biochemistry. For example, reserpine or cold exposure stress results in the transynaptic induction of tyrosine hydroxylase in the rat adrenal medulla (Costa and Guidotti, 1978). Similar long-lasting neuromodulatory and regulatory changes appear to occur in several of the polypeptide systems. Acute alterations in a variety of neurotransmitter and modulator systems may transiently occur (possibly explaining the negative results in many human studies of amine function) and trigger longer-lasting alterations in synaptic efficacy and behaviorally relevant set points. Olds (1976) has postulated and Chan-Palay et al. (1978) have found preliminary evidence that polypeptide neuromodulatory substances may be located in the same nerve cells containing biogenic amine transmitters and may be released with different time courses of effect.

PHARMACOLOGICAL DISSECTION OF LEVEL OF BIOCHEMICAL DEFECT IN MANIC-DEPRESSIVE ILLNESS

Consideration of the neurotransmitter-receptor level at which the routine symptomatic treatments of mania (neuroleptics) and depression (tricyclic antidepressants, MAOI's) act, compared to agents that are useful in both phases of the illness, may be important to the understanding of basic or etiological mechanisms. As illustrated in Table 5, these agents are useful in both the acute and the prophylactic treatment of the respective phases of the illness, but are not useful in, and may even exacerbate, the manifestation of the opposite mood phase. That is, the neuroleptic may worsen depression,and the antidepressants worsen or precipitate mania.

However, several agents act on both phases of the illness, and a comparison of these with the drugs acting on a single mood phase may yield important clues to the "deeper," more basic defects in manic-depressive illness. Lithium is therapeutic in both the manic and depressive phases, and preliminary evidence suggests that carbamazepine may likewise be effective (Okuma et aa.,l., 1973; Ballenger and Post, 1978 [Figure 12]). Lithium and carbamazepine also appear to have long-term prophylactic effects in both phases. (ECT is effective in both phases, but its prophylactic usefulness is questionable.)

The mechanisms of the antimanic effects of carbamazepine are largely unknown, although several biochemical changes have been reported in animals and man (Ballenger and Post, 1978; Post et al., 1978b). Carbamazepine is often the drug of choice in temporal lobe epilepsy, and animal and clinical data support the notion that it has more prominenet limbic compared to cortical anticonvulsant activity. Carbamazepine is a tricyclic which, like many tricyclic antidepressants, blocks reuptake of norepinephrine. However, carbamazepine also has an effect opposite to that of amphetamine on norepinephrine release. It blocks stimulated induced release of norepinephrine, a mechanism conceptually compatible with its antimanic effects. It also affects dopamine, acetylcholine, electrolyte, and cyclic nucleotide function. Are its limbic anticonvulsant effects related to the antimanic effects in man? Even if this is the case, what are the biochemical underpinnings of this effect?

Intriguingly, lithium is a simple univalent cation with a wide CNS distribution and many possible levels of molecular action. Biochemical actions shared by lithium and carbamazepine (and ECT) might lead one toward the more basic alterations in mania and depression. In this regard, the effects of lithium on limbic excitability (Delgado and DeFeudis, 1967) relative to those of carbamazepine would make an important comparative study and would lend support to the concept of limbic alterations in affective illness.

Our data (Ballenger and Post, 1978) and that of Okuma et al. (1973) also suggest, however, that some manic patients who are lithium nonresponders respond well to carbamazepine and vice versa. Thus, heterogeneity of biochemical alterations may also be implied by the pharmacological responses to these drugs and the dopamine agonists and antagonists (see above), and may lead to more precise psychobiological dissection of the manic syndrome.

ALTERNATE CONCEPTUAL APPROACHES
TO TRANSMITTER ALTERATIONS IN MANIA

The dopaminergic system will be discussed as a prototype for several alternative approaches to transmitter-receptor alterations postulated on the basis of pharmacological data. Although dopamine is the focus of this discussion, arguments may apply to other neurochemical systems. For example, there is a growing literature on the possible involvement of phenylethylamine in affective alterations (Sabelli and Giardina, 1973; Wyatt et al., 1977). An interaction of dopamine with other transmitters and modulators is also assumed throughout the discussion. There is pharmacological evidence in manic patients and in animal models that dopaminergic tone in balance with acetylcholinergic function is behaviorally relevant. The evidence for disturbed dopaminergic-acetylcholinergic balance in mania has been extensively reviewed by Janowsky (this volume) and Davis et al. (1978). In addition, dopaminergic-serotonergic balance could affect a variety of behavioral and cognitive disturbances observed in mania similar to those observed in animals models—including activation, exploration, sexuality, and appetite. Although the preliminary biochemical data in manic patients suggest that norepinephrine is increased (Post et al., 1978c), Antelman and Caggiula (1977) have postulated that low noradrenergic function may also facilitate some behaviors mediated by dopamine. GABA and a variety of peptide modulators interact with the dopaminergic system such that alterations in dopamine itself or related systems could alter symptoms observed in mania.

There are several ways to conceptualize negative data on HVA accumulations following probenecid in manic patients in relation to the role of dopaminergic mechanisms postulated on the basis of convincing, but indirect, pharmacological data.

Table 5. Pharmacological Spectrum of Effects in Affective Illness: Implications for Etiology and Pathogenesis

Agents	Mania Therap.[1] Effects	Mania Precip.[2] or Exacer.[3]	Depression Therap.[1] Effects	Depression Precip.[2] or Exacer.[3]	Postulated Mechanisms
Antimanic Agents Only					
Neuroleptics	++			✓	DA receptor blockade
Reserpine	++			✓✓	Amine depletion
α-methyl-p-tyrosine	++			✓	DA, NE depletion
Physostigmine	+			✓	↑ ACH tone; ↓ functional catecholamines or balance with acetylcholine
Antidepressant Agents Only					
Tricyclics		✓	++		↑ NE, 5HT (reuptake or receptor sensitivity)
Monoamine Oxidase Inhibitors (MAOI's)		✓	++		↑ NE, 5HT, DA
(Piribedil)		(✓)	(+)		↑ DA receptor activity; ↑ functional NE, 5HT (DA)

Combined Acute Effectiveness			
Electroconvulsive Therapy (ECT)	++	++	Pre- and postsynaptic effects on DA, NE, 5HT
Tryptophan	+	+	Enhanced 5HT
Combined Acute & Prophylactic Effectiveness			
Lithium	++	(++)	Mechanisms unknown: presumed common effects on neural substrates underlying both mood phases or state dependent biochemical effects such that different changes occur with the same drug depending on the initial values or set points.
Carbamazepine	++	(++)	

[1]Therap = Therapeutic
[2]Precip. = Precipitate
[3]Exacer. = Exacerbate

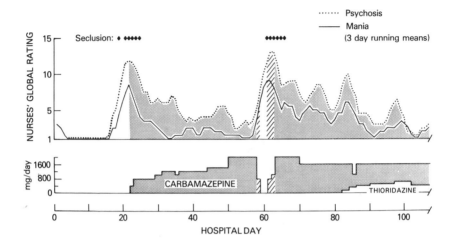

Fig. 12. Treatment with carbamazepine (Tegretol) resulted in marked improvement in this manic-depressive patient. During placebo substitution (cross-hatched and unshaded periods), the patient experienced an exacerbation of his manic psychosis. As carbamazepine was reinstituted during this double-blind trial, he again showed notable improvement (see Ballenger and Post, 1978, for details).

Receptor Alterations

Since HVA represents a measure of presynaptic dopaminergic metabolism, it is possible that dopaminergic *receptor* function is altered in mania and is not detectable by current clinical assessment techniques. That is, there could be increased dopamine receptor function in mania that would be reflected by either no change or actually a compensatory decrease in presynaptic dopamine turnover (Bunney et al., 1977). This formulation was also suggested by Bowers (1975) in relation to his findings of low HVA accumulation in acutely schizophrenic patients. Possible regional alterations in receptor mechanism are discussed below (sections E and F).

Altered Transport or Enzymatic Degration

Another explanation for the lack of increase in HVA could be that dopamine levels are actually increased in brain or cerebrospinal fluid, but the transport and disposal mechanisms for HVA do not allow this to be observed. Deficits in monoamine oxidase (Murphy et al., 1978) or catechol-o-methyl-transferase activity could also decrease degration of dopamine to dihydroxy-phenylacetic acid (DOPAC) and homovanillic acid (HVA), even though functionally available dopamine is actually increased. Deficits in monoamine oxidase, particularly in bipolar compared to unipolar patients, are intriguing in light of the apparent stability of the measure in the same patient over time, its genetic aspects, and its possible relationship in normals to a vulnerability to behavioral disorders (Murphy et al., 1978). Decreased deactivation by a genetically deficient MAO system of several endogenous neurotransmitter substrates released during stress, including dopamine, norepinephrine, or phenylethylamine, is a provocative concept in the study of vulnerability to mania. Biological alterations that are observed in the "well interval" or in the depressed state in bipolar patients may help dissect the role of predisposing, precipitating, and state-dependent correlative changes in mania.

Time-Dependent Effects

Another alternate view of negative HVA data is that HVA increases are present during an acute phase of manic episodes, but, similar to compensatory changes observed to a variety of pharmacological agents over time (Post and Goodwin, 1975), the HVA increases are attentuated with increasing duration of the manic episode. Mandell (1978) highlighted the redundant mechanisms for the regulation of tyrosine hydroxylase. Perhaps multiple feedback adaptations and compensatory changes are adequate to return an altered dopaminergic system toward normal. Arguing against this interpretation are the data presented in Table 4 of a rapidly cycling manic-depressive patient. In this individual studied multiple times during his manic and depressed phases, there was no consistent pattern of HVA increases in mania compared to the depressed phase even when this patient and several other rapid cyclers were studied within several days of the onset of their manic episodes.

HVA accumulations following probenecid were higher in manic compared to nonmanic patients treated with chlorpromazine, thioridazine, or pimozide (Post et al., unpublished manuscript, 1978). These data might suggest that activation of dopamine turnover following neuroleptic treatment is greater in manic patients even though the initial HVA accumulations were not significantly higher than in nonmanic patients.

It is also possible that HVA is *low* in the well interval state, and with the onset of mania HVA increases toward normal values, indicating a relative excess in dopaminergic function compared to baseline. Again, data in recovered manics compared to schizophrenics (Figure 6) and longitudinal data in individual patients are not supportive of this formulation.

Lag in Drug-Induced Onset and Offset of Mania

The possibility remains that dopamine is involved in the triggering and modulation of mania (based on the pharmacological evidence), but the alterations are either extremely transient or are mediated through and reflected biochemically in other neurotransmitter or modulatory systems. Consistent with this notion are the observations of repeated fortuitous induction of mania by amphetamine in the single patient described above (Gerner et al., 1977 [Figure 9]). On two occasions the patient became manic after amphetamine, not immediately following the intravenous infusions when dopamine and noradrenergic systems should have been maximally activated and when patients usually experience maximum intensity of euphoric or dysphoric activation, but the next day, some 32 to 34 hours later. This lag in onset may relate to the time required to induce or transport critical regulatory enzymes (Costa and Guidotti, 1978; Mandell and Knapp, 1978), affect receptor protein (Nathanson and Greengard, 1977) or peptide neuro-modulators (Chan-Palay et al., 1978).

As illustrated in Figures 8 and 9, there is a similar lag period of several days or more in manic "offsets" achieved by a variety of dopamine active pharmacological agents, including the relatively specific (pimozide) and nonspecific (chlorpromazine and thioridazine) neuroleptics, as well as lithium. Even electroconvulsive therapy, which has recently been shown to increase dopaminergic (and NE and 5-HT) receptor activity chronically but not acutely (Modigh, 1970, 1976; Green et al., 1977), appears to have a lag in onset.

Thus, similar to the manic onsets observed in Figure 9, longer-term regulatory changes may have to be induced by these therapeutic agents before improvement in manic symptoms is noted. This lag may be even longer for core psychotic symptoms in mania and schizophrenia. It is noteworthy that in patient #22 (Figure 13), all the onsets and offsets of mania during a medication-free interval were extremely rapid and dramatic, but those observed during lithium carbonate administration were slow and gradual (although of similar magnitude). In this patient, her spontaneous manic onsets and offsets were largely "all or none" phenomena, while those on lithium and neuroleptics were graded. Subsequently she experienced an essentially complete prophylactic response when treated with lithium alone as an outpatient. This observation might suggest that lithium initially was only indirectly affecting or modulating the critical biochemical mechanisms involved in this patient's manic episodes. The regulatory or reset mechanisms affected in mania may take time to be altered in the appropriate direction and magnitude. Pert et al. (1978) have demonstrated that chronic but not acute pretreament with lithium will block behavioral and receptor supersensitivity following neuroleptics. The time lags involved in this phenomenon may be clinically relevant and point to possible underlying mechanisms involving effects on "compensatory" dopamine receptor alterations.

Costa and Guidotti (1978) and Nathanson and Greengard (1977) emphasize the time course required for the transynaptic induction of new protein, a step requiring a cascade of sequential actions, involving (1) the receptor site; (2) adenylate cyclase; (3) activation of a protein kinase; (4) translocation of phosphorylated protein into the nucleus; (5) altered RNA; (6) new protein

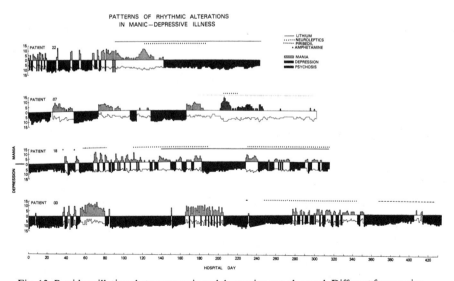

Fig. 13. Rapid oscillations between mania and depression are observed. Different frequencies are noted within and between patients. Many of the switches during medication-free intervals have an "all or none" pattern, especially in patients 22, 7, 33. During lithium treatment (alone and in combination with neuroleptics), the manic onsets and offset in patient #22 became more gradual.

synthesis; and finally (7), a new level of enzyme or receptor activity. Recent studies have reported that alterations in synaptic efficacy as observed in hippocampal posttetanic potentiation may involve changes in dendritic spines that are anatomically demonstrable (Lynch, 1978). Similarly, alterations in neurons have been induced by appropriate environmental-social manipulations during maturation (Globus and Coss, 1978). These possible anatomical reflections of altered synaptic function or plasticity could also require considerable time to produce, as well as to modify or reverse with appropriate drug or physiological treatments. Thus, exogenously or endogenously produced acute neurotransmitter alterations may be associated with a complex spatio-temporal sequence of changes leading to a new chronic baseline, which might be critical for behavioral regulation.

Regional Dopaminergic System in Relation to Manic Symptoms

Numerous investigators have suggested that dopaminergic areas in the mesolimbic system, particularly in the nucleus accumbens, may be more closely associated with increases in motor activity than the nigro-striatal system, which is more closely associated with stereotypic behavior (Costall and Naylor, 1977; Moore and Kelly, 1978; Scheel-Kruger et al., 1977; Cools, 1977; Ljungberg and Ungerstedt, 1977, 1978; LeMoal et al., 1977; Tassin et al., 1977). It is perhaps a fortunate coincidence for clinical neuroscientists interested in the study and therapy of Parkinson's disease that the caudate nucleus lines the walls of the lateral ventricles and provides a major contribution to the total amount of HVA in CSF, so that changes in Parkinson's disease are readily reflected in CSF. It is possible that alterations in mesolimbic or mesocortical dopamine areas more distant from the ventricular system would not be reflected in cerebrospinal fluid measures of dopamine metabolism.

The conceptualization of regional neurotransmitter systems possessing relatively different effects on behavior could lead to a speculative neuroanatomy of manic symptoms (Table 6). That is, alterations in neurotransmitter regulation and balance could affect different and successively higher levels of integrative function, such as the midbrain, striatal, hypothalamic, and limbic systems, as well as the cerebral cortex. Basic drive and arousal mechanisms may in part be set by midbrain and hypothalmic mechanisms, as would be the alterations in sleep and appetite. Motor mechanisms may be critically influenced at dopaminergic striatal and mesolimbic systems, while the mesocortical dopaminergic systems could also be linked to higher cognitive, social, and language disturbances of mania. To the extent that there are

**Table 6. A Speculative Neuroanatomy of Manic Symptoms:
Relative Regional Dopaminergic Tone in Balance with
Other Transmitter-Receptor Systems**

Manic Symptoms	Nigrastriatal	Hypothalamic	Mesolimbic	Mesocortical
Motor hyperactivity, stereo-typy, catatonic bizarre posturing	++	+	++	+
Appetite, sexuality, aggression	++	++	+	+
Mood: elation, irritability, anxiety, lability	+	+	++	++
Decreased need for sleep, excessive energy	+	++	++	+
Ideational hyperactivity, flight of ideas, idiosyncratic and clang associations			++	++
Religiosity, hypergraphia, grandiosity, delusions, hallucinations	+	+	++	+

regional specificities to transmitter receptor mechanisms, regional alterations in dopaminergic function could account for varying clinical pictures and the appearance and disappearance of different manic symptoms with different time courses. A related conceptualization is that dopaminergic influences on a given behavioral syndrome is more finely and discretely regulated at successively higher levels of the neuroaxis. In a fashion similar to that suggested for temperature regulation, striatal, limbic, and cortical dopaminergic mechanisms may all be involved in the regulation of psychomotor activation, but a finer tuning and higher level of integration, perhaps more linked to subtle psychosocial influences, would occur at a cortical compared to limbic or striatal level.

Different Dopamine Receptors in Relation to Manic Behavior

This view of an interaction of neurotransmitters acting on different neuroanatomical substrates would also be consistent with existing pharmacological data. Neuroleptics, reserpine, and alpha-methylparatyrosine (AMPT), an inhibitor of tyrosine hydroxylase, presumably are exerting their antimanic effects through decreasing functional catecholaminergic synaptic activity. Low doses of dopamine agonist compounds may also be inhibiting dopaminergic through selective activation of presynaptic receptors (Carlsson, 1975; Strombom, 1976; Aghajanian and Bunney, 1974). Data in a very small number of patients suggest that low doses of piribedil, apomorphine, or bromocriptine may have sedative or even antimanic effects on man (Post et al., 1977a, b). These data are comprehensible in an alternative of theoretical frameworks, however. Cools and van Rosum (1976) have suggested that some dopamine agonist compounds act on inhibitory as opposed to excitatory dopamine receptors in the central nervous system. Creese and Snyder's suggestion (1978) that antagonist and agonist conformations of the dopamine receptor may be interconvertible provide another mechanism for conceptualizing dual actions on dopaminergic mediated functional activity at a receptor level. Ljungberg and Ungerstedt (1977, 1978) suggest that different dopamine agonists and antagonists differentially affect limbic versus striatal mechanisms. Comparison of the antimanic effects of clozapine, sulpiride, thioridazine (all relatively more limbic), with pimozide and haloperidol (more striatal) would be of particular clinical and theoretical interest.

RAPID CYCLING IN MANIC-DEPRESSIVE ILLNESS: IMPLICATIONS OF A PARKINSON'S DISEASE MODEL

The known neurochemical alterations in Parkinson's disease present an interesting inverse biochemical model for mania. A prominent feature of Parkinsonian illness is a psychomotor retardation—difficulty in initiating both gross motor and linguistic sequences. In mania, the reverse obtains—there is often an inability to slow down or stop once activity or speech has been initiated. Nauta (1978) has emphasized the possible parallelisms and interactions between mesolimbic and cortical dopaminergic systems (possibly mediating motivational, affective, and cognitive function) and those of the nigrostriatal (relatively more closely associated with motor mechanisms).

The model of Parkinsonian illness may also be a useful one for conceptualizing possible transmitter-receptor mechanisms underlying the development of very rapid alterations in behavioral state. With chronic levodopa therapy of Parkinson's disease, patients experience an increased incidence of dyskinetic phenomena and ultimately the "on-off effect" or periods of time when Parkinsonian immobility rapidly alterate with severe dyskinesias (Figure 14). These dyskinetic and on-off phenomena emerge with increasing frequency and severity following increasing durations of levodopa or dopamine agonist treatment (DiMascio et al., 1973; McDowell and Barbeau, 1974; Klawans et al., 1975). To the extent that manic symptoms may be related to increased dopaminergic tone in striatal or mesolimbic and

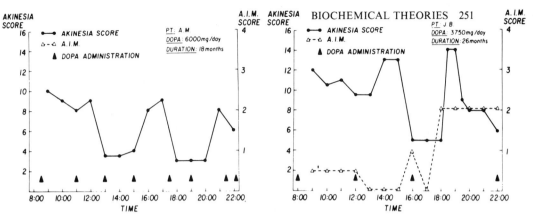

FIG. 3. Type one (first-stage) oscillations in performance.

FIG. 5. Type two (second-stage) oscillations in performance.

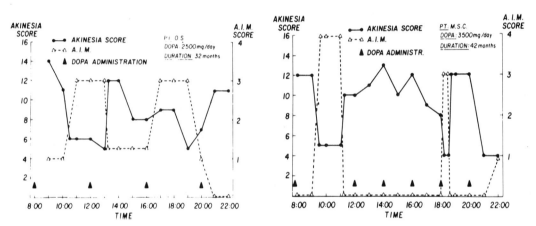

FIG 6 Type three (third-stage) oscillations in performance

FIG. 7. Type four (fourth-stage) oscillations in performance.

Fig. 14. Note increased amplitude of on-off oscillations in Parkinsonian patients treated with chronic levodopa. Severe akinesias and involuntary movements (A.I.M.) alternate. The evolution of these motor phenomena may be a useful model for rapidly cycling mood disorders highlighting increasing transmitter receptor dysregulation (from Barbeau, 1974).

mesocortical dopaminergic areas, the concept of progressive dopamine agonist supersensitivity might be a useful approach to rapidly recurrent manic illness or that alternating with severe depression. Repeated administration of a variety of indirect- and direct-acting dopamine agonists (Table 8) may lead to behavioral sensitization or a kindling-like facilitation of responsivity to subsequent agonist challenges.

Psychological side effects to long-term levodopa therapy of Parkinson's disease also evolve over time (Moskovitz et al., 1978) and may be an important lead to the biochemistry of mental and motor phenomena in

Table 7. Temporal Sequence of Psychomotor Pathology Following Chronic Repeated Dopaminergic and Stimulant Administration

Evolution of levodopa Side Effects in Parkinsonian Patients[1]

Psychological:
  normal → vivid dreams → daytime illusions → paranoid psychosis → confusional psychosis
Motor:
  immobility → improvement → dyskinesias → on-off oscillations of dyskinesias and immobility

Evolution of Psychomotor Stimulant Effects

Psychological (in man):
  normal → euphoria → dysphoria → paranoid psychosis → confusional psychosis
                                   (dyskinesias)
Motor (in animals):
  locomotor hyperactivity → mild stereotypy → intense stereotypy → motor inhibition → catalepsy
                                   (dyskinesias)

[1]From Klawans et a., 1975; Moskowitz et al., 1978

mania. Some Parkinsonian patients treated with levodopa experience increasingly vivid dreams that spill over into their waking life and finally develop into hallucinatory phenomena. A full-blown paranoid psychosis may emerge, and finally a confusional psychosis may occur. The emergence of a sequence of different symptoms over time in relationship to chronic dopaminergic treatment again highlights the progressive aspects of psychological and motor symptoms in mania.

The Parkinsonian model also directs attention to loss of normal regulatory and compensatory presynaptic neurotransmitter mechanisms in balance with postsynaptic receptor mechanisms. As the illness progresses, the dopaminergic defect is eventually associated with a receptor loss (measured by ^{3}H-apomorphine), and compensatory receptor (^{3}H-haloperidol binding) increases (Lee et al., 1978). Chronic levodopa therapy on top of this altered dopamine system may, then, be associated with increasing psychological and motor dysregulation, i.e., psychosis and dyskinesias. Eventually, the dyskinesias rapidly alternate with Parkinsonian immobility, possibly a reflection of the loss of integrated balance and regulation at the dopaminergic synapse. This might involve both unphysiological presynaptic mechanisms in response to levodopa therapy and unphysiological postsynaptic compensatory receptor alterations.

Might not increasingly severe and rapid mood swings in manic-depressive illness also relate to the progressive dysregulation of transmitter-receptor

Table 8. Evidence for Behavioral Sensitization to Repeated Dopamine Active Agents: Increases in Hyperactivity, Stereotypy, or Seizures*

Pretreatment	Increased Response to Test Agent
Amphetamine	Amphetamine, apomorphine
	NOT TO: morphine or cocaine
Cocaine	Cocaine
	NOT TO: amphetamine
Methylphenidate	Methylphenidate
Morphine	Cocaine
Lidocaine	Cocaine
Apomorphine	Apomorphine, amphetamine
Bromocriptine	Bromocriptine, amphetamine, apomorphine
Levodopa	Levodopa, amphetamine, apomorphine
Phenylethylamine (PEA)	Phenylethylamine (PEA)
Piribedil, S589 and Levodopa	Apomorphine
Electroconvulsive Shock	Methamphetamine, apomorphine, 5-methoxy NN dimethyltryptamine, clonidine, alcohol withdrawal
Amygdala Kindling	Lidocaine seizures, decreased cocaine effect, alcohol withdrawal

*For Selected References see Tables 1, 4 in Post and Ballenger, 1978.

feedback systems in a different biochemical-anatomical substrate? In 1904 Kraepelin observed the tendency for increased frequency of cycling in manic-depressive illness. "That in the course of time the duration and severity of the attacks have increased, while the intervals have become shorter and shorter, corresponds with the general experience of the disease [page 61]." Lundquist (1945) and Grof et al. (1974, 1978) have further documented these observations in large numbers of unipolar depressives and bipolar manic-depressive patients (see also Figure 10).

Hypothetically, low levels of dopamine might occur in mesolimbic-cortical systems initially as the result of stress (Thierry et al., 1976), a prior depression, a pharmacological intervention, or a genetic defect. This deficit state might then evoke a compensatory increase in dopamine receptor sites (Creese et al., 1977; Snyder et al., 1978), resulting in increased dopaminergic sensitivity (see Bunney and Post, 1977). Upon challenge of these supersensitive receptors with endogenous or exogenous dopaminergic agents, an increased activation or manic response might result. Repeated initiation of this sequence could gradually lead to severe overshooting of normally adaptive regulatory mechanisms (like the on-off phenomena during chronic levodopa therapy).

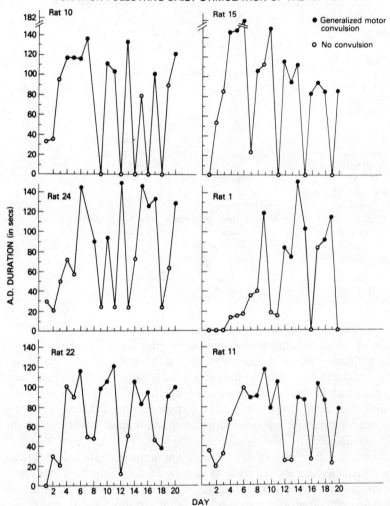

Fig. 15. Repeated once daily electrical stimulation of the amydala evokes increasingly long after-discharges, which eventually result in major motor seizures to a previous threshold stimulus (200 μamps for 0.5 seconds). Such a kindling procedure produces long-lasting changes in amygdala thresholds and excitability. Following repeated stimulation, some rats develop regular oscillations in amygdala after-discharge duration and seizures (Post et al., 1978a).

Perez-Cruet (personal communication, 1976) and Bridger et al. (1978) have demonstrated that HVA alterations in brain originally induced by drugs may be conditioned. Might not a similar conditioning of endogenous biochemical changes associated with repeated episodes of mania and depression predispose to further recurrences and biochemical changes?

The pharmacological sensitization and electrical kindling paradigms (Post and Kopanda, 1977; Post et al., 1978a [see Figure 15]) as well as the on-off phenomena in Parkinsonian patients may be useful models for the evolution of rapid cycling. In particular, they lead to the consideration of increasingly severe and maladaptive alterations in biochemical regulatory mechanisms.

If this conceptual framework is useful, it would predict that early prophylaxis of recurrent mood disorder might decrease the ultimate predisposition to rapid cycling. However, with the advent of efficacious long-term therapies, such as lithium carbonate and possibly carbamazepine (Okuma et al., 1973; Ballenger and Post, 1978), a definitive prospective study of patients off medication for long periods of time may be ethically difficult.

REFERENCES

Aghajanian, G.K., and Bunney, B.S. Central dopaminergic neurons: Neurophysiological identification and responses to drugs. In *Frontiers in Catecholamine Research,* E. Usdin and S.H. Snyder, eds. Pergamon, New York (1974), pp. 643–648.

Aghajanian, G.K., Cedarbaum, J.M., and Wang, R.Y. Evidence for norepinephrine-mediated collateral inhibition of locus coeruleus neurons. *Brain Res.* 136, 570–577 (1977).

Akiskal, H.S., and McKinney, W.T. Depressive disorders: Toward a unified hypothesis. *Science* 182, 20–29 (1973).

Akiskal, H.S., and McKinney, W.T. Overview of recent research in depression. Integration of ten conceptual models into a comprehensive clinical frame. *Arch. Gen. Psychiat.* 32, 285–305 (1975).

Antelman, S.M., and Caggiula, A.R. Norepinephrine-dopamine interactions and behavior: A new hypothesis of stress-related interactions between brain norepinephrine and dopamine is proposed. *Science* 195, 646–653 (1977).

Ashcroft, G.W., and Glen, A.I.M. Mood and neuronal functions: A modified amine hypothesis for the etiology of affective illness. *Adv. Biochem. Psychopharmacol.* 11, 335–339 (1974).

Ashcroft, G.W., Crawford, T.B.B., and Eccleston, D. 5-Hydroxyindole compounds in the cerebrospinal fluid of patients with psychiatric or neurological diseases. *Lancet* II, 1049–1050 (1966).

Ashcroft, G.W., Blackburn, I.M., Eccleston, D., Glen, A.I.M., Hardley, W., Kinloch, N.E., Lonergan, M., Murray, L.G., and Pullar, I.A. Changes on recovery in the concentrations of tryptophan and the biogenic amine metabolites in the cerebrospinal fluid of patients with affective illness. *Psychol. Med.* 3, 319–325 (1973).

Baldessarini, R.J. The basis for amine hypothesis in affective disorders. *Arch. Gen. Psychiat.* 32, 1087–1093 (1975).

Ballenger, J.C., and Post, R.M. Therapeutic effects of carbamazepine in affective illness: A preliminary report. *Commun. Psychopharmacol.* 2, 159–175 (1978).

Banki, C.M. Correlation between cerebrospinal fluid amine metabolites and psychomotor activity in affective disorders. *J. Neurochem.* 28, 225–257 (1977).

Birkmayer, W., Danielczyk, W., Neumayer, E., and Riederer, P. Nucleus ruber and L-DOPA psychosis: Biochemical post-mortem findings. *J. Neural Transm.* 35, 93–116 (1974).

Bond, P.A., Jenner, F.A., and Sampson, G.A. Daily variations in the urine content of 3-methoxy-4-hydroxyphenyl glycol in two manic-depressive patients. *Psychol. Med.* 2, 81–85 (1972).

Bowers, M.B. Central dopamine turnover in schizophrenic syndromes. *Arch. Gen. Psychiat.* 31, 50–54 (1974a).

Bowers, M.B. Lumbar CSF 5-hydroxyindoleacetic acid and homovanillic acid in affective sydromes. *J. Nerv. Ment. Dis.* 158, 325–330 (1974b).

Bowers, M.B. CSF acid monoamine metabolites as a possible reflection of central MAO activity in chronic schizophrenia. *Biol. Psychiat.* 11, 245–249 (1976).

Bowers, M.B., Heninger, G.R., and Gerbode, F.A. Cerebrospinal fluid 5-hydroxy-indoleacetic acid and homovanillic acid in psychiatric patients. *Int. J. Neuropharmacol.* 8, 255–262 (1969).

Bridger, W.H., Schiff, S.R., and King, J. Classical conditioning of dopamine neurons. Presented at the 131st Annual Meeting of the American Psychaitric Association, Atlanta, May, 1978. *New Research Abstracts #16.*

Brown, B.L., Salway, J.G., Albano, J.D.M., Hullin, R.P., and Ekins, R.P. Urinary excretion of cyclic AMP and manic-depressive psychosis. *Br. J. Psychiat.* 120, 405–408 (1972).

Brown, G.L., Goodwin, F.K., Ballenger, J.C., Goyer, P.F., and Major, L.F. CSF amine metabolites in human aggression. Presented at the 131st Annual Meeting of the American Psychiatric Association, Atlanta, May, 1978. *Sci. Proc. Am. Psychiatr. Assn.* 131, 88 (1978), Abstract #180.

Bunney, B.S. Central dopaminergic systems: Two *in vivo* electrophysiological models for predicting therapeutic efficacy and neurological side effects of putative antipsychotic drugs. In *Animal Models in Psychiatry and Neurology,* I. Hanin and E. Usdin, eds. Pergamon, Oxford (1977), pp. 91–105.

Bunney, W.E., Jr. Psychopharmacology of the switch process in affective illness. In *Psychopharmacology: A Generation of Progress,* M.A. Lipton, A. DiMascio, and K.F. Killam, eds. Raven, New York (1978), pp. 1249–1259.

Bunney, W.E., Jr., and Davis, J.M. Norepinephrine in depressive reactions. *Arch. Gen. Psychiat.* 13, 483–494 (1965).

Bunney, W.E., Jr., and Post, R.M. Catecholamine agonist and receptor hypothesis of affective illness: Paradoxical drug effects. In *Neuroregulators and Psychiatric Disorders,* E. Usdin, D.A. Hamburg, and J. Barchas, eds. Oxford Univ. Press, New York (1977), pp. 151–159.

Bunney, W.E., Jr., Post, R.M., Anderson, A.E., and Kopanda, R.T. A neuronal receptor sensitivity mechanism in affective illness (a review of evidence). *Commun. Psychopharmacol.* 1: 393–406 (1977).

Bunney, W.E., Jr., Goodwin, F.K., Murphy, D.L., House, K.M., and Gordon, E.K. The switch process in manic-depressive illness: II. Relationship to catecholamines, REM sleep, and drugs, *Arch. Gen. Psychiat.* 27, 304–309 (1972).

Carlsson, A. Receptor-mediated control of dopamine metabolism. In *Pre- and Postsynaptic Receptors,* E. Usdin and W.E. Bunney, Jr., eds. Marcel-Dekker, New York (1975), pp. 49–87.

Carman, J.S., and Wyatt, R.J. Alterations in cerebrospinal fluid and serum total calcium with changes in psychiatric state. In *Neuroregulators and Psychiatrric Disorders,* E. Usdin, D.A. Hamburg, and J.D. Barchas, eds. Oxford Univ. Press, New York (1977), pp. 488–494.

Carman, J.S., Post, R.M., Buswell, R., and Goodwin, F.K. Negative effects of melatonin in depression. *Am. J. Psychiat.* 133, 1181–1186 (1976).

Carroll, B.J. Limbic system-adrenal cortex regulation in depression and schizophrenia. *Psychosom. Med.* 38, 106–121 (1976).

Carroll, B.J. Neuroendocrine function in psychiatric disorders. In *Psychopharmacology: A Generation of Progress,* M.A. Lipton, A. DiMascio, and K.F. Killam, eds. Raven, New York (1978), pp. 487–497.

Casper, R.C., Davis, J.M., Pandey, G.N., Garver, D.L., and Dekirmenjian, H. Neuroendocrine and amine studies in affective illness. *Psychoneuroendocrinol.* 2, 105–113 (1977).

Chan-Palay, V., Jonsson, G., and Palay, S.L. Serotonin and substance P coexist in neurons of the rat's central nervous system. *Proc. Natl. Acad. Sci. USA* 75, 1582–1586 (1978).

Cohen, D.J., Shaywitz, B.A., Caparulo, B., Young, J.G., and Bowers, M.B. Chronic, multiple tics of Gilles de la Tourette's disease: CSF acid monoamine metabolites after probenecid administration. *Arch. Gen. Psychiat.* 35, 245–250 (1978).

Cools, A.R. Basic considerations on the role of concertedly working dopaminergic, GABA-ergic, cholinergic, and serotonergic mechanisms within the neostriatum and nucleus accumbens in locomotor activity, stereotyped gnawing, turning, and dyskinetic activites. In *Cocaine and Other Stimulants (Advances in Behavioral Biology, Vol. 21),* E.H. Ellinwood and M.M. Kilbey, eds. Plenum, New York (1977), pp. 97–142.

Cools, A.R., and van Rossum, J.M. Excitation mediating and inhibition-mediating dopamine-receptors: A new concept towards a better understanding of electrophysiological, bio-chemical, pharmacological, functional, and clinical data. *Psychopharmacologia* 45, 234–254 (1976).

Coppen, A.J., Prange, A.J., Jr., Whybrow, P.C., and Noguera, R. Abnormalities of indoleamines in affective disorders. *Arch. Gen. Psychiat.* 26, 474–478 (1972).

Corsini, G.U., Del Zompo, M., Manconi, S., Piccardi, M.P., Onali, P.L., and Mangoni, A. Evidence for dopamine receptors in the human brain mediating sedation and sleep. *Life Sci.* 20, 1613–1618 (1977a).

Corsini, G.U., Del Zompo, M., Manconi, S., Cianchetti., Mangoni, A., and Gessa, G.L. Sedative, hypnotic, and antipsychotic effects of low doses of apomorphine in man. In *Nonstriatal Dopaminergic Neurons (Advances in Biochemical Pharmacology, Vol. 16),* E. Costa and G.L. Gessa eds. Raven, New York (1977b), pp. 645–648.

Costa, E., and Guidotti, A., Molecular mechanisms mediating the transynaptic regulation of gene expression in adrenal medulla. In *Psychopharmacology: A Generation of Progress,* M.A. Lipton, A. DiMascio, and K.F. Killam, eds. Raven, New York (1978), pp. 235–246.

Costall, B., and Naylor, R. Mesolimbic and extrapyramidal sites for the mediation of stereotyped behavior patterns and hyperactivity by amphetamine and apomorphine in the rat. In *Cocaine and Other Stimulants (Advances in Behavioral Biology, Vol. 21),* E.H. Ellinwood and M.M. Kilbey, eds. Plenum, New York (1977), pp. 47–76.

Cramer, H., Goodwin, F.K., Post, R.M., and Bunney, W.E., Jr. Effects of probenecid and exercise on cerebrospinal-fluid cyclic AMP in affective illness. *Lancet* II, 1346–1347 (1972).

Creese, I., and Snyder, S.H. Behavioral and biochemical properties of the dopamine receptor. In *Psychopharmacology: A Generation of Progress,* M.A. Lipton, A. DiMascio, and K.F. Killam, eds. Raven Press, New York (1978), pp. 377–388.

Creese, I., Burt, D.R., and Snyder, S.H. Dopamine receptor binding enhancement accompanies lesion-induced behavioral supersensitivity. *Science* 197, 596–589 (1977).

Davis, G.C., Bunney, W.E., Jr., DeFraites, E.G., Kleinman, J.E., van Kammen, D.P., Post, R.M.,and Wyatt, R.J. Intravenous naloxone administration in schizophrenia and affective illness. *Science* 197, 74–77 (1977).

Davis, G.C., Bunney, W.E., Jr., Buchsbaum, M.S., DeFraites, E.G., Duncan, W., Gillin, J.C., van Kammen, D.P., Kleinman, J., Murphy, D.L., Post, R.M., Reus, V.I., and Wyatt, R.J. The use of narcotic antagonists to study the role of endorphins in normal and psychiatric patients. In *Endorphins and Mental Health Research*, E. Usdin, W.E. Bunney, Jr., and N.S. Kline, eds. MacMillan, New York (1978, in press).

Davis, K.L., Berger, P.A., Hollister, L.E., and DeFraites, E. Physostigmine in mania. *Arch Gen. Psychiat.* 35, 119–122 (1978).

DeLeon-Jones, F., Maas, J.W., and Dekirmenjian, H. Urinary catecholamine metabolites during behavioral changes in a patient with manic-depressive cycles. *Science* 179, 300–302 (1973).

Delgado, J.M.R., and DeFeudis, F.V. Effects of lithium injections in to the amygdala and hippocampus of awake monkeys. *Exp. Neurol.* 25, 255–267 (1967).

de Montigny, C., and Aghajanian, G.K. Sensitization of postsynaptic receptors by chronic pretreatment with tricyclic antidepressants: An iontophoretic study. *Soc. Neurosci. Abstr.* III, 248 (1977), Abstract #776.

Dencker, S.J., Malm, V., Roos, B.-E., and Werdinius, B. Acid monoamine metabolites of cerebrospinal fluid in mental depression and mania. *J. Neurochem.* 13, 1545–1548 (1966).

DeWeid, D. Peptides and behavior. *Life Sci.* 20, 195–204 (1977).

DiMascio, A.R., Castro-Caldas, A., and Levy, A. The on-off effect. In *Advances in Neurology*, Vol. 3, D.B. Calne, ed. Raven, New York (1973), pp. 11–22.

Ebert, M.H., and Kopin, I.J. Differential labelling of origins of urinary catecholamine metabolites by dopamine C^{14}. In *Transactions of the Association of American Physicians*, Vol. 88. William J. Dornian, Collingdale, Pennsylvania (1975), pp. 256–264.

Ebert, M.H., Post, R.M., and Goodwin, F.K. Effect of physical activity on urinary MHPG excretion in depressed patients. *Lancet* II, 766 (1972).

Ehrensing, R.H., and Kastin, A.J. Dose-related biphasic effect of prolyl-leucyl-glycinamide (MIF-I) in depression. *Am. J. Psychiat.* 35, 562–566 (1978).

Feldberg, W., and Sherwood, S.L. Effects of calcium and potassium injected into the cerebral ventricles of the cat. *J. Physiol.* 139, 408–416 (1957).

Gerner, R.H., Post, R.M., and Bunney, W.E., Jr. A dopaminergic mechanism in mania. *Am. J. Psychiat.* 133, 1177–1180 (1976).

Geyer, M.A., Segal, D.S., and Mandell, A.J. Effect of intraventricular infusion of dopamine and norepinephrine on motor activity. *Physiol. Behav.* 8, 653–658 (1972).

Geyer, M.A., Puerto, A., Menkes, D.B., Segal, D.S., and Mandell, A.J. Behavioral studies following lesions of the mesolimbic and mesostriatal serotonergic pathways. *Brain Res.* 106, 257–270 (1976).

Gillin, J.C., Mazure, C., Post, R.M., Jimerson, D.C., and Bunney, W.E., Jr. An EEG study of a bipolar (manic-depressive) patient with a nocturnal switch process. *Biol. Psychiat.* 12, 711–718 (1977).

Globus, A., and Coss, R.G. Spine stems on tectal interneurons in Jewel fish are shortened by social stimulation. *Science* 200, 787–789 (1978).

Gold, P., Reus, V.I., and Goodwin, F.K. Vasopressin in affective illness. *Lancet* (1978, in press).

Gold, P.W., Goodwin, F.K., Wehr, T., Rebar, R., and Sack, R. Growth-hormone and prolactin response to levodopa in affective illness. *Lancet* II, 1308–1309 (1976).

Goode, D.J., Dekirmenjian, H., Meltzer, H., and Maas, J.W. Relation of exercise to MHPG excretion in normal subjects. *Arch. Gen. Psychiat.* 29, 391–396 (1973).

Goodwin, F.K., and Beckmann, H. Urinary MHPG in subtypes of affective illness. *Sci. Proc. Am. Psychiatr. Assn.* 128, 95–97 (1975).

Goodwin, F.K., and Post, R.M. Studies of amine metabolites in affective illness and in schizophrenia: A comparative analysis. In *The Biology of the Major Psychoses*, D.X. Freedman, ed. Raven, New York (1975), pp. 299–332.

Goodwin, F.K., Post, R.M., Dunner, D.L., and Gordon, E.K. Cerebrospinal fluid amine metabolites in affective illness: The probenecid technique. *Am. J. Psychiatr.* 130, 73–79 (1973).

Goodwin, F.K., Rubovits, R., Jimerson, D.C., and Post, R.M. Serotonin and norepinephrine subgroups in depression. *Sci. Proc. Am. Psychiatr. Assn.* 130, 108–109 (1977), Abstract #180.

Gordon, E.K., and Oliver, J. 3-Methoxy-4-hydroxyphenylethylene glycol in human cerebrospinal fluid. *Clin. Chim. Acta* 35, 145–150 (1971).

Grahame-Smith, D.G., Green, A.R., and Costain, D.W. Mechanism of the antidepressant action of electroconvulsive therapy. *Lancet* I, 254–257 (1978).

Green, A.R., Heal, D.J., and Grahame-Smith, D.G. Further observations on the effect of repeated electroconvulsive shock on the behavioral responses of rats produced by increases in the functional activity of brain 5-hydroxytryptamine and dopamine. *Psychopharmacology* 52, 195–200 (1977).

Greegard, P. Possible role for cyclic nucleotides and phosphorylated membrane proteins in postsynaptic actions of neurotransmitters. *Nature* 260, 101–108 (1976).

Greenspan, K., Schildkraut, J.J., Gordon, E.K., Baer, L., Aronoff, M.S., and Durell, J. Catecholamine metabolism in affective disorders. II. MHPG and other catecholamine metabolites in patients treated with lithium carbonate. *J. Psychiatr. Res.* 7, 171–183 (1970).

Grof, P., Angst, J., and Haines, T. The clinical course of depression: Practical issues. In *Symposia Medica, Hoest,* Vol. 8: *Classification and Prediction of Outcome of Depression,* F.K. Schattauer, ed. Schattauer-Verlag, New York (1974), pp. 141–148.

Grof, P., Zis, A.P., Goodwin, F.K., and Wehr, T.A. Patterns of recurrence in bipolar affective illness. *Sci. Proc. Am. Psychiatr. Assn.* 131, 179–180 (1978), Abstract #349.

Halaris, A.E., and Freedman, D.X. Psychotropic drugs and dopamine uptake inhibition. in *The Biology of the Major Psychoses,* D.X. Freedman, ed. Raven Press, New York (1975), pp. 247–258.

Hullin, R.P., Salway, J.G., Allsopp, M.N.E., Barnes, G.D., Albano, J.D.M., and Brown, B.L. Urinary cyclic AMP in the switch process from depression to mania. *Br. J. Psychiat.* 125, 457–458 (1974).

Jenner, F.A., and Sampson, G.A. Daily variation of the urine content of 3-methoxy-4-hydroxyphenyl glycol in two manic-depressive patients. *Psychol. Med.* 2, 81–85 (1972).

Jenner, F.A., Sampson, G.A., Thompson, E.A., Somerville, A R , Beard, N.A., and Smith, A.A. Manic-depressive psychosis and urinary excretion of cyclic AMP. *Br. J. Psychiat.* 121, 236–237 (1972).

Jimerson, D.C., Gordon, E., Post, R.M., and Goodwin, F.K. Central noradrenergic function in man: Vanillylmandelic acid in CSF. *Brain Res.* 99, 434–439 (1975).

Jimerson, D.C., Post, R.M., Carman, J.S., van Kammen, D.P., Wood, J.H., Goodwin, F.K., and Bunney, W.E., Jr. CSF calcium: Clinical correlates in affective illness and schizophrenia. *Biol. Psychiat.* (in press, 1978).

Jimerson, D.C., Post, R.M., Reus, V.I., van Kammen, D.P., Docherty, J., Gillin, J.C., Buchsbaum, M., Ebert, M., and Bunney, W.E., Jr. Predictors of amphetamine response on depression. *Sci. Proc. Am. Psychiatr. Assn.* 130, 100–101 (1977), Abstract #170.

Judd, L.L., Janowsky, D.S., Segal, D.S., and Leighton, H.Y. Effects of naloxone on manic patients and normals. Presented at the 131st Annual Meeting of the American Pschiatric Association, Atlanta, May 1978. *New Research Abstracts,* #8.

Kirstein, L., Bowers, M.B., and Heninger, G. CSF amine metabolites, clinical symptoms, and body movement in psychiatric patients. *Biol. Psychiat.* 2, 421–434 (1976).

Klawans, H.L., Crosset, P., and Dana, N. Effect of chronic amphetamine exposure on stereotyped behavior: Implications for pathogenesis of L-dopa-induced dyskinesias. In *Advances in Neurology,* Vol. 9, D.B. Caline, T.N. Chase, and A. Barbeau, eds. Raven, New York (1975), pp. 105–112.

Knigge, K.M., Morris, M., Scott, D.E., Joseph, S.A., Notter, M., Schock, D., and Krobisih-Dudley, G. Distribution of hormones by cerebrospinal fluid. In *Fluid Environment of the Brain,* H.F. Cserr, J.D., Fenstermacher, and V. Fencl, eds. Academic Press, New York (1975), pp. 237–254.

Kraepelin, E. *Lectures in Clinical Psychiatry,* T. Johnstone, trans. and ed. Hafner, New York (1904, 1968), p. 61.

Kupfer, D.J., and Heninger, G.E.R. REM activity as a correlate of mood changes throughout the night: Electroencephalographic sleep patterns in a patient with a 48-hour cyclic mood disorder. *Arch. Gen. Psychiat.* 27, 368–373 (1972).

Kupfer, D.J., Weis, B.L., Foster, G., Detre, T.P., Delgado, J., and McPartland, R. Psychomotor activity in affective states. *Arch. Gen. Psychiat.* 30, 765–768 (1974).

Lee, T., Seeman, P., Rajput, A., Farley, I.J., and Hornykiewicz, O. Receptor basis for dopaminergic supersensitivity in Parkinsons's disease. *Nature* 273, 59–61 (1978).

LeMoal, M., Stinus, L., Simon, H., Tassin, J.P., Thierry, A.M., Blanc, G., Glowinski, J., and Cardo, B. Behavioral effects of a lesion in the ventral mesencephalic tegmentum: Evidence for invovement of A_{10} dopaminergic neurons. In *Nonstriatal Dopaminergic Neurons (Advances in Biochemical Pharmacology,* Vol. 16), E. Costa and G.L. Gessa, eds. Raven, New York (1977), pp. 237–245.

Lerner, P., Goodwin, F.K., van Kammen, D.P., Post, R.M., Major, L.F., Ballenger, J.C., and Lovenberg, W. Dopamine β-hydroxylase in the cerebrospinal fluid of psychiatric patients. *Biol. Psychiat.* (1978, in press).

Lewy, A.J., Wehr, T.A., and Goodwin, F.K. Melatonin and manic-depressive illness. Presented at the 131st Annual Meeting of the American Psychiatic Association, Atlanta, May 1978. *New Research Abstracts,* #6.

Lindstrom, L.H., Widerlov, E., Gunne, L.M., Wahlstrom, A., and Terenius, L. Endorphins in human cerebrospinal fluid: Clinical correlations to some psychotic states. *Actca Psychiatr. Scand.* 57, 153–164 (1978).

Ljungberg, T., and Ungerstedt, U. Different behavioral patterns induced by apomorphine: Evidence that the method of administration determines the behavioral response to the drug. *Eur. J. Pharmacol.* 46, 41–50 (1977).

Ljungberg, T., and Ungerstedt, U. Classification of neuroleptic drugs according to their ability to inhibit apomorphine-induced locomotion and gnawing: Evidence for two different mechanisms of action. *Pharmacology* 56, 239–274 (1978).

Lloyd, K.G., and Hornydiewicz, O. Effect of chronic neuroleptic or L-dopa administration on GABA levels in the rat substantia nigra. *Life Sci.* 21, 1489–1496 (1978).

Lundquist, G. Prognosis and course in manic-depressive psychoses. *Acta Psychiatr. et Neurol.* 35, 1–96 (1945).

Lynch, G.S. Hippocampal potentials and related events. presented during "Symposium III: Physiological Mechanisms Related to Learning and Memory" at the Annual Meeting of the Society for Biological Psychiatry, Atlanta, May 1978.

Maas, J.W., Fawcett, J.A., and Dekirmenjian, H. 3-Methoxy-4-hydroxyphenyl glycol (MHPG) excretion in depressive states. *Arch. Gen. Psychiat.* 19, 129–134 (1968).

Maas, J.W., Haffox, S.E., Landis, D.H., and Roth, R.H. A direct method for studying 3-methoxy-4-hydroxyphenylethylene glycol (MHPG) production by brain in awake animals. *Eur. J. Pharmacol.* 46, 221–228 (1977).

Maj., J. Dopaminergic drug effects upon serotonin neurons. *Curr. Dev. Psychopharmacol.* 3, 55–83 (1976).

Mandell, A.J. Redundant mechanisms regulating brain tyrosine and tryptophan hydroxylases. *Annu. Rev. Pharmacol. Toxicol.* 18, 461–493 (1978).

Mandell, A.J., and Knapp, S. Adaptive regulation in central biogenic amine neurons. In *Psychopharmacology: A Generation of Progress*, M.A. Lipton, A. DiMascio, and K.F. Killam, eds. Raven Press, New York (1978), pp. 205–216.

McCarley, R.W., and Hobson, J.A. Neuronal excitability modulation over the sleep cycle: A structural and mathematical model. *Scienc3* 189, 58–60 (1975).

McDowell, F., and Barbeau, A. (eds.) *Advances in Neurology*, Vol. 5. Raven Press, New York (1974).

Messiha, F.S., Agallianos, D., Clower, C. Dopamine excretion in affective states and following lithium carbonate therapy. *Nature* 225, 868–869 (1970).

Modigh, K. Electroconvulsive shock and postsynaptic catecholamine effects: Increased psycho-motor stimulant action of apomorphine and clonidine in reserpine pretreated mice by repeated ECS. *J. Neural Transm.* 36, 19–32 (1970).

Modigh, K. Long-term effects of electroconvulsive shock therapy on synthesis turnover and uptake of brain monoamines. *Psychopharmacol.* 49, 179–185 (1976).

Moller, H.J., Ehrich, H.M., Cording, C., Kissling, W., Schietsch, H.J., Riedel, E., and von Zerssen, D. Action of d-propanolol in mania. *Abstracts of the Proceedings of the Eleventh Congress of the Collegium Internationale Neuro-psychopharmacologium*, Vienna, July 9–14, 1978, p. 222.

Moore, K.E., and Kelly, P.H. Biochemical pharmacology of mesolimbic and mesocortical dopaminergic neurons. In *Psychopharmacology: A Generation of Progress*, M.A. Lipton, A. DiMascio, and K.F. Killam, eds. Raven, New York (1978), pp. 221–234.

Moskovitz, C., Moses, H., and Klawans, H.L. Levodopa-induced psychosis: A kindling phenomenon. *Am. J. Psychiat.* (1978, in press).

Murphy, D.L. L-dopa, behavioral activation, and psychopathology, In *Neurotransmitters* (Research Publications, Association for Ressearch in Nervous and Mental Disorders, Vol. 50), I.J. Kopin, ed. Raven, New York (1972), pp. 472–493.

Murphy, D.L., in Post, R.M., and Murphy, D.L. Research planning in biological psychiatry: Some general principles as exemplified in studies of cerebrospinal fluid metabolites and blood cell enzymes. In *Handbook of Psychopharmacology*, Vol. 1, H.M. van Praag, M.H. Lader, O.J. Rafaelsen, and E.J. Sachar, eds Marcel-Dekker, New York (1978, in press).

Murphy, D.L., Goodwin, F.K., and Bunney, W.E., Jr. Electrolyte changes in the affective disorders. Problems of specificity and significance. In *Recent Advances in the Psychobiology of the Depressive Illnesses*, T. Williams, M.L. Katz, and J. Shield, eds. Public Health Service Publication, Government Printing Office, Washington, D.C. (1972), pp. 59–70.

Murphy, D.L. Goodwin, F.K., and Bunney, W.E., Jr. The psychobiology of mania. In *American Handbook of Psychiatry*, Vol. VI, D. Hamburg and H.K.H. Brodie, eds. Basic Books, New York (1975), pp. 502–532.

Muscettola, G., Wehr, T., and Goodwin, F.K. Central norepinephrine response in depression versus normals. Presented at the 129th Annual Meeting of the American Psychiatric Association, Miama, May 1976.

Muscettola, G., Wehr, T., and Goodwin, F.K. Effect of diet on urinary MHPG excretion in depressed patients and normal control subjects. *Am. J. Psychiat.* 134, 914–916 (1977).

Nathanson, J.A., and Greengard, P. "Second messengers" in the brain. *Sci. Am.* 237, 108–119 (1977).

Nauta, J.H., and Domesick. V.B. Crossroads of limbic and striatal circuitry: Hypothalamic-nigral connections. In *Limbic Mechanisms: The Continuing Evolution of the Limbic System Concept*, K. Livingston and O. Hornykiewicz, eds. Plenum, New York (1978), pp. 75–93.

Okuma, T., Kishimoto, A., Inoue, K., Matsumoto, H., Ogura, A., Matsushita, T., Naklao, T., and Ogura, C. Antimanic and prophylactic effects of carbamazepine on manic-depressive psychosis. *Folia Psychiatr. Nerol. Jpn.* 27, 283–297 (1973).

Olds, J. Behavioral studies of hypothalamic functions: Drives and reinforcements. In *Biological Foundations of Psychiatry*, Vol. 1, R.G. Grenell and S. Gabay, eds. Raven, New York (1976). pp. 321–447.

Pappenheimer, J.R., Heisey, S.R., Jordan, E.F., and Downer, J.C. Perfusion of the cerebral ventricular system in unanesthetized goats. *Am. J. Physiol.* 203, 763–774 (1962).

Paul, M.I., Cramer, H., and Bunney, W.E., Jr. Urinary adenosine 3' 5'-monophosphate in the switch process from depression to mania. *Science* 171, 298–303 (1971).

Perez-Cruett, J. Personal communication, 1976.

Pert, A., Rosenblatt, J.E., Sivit, C., Pert, C.B., and Bunney, W.E., Jr. Chronic lithium prevents the development of dopamine receptor supersensitivity. *Science* 201, 171–173 (1978).

Post, R.M. Frontiers in affective disorder research: New pharmacological agents and new methodologies. In *Psychopharmacology: A Generation of Progress*, M.A. Lipton, A. DiMascio, and K.F. Killam, eds. Raven, New York (1978), pp. 1323–1335.

Post, R.M., and Goodwin, F.K. Simulated behavior states: An approach to specificity in psychobiological research. *Biol. Psychiat.* 7, 237–254 (1973).

Post, R.M., and Goodwin, F.K. Studies of cerebrospinal fluid amine metabolites in depressed patients: Conceptual problems and theoretical implications. In *Biological Aspects of Depression*, J. Mendels, ed. Spectrum, New York (1975), pp. 47–67.

Post, R.M., and Kopanda, R.T. Cocaine, kindling, and psychosis. *Am. J. Psychiat.* 133, 627–634 (1976).

Post, R.M., and Goodwin, F.K. Approaches to brain amines in psychiatric patients: A re-evaluation of cerebrospinal fluid studies. In *Handbook of psychopharmacology*, Vol. 13, L.L. Iverson, S.D. Iversen, and S.H. Snyder, eds. Plenum, New York (1978), pp. 147–185.

Post, R.M., and Ballenger, J.C. Models for the progressive development of psychopathology: Sensitization to electrical, pharmacological, and psychological stimuli. In *Handbook of Biological Psychiatry*, Vol. II, H.M. van Praag, M.H. Lader, O.J. Rafaelsen, and E.J. Sachar, eds. Marcel-Dekker, New York (in press, 1978).

Post, R.M., Cramer, H., and Goodwin, F.K. Cyclic AMP in cerebrospinal fluid of manic and depressive patients. *Psychol. Med.* 7, 599–607 (1977a).

Post, R.M., Squillace, K.M., and Pert, A. Rhythmic oscillations in amygdala excitability during kindling. *Life Sci.* 22, 717–726 (1978a).

Post, R.M., Jimerson, D.C., Goodwin, F.K., and Bunney, W.E., Jr. Dopamine and mania: Behavioral and biochemical effects of the dopamine receptor antagonist pimozide. Unpublished manuscript (1978).

Post, R.M., Kotin, J., Goodwin, F.K., and Gordon, E.K. Psychomotor activity and cerebrospinal fluid amine metabolites in affective illness. *Am. J. Psychiat.* 130, 67–72 (1973a).

Post, R.M., Gordon, E.K., Goodwin, F.K., and Bunney, W.E., Jr. Central norepinephrine metabolism in affective illness: 3-methoxy-4-hydroxyphenylethylene glycol in the cerebrospinal fluid. *Science* 179, 1002–1003 (1973b).

Post, R.M., Fink, E., Carpenter, W., and Goodwin, F.K. CSF amine metabolites in acute schizophrenia. *Arch. Gen. Psychiat.* 32, 1063–1069 (1975).

Post, R.M., Gerner, R.H., Carman, J.S., and Bunney, W.E., Jr. Effects of low doses of a dopamine-receptor stimulator in mania. *Lancet* I,203–204 (1976).

Post, R.M., Ballenger, J.C., Reus, V.I., Lake, C.R., Lerner, P., and Bunney, W.E., Jr. Effects of carbamazepine in mania and depression. Presented at the 131st Annual Meeting of the American Psychiatric Association, Atlanta, May 1978. *New Research Abstracts*, #7 (1978b).

Post, R.M., Stoddard, F.J., Gillin, J.C., Buchsbaum, M., Runkle, D.C., Black, K.E., and Bunney, W.E., Jr. Slow and rapid alterations in motor activity, sleep, and biochemistry in a cycling manic-depressive patient. *Arch. Gen. Psychiat.* 34, 470–477 (1977b).

Post, R.M., Lake, C.R., Jimerson, D.C., Bunney, W.E., Jr., Wood, J.H., Ziegler, M.G., and Goodwin, F.K. Cerebrospinal fluid norepinephrine in affective illness. *Am. J. Psychiat.* 135, 907–912 (1978c).

Post, R.M., Gerner, R.H., Carman, J.S., Gillin, J.C., Jimerson, D.C., Goodwin, F.K., and Bunney, W.E., Jr. Effects of a dopamine agonist piribedil in depressed patients: Relationship of pretreatment HVA to antidepressant response. *Arch. Gen. Psychiat.* 35, 609–615 (1978d).

Prange, A.J., Wilson, I.C., Lynn, C.W., Alltop, L.B., and Stikeleather, R.A. L-Tryptophan in mania: Contribution to a permissive hypothesis of affective disorders. *Arch. Gen. Psychiat.* 30, 56–62 (1974).

Prange, A.J., Nemeroff, C.B., and Lipton, M.A. Behavioral effects of peptides: Basic and clinical studies. In *Psychopharmacology; A Generation of Progress,* M.A. Lipton, A. DiMascio, and K.F. Killam, eds. Raven, New York (1978), pp. 441–458.

Prien, R.F., Caffey, E.M., Jr., and Klett, C.J. Factors associated with treatment success in lithium carbonate prophylaxis. *Arch. Gen. Psychiat.* 31, 189–192 (1974).

Purdy, R.E., Julien, R.M., Fairhurst, A.S., and Terry, M.D. Effect of carbamazepine on the *in vitro* uptake and release of norepinephrine in adrenergic nerves of rabbit aorta and in whole brain synaptosomes. *Epilepsia* 18, 251–257 (1977).

Randrup, A., and Braestrup, C. Uptake inhibition of biogenic amines by newer antidepressant drugs: Relevance to the dopamine hypothesis of depression. *Psychopharmacology* 53, 309–314 (1977).

Randrup, A., Munkvad, I., Fog, R., Gerlach, J., Molander, L., Kjellberg, B., and Scheel-Kruger, J. Mania, depression, and brain dopamine. *Curr. Dev. Psychopharmacol.* 2, 205–248 (1975).

Raskind, M.A., Weitzman, R.E., Orenstein, H., Fisher, D.A., and Courtney, N. Is antiduiretic hormone elevated in psychosis?: A pilot study. *Biol. Psychiat.* 13, 385–390 (1978).

Reus, V.I., Silberman, E., Post, R.M., Weingartner, H., and Bunney, W.E., Jr. D-amphetamine: Effects on memory in a depressed population. *Biol. Psychiat.* (1978, in press).

Roberts, E. Some thoughts about GABA and the basal ganglia. In *The Basal Ganglia,* (Research Publications, Association for the Research of Nervous and Mental Disorders, Vol. 55), M.D. Yahr, ed. Raven, New York (1976), pp. 191–203.

Rodriguez, E.M. The cerebrospinal fluid as a pathway in neuroendocrine integration. *J. Endocrinol.* 71, 407–443 (1976).

Roos, B.E., and Sjostrum, R. 5-Hydroxyindoleacetic acid (and homovanillic acid) levels in the CSF after probenecid application in patients with manic-depressive psychosis. *Pharmacol. Clin.* 1, 153–155 (1969).

Rotrosen, J.V. Neuroendocrine alterations in affective illness and schizophrenia. Presented at the Winter Conference on Brain Research, Keystone, Colorado, January 1978.

Sabelli, H.C., and Giardina, W.J. Amine modulation of affective behavior. In *Chemical Modulation of Brain Function,* H.C. Sabelli, ed. Raven, New York (1973), pp. 225–259.

Sack, R.L., and Goodwin, F.K. Inhibition of dopamine β-hydroxylase in manic patients. *Arch Gen Psychiat* 31, 649–654 (1974).

Sachar, E.J., Hellman, L., Fukushima, D.K., and Gallagher, T.F. Cortisol production in depressive illness. *Arch Gen Psychiat* 23, 289–298 (1970).

Scheel-Kruger, J., Braestrup, C., Nielson, M., Golembiowska, K., and Mogilnicka, E. Cocaine: Discussion on the role of dopamine in the biochemical mechanism of action. In *Cocaine and Other Stimulants (Advances in Behavioral Biology,* Vol. 21), E.H. Ellinwood and M.M. Kilbey, eds. Plenum, New York (1977), pp. 373–407.

Schildkraut, J.J. The catecholamine hypothesis of affective disorders: A review of supporting evidence. *Am. J. Psychiat.* 122, 509–522 (1965).

Schildkraut, J.J. Current status of the catecholamie hypothesis of affective disorders. In *Psychopharmacology: A Generation of Progress,* M.A. Lipton, A. DiMascio, and K.F. KIllam, eds. Raven, New York (1978), pp., 1223–1234.

Schildkraut, J.J., and Kety, S.S. Biogenic amines and emotion. *Science* 156, 21–30 (1967).

Schildkraut, J.J., Keeler, B.A., Papousek, M., and Hartmann, E. MHPG excretion in depressive disorders: Relationship to clinical subtypes and desynchronized sleep. *Science* 181, 762–764 (1973).

Segal, D.S., and Mandell, A.J. Behavioral activation of rats during intraventricular infusion of norepinephrine. *Proc. Natl. Aca. Sci. USA* 66, 289–293 (1970).

Shaw, D.M., O'Keefe, R., and MacSweeney, D.A. 3-Methoxy-4-hydroxyphenyl glycol in depression. *Psychol. Med.* 3, 333–336 (1973).

Shopsin, B., and Gershon, S. Pharmacology—toxicology of the lithium ion. In *Lithim: Its Role in Psychiatric Research and Treatment,* S. Gershon and B. Shopsin, eds. Plenum Press, New York (1973), pp. 107–146.

Shopsin, B., Wilk, S., Gershon, S., Davis, K., and Suhl, M. An assessment of norepinephrine metabolism in affective disorders. *Arch. Gen. Psychiat.* 28, 230–233 (1977a).

Shopsin, G., Wilk, S., Gershon, S., Roffman, M., and Goldstein, M. Collaborative psycho-pharmacologic studies exploring catecholamine metabolism in psychiatric disorders, In *Frontiers in Catecholamine Research,* E. Usdin and S.H. Snyder, eds. Pergamon Press, new York (1973b), pp. 1173–1179.

Sjostrom, R. Steady-state levels of probenecid and their relation to acid monoamine metabolites in human cerebrospinal fluid. *Psychopharmacologia (Berlin)* 25, 96–100 (1972).

Sjostrom, R. Cerebrospinal fluid content of 5-hydroxyindoleacetic acid and homovanillic acid in manic-depressive psychosis. *Acta Univ. Ups.* 154, 5–35 (1973a).

Sjostrom, R. 5-Hydroxyindoleacetic acid and homovanillic acid in cerebrospinal fluid in manic-depressive psychosis and the effect of probenecid treatment. *Eur. J. Clin. Pharmacol.* 6, 75–80 (1973b).

Sjostrom, R., and Roos, B.E. 5-Hydroxyindoleacetic acid and homovanillic acid in cerebro-spinal fluid in manic-depressive psychosis. *Eur. J. Clin. Pharmacol.* 4, 170–176 (1972).

Sloane, R.B., Hughes, W., and Haust, H.L. Catecholamine excretion in manic-depressive and schizophrenic psychosis and its relationship to symptomatology. *Can. Psychiatr. Assoc. J.* 11, 6–19 (1966).

Smith, C.C., TAllman, J.F., Post, R.M., van Kammen, D.P., Jimerson, D.C., Brown, G.L., Brooks, B.R., and Bunney, W.E., Jr. An examination of baseline and drug-induced levels of cyclic nucleotides in the cerebrospinal fluid of control and psychiatric patients. *Life Sci.* 19, 131–136 (1976).

Snyder, S.H., Banerjee, S.P., Yamamura, H.I., and Greenberg, D. Drugs, neurotransmitters, and schizophrenia. *Science* 184, 1243–1254 (1974).

Strom-Olsen, R., and Weil-Malherbe, H. Humoral changes in manic-depressive psychosis with particular reference to the excretion of catecholamines in urine. *J. Ment. Sci.* 104, 696–704 (1958).

Strombom, U. Effects of low doses of catecholamine receptor agonists on exploration in mice. *J. Neural. Transm.* 37, 229–235 (1976).

Subrahmanyman, S. Role of biogenic amines in certain pathological conditions. *Brain Res.* 87, 355–362 (1975).

Svensson, T.H., and Strombom, U. Discontinuation of chronic clonidine treatment evidence for facilitated brain noradrenergic neurotransmission. *Naunyn Schmiedebergs Arch. Pharmacol.* 229, 83–97 (1977).

Svensson, T.H., Bunnye, B.S., and Aghajanian, G.K. Inhibition, G.K. Inhibition of both noradrenergic and serotonergic neurons in the brain by the alpha-adrenergic agonist clonidine. *Brain Res.* 92, 291–306 (1975).

Sweeney, D.R., Maas, J.W., and Heninger, G.R. Anxiety, physical activity, and urinary 3-methoxy-4-hydroxyphenyl glycol. *Sci Proc. Am. Psychiatr. Assoc.* 130, 173 (1977), Abstract #289.

Tassin, J.P., Stinus, L., Simon, H., Blanc, G., Thierry, A.M., LeMoal, M., Cardo, B., and Glowinski, J. Distribution of dopamineric terminals in rat cerebral cortex: Role of dopaminergic mesocortical systems in ventral tegmental area syndrome. In *Nonstriatal*

Dopaminergic Neurons (Advances in Biochemical Pharmacology, Vol. 16), E. Costa and G.L. Gessa, eds. Raven, New York (1977), pp. 21–28.

Thierry, A.M., Tassin J.P., Blanc, G., and Glowinski, J. Selective activation of the mesocortical DA system by stress. *Nature* 263, 242–244 (1976).

van Kammen, D.P. γ-Aminobutyric acid (GABA) and the dopamine hypothesis of schizophrenia. *Am. J. Psychiat.* 134, 138–143 (1977).

van Praag, H.M. Significance of biochemical parameters in the diagnosis, treatment, and prevention of depressive disorders. *Biol. Psychiat.* 12, 101–131 (1977).

van Praag, H.M. 5-Hydroxytrophan prophylaxis in affective disorders. *Abstracts of the Eleventh Congress of the Collegium Internationale Neuro-psychopharmacologium,* Vienna, July 9–14, 1978, p. 237.

Veale, W.L., and Myers, R.D. Emotional behavior, arousal, and sleep produced by sodium and calcium ions perfused within the hypothalamus of the cat. *Physiol. Behav.* 7, 601–607 (1971).

Wehr, T.A. Phase and biorhythm studies of affective illness. In Bunney, W.E., Jr. (moderator), The switch process in manic-depressive psychosis, pp. 321–324. *Ann. Intern. Med.* 87, 319–335 (1977).

Weiss, B.L., Foster, F.G., Reynolds, C.F., and Kupfer, D.J. Psychomotor activity in mania. *Arch. Gen. Psychiat.* 31, 379–383 (1974a).

Weiss, B.L., Kupfer, D.J., Foster, F.G., and Delgado, J. Psychomotor activity, sleep, and biogenic amine metabolites in depression. *Biol. Psychiat.* 9, 45–54 (1974b).

Weston, P.G., and Howard, M.Q. The determination of sodium, potassium, calcium, and magnesium in the blood and spinal fluid of patients suffering from manic-depressive insanity. *Arch. Neurol. Psycyhiat.* 8, 179–183 (1922).

Wilk, S., Shopsin, B., Gershon, S., and Suhl, M. Cerebrospinal fluid levels of MHPG in affective disorders. *Nature* 235, 440–441 (1972).

Wyatt, R.J., Gillin, J.C., Stoff, D.M., Moja, E.A., and Tinklenberg, J.R. β-phenylethylamine and the neuropsychiatric disturbances. In *Neuroregulators and Psychiatric Disorders,* E. Usdin, D.A. Hamburg, and J.D. Barchas, eds. Oxford University Press, New York (1977), pp. 31–45.

Zerssen, D.V. β-adrenergic blocking agents in the treatment of psychoses: A report on 17 cases. In *Neuropsychiatric Effects of Adrenergic β-receptor Blocking Agents,* C. Carlsson, J. Engel, and L. Hansson, eds. Urban & Schwarzenberg, Munchem-Berlin-Wien (1976), pp. 105–114.

Ziegler, M.G., Lake, C.R., Wood, J.H., Brroks, B.R., and Ebert, M.H. Relationship between norepinephrine in blood and cerebrospinal fluid in the presence of a blood-cerebrospinal fluid barrier for norepinephrine. *J. Neurochem.* 28, 677–679 (1977).

Zuckerman, E.C., and Glaser, G.H. Anticonvulsive action of increased calcium concentration in cerebrospinal fluid. *Arch. Neurol.* 29, 245–252 (1973).

CHAPTER 14

Cholinergic Mechanisms in Mania and Depression: Questions of Specificity

David S. Janowsky and John M. Davis

INTRODUCTION

In 1972, Janowsky, Davis, and colleagues (Janowsky et al., 1972a) began to explore the possibility that underlying affective disorders are a complex balance or interaction between adrenergic and cholinergic factors. Mania was hypothesized to be a syndrome occurring secondary to relatively diminished central acetylcholine activity compared to normal or increased adrenergic (noradrenergic and/or dopaminergic) activity, and depression was postulated to be the opposite (Janowsky et al., 1972b).

The most obvious analogy to this hypothesis lies in the control of peripheral autonomic functions, such as heart rate, in which catecholaminergic and cholinergic activation cause opposite effects (Goodman and Gilman, 1970).

In this chapter, we will review the possible role of cholinergic factors in the regulation of affective disorders.

In addition, the results of studies exploring the adrenergic-cholinergic hypothesis of affective disorders may be helpful in clarifying whether or not mania is a specific disease or a symptom complex. Specifically, whether or not a centrally acting cholinergic drug has effects in patients with manic-depressive disease that are different from those occurring in other patient groups may be relevant. Thus, for example, if some of the effects of cholinergic drugs were very specific to the manic-depressive patient and did not occur in other affective disorder patients, such evidence would support the hypothesis that mania is a specific disease. Conversely, if all individuals receiving a cholinergic drug showed similar effects regardless of diagnosis, an argument for nonspecificity could be made.

One strategy used to study the role of cholinergic factors in affective disorders has utilized cholinesterase inhibitors as research tools. Since cholinesterase inhibitors block the activity of acetylcholinesterase, an enzyme responsible for the breakdown of acetylcholine, such blockade increases available acetylcholine in the periphery and in the brain. This increased acetylcholine is functionally active, causing central and peripheral biologic effects, and can be antagonized by various muscarinic anticholinergic agents. We (Janowsky et al., 1973a), as well as others (Gershon and Shaw, 1961; Rowntree et al., 1950; Bowers et al., 1964; Modestin et al., 1973a, 1973b; Davis et al., 1978; Davis et al., 1976b), have used administration of cholinesterase inhibitors to evaluate the role of acetylcholine in affective disorders. We have refined this strategy to utilize both a centrally acting cholinesterase inhibitor as an "active drug," and a noncentrally acting cholinesterase inhibitor as an "active placebo."

EARLY STUDIES USING CHOLINESTERASE INHIBITORS

In 1961, Gershon and Shaw (1961) reported several cases of individuals poisoned with cholinesterase inhibitor insecticides. Among other symptoms, these patients developed depression, as well as peripheral parasympathetic toxicity. Gershon and Shaw also noted a higher incidence of depression in those orchardists exposed to cholinesterase inhibitor insecticides.

Earlier, Rowntree et al. (1950) administered the irreversible cholinesterase inhibitor di-isopropylfluorophosphonate (DFP) to ten normal and nine manic-depressive patients. The normal subjects developed lassitude, irritability, apathy, depression, and slowness or poverty of thoughts, which appeared prior to the onset of peripheral cholinergic symptoms. Two remitted manic-depressive patients showed mental changes similar to the normals, while two hypomanic patients improved with DFP. Another hypomanic patient showed decreased manic symptoms and was minimally depressed after each of two courses of DFP, but relapsed upon DFP withdrawal; and one almost remitted hypomanic patient became floridly manic upon DFP withdrawal. Also, a depressed patient showed a significant increase in depression during DFP administration. Furthermore, Bowers et al. (1964) noted that the irreversible cholinesterase inhibitor EA 01701 caused depressed mood, decreased energy and enthusiasm, lethargy, and decreased friendliness in normal volunteers to whom it was given.

RECENT STUDIES USING CHOLINESTERASE INHIBITORS

More recently, we (Janowsky et al., 1973a, 1973b) have used intravenous physostigmine (a reversible cholinesterase inhibitor that is centrally acting) and neostigmine (a similar cholinesterase inhibitor that does not cross the blood brain barrier [Goodman and Gilman, 1970]) to continue the study of cental cholinergic mechanisms in affect disorder patients. Our strategy has been to pretreat each patient with an injection of methscopolamine (0.5–1.0mg IM), a noncentrally acting muscarinic anticholinergic agent, so that any peripheral cholinometic effects of physostigmine or neostigmine would be blocked, leaving only central effects as study variables. We have administered intravenous physostigmine (0.5–4.0 mg)—since this cholinesterase inhibitor crosses the blood brain barrier and exerts central cholinomimetic effects—and have administered neostigmine (0.5–3.0 mg) as an "active placebo," since this drug does not effectively enter the brain.

GENERAL EFFECTS OF PHYSOSTIGMINE AND NEOSTIGMINE

Physostigmine, unlike neostigmine, rapidly exerts behavioral effects in virtually all subjects who receive it. These consist of lethargy, anergy, feelings of tiredness, psychomotor retardation, feelings of being drained, the perception of having no thoughts or of decreased thoughts, a desire to be left alone, and social withdrawal (Janowsky et al., 1973a, 1973b). Subjects receiving neostigmine exhibit no such symptoms. These "inhibitory" effects of physostigmine occur within 10–15 min of administration, last between 30 and 90 min, and are rapidly antagonized by small doses of centrally active anticholinergic agents, such as atropine. The physostigmine inhibitory state often preceeds sensations of nausea and episodes of vomitting, both of which can be antagonized by such centrally acting anticholinergic agents as atropine (1.0 mg) or scopolamine.

MOOD DEPRESSANT EFFECTS OF PHYSOSTIGMINE

In addition to its nonspecific "inhibitory-anergic" effects, physostigmine, but not neostigmine, is capable of inducing a depressed mood (Janowsky et al., 1973a, 1973b), consisting of such symptoms as sadness, feelings of uselessness, and intensification of suicidal feelings in subjects who have preexisting depression or are manic. Thus, depressed mood, as contrasted with the more pervasive nonspecific anergic-inhibitory effects of physostigmine, can occur in manic or depressed manic-depressives, unipolar depressed patients, or schizoaffective patients following physostigmine infusion. This mood depressant effect contrasts with that caused by physostigmine in schizophrenic patients without an affective component to their illness

(Janowsky et al., 1973b), where only the physostigmine inhibitory syndrome, but not depression, develops.

More recently, K.L. Davis et al. (1976) administered physostigmine to 13 normal volunteers. Although a physostigmine inhibitory syndrome occurred frequently, depression was noted in only two subjects, one of whom was marijuana intoxicated and one of whom had a history of premenstrual depression. In contrast, K.L. Davis et al. (1978), like ourselves, noted the frequent occurrence of depressed mood in manic patients following physostigmine infusion. Thus, there is evidence to support the possibility that physostigmine selectively causes depressed mood in subjects with a preexisting affective disorder, in contrast to those who have no such disorder.

There is also some evidence indicating that physostigmine selectively induces depressed mood in patients who are euthymic but have a history of affective disorder. Oppenheim et al. (1979) has noted that euthymic manic-depressive patients who are receiving lithium become somewhat depressed when given intravenous physostigmine.

Modestin and his coworkers (1973a, 1973b) have added considerably to our knowledge concerning physostigmine's effect on psychiatric patients. After pretreatment with methscopolamine, these investigators administered 1.25 to 1.5 mg of physostigmine and neostigmine (i.v.), using a double-blind, counterbalanced order, cross-over design. In their sample of 24 depressed patients, 4 manic patients and 40 nonpsychotic, nondepressed control patients, physostigmine produced a substantial overall increase in depressive symptomatology (p < 0.01). Modestin et al. noted that after physostigmine infusion, some of their patients experienced a fair amount of depression, and others experienced only minimal depression. Unfortunately, they did not subdivide their patients into those with preexisting affective symptomatology and those without such symptoms. Thus, a comparison between physostigmine's mood depressant effects in subjects having and those not having affective symptoms was not possible.

Data from Modestin et al. (1973a, 1973b) are also helpful in clarifying whether or not the depressive symptoms noted following physostigmine infusion are secondary to physostigmine's physical side effects, such as nausea and vomiting. If physostigmine-induced depressive symptoms are a consequence of physical symptomatology, one would expect a correlation between the intensity of depressive symptoms and physical symptoms. When the results of Modestin et al.'s studies are summarized (1973a, 1973b), there is no such correlation. Also, it has been our observation that physostigmine's anergic-depressant effects precede, rather than follow or occur simultaneously with, its emetic and nausea-inducing effects. Thus, it is likely that physostigmine-induced depression is not simply caused by feeling physically ill.

DEPRESSANT EFFECTS OF ACETYLCHOLINE PRECURSORS

Consistent with the mood depressant effects of physostigmine in patients with an affective component to their illness, several anecdotal reports suggest that the acetylcholine precursors deanol and choline may, in some cases, cause depressed mood. Tamminga et al. (1976) reported that choline administration caused an atropine-reversible severe depressed mood in 2 of 4 tardive dyskinesia patients to whom it was given. Furthermore, Casey and Denney (1977) have observed depressed mood as a side effect in 4 of 5 tardive dyskinesia patients who developed affective symptoms after high-dose deanol administration. However, two of their subjects became agitated, with manic symptoms, after deanol administration. Whether or not these patients had a history of concurrent or previous depression was not indicated.

EFFECTS OF PHYSOSTIGMINE ON MANIC SYMPTOMS

Physostigmine exerts significant antimanic effects in hypomanic and manic patients. As in the studies utilizing depressed patients, we administered physostigmine to 11 manic or hypomanic patients (Janowsky et al., 1973a). Administration of physostigmine to these manic patients in most cases resulted in a dramatic reduction of manic symtoms, whereas placebo and neostigmine produced no changes. At baseline, the patients exhibited typical manic symptoms, such as rapidity of thought and speech, grandiose ideation, punning, and rhyming. Physostigmine rapidly converted the manic syndrome to one consistent with a psychomotor retarded depression. Patients appeared lethargic, as well as slowed in their movements. They were significantly less talkative, euphoric, active, cheerful, happy, friendly, or grandiose, and had a decrease in flight of ideas, as rated by the Beigel-Murphy Mania Scale (Beigel and Murphy, 1971). Patients also reported "inhibitory symptoms," such as feeling drained, being without energy, becoming apathetic, and having "no thoughts." Often, the manic patients' responses included depression, with crying, sadness, and similar signs of depressed effect. An example of the effects of physostigmine on manic symptoms is illustrated by the folowing case: A 43-year-old white woman with a history of bipolar manic-depressive illness showed hypomanic symptoms, including moderate talkativeness, flight of ideas, grandiosity, and cheerfulness during the placebo-baseline phase. She was energetic, friendly, and showed increased interactions, as well as occasional hostility. Administration of a total of 1.75 mg i.v. physostigmine caused the patient to show a marked decrease in her interactions, talkativeness, grandiosity, cheerfulness, and flight of ideas. She became withdrawn, wanted to be left alone, and was lethargic, stating that she lacked thoughts and was somewhat depressed. She complained of nausea five minutes after the onset of the above syndrome.

The observation that physostigmine decreases manic symptoms has been partially confirmed by others. Two of 4 manic patients studied by Modestin (1973a) showed a lessening of mania following physostigmine administration. More recently, K.L. Davis et al. (1978) reported that physostigmine had significant and dramatic antimanic effects in those manic patients who show low anger and irritability levels.

However, some controversy (Carroll et al., 1973; Shopsin et al., 1975) exists as to whether or not the "antimanic" effects of physostigmine are truly antimanic. Carroll et al. (1973) and Shopsin et al. (1975) found that while physostigmine caused a decrease in manic hyperactivity and talkativeness, no change in "thought disorder" occurred. As outlined by J.M. Davis et al. (1976), the key to whether or not physostigmine alleviates mania may rest with how an investigator clinically diagnoses mania. If the essence of mania is considered primarily to be the cognitive aspects of the syndrome, i.e., the grandiosity and expansive paranoia, then physostigmine probably exerts relatively weak or nonspecific effects. If mania is considered to be primarily a disturbance of rate of mental processes, i.e., increased talkativeness, cheerfulness, hyperactivity, and thoughts, then physostigmine is obviously effective as an antimanic substance.

In any case, it is important to note that the "decrease in rate" caused by physostigmine in manics and other patients is not just sedation. Barbiturates and sedative hypnotics, in contrast to physostigmine, are not particularly effective in controlling mania. A patient can be markedly sedated with these agents—i.e., sleepy, dysarthric, and ataxic—and still display a very high level of mania. In contrast, physostigmine causes only slight sedation and does not usually cause sleep, yet is dramatic in antagonizing many manic symptoms.

"REBOUND" EFFECTS IN MANICS
FOLLOWING PHYSOSTIGMINE ADMINISTRATION

Shopsin and Gershon, in collaboration with ourselves (Shopsin et al., 1975), studied physostigmine's effects on three severely manic patients at Bellevue Psychiatric Hospital in New York. These patients were given relatively high intravenous doses of physostigmine. All developed the "physostigmine inhibitory syndrome" in addition to a decrease in certain manic symptoms (activity, cheerfulness, flight of ideas, tangentiality, pressure of speech, talkativeness, etc.). Manic grandiosity was at best equivocally decreased. However, most impressively, in two subjects, a rebound into a "hypermanic state" occurred. This "rebound" was noted approximately 2 hours following physostigmine administration, and lasted up to 4 hours. In the two patients in whom "rebound" was noted, a marked exacerbation and intensification beyond baseline levels of the manic state occurred, with emergence for the first time of obvious primary process behavior.

A nonspecific rebound phenomena may exist with respect to physostigmine. In Fibiger et al.'s animal studies (1971), physostigmine initially caused behavioral inhibition, followed several hours later by a rebound increase over baseline in locomotor activity. Fibiger et al., suggest that the rebound phenomena may be due to an unmasking of compensatory adrenergic activity, as physostigmine activity decreases over time. In man, the observation of a rebound phenomena following physostigmine in manic patients has not been observed in other than manic subjects. Thus, rebounding as described above is not a normal feature following physostigmine infusion. The fact that rebounding did occur in several manic patients would suggest that these patients may have a specific biochemical vulnerability to rebound. Such a vulnerability could be postulated to be due to a hyperreactive dopaminergic system, a possible defect in mania (Shopsin et al., 1975).

ANTAGONISTIC EFFECTS OF METHYLPHENIDATE AND PHYSOSTIGMINE

Methylphenidate, presumably a central norepinephrine- and dopamine-releasing agent, and physostigmine appear to exert behaviorally opposite effects in rodents (Janowsky et al., 1972c) and in man (Janowsky et al. 1973c). Methylphenidate causes increases in locomotion and in stereotypy in rats. It causes increases in thinking, talkativeness, and interactions in humans. It usually increases manic symptoms in manic patients, including flight of ideas, talkativenes, elation, and, when present, manic grandiosity and paranoia; these effects contrast with the effects of physostigmine. In schizophrenic patients, methylphenidate causes, as in manic patients, a generalized increase in talkativeness and interactions. However, in schizophrenic patients with preexisting psychotic symptoms, methylphenidate usually causes a significant increase in such psychotic symptoms as delusions, hallucinations, and bizarre behavior (Janowsky et al., 1973c).

A pharmacologic model for naturally occurring adrenergic and cholinergic central nervous system interactions may be found in the interaction of physostigmine and methylphenidate. We have noted (Janowsky et al., 1972c) that methylphenidate-induced psychostimulation in rats (running and gnawing behavior) and in various types of psychiatric patients (1973c) can be antagonized by physostigmine, but not by neostigmine. Conversely, the inhibitory syndrome, caused by physostigmine in rats and in man, can be antagonized by methylphenidate. Specifically, manic patients whose mania is further increased by methylphenidate can have this increased activation turned off by physostigmine. This antagonism can include attenuation of methylphenidate effects on manic grandiosity, as well as effects on manic mood and rate disturbances. Similarly, physostigmine can antagonize the activation of psychotic symptoms occurring in schizophrenic patients following methylphenidate infusion.

Thus, behavioral and psychosis activation, induced by the psychostimulant methylphenidate, are antagonized by physostigmine; and behavioral inhibition, induced by physostigmine, is antagonized by methylphenidate. The effects of physostigmine and methylphenidate as they interact with each other in man could suggest a pharmacologic model in which behavior may range from activation (increased thoughts, cheerfulness, talkativeness, emotionality) to inhibition (decreased thoughts, dysphoria, lethargy, and anergy). Thus, at a given time in a given individual, relative adrenergic-cholinergic balance could determine a person's behavioral state on an activation-inhibition contiuum. Clinically, such a continuum could determine a normal individual's relative aggressiveness, talkativeness, and activation. In the schizophrenic, the intensity of symptoms, such as degree of autism, could be determined by the latter balance. In the manic-depressive, such a balance could determine whether the patient was activated and manic, or motor-retarded and depressed.

CHOLINERGIC AND ANTICHOLINERGIC EFFECTS OF PSYCHOTROPIC AGENTS

Although much literature has focused on the adrenergic and anti-adrenergic effects of psychoactive drugs (Schildkraut, 1965; Davis, 1970) to explain the etiology of affective disorders, an argument can be made for the importance of the cholinergic-anticholinergic effects of these drugs. Janowsky et al. (1972b) have reviewed data indicating that most physical antidepressant therapies—including (1) electroconvulsant therapy, (2) the tricyclic antidepressants, (3) the monoamine oxidase inhibitors, and (4) the short-term effects of the psychostimulants—are associated with decreased cholinergic activity, in addition to increased adrenergic activity. Conversely, such anti-adrenergic drugs as reserpine, propranolol, and alpha-methyldopa, all of which can precipitate lethargy and depression in predisposed individuals, have prominent central and peripheral cholinergic side effects. Similarly, guane-thidine, which is reported not to cross the blood brain barrier and is not a prominent mood depressant, has prominent peripheral cholinergic side effects. Interestingly, as will be commented upon later, much literature suggests that the mood depressant effects of antiadrenergic drugs may be specific rather than nonspecific. For example, individuals developing depression following reserpine therapy usually have prior and/or family histories of depression.

Conversely, certain adrenergic drugs, such as the tricyclic antidepressants, MAO inhibitors, and L-dopa, are, under certain conditions, selectively capable of inducing manic symptoms in manic-depressives or of switching a bipolar patient from a depressed state to a manic or mixed manic-depressive state.

DISCUSSION

Although we have presented evidence suggesting that shifting central adrenergic-cholinergic balance regulates affect in man, evidence not supportive of a role for acetylcholine in affect regulation does exist. Anticholinergic agents are not particularly effective antidepressant agents (Safer and Allan, 1971); and no obvious relationship between the degree of central anticholinergic activity of a given tricyclic antidepressant and clinical efficacy or potency exists (Snyder and Yamamura, 1977). Furthermore, to date, there is no truly direct evidence that cholinergic mechanisms are abnormal in naturally occurring affective states.

Is is also important to refine the concept of "adrenergic-cholinergic" balance. Much evidence suggests that cholinergic and adrenergic neurotransmitters are in dynamic equilibrium and exert mutual feedback on each other. Blocking dopaminergic receptors with neuroleptics leads to an increase in acetylcholine turnover (Stadler et al., 1973; Trabucchi et al., 1975), as does depletion of monoamines with reserpine (Sulser et al., 1964). Conversely, L-dopa, amphetamine, and norepinephrine acutely decrease acetylcholine turnover and output (Trabucchi et al., 1975; Gorney et al., 19776). Furthermore, compensatory adrenergic hyperactivity may occur following chronic cholinergic stimulation; the converse may occur following adrenergic activation (Mandell and Knapp, 1971).

Specificity Questions

At this point, it is appropriate to return to the question of whether or not mania is a specific disease or a nonspecific cluster of symptoms.

Specificity of Manic-Depressives *vs.* Normals and Affect Disorder Patients in General

Much literature suggests that the mood depressant effects of anti-adrenergic drugs are specific to affect disorder patients. Individuals developing depression following reserpine therapy usually have prior histories of some form of depression and/or a family history of depression. However, no information suggests that one type of depressive patient is more vulnerable to the mood depressant effects of reserpine than is another type. Similarly, adrenergic drugs generally nonspecificially alleviate depression, regardless of subtype.

In contrast, various adrenergic drugs, including L-dopa, are selectively capable of inducing or intensifying manic symptoms in manic-depressive patients (Murphy et al., 1971; Bunney et al., 1972). Significantly, patients with a prior history of bipolar manic-depressive illness are most vulnerable to the mania-activating effects of these drugs. Similarly, Wald et al. (1978) demonstrated that methylphenidate selectively activates manic symptoms in euthymic manic-depressives treated with lithium. This later information tends to support a specificity hypothesis for manic-depressive patients, as contrasted to other affect disorder patients and normals.

As with psychotropic drugs in general, not everyone becomes depressed when receiving low doses of physostigmine, although anergic symptoms are very common. Normal volunteers and schizophrenics without affective symptoms usually do not become depressed after receiving physostigmine. In contrast, manics, whether or not they are actively manic, depressives without a manic component to their illness, or schizoaffectives, frequently become depressed when they receive physostigmine. Thus, individuals with at least an endogenous affective component to their illness seem to react to physostigmine with a depressive syndrome.

The effects of physostigmine on manic symptoms may shed some light on the differences or similarities among manic-depressives and other subject groups. If physostigmine were to cause a decrease in euphoria, talkativeness, and flight of ideas only in manics, disease specificity might be inferred. Unfortunately, such is not the case. Although there is no question that physostigmine decreased many aspects of the manic syndrome, its effects on many of the behavioral target symptoms of mania are not limited to manics alone.

In contrast, the observation of rebound phenomena following administration of physostigmine in manic patients may hint at manic "specificity." The fact that rebounding did selectively occur in several manic patients would suggest that manic patients may have a specific biochemical tendency to rebound.

One way of considering the "specificity" of mania as well as depression is to consider depressives and manics from the perspective of pharmacologic or neurotransmitter vulnerability. Possibly, depressives in general are relatively more vulnerable to cholinergic influences, whereas manic-depressives are specifically vulnerable to adrenergic and cholinergic influences. Perhaps anyone, given enough acetylcholine or adrenergic agent, would tend to become depressed or manic respectively. Since all humans have the capacity to show changes in speed of thinking, positive or negative mood, and feelings of importance, and since such factors can be shifted by chemically increasing adrenergic or cholinergic activity respectively, what may be different in the manic-depressive or the depressive pateint may be quantitative rather than qualitative. Thus, the manic may be but an extension of normality.

If manic behaviors represent an adrenergic predominance, and depressive behaviors represent a cholinergic predominance, then the unique difference of the manic patient may be that there is no cholinergic constraint to the limits of euphoria, no mobilization of catecholamines when sadness and depression intervene. Perhaps, then, the homeostatic mechanisms in the central nervous system of the manic-depressive patient are faulty. Such a homeostatic imbalance of adrenergic and cholinergic factors could explain the excessive activation and inhibition occurring in these patients, as compared to nonaffect disorder subjects.

Specificity of Mania vs. Schizophrenia

Considering the question of whether mania is a definable illness or a symptom complex on one end of a continuum ranging through schizoaffective syndromes to schizophrenia, the following is relevant: With respect to conventional psychotropic drugs, anti-adrenergic drugs exert both antipsychotic effects in schizophrenics and "antimanic" effects in manics. Conversely, increasing adrenergic activation can activate both manic and schizophrenic psychotic symptoms. This nonspecificity of effect would suggest that mania is in a continuum with schizophrenia rather than a specific illness. Although the behavioral symptoms may differ, the fact that antiadrenergic and adrenergic agents respectively decrease and activate symptoms in manics and schizophrenics would suggest that both disordis have a common underlying adrenergic pathophysiologic etiology.

Similarly, results using physostigmine do not distinguish between mania and schizophrenia as such. If schizophrenics have an affective component to their illness, they often show depression after physostigmine infusion, as do manics and depressives. However, the quality of manic grandiosity, and schizophrenic delusions and hallucinations, is not significantly changed by physostigmine, although the intensity of these psychotic symptoms in both diagnostic groups may be muted by physostigmine. Furthermore, both diagnostic groups show similar anergic symptoms following physostigmine infusion. Similarly, both manic and schizophrenic symptom activations following methylphenidate infusion are effectively antagonized by physostigmine.

The effect of a cholinomimetic agent—which, like manic rebound following physostigmine infusion, may differentiate schizophrenics from manics, thus indicating manic diagnostic specificity—is found in the differential effects of DFP on mania and schizophrenia (Rowntre et al., 1950). This irreversible

JANOWSKY AND DAVIS

cholinesterase inhibitor, given chronically, caused manics to improve, while schizophrenics became dramatically more psychotic.

Therefore, in conclusion there is evidence from adrenergic and cholinergic precursor studies for both sides of the question of whether or not mania is a definable illness rather than a symptom complex at one end of a continuum with schizophrenia. The majority of evidence suggests that precursor strategies do not effectively differentiate mania from schizophrenia, except by increasing or decreasing already existing symptoms. Thus, most, but not all, such studies suggest that mania and schizophrenia are symptom complexes that pharmacologically respond similarly, at least to adrenergic and cholinergic agents. However, the observation of Rowntree et al. (1950) showing divergent effects of DFP in manics and schizophrenics is intriguing, and is worthy of replication and extension.

With respect to the use of adrenergic and cholinergic agents to differentiate manic patients from other affect disorder patients and from nonaffect disorder patients, it would appear that most affect disorder patients are equally vulnerable to the depressant effects of cholinergic drugs, when contrasted to nonaffect disorder subjects. Manic-depressives may be selectively more vulnerable, as are schizophrenics, to the psychosis-activating effects of adrenergic agents.

REFERENCES

Beigel, A., and Murphy, D.L. Assessing clinical characteristics of the manic state. *Am. J. Psychiat.* 128, 688–694 (1971).

Bowers, M.B., Goodman, E., and Sim, V.M. Some behavioral changes in man following anticholinesterase administration. *J. Nerv. Ment. Dis.* 138, 383–389 (1964).

Brown, H. Some anticholinergic-like behavioral effects of tran (-)-Δ^8 tetrahydrocannabinol. *Psychopharmacologia (Berl)* 21, 294–301 (1971).

Bunney, W.E., Goodwin, F.K., and Murphy, D.L. The "switch process" in manic-depressive illness. *Arch. Gen. Psychiat.* 27, 312–317 (1972).

Carroll, B.J., Frazer, A., Schless, A., and Mendels, A. Cholinergic reversal of manic symptoms. *Lancet* I, 427–428 (1973).

Casey, D.E., and Denney, D. Pharmacological characterization of tardive dyskinesia. *Psychopharmacology* 54:1–8 (1977).

Davis, J.M. Theories of the biological etiology of affective disorders. *Int. Rev. Neurobiol.* 12, 145–175 (1970).

Davis, J.M., Janowsky, D.S., Tamminga, C., and Smith, R.C. *Cholinergic Mechanisms and Psychopharmacology,* (D.J. Jenden, ed.) Plenum, New York (1976).

Davis, K.L., Hollister, L.E., Overall, J., Johnson, A., and Train, K. Physostigmine: Effects on cognition and affect normal subjects. *Psychopharmacology* 51, 23–27 (1976).

Davis, K.L., Berger, P.A., Hollister, L.E., and Defraites, E. Physostigmine in Mania. *Arch. Gen. Psychiat.* 35(1), 119–122 (1978).

El-Yousef, M.K., Janowsky, D.S., Davis, J.M., and Rosenblatt, J.R. Induction of severe depression by physostigmine in marijuana-intoxicated individuals. *Br. J. Addict.* 68, 321–325 (1973).

Fibiger, J.D., Lynch, G.S., and Cooper, H.P. A biphasic action of central cholinergic stimulation on behavioral arousal in the rat. *Psychopharmacologia* 20, 366–382 (1971).

Gershon, S., and Shaw, F.H., Psychiatric sequelae of chronic exposure to organophosphorous insecticides. *Lancet* I, 1371–1374 (1961).

Goodman, L.S., and Gilman, A. eds. *The Pharmacological Bsis of Therapeutics,* 4th ed. Collier-MacMillan, Toronto (1970).

Gorny, D., Billewicz-Stankiewicz, J., Zajqczkowska, M., and Kutarski, A., Effect of noradrenaline on the content, synthesis and catabolism of acetylcholine in the brain. *Acta Physiol. Pol.* 27, 55–62 (1976).

Janowsky, D.S., Davis, J.M., El-Yousef, M.K., and Sekerke, H.J. Acetylcholine and depression. *Psychosom. Med.* 35(5), 568 (1973b).

Janowsky, D.S., El-Yousef, M.K., and Sekerke, H.J. Antagonistic effects of physostigmine and methylphenidate in man. *Am. J. Psychiat.* 130, 1370–1376 (1973c).

Janowsky, D.S., El-Yousef, M.K., Davis, J.M., and Sekerke, H.J. A cholinergic-adrenergic hypothesis of mania and depression. *Lancet* II, 632–635 (1972b).

Janowsky, D.S., El-Yousef, M.K., Davis, J.M., and Sekerke, J.H. Parasympathetic suppression of manic symptoms by physostigmine. *Arch. Gen. Psychiat.* 28, 542–547 (1973a).

Janowsky, D.S., El-Yousef, M.K., Davis, J.M., et al. Cholinergic antagonism of methylphenidate-induced stereotyped behavior. *Psychopharmacologia* 27, 295–303 (1972c).

Janowsky, D.S., El-Yousef, M.K., Davis, J.M., Sekerke, H.J., and Hubbard, B.J. Cholinergic antagonism of manic symptoms. *Lancet* I 1236–1237 (1972a).

Mandell, A.J., and Knapp, S. The effects of chronic administration of some cholinergic and adrenergic drugs on the activity of choline acetyl-transferase in the optic lobe of the chick brain. *Neurophramacology* 10, 513–516 (1971).

Modestin, J.J., Hunger, R.B., and Schwartz, R.B. Uber die depressogen Wirkung von Physostigmin. *Arch. Psychiatr. Nervenkr.* 218, 67–77 (1973a).

Modestin, J.J., Schwartz, R.B., and Hunger, J. Zur frage der beeinflssung schizophrener symptome physostigmin. *Pharmakopsychiatrie* 9, 300–304 (1973b).

Murphy, D.L., Brodie, H.K.H., Goodwin, F.K., et al. Regular induction of hypomania by I -dopa in "bipolar" manic-depressive patients. *Nature* 229, 135–136 (1971).

Oppenheim, G., Ebstein, R.P., and Belmaker, R.H. The effect of lithium on physostigmine-induced behavioral syndrome and plasma cyclic GMP. *J. Psychiat. Res.* 15, 133–138 (1979).

Rosenblatt, J.E., Janowsky, D.S., Davis, J.M., and El-Yousef, M.K. The augmentation of physostigmine toxicity in the rat by Δ^9-tetrahydrocannabinol. *Res.Comm. Chem. & Pharmacol.* 3(3), 479–482 (1972).

Rowntree, D.W., Neven, S., and Wilson, A. The effects of diisoprophylfluorophosphonate in schizophrenic and manic depressive psychosis. *J. Neurol. Neurosur. Psychiat.* 13, 47–62 (1950).

Safer, D.J., and Allen, R.P. The central effects of scopolamine in man. *Biol. Psychiat.* 3, 347–355 (1971).

Schildkraut, J.J. The catecholamine hypothesis of affective disorders: A review of supporting evidence. *Am. J. Psychiat.* 122, 509–522 (1965).

Shopsin, B., Janowsky, D.S., Davis, J.M., and Gershon, S. Rebound phenomena in manic patients following physostigmine. *Neuropsychobiology* 1, 180–187 (1975).

Snyder, S.H., and Yamamura, H.I. Antidepressants and the muscarinic acetylcholine receptor. *Arch. Gen. Psychiat.* 34, 236–239 (1977).

Stadler, H., Lloyd, K.G., Gadea-Cira, M., and Bartholini, G. Enhanced striatal acetylcholine release by chlorpromazine and its reversal by apomorphine. *Brain Res.* 55, 476–480 (1973).

Sulser, F., Bickel, M.H., and Brodie, B.B. The action of desmethylimipramine in counteracting sedation and cholinergic effects of reserpine-like drugs. *J. Pharmacol. Exp. Ther.* 144, 321–330 (1964).

Tamminga, C., Smith, R.C., Chang, S., Haraszti, J.S., and Davis, J.M. Depression associated with oral choline. *Lancet* II, 905 (1976).

Trabucchi, M., Cheney, D.L., Racagni, G., and Costa, E. In vivo inhibition of striatal acetylcholine turnover by L-dopa, apomorphine and (+)-amphetamine. *Brain Res.* 85, 130–134 (1975).

Wald, D., Ebstein, R.P., and Belmaker, R.H. Haloperidol and lithium blocking of the mood respose to intravenous methylphenidate. *Psychopharmacology* 57, 83–87 (1978).

CHAPTER 15

Manic-Depressive Illness and Cognitive Immaturity

Gabrielle A. Carlson

INTRODUCTION

The onset of the manic phase of bipolar manic-depressive illness (MDI) appears to be very uncommon in childhood (Anthony and Scott, 1960). It is known that the incidence of mania begins to increase in late latency years (Anthony and Scott, 1960) and then postpubertally to a peak in the third decade (Perris, 1968), but its rarity in childhood has yet to be explained. One hypothesis suggests that the cognitive and psychodynamic maturity necessary to sustain and express severe depression, and hence its defense, mania, is not present until adulthood (Anthony, 1975). Interestingly, a somewhat similar observation has been made for the other major psychosis, schizophrenia— that is, according to some (Rutter, 1972; Lester, 1978), the adult form of schizophrenia is rare in early childhood (before age 7), and again, one suggested explanation is that true delusions and thought disorder cannot exist before a child has reached a certain stage of cognitive maturity enabling him to use deductive logic.

The question remains, then: How do cognitive maturation and the psychoses, in this case MDI, interact? Does this interaction explain the rarity of bipolar MDI in young children?

Unfortunately, it is not possible to answer these questions definitively. First, a cross-sectional examination of the interaction between IQ and bipolar MDI is hampered because those few studies carried out on depressed patients fail to note whether such patients are unipolar or bipolar (Mason, 1956). Also, there are no studies correlating IQ with types of symptoms during depression (Miller, 1975). Additionally, studies of cognitive functioning during mania are limited by the uncooperativenes of the patient in his distractible, hyperkinetic, and frequently unstable state. Finally, longitudinal studies of IQ before, during, and after an episode of depression or mania are lacking (Miller, 1975). So the question of specific influence of bipolar MDI on IQ (in contrast to depression per se and IQ) is unexplored.

One paradigm for understanding possible interactions between cognitive maturity and the phenomenology of bipolar MDI exists in studying those few bipolar children who are chronologically immature (i.e., prepubértal) but functioning age-appropriately, and those bipolar adults who are biologically mature but functioning intellectually at a much younger age equivalent—i.e., patients with mental retardation (MR). Assuming their levels of cognitive functioning are approximately equivalent, we can look for similarities and differences in their signs and symptoms, and further assume that similarities are due to cognitive immaturity and differences to some other variables.

The infrequency of prepubertal MDI and of combined MR and MDI would necessitate a long-term, multi-institutional cooperative study to develop the number of patients needed for such a study. Over the years, however, there have been a number of case reports in the literature in both populations to permit at least an initial examination of this paradigm.

METHOD

The Diagnostic and Statistical Manual of Mental Disorders (DSM III, 1978) was used to make the diagnosis of episodic affective disorders as well as of mental retardation. Since the clinical data reported in the cases reviewed were not systematic, it was abstracted as follows: (1) Signs and symptoms of mania and depression were noted under four basic categories—affect, thought content and process, psychomotor and vegetative disturbances. (2) Categories of mental retardation were borderline (IQ 68–83, though this is no longer considered mental retardation in DSM III); mild (IQ 52–67), cognitively functioning at maturity at the approximate equivalent of a sixth-grader; moderate (IQ 36–51), functioning around the second-grade level; severe/profound (IQ below 36), functioning only to a very limited extent with speech and self-care. Finally, the results of this symptom review were compared to signs and symptoms of MDI in cognitively normal adults (Winokur et al., 1969).

RESULTS: MR AND MDI

A total of 21 case reports of mental retardation and MDI were found with sufficient information to make an estimate of cognitive functioning and a verification of the affective disorder diagnosis (Reid 1972; Reid, 1976; Reid and Naylor, 1976; Van Krevelen and Van Voorst, 1959; Kelly et al., 1969;

Hurd, 1888; Roith, 1961; Herskowitz and Plesset, 1941; Sovner, 1975). Fourteen were male, 7 were female. Twelve patients were bipolar, 6 were unipolar (no report of mania), and 3 were mixed (components of mania and depression simultaneously).

Intellectually, the sample contained 2 borderline, 8 mild, 6 moderate, and 4 severely retarded patients. One patient was functionally retarded secondary to a deteriorating organic brain syndrome (OBS), and had no IQ score given.

The mean age of MDI onset in bipolar mentally retarded patients was 20 (range 15–46), and for unipolar 37.3 (range 26–50). Data were insufficient to gauge duration of episodes or severity. Some patients were functioning outside the hospital until the onset of their psychiatric symptoms; the more severely retarded patients had been chronically institutionalized for other reasons, and thier affective disorder was noted incidentally.

Of the 11 bipolar cases that reported family history, the presence of affective disorder in relatives was noted in 5. In 7 of the 10 patients who received lithium, the drug produced partial to complete remission of affective symptoms; in 2 of these 7 (Annell, 1969; Sovner, 1975), patients' cognitive performance was improved sufficiently to move them from "backward" to normal classes (mild to borderline IQ). Of the 3 remaining lithium-treated cases, one was the OBS case mentioned above (who showed no respone to lithium), the second was unable to tolerate therapeutic lithium levels without becoming toxic, while in the third the effects of the lithium were not mentioned. In the unipolar and mixed patients, lithium, tricyclic, and MAO-inhibitor antidepressants and ECT were effective in terminating affective episodes. Of three patients without drug treatment, one spontaneously remitted (Reid, 1976), one was described in 1888, prior to the availability of drugs or ECT (Hurd, 1888), and one report mentioned no treatment (Herskovitz and Plesset, 1941).

Affective, thought, psychomotor, and somatic components were distributed throughout all IQ ranges. Thought disorder was generally not reported in the most severely retarded patients with little speech. In less retarded patients, affective thought content reflected preoccupations consistent with patients' functional immaturity. Also, patients were usually described as looking depressed rather than reporting dysphoric mood. Symptom differences otherwise did not vary substantially with IQ, but very much resemble qualitatively the symptoms of MDI in intellectually normal adults. There was no consistent pattern of missing data; when a factor was not noted, however, it was impossible to know if the patient lacked the sign or symptom, or whether it was overlooked or simply not reported. For this reason, statistical comparisons among the children, MR, and cognitively normal adults are impossible.

Table 1. Frequency of Signs and Symptoms in Study Population

DEPRESSION

| | | Mentally Retarded | | | Cognitively Normal Adults |
		Unipolar	Bipolar	Children	
N		9	11	15	33 episodes
Emotional Signs and Symptoms		89%	91%	100%	100%
Thought Disturbance	Depressive Content	78%	63%	60%	97%
	Slowed thinking Poor concentration	22%	18%	0%	91%
Psychomotor Symptoms	Retardation	66%	82%	50%	76%
	Agitation	22%	0%	40%	not given
Vegetative Symptoms		100%	55%	53%	100%

MANIA

N			11	19	100 episodes
Emotional			75%	100%	98%
Thought Disturbance	Manic content		45%	21%	48%
	Flight of ideas Distractibility		27%	84%	100%
Psychomotor	(hyperactivity hyperverbosity)		100%	100%	100%
Vegetative Symptoms			58%	57%	90%

Tables 1 and 2 report the frequency of signs and symptoms of mania and depression in these retarded subjects. In all cases, these phenomena represented clear alterations in the patients' usual behavior patterns. Careful behavioral observations were necessary in the severely retarded to determine the precise onset of each episode; this did not seem to be problematic in the other patients with higher levels of functioning.

Table 2. Clinical Findings of MDI in Retarded Adults and Children

Manic-Depressive/Mentally Retarded	Children
Emotional Symptoms	
Depression: Looked depressed, anxious, tearful	Irritable, frequently crying; depressed appearance *per se* not noted
Mania: Called cheerful, excited, playful, hostile	Irritable, emotionally labile (elation in only 25% of cases)
Thought Content	
Depression: Preoccupations with death, destruction suicide, guilty · obsessions, hypochondriacal delusions, ideas of reference, low self-esteem, auditory hallucinations*	Not described in younger children; in older children: feeling of worthlessness, guilt, death preoccupation, paranoia, phobias
Mania: Grandiosity, hypersexuality, auditory hallucinations*	Grandiosity, paranoia (in older children)
Thought Process	
Depression: Slow, diminished or absent speech, confused speech	Not Noted
Mania: Rapid speech, hyperverbosity, distractibility, flight of ideas	Distractibility, flight of ideas, incoherence
Psychomotor Behavior	
Depression: Psychomotor retardation; withdrawn and disinterested in usual activities	Younger half were "agitated"—temper tantrums, fighting, destructive behavior; older children withdrawn, apathetic
Mania: Hyperactive, frenetic, noisy, destructive, dissheveled	Hyperactivity reported in all cases
Vegetative/Somatic Symptoms	
Depression: Anorexia, food refusal, insomnia, somatic complaints	Insomnia, anorexia
Mania: Lack of sleep	Sleeplessness

*Auditory hallucinations occurred during both manic and depressed phases in one patient.

MDI IN CHILDHOOD

Nineteen cases of probable bipolar affective disorder were found in youngsters age 12 or younger (Weinberg and Brumback, 1976; Brumback and Winberg, 1977; Barrett, 1931; McHarg, 1954; Feinstein and Wolpert, 1973; Warneke, 1975; Varsamis, 1972; McKnew and Cytryn, 1974; Kasanin, 1931) with enough data presented to enable a clear diagnosis (since puberty per se was not usually mentioned, 12 was the upper age limit); 14 were male, 5 were female. Onset of first affective symptoms ranged from 15 months to 12 years, with a mean of 9 years; 52% of the children were between ages 9 and 12. All children were having sufficient problems to come to psychiatric attention. In 10 cases a manic episode occurred first (4 had only a manic episode), while 9 had a depressive episode first. There was a family history of manic-depressive illness or cyclothymia in all but one case. Lithium therapy was successful in 4 of 8 cases in which it was initially tried (Feinstein and Wolpert, 1973; Warneke, 1975; Brumback and Weinberg, 1977). The remaining patients either were seen before the availability of lithium or were treated with other drugs. In 3 of 4 unsuccessful cases, lithium worsened depressive symptoms. In one, the drug produced an epileptiform EEG (Brumback and Weinberg, 1977).

Sign and symptom manifestations are again presented in Tables 1 and 2. In bipolar children, affective disturbances were manifested more by irritability and crying than by a depressed or elated appearance. Where depression and elation were noted, the children were much more likely to be older (ages 9 to 12) at onset of illness. In depressed children, agitation was present as often as psychomotor retardation, which, when seen, was found ony in the older children.

In older children, content disturbances were also seen more often in depression than in mania (content disturbances in young children were rare in either phase); disorders of form, however, were very frequent in mania and rare in depression. This is possibly explained by the relative infrequency of psychomotor retardation (which seems associated with slowed thinking) in children. In summary, there seems to be a change in quality of symptoms from younger children to children over age 8.

DISCUSSION

The methodology used in this review admittedly has several limitations. The literature on mental retardation and manic depressive illness spans many yers (1888–1976), and the meanings of diagnostic terms have changed; additionally, the quality of observations and consistency of reporting them varies. Nonetheless, in the cases reported, the symptom description, mention of lithium response, and occasional mention of family history allows confidence in the diagnosis of MDI, if not the specific symptom enumeration.

The literature dealing with childhood manic-depressive illness suffers not only from the aforementioned problems but also from lack of follow-up. There is some question of accuracy of diagnosis in the youngest patients; this problem will remain unanswered until follow-up studies to ascertain the continuity of this illness with adult MDI have been completed. Follow-up, of course, is made additionally difficult because of the long natural history of the illness, persisting essentially through the climacteric. In 6 cases reported here, however, that continuity has been established (Barrett, 1931; Warneke, 1975; Varsamis, 1972; McKnew and Cytryn, 1974).

Keeping the above caveats in mind, several findings in the present study are suggestive and worthy of more systematic examination. From this review, it would appear that the signs and symptoms of mania and depression in mentally retarded adult patients conspicuously resemble those of the general manic-depressive population (Winokur et al., 1969). Moreover, the 70% positive lithium response and successful treatments with antidepressants and ECT do not distinguish this population from the intellectually normal (Baastrup and Schou, 1967).

We might predict, then, if cognitive immaturity alone is responsible for modifying the symptoms of MDI, that the symptoms presented in the 19 children should also be less sophisticated versions of adult symptoms but otherwise similar. Although the frequency of symptoms in the broad categories is similar to that seen in the retarded group, the quality of symptoms in the children differs to some extent. As noted previously in children, irritability and crying are seen more frequently than a depressed or elated appearance, or reports of sadness or euphoria. This differs from retarded patients who appear frankly depressed and are at least as often reported to be elated as irritable, regardless of IQ. In adult mentally retarded subjects, regardless of IQ, psychomotor slowing predominated, whereas psychomotor retardation was seen only in the older children.

In both the verbal mentally retarded patients and older children, affective preoccupations were noted; these were absent in younger children. Interestingly, distractibility and hyperactivity were seen during mania in all populations.

Vegetative/somatic symptoms were the most inconsistently reported findings in both children and mentally retarded groups; thus, it is impossible to know if this reflects underoccurrence or underreporting. Reid and Naylor (1976) noted that special attention must be paid to the biologic rhythms in the severely retarded, where language-related signs and symptoms are less discernible. If we postulate that episodic behavior disorders in children are a "form fruste" of bipolar MDI, special attention may have to be paid to their eating and sleeping patterns as well.

We conclude, then, that although cognitive immaturity modifies the manifestations of MDI to some extent, there seem to be qualitative differences that increasing chronologic age superimposes. These maturational changes seem to occur in the cognitively normal around 8 or 9 years of age, and account for the more "adult-like" affective symptoms of the later latency-age child. In contrast, there is no change in symptom manifestations of MDI between the moderately and mildly retarded, as one would have predicted if cognitive development alone accounted for the changes. A similar maturational phenomenon in a different population has been reported by Rutter et al. (1967), who noted in his 10–15 year follow-up of patients with infantile psychosis that severe overactivity in childhood frequently becomes underactivity in adolescence.

In summary, this review suggests that immature cognitive functioning affects the content of manic or depressive preoccupations, and possibly the patient's awareness of his mood state; it does not, however, seem to determine the presence or absence of mania and depression, nor does it explain other age-related symptom disparities between young children and adults. Although more definitive research is needed to substantiate this observation, it is further felt that other reasons must be sought to explain the relative absence of bipolar MDI in childhood and its increasing incidence with biologic maturity.

REFERENCES

Adams, G., Kovowitz, J., and Ziskind, E. Manic-depressive psychosis, mental retardation and chromosomal rearrangement. *Arch. Gen. Psychiat.* 23, 305–309 (1970).

Annell, A. Lithium in the treatment of children and adolescents. *Acta Psychiat. Scand. Supp. 207* 19–30 (1969).

Anthony, E.J. Childhood depression. In *Depression and Human Existence*, E.J. Anthony and T. Benedek, eds. Little, Brown, Boston (1975), pp. 253–254/

Anthony, J., and Scott, P. Manic-depressive psychosis in childhood. *Child Psychol. & Psychiat.* 1, 53–72 (1960).

Baastrup, P.C., and Scou, M. Lithium as a prophylactic agent. *Arch. Gen. Psychiat.* 16, 162–172 (1967).

Barrett, A.M. Manic depressive psychosis in childhood. *Int. Clin.* 3, 205–217 (1931).

Brumback, R.A., and Weinberg, W.A. Mania in childhood. II. Therapeutic trial of lithium carbonate and further description of manic-depressive illness in children. *Am. J. Dis Child* 131, 1122–1126 (1977).

Diagnostic and Statistical Manual of Mental Disorders (DSM III), American Psychiatric Association, January 1978 draft.

Feinstein, S.C. and Wolpert, E.A. Juvenile manic-depressive illness. *J. Am. Acad. Child Psychiat.* 12, 123–136 (1973).

Forssman, H., and Walinder, J. Lithium treatment on atypical indication. *Acta Psychiat. Scand. Suppl. 207* 34–40 (1969).

Herskovitz, H.H., and Plesset, M.R. Psychoses in adult mental defectives. *Psychiat. Quart.* 15, 574–588 (1941).

Hurd, M. Imbecility with insanity. *J. Insanity* 45, 261–269 (1888).

Kasanin, J. The affective psychoses in children. *Am. J. Psychiat.* 10, 897–926 (1931).

Kelly, J., Koch, M., and Buegel, D. Lithium carbonate in juvenile manic-depressive illness. *Dis. Nerv. Syst.* 37, 90–92 (1976).

Lester, E.P., and LaRoche, C. Schizophreniform psychoses of childhood: Therapeutic considerations. *Compr. Psychiat.* 19, 153–159 (1978).

Mason, C.R. Pre-illness intelligence of mental hospital patients. *J. Consult. Psychol.* 20, 297–300 (1956).

McHarg, J.F. Mania in childhood. *Arch. Neurol. & Psychiat.* 72, 531–539 (1954).

McKnew, D.H., Jr., and Cytryn, L. Clinical and biochemical correlates of hypomania in a child. *J. Am. Acad. Child Psychiat.* 13, 576–585 (1974).

Miller, W.R. Psychological deficit in depression. *Psycholog. Bull.* 82, 238–260 (1975).

Payne, R. The psychotic subnormal. *J. Ment. Subn.* 26, 25–34 (1968).

Perris, C. The course of depressive psychoses. *Acta Psychiatr. Scan.* 44, 238–248 (1968).

Reid, A.H. Psychoses in adult mental defectives. I. Manic Depressive Psychosis. *Brit. J. Psychiat.* 120, 205–212 (1972).

Reid, A.H. Psychiatric disturbances in the mentally handicapped. *Proc. Roy. Soc. Med.* 69, 509–512 (1976).

Reid, A.H., and Naylor, G.J. Short-cycle manic depressive psychosis in mental defectives: A clinical and physiological study. *J. Ment. Defic. Res.* 20, 67–76 (1976).

Roith, A.J. Psychotic depression in a mongol. *J. Ment. Subn.* 7, 45–47 (1961).

Rutter, M. Childhood schizophrenia reconsidered. *J. Aut. & Child Schizo.* 2, 315–337 (1972).

Rutter, M., Greenfield, D., and Lockyer, L. A five to fifteen-year follow-up study of infantile psychosis. II. Social behavioral outcome. *Brit. J. Psychiat.* 113, 1183–1199 (1967).

Sovner, R. The diagnosis and treatment of manic-depressive illness in childhood and adolescence. *Psych. Opinion* 37–42 (1975).

Van Krevelen, D., and Van Voorst, J. Lithium in the treatment of a cryptogenetic psychosis in a juvenile. *Acta Paedopsychiatrica* 26, 148–152 (1969).

Varsamis, J. Manic depressive disease in childhood. *Can. Psychiatr. Asson. J.* 17, 279–281 (1972).

Warneke, L. A case of manic-depressive illness in childhood. *Can. Psychiatr. Assn. J.* 20, 195–200 (1975).

Weinberg, W.A., and Brumback, R.A. Mania in childhood. *Am. J. Dis. Child* 130, 380–385 (1976).

Winokur, G., Clayton, P., and Reich, T. *Manic Depressive Illness.* C.V. Mosley, St. Louis (1969), pp. 122–125.

CHAPTER 16

Social, Cultural, and Epidemiologic Aspects of Mania

Dinshah D. Gagrat and Herzl R. Spiro

Mania produces marked social consequences that in turn are significant in the management of the disorder. Symptoms of the disorder are shaped by social and cultural determinants. Moreover, such determinants may serve as predisposing, precipitating, or even pathogenetic factors in the disorder.

The literature of the 1950's created hope that psychosocial factors related to this disorder could be elucidted and understood (Cohen et al., 1954; Gibson, 1958; Gibson et al., 1959). The 1960's and 70's have shown far more progress in elucidating somatic factors and in pharmacologic treatment than in fulfilling these early hopes. Perhaps the signal exception to this statement is in a number of epidemiologic studies undertaken in the last two decades. Through understanding of the patterns of incidence and prevalence of the disorder may come increased understanding of social contributing factors and cultural aspects of the disease. There are, however, major methodologic problems in studying mania as an isolated phenomenon. Manic episodes tend to be of short duration. When the marker symptom for a disease is manifest only for brief periods of time, random sample epidemiologic studies become difficult. Moreover, the point prevalence of the disease is low enough so that the numbers of normal subjects who must be screened reach figures tht render survey epidemiologic research difficult or impossible. For purposes of this report, we shall consider the literature both on unipolar manic disease and bipolar affective disorders. By definition, bipolar affective disorders involved manic episodes. Epidemiologic studies of mania alone are virtually absent from the literature with the exception of a few studies that will be summarized below.

This chapter begins with a consideration of psychiatric epidemiology as it applies to the bipolar affective disorders. Risk factors, course and outcome, and predisposing genetic factors are considered in this epidemiologic section. The second section of the chapter deals with premorbid social factors and life events. The third section considers social and family factors. The fourth considers cultural factors, and the final sections take into account the social consequences of the disorder.

EPIDEMIOLOGY OF MANIA
AND BIPOLAR AFFECTIVE DISORDERS

Psychiatric epidemiology is that branch of psychiatric research that investigates the distribution of mental disorder in the population (Robins, 1978). Epidemiologic studies may be directed at detecting the incidence of a disorder (the appearance of new cases); the point prevalence of a disorder (the number of case appearing at any given point in time); or the yearly prevalence (the number of cases appearing in any given year). By comparing the pattern and distribution of mental illness in different populations, utilizing studies of incidence and prevalence, clues may be obtained leading to the detection of factors that may increase or decrease the severity of the illness. The best-known psychiatric example is probably Goldberger's use of epidemiologic clues to explain, control, and prevent pellagra (Parsons, 1952). Epidemiologic methods have been utilized to make inferences about social and cultural factors in various psychiatric disorders. Of course, the prevalence and incidence of a disorder can only be correlated with social and cultural factors, and direction of causation cannot be stated from correlative information. The fact that illness A occurs in the presence of event B does not, in and of itself, tell one whether the illness caused the event or the event caused the illness. Any consideration of mania must take into account not only potential social predisposing factors, but also social consequences. Epidemiologic studies do not, in and of themselves, differentiate cause from consequence.

Moreover, there is no guarantee that epidemiologic approaches will be effective in disorders like mania. There has been a shift to a multifactorial mode of explanation wherein no single antecedent factor is considered necessary or sufficient to explain an illness (Weismann and Klerman, 1978). Our current state of knowledge lends more credence to a multifactorial explanation for mania than to a unitary simple and sovereign cause approach to the disease. Any time that somatic, psychodynamic, behavioral, social, and cultural factors interact both as causes and consequences, complexity rises to levels that defy understanding. Nonetheless, the difficulty of the research problem is no reason to avoid study. One can take comfort from the Mishanaic sage who said, "It is not incumbent upon one to complete the task, but it is incumbent to begin." In considering the psychiatric epidemiology of mania, let us trace some beginnings.

METHODOLOGIC ISSUES

The literature on the epidemiology of the affective disorders has been described as "contradictory, vague, and confusing," and while all psychiatric research faces problems of diagnosis and case identification, affective disorders seem to epitomize these difficulties (Turns, 1978). The diagnostic criteria used to differentiate manic disease from other functional psychoses such as schizophrenia are vague, subject to differing interpretation in different nations, and insufficiently rigorous to support rigorous research. Even psychiatrists in the same hospital and in the same geographic region diagnose schizophrenia and manic-depressive psychosis in widely disparate ratios and employ different criteria and standards (Rosenthal, 1970). The differences between countries and cultures are very, very great. Thus, in reporting cross-cultural studies, one never knows whether the epidemiologic findings reflect cultural differences among the psychiatrists or among the patients. One study (Cooper, 1969) would seem to suggest that the apparent difference in the frequency of schizophrenia and affective disorders between the United States and the United Kingdom was largely a result of physicians' diagnostic bias rather than of a true difference in disease distribution. American psychiatrists tend to diagnose schizophrenia in patients who would be considered depressed or manic in England (Wing et al., 1974). Rosenthal (1962) points out that the ratio of schizophrenia to manic-depressive diagnosis varies considerably in the major twin studies based on samples of hospitalized twins. More recently, Carlson and Goodwin (1973) have shown that symptoms indistinguishable from acute schizophrenia can occur during the course of mania. Abrams and Taylor (1976) have demonstrated that catatonia, thought to be pathognomonic for schizophrenia, occurs with great frequency in diagnosable affective disorders (usually mania) when thorough research diagnostic criteria are applied. There is increasing evidence that cross-sectional observations are not reliable in making a diagnosis utilized by themselves (Carlson and Goodwin, 1973). Longitudinal sequential analysis of changing symptom patterns may be required to make a definitive diagnosis of schizophrenia or of manic-depressive disease. For the epidemiologist doing random samples, this presents an overwhelming problem. Moreover, given the fragmentary nature of most treatment systems, diagnosis is much more likely to be based on a horizontal histologic slice than a thorough longitudinal study.

This methodologic problem must be taken into account in interpreting any data. The researcher who begins with any systematic bias has ample opportunity to produce results that will support that bias. When the markers that delineate the presence of disease can be interpreted in so many manners, scientific epidemiologic study becomes virtually impossible. A desirable direction for future epidemiologic research is the delineation of specific markers for determining the presence of the disorder under study.

GENERAL PREVALENCE AND INCIDENCE

Most of the studies that are reported are actually yearly prevalence studies. Some of the purported discrepancies in prevalence rates for manic-depressive disease are related to the confusion between point prevalence and yearly prevalence. In a disorder of short duration, such as mania, yearly prevalence rates could be anywhere from twice as high to ten times as high as point prevalence rates. Prevalence rates vary a great deal, as is demonstrated in Table I. For example, Book (1953) found only two clear-cut cases of manic depressive psychosis in a population of 9,000 inhabitants of a province in northern Sweden. In contrast, von Tomassen (1938) reported an incidence of seven per cent or one-hundred times the Swedish rate. Other studies, (Sjogren, 1948; Fremming, 1952; Stenstedt, 1952; Slater, 1953; Kallman, 1959; Helgason, 1964), fall between these two values. Rosenthal summarizes the literature up to 1970 as showing an average rate for manic depressive disease as 0.7% per year. Studies of point prevalence are lacking.

The main epidemiologic method in the study of mania has been the use of hospital and psychiatric clinic records as the numerator, and the populations served by the hospitals or clinics as the denominator. The approach itself is fraught with peril. It should be emphasized that the literature truly summarizes diagnosed manic-depressive disease and may seriously underestimate the actual rate of manic-depressive disease. The primary cultural differences may not be related to culture buffering the individual from ever developing the disease. More likely, cultural differences result in the likelihood of any individual with the disease coming to medical attention and thus being included in the sample. Point prevalent studies for a short-duration disorder with a yearly prevalence of 0.7% would require the screening of very, very large numbers of persons. The research problem is thus much more formidable than the problem of studying schizophrenia. It would be rare to find a manic whose episode of illness extended beyond a month. Even allowing for a mean duration of the manic episode being two months, the point prevalence rate would be of the order of .2% if the yearly prevalence in the population at large was 1.0%. This means that one must screen a thousand

Table 1. Prevalence and Incidence
Manic-Depressive Psychosis in the
General Population

Author	Year	Location	Prevalence %
Von Tomasson	1938	Iceland	7.00
Stromgren	1938	Denmark	0.58–0.70
Sjogren	1948	Sweden	0.75–0.80
Fremming	1951	Denmark	1.40–1.88
Stenstedt	1952	Sweden	0.48–0.58
Slater	1953	England	0.50–0.80
Book	1953	Sweden	0.07
Kallman	1959	New York	0.40
Helgason	1964	Iceland	Male 1.80–2.18 Female 2.46–3.23
Dube and Kumar	1973	India	Male 0.65 Female 0.76

AUTHOR	YEAR	LOCATION	INCIDENCE/ 100,000
Muller et al.	1968	Switzerland	4.50–5.60
Leff	1976	Denmark London	2.60

people to find two active cases. Epidemiologic studies of several hundred thousand people at a time would be required to find the natural point prevalence in the population at large. Moreover, it is questionable whether current epidemiologic research instruments would be reliable in such studies. This perhaps explains why the definitive study, either of mania or of bipolar affective disease, has yet to be performed.

The variation in the prevalence of the disorder is likely to reflect multiple factors. We have emphasized differences in diagnostic practices and in rates of hospitalization and treatment. Once these artifacts are dealt with through rigorous research design and instrument development, it will be possible to determine what national differences, climate differences, family differences, social class differences, cultural differences, etc., exist in prevalence rates.

Efforts have been made to develop an age-corrected expression of morbidity independent of the mortality rate that predicts the likelihood of any given individual experiencing bipolar affective disease during his or her lifetime. In Western nations, this rate is 1–2%. (Klerman, 1978; Klerman and Barrett, 1973).

RISK FACTORS

For affective disorders in general, a fairly consistent finding is that females are more at risk than males (Böök, 1953; Klerman, 1978; Merrel, 1951, Cadoret et al., 1970). However, although Winokur et al. have reported a female–male ratio of 2:1 for manic-depressive illness, others (Klerman, 1978) state that the sex difference is less marked for manic-depressive illness, and Goetzl et al. (1974) found parity for the sex ratios. Moreover, these findings are not necessarily applicable to other cultures (Rao, 1970). The risk generally seems to increase with age (Turns, 1978); the peak admission rate for manic-depressive illness occurs in patients aged 45 to 64. If hospital admission data for manic-depressive illness is used, the annual first admission rate for males is 8 to 10 per 100,000, with peak incidence between ages 55–64. For women, the first admission rate is 15 to 20 per 100,000 with peak incidence at age 60–69 (Klerman, 1978).

Manic-depressive illness was first reported to be a disorder of the upper and middle class (Farris & Dunham, 1939). However, Dohrenwend and Dohrenwend (1969, 1974) reviewed seven epidemiological studies that reported data on schizophrenic and manic-depressive illness according to class. In contrast to schizophrenia, none of the studies showed the highest rate of manic-depressive illness in the lowest class. Although Tietze et al. (1941) found some support for a direct relationship between class and rate of manic-depressive illness, this is not a consistent finding (Dohrenwend and Dohrenwend, 1969; Klerman, 1978). Nevertheless, there is some relationship between social class and manic-depressive illness if educational achievement and occupational level are used as indices of social status (Klerman, 1978). Hence, Odegaard's statement (1956) that "the incidence of affetive psychoses is higher in higher social strata, but the trend is neither strong nor constant" seems to summarize the data.

Manic-depressive illness also seems to be more common in rural areas and in cities with populations under 20,000 (Kaplan and Sadock, 1973). It seems the incidence of manic-depressive illness has decreased markedly in the last 50 years (Cohen, 1975), decreasing from 12% of first hospital admissions in 1933 to 1–5% in 1968. Kaplan and Sadock (1973) have attributed this not only to changes in diagnostic patterns and increased populations, but also to changes in social values. They hypothesize that as the closed class system of Catholic Europe gave way to the more open system of the Renaissance, responsibility (and the guilt associated with it) became widespread. At the same time, the

Protestant work ethic spread through Norhern Europe and from there to the colonies, so that the virtues of discipline played an important role in early American culture. However, with the population increasing and the value of this work ethic eroding, the type of family dynamic associated with manic-depressive illness has decreased.

COURSE AND OUTCOME

Manic-depressive illness has been extensively studied with regard to age of onset, natural course, and outcome. Perris (1966) studied 138 biplar patients, 139 with unipolar depression, but found 17 patients only with mania alone. However, Abrams and Taylor (1974) found tht unipolar manic patients (having at least one hospitalizåtion for mania but no episodes of depression) comprise as much as 28% of patient samples selected on the basis of a current manic episode. Recent evidence indicates that these patients should be included within bipolar disorder, because when compared with bipolar manics, they are identical in terms of symptomatology, demographic data, family history, and response to treatment (Depue and Monroe, 1978). The only difference between the two types of mania appears to be tht unipolar manics have a significantly later mean age of onset of the first episode (10–12 years later). However, since follow-up data on these patients is not as yet available, it is still possible that some of these patients will eventually have a depressive episode. If the patient has a family history for bipolar disorders, admissions for mania are more frequent and severe than are admissions for depression; the reverse, however, applied to patients who have a negative family history (Mendlewicz et al., 1972). Perris (1973) suggested that in order to distinguish between unipolar and bipolar patients, that unipolar cases be defined as having three depressive episodes with no manic episodes. However, Dunner et al. (1976) have shown that 80% of bipolar patients are either initially hospitalized for mania or develop mania during or shortly after their first hospitalization. Hence, they suggest that for research purposes, patients be classified as unipolar only if they have been followed for six months after their initial depression to ensure that this was not a manic-depressive attack.

There are several studies that report on the clinical course of unipolar and bipolar disorders (Angst et al., 1973; Brodie and Leff, 1971; Gershon et al., 1971; Winokur et al., 1968). Their findings are, for the most part, similar (Depue and Monroe, 1978). Angst et al. (1975) studied 1,027 cases consisting of 634 unipolar patients and 393 bipolar patients. Analyses were computed on episodic data that spanned many years, and they found that 64% first entered the hospital 15 years earlier. The equivalent percentages for unipolar patients were 61% and 42%, respectively. First onset bipolar episodes occurred predominantly between 26–29 years of age. The median age of first onset was 30 years, and 88% of the cases had an age of onset of less than 49 years. These values were similar to those found by Perris (1966) and Gershon et al. (1971).

The most valuable information as to the natural course of the disease comes from studies carried out before the introduction of effective treatment (Turns, 1978). Wertham (1929) reviewed 2,000 cases and reported that the modal duration of a first manic attack was between 2 and 6 months. Lundquist (1945) found that 75% of patients who became ill prior to age 30 were well by the tenth month. Those becoming ill later in life had longer episodes. Perris (1966) found that bipolar patients with a first episode of mania had a higher proportion of manic than depressive eipisodes. Pollack (1931), reporting on 8,000 manics who were followed for 10 years, found that of all first-episode manics, 50% had no recurrence, 30% had two relapses, and 20% had three attacks or more. Also, early onset was closely related to likelihood of relapse.* Angst et al. (1975) reported that although there was great individual variablity in the number of episodes, there was a trend for both unipolar and bipolar patients to show an increase in the number of episodes in the first 10 years of the disorder. Their data showed that for the majority of patients, the recurrence of episodes was limited to the first 20 years of the disorder. Winokur (1975) supports the idea of a limitation on the number of episodes, and although this has not been determined in many studies, it is a hypothesis that warrants future investigation (Depue and Monroe, 1978).

Kallman found the hereditary factor to be greater in manic-depressive illness than in schizophrenia. Although he suggested a dominant-single-gene theory, Slater and Tsuang (1968) concluded that his data favored a polygenic theory. On the other hand, because of the fact that females outnumber males with bipolar disorder, a theory of transmission by an X-linked dominant gene has been postulated (Cadoret and Winokur, 1968; Mendlewicz et al., 1972). However, there are a large number of studies reporting father-son transmission (Gershon et al., 1971; Hays, 1976). Since the father cannot pass an X-linked gene to a son, but only to a daughter, such transmission is incompatible with X-linkage being the sole etiological basis. Nevertheless, the evidence supports the involvement of dominant X-linked inheritance in at least a subgroup of bipolar disorders. Stabenau (1977) reviewed the evidence and felt that there is an overall lean toward a polygenic model. Allen (1976) reviewed the twin literature on affective illness. His data suggest that because

---

*Braftos and Haug (1968) more recently showed that 19 out of 40 patients did not relapse in the six years following their first attack.

monozygotic concordance in bipolar twins (72%) is significantly higher than unipolar monozygotic concordance (40%), genetic factors may be more important in the development of bipolar illness as opposed to unipolar illness.

PREMORBID FACTORS: LIFE EVENTS

For manic-depressive illness, there seems to be a consistent correlation of a personal object loss (either real or threatened) with a predisposition to mania and depression (Stabenau, 1977). Many studies have found a significant early loss, especially of parents, retrospectively (Leff et al., 1970; Paykel et al., 1970; Thompson and Hendrai, 1972). On the other hand, equally well-controlled studies have not borne out this relationship (Cadoret et al., 1972; Hudgens et al., 1967; Morrison et al., 1968). Reviewing the data, Klerman (1978) feels that the research consistently confirms the existence of a relationship between life events and depression. When these life events are classified as desirable or undesirable, a greater number of undesirable events are associated with depression (Paykel, 1974). Bunney et al. (1972) studied, retrospectively, eight patients who "spontaneously" switched from depression to mania. A careful review of all available clinical data demonstrated a high frequency of environmental events that were classified as stressful in the period immediately preceding mania. Leff et al. (1976) reviewed the histories collected during a recent cross-national epidemiological study of mania and found a surprisingly high number of patients who had a history of stressful life events preceding the onset of their symptoms. Thus, clinical experience and systematic study both support an association between environmental stress and the development of depressive or manic episodes (Goodwin and Bunney, 1973).

SOCIAL AND CULTURAL FACTORS

Murphy (1976) has shown that very similar kinds of abnormal behavior appear to be labeled "abnormal" in very diverse cultures, and concludes that symptoms of mental illness are manifestations of types of affliction shared by all mankind, rather than simply violations of the social norms of certain groups. Dohrenwend and Dohrenwend (1974) point out that there are different symptom manifestations in different cultures of types of psychopathology that are otherwise familiar to us, and also state that types of psychopathology are probably differently distributed in contrasting cultural settings. These may provide important clues as to etiology. Manic-depressive illness is proportionately higher among Jews and the Irish, and very much higher among the Hutterites, a small religious sect in the United States and Canada. The Fiji Islands were found to have a high rate of manic-depressive illness as compared to schizophrenia (a fact that Kraepelin had noted). Asian societies, on the other hand (especially where Hinduism or Buddhism is predominant), have traditionally had a higher rate of schizophrenia. In India, males living in joint families had a higher prevalence rate than those living in nuclear families (Dube & Kumar, 1973), and prevalence rates were higher for Indian refugees than nonrefugees. In a clinical study of affective disorders in Iraq, Bazzoui (1970) demonstrated cultural differences in the presentaion of the affective disorders. The average Iraqi patient describes his depression in somatic terms, and the patient is unaware of his mood, as depression is conceptualized not as an emotional disturance, but as a physical abnormality affecting various body organs. Most manic patients similarly displayed irritability, hyperactivity, and aggressive trends, elation being present in roughly only a third of his sample.

A high proportion (75%) of the hypomanic patients demonstrated paranoid ideation, and there was a similarly high proportion of violent behavior. Bazzoui explained these differences on the basis of a culture wherein the "higher" defense mechanisms such as repression and sublimation are only partially developed. As a result, there was reversion very easily to more firmly established primitive modes of behavior. He also points out that the change from a tribal system with a shame-directed moral code to a guilt-oriented system with introjected values is not as yet complete in Iraq, and demonstrates that this might be responsible for the absence of a depressed or elated mood in his patient population as a sense of personal responsibility and the development of a superego with the ability to feel guilt must occur before a person can experience depression or elation (Bazzoui, 1970).

It is generally accepted that manic-depressive patients seem to have a specific family dynamic (Kaplan and Sadock, 1973). Gibson et al. (1959) found that in a detailed analysis of 12 manic-depressive patients, the most consistent observation was that each family was set apart in its social environment by several factors that singled it out as different. This varied from social or economic difference to difference arising from mental illness in a parent. All the families were acutely aware of this social difference and reacted to it by attempts to maintain or raise the family's prestige by "excessive literal adherence to conventional standards of proper behavior" (Gibson et al., 1959). The children have been desribed as being designated the "family redeemers" (Kaplan & Sadock, 1973), and the manic-depressive patient is frequently the best endowed member of the family (Cohen et al. 1954; Gibson, 1958). There is a background of intense envy and competitiveness (Cohen et al., 1954). The child conceives of his worth as being proportional to his degree of success in being conventionally good; he comes to fear that family catastrophe would result from lack of conformity, feels that he would then himself be completely rejected and abandoned (Gibson et al., 1959). A less consistent observation (Cohen et al., 1934; Gibons, 1958; Gibson et al., 1959) was the finding that the mother was the more driving and ambitious parent, while the father was not only ineffectual but also blamed by the mother for the family difficulties. Gibson et al. (1959) stressed that their findings, although corroborated by a second study involving patients from other social classes and a control group of schizophrenics (Gibson, 1958), must be interpreted with caution. They stressed that much further research was required before a definitive statement could be made. This description of family dynamics, nevertheless, is of great interest, and there is some evidence from epidemiological studies to support it.

Eaton and Weil (1955), for instance, extensively studied the Hutterites, an ethnic enclave of about 8,500 people who have lived for over 90 years in Canada and the United States. The society is highly effective in supporting its members from "the cradle to the grave" (Dohrenwend and Dohrenwend, 1974). Nevertheless, Eaton and Weil found a rate of psychosis that ranked the Hutterites as the third highest of ten different populations with which they were compared. Moreover, they found an extemely high rate of manic-depressive psychoses—the highest of the ten studies. They postulated that the extreme cohesiveness of the Hutterites, which may contribute to their low frequency of schizophrenia, may be significant for the high proportion of manic-depressive disorder. The Hutterites are "extreme in their emphasis on communal cohesiveness" (Eaton and Weil, 1955). There is a great deal of emphasis on religion, duty to God and society, and a tendency to internalize aggressive drives. Moreover, the childhood development and normative socialization process of the Hutterites resembles, to a great degree, the description of family dynamics quoted above. They come from large families with multiple parental figures who share the responsibility for the child, and there is no single significant adult to whom the child can relate meaningfully. This has been described by Fromm-Reichmann (1949) as typical of manic-depressive families. Moreover, since they are an isolate minority group for whom it is very necessary to maintain certain standards, often the child's relationship with the adults is determined by the purpose for which the child is needed, the needs of the group taking precedence over the wants of any individual. It is easy to see how this fits in with the description of family dynamics given above.

Leff et al. (1976), in a cross-national epidemiological study of mania, found a high proportion of West Indian immigrants in their London sample. They felt that the excess was of such sufficient degree that it could not be accounted for either by sampling errors or by underestimates of the West Indian population.

This again tends to support the view that manic-depressive illness seems to occur more frequently in families that are "different" from their social environment. The authors do give other explanations that may fit the facts; for instance, patients with a manic-depressive constitution may have a certain drive and initiative, making them more likely to emigrate, or West Indians as an ethnic group may be particularly liable to mania (although no reliable data are available as to this possibility). Odegaard's well-known study (1936) compared the rates of mental illness (especially schizophrenia) among Norwegians who emigrated to Minnesota with those who stayed at home. Having found higher rates among the immigrants, he concluded that those who were most prone to schizophrenia tended to emigrate. Braatoy (1937) challenged this interpretation, stating that the discrepancy might well be explained in terms of environmental stresses, and it seems the same controversy remains about manic-depressive illness.

SOCIAL CONSEQUENCES

Most studies indicate that bipolar patients suffer from a greater total number of episodes and somewhat worse marital impariment than unipolar patients (Depue and Monroe, 1978). Brodie and Leff (1971), for example, studied 30 unipolar-bipolar pairs of patients matched for age and sex. They found that although about 8% of the unipolar patients had marriages that ended in divorce, 57% of the bipolar group had marital failure. Since the authors also found that divorce occurred only after a manic attack and never before a bipolar patient had experienced at least one period of mania, they suggested the possiblity that manic symptoms might be incompatible with stable marriage. Similarly, Janowsky et al. (1970) found that the discussion of separation in the marriages of bipolar patients occurred so frequently as to be almost a diagnostic differentiator between manic-depressive illness and unipolar depression. In attempting to explain the reason for this, they note that depression is usually viewed by the spouse as an illness over which the patient has no control. In contrast, when the patient is manic, there is always an underlying feeling that the manic can control his actions and does not do so simply out of selfishness and lack of consideration. This is accentuated by the manic's periods of seeming reasonableness when logical discussions take place. When, a short time later, the manic has ignored and distorted all plans, the spouse feels cheated. The spouse also rapidly becomes a buffer between the patient and the community, having to deal with irate neighbors, creditors, and so on; this causes much embarrassment. In addition to all this, the manic patient is often prone to infidelity, which is seen as a final affront by the spouse, leading to divorce. Other studies (Mayfield and Coleman, 1968;

Reich et al., 1974) support the idea that mania in particular is responsible for poor marital functioning by showing that alcohol abuse is more highly associated with manic than depressive symptoms. Lastly, Dunner et al. (1976) found that the rate of completed end attempted suicide was significantly higher in bipolar than in unipolar patients.

The difficulty of treating manic individuals with psychotherapy is well known (Gibson et al., 1959; Janowsky et al., 1970). Although patients treated with lithium can make use of psychotherapy or family therapy (Fitzgerald, 1972), the drug does not solve all problems. Even when effective, family friction continues to exist with mood swings "no longer the convenient scapegoat" (Janowsky et al., 1970). However, Demers and Davis (1971) indicate that lithium therapy in the patient can help the spouse and the marriage as well. It is emphasized that for therapy to be effective, inter-personal issues must be emphasized from the start, and psychotherapeutic nihilism and excessive reliance on medication may hinder a good therapeutic relationship.

Prevention in psychiatry has become an increasingly recognized concern over the last 30 years, with the increasing awareness of the cost that psychiatric impairment entails for the individual and society. In psychiatry, the concept of prevention has been defined in terms derived from public health. Primary prevention is concerned with the removal of those factors that cause or contribute to the incidence of disease; secondary prevention aims at reducing the duration of those disorders that do occur through early diagnosis and prompt and effective treatment, whereas teritary prevention is directed towards decreasing impairment and the extent of residual effect following the illness. We do not yet know the necessary and sufficient conditions for preventing psychiatric disease (Adler et al., 1978). Caplan (1967) has the most influential theory of prevention in psychiatry, and emphasizes the causal importance of stress. Nevertheless, our ability to predict individual pathology and to define vulnerability to stress remains limited (Adler et al., 1978). Moreover, such primary prevention as Caplan recommends is nonspecific in aims and method. In mania, as with other psychiatric disorders, the state of our knowledge is insufficient to really consider primary prevention in any meaningful way.

In a recent overview, Dunham (1976) has concluded that the process through which societal and cultural factors play an etiological role in the development of the psychoses still remains to be clarified. It is hoped, however, that with the incorporation of recent advances in genetics, neuro-biology, psychopharmacology, and psychopathology into the epidemiolog-ical studies, we shall obtain new knowledge of the distribution of mental disorders in the community, and we shall come closer to this goal.

REFERENCES

Abrams, R., and Taylor, M.A. Unipolar mania: A preliminary report, *Arch. Gen. Psychiat.* 30, 441–443 (1974).

Abrams, R., and Taylor, M.A. Catatonia: A prospective clinical study. *Arch. Gen. Psychiat.* 33, 579–581 (1976).

Adler, D.A., Levinson, D.J., and Astrachan, B.M. The concept of prevention in psychiatry. *Arch. Gen. Psychiat.* 35, 786–789 (1978).

Allen, M.G. Twin studies of affective illness. *Arch. Gen. Psychiat.* 33, 1476–1478 (1976).

Angst, J., Baastrup, P., Hippius, H., Poldinger, W., and Weis, P. The course of monopolar depression and bipolar psychoses. *Psychiat. Neurolog. et Neurochir.* 76, 489–500 (1975).

Babigian, H., Gardner, E., Myles, H., and Romano, J. Diagnostic consistency and changes in the follow-up of 1215 patients. *Am. J. Psychiat.* 121, 895–901 (1965).

Bazzoui, W. Affective disorders in Iraq. *Br. J. Psychiat.* 117 (537), 195–203 (1970).

Böök, J.A. A genetic and neuropsychiatric investigation of a north Swedish population with special regard to schizophrenia and mental deficiency. *Acta Gent. et Stat. Med.* 4, 1–139 (1953).

Braatoy, T. Is it possible that the sociological situation is a factor in schizophrenia. *Acta Psychiatr. Neurol.* 12, 109–138 (1937).

Braftos, O.I. and Haug, J. The course of manic depressive psychosis: A follow-up investigation of 215 patients. *Acta Psychiatr. Scand.* 44, 89 (1968).

Brodie, H., and Leff, M. Biopolar depression: A comparative study of patient characteristics. *Am. J. Psychiat.* 127, 1086–1090 (1971).

Brown, G.W., Birley, J.L.T. Crises of life changes and the onset of schizophrenia. *J. Health Soc. Behav.* 9, 203–214.

Bunney, W.E., Murphy, D.L., Goodwin, F.K. and Gorge, G.F. The "switch process" in manic-depressive illness. 1. A systematic study of sequential behavior change. *Arch Gen. Psychiat.* 27, 295–302 (1972).

Cadoret, R., and Winokur, G. X-linkage in manic-depressive illness. *Ann. Rev. MEd.* 26, 21–25 (1975).

Cadoret, R.J., Winokur, G., and Clayton, P.J. Family history studies. VII. Manic-depressive disease vs. depressive disease. *Br. J. Psychiat.* 116, 625–635 (1970).

Cadoret, R., Winokur, G., and Dorzab, I. Depressive disease: Life events and onset of illness. *Arch. Gen. Psychiat.* 26, 133–136 (1972).

Caplan, G., and Grunebaum, H Perspective on primary prevention: A review. *Arch. Gen. Psychiat.* 17, 331–346 (1967).

Carlson, G.A., and Goodwin, F.K. The stages of mania. *Arch. Gen. Psychait.* 28, 221–228 (1973).

Cohen, M.B., Baker, G., Cohen, R.A., Fromm-Riechmann, F., and Wigert, E.V. An intensive study of twelve cases of manic-depressive psychosis. *Psychiatry* 17, 103–137 (1954).

Cohen, R.A. Manic-depressive illness. In *Comprehensive Textbook of Psychiatry*, 2nd ed., A.M. Freedman, H.I. Kaplan, and B.J. Sadock, Williams & Wilkins, Baltimore (1975).

Cooper, J., Kendell, R.E., and Garland, B.J., et al Cross-national study of diagnosis of the mental disorders: Some results from the first comparative investigation. *Am. J. Psychiat.* (Supp. 125), 21 (1969).

Demers, R.G., and Davis, L.S. The influence of prophylactic lithium treatment on the marital adjustment of manic-depressives and their spouses. *Compr. Psychiatr.* 12, 348 (1971).

Depue, R.A., and Monroe, S.M. The unipolar-bipolar distinction in the depressive disorders. *Psychol. Bull.* 85 (5), 1001–1029 (1978).

Dohrenwend, B.P., and Dohrenwend, B.S. *Social Status and Psychological Disorder: A Casual Inquiry.* Wiley-Interscience, New York, (1969), p. 28.

Dohrenwend, B.P., and Dohrenwend, B.S. Social and cultural influences on psychopathology, *Ann. Rev. Psychol.* 25, 417–451 (1974).

Dohrenwend, B.P., and Dohrenwend, B.S. Psychiatric disorders in urban settings. In *American Handbook of Psychiatry,* S. Arieti, ed. (1974).

Dube, K.O., and Kumar, N. An epidemiological study of manic-depressive psychosis. *Acta Psychiat. Scand.* 49(6), 691–697 (1973).

Dunham, W.H. Society, culture and mental disorder. *Arch. Gen. Psychiat.* 35, 147–156 (1976).

Dunner, D.L., Gershon, E.S., and Goodwin, F.K. Heritable factors in the severity of affective illness. *Bio. Psychiat.* 11, 31–42 (1976).

Dunner, D.L., Fleiss, J.L., and Fieve, R.R. The course of development of mania in patients with recurrent depression. *Am. J. Psychiat.* 133, 905–1508 (1976).

Eaton, J.W., and Weil, R.J. *Culture and Mental Disorders.* Free Press, New York (1955).

Farris, R.L., and Dunham, H.S. *Mental Disorders in Urban Areas: An Ecological Study of Schizophrenia and Other Psychoses.* Chicago Univ. Press (1939).

Fitzgerald, R.S. Mania as a message: Treatment with family therapy and lithium carbonate. *Am. J. Psychother.* 26(4), 547–554 (1972).

Fremming, K.H. The expectation of mental infirmity in a sample of the Danish population. In *English Society Occasional Papers on Eugenics, 7.* Cassell, London (1952).

Fromm-Riechmann, F. Intensive psychotherapy of manic-depressive. *Confina Neurologica* 9, 159 (1949).

Gershon, E., Dunner, D., and Goodwin, R. Toward a biology of affective disorders. *Arch. Gen. Psychiat.* 25, 1–15 (1971).

Gibson, R.W. The family background and early life experiences of the manic-depressive. *Pat. Psychiat.* 21, 71–90 (1958).

Gibson, R.W., Cohen, M.B., and Cohen, R.A. On the dynamics of the manic-depressive personality. *Am. J. Psychiat.* 119, 1101–1107 (1959).

Goetzel, R., Green, K., Whybrow, P., and Jackson, R. Linkage revisisted: A further family study of manic-depressive illness. *Arch. Gen. Psychiat.* 31, 665–672 (1974).

Goodwin, F.K., and Bunney, W.E. A psychobiological approach to affective illness. *Psychiatr. Annals,* 3, 19–53 (1973).

Hays, P. Etiological factors in manic-depressive psychoses. *Arch. Gen. Psychiat.* 33, 1187–1188 (1976).

Helgason, T. Epidemiology of mental disorders in Iceland. *Acta Psychiatr. Neurol. Scand. Supp. 173* (1964).

Hudgens, R., Morrison, J., and Barracha, R. Life events and onset of primary affective disorder. *Arch. Gen. Psychiat.* 16, 134–145 (1967).

Janowsky, D.S., Leff, M., and Epstein, R.S. Playing the manic game. *Arch. Gen. Psychiat.* 22, 252–261 (1970).

Kallman, F.J. The genetics of mental illness. In *American Handbook of Psychiatry,* Vol. 1, S. Arieti, ed. Basic Books, New York (1959).

Kaplan, H.S., and Sadock, B.I. An overview of the major affective disorders. *Psychiatr. Annals* 3(8), 13–52 (1973).

Klein, D., and Davis, J. *Diagnosis and Drug Treatment of Psychiatric Disorders.* Williams & Wilkins, Baltimore (1969), pp. 187–297.

Klerman, G.L. Affective disorders. *The Harvard Guide to Modern Psychiatry,* M. Armand and Nichol, Jr., ed. Bel. nap Press, Harvard Univ. Press (1978).

Klerman, G.L., and Barrett, J.E. The affective disorders: Clinical and epidemiological aspects. In *Lithium; Its Role in Psychiatric Research and Treatment,* S. Gershan and B. Shopsin, eds. Plenum, New York (1973) pp. 201–236.

Landis, C., and Page, J.D. *Modern Society with Mental Disease.* Farrar and Rhinehart, New York (1938).

Leff, J.P., Fischer, M., and Bertelsen, A. A cross-national epidemiological study of mania. *Br. J. Psychiat.* 129, 428–437 (1976).

Leff, M., Roatch, J., and Bunney, W.J. Environmental factors preceding the onset of severe depressions. *Psychiat.* 33, 293–311 (1970).

Lundquist, G. Prognosis and course in manic-depressive psychoses. *Acta Psychiatr. Neurol. Suppl. 35* (1945).

Mayfield, D.C., and Coleman, L.L. Alcohol use and affective disorder. *Dis. Ner. Sys* 29, 467–474 (1968).

Mendlewicz, J., Fieve, R., Rainer, J., and Fleiss, J. Manic-depressive illness: A comparative study of patients with and without a family history. *Br. J. Psychiat.* 120, 523–530 (1972).

Merrel, D.O. Inheritence of manic-depressive psychosis, *A.M.A. Arch. Neurol. Psychiatr.* 66, 272–279 (1951).

Morrison, J., Hudgens, A., and Barracha, R. Life events and psychiatric illness. *Br. J. Psychiat.* 114, 423–432 (1968).

Muller, C., Loren, J., Eisert, M. Etude sur la frequence d'apparition de la manie. *Soc. Psychiat.* 3, 133–135 (1968).

Murphy, J.M. Psychiatric labeling in cross-cultural perspective. *Science* 191, 1019–1029 (1976).

Odegaard, O. Emigration and mental health. *Ment. Hyg.* 20, 546–553 (1936).

Odegaard, O. The incidence of psychoses in various occupations. *Int. J. Soc. Psychiat.* 2, 85–104 (1956).

Parsons, R.P. Joseph Goldberger and Pellagra. In *Great Adventures in Medicine*, S. and H., eds. Dial, New York (1952), pp. 586–605.

Paykel, E.A. Recent life events and clinical depression. In *Life Stress and Illness*, E.K. Gunderson and R.H., Rake eds. Charles Thomas, Springfield, Illinois (1974).

Paykel, E., Myers, J., Dievet M., et al. Life events and depression. *Arch. Gen. Psychiat.* 21, 753–776 (1970).

Perris, C., ed. A study of bipolar (manic-depressive) and unipolar recurrent psychoses. *Acta Psychiatr. Scand. Suppl. 194* 42, (1966).

Perris, C. The genetics of affective disorders. In *Biological Psychiatry*, J. Mendels, ed. Wiley-Interscience, New York (1973).

Pollack, H. Recurrence of attacks in manic-depressive psychoses. *Am. J. Psychiat.* 11, 567 (1931).

Rao, A.V. A study of depression as prevalent in South India. *Transcult Psychiatr. Res. Rev.* 7, 116 (1970).

Reich, L.H., Davies, R.K., and Himmelhock, J.M. Excessive alcohol use in manic-depressive illness. *Am. J. Psychiat.* 131, 83–89 (1974).

Robbins, L.N. Psychiatric epidemiology. *Arch. Gen. Psychiat.* 35, 697–702 (1978).

Rosenthal, D. Problems of sampling and diagnosis in the major twin studies of schizophrenia. *J. Psychiatr. Rev.* 1, 116–134 (1962).

Rosenthal, D. *Genetic Theory and Abnormal Behavior*. McGraw-Hill, New York (1970) p. 205.

Sjögren T. Genetic-statistical and psychiatric investigations of a west Swedish population. *Acta Psychiatr. Neurol. Supp. 52* (1948).

Slater, E., Maxwell, J., and Price, J.S. Distribution of ancestral secondary cases in bipolar affective disorders. *Br. J. Psychiat.* 118, 215–218 (1971).

Slater, E., and Tsuang, M. Abnormality of paternal and maternal sides: Observations on schizophrenia and manic-depression. *J. Med. Genet.* 5, 197–199 (1968).

Stabenau, J.R. Genetic and other factors in schizophrenia, manic-depressive and schizo-affective disorders. *J. Nerv. & Ment. Dis.* 164(3), 149–167 (1977).

Stenstedt, A. A study in manic-depressive psychosis: Clinical, social and genetic investigations. *Acta Psychiatr. Neurol. Scand. Supp. 79* (1952).

Thompson, K., and Hendrai, H. Environmental stress in primary depressive illness. *Arch. Gen. Psychiat.* 26, 130–132 (1972).

Tietze, C., Lemkau, P., and Cooper, M. Schizophrenia, manic-depressive psychosis and socioeconomic status. *Am. J. Sociol.* 47(2) (1941).

Turns, D. The epidemiology of major affective disorders. *Am. J. Psychother.* 32, 5–19 (1978).

Von Tomassen, H. Further investigations on manic-depressive psychosis. *Acta Psychiatr. Neurol.* 13, 517–526 (1938).

Weismann, M., and Klerman, G.L. Epidemiology of mental disorders. *Arch. Gen. Psychiat.* 35, 705–712 (1978).

Werthman, F. A group of benign chronic psychoses: Prolonged manic excitements. *Am. J. Psychiat.* 9, 17 (1929).

White, R., Schlagenhauf, G., and Tupin, J. The treatment of manic-depressive states with lithium carbonate. *Am. Psychiatr.* 5, 230–242 (1966).

Winokur, G., Clayton, P.J., and Riech, T. *Manic-depressive disease.* C.V. Mosby, St. Louis (1969).

Wing, J.K., Cooper, J.E., and Sartorious, N. *The Measurement and Classification of Psychiatric Symptoms.* Cambridge Univ. Press, London (1974).

CHAPTER 17

Psychoanalytic Studies of Mania

Dov R. Aleksandrowicz

INTRODUCTION

The past 20 years have witnessed impressive advances in neurobiology, such as studies on physiology of sleep and dreaming, genetics of mental illness, and the role of neurotransmitters in normal and deviant behavior. Such studies open up new and exciting perspectives for psychoanalytical observations with data derived from biological studies (Aleksandrowicz, 1977; Hartmann, 1973). Such seems also to be the case of manic-depressive psychosis. Its inexplicable recurrent course, the profound derangement and depression of vital functions such as sleep and hunger during mania, and the patient's own perception, during remissions, of his illness as being alien to his own self; all seem to indicate that a biological disorder underlies or accompanies the illness (Jacobson, 1953). Such an assumption is strongly supported by the recent studies on the biology of mania and depression reviewed in this volume. On the other hand, during the last 60 years considerable information has been gathered on the psychological processes occurring during, triggering off, and predisposing to manic-depressive psychosis. Beginning with Karl Abraham's (1912) and Freud's (1917) early papers, many psychoanalysts have been studying patients with mania (Dooley, 1921; Lewin, 1950, 1959; Cohen et al., 1954; Gibson et al., 1959; Freeman, 1971) and/or depression (Rado, 1928; Jacobson, 1953; Klein, 1935, 1940; Bowlby, 1963) both during the mood-swings and during remissions. Those analysts have attempted to correlate their observations with the psychoanalytic theory of personality and of mental development.

The data derived from psychoanalytic observations differ considerably from any other set of data, and it will be useful to review briefly the unique features of the method and the theory. The psychoanalytic technique consists of an intense, systematic introspection, conducted in a healing setting (the therapeutic situation) and assisted by a trained therapist. The introspection is facilitated by frequent, regular sessions, restriction of external stimuli (use of couch), and last but not least, an attitude of benevolent interest and emotional neutrality on the part of the therapist. The introspection is focused on fantasies, wishes and needs (including thoughts the subject is not aware of), and those defences that we all erect against unconscious wishes and fantasies. The analysis is particularly concerned with fantasies and wishes directed at the therapist (transferences), since experience has shown that these reflect long-repressed events and fantasies of childhood, which play a critical role in the formation of psychoneurotic symptoms and other types of maladaptive behavior.

The psychoanalytic technique is therefore particularly well suited to the study of inner psychic life (as opposed to overt behavior), including those processes of which the subject was not previously aware, and it permits a historical reconstruction of one's emotional development and interpersonal relationship.

Psychoanalytic theory describes mental life in terms of mutually complimentary models:

a. The *topographic* model refers to the accessibility of ideas to awareness. Ideas may be "conscious"; "preconscious," i.e., easily brought into awareness; or "unconscious," i.e., repressed.

b. The *dynamic* model refers to conflicts between opposing forces; e.g., a wish to be nurtured and protected may be opposed by a wish to be strong, independent and proud. The conflict may result in a compromise behavior; e.g., a person may choose a masculine, seemingly active role in an organization which offers economic security and clear guidelines for decision making, such as the military. The conflict may often result in repression of one wish and exaggeration (reaction formation) of the opposing one. Thus, intense and promiscuous heterosexual activity may be a defence against repressed homosexual wishes.

c. The *economic* model refers to the relative dominance of drives, wishes, and other psychic functions, or their being invested with "psychic energy," or "cathected." For instance, being in love involves a greatly heightened interest in the object of love and reduces interest in all other people and even in one's own gains. We consider, therefore, the mental image of the loved person to be invested with an unusually high psychic energy. Some analysts consider the term "psychic energy" a mere figure of speech, while others assume the presence of an underlying physical process and hope that "psychic energy" will eventually be found correlated with activation of specific neural structures.

d. The *structural* model describes three psychic "organs," or clusters of functions: The Id is the reservoir of instinctual drives, derivatives of biological needs, primarily the sexual and the aggressive drives. The ego encompasses the integrative functions, such as control and channelization of drives, perception and judgment of reality, learning and memory. The superego represents the moral and social values and norms acquired by absorbing the injunctions and example of parents and other important and admired figures.

e. The *genetic* model describes the development of personality through the reciprocal influence of innate endowment (Aleksandrowicz and Aleksandrowicz, 1975 a, b) and the early environment, particularly parents. It refers to "oral," "anal," and "oedipal" (or "phallic") stages, preceding "latency" (middle childhood), adolescent, and adult stages.

f. The *object relationship* theory of M. Klein and her followers emphasizes that the very early experiences of the infant in relation to parenting figures (joy, rage, or anxiety) become incorporated into the psychological makeup and determine one's way of coping with life and the more subtle aspects of relationship to others.

It is useful to keep in mind that some psychoanalytic formulations refer to behavioral and subjective observation while others refer to abstract constructs. The former are verifiable, while the latter, useful as they may be, are not verifiable. For instance, the statement "Feelings of unworthiness are usually accompanied by unconscious or partly conscious grandiose wishes and fantasies" can be confirmed (or disproved) by observation. On the other hand, the statement "Feelings of unworthiness are produced by a harsh, punitive superego" cannot be verified or disproved empirically. Let us assume that we find a patient who feels worthless and yet acts like a despicable rascal, i.e., shows little overt influence of a system of moral values, which a superego is supposed to be. Instead of abandoning our formulation, we can now modify it and add, "A harsh, punitive superego may be inconsistent and corruptible." Useful as such formulations are for the therapist, they do not lend themselves well to integration with other frames of reference. Since our discussion aims at comparing psychoanalytic formulations with other sets of hypotheses, we will emphasize more the empirical, verifiable psychoanalytic statements.

This very brief diversion into basic concepts of psychoanalysis will help us to examine the different ways in which psychoanalytic data contribute to the understanding of manic illness.

THE NATURE OF PSYCHIC DISORGANIZATION DURING MANIA

Abraham (1924) and Freud (1917) were impressed by the abundance in manic patients of feelings and fantasies derived from the oral stage of development, i.e., when sucking and ingesting is a dominant source of sensual pleasure. Patients would talk of "gobbling up the world" or similar expressions. Later studies confirmed those observations (Rado, 1928; Lewin, 1950; Klein, 1935, 1940). Thus a regressive link was established between mania (and depression) and an early developmental stage, though the implications of the regression were not all too clear. In terms of the structural model in depression, the superego becomes overly dominant and harsh, while in mania it becomes absorbed into the rest of the personality, and the triumphant id finds an almost unlimited outlet.

Freud's most important contribution was pointing out the phenomenological and psychological similarities between the normal process of mourning and the abnormal state of psychotic depression (Freud, 1917), and the importance of loss of a love object in the latter condition, as well as in the former. He demonstrated that the loss of a love object in depression may not be a realistic loss, but a symbolic one—i.e., loss of an ideal, or disappointment, rejection by a love object. In each case the depresed patient will respond in a manner similar to the bereaved: Rather than relinquishing the lost object, he will set up a mental image or representation thereof and invest it with an enormous amount of psychic energy, depleting all other endeavors and relationships. The mourner is usually aware of this investment of feelings in the image of the departed. He may be less aware of the tendency of this mental image to become gradually absorbed in the self-image, by process of identification or introjection. Indeed, the bereaved patient's oral fantasies often hint at or describe infantile, cannibalistic fantasies of ingesting the lost beloved (Abraham, 1924).

The most important feature of melancholia is the overwhelming aggression directed against oneself: self-reproach, guilt, and suicidal tendencies. Freud (1917) was able to demonstrate that the source of this murderous agression is the rage against the lost object, consisting of previously repressed resentment but mainly of reproach for being rejected or abandoned. Since the representation of the lost object merges (by identification) into the self, the rage is thus deflected against the self and the patient is able to remain unaware of his unacceptable anger against the love object.

Freud assumed that in mania the lost object is rapidly relinquished (though he could not explain why) and a vast amount of psychic energy becomes free to be invested upon the self and the surrounding world.

Lewin (1950) made a thorough study of the psychoanalytic literature on mania, adding his own observations. He presents detailed evidence of the profound psychic regression occurring during mania. He also points out the importance of *denial* both of psychic pain and of unpleasant external reality. His main thesis is that elation and mania are derivatives of the bliss experienced by the satiated infant, but such a conclusion is open to serious question. Some states of elation and ecstasy, notably those described by the mystics (Lewin, 1950) may well resemble infantile bliss to the extent that our intuitive understanding of it is at all accurate. Mania, however, includes the important elements of hypervigilance and hyperactivity, for which Lewin is not able to account satisfactorily. Nor is mania a blissful condition: It is usually accompanied by anxiety, fearful fantasies, and, paradoxically, depressed thoughts (Machover and Wexler, quoted by Bellak, 1952, p. 104; Kotin and Goodwin, 1972). M. Klein (1940) makes a more credible assumption comparing mania with the sense of triumph and omnipotence with which the very young child presumably attempts to overcome the "primal depression." According to her, a depressive state is a normal developmental phase, occurring toward the end of the first year of life and caused by weaning and gradual weakening of the deep bond between the infant and the mothering figure. Depression and the defence against it, i.e., mania, would represent a reactivation of the corresponding infantile state. Articulate as Klein's arguments are, they are based on extrapolations from analyses of older children and adults, and represent hypotheses difficult to confirm or disprove.

Psychoanalytic investigations of the dynamics of depression and mania raise the question of etiology: Are the psychological processes the *cause* of the extreme change of mood? Freud (1917), while describing psychotic depression as an abnormal reaction to loss, is careful not to draw etiological conclusions beyond describing the importance of ambivalence and repressed hate. He is even more cautious in regard to mania, and recognizes that the economic description (i.e., freeing of energy) does not account adequately for the condition. Some later analytic writers (Freeman, 1971) emphasize that the manic symptoms serve as a defence against unacceptable drives and thus imply psychological causation of mania. In the last analysis, the question reduces itself to the following: Why do specific psychological stresses—e.g., object loss—unleash in some people an extreme derangement like a manic attack?

THE RELATIONSHIP BETWEEN MANIA AND DEPRESSION

One of the puzzling features of manic-depressive psychosis is the bipolar nature of the illness. If the symptoms are manifestation of a biochemical deviation in the CNS, then one would expect the deviation during mania to be the opposite of that underlying depression, and so indeed many investigators assume. This, however, leaves a number of questions unanswered: Why should so many patients be susceptible to both? Why are some drugs effective against both syndromes? Why are features of one phase of the disorder present during the opposite phase? (Winokur et al., 1969). In many manic patients symptoms of depression seem to *increase* at the same time as symptoms of mania (Kotin and Goodwin, 1972). Psychoanalysts have demonstrated that on the psychological level elation and depression are closely related. Carlisle (quoted by Bellak, 1952, p. 100) described depressions following success, and one can often observe elation arising in a context that would more likely be expected to cause depression, such as a loss or a blow to self-esteem. It is assumed that elation is a defence against depression, an attempt to deny and ward off psychic pain. Psychoanalytic technique is particularly well suited to discover underlying depressive content, as the following vignettes illustrate:

a. The patient was an ambitious and successful industrial engineer in his forties, who suffered a coronary infarction while in psychotherapy. At that time he suffered frustrating business reverses and was experiencing difficulties in his personal life. During recovery from the infarction the patient became mildly euphoric, was telling jokes to visiting friends, and found the anxious concern of his relatives rather amusing. He reported a dream in which "knights dressed in black and white were slowly marching up a flight of stairs." The initial association led to a Pelican paperback with humorous content, read the day before. Later associations led to "knights" being prominent military people with whom he had been associated and the patient's satisfaction of having acted decisively and effectively some days before his illness. However, further associations led to a very different and less cheerful train of thought: his father's funeral, the illness of the patient's analyst, and thoughts about his own life expectancy being reduced.

b. A college student in her mid-thirties was approaching her graduation with joyful expectation, planning a long-due visit to her family and exploring career opportunities. She was emotionally a very unstable person with major problems in her love life and previous severe depressions leading on one occasion to a serious suicidal attempt. A few days before her final examination she dreamt of seeing the face of a close friend all wrinkled up. Her first thoughts were of becoming like her admired friend: beautiful, self-confident, and well liked. Then the patient realized that the forthcoming graduation reminded her that she was much older than her schoolmates. She realized her loneliness and thought that in a few years she would lose her still youthful appearance and no longer be able to get the little affection she was now receiving by being sexually desired. Her thoughts of suicide returned with renewed strength.

Thus euphoria and even mania may be a defence against depression. The opposite situation, depression as defence against mania, also occurs, though it seems to have been generally overlooked in the literature. Kohut (1971, p. 97) describes people with impaired psychic homeostasis whom an intense aggressive self-satisfaction can stimulate to the point of danger of manic excitement. They then develop various symptoms to avoid it. Kohut does not mention depression, but the following vignette illustrates it:

The patient was a student in his late twenties, very intelligent and endowed with keen psychological insight, in treatment because of alcoholism and difficulties in interpersonal relationships. He reported that drinking was the only way to cope with a dilemma posed by his enormous ambition. He found himself driven to constantly prove his superiority and gain dominance over others. Failure made him feel dejected and worthless, but success brought on a brief, mounting elation, followed by panic and then depression. He realized that elation was accompanied by megalomanic fantasies of possessing enormous physical power (his favorite hobby was weight-lifting), which enabled him to literally rip the whole world apart. He was seized with terror and visions of having wreaked a cosmic destruction and of being left all alone in a cold, empty universe. Then depression would set in and he would relax; depressed, he felt safe. Thus, for some patients the pain of depression and sense of low self-esteem seem to be intolerable, and they retreat into mania to deny and ward off depression. Other patients are so threatened by manic excitement and agressive grandiose fantasies that they seek refuge in depression, as a last resort to curb their uncontrollable drives.

In psychoanalytic terms, mania and depression represent not only opposite moods, but also polar extremes of drive control, i.e., hyperinhibition and hyperrelease. Therefore, the substitution of one for the other can easily be understood as an effect of the organism's homeostatic efforts. Both states represent inadequate, desperate means of maintaining internal balance, and the interplay between internal psychic forces and environmental circumstances will dictate which of the two conditions will be less threatening.

PERSONALITY OF BIPOLAR PATIENTS

Patients with manic-depressive illness are often described as "oral" personalities. However, this is a feature of many other people with psychological difficulties, such as people with infantile personalities, anorexia nervosa and/or obesity, and alcoholics, to mention just a few. Rado (1928) was the first one to point out that bipolar patients tend to be particularly sensitive and to crave other people's approval, support, and affection. Their self-esteem is easily increased or lowered by others' attitudes. Later, psychoanalytic studies (Jacobson, 1953; Cohen et al., 1954; Gibson et al., 1959) confirmed amply Rado's descriptions. Patients susceptible to bipolar illness seem to develop a peculiar set of interpersonal relationships. They show an intense need to be accepted by society, their value system is oriented toward gaining approval, and many of them present an affable facade, cherishing a large number of superficial "friends." Those friendships lack depth, and the patient seems singularly lacking in empathy toward others' feelings and devoid of psychologic subtlety (Gibson et al., 1959).

In the center of the patient's life, there usually is one greatly admired person (or ideal) on whose approval the patient's gratification and security depend. The patient may even sacrifice his own ambition and self-sufficiency to gain that approval, and struggles to repress envy and competitive resentment toward the object of his admiration and dependency. The patient seems particularly concerned with his or her own and others' envy (a largely unconscious apprehension), and some patients seem to maintain a self-defeating life style in order to avoid the real or imagined envy of other people (Cohen et al., 1954). Cohen and her associates (1954) attributed these personality features to the patients' family background, characterized by strong emphasis on success and social conformity and by being emotionally accepted only if and when serving the ambitious goals of one or both parents. They were also impressed by unusual competitiveness and envy on part of the patients' siblings.

The depressive or the manic attacks are precipitated by the loss of the all-important object, usually because the patient feels rejected, rebuked, or not appreciated. This loss need not be a conspicuous, obviously stressful life event. Cohen and her coworkers (1954) pointed out that even a change in the patient's appraisal of existing relationships may be subjectively experienced as loss of love, and so can, paradoxically, a promotion. People susceptible to bipolar illness rely heavily on denial, and therefore one can expect them to overlook the occurrence or significance of psychologically painful events. It is no surprise, therefore, that searches for precipitating events, such as reviewed by Dunner and Hall (this volume) often do not reveal it. According to Clancy et al. (quoted by Dunner and Hall, this volume), "physical" precipitating events are more often reported by bipolar patients. This is also expected, since bipolar patients are sensitive to social "desirability" (Donnelly and Murphy, 1973), and it is somehow more dignified, in the eyes of many, to become mentally ill after a physical mishap, such as illness or accident, than after an emotional setback.

Interestingly enough, the psychoanalytic investigations of the personality of patients with bipolar illness have been confirmed in part by investigators using experimental, quantitative methods (Donnelly and Murphy, 1973; Donnelly et al., 1976). Bipolar patients seem to be environment-directed, sensitive to social cues, "field-dependent," and sensitive to being judged by others. It may be concluded that people susceptible to bipolar illness show features of a narcissistic personality of a certain type. Narcissism refers to the emotional attitude toward one's own self. A considerable amount of "healthy" self-love is necessary for emotional well-being and perhaps for survival. Kohut (1971), Kernberg (1975), and others have studied in detail the development and vicissitudes of narcissistic needs and wishes in normal and deviant personality structure. Ambition, greed, idealism, ruthlessness, and exhibitionism all reflect narcissistic strivings, some ethically acceptable, others less so. Self-esteem depends on the degree of satisfaction of one's narcissistic needs. The infant's narcissistic needs are provided by means of physical care and emotional nurture by tne mothering adults. His narcissistic frustrations are the inevitable result of cognitive growth; the developing assessment of reality makes him realize gradually and repeatedly how small and helpless he really is and stirs up feelings of envy and helpless rage. The very young child apparently finds consolation in fantasies (or hallucinations?) of omnipotence, of which traces are found later in play, stories of magic power, and dreams. He also finds consolation in the love of the parents, whose wisdom and power he idealizes.

These modes of consolation determine the three principal styles of coping for people whose narcissistic needs are strong. Some people strive for gratification from reality, i.e., make their fantasy come true: amass power or money, command attention by behavior, "collect" sexual successes. Other narcissists retreat into haughty emotional isolation, buttressed by conscious or unconscious fantasies of grandeur. The third group of people seek narcissistic support from being approved of, liked, or held in esteem. Indeed, many such people are well liked and respected. To the extent that narcissism is equated with self-love and being self-centered, these people may appear the opposite—i.e., selfless and exceedingly considerate of others. A more careful analysis, however, shows that the selflessness and concern for others' feelings result from the persistent need to be accepted and approved of and therefore to ultimately serve a narcissistic need. The narcissistic structure is revealed when these people suffer a rebuke, disappointment, or even worse, a permanent loss of the person or object (such as career) providing the primary source of narcissistic needs. Their need to be liked inhibits the overhwelming inner rage to the point that the subject is usually not aware of it. Instead, depression or mania may follow, giving vent, indirectly, to the enormous pent-up aggression. In depression the aggression is primarily turned inward, against the self (even though some of it remains directed at the environment; many depressed patients are irritable or annoyed). In mania, the aggression is directed outward. Manic patients, however, are not only irritable and controlling (i.e., aggressive), they also bestow their love generously, if indiscriminately. It seems that the manic patient, having lost his primary source of security, his love object, now intensifies, to the point of grotesque, the shallow, unempathetic relationships he maintained with everybody else, "seeking like a ravenously hungry man for new object cathexes" [Freud, 1917].

The narcissistic personality of the type seen in bipolar patients is vulnerable, susceptible to the impact of environment and the caprice of fate. Depression and elation are indices of the narcissistic balance, and therefore narcissistically vulnerable people are subject to mood swings. The extreme state of mania and psychotic depression seem, however, to require an additional postulate. In most vulnerable narcissistic patients, the mood swings, whether resulting from frustration or gratification, are self-limiting. It seems probable that in bipolar patients the regulatory mechanism is somehow absent, and we observe instead a self-perpetuating derangement resembling the "positive feedback" phenomenon. At our present state of knowledge, it is pure speculation to consider the failure of mood regulation to be primarily psychological or biological defect, to be genetically determined or related to early environment (Gibson et al., 1959). We begin to realize now that it is not an either-or issue. Environmental influences can have lasting biological effects (Henry et al., 1972), and innate qualities affect the environment one is developing in (Korner and Gronstein, 1967; Aleksandrowicz and Aleksandrowicz, 1975b).

In conclusion, present evidence suggests that bipolar patients tend to have a vulnerable narcissistic personality sensitive to environmental cues ("field dependent") and relying on a significant person's approval for narcissistic balance. They also seem to lack the capacity to limit the mood swings that reflect the narcissistic balance. Whether these features are primarily biological or psychological deviations is still a matter of speculation. Most likely they are both and result from an interaction between genetic and environmental determinants.

MANIC-DEPRESSIVE ILLNESS AND SCHIZOPHRENIA

In the absence of definite understanding of etiology, the question of distinct disease entity versus continuity cannot be answered. Psychoanalytic investigations, however, show that in typical cases the two conditions are psychologically sharply separated. "Preschizophrenic" or "schizoid" personalities are typically introverted, "field-independent" persons often intensely aware of their fantasy life and highly responsive to inner cues. In more severe cases, these people tend to withdraw emotionally and become different, cold and dreamy. The bipolar patients, in contrast, are "field dependent," responsive to social cues, intolerant of internal stress and avoiding inner cues by means of denial or "flight into reality" (Dooley, 1921; Cohen et al., 1954).

When the schizoid patient suffers a decompensation—i.e., psychotic episode—his contact with outer reality is lost to a greater or lesser degree, and he populates the environment with fragments of his inner world—memories, wishes, fears, and thoughts, thus creating the "cursorily improvised" world aptly described by Justice Schreber (Freud, 1911, pp. 12–34). The manic patient's world instead is flooded and distorted by his grandiosity, but contact with physical reality is maintained and so is his interest in other people, even though the narcissistic nature of the relationship becomes more grossly visible. Thus, on a psychodynamic level there are clear-cut differences between the schizoid and bipolar prepsychotic personalities, and also between the two corresponding psychotic states. Moreover, from a psychoanalytic point there is no need to assume a continuity between manic-depressive psychosis and schizophrenia because of the "mixed" or "borderline" cases or the presence of symptoms of one disease in a case of the other illness (e.g., grandiose ideas in schizophrenia or paranoid thinking in mania). In both conditions there is a severe regression and emergence of psychological processes belonging to very early developmental stages. Development, however, is a continuous process, and developmental stages overlap and also "telescope" into later stages. Therefore, regression can and does cause emergence of processes belonging to different periods of development. Phenomenological overlap need not indicate etiological unity, though it may.

In conclusion, psychoanalysis cannot resolve the issue of discrete versus continuous etiology of schizophrenia and bipolar illness. Psychoanalysis does, however, differentiate sharply between predisposing personalities of the two conditions, and it can explain the overlap of symptoms even if the two diseases are assumed to be separate entities.

THERAPEUTIC IMPLICATIONS

The effectiveness of psychotropic medication in bipolar illness raises the issue of whether psychotherapy is useful in those patients and whether medication and psychotherapy help or hinder each other. Psychotherapists and psychoanalysts are wary of prescribing psychoactive drugs during treatment and they have good reasons to be so. The case of schizophrenia, manic-depressive or unipolar depressive psychosis, and of borderline conditions, however, are entirely different. For the purpose of this study we will limit our discussion to bipolar illness. The model suggested here—i.e., that the illness results from a combination of vulnerable narcissistic peronality and failure of mood-regulating mechanism—opens possibilities for both biological and psychological treatment. Mood deviations respond well to drugs and can be prevented by medication. On the other hand, personality structure is not (yet) amenable to any intervention except patient systematic psychotherapeutic exploration. Many manic patients in remission are not good candidates for intense psychotherapy or psychoanalysis (Dooley, 1921). They form a therapeutic relationship easily because they are eager to please and grateful for the therapist's interest. The relationship, however, is narcissistically motivated, tends to remain shallow and rigid. The manic patient rarely is introspective even during remission and treatment tends to be interrupted by "flight into reality" (Dooley, 1921). Some of those patients can benefit from psychoanalysis; others benefit more from a less intense supportive psychotherapy. In my experience the prospects of psychotherapy are not improved by refraining from adequate psychotropic medication. The inhuman suffering inflicted by psychotic depression or mania does not increase the motivation to engage and persist in psychotherapy, in contrast to the anxiety of neurotic patients, which does. Quite the opposite is true: The mood swings and accompanying denial constitute rigid, impenetrable resistance, rendering psychotherapy arduous and sterile. The following case demonstrates the risk of purely psychological approach:

A physician in his thirties was suffering from severe, recurrent unipolar depression. The psychotherapist trying to explore the underlying conflicts urged the patient to refrain from using the "crutches" of antidepressant medication. The patient found himself torn between the wish to please his therapist and intolerable depression, and committed suicide.

In conclusion, at the present state of knowledge, the bipolar patient should receive adequate biological treatment. Once the mood is stabilized the patient and his therapist should decide whether psychological exploration is needed, and if so, what kind of psychotherapy should be recommended. Attempts to control severe mood swings by psychological means alone are of questionable value, risky, and undefensible at our present state of art. On the other hand, there is clinical evidence that in some patients skillfully conducted psychotherapy or psychoanalysis helps to avert the recurrence or reduce the severity of manic or depressive attacks (Abraham, 1912; Gibson et al., 1959). Moreover, many bipolar patients experience more difficulties in interpersonal relationships during remissions than they care to admit. Donnelly et al. (1976) found that bipolar patients tend to underrate their difficulties and symptoms even when depressed, a fact that should be taken into account when interpreting surveys of social adjustment, such as reviewed by Dunner and Hall (1978). This is not surprising in view of the bipolar patient's denial and emphasis on social desirability. It seems that recommendation for psychotherapy or against it can best be made only if the patient has established enough trust in the therapist to overcome some of those impediments.

CONCLUSION

Mania is a puzzling condition for the clinical psychiatrist, psychoanalyst, and neurobehavioral scientist alike. It is clear, however, that neither purely psychological nor purely behavioral or biochemical hypotheses can fully account for the facts known about mania. Therefore, further study of bipolar disease should prove fertile ground for examining the intricate and complex relationship between subjective experience and observable behavior, between intrapsychic process and neurochemical event.

REFERENCES

Abraham, K. Notes on the psycho-analytical investigation and treatment of manic depressive insanity and allied conditions (1912). In *Selected Papers on Psycho-Analysis*. Basic, New York (1953), pp. 137–156.

Abraham, K. A short study of the development of the libido, viewed in the light of mental disorders (1924). In *Selected Papers on Psycho-Analysis*. Basic, New York (1953), pp. 418–480.

Aleksandrowicz, D.R. Are there precursors to repression? *J. Nerv. Ment. Dis.* 164(3), 191–197 (1977).

Aleksandrowicz, M.K., and Aleksandrowicz, D.R. The case history of a happy child. *Child Psychiat. & Hum. Dev.* 5(3), 174–181 (1975a).

Aleksandrowicz, M.K., and Aleksandrowicz, D.R. The molding of personality. *Child Psychiat. & Hum. Dev.* 5(4), 231–241 (1975b).

Aleksandrowicz, M.K., and Aleksandrowicz, D.R. Precursors of ego in neonates: Factor analysis of Brazelton Scale data. *J. Am. Acad. Child Psychiat.* 15(2), 257–268 (1976).

Bellak, L. *Manic-Depressive Psychosis and Allied Conditions.* Grune & Stratton, New York (1952)

Bowlby, J. Pathological mourning and childhood mourning. *J. Am. Psychoan. Assn.* 11, 500–541 (1963).

Cohen, M.B., Baker, G., Cohen, R.A., Fromm-Reichmann, R., and Weigert, E.V. An intensive study of twelve cases of manic-depressive psychosis. *Psychiatry* 17:103–138 (1954).

Donnelly, E.F., and Murphy, D.L. Social desirability and bipolar affective disorder. *J. Consult. & Clin. Psychol.* 41(3), 469 (1973).

Donnelly, E.F., Murphy, D.L., and Goodwin, F.K. Cross-sectional and longitudinal comparisons of bipolar and unipolar depressed groups. *J. Consult. & Clin. Psychol.* 44(2), 233–237 (1976).

Dooley, L. A psychoanalytic study of manic-depressive psychosis. *Psychoan. Rev.* 8, 32–72 and 144:167 (1921).

Freeman, T. Observations on mania. *Int. J. Psychoan.* 52, 479–486 (1971).

Freud, S. Psycho-analytic notes on an autobiographical account of a case of paranoia (dementia paranoides) (1911). In *Standard Edition*, Vol. XL1. Hogarth, London (1958), pp. 9–82 (case history pp. 12–34).

Freud, S. Mourning and melancholia (1917). In *Standard Edition*, Vol. XIV. Hogart, London (1957), pp. 243–258.

Gibson, R.W., Cohen, M.B., and Cohen, R.A. On the dynamics of the manic-depressive personality. *Am. J. Psychiat.* 115, 1101–1107 (1959).

Hartmann, E.L. *The Functions of Sleep,* Yale Univ. Press (1973).

Henry, J.P., Ely, D.L., and Stephens, P.M. Changes in catecholamine-controlling enzymes in response to psychosocial activation of the defence and alarm reactions. In *Physiology, Emotion and Psychosomatic Illness,* Ciba Foundation Symposium 7, R. Porter and J. Knight, eds. Elsevier, Amsterdam (1972).

Jacobson, E. Contribution to the metapsychology of cyclothymic depression. In *Affective Disorders,* P. Greenacre, ed. International Univ. Press, New York (1953), pp. 49–83.

Klein, M. A contribution to the psychogenesis of manic-depressive states. *Int. J. Psychoan.* 16, 145–174 (1935).

Klein, M. Mourning and its relation to manic-depressive states. *Int. J. Psychoan.* 21(2), 125–153 (1940).

Kohut, H. *The Analysis of the Self.* International Univ. Press, New York (1971).

Korner, A.F., and Grobstein, R. Inidividual differences at birth. *J. Am. Acad. Child Psychiat.* 6, 676–690 (1967).

Kotin, J., and Goodwin, F.K. Depression during mania: Clinical observations and theoretical implications. *Am. J. Psychiat.,* 129(6), 679–686 (1972).

Levitan, H.L. Dreams preceding hypomania. *Int. J. Psychoan. & Psychother.* 1(4), 50–61 (1972).

Lewin, B.D. *The Psychoanalysis of Elation.* Norton, New York (1950).

Lewin, B.D. Some psychoanalytic ideas applied to elation and depression. *Am. J. Psychiat.* 116, 38–43 (1959).

Rado, S. The problem of melancholia. *Int. J. Psychoan.* 9, 420–438 (1928).

Winokur, G., Clayton, P.J., and Reich, T. *Manic-Depressive Illness.* C.V. Mosby, St. Louis (1969).

CHAPTER 18

Psychodiagnostic Assessment
And Psychological Function in Mania

Uriel Last

Only a surprisingly meager volume of literature has ever been published on psychodiagnosis and psychological function in mania. The reason for this state of affairs may be understood after examining briefly some basic features of clinical assessment in general and mania in particular.

Personality assessment procedures may be characterized by the following criteria: (a) identity of data producer (subject or examiner), (b) awareness by the subject of being assessed, and (c) type of task assigned to data producer. All common psychodiagnostic procedures require the assessed subject to produce the data under consideration, while the subject is usually aware of being assessed, and the task assigned varies with the specific assessment procedure. The subject may be asked to describe himself, as in the Minnesota Multiphasic Personality Inventory (MMPI); he may be asked to report his current experiencing, as in the Rorschach technique; or he may be required to perform accurately and display capabilities, as on various intelligence scales or grapho-motor tests.

Clinical assessment methods, on the other hand, rest heavily on two other sources of information, namely objective observation and reference to prior behavior, including personal and familial history. When gathering these kinds of data, the assessed subject is usually not required to produce anything, nor is he aware that he is subjected to assessment.

Considering the typical behavior patterns of mania, such as inability to remain still, failure to filter trivial stimuli, irritability, and assaultive or dominating behavior (Carpenter and Stephens, this volume), one can imagine why manic patients in an acute phase are usually unable to assume a role of a subject in an assessment session.

This state of affairs leads, of course, to preference, on practical grounds, of clinical-psychiatric assessment methods—mainly observational procedures like Beigel et al's. (1971) and Young et al's. (1978) rating scales—to psychodiagnostic methods.

Traditionally, psychodiagnostic assessment techniques have been employed for three purposes: (1) diagnostic appraisal, (2) psychodynamic uncovering, and (3) evaluating efficacy of treatments. The present review will critically examine the literature on psychodiagnostic techniques as applied to mania, and judge whether such techniques have indeed been useful for the purposes assigned to them.

The review will cover (a) grapho-motor assessment in mania, using the Bender Gestalt Test and the Draw A Person Test; (b) assessment of cognitive functioning in mania, stressing the Wechsler scales; (c) MMPI in mania; (d) projective techniques in mania, stressing the Rorschach and the Thematic Apperception Test (TAT); (e) thought and speech assessment in mania.

GRAPHO-MOTOR ASSESSMENT

Despite the wide use of the Bender Gestalt Test and the Draw A Person Test for psychodiagnostic purposes, only very little systematic knowledge is available in regard to manics' performance on these grapho-motor tests.

Hutt (1977) mentions confused sequence of Bender-Gestalt reproductions to indicate severe disturbance and to be characteristic of manic or hypomanic conditions. Hutt's statement is corroborated by a single study on sequential style of Bender Gestalt performance conducted by Donnelly and Murphy (1974), who compared sequential performance of bipolar depressives and unipolar depressives. Bipolar subjects tended to exhibit irregular sequence, which was interpreted to indicate lack of impulse control. Unipolar subjects, on the other hand, tended to show overly methodical sequence, presumably an indicator of rigid impulse control.

Despite the inclination of manic patients to engage in drawing, Machover (1949) comments only on very few characteristics of their Draw A Person performance, amongst them their tendency to draw large expansive figures and to spontaneously write on or identify their drawings.

Grapho-motor testing, which elicits mainly expressive behavior, might be a relatively easy way to collect systematic behavioral data that is amenable to both quantitative and qualitative analysis. Grapho-motor behavior obviously could also serve in diagnosis of mania, due to ease of administration and the minimal tester-testee interaction needed. These features are highly necessary when one is concerned with eliciting relevant test data from a manic patient. This state of affairs calls for a systematic study of grapho-motor behavior in which manic patients will be compared at least with normal controls and schizophrenics in order to find out by a blind design whether typical manic grapho-motor pecularities can be identified.

ASSESSMENT OF COGNITIVE FUNCTIONING

Rabin (1965), in a review of the diagnostic use of intelligence tests, concludes that "the data reported in the literature tend to indicate that in the psychoneuroses and in the manic depressive disorders there is no reduction in intellectual functioning. Over all indices of intelligence such as IQ, MA, and vocabulary levels show that these groups do about as well or better than the normals [p. 481]." This conclusion was formulated on the basis of reviewing research data collected with the Stanford-Binet Scale.

The most frequently used intelligence scales in clinical practice today are, however, Wechsler's scales. Various attempts had been made to determine a specific profile of Wechsler subtests for manic disorders. The results have been disappointing. Rabin (1942) compared Wechsler Bellevue scale performances of schizophrenics, manics, and normal controls. He reported manics to have higher performance IQ's than verbal IQ's, while the opposite was true for schizophrenics. On the other hand, Gilliand et al. (1943) found that manic patients did slightly worse on most performance tests, although their scatter did not differ significantly from the scatter of normal controls. However, their subjects were preselected on the basis of favorable test attitudes, a fact that raises questions in regard to the representativeness of their manic group. Waldfogel and Guy (1951) reported patients with affective disorder to show similar subtest scatter on the Wechsler Bellevue Intelligence Scale regardless of whether they were classified as manic or depressive. The typical pattern was higher vocabulary IQ than performance IQ. These authors were, however, sensitive to the fact that the mentioned pattern was a function of age, and concluded that its diagnostic value is thereby diminished. An additional attempt to delineate specific subtest Wechsler Bellevue patterns characteristic of defined nosological groups is reported by Wittenborn and Holzberg (1951a). Comparing paranoid schizophrenics, alcoholic psychotics, psychopaths, and manics, they concluded that the Wechsler Bellevue subtest scores are of no practical diagnostic value. A recent study utilizing the WAIS (Brown, 1967) did not find any significant differences between verbal IQ and performance IQ for manics.

The depressive phase of manic-depressive psychosis is better documented in the literature on intellectual functioning, but with the disadvantage that only rarely is there a distinction between what now is labeled bipolar and unipolar illness. The depressive phase of manic-depressive illness, like other depressed states, is marked by one feature amongst others, which may have vast impact on performance subtests of the Wechsler—namely psychomotor slowing and inertia. Success on Wechsler performance tests is heavily determined by psychomotor speed, a fact that makes for retardation in action of depressed patients on the performance scales in general and especially on the digit symbol subtest (Rapaport et al., 1968).

Despite the failure to document a specific pattrn for mania on the Wechsler, the test allows ample opportunity for manic patients to reveal on various subtests, such as comprehension, similarities, information, and vocabulary, some of the typical features of mania, like flighty ideation and uncontrolled emotionality.

THE MINNESOTA MULTIPHASIC PERSONALITY INVENTORY (MMPI) IN MANIA

The MMPI is aimed at portraying a personality pattern and not a transitory state of affairs. This objective has, of course, implications both for labeling the pertinent MMPI scale Ma (hypomania, not mania) and in the process of its validation.

Many of the characteristic features of the hypomanic patient are portrayed in the 46 items of self-report comprising the Ma scale. The main features covered by questions on the scale are grandiosity, excitement, and the activity level so characteristic of the hypomanic person. The criterion subjects for validating the scale were difficult to obtain partly because of the nature of the psychiatric setting in which the initial validation research was conducted and partly because of the untestability of manic patients during an acute episode. Only a small group of 24 patients was used in the process of selecting the items for the Ma scale. Subsequent research has proven these items to be discriminating and the whole scale to be dependable (Welsh and Dahlstrom, 1951; Dahlstrom et al., 1972).

The potential usefulness of the MMPI in general and the Ma scale in particular for diagnosis of affective disorder is exemplified by a series of studies from N.I.M.H. Donnelly and Murphy (1973) tried to differentiate hospitalized patients with a bipolar affective disorder from hospitalized patients suffering from a unipolar affective disorder. Both types of patients were assessed during a depressive episode. Significant differences between the MMPI profiles of a unipolar group and a well-matched bipolar group were found. Unipolar patients scored higher on the D (depression) scale and on the Pt (psychasthenia) scale, while bipolar patients scored higher on the Ma scale. A similar trend of bipolars being higher on Ma scale during admission because of a depressive episode is also evident in a later study (Donnelly et al., 1976). In a third study with bigger samples (Donnelly et al., 1976), the Ma scale did not, however, differentiate between bipolar and unipolar patients. The two groups differed on a whole array of the ten MMPI clinical scales: Hs (Hypochondriasis) scale, D (depression) scale, Hy (Hysteria) scale, Pa (paranoia) scale, Pt (psychasthenia) scale, Sc (schizophrenia) scale, and Si (social introversion) scale. On all these scales the unipolar group scored significantly higher than the bipolar group. Most of these trends were already evident in the initial study (Donnelly and Murphy, 1973), but did not reach significance. Taken together, these studies show that newly hospitalized unipolar and bipolar depressive patients report remarkably different experiences of depression and other psychopathology. Bipolar groups of patients, when compared with unipolar groups, tend to report less psychopathology in general, as indicated for the aforementioned list of MMPI scales. They also tend to score above average on the Ma and Pd (psychopathic deviation) scales both at admission and at remission (Donnelly et al., 1976), and special mention must be given again to their consistent tendency to score significantly low on D (depression) scale.

Interestingly, when bipolar depressives are compared with unipolar depressives on behavioral ratings of depression, no difference emerges. It thus seems that the subjective experience of depression (manifested in the MMPI D scale) is uncorrelated with objective clinical assessments of depression for bipolars. It is, however, significantly correlated for unipolar subjects (Donnelly and Murphy, 1973). It must also be noted that MMPI group differences between bipolar and unipolar depressive patients are almost exclusive to the acute depressive phase (admission) and dissipate towards remission. This results from the fact that after recovery from the depressive episode, there is a shift within the unipolar group toward less reported psychopathology on most clinical scales on the MMPI. The score elevation on the clinical scales is thus phase-specific for unipolar patients. The clinical MMPI profile of bipolars resembles at admission a normal profile without too much change at remission. On the other hand, Donnelly et al. (1976) call attention to elevated Ma and Pd scores as phase-independent features of the bipolars' MMPI profile both at admission and at remission. These scores reflect personality characteristics of overactivity and impulsivity as enduring features of bipolar patients. One possible outcome of these NIMH studies could be the formulation of typical MMPI profiles for unipolar and bipolar depressives against which individual patients' profiles could be compared to determine diagnosis with minimized probable error. This would be attained, of course, only after more replication studies are conducted and confirmed with additional criterion groups.

ASSESSMENT WITH PROJECTIVE TECHNIQUES

Rorschach's (1921) original data on mania were based on responses of only 14 manic-depressive patients. Despite this small number, the syndromes that he elaborated for the various phases of the bipolar illness are regarded by an expert like Bohm (1958) as being "among the best validated of the foundation stones on which the entire Rorschach diagnostic procedure rests [p. 277]."

The main features of the depressive phase of bipolar affective illness are sharply portrayed by Rorschach (1921) and summarized by Bohm (1958). The following indicators are claimed to be the typical markers on the Rorschach for depression: below average number of responses, a lengthened response time, elevated accurate perception of form (F percent is 80–100), rather rigid sequence, poor approach, lowered W (0–3), decreased variability in content (A percent 60–80), lowered original perception (0–10%), and above all, constricted experience balance—namely, decreased number of M responses (almost zero) with complete absence of color responses.

Rorschach's syndrome for manic mood disorder (hypomania) is the polar contrast of the depressive syndrome: number of responses is above average, response time is shorter than average, form perception becomes poorer (F percent 60–70), sequence is loose, approach is richer, number of W responses is elevated (8–10), variation in content increases (A percent 40–50), originals increase in number (20–30%), but are rather poor in quality, and most important, experience balance is dialated—namely an increased number of both M responses (3–5) and color responses are found (on an average 1–2 FC, 2–3 CF, and 1–2 C). Bohm notes, however, that if the disorder increases to reach the phase of genuine mania, then form perception becomes even poorer (F percent 50–70), and number of W responses decreases. The approach therefore becomes poorer again, and the variability of contents is somewhat less than in the hypomania phase (A percent 50–70). Originals are correspondingly also lower (10–30%), but the experience balance grows more dialated through increase of both M responses (5M and more) and color responses (1–3 FC, 2–3 CF, 1–3 C). Number of responses and response time are about the same as in the hypomanic phase. Qualitatively, new features may be added to the genuine manic record in the form of DW and successive combinatory W, at times confabulatory-combinatory ones (Bohm, 1958, p. 578).

The first large Rorschach study devoted exclusively to the issue of manic-depressives' functioning was conducted by Levy and Beck (1934), who compared Rorschach responses during depressive phase with responses during manic phase. The contrast on Rorschach functioning for both phases was found to be in overall agreement with the psychogram portrayed by Bohm. The most authoritative study conducted on Rorschach scores in mania was reported by Schmidt and Fonda (1954). These authors compared data obtained from 42 manic-depressives and 42 matched schizophrenics, with data published on normals by Beck et al., (1950). When compared to normals, manics were reported to respond more rapidly, show greater emotional dialation (Beck's Lambda Index), and discharge more intellectual energy through organizational activity (Beck's Z score). In full accord with Bohm's scheme of responding in mania, subjects in this study manifested higher W and less A%, when compared with normals. Their being frankly psychotic was mirrored in inferior perceptual accuracy (Ft% = 62) and in their inadequate sharing of conventional modes of thinking (low P).

Emotional responsiveness was evident through higher available affective energy, as reflected in the Sum C index. In particular, manics exceeded normals in pure color responses, in FC responses, as well as in Y responses, which stand as usually interpreted for dysphoric affects. On the other hand, they gave considerably less V responses, which stand for ability of detachment and critical self-appraisal. Schmidt and Fonda's study seems to be a rare opportunity that could have provided definite data on the pecularities of manics' psychological functioning. However, the normal controls were not a matched comparative group but a normative standardization sample. The adequacy of such a comparison is, of course, questionable on methodological grounds. The differential diagnostic aspect of their study, namely the comparison of manic patients with well-matched schizophrenics (on the basis of age, sex, and total number of Rorschach responses), is up-to-date, a good intance of study of differential psychodiagnosis in psychosis. They found manic scores to be higher than schizophrenics' for Sum C, indicating affective impetus; Z, indicating intellectual synthetizing capacity; and H and M scores, indicating interest and involvement in the human and interpersonal domain. Manics were also significantly lower on time parameters of Rorschach performance (TIR and TR), which indicates their psychological agility and drive pressure.

Another pertinent line of evidence is supplied by Wittenhorn and Holzberg (1951b). They, however, found that only one Rorschach score, the CF, was associated with differential diagnosis indicating mania, while other scores, including FC, C, and Sum C, which also indicate affective responsivity, were not. Wittenborn and Holzberg compared in their study manics, paranoid schizophrenics, involutional simple schizophrenics, and depressives. The crucial importance of a color factor in the Rorschach diagnosis of mania was corroborated also in a study by Donnelly et al. (1975). Their procedure of administering the Rorschach was not followed, unfortunately, by standard inquiry, and therefore responses were not amenable to the usual quantitative analysis. Comparing bipolar and matched unipolar depressive patients, they found that bipolar subjects tended to respond with primary color responses (color naming and color symbolism), while such responses were totally absent in records of unipolar subjects. Another evident tendency of bipolar subjects was their inclination to refer to color, namely to mention the word "color" without any further elaboration. The overresponsiveness to color manifested by bipolar patients may imply what the authors state as "proneness to impulsivity," a feature that in their opinion is part of the permanent make-up of these personalities, whose prevailing mood at the time of assessment was depressive.

Donnelly et al. noted a second feature besides the primary responsiveness to color as characteristic of bipolar subjects' response style to the Rorschach. This feature they label as "global approach," which is seen in bipolars' selective recognition of and attention to the more obvious qualities of the stimuli without associational integration with inner experience. This "global approach" may be seen, for example, in frequent production of amorphous percepts, and reveal, in their opinion, a kind of "perceptual noninvolvement," which stands also for neurotic noninvolvement, and an apparent lack of dysphoric affects and conflictual contents. Rorschach productions of unipolar depressive patients are, on the other hand, characterized by "perceptual involvement," namely the projection of inner experience onto the test stimuli, thus disclosing considerable degree of neurotic concern. These differential response styles in bipolar depressives as compared with unipolar depressives may result in more apparent psychopathological disorder manifested in unipolar patients' Rorschach records.

The two response pecularities of bipolar depressive patients described by Donnelly et al. are compatible with Klopfer and Spiegelman's statement (1956) describing manic functioning as characterized by free use of color stimuli and by avoidance of actual breaks in reality testing through the use of sweeping indefinite or semidefinite responses. These characteristics have some bearing on the important issue of differential diagnosis between mania and schizoaffective disorder. Both manic and schizoaffective subjects tend to produce an overflow of color and movement responses. But whereas manics' minus elements in movement repsonses lack bizarre quality, and minus form level responses are produced by carelessness and lack of effort, schizoaffective subjects mirror their schizophrenic ego disturbance in bizarre content and through violation of the reality depicted in the blots.

Turning to Rorschach content, manic tendencies are commonly reflected in fantasy productions associated with obvious reliance on the mechanism of denial. Schafer (1954) conceptualized manic disturbance as largely defined by behavioral and affective patterns that result from excessive operation of denial. This psychodynamically derived notion was tested for validity by Welch et al. (1961), utilizing Thematic Apperception Test (TAT) stories and comparing hypomanic with depressive patients. TAT stories were scored for depressive material (D variables) and for denial of depressive material (M variables). Results indicated that D scores were not related to diagnosis, but M scores were related as hypothesized. In addition to these content-related differences, some stylistic features of hypomanic patients' stories emerged.

Their stories were significantly longer and were judged as expansive in regard to space and time setting.

Diagnostic application of the research results described in this section must of course be tentative and careful. Some of the reviewed investigations were conducted in an era when sensitivity to the need for blind studies was not great. All studies, even when conducted with fairly matched comparison groups, report group differences rather than frequencies of differences within matched pairs of subjects. Suitability of these results for diagnosis of individual cases is therefore questionable. The usual recommendation of "more research is needed" must be implemented before definite questions like "Can an euthymic bipolar patient be distinguished from a recovered schizophrenic?" or "can an acute manic be distinguished from a frankly psychotic schizophrenic?" could be answered affirmatively with a considerable degree of confidence. Meanwhile, psychodiagnostic conclusions, as far as they are empirically based, are more of a probabilistic nature.

THOUGHT AND SPEECH ASSESSMENT IN MANIA

The salient feature of the thought process in mania is thought pressure. Thought pressure is evidenced as an overflow of associative activity where ideas are generated faster than they can be elaborated and meaningfully integrated. This stylistic speed characteristic implies, of course, some qualitative attributes of manic thinking. One such attribute is overinclusion, which for a long time since Cameron (1946) introduced the term was regarded as pathognomonic of schizophrenia. Eysenck (1960) questioned critically this pathognomonicity and claimed that it has not been demonstrated that abnormal overinclusion is specific to schizophrenia. He suspected that overinclusion might be equally frequent in manic-depressive patients and therefore could be regarded as a general characteristic of psychosis rather than as a schizophrenic marker. The plausibility of such a hypothesis was based on an early study (Eysenck, 1952), where normals, schizophrenics, and manic-depressives were compared on a large battery of tests, which were preselected under the assumption that they would differentiate between the two psychotic groups. Factor analysis revealed one factor that could account for the differences observed between the three groups. This factor was labeled "psychoticism."

A second factor independent of "psychoticism" that was expected to be found failed, however, to emerge and to differentiate between the two psychotic groups. Thus, Eysenck found manic-depressives to be highest on psychoticism, normals lowest, and schizophrenics occupying an intermediate position.

Eysenck's position has been recently confirmed in a study that directly compared overinclusive thinking in manic and in schizophrenic patients. Andreasen and Powers (1974) evaluated manics, schizophrenics, and normal controls using a battery of tests for overinclusive thinking. Manics manifested significantly more overinclusive thinking when compared with schizophrenics and with normals. Schizophrenics, however, tended to be underinclusive, even when compared with normals. These authors suggested that overinclusion is not specific to schizophrenia and that it may be associated with illness, which remits or has a good prognosis. This hypothesis was corroborated in another study by these authors (Andreasen and Powers, 1975). In this study manic patients were compared with schizophrenics and with creative writers on the Goldstein-Sheerer Object Sorting Test. Writers and manic subjects tended to demonstrate more behavioral and conceptual overinclusion. Manic subjects showed more idiosyncratic thinking, while writers showed substantially more richness. Schizophrenics were characterized as underinclusive rather than overinclusive, and showed less bizarreness and richness in thought when compared to manics and creative writers.

If overinclusion is regarded as an index of thought disorder, then it seems as if manic subjects do have a more florid thought disorder than schizophrenics. Similar results were found in another related study (Andreasen et al., 1974), where 42 clinicians examined proverb interpretations and samples of writing from two schizophrenics, two creative writers, and two manic subjects. The clinicians tended to diagnose thought disorder more frequently in the manic subjects and in the creative writers than in schizophrenic subjects. Moreover, suspected diagnoses based on this material failed to correlate with clinical diagnoses.

When taken together, the presented data call, of course, for a comprehensive reevaluation and revision of current thinking about the nature and significance of thought disorder. One plausible explanation of the contradiction between the traditional view associating thought disorder with schizophrenia and these recent findings is implied in a study conducted by McPherson et al. (1973). These authors compared a well-defined subgroup of thought-disordered schizophrenics with non-thought-disordered schizophrenics, with manic subjects, and with depressives on four measures of thought disorder based on the Bannister-Fransella Grid Test of Thought Disorder. On all measures thought-disordered schizophrenics gained poorer scores, while all other groups did not differ from one another. Thus, thought disorder as testable by the above methods may be characteristic of some schizophrenics, but not of all, and manic patients may manifest thought disorder not less than some schizophrenics.

A new trend in research utilizing psycholinguistic methodologies has also been applied to the study of mania. Durbin and Martin (1977) observed and analyzed verbal behavior of six manic patients, finding preseveration of basic speech capacities, including the ability to comprehend and generate grammatical sentences and to utilize highly complex linguistic transformations. However, they noted a disruption in the ability of manics to properly utilize linguistic features that enable them to maintain a meaningful progression of thought in discourse. Andreasen and Pfohl (1976) found manic speech when compared with depressive speech to be more colorful and concrete and to show more concern with things than with people. These features and additional characteristics of manic speech derived either by psycholinguistic techniques or by content analysis do not have, however, any specific bearing on thought disorder. From a contextual point of view, manics tended to use more words reflecting a concern with power and achievement. From a psycholinguistic point of view, manics did not show, contrary to what was anticipated, more varied word choice, more complexity of sentence structure, or greater-type token ratio.

DISCUSSION

When may psychodiagnostic testing be useful in the study and treatment of mania?

First, psychodiagnostic assessment procedures may be valid devices for differentiating between bipolar and unipolar depression. Bipolar depressive patients display some mania-related traits even in their depressed phases on a whole array of psychodiagnostic procedures reviewed above. The data available up-to-date should be regarded as preliminary, which must be replicated and validated against various representative criterion of groups of unipolar and bipolar depressives. Only after such a process would it be appropriate to apply with certain confidence these findings for individual diagnosis.

Second, psychodiagnostic testing may contribute to differential diagnosis of mania as opposed to schizoaffective disorder. Weiner (1966), advocating the use of the Rorschach for this purpose, claims that from a quantitative point of view, encompassing variables like speed of reaction, length of record, dialation of contents, and affect-indicating determinants, there may be no apparent difference between mania and schizoaffective disorder. It is the infusion, he states, of the manic response pattern with elements of primary disturbances of reasoning and reality testing that differentiates the two. No specified variables or research data are, however, supplemented to this general claim. Another differentiating feature concerns the clinical impression, which has also some empirical psychodiagnostic evidence (Welch et al., 1961), that manic subjects rely excessively on the use of denial as defense mechanism.

These two specific marker phenomena in the Rorschach record might thus aid in identifying typical psychological processes specific for mania and in distinguishing it from schizoaffective disorder. However, the empirical validation of this twofold psychodiagnostic notion is still a task to be accomplished.

Third, psychological assessment using tests of thought disorder has helped reveal several diagnostic misconceptions, including the notion that thought disorder is pathognomonic of schizophrenia. Such findings may contribute to improvement in diagnosis and to prevention of misdiagnosis.

In what ways are present psychodiagnostic procedures of limited value for both clinician and researcher?

First, no psychodiagnostic instrument has yet been validated against criteria of family history, treatment response, or prognosis in the manner that clinical psychiatric diagnosis is now being evaluated. Questions may be raised, like (a) do Rorschach signs of mania correlate with family history of mania versus schizophrenia in atypical psychoses, (b) do Rorschach signs of mania or MMPI profiles of bipolar illness predict lithium response or suggest outcome characteristic of mania rather than schizophrenia?

Second, psychodiagnostic assessment has not been applied systematically to the intermorbid state. While clinicians often adhere to the notion of psychodiagnosis being a sort of psychiatric "X-ray" that may uncover psychopathology hidden from clinical examination, no data is available to prove that an euthymic manic-depressive can be distinguished in any reliable way from a recovered schizophrenic by psychodiagnostic means.

The third and most critical present limitation of psychodiagnostic assessment relates to validating criteria. If psychodiagnostic assessment is to be of use for psychiatric research and treatment planning in mania, an attempt must be made to aspire for more than mere psychiatric or psychodynamic diagnosis of a particular case. Further research should attempt to use psychodiagnostic procedures to predict outcome of treatment, thereby extracting and utilizing measurements that the psychiatric examination overlooks. Unfortunately, however, this possibility is only a promise of the future, and the present-day clinician should not hope to rely on psychodiagnostic assessment to solve the serious diagnostic and pragnostic problems he encounters when dealing with mania.

REFERENCES

Andreasen, N.J.C., and Pfohl, B. Linguistic analysis of speech in affective disorders. *Arch. Gen. Psychiat.* 33, 1361–1367 (1976).

Andreasen, N.J.C., and Powers, Pauline S. Overinclusive thinking in mania and schizophrenia. *Br. J. Psychiat.* 125, 452–456 (1974).

Andreasen, N.J.C., and Powers, Pauline S. Creativity and psychosis: An examination of conceptual style. *Arch. Gen. Psychiat.* 32, 70–73 (1975).

Andreasen, N.J.C., Tsuang, M.T., and Canter, A. The significance of thought disorder in diagnostic evaluations. *Comp. Psychiat.* 15, 27–34 (1974).

Beck, S.J., Rabin, A.I., Thiesen, W.G., Molish, H., and Thetford, W.N. The normal personality as projected in the Rorschach test. *J. Psychol.* 30, 241–298 (1950).

Beigel, A., Murphy, D.L., and Bunney, W.E. The manic state rating scale. *Arch. Gen. Psychiat.* 25, 256–262 (1971).

Bohm, E. *A Text Book in Rorschach Test Diagnosis.* Grune & Straton, New York (1958).

Brown, O. Relation of WAIS verbal and performance IQs for four psychiatric conditions. *Psychol. Rep.* 20, 1015–1020 (1967).

Cameron, N.S. Experimental Analysis of Schizophrenic Thinking in Language and Thought. In *Schizophrenia*, J.S. Kasanin, ed. Univ. of California Press, Berkeley (1946) pp. 50–64.

Dahlstrom, W.G., Welsh, G.S., and Dahlstrom, L.A. *An MMPI Handbook*, Vol. I. Univ. of Minnesota Press, Minneapolis (1972).

Donnelly, E.F., and Murphy, D.L. Primary affective disorder: MMPI differences between unipolar and bipolar depressed subjects. *J. Clin. Psychol.* 29, 303–306 (1973).

Donnelly, E.F., and Murphy, L. Primary affective disorder: Bender Gestalt sequence as an indicator of impulse control. *Percep. & Motor Skills* 38, 1079–1082 (1974).

Donnelly, E.F., Murphy, D.L., and S cott, W.H. Perception and cognition in patients with bipolar and unipolar depressive disorders. *Arch. Gen. Psychiat.* 32, 1128–1131 (1975).

Donnelly, E.F., Murphy, D.L., and Goodwin, F.K. Cross sectional and longitudinal comparisons of bipolar and unipolar depressed groups on the MMPI. *J. Consult. Clin. Psychol.* 44, 233–237 (1976).

Donnelly, E.F., Murphy, D.L., Waldman, I.N., and Reynolds, T.D. MMPI differences between unipolar and bipolar depressed subjects: A replication. *J. Clin. Psychol.* 32, 610–612 (1976).

Durbin, M., and Martin, R.L. Speech in mania: Synthetic aspects. *Brain and Language.* 4, 208–218 (1977).

Eysenck, H.J. Schizothymia—cyclothymia as a dimension of personality. *J. Pers.* 20, 345–384 (1952).

Eysenck, H.J. *Experiments in personality.* Vol. II, Routledge & Kegan, Paul, London (1960).

Gilliland, A.R., Wittman, P. and Goldman, M. Pattern and scatter of mental abilities in various psychoses. *J. Gen. Psychol.* 29, 251–254 (1943).

Hutt, M. *The Hutt Adaptation of the Bender Gestalt Test.* Grune & Straton, New York (1977).

Klopfer, B., and Spiegelman, M. *Differential diagnosis, in developments in the Rorschach technique.* Vol. II. *Fields of Application*, B. Klopfer, ed. Harcourt, Brace, New York (1956).

Levy, D.M., and Beck, S.J. The Rorschach test in manic depressive psychosis. *Amer. J. Orthopsychiat.* 4, 31–42 (1934).

Machover, K. *Personality Projection in the Drawing of the Human Figure.* Charles C. Thomas, Springfield, Illinois (1949).

McPherson, F.M., Blackburn, Ivy M., Draffan, Joan W., and McFadjen, M. A further study of the Grid test of thought disorder. *Brit. J. Soc. & Clin. Psychol.* 12, 420–427 (1973).

Rabin, A.I. Differentiating psychometric pattern in schizophrenia and manic-depressive psychosis. *J. Abn. Soc. Psychol.* 37, 270–272 (1942).

Rabin, A.I. *Diagnostic Use of Intelligence Tests in Handbook of Clinical Psychology*, B.B. Wolman, ed. McGraw-Hill, New York (1965), pp. 477–497.

Rapaport, D., Gill, M.M., and Schafer, R. *Diagnostic Psychological Testing.* International Univ. Press, New York (1968).

Rorschach, H. *Psychodiagnostics* (1921), 5th ed. Hans Huber Bern (1942).

Schafer, R. *Psychoanalytic Interpretation in Rorschach Testing.* Grune & Stratton, New York (1954).

Schmidt, H.O., and Fonda, C.P. Rorschach scores in the mania state. *J. Psychol.* 38, 427–437 (1954).

Waldfogel, S., and Guy, W. Wechsler-Bellevue subtest scatter in the affective disorders. *J. Clin. Psychol.* 7, 135–139 (1951).

Weiner, I.B. *Psychodiagnosis in Schizophrenia.* Wiley, New York (1966).

Welch, B., Schafer, R., and Dember, Cyntia. TAT stories of hypomanic and depressed patients. *J. Proj. Tech.* 25, 221–232 (1961).

Welsh, G.S., and Dahlstrom, W. *Basic Readings on the MMPI in Psychology and Medicine.* Univ. of Minnesota Press, Minneapolis (1956).

Wittenborn, J.R., and Holzberg, J.D. The Wechsler-Bellevue and descriptive diagnosis. J. Consult. Psychol. 15, 325–329 (1951).

Wittenborn, J.R., and Holzberg, J.D. The Rorschach and descriptive diagnosis. *J. Consult. Psychol.* 15, 460–463 (1951).

Young, R.C., Biggs, J.T., Ziegler, V.E., and Meyer, D.A. A rating scale for mania: Reliability, validity and sensitivity. *Br. J. Psychiat.* 133, 429–435 (1978).

CHAPTER 19

Social Adjustment and Psychological Precipitants in Mania

David L. Dunner and Kathleen S. Hall

The purpose of this chapter is to discuss social adjustment in patients with bipolar affective disorder and the possible role of life events as etiologic factors in the onset of the initial or subsequent episodes in bipolar patients. We define bipolar affective disorder as a primary affective disorder (Feighner et al., 1972). Patients who have been hospitalized at least once for a manic episode (Dunner et al., 1970, 1976a) are termed "bipolar 1." Bipolar 1 patients tend to be different from other patients with primary affective disorder, using clinical, biological, pharmacological, or genetic data (Fieve and Dunner, 1975). Bipolar 1 patients can be studied while manic or hypomanic, depressed or euthymic, or prior to the onset of these mood states. The bipolar 1 patients we report in this chapter have been attending the lithium clinic of the New York State Psychiatric Institute, and most were studied while being treated with lithium carbonate for prophylaxis of recurrent affective episodes (Fieve, 1975).

SOCIAL ADJUSTMENT IN BIPOLAR PATIENTS

Mania and depression create severe disruption in the lives of patients and their families. However, the measurement of this disruption has presented a problem. Furthermore, the separation of affectively ill patients into unipolar and bipolar subtypes has been relatively recent, and studies relating to this separation have been primarily studies of pharmacological and genetic differences rather than studies of social assessment. Thus, few investigations have been concerned with the study of social adjustment in bipolar patients, and such studies have tended not to use systematic assessment of social function.

Weissman (1975) has defined social adjustment as the interplay between an individual and his social environment. Numerous instruments to define and measure social adjustment have been proposed, and these have been reviewed by Weissman. She noted that instruments to assess social adjustment should cover role functioning in broad social areas and should have discretely defined anchor points. Weissman (1975) discussed the relative advantages of 15 scales used to assess social adjustment and selected one of these instruments for her own studies of depressed patients (Weissman and Paykel, 1974). This scale, the "Social Adjustment Scale [SAS]," is a modification of an instrument developed by Gurland et al. (1972), and can be used to interview patients or as a self-report instrument (SAS-SR).

The SAS-SR is a self-administered questionnaire with several questions in six social areas (work, leisure time, extended family, marital, parental, and family unit). Each question is scored on a 1 to 5 scale—1 being excellent adjustment and 5 being poorest adjustment—and the mean adjustment for each of the six areas is calculated along with a grand mean for all areas. Weissman and Paykel (1974) showed that depressed outpatients had about a one-point mean change in social adjustment in most areas when compared to their euthymic state. Furthermore, they described statistically significant differences in social adjustment between euthymic depressives and psychiatrically well controls. They did not separately report data on bipolar depressives (their sample was described as mostly unipolar), and to our knowledge, there is no data regarding the SAS-SR in patients who are manic or hypomanic.

We administered the SAS-SR to 78 bipolar 1 patients who were attending our lithium clinic (Dunner et al., 1977). The mood of patients was assessed by trained rating teams, and patients who were minimally depressed or hypomanic were not considered as euthymic even though such patients may not have had required medication in addition to lithium for their mood disorder. Our results (Table 1) revealed somewhat consistent mood effects, with depressed bipolar 1 patients showing worse adjustment in each area as compared to euthymic bipolar 1 patients except for marital adjustment.

Table 1. Social Adjustment Among Bipolar Patients

Area of Adjustment	Depressed	Hypomanic	Euthymic
Work	1.75 ± .60	1.62 ± .58	1.61 ± .71
Leisure time	2.69 ± .68	2.01 ± .51	2.04 ± .55
Extended family	1.89 ± .77	2.25 ± .97	1.57 ± .45
Marital	1.92 ± .56	2.01 ± .17	1.99 ± .64
Children	1.70 ± .54	2.00	1.64 ± .63
Family unit	2.38 ± .89	1.89 ± .51	1.64 ± .66
Grand mean	2.14 ± .60	2.08 ± .50	1.80 ± .42

Numbers refer to mean ratings from the SAS-SR ± S.D.

Patients who were rated as hypomanic tended to show social disruption but not as marked as depressed patients. However, none of these differences in mean SAS-SR ratings achieved statistical significance, either between depressed versus euthymic or depressed versus hypomanic bipolar 1 patients. This is in slight contrast to the data from our overall clinic population of 169 patients, which included unipolar patients and which did reveal significant differences between euthymic and depressed patients except for parental adjustment. It should be noted that we studied no patients who were severely or even moderately manic or severely depressed. It is likely that the degree of social impairment would correlate with severity of the mood disorder (Weissman et al., 1974) and that more severely ill bipolar manic or depressive patients would show greater social impairment. Furthermore, most of our bipolar 1 patients were being treated with lithium and may have had a reduction in severity of depressed or hypomanic symptoms because of this treatment (Fieve et al., 1976). However, our data would indicate that lithium-treated bipolar 1 patients do not experience severe disruptions in social adjustment (as measured by the SAS-SR) when hypomanic or depressed. This may be in contrast to unipolar depressives, where such social disruption may be found more easily (Weissman and Paykel, 1974).

Social impairments are also not clearly discernable in euthymic bipolar 1 patients. Weissman (unpublished data) applied the SAS-SR to over 300 psychiatrically well community controls. Mean ratings for each social area were about 1.5. Although our patients showed statistically significant differences in all six areas of social adjustment as compared to Weissman's controls, the actual differences in the mean adjustment scores were within 1 rating point. Thus, our patients usually answered the questions with a 1 or 2 rating (excellent or very good adjustment). Weissman and Paykel (1974) have suggested that outpatients with a history of recurrent unipolar depression should be treated with maintenance therapy (medication and / or psychotherapy) in order to improve their social adjustment. We feel that the social adjustment of our patients (as measured by the SAS-SR) is not meaningfully different than controls and that psychotherapy should not be imposed on all patients but should be available for patients with meaningful social disruption.

One particular area of concern to clinicians treating bipolar patients is marital adjustment, and Davenport et al., (1975) have suggested that married bipolar patients respond well to couple therapy in the interval shortly after one spouse has had a manic episode. They suggested that such therapy leads to a healthier marriage and also to better patient compliance regarding taking lithium.

The need for couple therapy has been questioned by us (Dunner, 1976b) after assessment of the marital status and marital adjustment of our bipolar patients (Dunner et al., 1976c). We noted that our bipolar patients had similar frequency of nonmarriage as psychiatrically well controls and that the incidence of divorce among those patients who had married was also similar to controls (Dunner et al., 1976c). We noted that several marriages were of greater than 30 years' duration in spite of the occurrence of severe and disruptive manic and depressive episodes. In assessing marital adjustment with the SAS-SR, we noted that married patients and their spouses had a high correlation of ratings for overall marital adjustment (Ruestow et al., 1978). We did find that younger female patients tended to feel more dependent on their husbands than did older patients or well wives. Furthermore, in those instances where husband and wife were both psychiatrically ill, the marital adjustment was rated as worse than when only one spouse had a psychiatric history (Ruestow et al., 1978).

Based on our data, we have suggested that the social adjustment of bipolar patients is not necessarily aberrant and that psychotherapy in addition to lithium treatment should not be proposed to all patients with bipolar illness (Dunner et al., 1977). The natural history of bipolar illness is toward return to normal function between affective episodes. The use of lithium tends to lengthen the asymptomatic interval between these episodes as well as reduce the severity of the episodes themselves (Stallone et al., 1972; Dunner et al., 1976d). Thus, it is not surprising that measured social adjustment in euthymic bipolar patients was not found to be meaningfully disturbed. Those disruptions in social adjustment that occur due to manic and depressive relapses in these patients seem to resolve as the relapse is treated with appropriate medication. The use of supportive psychotherapy during these relapses seems appropriate. More intensive psychotherapeutic intervention should be employed when specifically indicated, such as the occurrence of complaints of interpersonal and/or other difficulties by euthymic bipolar patients or their families.

PSYCHOLOGICAL PRECIPITANTS IN MANIA

In search for etiological factors of manic-depressive illness, research has focused upon environmental and social factors in addition to genetic and biological characteristics of patients. The environmental approach is generally referred to as "life-events" research and attempts to assess the temporal relationship, if any, between change in a person's life situation and the onset of psychiatric symptoms. The assumption is that change in the life situation requires adaptation and such adaptation may be stressful—thus the frequently used term *stressful life events*. This approach is based upon the work of such researchers as Selye (1956), Cannon (1929), and Meyer (1951), who demonstrated that emotions can evoke metabolic changes. Life-events research has proven to be especially appealing to the study of affective disorders, due perhaps to the striking similarity between affective symptoms and extremes of the normal range of emotions. Although there is a considerable volume of life-events research on affective disorders, there is very little information specifically regarding mania.

The 1954 study of Cohen et al. reported an intensive psychoanalytic study of 12 cases of manic-depressive illness. They emphasized the importance of interpersonal relationships and life events as precipitants of episodes of depression or mania. They concluded: "The manic attack is similar to the depressive in following a precipitating incident which carries the meaning of loss of love [Cohen et al., 1954, p. 122]." They further point out that the precipitating effect is the same whether the loss is real or imagined.

Cassidy et al. (1957) took a different approach to the question in their study of 100 manic-depressive patients. In a retrospective evaluation of events preceding hospitalization, 50 of the 100 patients reported some event they felt may have caused or precipitated their symptoms. Further information revealed that 28 of the 50 had symptoms prior to the reported event. Of the remaining 22 patients, only 4 reported discrete events that occurred less than several years prior to hospital admission. Of the 100 patients in the Cassidy study, only 6 were hospitalized for mania; the investigation of precipitating factors did not separately report on these 6 manic patients. Cassidy and his colleagues concluded that although precipitating events were rare in their sample, events that were a consequence of the illness were common.

Hudgens and his colleagues (1967) compared life events in 40 affectively ill patients with 40 controls. Theirs was a retrospective assessment of life events estimated to have occurred from one to three months prior to onset of symptoms. Six of the 40 patients were manic. The manic patients reported the following: Two reported no events prior to illness, one reported an event 6 months prior to symptoms (going away to college), two reported that some symptoms preceded an event but the fully symptomatic illness followed within 6 months of the event (wife seriously ill, only child married), and one reported illness fully developed before the event but exacerbation followed the event (fractured arm). They concluded that by the method they used no evidence was found to suggest that life events were related to the onset of mania or depression. Benson (1976) described three cases in which psychological stress was the cause of lithium prophylaxis failure.

The above studies examined the relationship between life events and episodes of manic-depressive illness. Okuma and Shimoyama (1972) looked at precipitating factors for the initial onset of illness and subsequent episodes. They found that 47 of their 75 male patients and 45 of 57 female patients reported at least one episode of illness to have been preceded by external factors. Problems related to job performance, especially change of job or increased job responsibility, were precipitating factors frequently reported by men, while women reported problems concerning reporductive function. The authors did not separately analyze episodes of mania and depression. Their sample reported a decline in ratio of episodes precipitated by external factors as episodes were repeated during the course of the illness. Patients in their sample who reported episodes with precipitating factors reported fewer episodes with precipitating factors than without such precipitating factors.

Dunner et al. (1978) looked at the association of life events with the onset of illness and with subsequent episodes of illness in 79 bipolar 1 manic-depressive patients. Thirty-five of the 79 subjects experienced an episode of mania at the onset of illness. Of this group a greater percentage of males than females reported life events preceding illness onset: 16 of 22 men reported events while 4 of 9 women reported events. Difficulties at work and interpersonal conflict were reported most frequently by this group of patients. Of the 44 patients who experienced depression at onset of illness, 5 of 19 men reported events, while 16 of 25 women reported events. Here, as in the Okuma and Shimoyama study, women reported events related to reproductive function (8 reported childbirth as the preceding event). Reporting for subsequent episodes was also similar to the Okumo study in that fewer events were reported for subsequent episodes than for onset episode. Of the 12 patients who reported events for subsequent episodes, only 5 also reported events for onset episodes.

A prospective study of life events and episodes of illness is being conducted on these patients. The preliminary report of this study (Hall et al., 1977) described 38 bipolar 1 manic-depressive patients who recorded life events at each regular lithium clinic visit over a period of 10 months. All were on maintenance levels of lithium. During this period 6 of the patients became manic (2 severe enough to be hospitalized), 8 became depressed, 3 had episodes of mania and depression, and 21 remained well. No significant differences were found in the types or numbers of events reported by patients who experienced episodes and by those who remained well except that patients who experienced a manic episode reported significantly more events related to employment in their well visit prior to episode onset than did patients who remained well or who became depressed.

The studies described here attempted to assess the relationship, if any, between external precipitating factors and episodes of illness in patients with manic-depressive illness. Only three of the studies reported data specifically for episodes of mania, and these each used a different research method. These data are inconclusive regarding the issue of external precipitants of mania.

The authors feel the question bears further consideration and a prospective approach is the most promising.

PRECIPITANTS AND OTHER PSYCHOSES

Is there evidence to support the notion that precipitants of mania are different from precipitants of other psychoses? What is the evidence for precipitating life events and other psychoses? There have been few studies comparing affective disorder patients with schizophrenic patients with regard to life events.

Clancy et al. (1973) reviewed patient records of 525 hospitalized patients in search of precipitating factors. Their sample compared 200 schizophrenic patients with 325 with affective disorder (100 bipolar, 225 unipolar). Preceding events were counted only if they occurred within 3 months prior to onset of illness. Patients with preceding events were in the minority in all three diagnostic categories: 39% of unipolar, 27% of bipolars, and 11% of schizophrenics had recorded preceding events. Type of event differed significantly between diagnostic categories, but the authors did not discuss in detail events included in their categories. Their categories were psychological, physical, social, and a combination of the three. Unipolar patients reported significantly more psychological events, while bipolar reported significantly more physical. Postpartum was counted as a separate category and was reported by all diagnostic groups with no significant difference. The authors concluded that they saw a trend for more precipitating factors among affective disorders, with unipolar tending to have more than bipolar (Clancy, 1973).

The 1974 study of Jacobs et al. compared life events 6 months prior to onset of illness in 50 schizophrenic and 50 depressed patients. Depressed patients were not further grouped into unipolar and bipolar categories. The depressives reported more events in the categories of exits from the social field and more undesirable events than did the schizophrenics (Jacobs et al., 1974).

The research reviewed in this chapter includes investigations of precipitants of initial onset of psychiatric illness in subjects who were previously well, and the altogether different research area, precipitants of episodes during the course of previously diagnosed illness. The problem of ascertaining initial onset of illness is a difficult one. This may be more of a problem with the insidious onset of schizophrenia than with the affective disorders, in which onset of illness tends to be more circumscribed. This is a serious problem in the comparison of studies of the two diagnostic categories. One approach to this problem regarding onset of illness would be a prospective research design in which a longitudinal study of offspring of patients with schizophrenia and affective disorder would be followed regarding life events. These children are at greater risk of developing disorder than the general population. A prospective study would permit early diagnosis, and initial onset would be more accurately determined.

Investigations of precipitating events during the course of psychiatric illness vary in definition of an episode. Onset of symptoms may be insidious and therefore problematic to such studies. This problem may confound life-events findings, especially in retrospective studies, due to the fact that patients themselves may be searching for an explanation of their episode. This "direct contamination" [Brown, 1974, p. 218] raises serious question of the retrospective approach. Affective disorders, especially bipolar types, may be characterized by essentially discrete episodes in which there are periods of normal functioning between episodes. Symptoms of mania or hypomania may be quite dramatic at onset, and therefore this diagnostic category logically lends itself to the study of life events. Depression symptoms may have equally discrete onset in bipolar patients. Patients seen at regular intervals, as those attending maintenance clinics, provide the researcher an opportunity to more accurately monitor episode onset.

The complex and numerous methodological problems in the study of life events have been discussed by several authors (Brown et al., 1973; Dohrenwend and Dohrenwend, 1974; Rabkin and Streuning, 1976; Uhlenhuth et al., 1977; Dohrenwend and Dohrenwend, 1978). Issues previously discussed in the literature will not be reviewed in this chapter. The authors will report some methodological issues encountered in their ongoing prospective study of bipolar patients that have not been discussed elsewhere.

It appears that physical ailments take precedence in subjects' recording of events. When patients record physical illnesses, many seem to underreport other events. These other events come to the attention of the researchers during the standard life-events interview that follows the completion of the self-administered Schedule of Life Events.

Life-events researchers have given considerable attention to the issue of the time interval appropriate for study: A pattern of repetitive recording of certain events in some of our subjects may provide a clue to the length of time people respond to events. Several patients in our prospective study have recorded events repeatedly as "new" beyond the appropriate reporting period. An example of this is Mr. A., who recorded "change of residence" at three successive clinic visits. Mr. A changed his residence in early October and recorded the event as "new" in October, November, and December. This "error" was not due to Mr. A's misunderstanding instructions, as he had been correctly completing the Schedule of Life Events on a regular basis for two years prior to the change of residence. This pattern of recording has occurred in other apparently discrete events, such as retirement and abortion. By making continued reference to an event, Mr. A. may be indicating the perceived duration of its effects. If stressful life events are processes rather than discrete events, perhaps researchers should be measuring process. Viewing life events as processes rather than discrete experiences raises the problem of quantification over time.

Lack of events may be a source of stress. The Schedule of Life Events in use in the authors' study provides space for patients to indicate events they anticipate happening during the interval to their next clinic visit. Instances in which anticipated events do not occur may be experienced as stressful. In an ongoing study of the course of psychiatric illness, lack of events may be especially important. During the course of bipolar illness, the patient's life may be disrupted by mild episodes of hypomania or depression, or periodic hospitalization. Patients expect to return to work and reestablish disrupted family ties after such episodes. It may therefore be important to measure patients' expectations and subsequent realization or lack of realization of events.

In summary, the assessment of social adjustment and the role of stressful life events in relation to affective illness has received considerable research attention over the past several years. Only recently have these research efforts been focused toward bipolar affective illness. Furthermore, awareness of methodological problems in studies of social adjustment and life stress has brought forth the need to redesign such research efforts. Such studies as those involved in the prospective evaluation of the development of illness in children of bipolar subjects may further illuminate these research areas.

REFERENCES

Benson, R. Psychological stress as a cause of lithium prophylaxis failure: A report of three cases. *Dis. Nerv. Syst.* 37, 699–700 (1976).

Brown, G., Sklair, F., Harris, T.O., and Birley, J.L.T. Life-events and psychiatric disorders. 1. Some methodological issues. *Psychol. Med.* 3, 74–87 (1973).

Brown, G. Meaning, measurement, and stress of life events. In *Stressful Life Events: Their Nature and Effects*, B.S. Dohrenwend and B.P. Dohrenwend, eds. Wiley, New York (1974), pp. 217–243.

Cannon, W.B. *Bodily Changes in Pain, Hunger, Fear and Rage.* D. Appleton, New York (1929).

Cassidy, W.L., Flanagan, N.B., Spellman, M., and Cohen, M.E. Clinical observations in manic-depressive disease: A quantitative study of one hundred manic-depressive patients and fifty medically sick controls. *JAMA* 164, 1535–1546 (1957).

Clancy, J., Crowe, R., Winokur, G., and Morrison, J. The Iowa 500: Precipitating factors in schizophrenia and primary affective disorder. *Compr. Psychiat.* 14, 197–202 (1973).

Cohen, M.B., Baker, G., Cohen, R.A., Fromm-Reichmann, F., and Weigert, E.V. An intensive study of twelve cases of manic depressive psychosis. *Psychiatry* 17, 103–137 (1954).

Davenport, Y., Ebert, M.H., Adland, M.L., and Goodwin, F.K. Lithium prophylaxis: The married couples group. *Sci. Proc Am. Psychiatr. Assn.* 128, 66–67 (1975).

Dohrenwend, B.S., and Dohrenwend, B.P. *Life Events: Their Nature and Effects.* Wiley, New York (1974).

Dohrenwend, B.S., and Dohrenwend, B.P. Some issues in research on stressful life events. *J. Nerv. ment. Dis.* 166, 7–15 (1978).

Dunner, D.L., Gershon, E.S., and Goodwin, F.K. Heritable factors in the severity of affective illness. Presented at the Annual Meeting, American Psychiatric Association, San Francisco, May 1970. *Sci. Proc. Am. Psychiatr. Assn.* 123, 187–188 (1970).

Dunner, D.L., Gershon, E.S., and Goodwin, F.K. Heritable factors in the severity of affective illness. *Biol. Psychiat.* 11, 31–42 (1976a).

Dunner, D.L. Affective illness and the family (Panel). Presented at the Annual Meeting, American Psychiatric Association, Miami, May 1976. *Sci. Proc. Am. Psychiatr. Assn.* 129, 339–340 (1976b).

Dunner, D.L., Fleiss, J.L., Addonizio, G., and Fieve, R.R. Assortative mating in primary affective disorder. *Biol. Psychiat.* 11, 43–52 (1976c).

Dunner, D.L., Igel, G., and Fieve, R.R. Social adjustment in primary affective disorder. Presented at the VI World Congress of Psychiatry, Honolulu, Aug. 28–Sept. 3, 1977. Abstracts, p. 251 (1977).

Dunner, D.L., Patrick, V., and Fieve, R.R. Life events at the onset of bipolar affective illness. Submitted for publication (1978).

Feighner, J., Robins, E., Guze, S., Woodruff, R.A. Jr., Winokur, G., and Munoz, R. Diagnostic criteria for use in psychiatric research. *Arch. Gen. Psychiat.* 26, 57–63 (1972).

Fieve, R.R., and Dunner, D.L. Unipolar and bipolar affective states. In *The Nature and Treatment of Depression,* F.F. Flack and S.C. Draghi, eds. Wiley, New York (1975) pp. 145–166.

Fieve, R.R. The lithium clinic: A new model for the delivery of psychiatric services. *Am. J. Psychiat.* 132, 1018–1022 (1975).

Fieve, R.R., Dunner, D.L., Kumberaci, T., and Stallone, F. Lithium carbonate prophylaxis of depression in three subtypes of primary affective disorder. *Pharm. Psychiatr. Neuro. Psychopharmakol.* 9, 100–107 (1976).

Gurland, B., Yorkston, N., Stone, A.R., Frank, J.D., and Fleiss, J.L. The structured and scaled interview to assess maladjustment (SSIAM): Description, rationale and development. *Arch. Gen. Psychiat.* 27, 259–264 (1972).

Hall, K.S., Dunner, D.L., Zeller, G., and Fieve, R.R. Bipolar illness: A prospective study of life events. *Compr. Psychiat.* 18, 497–502 (1977).

Hudgens, R.W., Morrison, J.R., and Barchha, R.G. Life events and onset of primary affective disorders. *Arch. Gen. Psychiat.* 16, 134–145 (1967).

Jacobs, S.C., Prusoff, B.A., and Paykel, E.S. Recent life events in schizophrenia and depression. *Psychol. med.* 4, 444–453 (1974).

Meyer, A. The life chart and the obligation of specifying positive data in psychopathological diagnosis. In *The Collected Papers of Adolph Meyer,* Vol. 11, *Medical Teaching,* E.E. Winters, ed. Johns Hopkins Press (1951).

Okuma, T., and Shimoyama, N. Course of endogenous manic-depressive psychosis, precipitating factors and premorbid personality—a statistical study. *Fol. Psychiatr. et Neurol. Jpn.* 26, 19–33 (1972).

Rabkin, J.G., and Streuning, E.L. Life events, stress and illness. *Science* 194, 1013–1020 (1976).

Ruestow, P., Dunner, D.L., Bleecker, B., and Fieve, R.R. Marital adjustment in primary affective disorder. (Submitted for publication, 1978.)

Selye, H. The Stress of Life. McGraw-Hill, New York (1956).

Stallone, F., Shelley, E., Mendlewicz, J., and Fieve, R.R. The use of lithium in affective disorders. III. A double blind study of prophylaxis in bipolar illness. *Am. J. Psychiat.* 130, 1006–1010 (1972).

Uhlenhuth, E.H., Haberman, S.J., Balter, M.D., and Lipman, R.S. Remembering life events. In *The Origins and Course of Psychopathology: Methods of Longitudinal Research,* J.S. Strauss, H.M. Babigian, and M. Roff, eds. Plenum, New York (1972) pp. 117–133.

Weissman, M.M., and Paykel, E.S. *The Depressed Woman: A Study of Social Relationships.* Univ. of Chicago Press (1974).

Weismann, M.M. The assessment of social adjustment: A review of techniques. *Arch. Gen. Psychiat.* 32, 357–365 (1975).

Weismann, M.M., Klerman, G., Paykel, E.S., Prusoff, B., and Hanson, B. Treatment effects on the social adjustment of depressed patients. *Arch. Gen. Psychiat.* 30, 771–778 (1974).

CHAPTER 20

Psychosocial Aspects of
The Management of Mania

A. Kaplan De-Nour

The impact of the manic patient on his surroundings, be it family or psychiatric staff, is great. The transactions and the interaction of the manic patient with them often influence their emotional condition as well as their ability to function. These psychosocial reactions of family and staff to the manic patient can interfere with the proper management of the patient. Thus, a vicious circle may begin and accelerate dangerously. Identification of all of these psychosocial factors and reactions will improve the management of the patient and, ultimately, the outcome of treatment.

MARITAL RELATIONS OF THE MANIC PATIENT

The spouse's intolerance of manic episodes is commonly observed in clinical practice. This intolerance is not necessarily related to the severity of the manic episode, because the spouse often "cannot stand" even the mild hypomanic condition. The spouse's awareness of this intolerance as well as the readiness to discuss it is often surprising. He or she usually complains that the hypomanic patient disregards his or her needs and wishes, and is inclined to be critical, abusive, and humiliating. Some say that when hypomanic, the patient transmits to them the feeling of not needing them and of being far superior to them. On the other hand, when normal or preferably even somewhat depressed, the spouse feels needed and important.

This common clinical observation is supported by the high divorce rate of the manic patients. Brodie and Leff (1971) studied the marital stability of bipolar patients compared to that of unipolar (depressed) patients and found that while only 8% of unipolar patients' marriages ended in divorce, 57% of the bipolars' marriages ended in divorce. Furthermore, in that study they found that divorce in the bipolar patients occurred only after manic attacks and summarized that "these findings suggest the probable incompatibility of manic symptoms with stable marriage." In that study, three possible factors are described as responsible for the failure of marriage: (1) Lack of a male parent figure in the home of the majority of the few female bipolar patients; (2) the inability of the well spouse to tolerate bipolar illness, but without giving details of what this "inability" includes; and (3) "The manic patient's acting out of his counterphobic defense against his dependency needs by seeking divorce from a spouse who might be most acceptable to him when he was nonmanic."

Not all studies describe such extreme incompatibility. Greene et al. (1976) studied 100 couples, 40 of them unipolar depressive, 18 unipolar manic, and the other 42 bipolar patients; 11% of their patients divorced and 60% of the marriages were considered to be "intermittently incompatible." In their results, however, they do not distinguish between the patients with manic episodes and those without such episodes, and therefore their findings are not comparable to Brodie's study.

Another study (Ablon et al., 1975) found that the stability of marriage of manic men is higher than that of manic women: 86% of bipolar men remained married, compared to only 59% of the bipolar women. In that study it was suggested that "these men partially, or in a poorly differentiated way, identified with their weak and absent fathers and married dominant women like their mothers." Some studies that indicate a selection of overcontrolling spouse (e.g., Greene et al., 1976), support Ablon et al.'s suggestion (1975). As mentioned (Brodie and Leff, 1971), lack of a male parent figure was found in the majority of the female bipolar patients. In the study of nearly 50 bipolar patients (Ablon et al., 1975), this suggestion was only partially supported: About 35% of bipolar men and women patients lost their mothers before the age of 16; just over 75% of the bipolar men and about 60% of the bipolar women lost their fathers before that age. Yet, the authors' explanation is along similar lines to that of the male patient: "It appears that in identification with a dominant mother and her way of life, bipolar women marry weak or absent men like their fathers."

In order to understand the marital relations of the manic patient, one has to learn about the basic needs of patient and spouse to understand the interpersonal meaning of the manic symptoms as well as the reactions of the spouse to the manic symptoms. A number of efforts to study these questions have been made. Janowsky et al. (1970) observed that the spouses of manic patients are often motivated to dissolve the marriage. In that sample there were 11 married patients, and 10 spouses considered divorce; these thoughts were most prominent when the patients were manic, but continued also when the patients were depressed. In that report a vivid description is given about what makes the life of the manic's spouse so difficult.

1. The manic phase is often perceived as a willful, spiteful act, and not as an illness. "There is always an underlying feeling that the manic can control his actions, and does not do so out of maliciousness, selfishness and lack of consideration." One might add that at least three factors combine and lead to this perception: The manic often has periods of seeming reasonableness. He seems to enjoy his condition (at least in the beginning of the episode), and it is difficult indeed to identify pleasure with disease. Furthermore, the manic often "brings" the attack upon himself and by that strengthens the spouse's attitude that the manic phase is a willful, spiteful act.

2. The spouse often agrees to all kinds of concessions: "When shortly thereafter the manic has distorted or ignored all plans, the spouse feels duped."

3. The spouse is seen as a hostile opponent.

4. The spouse is not only the major recipient of the patient's anger, but also the major object for displacement and projection: The spouse is blamed for all failures, problems, etc.

5. The spouse is experiencing progressively diminished self-esteem. Added to that is the problem of marital infidelity, which is one of the common manifestations of the manic patient.

6. The spouse has to act as a buffer between the patient and the community. He or she is very likely to be frustrated in this role as he or she cannot control the patient, and is severely blamed and berated by the patient for trying to control, and by the community for failing to control, the manic behavior.

Yet the question remains why some spouses do not divorce. Different partial answers are to be found in the literature. Ablon et al. (1975), who did not report an extremely high divorce rate, explained the survival of marital relations in the following way: "In the face of their great dependency needs, they appeared to select spouses who would help them defend against the conscious awareness of these needs. For most couples, this perpetuation, and at the same time denial of passivity and dependency, acted to maintain the marriage."

Greene et al. (1976) tried to understand the interpersonal system. They found that the majority of the dyads (61%) were of an extroverted person married to a controlling one, and said: "This strongly suggests that the person with a primary affective disorder consciously and/or unconsciously selects an over-controlling partner to help cope with the severity of his/her mood swings, whereas the over-controlled, usually obsessive-compulsive, personality seeks the spontaneity of emotional expression of the PAD (primary affective disorder) personality. The preponderance of the controlling-extrovert dyad supports the notion of a deep symbiotic attachment that takes place when a PAD spouse is involved and suggests a reason for the low incidence of divorce found in this type of marriage."

As mentioned earlier, these findings are contrary to all other studies that show high divorce rates and that indicate that the manic patient does not fulfill the needs of his or her spouse. Yet, one can infer even from this study that the manic patient has strong dependency needs. It is by now accepted that the manic patient indeed has strong dependency needs (Cohen et al., 1954; Gibson et al., 1959; Janowsky et al., 1970; Wadeson and Fitzgerald, 1971; Fitzgerald, 1972). In the depressed condition, the patient expresses, among other things, his need to be taken care of. In the manic condition, these dependency needs are often expressed only indirectly, while overtly the patient is controlling.

Interesting information was gathered about the marital relations of four couples by conjoint psychiatric art evaluations (Wadeson and Fitzgerald, 1971). Amazing similarity in the drawings of each couple was found, and a lack of differentiation between patient and spouse. In that study strong dependency needs were found in the manic patients, complemented by a desire for strength in the spouse. Surprisingly, however, in all of the couples the manic patient was the dominant partner, providing most of the leadership, while the behavior of the spouse was very passive. It was observed in the sessions that the passivity and lack of responsiveness of the spouse escalated the patient's provocativeness. Furthermore, it was found that the spouses, too, had very strong dependency needs and wishes for strength in partner. The main difference found was that the patients were and had been, prior to illness, more dominant and controlling and the spouses more passive and compliant. To quote: "This problem can be summed up as mutual dependence and inadequate sense of coping expressed complementarily—verbally and psychopathologically by the patients, and in the behavior and words, but indirectly, by the reluctantly but heroically coping spouses. It may be this sort of mutual dependency which keeps these couples together despite the tremendous strains placed on married life by manic behavior....A relevant issue for future study in mania is that extent of mutual dependency might differentiate those marriages which endure from those ending in divorce." One can completely agree with the last statement. However, although that study was reported seven years ago, no additional work was done in that direction.

Few studies have actually tried to assess the patient-spouse interrelations or how one partner perceives the other in various stages of mania or depression. Ludwig and Ables (1974) followed up one couple for about eight months. In that study the patient rated himself daily on mania and depression scales and was rated daily on these scales by spouse. In addition, the patient rated his wife daily on positive and negative attributes scales, and the spouse rated herself daily on these scales. Some very interesting results are to be found in this study, which demanded unusual cooperation from both patient and spouse.

1. There was high and significant correlation between spouse's and patient's ratings on the mania scale. In other words, partners agreed on patient's mania.

2. Surprisingly, spouse's rating of patient's depression did not correlate with patient's own rating of depression. The correlation was negative but not significant.

We would have expected the opposite: One could expect that denial distorts patient's assessment of his condition in the manic phase. On the other hand, one could expect that during the depressed phase, patient would be more aware of his condition. The present findings can be explained in another way, i.e., that the spouse's acuteness as observer changes.

3. The change of patient's attitudes to spouse along with change in mania-depression found partial confirmation: When patient was depressed, he perceived significantly less negative attributes in spouse, and when manic, the negative attributes of the spouse significantly increased. In other words, the tendency of the manic patient to abuse and blame his partner was confirmed.

4. More surprising even is the finding that spouse's self-esteem indeed changed along with patient's condition. When patient was manic, spouse's estimation of her own negative attributes increased and of her own positive attributes decreased. It seems, therefore, that the manic patient actually manages to demolish the self-esteem of the spouse.

We would like to stress that these two findings—mainly that the manic patient views his spouse in negative terms and that spouse's self-esteem is lowered—should receive appropriate attention when treatment is considered.

Another study (Demers and Davis, 1971) tried to analyze the problem of the influence of the disease on marital relations in retrospect, i.e., when patients were stabilized on lithium. The only statistically significant finding was that spouses rated the patients as having significantly less negative attributes while on lithium compared to their condition before stabilization on lithium. It is worthwhile to note that only 43% of the patients rated their marriage as improved when on lithium, compared to 77% of the spouses. This might be viewed as indirect evidence that the spouse suffers more from the disturbed marital relations than the patient.

Taking into consideration all the available information, the question still remains: Why do some, probably many, of the manic marriages end in divorce while others do not. One may suggest that it depends to a great extent on the personality of the spouse, or, one might even say, on the psychopathology of the spouse. Certain traits or needs would make the spouse remain with the manic patient and at times even enjoy the situation. Conscious or unconscious guilt feelings may well make the spouse stick it out; direct or vicarious gratification, especially from the patient's hypersexuality, might be another reason, as well as conscious or unconscious need to control. Furthermore, it might be that the patient's "type" of mania is an important factor: As described, one is of elation and grandiosity and the other of destructiveness and paranoia. It would seem likely that the marriages of the second type are much more likely to end in divorce than those of the first.

Limited attention has been paid to the fact that fear of recurrent attacks is an additional stress for patient and spouse. None of the reviewed studies mentioned another extremely important source of stress: What does the knowledge relating to heredity do to marital relations? In group therapy with bipolar patients and spouses, many sessions were concentrated on the difficulties and disappointments with children. Yet, it seems that so far, this impact of fear, guilt, and blame on marital relations was not studied.

All of these factors—i.e., the special marital relations of the manic patient and the impact of the mania on the spouse—have to be taken into account in the psychosocial management of the manic patient. One may suggest that any treatment program that ignores these facets of mania is doomed to have only limited success.

INTERPERSONAL RELATIONS OF THE MANIC PATIENTS

This division into marital relations and interpersonal relations is somewhat artificial. Gibson et al. (1959) commented on "there being a notable lack of subtlety and of awareness of their own or of the feelings of others in their interpersonal relations." Others (Carlson and Goodwin, 1973) mentioned the manipulativeness of the manic patient, which was one of the few manic symptoms found in *all* patients. Yet, Beigel et al. (1971) did not include it in his manic scale at all. Nor did Feighner et al. (1972) include any of the interpersonal transactions in the diagnostic criteria for mania. Lipkin et al. (1970) commented that "manics tend to be quite irritating or may elicit a warm and humorous response.... When the manic is belligerent and hostile, he easily produces anger in others." However, except for Janowsky et al (1970; 1974), no author paid systematic attention to this aspect of the manic psychopathology. Because of the extremely important implications for the clinical management of the patients, these two fascinating reports will be presented in some detail. In the first report five types of activity were observed:

Type 1 is "manipulation of self-esteem of others; sensitivity to issues of self-esteem in others with the increasing or lowering of another's self-esteem as a way of exerting interpersonal leverage." Manic patients successfully appeal to the self-esteem of people, including therapists, make them feel good, and often "stimulate rescue fantasies and appeal to one's narcissism." What is often overlooked is that what the manic gives, he can as easily take back. "The relationship is made open for exploitation by the patient who titrates esteem offered against demands met."

Type 2 activity described by Janowsky et al. (1970) is "perceptiveness to vulnerability and conflict; the ability to sense, reveal and exploit areas of covert sensitivity in others." One should stress that the manic patient is an expert in sensing not only the individual vulnerability, but also areas of group conflict. The manic patient often turns covert group conflict into overt conflict. The manic patient will often divide the staff of a department and play one against the other. "Thus, the manic patient is able to bring out the worst characteristics of individuals in a group, leading to fragmentation of working relations." (Janowsky et al., 1970). It should be added that the tendency to manipulate and try to split the therapists was observed also in group psychotherapy (Ablon et al., 1975).

Type 3 activity is "projection of responsibility; the ability to shift responsibility in such a way that others become responsible for the manic's actions."

Type 4 activity is "progressive limit testing, the phenomenon whereby the manic extends the limits imposed on him, upping the ante." This activity or maneuvering is crucial: "The first of a series of requests may seem quite reasonable. However, once a minor concession is made and it is established that a limit may be challenged, the manic patient very gradually increases the 'ante.' Each step appears to be a minor addition and in itself seems quite reasonable. Each incremented request is stated in such a way as to make the other person feel that if he does not meet the patient's demands, he is rigid, unfair, petty and unreasonable." Every clinician has faced the above-described situation.

The fifth type of activity—alienating family members was reviewed in the discussion of marital relations.

In a later work, Janowsky's group (1974) measured some of these "interpersonal-interactional" characteristics; nurses rated patients on six items: testing of limits, projection of responsibility, sensitivity to other's soft spots, attempts to divide staff, flattering behavior, and ability to evoke anger. The sum of the six items created "Manic Interpersonal Interaction Scale" (MIIS) score. On each of the six items, as well as on the MIIS, the manic patients scored significantly higher than schizoaffective and schizophrenic patients. High intercorrelations were found among all items as well as between each item and global manic rating. Furthermore, when patients remitted, the scores on each of the six items separately as well as on the MIIS diminished dramatically. The differences between the scores of the acutely ill and those of the remitted patients were of high statistical significance.

Thus, it seems that the interpersonal relations, or maneuvers, of the manic patients are part and parcel of the manic episode and change or decrease with remission. These transactions, as described, may lead to countertransference reactions and can cause havoc in the treating team. The psychiatrist as well as the staff of the department of psychiatry has to be aware of these maneuvers and to take them into consideration when the overall psychosocial treatment of the manic patient is planned.

CLINICAL MANAGEMENT

The clinical management of the manic patient always includes outpatient as well as inpatient treatment. Optimally, it should be done by one flexible psychiatrist who can change the tactics of treatment according to the changes in the patient's condition. When treating a manic patient, one should expect changes, at times extreme changes. Furthermore, one has to be aware at all times that some of the changes are due to the nature of the disease process. Changes, however, may also be caused by emotional or medical stresses. Patient's condition may change because of failure in following the medical regimen for a variety of reasons, e.g., preference for the hypomanic state, provocation by family members, or even sudden change in diet, such as high sodium input. A psychiatrist treating manic patients should, therefore, fulfill a number of criteria:

1. He should be well versed in the biological aspects of the treatment, including the possible side effects and toxicity of lithium therapy.
2. He should be a competent psychotherapist and able to understand the psychodynamic process in the patients and the spouses.
3. He should be flexible and able to change techniques and tactics according to changes in patients' and family's condition.
4. He should be able to switch from outpatient to inpatient treatments without regarding hospitalization as punishment for the patient, rejection of patient, or proof of his own failure.
5. He should be able to sustain a neutral therapeutic relationship with patient and family without taking sides and without sliding into the extremely complicated antitherapeutic relationship which the manic patient would try to establish.

Indications for hospitalization are a major issue in the management of mania. It seems that often the manic patient gets hospitalized only when he is already severely disturbed. A number of factors seem to delay hospitalization:

1. The manic periods of seeming reasonableness were mentioned. Like family, the psychiatrist is often inclined to make plans and bargains with the patient—

e.g., to increase medication, to see the patient more often, etc.—in an effort to avoid hospitalization.

2. The rescue fantasies and the psychiatrist's need to remain the good guy were mentioned. These nonprofessional attitudes may well induce the therapist to make heroic efforts to avoid hospitalization.

3. The patient's testing of limits starts before hospitalization, and his request—"Doctor, give me only a couple of days more"—often succeeds. Once a concession is made, the "ante" is increased and the days turn into weeks.

4. Patient's refusal to be hospitalized usually is put not as a point-blank refusal but as "let us wait a bit." The psychiatrist, hoping to maintain the patient's cooperation (which is often an illusion), is tempted and finds it difficult to overcome the patient's refusal.

5. Manic patients, at least in the earlier or middle stages of the episode, do not fulfill the criteria for commitment that exist in most countries: The patients are often physically dangerous neither to themselves nor to others.

All of these factors often combine, and the end result is that the patient is brought into the hospital in an extremely disturbed condition. The orientation and attitudes of modern psychiatry is another factor that may delay hospitalization. In many centers and services, the emphasis is on community psychiatry, and one attempts to avoid hospitalization as much or as long as possible. This approach, on the whole, proved itself, and many patients, including schizophrenic patients, benefit from this change from hospital to community-oriented treatment. It seems, however, that such policy should not be applied to the manic patient. There are a number of indications showing why the manic patient, contrary to the majority of other patients, should be hospitalized as soon as the manic episode begins:

1. Many manic patients enjoy their condition, especially in its early stages and especially if they are of the euphoric type. It is the time when they feel best. Even after a number of severe episodes, they often believe that "this time" they will stay in the hypomanic state. They are, therefore, not to be trusted: They are inclined to abuse medication, take as little as possible or nothing at all, as well as cheat and lie about it in order to "protect and prolong the good period." This lack of compliance is an indication for early hospitalization.

2. As described, some patients accelerate very quickly into severe conditions. Since one cannot predict the rate of acceleration, it is good policy to regard all patients as high risk.

3. The manic and even the hypomanic patient easily gets involved in acts that compromise him and/or his family. He should be protected from his indiscretions and his grandiose plans. The only way to do so is to hospitalize him.

4. The impact of the manic on his family was described at length. The family should be spared all that, both to reduce the immediate amount of suffering and to enhance the chances of future relations. The patient, therefore, should be separated from his family, and the only logical way of doing it is hospitalization.

This attitude recently found support: Bleuler (1977) wrote: "I frequently see that younger psychiatrists have no idea what a terrible burden it is for the family to care for a manic member. I have seen many cases in which the patient has ruined the happiness, the social position of himself and of his family for good—as he had not been hospitalized at the right time." One can, therefore, strongly recommend "sparing" the family, but certainly not playing along with the family's rejection.

5. While psychiatrists often consider the damage that can be caused by the patient's elation and grandiosity, the other dangers are often forgotten. As described at length, many manic patients are assaultive and most manic patients are depressed. The psychiatrist, therefore, has to keep in mind that the manic patient may cause direct physical harm to his surroundings as well as to himself. This strong combination of elation and depression should be regarded as another indication for early hospitalization. It is suggested, therefore, that contrary to what is now the accepted attitude in psychiatry, it is best to hospitalize the manic patient in the early stages of the episode. Often it is a "strange" psychiatrist and not the patient's therapist that has to make that decision. In other words, someone who is not involved in the highly complicated interpersonal maneuvers of the patient can, with greater ease, reach a neutral decision and stand firmly by it. One should add that quite often when the manic patient is faced with a firm, unambivalent decision that he has to be hospitalized, he will agree to it.

The inpatient treatment of the manic patient includes at least three facets: medical treatments, attitudes of the staff, and psychotherapeutic interventions with patient and/or spouse. Yet, a number of problems should be mentioned: The manic patient often refuses to take medication. In many cases the objection is based on his feeling well and the wish to protect and prolong this feeling. In some cases this objection is colored by paranoid ideation, which may be stated mildly as "you try to spoil my fun," or more directly, as "you want to harm me." Furthermore, one should keep in mind that the manic patient will use all of his interpersonal maneuvers to avoid medication: He will try to split the team and find "allies" to support his objection to medication. He will test the limits by bargaining about amounts or about the schedule of medication. He will seem reasonable and try to bribe the physician by "I will take the stuff before I go to bed, I promise you," etc. The patient's objections to neuroleptics will be even greater than to lithium, since he feels the effects much faster. The psychiatrist, therefore, is often faced with a psychotic patient who refuses medication. However, the handling of medication to the manic patient also reveals the psychotherapeutic staff's attitudes. The way medication is handled will also spell out to him whether he can play with the psychiatrist's self-esteem, whether he can split and divide the staff, and whether he can, in fact, break limits. Therefore, once a decision about medication is reached, it should be carried out promptly with minimal bargaining. Often, if the patient receives this clear-cut message about medication, he will comply. In some cases force has to be used, and once more it is recommended that when indicated, it should be done without hesitation and too much deliberation.

ECT is another efficient tool for management of the manic and specifically the severely disturbed manic (McCabe, 1976). It seems that for quite a number of years, ECT was used sparingly and was regarded by the medical staff as "aggressive" treatment. It should be noted, therefore, that there are very few contraindications to ECT and very few complications. Furthermore, often the manic patient, like the overly depressed patient, does not object very much, and at times even welcomes ECT. Therefore, a few ECT's in the acutely manic patient can save the patient and the department a great deal of suffering.

Once in the hospital the manic patient can wreck havoc among the medical staff. Special sessions should be held with staff to discuss and work through the impact of patient's behavior on their self-esteem and solidarity. Staff should be aware of the patient's mastery in playing one against the other and in getting permission for things forbidden by another.

In some departments there is a team treating a group of patients. This has to be changed for the manic patient, as it is extremely important that only one psychiatrist be in charge of the manic patient. In addition to the other requirements for such a psychiatrist mentioned at the beginning of this section, he should also be accepted as an authority by the staff and all decisions should be taken by him. Janowsky et al. (1970) recommended: "We have found that the unambivalent, firm and rather arbitrary setting of limits and controls is most useful in decreasing manic symptomatology. It seems that when the manic is unable to successfully divide staff members, exploit areas of conflict and vulnerability and exceed set limits, his manipulative and uncontrolled behavior decreases." This seems to be true of manic behavior in general as well as of compliance with medication. In the acute state the patient should not be included in patients' group activities. His provocative behavior is often a welcome stimulus to a withdrawn group, but the patient himself is often provoked into more uncontrolled behavior. While the patient is acutely manic, sessions with him should be frequent—at least once a day, preferably twice and brief, 10 to 15 minutes. The sessions should be at prearranged times and the schedule adhered to—this is another important facet to setting limits. In sessions, topics should concentrate on daily management problems.

Such an approach implies that the goals of inpatient psychotherapy are:

1. Establishing a good working relation that in the inpatient department will help set limits and in the outpatient department ensure, as much as possible, continuation of maintenance treatment.

2. Identification of stress factors that may precipitate an acute episode. This can be regarded as the second stage of psychotherapy. It commences in the

inpatient service once the patient is more organized and has to be continued in the outpatient service.

However, there are different opinions about inpatient psychotherapy with the manic patient (Fitzgerald, 1972): "The patient's interpersonal difficulties must be treated by starting psychotherapy at the beginning of hospitalization even though the patient may seem unavailable because of mania." In that study, for example, meetings with the patient were held both informally as well as in the office. The author also recommends frequent visits by relatives (including children) and conjoined therapy from the very beginning of hospitalization. "It is helpful to make as a condition of admission and treatment that the spouse and other relatives be available from the start to meet once or twice weekly in conjoint meetings with the patient and therapist(s)." In that report, however, one also finds a warning that "the therapist must be flexible and realize that at times a family approach may not be indicated. Occasionally, attempts to bring family members together with the patient meet with reexacerbation of illness in the patient and difficulties for the relatives."

The family approach, however, is not accepted by all clinicians. Some suggest that in the first stages of acute hospitalization it is best to limit patient's contact with his family. The family often seems to be provoking the manic behavior and is abused by the patient. A vicious circle is then likely to start: The family feels angry, which leads to overcompensation and/or reaction formation with increased need to be with patient, which leads to additional humiliation, etc. These are also the reasons why couple interviews or psychotherapy are to be avoided in the acute stage. The contact with the family is limited: The family is seen by the psychiatrist in order to alleviate guilt feelings and to try to identify what "brought on" the attack. In many departments the routine is that families are seen by the social worker and patients by the psychiatrist. In the case of the manic patient, it is best to avoid this routine: Such routine adds to the patient's opportunities to divide staff.

Inpatient treatment of the manic patient should be regarded as an interim in the long-term treatment of the manic patient. Hospitalization, therefore, should not be prolonged. Once the patient is stabilized on lithium and symptom-free, he should be discharged from the hospital. Need for continuation of individual or family psychotherapy should not be an indication for continuation of hospitalization.

A lithium clinic was described by Fieve (1975). In that clinic, initial diagnosis is done independently by two psychiatrists and the patient is then seen once a week until stabilized on lithium and clinically well. After that patients come every four weeks for serum lithium monitoring and clinical evaluation, behavior and mood rating. "The patient load is handled by one supervising psychiatrist, four or five paramedical personnel and rating teams." The rating teams, which consist of a psychiatric nurse and one or two aids, interview each patient, usually in pairs, and often varies "so that no patient is seen frequently by the same staff members." The author stresses that not only does the briefly described model save manpower, but that it actually changes the traditional model of patient problem and psychiatrist. "Our focus in the clinic is on the presence or absence of affective episodes and the staff makes little attempt to deal with the interpersonal or intrapsychic problems of the patients, except as they relate to mood."

A somewhat different lithium clinic was described in England (Hullin et al., 1972). They see the patients after hospitalization every four weeks. When stability is maintained for at least six months, visits to the lithium clinic decrease to once in six weeks, and later to once in eight weeks. At each visit, in addition to a number of biochemical determinations, "the psychiatric state of the patient was briefly assessed, and the patient was given enough tablets to cover treatment until next appointment." In addition, each patient was seen concurrently by the referring consultant psychiatrist in outpatient clinics. "The frequency of the outpatient appointment schedule was determined by each consultant psychiatrist according to his usual practise." In other words, the lithium maintenance was completely separated from any other psycho-therapeutic interventions.

In some aspects similarities can be found between the two clinics: They have concentrated on administration of lithium (although in the first-mentioned report it is stated, in brackets, that other services, including social work, nursing, and referrals, were provided). This division between lithium treatment and other aspects of management has to raise questions. It has been repeatedly described that mania is also a message and that the manic interpersonal transactions interfere with treatment. Such clinics, especially the one described by Fieve (1975), are certainly efficient but seem to disregard the psychosocial aspects of mania.

Lithium clinics organized as patient groups seem to be a common practice, though rarely described (Davenport et al., 1977). In such a setup the group meets once a month and a group session is held (in addition to the biochemical determinations, which are done at the same time). The advantage lies in the fact that the group serves as a supportive system and encourages adherence to the maintenance. Furthermore, it enables crisis intervention. Usually in these clinics there is no clear-cut policy about other psychiatric treatments, and some of the patients in the group also receive other psychotherapeutic treatments while others do not. This lack of well-defined indications and interventions hampers comparison of outcome.

One study (Davenport et al., 1977) attempted to compare results of various lithium maintenance follow-ups. Three groups of patients were compared: The first was patients stabilized on lithium who were referred to community service and were supposed to, but usually did not, receive individual psychotherapy; the second was a lithium-monitored group which also included crisis intervention but no regular psychotherapy; and the third modality of treatment was regular couples group psychotherapy (in addition to lithium maintenance). In that study the couples group psychotherapy was found to be by far the superior modality of treatment: In that group there were neither rehospitalizations nor marital failures. In the community-referred patients, almost 40% were rehospitalized after a mean of 2.8 years, and in the lithium-monitored group, 20% were rehospitalized after a mean of 3.2 years. Marital failure was also common in both modalities of treatment: It occurred in nearly 25% of the community-referred group and nearly 55% of the lithium-monitored group. The patients in the couples psychotherapy were doing significantly better in social functioning than the community group. The lithium-monitored group scored on social functioning nearly as well as the couples group psychotherapy. One of the problems in that study was that the patients in the couples psychotherapy were significantly older than the other two groups and were married for a significantly longer time. One could argue, therefore, that this and not the modality of treatment is the reason for the marital stability of that group. Along the same lines, one can argue that the two groups treated by very different methods but in the same outpatient clinic did as well in social functioning. One cannot, however, ignore the fact that the couples group psychotherapy had no rehospitalization, while in the other two modalities, rehospitalization was quite high. One can suggest, therefore, that the spouse may be a very important factor in "bringing on" attacks that require rehospitalization. The details of the content of this couples group psychotherapy is to be found in two papers, Ablon et al., 1975, and Davenport et al., 1977. The mutually disturbed marital relations of the manic patient supports this suggestion that "something" should be done with or for the spouse. Some (Greene et al., 1976) actually recommend psychotherapy for the spouse: At times the psychotherapy recommended was of supportive character and at other times it was dynamic treatment. One of the aims of that treatment has been "to turn the non-PAD spouse into an assistant therapist and train him for the task of managing the marital system during a PAD crisis." Considering the described psychopathology of the "non-PAD spouse," one can doubt whether turning him into an assistant therapist is indeed indicated.

There seems to be an agreement that heterogeneous group psychotherapy is not indicated for the manic patient (Greene et al., 1976). Some put it even more strongly and suggest that the presence of a bipolar patient in a group is one of the "worst calamities" to befall the group (Yalom, 1970). There also seems to be agreement that individual dynamic psychotherapy with the manic patient is not indicated (Cohen, 1954; Davenport et al., 1977). Many clinicians do perform a variety of individual psychotherapies, but not in a controlled or reported method.

This brief review of opinions as to what outpatient management of the manic patient should include in addition to lithium maintenance highlights the extent of the problem. It raises the question whether there is indeed one preferable modality of treatment. Some outlines can be drawn, although there is no consensus even about such outlines: Contact with the patient should be maintained in the form of individual or group sessions; the psychiatrist should have dynamic understanding of the patient and know more specifically about internal or external stresses that may precipitate an attack. Yet, dynamic psychotherapy has not, so far, proved itself. A group of manic patients reinforces desired behavior, including compliance with medication. Contact with the family should be maintained and probably switch at times from supportive to dynamic to conjoint treatment. Review of recent literature about the outpatient management of the manic patient stresses three major issues: The first is that although lithium maintenance certainly reduces rehospitalization, the overall management of the manic patient is still an acute problem. The second issue is that the psychiatrist must be extremely flexible, with no preconceived ideas. The last issue is the dire need for well-controlled clinical studies that may provide evidence about the relative efficacy of various psychosocial approaches to the management of mania.

REFERENCES

Ablon, S.L., Davenport, Y.B., Gershon, E.S., and Adland, M.L. The married manic. *Am. J. Orthopsychiat.* 45, 854–866 (1975).

Beigel, A., Murphy, D.L., and Bunney, W.E. The Manic-State Rating Scale. *Arch. Gen. Psychiat.* 25, 256–262 (1971).

Bleuler, M. Personal communication, 1977.

Brodie, H.K.H., and Leff, M.J. Bipolar depression—a comparative study of patients' characteristics. *Am. J. Psychiat.* 127, 126–130 (1971).

Carlson, G.A., and Goodwin, F.K. The stages of mania—a longitudinal analysis of the manic episode. *Arch. Gen. Psychiat.* 28, 221–228 (1973).

Cohen, M.B., Baker, G., Cohen, R.A., Fromm-Reichmann, F., and Weigert, E.V. An intensive study of 12 cases of manic depressive psychosis. *Psychiatry,* 17, 103–137 (1954).

Davenport, Y.B., Ebert, M.H., Adland, M.L., and Goodwin, F.K. Couples group therapy as an adjunct to lithium maintenance of the manic patient. *Am. J. Orthopsychiat.* 47, 495–502 (1977).

Demers, R.G., and Davis, L.S. The influence of prophylactic lithium treatment on the marital adjustment of manic-depressives and their spouses. *Comp. Psychiat.* 12, 348–353 (1971).

Feighner, J.P., Robins, E., and Guze, S.D. Diagnostic criteria for use in psychiatric research. *Arch. Gen. Psychiat.* 20, 57–63 (1972).

Fieve, R.R. The lithium clinic: a new model for the delivery of psychiatric services. *Am. J. Psychiat.* 132, 1018–1022 (1975).

Fitzgerald, R.G. Mania as a message: Treatment with family therapy and lithium carbonate. *Am. J. Psychother.* 26, 547–554 (1972).

Gibson, R.W., Cohen, M.B., and Cohen, R.A. On the dynamics of the manic depressive personality. *Am. J. Psychiat.* 115, 1101–1107 (1959).

Greene, B.L., Lustig, N., and Lee, R.R. Marital therapy when one spouse has primary affective disorder. *Am. J. Psychiat.* 133, 827–830 (1976).

Hullin, R.P., McDonald, R., and Allsopp, M.N.E. Prophylactic lithium in recurrent affective disorders. *Lancet,* 1044–1049 (1972).

Janowsky, D.S., Leff, M., and Epstein, R.S. Playing the manic game. *Arch. Gen. Psychiat.* 22, 252–261 (1970).

Janowsky, D.S., El-Yousef, M.K., and Davis, J.M. Interpersonal maneuvers of manic patients. *Am. J. Psychiat.* 131, 250–255 (1974).

Ludwig, A.M., and Ables, M.F. Mania and marriage: The relationship between biological and behavioral variables. *Compr. Psychiat.* 15, 411–421 (1974).

McCabe, M.S. ECT in the treatment of mania: A controlled study. *Am. J. Psychiat.* 133, 688–691 (1976).

Wadeson, H.S., and Fitzgerald, R.G. Marital relationship in manic-depressive illness. *J. Nerv. Ment. Dis.* 153, 180–196 (1971).

Yalom, I.D. *The Theory and Practice of Group Psychiatry.* Basic, New York (1970), pp. 305–306.

CHAPTER 21

Forensic Aspects of Mania

Haim Dasberg and H.Z. Winnik

DANGEROUSNESS AND CRIMINALITY

Dangerousness has been defined as the capacity to commit violent antisocial acts. Strictly speaking, the concept of dangerousness should not be confounded with aggressiveness, violence, or hostility. A dangerous person should not simply indicate anyone whom we would prefer not to meet in a lonely street at night. The threatening harm to society of a dangerous individual should be likely and substantial, not just probable. Thus, the frequently rated symptom of "assaultiveness" by research psychiatrists (in 75% of manic cases by Carlson and Goodwin, 1973; in 45% of cases by Taylor and Abrams, 1975), "combativeness" (Good, 1978), or "outward hostility" (Blackburn, 1974) are probably not signs of dangerousness in the legal sense.

It is important to evaluate the degree of dangerousness in mental illness, where it is generally overestimated. But in spite of a remarkable literature, there are at present no operational criteria for such an evaluation, and it seems that ultimately it is based upon a subjective impression (Halleck, 1967). Scott (1977), in a study on assessing dangerousness, found that the link between crime and mental illness is not strong.

Clement et al. (1972) compiled some data as guides in the evaluation of dangerous patients as follows: (1) Severe head injury and/or severe headaches in childhood. (2) Physical assault and/or abuse during childhood. (3) Alcoholic parents. (4) Stubborness and temper tantrums in childhood and/or emotional deprivation. (5) General criminogenic factors of a social nature, like poverty, overcrowded housing, broken homes in childhood, and a history of antisocial acts. (All these criteria are not typical for the manic or the manic-depressive patients.)

As an illustration of how uncertain the evaluation of dangerousness is, a study by Steadman and Cocozza (1975) may be cited. They compared a group of 154 felons that were judged dangerous with a group of 103 not considered dangerous. The follow-up study three and a half years after release from prison showed that both groups were remarkably similar as to rearrest, rehospitalization and violent behavior. It would therefore seem that the criteria for future violent crimes in mental patients who became criminal are not very convincing, prior crimes (Silving, 1967) having more predictive value than psychological or biological factors. The best indicator for future behavior is past behavior; this saying seems to be valid in the evaluation of dangerousness too.

As to the criminality of mental patients in general, and manic patients in particular, the relevant studies (Rollin, 1963, 1965, 1977; Gunn, 1977; Orr, 1978; Steadman et al., 1978b) found that the rate of arrest in mental patients is similar to the rest of the population. It is the previous arrest rate—alike in the general population, expatients, or ex-convicts—that determines future criminality, not the fact of having been a mental patient. This is especially true for the functional psychoses, including mania.

Guze et al. (1969) in the United States found that affective illness is not associated with serious crime. Ambulatory psychiatric patients do not commit more offenses than the general population in the United States (Guze, 1976). In a comprehensive study, Böker and Häffner (1973) compared the percentage of criminals in the whole population of Germany with the percentage of criminals in the hospitalized mentally ill population over the decade 1955–1964, and found that the rate of criminality of both populations is similar. Fifty percent of the psychologically sick offenders were admitted for the first time after committing the offense, and 40% committed their first offense in the six-month period after their release from the hospital; therefore, the authors advise a close follow-up, maintenance treatment, information to families and social workers, at least over this critical period.

According to Aito Ahto (1951), the Finnish author, scientific research increasingly shows that mental illness as a cause of criminal activity is not a significant factor. Some recent reports (Steadman et al., 1978a) of an increased number of patients with prior and subsequent arrests might be explained as increase of admissions from a group of highly disadvantaged individuals that "bounce back and forth" among prison, hospital and a rejecting community (Rollin, 1977). Gunn (1977) calls them "the stage army tramping around and around." Breakdown by diagnosis shows that most of them are psychopaths, addicts, alcoholics, and intellectually subnormal persons. The less serious offenders are chronic schizophrenics, while affective disorders play a minor role among these criminal expatients (Rubin, 1972). Böker and Häfner in the aforementioned study came to the conclusion that the risk of affective psychotics committing violent offenses is 6 of 100,000, and only one tenth of that of schizophrenic patients.

Hospital referrals from the police, mentioned in the study of Sims and Symonds (1975), reveal that 12% of them were manic-depressive. In another British study (Bowden, 1978b), out of 105 remanded in custody for medical expertise, less than 2% were manic-depressive, although reevaluated following hospital treatment a larger proportion than expected turned out to be manic-depressive (19% of 82 cases), a fact pointing to the occurrence of unrecognized affective diseases among criminal offenders. The few studies dealing separately with the criminality of manic patients support the conclusion that criminality of manic patients is rare, according to the dictum "le maniaque fait généralement plus de bruit que de mal" (the manic makes more noise than harm). He prefers the so-called "non-violent" crimes, like joy-riding, fraud, shoplifting, not paying taxi fares, giving false alarms, sexual demeanors. An example out of many may be given: A typical manic patient, accused of stealing an automobile, stated that he knew that the owner of the car, being his friend, would not only allow him to use it but would even give it as a present. According to Woods (1972), criminal violence in mania is even less frequent than in depression. Binns et al. (1969a, 1969b) reported that out of 92 individuals admitted by court order at Lavendale Hospital in the year 1965–1966, only 6 suffered from hypomania, and their offenses were not violent (shoplifting, breach of peace, etc.). Macdonald (1959) reports that even among nonviolent offenders, the manic patients constitute a minority of 25% of mentally abnormal check offenders, whereas 7.8% of mentally ill patients involved in traffic accidents were manic-depressives (mania not being separately noted [Kastrup et al., 1978]). Witter (1973) in Germany noted that out of 950 psychiatric expertises made by him, only 20 delinquent offenses (less than 2%) were committed in the manic phase. In the forensic clinic of Cologne, only 6 cases of mania were observed in the last 20 years, and 20 cases in the last 10 years in Göttingen (Bresser and Langelüddeke, 1976). In Jerusalem, of 150 offenders admitted to the Ezrath Nashim Hospital for psychiatric opinion over the last 10 years, only 2% were manic (Dasberg, unpublished). Stierlin in Basle (1956) selected material from 73 psychiatric clinics and hospitals in Europe, and stated that out of 773 aggressive inmates, only 29 were "cyclophrenic." He remarks justly that people who commit a petty larceny are much less likely than heavy offenders to be examined by a psychiatrist. Aito Ahto (1951) surveyed 216 dangerous habitual criminals who were psychically disturbed. Not a single case of manic-depressive was among them.

There has been no study concerned with psychiatric diagnosis in a consecutive group of offenders appearing in a particular court (Gunn, 1977). Thus we do not know how often an unrecognized manic person is prosecuted or convicted.

In typical mania two thirds of the hospital admissions occur within a month of onset (Winokur, 1978), but nonhospitalized, nontypical, misdiagnosed, or unrecognized manic offenders probably do not receive proper forensic attention at all. Studies of emergency-room cohorts support the notion that only very few manics are promptly hospitalized (Skodol, 1978; Robins et al., 1977). From clinical practice it is known that many manic-like offenders are kept away from the authorities by embarrassed families who compensate the losses incurred by their sick relatives. This is obviously possible only as long as no major offenses have been committed.

Good (1978) mentioned undiagnosed or misdiagnosed mania in sociopathic families with manic patients, and antisocial acts of first offenders who are not overtly manic-depressive. Once in prison, these patients become "invisible," because the corrective milieu in prison may serve as a strong and effective therapeutic agent. Reviewing 100 consecutive cases referred for psychiatric evaluation at the Massachusetts Correctional Institute, Good (1978) found three such cases (3%) of "masked mania" (seven of masked depression). According to Bowden (1978a), manic-depressive illness is underdiagnosed in the offender population when kept in the remand setting. Herjanic et al. (1977) found that female offenders were less likely than male offenders to receive psychiatric evaluation, but still 13% of the female offenders had affective disorders, as compared to only 4% of the males. The question can be asked: Are criminal males underdiagnosed for affective illness?

There are manic murderers too, but not many. Asuni (1969) failed to find a single manic patient in 30 cases of homicide sent to his hospital. The same is valid for the material of Sayed et al. (1969), who report on 32 insane murderers in Scotland. Good (1978) reviews 23 studies on criminal populations; the percentage of mania is about 2%. Special mention should be made of East's report (1936) on 300 insane murderers admitted to the Broadmoor Criminal Lunatic Asylum in England: 6.7% of these inmates were diagnosed as mania, a relatively high proportion.

Schipkowensky (1968) reviewed the 600 offenders seen at the Sofia University Institute of Psychiatry in 1932–1956 (over 25 years). Forty-five offenders suffered from "Cyclophrenia"—30 of them from manic states (1.5%). Only three of them committed severe offenses which resulted in the death of the victim. Schipkowensky streses that the offenses of manic patients are mostly trivial, of a nonviolent nature. He quotes Lombroso's finding of 22.5% manics in his sample of criminals and a similar statement of Krafft-Ebing, and explains it as apparently reflecting the fact that at the turn of the century the majority of the psychiatrists included different clinical pictures under the headings of mania and melancholia.

Suicidal acts happen in mania but are rare events. Holding and Barraclough (1975) found that among 134 recent deaths recorded as open verdicts by a London coroner, there were 73% mental cases of suicide or accident, but only one case of recent mania. Occasional occurrences of suicide in mania remind us that depressive trends of thought and feelings are not uncommon in manic states and are already mentioned in Kraepelin's classic description (1913).

Even the so-called angry manic ("zornige Manie" of Kraepelin), more typical for its onset in the fifth decade of life, is not characterized by committing the so-called indexed offenses; even in cases of bodily assault, the injuries are generally slight. These patients usually exhaust their aggressive affective tension in threats and acts which do not result in severe harm or destruction of the adversary. Apparently their vivid and often strong empathic feelings to fellow beings and the mature age have an inhibitory effect on their agressive tendencies.

In conclusion we can say that the criminality of manic patients is relatively low. Factors connected with the social situation and the premorbid personality largely outweigh those of the mental disturbance as determinants of antisocial, criminal, and violent activity. In the case of antisocial activity, manic patients belong to the group of temporary or occasional offenders, and not to the group of professional or habitual criminals.

FORENSIC DELIBERATIONS

In the common law, responsibility requires (a) the existence of a connection between the act of the offender and the offense, i.e., the existence of the *"actus reus"*; (b) that the offender's behavior when committing the act be proven intentional or volitional, i.e., the existence of the *"mens rea."*

At court the prosecution has to prove that *mens rea* and *actus reus* apply in a case of criminal offense. The offender is not responsible if *mens rea* was not extant when committing the offense. For the assessment of responsibility, most of the civilized countries have their specific rules. In the Anglo-Saxon countries starting in 1843, the MacNaughton rules prevailed. These were replaced by other, more liberal ones during the last decades, such as the principle of the irresistible impulse in cases of mental illness. They define the conditions required in order to establish when a mentally ill person should not be held responsible for his criminal act.

In spite of the fact that in clinical psychiatry there is no place for a concept like responsibility, psychiatrists are entrusted to give an opinion on the responsibility of criminal offenders. This is despite the advice given by the 1926 Committee on Legal Aspects in Psychiatry to change the legal procedure and exempt psychiatrists from the necessity of pronouncing upon intangible subjects of religious, moral, and legal tradition, such as responsibility and punishment (Menninger, 1959; Sasz, 1963).

The manic patient is often unaware that he is acting contrary to the law or to the accepted standard of behavior; he does not know that he ought not to do the act he is doing. This is self-evident in cases of acute, delusional, delirious mania, where the patient is unable to control his impulses, and where he overestimates, is reckless, disregards dangers, and is inaccessible to logical arguments and deliberations.

From the foregoing, the conclusion has to be drawn that regardless of the etiological factors or the psychopathological principles adopted by various psychiatrists, from the forensic point of view the acute forms of mania render the individuals suffering from them not responsible for actions performed during the manic attack. Such an individual is also not fit to stand trial as long as he is in the manic state, because "he cannot appraise the outcome of the trial situation, cannot make decisions on receiving advice; he is unable in most instances to maintain a collaborative relationship with his attorney. He cannot tolerate the stress of the trial and will not refrain from irrational and unmanageable behavior during the trial" [GAP Report, 1974].

The success of the new psychopharmacological treatment of mania, e.g., with lithium salts, having not only curative but also preventive effects, may raise the question whether interrupting the preventive treatment, when followed by a violent criminal offense, might not require prosecution and in certain cases conviction—for instance, in those cases where the interruption of the treatment was done with the intention of facilitating the prohibited act, which is therefore done with a *mens rea* (and especially in cases of previous criminal acts in the personal history). The following case may be an illustration: A female patient, overdependent on a too dominant husband, repeatedly escaped into mania by discontinuing her lithium treatment. This forced her husband "to surrender," to take care of her, and finally to bring her to the hospital.

It goes without saying that in similar cases we have to consider whether the seemingly voluntary interruption of the treatment per se is the first sign of the impending manic attack.

Undiagnosed mania often becomes a serious problem in court. The judges, the members of the jury, and the lawyers are again and again misled by the irrational optimism and the rationalization of the elated, manic, or hypomanic defendant, and when they are provoked by his manic outbursts, they tend to interpret it as contempt of court.

A quite serious problem is connected with offenses perpetrated in hypomanic states. Then, often, the exploits are begun with a certain measure of volition or choice, but in the later stages of their activity, the patients continue by yielding to temptations where so-called normal people would refrain. It is then most difficult—if not impossible—to draw a line between hypomania, where some, though reduced, control to resist impulses and temptations does exist, and a manic state, in which impulsivity can no longer be resisted and the perpetrator of an antisocial act has to be considered irresponsible and therefore not punishable. On biological and genetic grounds it seems that recurrent hypomania in known bipolars and in cases with family histories positive for affective disease is a form of mania. The habitual hypomanic, lacking a biological background, remains a diagnostic and forensic dilemma. Some legal systems in Europe, where the principle of diminished responsiblity is acknowledged, give the court the expedient to apply this principle by giving a lighter sentence.

INVOLUNTARY COMMITMENT

Involuntary commitment to a hospital should involve a very small number of manic patients. In most civilized countries it requires a medical certificate issued by physicians not associated with the hospital to which the patient is being sent.

In cases of emergency or involuntary hospitalization, the duration of hospitalization should be relatively short, two days to several weeks, according to the country. Long-term involuntary hospitalization requires, in most countries, a detailed and well-founded medical report of the hospital or of a recognized psychiatrist to be submitted to the court or the respective authorities, and generally involves a judicial decision. A medical reexamination and reconsideration of the involuntary admitted cases is desirable, especially in the rare manic cases, considering the ups and downs so characteristic for this illness even in its chronic forms.

In acute manic illness, mainly in its delirious and delusional forms, involuntary hospitalization may be unavoidable, especially where the manic behavior involves a serious degree of dangerousness to a person, to his property or to other people. In many manic cases, however, involuntary admission to a hospital is probably not justified from a strictly legal point of view, even when behavior is very disturbing.

Disregarding for a while the purely legal aspect, it has to be stressed that involuntary admission generally does not inflict any harm to these patients. They are clearly in need of treatment, although they are not capable of understanding and admitting it. It is surprising how often severely disturbed manic patients quiet down after admission to a hospital, so that they can be managed in an open ward, especially if the staff is well trained and the staff/patient ratio is sufficient. Physical restraint, even in involuntary admitted cases, is therefore generally not necessary except in rare cases of dangerous assault or in suicidal attempts. As to the evaluation of the degree of dangerousness of manic patients, we refer the reader to the comments above, but would add that the attempt of Beigel and Murphy (1971) to single out a subgroup of more destructive manic patients seems to be noteworthy. The patients of this group show higher scores in their MS scale relating to paranoia and threatening and destructive behavior. This so-called P-D (paranoid-destructive) group is characterized as follows: (a) moving from one place to another; (b) making threats; (c) seeking out others; (d) being combative, destructive. If the validity of this test can be confirmed, it may be of help in decisions connected with the discharge of dangerous patients. Clearly, there is a subtle difference between taking care of a patient, even in the form of involuntary admission to a hospital, and the conscious or semiconscious wish to get rid of an individual who does not know how to behave. This is one of the reasons why it is so difficult to formulate guiding rules beyond the usual criterion of dangerousness. Infringement of personal freedom and abuse of psychiatry are dangers that always lurk round the corner.

Gove and Fain (1977) demonstrated that involuntarily admitted patients do not differ from voluntarily admitted ones as to the emotional difficulties after being released from the hospital; neither is the effect of social labeling attributed to having been a committed patient a detrimental factor in the subsequent course of the illness. Our concluding comment on involuntary admission would be as follows: Legally this step is rarely justified in manic patients; psychologically it is seldom harmful.

OTHER LEGAL ASPECTS OF FORENSIC PSYCHIATRY

In modern society every adult person is presumed to be mentally competent in all spheres of social life. This mental competence refers to the degree of mental soundness consistent with the ability to carry out certain civil acts of a judicial nature. Mental competence is presumed unless there is clear evidence of incapacity, which has to be assessed by the authorities concerned, and this means competency not only as such, but also to what degree it affects particular issues or social functions, such as managing one's property, signing a contract, driving a car, making a valid will, etc. This is in addition to the aforementioned problems of responsibility and of the fitness to stand trial. In this section three of these issues of civil law will be mentioned: guardianship, testamentary capacity, and credibility of witnesses.

The ownership of property is one of the basic rights in our civilization. We are granted the right to dispose of that property as we wish so long as the rights of others are not violated. (The same is valid regarding our whereabouts, our mobility, and the right to dispose of matters concerning our body.)

It is customary, if a person lacks the capacity to manage his own affairs, for the court, after taking evidence of that issue, which in cases of mental illness includes a psychiatric opinion, to appoint a guardian or a trusteeship to take care of the patient's interests and to act on behalf of the ward.

One of the fundamental concerns in that respect is the person's state of awareness and his capacity to comprehend the significance of the specific issue or of the particular commitment he was making at the time he was carrying it out.

In full-blown mania one cannot avoid placing the patient under the care of a guardian. Trusteeship seems to be insufficient to prevent damage to his family and his property. But in many cases one can dispense with creating a guardianship, namely in cases where the patient is protected by members of his family before being hospitalized and in favorable cases when the patient, at his discharge, has improved so that he is again able to function in society and to manage his affairs. The guardianship, when created, should be a temporary measure, bearing in mind the frequent variations in the manic states, even the chronic ones.

Wills are the instruments by which we dispose of our property after death. Only rarely are wills challenged by questioning their testamentary dispositions through allegations of manic illness of the testator. Such allegations are mostly made on the basis of senile dementia or chronic, intractible, deteriorating psychosis.

The assessment of the mental state of the testator generally has to be made retrospectively after his death. Informants in such cases are often not reliable. In order to establish mental ability to make a testament, it must be shown that the testator, at the time of making the will, understood the nature and the position of his property and the natural objects of his bounty.

In making a will, the manic sometimes lacks this capacity, namely to understand who the persons are that should be the objects of his natural bounty, and he makes his will under undue influences, sometimes out of contact with reality, therefore not following his own inclinations and not determined by reasonable deliberations. Considering the fluctuations in manic illness, it is difficult, if not impossible, to reconstruct the psychic state prevailing at the time the manic patient made the will and its influence on his testamentary capacity. The psychiatric opinion is, therefore, in these rare cases, often determined by intuition and experience.

A witness may not be competent to testify by virtue of his mental state. This may stem from the presence of a manifest emotional disturbance. Assessment of credibility in giving evidence as witness is with increasing frequency entrusted to psychiatrists, especially as to the reliability of chief witnesses. In cases of outspoken mania it is evident—even without asking the psychiatrist —that the person is unfit for witness. In other cases the decision is difficult, since a person can have the capacity to talk about some subjects with perfect

374 DASBERG AND WINNIK

accuracy but may become thoroughly deranged and disorientated in relation to other topics. In cases of hypomania the decision is no less difficult. When psychiatric testimony is required, it should be based upon complete knowledge of the case and of the subject of the trial. In some of the cases the witness has to be accepted under the condition that his testimony refers only to material which can be verified objectively.

CONCLUSION

Clinical psychiatry as a branch of medicine on the one hand and legal tradition on the other are incongruent systems of thought. Responsibility in the legal sense is grounded on free will and on knowing what is wrong. It is an all-or-none concept. But clinical thought recognizes gradual transitions on a continuum from normal to abnormal, and in descriptions of pathological states there is no place for ethical values.

The sequence euthymia-elation-hypomania-mania is the most typical example of a biological and psychological continuum. One of its main psychodynamic features is defiance, which may be incorrigible in the extreme state. It is difficult for psychiatrists to translate clinical multifaceted phenomena into the unequivocal terms of law, especially in the case of mania. However, in spite of this difficulty, it seems clear that regardless of the wide variations of psychopathological principles adopted by different psychiatrists, the typical manic patient is not criminally responsible. Neither is he competent to stand trial. The matter starts to be problematic in cases of nontypical mania.

REFERENCES

Abraham, K. Versuch einer Entwicklungsgeschichte des Libido auf Grund des Psychoanalyse seelischer Störungen. In *Neue Arbeiten for ärztlichen Psychoanalyse* (1924) or in *Selected Papers of Psychoanalysis*. Basic, New York (1953).

Aito Ahto. Dangerous habitual criminals. *Acta Psychiatr. Neurolog. Suppl. 69* (1951).

Asuni, T. Homicide in western Nigeria. *Br. J. Psychiat.* 115, 1105–113 (1969).

Beigel, A., and Murphy, D.L. Assessing clinical characteristics of the manic state. *Am. J. Psychiat.* 128, 689–697 (1971).

Binns, J.K., Carlisle, J.M., Numme, D.M., Park, R.H., and Todd, N.A. Remanded in hospital for psychiatric examination: Section 54—Mental Health Act (Scotland) 1960. *Br. J. Psychiat.* 115, 1125–1132 (1969a).

Binns, J.K., Carlisle, J.M., Numme, D.M., Park, R.H., and Todd, N.A. Remanded in custody for psychiatric examination: A review of 83 cases. *Br. J. Psychiat.* 115, 113–1139 (1969b).

Blackburn, I.M. The pattern of hostility in affective illness. *Br. J. Psychiat.* 125, 141–145 (1974).

Böker, W., and Häfner, H. *Gewaltaten Geistesgestörter*. Springer Verlag, Heidelberg (1973).

Bowden, P. Men remanded in custody for medical reports: The selection for treatment. *Br. J. Psychiat.* 132, 320–331 (1978a).

Bowden, P. Men remanded in custody for medical reports: The outcome of the treatment recommendation. *Br. J. Psychiat.* 132, 332–338 (1978b).

Bresser, P.H., and Langelüddeke, A. *Gerichtliche Psychiatrie*, 4th ed. W. De Gruyter, Berlin (1978), pp. 189–197.

Carlson, G.A., and Goodwin, E.K. The stages of mania (A longitudinal study of manic episodes). *Arch. Gen. Psychiat.* 28, 221–228 (1973).

Clement, C.E., Hyg, M.S., and Ervin, F.R. Historical data on the evaluation of violent subjects. *Arch. Gen. Psychiat.* 27, 621–624 (1972).

East, W.N. (cited in M.I. Good). *Medical Aspects of Crime.* P.B. Blakiston, Philadelphia (1936), p. 378.

Feighner, J.P., Robins, E., Guze, S.B., Woodruff, R.A., Winokur, G., and Munoz, R. Diagnostic criteria for use in psychiatric research. *Arch. Gen. Psychiat.* 26, 57–63 (1972).

Group for the Advancement of Psychiatry. *Misuse of Psychiatry in the Criminal Courts: Competency to stand trial,* Vol. 8, Report No. 89 (1974).

Good, M.I. Primary affective disorder, aggression and criminality: A review and clinical study. *Arch. Gen. Psychiat.* 35, 954–960 (1978).

Gove, W.R., and Fain, T. A comparison of voluntary and committed psychiatric patients. *Arch. Gen. Psychiat.* 34, 669–676 (1977).

Gunn, J. Criminal behaviour and mental disorder. *Br. J. Psychiat.* 130, 317–329 (1977).

Guze, S.B., Goodwin, D.W., and Crane, J.B. Criminality and psychiatric disorder. *Arch. Gen. Psychiat.* 20, 583–591 (1969).

Guze, S.B. *Criminality and Psychiatric Disorder.* Oxford Univ. Press, New York (1976).

Halleck, S.L. *Psychiatry and the Dilemma of Crime.* Harper & Row, New York, and Hoeber medical Books, New York (1967).

Herjanic, M., Hem, F.A., and Vanderpearl, R.H. Forensic psychiatry: Female offenders. *Am. J. Psychiat.* 134, 556–558 (1977).

Himmelhoch, J.M., Mulla, D., Neill, J.F., Detre, T.P., and Kupfer, D.J. Incidence and significance of mixed affective states in bipolar populations. *Arch. Gen. Psychiat.* 33, 1062–1066 (1976).

Holding, T.A., and Barraclough, B.M. Psychiatric morbidity in a sample of a London coroner's open verdicts. *Br. J. Psychiat.* 127, 133–143 (1975).

Kastrup, M., Dupont, A., Bille, M., and Lund, H. Traffic accidents involving psychiatric patients. *Acta Psychiat. Scand.* 68, 30–39 (1978).

Kraepelin, E. *Psychiatrie. Ein Lehrbuch für Studierente,* 8th ed. J. Barth, Leipzig (1913).

Leff, J.P. Fischer, M., and Bertelsen, A. A cross-national epidemiological study of mania. *Br. J. Psychiat.* 179, 428–442 (1976).

Liebowitz, J.H., Rudy, V., Gershon, E.S., and Gillis, A. A pharmacogenetic case report: Lithium-responsive postpsychotic antisocial behavior. *Compr. Psychiat.* 17, 655–660 (1978).

Lewin, B.D. *The Psychoanalysis of Elation.* Norton, New York (1950).

McDonald, J.M. A psychiatry study of check offenders. *Am. J. Psychiat.* 126, 438–442 (1955).

Menninger, K. *A Psychiatrist's World: Selected Papers,* B.H. Hall and M.E. Kenworthy, eds. Viking, New York (1959), pp. 729–736.

Orr, H.J. The imprisonment of mentally disordered offenders. *Br. J. Psychiat.* 133, 194–199 (1978).

Robins, E., Gentry, K.A., Munoz, R.A., and Marten, S. A contrast of the three more common illnesses with the ten less common in a study and 18 months follow-up of 314 psychiatric emergency room patients. *Arch. Gen. Psychiat.* 34, 259–265 (1977).

Rollin, H.R. Social and legal repercussions in the Mental Health Act 1959. *Br. Med. J.* (I) 786–788 (1963).

Rollin, H.R. Unprosecuted mentally abnormal offenders. *Br. Med. J.* (I) 831–835 (1965).
Rollin, H.R. (editorial). "De-institutionalization" and the community: Fact and theory. *Psychol. Med.* 7, 181–184 (1977).
Rubin, B. Prediction of dangerousness in mentally ill criminals. *Arch. Gen. Psychiat.* 27, 621–629 (1972).
Sayed, Z.A., Lewis, S.A., and Brittain, R.R. An EEG and psychiatric study of 32 insane murderers. *Br. J. Psychiat.* 115, 1115–1124 (1969).
Sasz, T. *Law Liberty and Psychiatry.* MacMillan, New York (1963).
Schipkowensky, N. Affective disorders, cyclophrenia and murder. In *The Mentally Abnormal Offender,* A.V.S. de Renak and R. Porter, eds. J.S.A. Churchil, London (1968).
Scott, P.P. Assessing dangerousness in criminals. *Brit. J. Psychiat.* 131, 127–142 (1977).
Silving, H. *Constitutional Elements of Crime.* Charles C. Thomas, Springfield, Illinois (1967), p. 263.
Sims, C.P., and Symonds, R.C. Psychiatric references from the police. *Br. J. Psychiat.* 127, 171–178 (1975).
Skodol, A.E., and Karasu, T.B. Emergency psychiatry and the assaultive patient. *Am. J. Psychiat.* 135, 202–205 (1978).
Sosowsky, L. Crime and violence among mental patients reconsidered in view of the new legal relationship between the state and the mentally ill. *Am. J. Psychiat.* 135, 33–42 (1978).
Steadman, H.G., Cocozza, J.G., and Melick, M.E. Explaining the increased arrest rate among mental patients: The changing clientele of state hospitals. *Am. J. Psychiat.* 135, 816–828 (1978a).
Steadman, H.J., Benderwyk, D., and Ribner, S. Comparing arrest rates of mental patients and criminal offenders. *Am. J. Psychiat.* 135, 1218–1220 (1978b).
Steadman, H.G., and Cocozza, J.G. Researchers challenge prediction of dangerousness of offenders. *Psychiat. News* 10, 13, 1975.
Stierlin, H. *Der Gewalttätige Patient.* S. Karger, Basel (1956).
Taylor, M.A., and Abrams, R. Acute mania: Clinical and genetic study of responders and nonresponders to treatment. *Arch. Gen. Psychiat.* 32, 863–865 (1975).
WHO. *Forensic Psychiatry: Report on a working group.* Siena, 1975, Distributed by the Regional office for Europe WHO, Copenhagen (1977).
Winokur, G. Duration of illness prior to hospitalization (onset) in the affective disorders. *Neuropsychobiology* 2, 87–93 (1976).
Witter, H. *Handbuch der Forensichen Psychiatry,* H. Göppinger and H. Witter, eds. Springer Verlag, Berlin (1972), pp. 969–971.
Woods, S.M. Psychotherapy of pseudohomosexual panic. *Arch. Gen. Psychiat.* 27, 255–258 (1972).
Ziskind, E., Sommerfeld, E., and Jens, R. Can schizophrenia change to affective psychosis. *Am. J. Psychiat.* 128, 331–335 (1971).

CHAPTER 22

Mania and Creativity

Nancy C. Andreasen

> ...for aught we know to the contrary, 103° or 104° Fahrenheit might be a much more favorable temperature for truth to germinate and sprout in, than the more ordinary blood-heat of 97 or 98 degrees.
> —William James, *Varieties of Religious Experience*

Vincent Van Gogh died at 37 by suicide, having suffered during his last years from intermittent episodes of mania and depression, and having completed more than 300 paintings during the last year and a half of his life. His singular style ushered in the era of experimentation loosely known as "modern art," and many of his best works were produced during his last years, when he was intermittently psychotic. Martin Luther experienced terrible periods of despair, but also periods of manic energy and prodigious productivity; his despair over not being able to satisfy the demands of his conscience led him to propose the importance of "faith" rather than "works," and once the *Ninety-five Theses* had launched the Reformation, he turned his enormous energies toward writing dynamically convincing theological tracts to support his position. His alternations of mood thus may have changed the course of history. Sylvia Plath died by suicide in the midst of a recurrent depression. During the months that preceded her depression, she had a burst of productivity in which she worked late into the night or early in the morning creating poems such as "Death & Co.," which one critic has described as having reckless energy and "weird jollity [Alvarez, 1970, p. 31]." Perhaps her depression was preceded by a period of hypomania, which permitted her to write so freely, creatively, and prolifically. Both her life style and her poetic style have had a potent effect on modern literary attitudes, overturning the rationalism of Eliot and the New Critics and introducing an emphasis on the personal and emotional, sometimes called the "Confessional School."

To these examples might be added many others. A variety of artists, writers, statesmen, philosophers, and scientists have suffered from disorders of mood, leading many different investigators to speculate on the association between "genius and insanity." The work of these investigators suggests a large number of questions and a few answers (Ellis, 1926; Juda, 1949; McNeil,

1969, 1971; Galton, 1892; Lombroso, 1891; Karlsson, 1970). Is there an association with mood disorder? Do mood disorders enhance or detract from creativity? Does the association suggest any hypotheses about the origins of either creativity or mood disorders?

IS THERE AN ASSOCIATION?

Several studies of the association between creativity and psychiatric illness are summarized in Table 1. Although there is considerable variation from one study to another, these investigations indicate a relatively high rate of psychiatric illness in creative and eminent persons. Further, a number of studies have also indicated a familial association between psychiatric illness and creativity :(Karlsson, 1970; McNeil, 1969, 1971; Juda, 1949; Ellis, 1926; Andreasen and Canter, 1974, 1975). Both the family study design and the adopted offspring design have been used. These studies have indicated a higher rate of both psychiatric illness and creativity in the relatives of creative persons than would be expected in the general population. The psychiatric illnesses observed in the relatives have usually been affective disorder or some type of personality disorder.

Studies of the association between creativity and psychiatric illness have, however, tended to suffer from a number of significant problems in conceptualization or design that complicate interpretation or decrease generalizability. Ideally, research on creativity should include methodological refinements such as identification of an appropriate sample of creative subjects, use of adequate measures to evaluate illness, firsthand interviews with all creative subjects, and provision of an adequate control group. Ellis, for example, drew his sample from names listed in the British *Dictionary of National Biography,* thereby including many individuals who were famous, but not necessarily creative. Juda relied heavily on anecdote and used relatively primitive nosology. Very few of the studies have used structured interviews and diagnostic criteria.

Table 1. Prevalence of Psychiatric Illness in Creative and Eminent Persons

	Ellis (1926) "British genius"	Judas (1949) Artists	Scientists	Andreasen and Canter (1974, 1975) Writers	Controls
Personality disorder	5%	27.4%	14.4%	60%	13%
Schizophrenia	4.2%	2.7%	0%	0%	0%
Affective disorder	8%	0%	3.9%	67%	13%
Alcoholism	—	2.7%	0.6%	40%	13%
Organic conditions	—	6.2%	6.6%	0%	0%
Suicide	—	1.8%	1.6%	—	—
Imprisoned	16%	—	—	0%	0%

Andreasen and Canter (1974, 1975) incorporated these methodological advances in their studies, providing a careful operational definition of creativity and a matched control group, and using structured firsthand interviews and diagnostic criteria on both creative subjects and controls. Their work is, however, restricted solely to creative writers, and it is not necessarily generalizable to other types of creative individuals, such as musicians, scientists, painters, and philosophers. They interviewed 15 writers who had served on the faculty of the University of Iowa Writers Workshop, the oldest creative writing program in the United States and probably the most distinguished. Its faculty has included such writers as John Cheever, Robert Lowell, Rober Coover, John Irving, Philip Roth, Kurt Vonnegut, Stanley Elkin, Vance Bourjaily, Anthony Burgess, Angus Wilson, and Paul Engle.

Their data, summarized in Table 2, suggest a striking association between affective disorder and creativity. Two thirds of the writers had experienced a major affective illness, including two who had suffered from severe manias requiring prolonged and repeated hospitalizations. Nine writers met criteria for cyclothymia as specified in the study (recurrent alternations of mood from high to low, with each episode lasting less than three weeks and characterized by at least four manic and four depressive symptoms). Since all nine writers receiving a diagnosis of cyclothymia by definition had had periods of hypomania, a total of 60% therefore experienced some type of manic or hypomanic syndrome. Thus there appears to be a close association between literary creativity and affective disorder, and more specifically an association with mania or hypomania as well. Although some writers also suffered from alcoholism or drug abuse, the association with mood disorders was far stronger.

DO MOOD DISORDERS ENHANCE OR DETRACT FROM CREATIVITY?

Because of the suicide of Sylvia Plath and of other fine modern writers, such as Hemingway and Virginia Woolf and Anne Sexton, some writers and

Table 2. Prevalence of Psychiatric Illness in Workshop Writers and Controls

| | Writers (N = 15) | | Controls (N = 15) | | |
	N	%	N	%	P*
Major affective disorder	10	67	2	13	.02
Bipolar affective disorder	2	13	0	0	—
Unipolar major depressive disorder	8	53	2	13	.05
Cyclothymic personality	9	60	2	13	.05
Alcoholism	6	40	1	7	—

*P values determined by Fisher Exact Test (2-tailed).

literary critics have begun to think that the relationship between creativity and mood disorder is even a necessary one. Some have romanticized and idealized affective disorder and the suicidal urge, seeing it as providing a reservoir of intense inner experience from which the writer can draw when he wishes to create. Further, the increased energy and flight of ideas that occur during hypomanic periods could also enhance creativity.

It is very improbable, however, that significant creative advances could be made during periods of either severe depression or severe mania. The Workshop writers consistently indicated that they were unable to work when they were depressed or under the influence of drugs or alcohol; the two writers who had experienced severe manias also indicated that the work produced during mania was of poor quality. Often even the hypomanic periods were not useful to creativity, since distractability, poor concentration, and increased sociability detracted from the creative drive. Creative individuals working in other fields have also stated that they were unable to work during periods of depression. For example, the painter Raphael Soyer has said, "I know that when I am depressed it is harder for me to work [Rosner and Abt, 1970, p. 274]." Composer Aaron Copeland has stated, "Too much depression will not result in a work of art because a work of art is an affirmative gesture [Rosner and Abt, 1970, p. 283]."

Nevertheless, disturbances in mood, including both depression and mania, may work to enhance creativity in some respects, even if creativity cannot occur during episodes of severe affective disorder. Sir George Pickering has hypothesized that periods of physical illness may be useful to creative individuals, since they provide an incubation period in which ideas may be developed (Pickering, 1974). He has illustrated this hypothesis by referring to the lives of Darwin, Freud, Proust, Florence Nightingale, and Mary Baker Eddy. This hypothesis may also apply to the incubation period provided during episodes of depression. Virginia Woolf, for example, felt that her periods of severe depression eventually enhanced her creativity even though she rarely wrote while depressed, since she often developed ideas for her novels while lying in bed in a state of depression. Further, the intense experience of suffering that occurs during a depressive episode may enhance the creative individual's understanding of the human condition. Some of our finest literature describes the experience of depression and despair: the soliloquies of Hamlet, Keats' "Ode to Melancholy," the sonnets of Hopkins, Milton's "Il Penseroso," or Goethe's "Sorrows of Young Werther." In painting, one thinks of the work of Munch, Rembrandt, or Van Gogh.

The interaction between periods of elation and creativity is even more complex. On the one hand, the creative process may itself generate a sense of euphoria and excitement. To create, discover, or invent something often leads to an intense elevation in mood. Much has been written about the fact that breakthroughs in science are more typically the result of an intuitive insight than of careful and detailed analysis (Koestler, 1964; Kuhn, 1970). Kekulé discovered the organic ring in chemistry after having an imaginative vision of a serpent biting its tail, and he has described other instances of insights about organic chemistry occurring as intense moments of insight that led him to work furiously through the night to describe and record them. Faraday, who apparently suffered from a severe psychotic depression in his later years, described the nature of light and electromagnetic forces as a result of intuitive visions and thereby developed the foundations of one branch of physics without even the slightest training in mathematics. Poincaré has described how he discovered the nature of Fuchsian functions, after having spent two weeks trying to disprove their existence through analytical reasoning, during a "wild night of excitement" during which ideas crowded into his mind and combined themselves in new and unusual ways (Vernon, 1970, pp. 77–78). Paul Saltman, a molecular chemist, describes the euphoria generated by this intuitive creative process as follows: "Those days when everything is hitting and you're seeing new relationships and each experiment works—this is a wonderful, wild whole life [Rosner and Abt, 1970, p. 130]." Thus, it is not surprising that creative individuals describe periods of euphoria and elevated mood. Experiencing a "high" is often a natural consequence of the creative process.

On the other hand, some creative individuals may also have a tendency toward mood swings that do not result from creative effort but may enhance it indirectly. A substantial number of the Workshop writers described such mood swings. Some of their periods of hypomania were clearly counterproductive. The increased energy that they experienced could not be focused and controlled so that it could be expressed creatively, and so that energy was dissipated in social or personal outlets. Nevertheless, some periods of hypomania may lead to increased creativity during the hypomanic period itself, and in other instances it may provide an incubation phase during which ideas are developed which can then be explored during a period of neutral mood. The form in which the creative individual works may help determine whether he or she can create during a period of hypomania. For example, painting could be enhanced by hypomania since it is more physical than intellectual; writing, especially of longer works, which demand sustained effort over a number of months, is less likely to be enhanced by hypomania, although shorter works, such as poems, might be produced during a hypomanic period. In religion or politics, decisions that require an absolute sense of confidence or certainty may be made during a hypomanic period and later implemented. One thinks of the careers of Oliver Cromwell, Napoleon, or both Roosevelts. Hitler apparently used amphetamines to artificially sustain the hypomanic energy that he needed to achieve his political goals.

In actuality, many creative individuals probably experience periods of both mild euphoria and mild depression. That is, they have personalities that tend to be cyclothymic. Although the work of Juda and McNeil used European nosology and did not employ the term *cyclothymic,* their high prevalence of personality disorder among creative individuals may reflect this basic tendency. American studies of the personality of creative individuals, although most do not use a formal diagnostic approach, imply that the creative person tends to experience extremes of mood and energy, which might be called bipolar or cyclothymic. These studies, which have examined a variety of creative individuals, such as architects or writers, and have employed standard personality tests, suggest that the creative individual tends to be adventuresome, self-assertive, nonconforming, independent, and fond of challenges; on the other hand, he is also socially detached, introspective, and sensitive (Barron, 1963, 1969, 1972; Drevdahl and Cattell, 1958; Roe, 1946; MacKinnon, 1965). These personality traits, which appear superficially contradictory, imply that the creative individual has an underlying personality that is by nature bipolar. This complex interaction of personality traits may enhance creativity over the long run by giving the creative individual a combination of energy and confidence to create, but also sensitivity to understand the human condition and the universe, and self-criticism to judge the product of his own effort.

IS THERE AN ETIOLOGICAL RELATIONSHIP BETWEEN CREATIVITY AND AFFECTIVE DISORDER?

Although it is by no means definitive, considerable evidence has been amassed which suggests that the association between creativity and affective disorder is familial. That is, psychiatric illness, especially affective disorder, tends to run in the families of creative individuals, and further, creativity tends to run in the families of creative individuals as well. The results of two of these studies are summarized in Table 3, and additional evidence has been provided by the work of Karlsson (1970) and McNeil (1969, 1971). The basic hypothesis that both genius and psychiatric illness run in families can be traced back to the work of Lombroso (1891) and Galton (1892), who supported their theories with a number of case histories and family pedigrees but did not collect systematic data. A familial pattern does not, of course, imply that the traits passed through generations are genetically determined. McNeil's study, which used the adopted-offspring design and therefore provided a purer test of a genetic hypothesis, did yield positive results. He began with adopted persons who were either highly creative (had achieved national recognition for their work) or were somewhat creative (pursued

Table 3. Psychiatric Illness in the Relatives of Creative Individuals

| | Juda (1949) | | | | Andreasen and Canter (1974, 1975) | | | |
| | Siblings | | Parents | | Siblings | | Parents | |
	Artists	Scientists	Artists	Scientists	Writers	Controls	Writers	Controls
Personality disorder	13.6%	8.6%	13.3%	5.6%	0%	0%	0%	0%
Schizophrenia	1.1%	1.3%		0%	2.5%	0%	0%	
Affective disorder	0.7%	0.9%	2.9%	.3%	10%	0%	13%	3%
Alcoholism	—	—	—	.6%	0%	2.4%	7%	3%
Suicide	—	1.7%	—	.8%	2.5%	0%	3%	0%
Creativity	10.8%	3%	—	—	25%	13%	20%	0%
Undiagnosed psychoses	1.5%	1.4%	—	—	10%	0%	0%	0%

creative occupations, such as journalism or teaching music). He then studied the prevalence of illness in the adopted person and of both illness and creativity in their biological parents and their adoptive parents. He found that 30% of the highly creative probands were psychiatrically ill, as were 28% of their biological parents, while only 5% of the adoptive parents were ill. The rates were somewhat lower for the less creative subjects and their relatives.

If there is an hereditary trait or set of traits that predispose to psychiatric illness and creativity, what might they be? One plausible hypothesis is that at least some creative individuals and some people suffering from affective disorder have a constitutional sensitivity to a wide range of stimuli, which is sometimes referred to as "input dysfunction." Individuals with input dysfunction have a defect in the cognitive mechanism which filters stimuli. Thus, at times they are flooded with stimuli that may be either painful or productive, and they are constitutionally unable to tune down or tune out these stimuli when they are noisy or inconvenient.

One study of cognitive style and affective disorders in creative individuals has provided some support for this hypothesis (Andreasen and Powers, 1975). The cognitive style of manics, schizophrenics, and creative writers was compared using the Goldstein-Sheerer object-sorting test. The writers tended to resemble the manics in conceptual style, in that both showed relatively increased behavioral and conceptual overinclusion. Overinclusive thinking is considered to be a manifestation of input dysfunction and difficulty in filtering stimuli. The writers and manics differed in the nature of their overinclusive thinking, however, in that the manics showed more idiosyncratic thinking and the writers more richness. The schizophrenic patients, on the other hand, tended to be underinclusive and idiosyncratic.

Subjectively, the writers also described themselves as easily flooded with stimuli, which they often had difficulty in tuning down or out. For example, many complained that they tended to be excessively sociable and that they needed to consciously isolate themselves from other people in order to complete their work. Many writers choose to write routinely every morning before beginning their contact with other people, a habit that may reflect a tendency to become overstimulated when outside a relatively secluded and protective environment. Other details of their histories indicate an intellectual and social restlessness, which is also suggestive of difficulty in filtering stimuli: many interests and hobbies, experimentation with various kinds of work, and a high level of sexuality. Their tendency to use alcohol and other drugs that act as central nervous system depressants may reflect a need to find a means for tuning down their excessive sensitivity to stimuli.

The hypothesis of input dysfunction is only suggested for its heuristic value. Its potential usefulness lies in the fact that it is a potentially hereditary trait, which would predispose to both creativity and mood disorder, thereby explaining the data that indicate that creativity and mood disorder tend to run together in families. Further, it is an hypothesis that can be tested through various indices of cognitive and autonomic functioning.

SUMMARY

Several lines of evidence imply that there is a relationship between affective disorder and some forms of creativity. The evidence includes a familial clustering of affective disorder and creativity, existence of the clinical syndrome of both mania and depression in creative individuals, and personality traits suggestive of cyclothymia in creative individuals. Much remains to be learned, however, about the nature of the association. The evidence to date is strongest in demonstrating the association in creative writers. The relationship needs to be explored further in other forms of creativity. In addition to further studies to examine the strength and extent of the relationship, more studies are also needed to explore the exact nature of the interaction between creativity and mood disorders. This interaction has significant implications for both etiology and treatment.

REFERENCES

Alvarez, A. *The Savage God: A Study of Suicide.* Random House, New York (1970), p. 31.

Andreasen, N.C., and Canter, A. The creative writer: Psychiatric symptoms and family history. *Compr. Psychiat.* 15, 123–131 (1974).

Andreasen, N.C., and Canter, A. *Genius and Insanity* revisited: Psychiatric symptoms and family history in creative writers. In *Life History Research in Psychopathology,* Vol. 4, R. Wirt, R. Winokur, G. and Roth, M. eds. Univ. of Minnesota Press, Minneapolis (1975), pp. 187–210.

Andreasen, N.C., and Powers, P.S. Creativity and psychosis. *Arch. Gen. Psychiat.* 32, 70–73 (1975).

Barron, F. *Creativity and Psychological Health.* D. Van Nostrand, Princeton, New Jersey (1963).

Barron, F. *Creative Person and Creative Process.* Holt, Rinehart & Winston, New York (1969).

Barron, F. *Artists in the Making.* Seminar Press, New York (1972).

Drevdahl, J.E., and Cattell, R.B. Personality and creativity in artists and writers. *J. Clin. Psychol.* 14, 107–111 (1958).

Ellis, H.A. *A Study of British Genius.* Houghton Mifflin, Boston (1926).

Galton, F. *Hereditary Genius.* Macmillan, London (1892).

Juda, A. The relationship between high mental capacity and psychic abnormalities. *Am. J. Psychiat.* 106, 296–307 (1949).

Karlsson, J.L. Genetic association of giftedness and creativity with schizophrenia. *Hereditas* 66, 177–182 (1970).

Koestler, A. *The Act of Creation.* Dell, New York (1964).

Kuhn, T.S. *The Structure of Scientific Revolutions,* 2nd ed. Univ. of Chicago Press (1970).

Lombroso, C. *The Man of Genius.* Walter Scott, London (1891).

MacKinnon, D.W. Personality and the realization of creative potential. *Am. Psychol.* 20, 273–281 (1965).

McNeil, T.F. *The Relationship Between Creative Ability and Recorded Mental Illness.* Unpublished doctoral dissertation, Univ. of Michigan, Ann Arbor (1969).

McNeil, T.F. Prebirth and postbirth influence on the relationship between creative ability and recorded mental illness. *J. Pers.* 39, 391–406 (1971).

Pickering, G. *Creative Malady.* Oxford Univ. Press, New York (1974).

Roe, A. The personality of artists. *Ed. Psychol. Meas.* 6, 401–408 (1946).

Rosner, S., and Abt, L.E., eds. *The Creative Experience.* Grossman, New York (1970).

Vernon, P.E., ed. *Creativity: Selected Readings.* Penguin, Harmondsworth, Eng. (1970).

CHAPTER 23

The Hypomanic Personality in History

Mortimer Ostow

Hypomanic personality differs from other states of mind in the manic-depressive group in that it is not only not pathologic, but in many instances it seems to confer an advantage. The psychiatrist encounters it as the interim personality of many patients whom he relieves of manic or depressive episodes. He also encounters it among relatives of his manic-depressive patients. He encounters it too among the more successful of his friends and acquaintances.

An early description of the hypomanic personality was given, I believe, in the Book of Genesis. Joseph is recognized by his father as aspiring to dominate his siblings and parents. (It is interesting that the first two dreams of the Joseph cycle are interpreted by his father, Jacob, and are the only two dreams that are interpreted as unconscious—or at least unacknowledged— wish fulfillments of the dreamer, rather than supernaturally inspired prophecies. In fact, they were fulfilled.) He had already become his father's favorite.

In the biblical story there followed a number of vicissitudes, literally ups and downs. He was his father's favorite. Then he was abandoned in the pit. Then he became the steward of the house of Potiphar. Then he was incarcerated in the dungeon. And finally he became the vizier of Pharoah. I should like to suggest that what in the biblical story are given as ups and downs in life experience symbolically represent episodes of depression separated by intervals of hypomanically tinged success. The Bible says of Joseph that he was a successful man. Finally, by virtue of his industry, intelligence, and charm, in a society in which mobility was severely limited, if nonexistent, he became second only to Pharoah. In the end, his brothers did bow down to him as he had anticipated in his childhood dreams.

It is the hypomanic's consistently high level of activity that impresses his friends. His work occupies him during most of his waking hours. He takes few vacations, and when he does, he manages to use them to further his endeavors. Hypomanics, despite their busyness with their principal activity, seem to be able to participate in a number of peripheral endeavors. One finds

387

them often at the forefront of community activities. While the energy of the hypomanic personality is usually reflected in physical action, it can often find major expression in intellectual or artistic work.

The individual with hypomanic personality can appear relatively youthful for his age. Not only does he look youthful, but he actually gives the impression of indefatigable busyness.

While at times such individuals can become angry, they usually present a cheerful and pleasant appearance. Moreover, they convey an air of self-confidence and courage, expressed at least partly by an erect carriage. In fact they are both confident and courageous. They look optimistically toward the future, and if their judgment is biased, it is biased in the direction of assuming that success will be achieved more easily than most people would think. Despite their optimistic bias, they are able to form realistic assessments.

There is probably no significant correlation between the hypomanic quality and intelligence. However, an impression of good intelligence is usually created by the combination of busyness, courage, optimism, and pleasantness. When the individual with hypomanic personality also possesses good intelligence, he is likely to achieve unusual success.

The hypomanic personality exhibits problems primarily in the area of object relations. While his charm and success often attract people to him, and while he enjoys being admired and desired, he generally cannot return the love that is offered to him. In most instances, he understands the meaning of fidelity and can remain faithful to spouse and to friends. However, he seems to lack the capacity for intimacy, so that despite his attractiveness, generosity, and popularity, he is seldom a good parent or spouse.

He has a need to have his impression of omnipotence and omniscience confirmed by others. Therefore, he may attempt to please them as well as to impress them. Moreover, he does not tolerate criticism well. Although he may attempt to conceal it, he does have the need to triumph over and to control others. Often, therefore, he finds himself competing for leadership with others, and attracting followers. His self-confidence, attractiveness, his need for followers and their admiration, taken together create the potential for leadership. When a leader possesses these special qualities that attract followers to him, he is said to be a charismatic leader. The term *charism* in theological language refers to a special gift or grace.

Among the changes most pronounced in the swings between mania and depression is the scope of the imagination. The truly depressed patient is imprisoned in current reality, which he sees as frustrating, uncongenial and unchangeable. He will frequently say that he sees the future stretching before him in an unrelieved, monotonous sameness. It reminds him of the eternal sameness of death. The same individual, when euphoric, finds the here and now not in the least restricting. His imagination sees possibilities of change and improvement and ultimate gratification. As contrasted with the individual who is neither manic nor depressed, the depressive individual will be unable to see the obvious potential in a situation, while the truly manic will see possibilities that are utterly unrealistic. The individual with hypomanic personality will see potentialities beyond those that are visible to the nonhypomanic; yet they will be sufficiently realistic to warrant being taken seriously. This perceptiveness and imaginativeness relate to problem-solving in whatever area of interest. They may also lead to the creation of imaginative images of reality, which will possess esthetic appeal for others. It is this ability which the creative individual cherishes and which is taken from him by a tranquilizing drug. He misses it and in many instances is willing to risk relapse into psychosis by omitting the therapeutic drug rather than to accept the deprivation of his ability to imagine. Reality, after all, does hem us in, and while it offers opportunities for gratification, it more effectively frustrates the fulfillment of most of our wishes. Realistic fantasy—that is, imagination— can suggest ways of overcoming realistic frustration in some instances, and can permit the enjoyment of escape into the magical world of the arts in others. Depression and the tranquilizing drugs that facilitate depression both suppress this capacity for imagination, while the manic tendency, of whatever extent, normal or abnormal, as well as the antidepression drugs that facilitate that tendency, promote imagination and fantasy. Schizophrenia and the hallucinogenic drugs make fantasy replace reality and even usurp the sense of reality.

The individual with hypomanic personality contributes much to society by virtue of his industriousness and his creativity. In addition, because he possesses so many attributes of leadership, he is often accepted as a leader. Problems arise, however, when the hypomanic personality is recurrently interrupted by episodes of mania or depression or both. The more serious problem is mania. The reason is that the leader is taken seriously simply by virtue of his leadership. Strange ideas that manic relapse induces might at first be interpreted as the result of greater perspicacity and wisdom. It may take some time before the public realizes that their leader is ill. For a while they struggle to accommodate themselves to his illusions and delusions so that they will not have to repudiate him.

When the hypomanic leader becomes depressed, the consequences are not so serious. He merely becomes less active, or completely inactive for a while, but seldom does anything that might injure others, unless the manic-depressive tendency is accompanied by a schizophrenic or paranoid quality. In that case, the leader may perceive his own depression as an incipient universal apocalypse, just as the schizophrenic does. If that is the case, he may lead his followers into some self-destructive struggle, failing to distinguish between his personal catastrophe and that of his community.

The history of the Sabbatian movement of the seventeenth century provides us with an instructive contrast between the individual with hypomanic personality and the individual in an episode of hypomanic illness or manic psychosis. In 1665 and 1666 a large proportion of the members of the Jewish communities of Europe, the Middle East, and north Africa acknowledged the arrival of a "messiah" in the person of a Turkish Jew, Shabbatai Zvi. The episode followed and brought to a climax 150 years of mystical and religious study and philosophy. It shifted the scene of anticipated redemption from the individual spirit to external political reality. Why so many Jews of diverse cultures and occupations and of widely differing social and economic status were so ready to disrupt daily life and prepared to depart for Palestine to participate in messianic redemption is difficult to understand. In any case, it is clear that the moving force lay in the readiness of the responders rather than in any external compulsion or in any attraction exerted by the leaders of the movement that would be found irresistible by reasonable people in normal times. What is interesting from our point of view is that the movement was led by two men, Shabbatai Zvi and a younger man who has come to be known as Nathan of Gaza.

Shabbatai Zvi, the messiah, was a rabbinic scholar, born in 1626, in Smyrna (Izmir), to a well-to-do family, probably Ashkenazic in origin. He occupied himself with religious and mystical studies, and led a life of asceticism, as did many others at that time and place. The biographical details that we possess leave little doubt that he suffered manic-depressive illness. Contemporaries describe what we recognize as classical episodes of both mania and depression. During melancholic episodes, he would withdraw into solitude, and his behavior did not occasion much comment. However, during his manic episodes, he engaged in characteristically grandiose and unconventional behavior.

Since he lived within a totally religious milieu, his delusions and provocations took religious form. He violated religious customs and laws publicly and noisily, and introduced bizarre and forbidden variations of ritual practice. He justified these innovations by characteristic manic word-play on classical texts. It is not known whether he actually declared himself a messiah before 1665.

At first his behavior was tolerated in his community because it was regarded as some sort of deviance, perhaps a manifestation of illness, and also because his interval behavior was characterized by dignity, asceticism, and studiousness. Ultimately, he was banished from his native Smyrna, then from Salonika, and then from Constantinople.

Shabbatai Zvi might have lived and died unrecorded in history had it not been for the efforts of another rabbinic scholar about 17 years younger, Nathan of Gaza. Nathan was celebrated as a brilliant scholar and a "prophet" who could understand people's problems and prescribe kabbalistic remedies. In February 1665, Nathan, who was then 20, described an ecstatic vision of Shabbatai Zvi, whom he had not yet met, as the messiah. In April of the same year, having heard of Nathan's ability to provide remedies for the troubled, Shabbatai Zvi consulted him, hoping to find some relief for his illness. The two men spent many days together, conversing and exchanging views. Ultimately Nathan persuaded Shabbatai that not only did he not require a remedy, but that he was truly the long-awaited messiah. At the end of May, in a state of manic elation, Shabbatai publicly proclaimed himself the messiah, and he acted the role whenever he was manic. At other times he was diffident but did not disavow his claim. The latter was accepted by amazingly large numbers of people, including some who knew him, but also by many who had merely heard of him by letter. It was Nathan rather than Shabbatai who instigated diffusion of the messianic claim, who called upon all Jews to initiate a preparatory effort of repentance, who created new prayers and liturgical recitations appropriate to the event, and who provided a revision of kabbalistic theory to accommodate the new situation created by the arrival of the messiah.

To complete the story, Jews all over the world responded to the proclamation by preparing to leave their homes for Palestine once the messiah had assumed political powers, as he promised he would. Shabbatai Zvi was arrested by Turkish authorities in February 1666. He was held in prison, first in Constantinople and then in the fortress of Gallipoli. Here he continued to play the role of messiah whenever he was in a state of manic elation, and continued to impress many of his followers who visited him there. Because the messianic furor continued to unsettle the Jews of Turkey, Shabbatai Zvi was removed to Adrianople, and there he was induced to apostasize to Islam by threats and promises. It is interesting that the messianic movement was not damaged by the incarceration of the messiah; it lost only some of its adherents after his apostasy, and retained a faithful few even after his death in exile in 1675. Just as Paul transformed a crucified messiah into a more powerful symbol than the living one had been, so Nathan transformed an incarcerated and then apostasized messiah into a powerful symbol with a similar promise of redemption upon his reappearance.

What is of interest from our point of view is the contrast between the two men Shabbatai Zvi and Nathan. Shabbatai Zvi was the messiah, but he was passive and ineffective. During the intervals of freedom from illness, he was inactive. When manic, he was so psychotic and disorganized that he could accomplish nothing. Nathan, on the other hand, was the leader, guiding light, and theoretician of the messianic movement who, if Shabbatai Zvi had not been available, might have organized the same movement around the person of someone else.

When not elated, Shabbatai was described as possessed of personal charm, conveying an impression of nobility, kind, dignified, and tactful. Yet he failed on his own to establish a coterie of followers. At times he gave the impression of being ascetic and saintly. Even when not depressed, he preferred solitude. But he was passive, lacking in initiative, and unable to form and execute long-range plans. When he was neither manic nor depressed, he did not retain enough of the manic drive or imagination to achieve anything remarkable.

Nathan, on the other hand, exhibited none of the manic or depressive swings. He is described (by Scholem) as possessor of "visionary power, intellectual capacity, and untiring energy." His qualities include "tireless activity, unwavering perseverance without manic depressive ups and downs, originality of theological thought, and considerable literary ability." One of those who visited Nathan after the proclamation of Shabbatai Zvi as messiah recorded his experience as follows (Scholem, 1973, p. 260): "When I stood before Nathan the prophet all my bones shook, although I had known him before, for his countenance was completely changed. The radiance of his face was like that of a burning torch, the color of his beard was like gold, and his mouth which [formerly] would not utter even the most ordinary things, now spoke words that made the listeners tremble. His tongue speaks great things...and the ear can hardly take in that which comes out of his mouth with a wonderful eloquence. And verily, every moment he tells new things, the like of which have not been heard since the day that the Law was given on Mount Sinai." Allowing for the enthusiasm of the believer, the contagious excitement of the situation, and the hyperbole of the then-current literary fashion, Nathan's impressiveness nevertheless comes through. This combination of a consistently high level of activity, imaginativeness, creativity, charisma, ambition, an interest in accomplishing things in the world, concern with community, an ability to convert misfortune into advantage, leadership, consistently high morale, strongly suggests that Nathan's was what we have been calling a "hypomanic personality."

Nathan and Shabbatai Zvi shared the same antinomian tendency. Shabbatai expressed his only during states of manic elation, at least at first. Even after he announced himself as messiah, his posturing was greatly diminished during nonpsychotic intervals, and there were some hints that in melancholic episodes he detached himself from the whole project. Nathan's antinomianism expressed itself in his sponsoring Shabbatai's claims and in leadership of the movement, which in many respects violated normal Jewish practice. However, he was not so uninhibited as to follow Shabbatai into apostasy. In other words, Shabbatai, in his manic episodes, personified Nathan's antinomianism, and Nathan used Shabbatai to give vicarious expression to this tendency without going to the same extremes. It is interesting that when led—or rather, misled—by a charismatic hypomanic, large numbers of thoughtful and reasonable people can take seriously the delusional behavior of a psychotic. Evidently the qualities of the hypomanic personality compel the ordinary person to respect and to defer to him, and to accept his influence.

What we learn from the comparison of these two men is that the same psychic process that in pathologic degree creates gross and disabling psychosis, when limited, can give rise to superior psychic function and a potential for leadership.

REFERENCE

Scholem, Gershom S. *Sabbatai Sevi, The Mystical Messiah* (Boilingen Series XCIII). Princeton Univ. Press (1973).

Index